# Children's Britannica

# CHILDREN'S BRITANNICA

## Volume 7

### Epic—Furs

ENCYCLOPÆDIA BRITANNICA INTERNATIONAL, LTD
LONDON

First edition 1960

Second edition 1969



SBN 85229 018 7

*Printed in England by Hazells Offset Limited, Slough*
*and bound by*
*Hazell Watson & Viney Limited, Aylesbury & Cymmer*

**EPIC.** An epic is a long narrative or story-telling poem, usually about the adventures and prowess of a single hero, in which brave and noble deeds are described. The stories of many epics had probably been told over and over again by minstrels before they were written down.

The greatest of all are the ancient Greek epics of Homer, the *Iliad* and the *Odyssey*, which were based on stories handed down from one generation to the next. Homer's epics have been taken as a model by many later writers. *Beowulf* was written in England in Anglo-Saxon times. In French there is the *Chanson de Roland* (Song of Roland), in German the *Ring of the Nibelungs* and in Spanish the *Chronicle of the Cid*.

Poems such as Virgil's *Aeneid*, written in Latin, and the two great English epics, Milton's *Paradise Lost* and Spenser's *Faerie Queene*, are sometimes called secondary epics because they were not first handed down by word of mouth but were created by the authors, although based on stories and ideas already well known.

**EPIDEMIC.** Many diseases are caused by small living things, such as bacteria and viruses, which pass from one person to another. (See BACTERIA and GERMS.) If a disease spreads to a fairly large number of people, over a fairly wide area, it is said to be epidemic (adjective) or an epidemic (noun). Throughout history there have been epidemics of various diseases, and scientists have studied their causes carefully and the ways to defeat them.

Some of the worst epidemics in the past were caused by the fact that human excrement, or waste matter, was not disposed of through sewers, and its disease germs passed into water used for drinking. Other diseases have been spread by infected milk, and by food contaminated by dirty hands or germ-carrying flies. Until about a century ago thousands of people died from cholera each year in England, and once a single infected well near Piccadilly Circus, London, caused 485 deaths in ten days. It was the closing of this well by sealing off the pump that led to the development of public health measures in Great Britain. In 1885 there was a famous epidemic of typhoid in Plymouth, a town in Pennsylvania, United States, where one out of every eight people was infected. Nowadays, with efficient sewerage systems, ample supplies of clean water and the pasteurization of milk (see MILK), epidemics of this sort rarely occur except in less-developed countries.

Other diseases are spread by insects. Plague (see BLACK DEATH) is spread by rat fleas, typhus by lice and malaria by mosquitoes. In many countries these diseases have been wiped out by greater personal cleanliness, the careful control of rats and the draining of marshes where mosquitoes breed. However, there are other countries which still have serious epidemics, and in India several million people suffer from malaria each year.

Some serious diseases are spread by germs in the tiny droplets of moisture that pass into the air when we breathe, cough or sneeze. Smallpox is one of them, but it can be controlled by vaccination, on which there is a separate article. Diphtheria has also been defeated, largely by the giving of special injections in early life. As recently as 1941 there were over 50,000 cases in England and Wales, but in the five years 1961–1965 fewer than 150 cases were reported. Other diseases spread by droplet infection include tuberculosis, influenza and even the common cold.

For some years diseases such as poliomyelitis ("polio") were quite common in Britain, but in general the threat of epidemic disease has been greatly reduced by medical science, health education and the increasing use of preventive injections.

**EPIDIASCOPE.** The ordinary projector or *diascope* takes a transparent slide or film strip and passes light through it to a lens which throws a much larger picture on a screen some distance away (see LENS); a cinema projector is of this kind. An *episcope* is a projector which throws an image of a picture postcard or page of a book or drawing; it does this by lighting up the postcard or drawing very brightly and then throwing the reflected light through a lens on to the screen. Because much of the light is absorbed by the postcard or drawing and not reflected, the picture seen on the screen is less bright than that from a diascope; nevertheless the episcope is valuable to a teacher or lecturer who can use it to show pictures or diagrams from a book to a large audience. When the two instruments are combined in one, with a simple

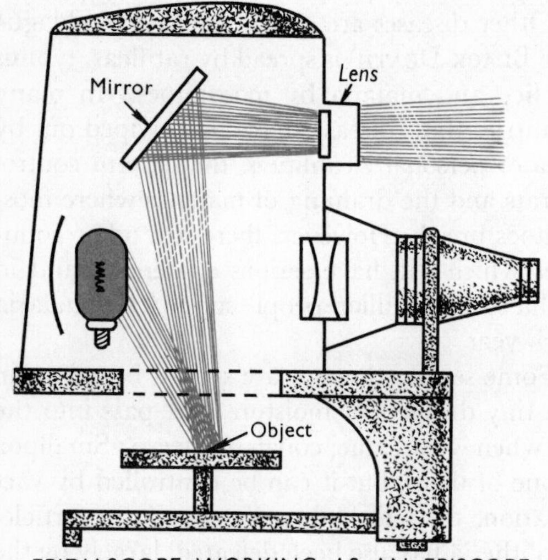


EPIDIASCOPE WORKING AS AN EPISCOPE FOR PROJECTING OPAQUE OBJECTS

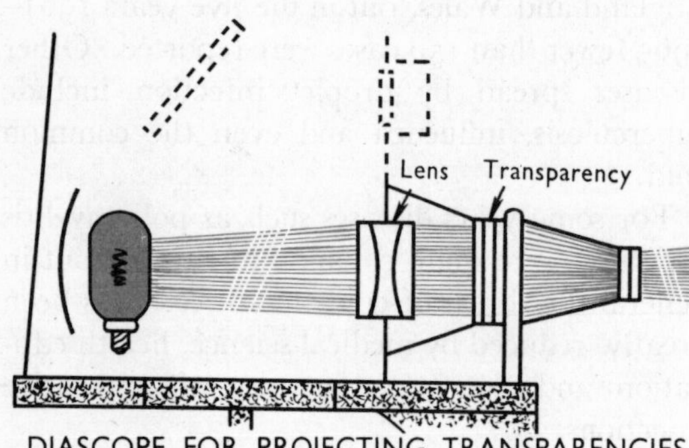


DIASCOPE FOR PROJECTING TRANSPARENCIES

**The upper diagram shows how a page in a book is projected. The lower one shows the method for a transparency.**

way of changing from one to the other, the combination is called an *epidiascope*.

The old name for a diascope was "magic lantern", because in the days when it was first used it seemed magical that a picture could be thrown on to a screen in a darkened room.

**EPIGRAM.** An epigram is a short saying that expresses some striking thought in very few words. Epigrams are often witty and clever too. In fact, one epigram describes very well what this kind should be like:

> What is an epigram? a dwarfish whole,
> Its body brevity and wit its soul.

The Greek poets often used the epigram for making short and delicate compliments, like this one written to a lady to suggest that she was sweeter even than the sweet-smelling plant called myrrh:

> I send thee myrrh, not that thou mayest be
> By it perfumed, but it perfumed by thee.

The Romans, however, more often used epigrams to make stinging remarks about people they disliked. One by the poet Martial to another author says:

> In spite of hints, in spite of looks,
> Titus, I send thee not my books.
> The reason, Titus, canst divine?
> I fear lest thou shouldst send me thine.

("Divine" means guess.)

Both complimentary and cutting (sarcastic) epigrams have been written in English. Some of the poets who lived in the 17th century, especially Robert Herrick, were very fond of them. Some of the best English epigrams were written by the 18th-century poet Alexander Pope; many of his were not written as separate little verses but came into his longer poems. Epigrams need not be in verse, for shortness and wit can also be effective in prose. The plays of Oscar Wilde are full of this sort.

**EPITAPH.** An inscription on a tomb, written in prose or verse, is called an epitaph. There were times when the writing of epitaphs was very popular, but today they are not very often used except on the tombs of great men.

It was the Greeks who started verse epitaphs and they wrote beautiful and dignified ones. An epitaph on Alexander the Great, who conquered many kingdoms in his lifetime, says:

> Here a mound is sufficient for the man for whom
> the world was not enough.

Soldiers who had fallen in battle sometimes had epitaphs written for them. This one is about the Spartan heroes who died fighting the Persians at the battle of Thermopylae:

> Go tell the Spartans, thou that passest by,
> That here, obedient to their laws, we lie.

Roman epitaphs were more like our own. They told who the dead man was and requested the passer-by to leave his bones undisturbed. An English epitaph that makes a request of this kind is the one on Shakespeare's tomb at Stratford-on-Avon, supposed to have been written by the poet himself:

> Good friend, for Jesus' sake forbear
> To dig the dust enclosed here;
> Blest be the man that spares these stones,
> And curst be he that moves my bones.

Some of the epitaphs written by poets were intended to criticize the dead man, if he was one whom the poet disliked. An example is this one by Alexander Pope:

> Here lies Lord Coningsby—be civil.
> The rest God knows; so does the devil.

Epitaphs are sometimes funny. A French one, for instance (translated into English here), was written by a husband for the tomb of his wife, at whose death he must have breathed a sigh of relief:

> Here lies my wife; and, Heaven knows,
> For her *and* me a just repose.

A true and dignified epitaph is found on the tomb of Sir Christopher Wren in St. Paul's Cathedral, the building he designed himself. It is in Latin, but the translation is:

> If you seek his monument, look about you.

**EPSTEIN, Sir Jacob** (1880–1959). A famous sculptor of the 20th century is Jacob Epstein. There has been a great deal of argument about his works; some people admire them tremendously but others dislike them very much indeed. He was born in New York, the son of Russian and Polish parents, and studied sculpture first in New York and then in Paris. In 1905 he came to London and from then onwards many of his works were created in England. In 1954 he was knighted for his work.

Epstein's sculpture can be divided into two main kinds: portraits modelled in bronze and large stone figures which are not modelled from real people and usually have some special meaning, sometimes a religious one. Not many people disagree about the portrait busts (a sculpture of a person's head and shoulders is called a *bust*), for they give a real feeling of what the people portrayed look like, and of what sort of people they are. Epstein made portraits of many famous people, including Sir Winston Churchill, the writers Bernard Shaw and Joseph Conrad, and the great mathematician Albert Einstein.

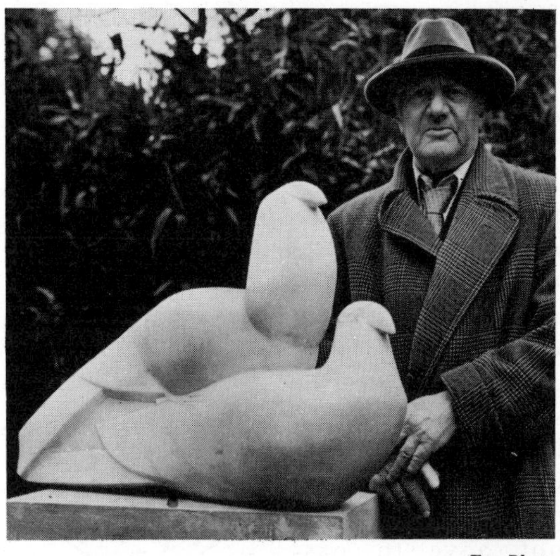

*Fox Photos*
Sir Jacob Epstein with his marble group, "The Doves".

Among Epstein's important larger sculptures which gave rise to much argument are two huge figures, standing for "Day" and "Night", over the entrances to the Underground station at St. James's Park in London, for Epstein showed them in quite a different way from what many people expected and thought right. Another well-known sculpture is a statue of Adam. In 1957 Epstein's huge figure of "Christ in Majesty", made in aluminium and coloured silver, was set up high over an arch in Llandaff Cathedral in Wales.

**EQUATOR.** The imaginary line passing round the earth midway between the poles is called the equator. Its name comes from the

Latin word for "equal", and it divides the earth into two equal parts called the northern and southern hemispheres.

Latitude is measured north or south from the equator, so the equator itself is in latitude 0 degrees and the poles are 90 degrees north and south. The parallels of latitude are imaginary circles parallel to the equator (see LATITUDE AND LONGITUDE). Two important parallels are the northern and southern tropics (Cancer and Capricorn), 23½ degrees (1,615 miles) from the equator. The lands between them are said to be "in the tropics", or sometimes called inter-tropical lands. (See TROPICS.) The belt between the two tropics is called the torrid zone (torrid means very hot). Lands within about ten degrees (690 miles) of the equator are called equatorial lands.

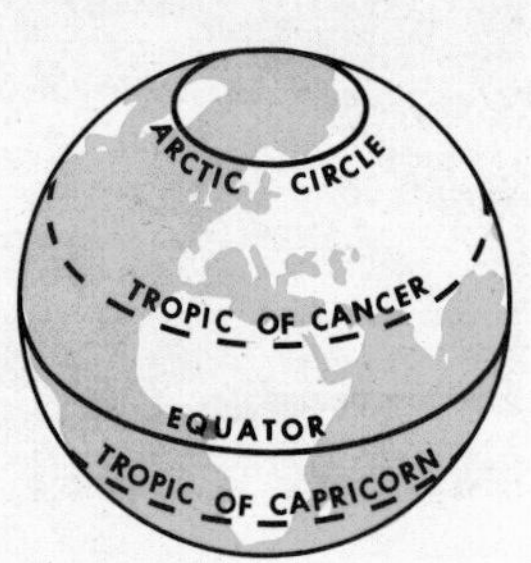


In the torrid zone the sun reaches its greatest height and sends its rays vertically down on the earth. As the rays do not have to pass through such a thick layer of air as they do when the sun is not overhead, this also makes them hotter.

At the equator, the days and nights are always equal in length. The sun rises at about six in the morning and sets at about six in the evening. It seems to rise and set more suddenly than in other latitudes so there is scarcely any morning or evening twilight.

There is of course nothing to mark the line of the equator, but sailors can tell when they cross it by observing the sun and stars (see NAVIGATION). Often when a ship "crosses the line" the sailors have a kind of comic ceremony, described in the article CROSSING THE LINE.

The equator measures 24,902 miles round. Some of the places on or near the equator are Singapore, Nairobi (Kenya), Kisangani (Democratic Republic of the Congo), Belem (Brazil) and Quito (Ecuador).

**EQUATORIAL GUINEA.** Just north of the equator on the West African coast is a region rather larger than Wales, bounded by the republics of Cameroun and Gabon. Together with the large island of Fernando Poo, which lies in the Gulf of Guinea, the region forms the Republic of Equatorial Guinea. The people are Negroes, many of those in Fernando Poo being Bantus. The chief products are cocoa, coffee and timber. Equatorial Guinea was formerly a Spanish possession. It became independent in 1968. The capital is Santa Isabel on Fernando Poo and the population is about 280,000.

**ERASMUS, Desiderius** (?1466–1536). Although we know that Erasmus was born in the Netherlands there is uncertainty as to whether Rotterdam or Gouda was his birthplace; the year of his birth is thought to have been 1466.

At this time people throughout Europe were beginning to be more interested in learning than they had been for centuries, and scholars were finding out about the achievements of the ancient Greeks and Romans, whose history and literature had been ignored and forgotten for hundreds of years. This knowledge gave men new ideas and encouraged them to be more critical than their fathers and grandfathers had been. Therefore it is not surprising that, at this time, people were beginning to criticize the church, for many of the monks and priests were not good Christians and were often narrow-minded in their teaching.

Erasmus supported both these movements for greater knowledge, and shared their belief that men should think for themselves and not just take on trust what they were taught. He was one of the greatest scholars of his time and devoted his life to the telling of the truth as he saw it. Although he never became a Protestant his work did much to inspire the Reformation, a movement in which many people became Protestants (see REFORMATION).

His guardians wanted him to become a monk and had him educated by the monks. Later he entered a monastery and became a priest but he was so disgusted by what he considered to be the petty, or small-minded, behaviour in monasteries that he decided to go out into the world as a scholar and teacher. In his book *The Praise of Folly* he makes fun of the superstition and ignorance of bad monks and priests.

Eric's settlements were on the west coast of Greenland—then, as now, a safer place for human beings than the east.

One of his aims was to enable the gospels to be read in the language in which they were originally written—Greek—for the only available version was a Latin translation, known as the Vulgate, which contained mistakes. His edition of the New Testament, published in 1516, was the first to be published in Greek. He also wanted to have the scriptures translated into the languages that ordinary people spoke so that they could read them in their own language, without having to rely on a priest for their knowledge of Christianity.

Erasmus worked and studied in France, England, Italy, Switzerland, the Netherlands and Germany. He first visited England in 1498 and afterwards spent much time there and made many friends, among them Sir Thomas More, on whom there is an article. One of the few foreigners to praise the English climate, Erasmus criticized the English for not opening their windows. Although he taught divinity at Queen's College, Cambridge, he never learnt English and always wrote and spoke Latin. His books on religion, education and other subjects were famous all over Europe for their wisdom, generous outlook and humour.

**ERIC THE RED** was the Viking who discovered and named Greenland. He is also the hero of the Icelandic saga *Eric the Red* (the article SAGA explains what kind of story a saga is). He was a Norseman, a subject of the king of Norway, and his explorations were part of a general movement of Norse conquest and settlement that took place in northern Europe in the early middle ages. As well as plundering and later settling in Britain and Normandy, these great sailors founded colonies in Iceland. Eric (or Eirik) settled in Iceland with his family but after a serious quarrel with his neighbours he had to leave Iceland. He sailed westwards in 982 and arrived on the coast of Greenland where he spent three years exploring, hunting and fishing. Afterwards he returned to Iceland to collect more Norsemen to found a settlement in Greenland. Eric had given the new island this attractive name, hoping that it would encourage people to settle there; it was certainly a more pleasant name than Iceland. He again set off with 25 ships and 14 of them reached Greenland. In 986 a colony was founded. In time there were two colonies, on the west coast at Ericsfiord (near Godthaab) and on the south coast at Brattahlid (near Julianehaab). Eric seems to have spent the rest of his life in Greenland. He and his wife Thjodhild (who had been converted to Christianity) had two children. The elder, Thorstein, spent his life mainly in Norway but the younger son Leif became as famous for exploring as his father.

Leif Ericsson went to the court of the king of Norway in 999 and then returned to Greenland on the king's orders, to encourage the Vikings to become Christians. On his way back he was driven off course by bad weather. His ship passed south of Greenland and came to the coast of North America. Arriving in A.D. 1000 he was almost certainly the first European to discover America. The first land sighted was called by the Vikings Vinland or Wineland. It must have been on the fertile eastern coast somewhere between Cape Cod and Nova Scotia. The Vikings noticed that the area was warmer and more fruitful than Greenland and they took back with them samples of wild wheat, vines and maple wood. They sailed northwards up the coast and finally returned to Greenland.

The following year Leif's brother Thorstein tried unsuccessfully to reach these new lands. The next Norseman to reach America was Thorfinn Karlsefni, who left Greenland in 1003 with three ships to reach Vinland. He sailed down the eastern coast, naming the bleak northern Labrador coast Helluland (Flagstoneland) and the wooded lands further south Markland (Forestland). He tried to found a colony but trouble broke out with the Eskimoes and the Norsemen returned to Greenland in 1006. Later there were probably occasional visits to Markland for timber but there was no settlement.

The Greenland colonies of Eric the Red flourished for many years. The western colony was given up about 1350 but the southern colony survived until the 16th century.

**EROS** was the Greek god of love. Nearly all the stories told about him tell how he made people fall in love with one another: the most important one is told in the article CUPID AND PSYCHE. (Cupid was the name the Romans gave to Eros.) He was the son of Zeus, the king of the gods, and Aphrodite, the goddess of love and beauty. The Greeks thought of Eros either as a handsome young man or as a pretty child, usually with wings and a bow and arrow.

In Piccadilly Circus in London there is a statue that was put up in 1893 in memory of Lord Shaftesbury, the 19th century reformer. This statue is known as Eros, but it is said that the sculptor thought of the statue as Charity, flying swift as an arrow to help people.

**EROSION.** The word "erosion" means "gnawing away" and is used to describe the gradual wearing away of rocks and soils by such things as ice, frost, wind and water. It is going on everywhere and all the time. Although some of these actions hardly show, and a hill may look the same now as it did a year ago, over the course of ages the change is great. In other cases, great changes may happen in a few years.

### Heat and Cold

In hot deserts the great difference between the temperature of day and night has a strong effect on the rocks. By day, the enormous heat of the sun makes them expand, or grow bigger; at night, the temperature falls suddenly and the rocks contract, or grow smaller, so quickly that they split and pieces break off.

Cold weather on its own produces great changes through the action of frost and ice. When water in the crevices of the earth freezes it expands and breaks off fragments of rock. This process can be seen most clearly in chalk or limestone country and even on the hard granite rocks of the Dartmoor tors. A far more drastic effect was produced by the glaciers that spread over most of Britain during the Ice Age (see ICE AGE). As they moved slowly southwards they ground down the rocks, carrying stones and boulders with them, and making scratches that can still be seen in the English Lake District and elsewhere. In regions that are still cold—either because they are high or because they are far from the equator—glaciers are still eroding the surface of the Earth.

### Water

The sea is perpetually wearing away the coast. The North Sea scours the east coast of

Great Britain and, for example, in the Lowestoft area has carried away so much of the cliffs that houses once far from their edge have fallen into the sea. In order to prevent this type of erosion coasts are often protected by groynes and walls.

Water in Nature is never pure. It contains carbon dioxide and so can dissolve calcium carbonate, the substance that forms chalk and limestone. (This is the "fur" in a kettle; the carbon dioxide escapes when the water is heated and the calcium carbonate then takes on a solid form.) Some rocks are made up of grit or stones cemented together; if this cement is calcium carbonate or other material which can dissolve in a similar manner, it can be washed away by the water and then the rock begins to crumble. Erosion easily follows.

Soil is eroded by rain, especially by the torrential rain that falls at certain times in the regions that have no rain for most of the year and receive all their rain in a month or two. The large raindrops hit the ground with great force and break up the soil. If the water is not absorbed in the earth it forms streams which gather power as they go, scooping out deep channels along which later water rushes down, carrying everything before it. The water must therefore be prevented from flowing away. In order to do this the land must be farmed along its contours; that is, it must be ploughed and cultivated round a hill instead of from top to bottom; banks and terraces must be built and the soil be left rough so that the water will sink into it more easily. This sort of farming is seen in parts of southern Europe and Asia. As the trouble may begin above the cultivated area, it is necessary to protect the tops of the hills by planting trees, whose roots and fallen leaves help to hold up the water till it sinks into the ground—to break out lower down as springs. The good work done by trees can be seen by what happened in the valley of the Tennessee River, in the United States, when they were cut down by men eager to cultivate the land. After a time the soil became loose, leaving bare rock. The Tennessee Valley Authority—a vast organization set up to repair the damage and to build dams on the river—has succeeded in making the area fertile once more.

## The Wind

The wind is a powerful eroding agent. In desert countries it picks up sand and drives it with great force against the rocks, breaking off tiny particles all the time. Or it may carry off soil as well as sand—which is what has happened in the Sahara area, parts of which were once fertile land. Very large particles are not lifted up but are blown along the ground and, in certain places, form sandhills or dunes. These can be seen both in the hot deserts and along the coast of Great Britain.

One way of preventing sand being blown is to plant trees to lessen the action of the wind. An even better method is to plant strips of grass between strips of cultivated land so that the blown sand will be caught in the grass. It has also been found that if the soil is left rough it is far less likely to blow away.

### Bad Farming

Grass roots build up the fine soil particles into crumbs that are not easily eroded, and the roots and leaves of all plants by decaying in the soil form sticky substances that have the same effect. However, when the soil is kept free from vegetation for fairly long periods, especially if it is thoroughly tilled, the crumbs get broken down and the fine particles are easily blown away by strong winds. This happens at times in the eastern counties of England. It caused terrible losses for the early farmer settlers in North America, South America and Australia, who had no means of knowing anything about the formation and destruction of soil crumbs. In the United States the famous "Dust Bowl" was created by the unsuitable farming methods of the 1890s and early 1900s, in the states of Kansas, Texas and Oklahoma. Appalling dust storms occurred and thousands of farmers were ruined by them. As a result of these happenings the United States took the lead in tackling the problem of erosion and set up the Soil Conservation Service. The farmers of a region meet its experts and, together, they make a plan for the care and use of the soil; if the plan is accepted by a majority of the farmers they are all bound to carry it out. This system has been widely adopted in the Commonwealth.

In parts of Africa special difficulties arise over the use of land because the tribal and social customs of the people may be involved. In some tribes, for instance, a man's social position depends on the number of cattle he has. There are many more cattle in Africa now than there were 30 years ago, and every blade of grass is eaten, leaving the soil bare and easily eroded. In order to prevent erosion many miles of banks and terraces have been built, farmers have been encouraged to cultivate their land along the contours, and the land on which cattle have grazed a great deal has been closed for two or three rainy seasons to give it a rest.

Scientists now know how to check the erosion of the soil. The ways of doing this are simple to understand, but are difficult to carry out because success depends on the co-operation of the people of an entire region. Neighbouring countries often have similar problems, and therefore arrange to work together against erosion. The United Nations Food and Agriculture Organization sends experts in soil conservation to the developing countries.

**ERRAND BOY.** Before the telephone was invented people living fairly near to one another often needed to send messages to each other quickly, either on business or because of some personal emergency. Boys ready to take an errand could easily be found in most streets and in great cities such as London there were even organized services of messenger boys who performed all kinds of jobs.

In the first half of this century, errand boys were employed by shops, at a small weekly wage, to deliver such things as groceries and meat to customers' homes. They rode special bicycles with big baskets mounted over the front wheel. But now errand boys and their bicycles are rarely seen.

**ERSE,** or Irish, is the first official language of the Republic of Ireland. (The other official language there is English.) Erse is one of the Celtic languages and is very like Scottish Gaelic, which is spoken in the Highlands of Scotland, and Manx, the old language of the Isle of Man. Indeed, Erse was introduced into Scotland from Ireland in about A.D. 500, and Scottish Gaelic did not become a distinct language until the 16th century. Many writings of all kinds have come down in manuscripts written in the Erse of former times. They include stories of the ancient heroes Conchobar and Cuchulainn and of Finn and Ossian.

In the past, governments often tried to do away with the Irish speech and prevent books from being written in Erse, but since 1920, when the Irish Free State was formed, the speaking of Erse has been much encouraged, as well as the study of the old literature and the writing of new poems, stories and novels. (See IRELAND.)

**ESCALATOR.** In underground railways and some big shops, escalators or moving stairways are used to take people up and down instead of ordinary staircases or lifts.

The escalator is made up of a set of steps attached to endless chains which pass round toothed wheels at the top and bottom of the stairway; the wheel at the top is driven by an electric motor and therefore when the motor is started all the steps move up (or down) together, as well as a flexible handrail for the passengers to hold on to. For the last few feet of their travel at top and bottom the steps flatten out and move forward without rising or falling. The steps have ribs running from front to back and a metal comb fastened to the fixed part of the landing has sloping teeth which fit between the ribs. Thus if a person fails to step off at the end his feet are carried gently on to the fixed comb on the landing without tripping him up.

In most places there is one escalator for going up and another for going down, but in some places there are three.

Many of the London Underground stations have escalators. Those at Leicester Square for instance have a vertical rise of 81 feet. The slope is usually such that a passenger is carried two feet forwards for every foot up or down. An escalator running at 90 feet a minute with two passengers on each step will carry 8,000 people an hour, or even 11,500 if they help by walking. The escalator is to be preferred to the lift when the height is not too great and it also has the advantage that passengers are not kept waiting. The escalators at the Tyne tunnel, Newcastle upon Tyne, can be used by people having bicycles with them. The travolator at the Bank station in London has two moving platforms, each of which forms a continuous gentle slope instead of steps.

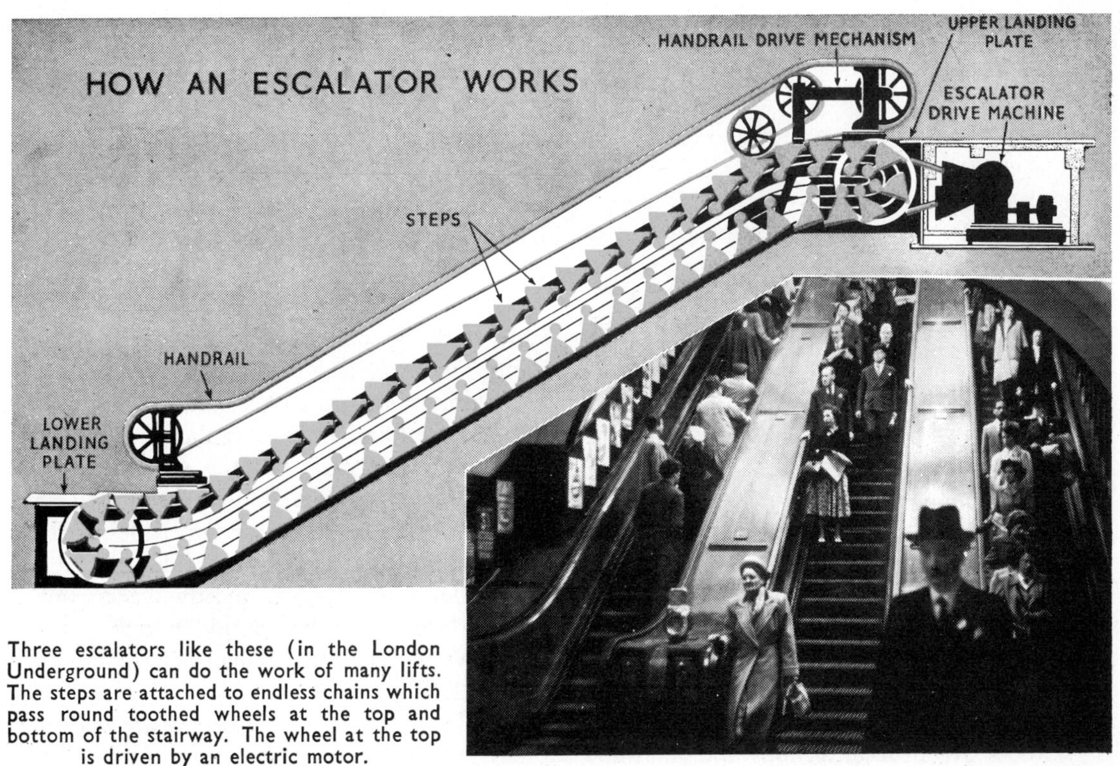


Three escalators like these (in the London Underground) can do the work of many lifts. The steps are attached to endless chains which pass round toothed wheels at the top and bottom of the stairway. The wheel at the top is driven by an electric motor.

**ESKIMOES** live in Greenland, northern Canada and Alaska and number about 50,000. They speak more or less the same language and they live by hunting, fishing and gathering roots during the short summers. Almost all Eskimoes have copper or yellow skins, and rather flat faces and straight, coarse black hair, and they are usually not very tall. However, in Greenland, for example, where the women have married European men, their children may have fair hair. Like American Indians they have clearly come from Siberia long ago and either there, or in North America, they have learnt to live and make the best use of a region of ice and snow. They crossed to Alaska by way of the Bering Strait about 3,000 years ago and spread across Canada into Greenland. They first met Europeans in about A.D. 1000 when the Norsemen reached the American continent. Today many are Christians.

Most people think that all Eskimoes live in houses made of snow, but this is not true. Today probably not more than a quarter of the Eskimoes live in snowhouses, most of which are found in the northwestern part of Greenland.

*Polar Photos*

An Eskimo boy with a small snowhouse that he has built.

The majority of Eskimoes now live in houses made of stone, wood, tar paper or skins. Many people also think that the Eskimoes use the word *igloo* only to describe a house made of snow, but in fact they call any building by this name.

Eskimoes live in small groups and the inner walls of their houses are hung with skins of seals, the way into them being through an underground passage instead of a door. This passage helps to keep in the heat and keep out the draught. The Eskimoes keep their homes warm by fires, for which blubber (fat from whales and other animals) is used as the main fuel. Within the Arctic Circle, where most of the Eskimoes live, the winters are long and dark and to light their houses they use modern kerosene lamps. Before they were able to obtain these lamps from traders they had to use ordinary oil lamps, the fuel for which was made from animal fat.

Since it is too cold and barren where the Eskimo lives for him to be able to grow crops, he must feed himself by fishing or hunting such animals as seals, whales, hares, caribou (a kind of wild reindeer) and bears. The Eskimoes are very clever hunters, and the way in which they catch the seals is especially skilful. The seals under the ice keep a breathing hole open through the ice by the warmth of their breath and the skilled hunter watches and knows when the seal is at the hole. He then thrusts down a spear and, if successful, fixes the seal on the point of the spear, after which he digs the animal out. In summer the seals bask on the rocks and the hunter kills them more easily. In the sea between Greenland and Canada the Eskimoes sometimes catch whales. Where it is possible, the men hunt the walrus, the musk ox and the caribou. The Canadian government has brought reindeer from Asia to northern Canada to mix with the caribou.

The *kayak*, a narrow canoe pointed at both ends, is the special Eskimo boat. It holds one hunter, who paddles it along. Many years ago an Eskimo man in a kayak paddled all the way to north Scotland from Greenland. Women do not travel in kayaks, but the *umiak*, another, broader, kind of boat used by Eskimoes, especially in west Greenland, is sometimes used for taking about the women and children.

On land the Eskimo mostly walks, but if suitable wood can be found he may have a sledge, which is pulled by teams of Eskimo dogs, often called huskies.

The hardy and cheerful people are very hospitable to stray hunters who may want food and

Courtesy, Canadian High Commissioner

Above: Eskimoes on the way to new hunting and fishing grounds. Right: Father and son with a white fox pelt.

shelter. They eat fat for warmth and an Eskimo wife may give her husband spoonfuls of liquid fat as a preparation for a hunting expedition. The women are expert in sewing skins together so that neither wind nor water can get in at the seams. They used to do this with needles made of bone or ivory but now they often have proper steel needles. Their clothing is chiefly made of sealskin and the skin can be turned with the fur outside or inside, according to need. Bone and walrus ivory are often used for ornaments. The people are very clever at making pictures by scratching an ivory surface and these may be seen in many museums. The Eskimoes pass the long winters when they are forced to stay so much in their huts by making these things and by telling each other stories.

**ESSAYS.** A short piece of writing, or composition, on any one subject is called an essay. When he writes an essay, an author shows in it his own feelings and ideas and describes the world as he himself sees it. Even if several people write an essay about the same subject, the finished essays will probably be quite different. In fact the more an essay shows what the author thinks and what sort of person he is, the better it is.

The first person to write essays was a Frenchman in the 16th century called Michel de Montaigne. He called his short writings "essays" because in each of them he was trying to explore some subject that interested him. (*Essayer* is the French word meaning "to try".) All sorts of things may become the subjects of essays—people, places, serious ideas about the world, an author's memories of things that he has done, or even jokes. Charles Lamb wrote one of these joking essays, called "A Dissertation upon Roast Pig" which tells the story of how a Chinese boy who was fond of playing with fire became the first person in the world to know the beautiful taste of roast pork and crackling!

When you have to write an essay yourself, it is a good plan to begin by jotting down the ideas that come into your head when you start to think about your subject, whatever it may be. The next step is to arrange these in order, so that the person who reads the essay will be led on from one to another and not get so muddled that he cannot understand what you are trying to say. An essay writer always tries to start off in a way that makes the reader want to go on reading —with a sentence that has something really interesting to say. The ending of an essay is important too, so that the reader is not disappointed but feels that the thought-journey he has taken with the author was really worth while. In writing your own essays, think carefully about the beginnings and endings and make them as interesting as you can.

Think, too, about arranging what you have to say in paragraphs. When you start on a new idea in your essay, you should begin a new paragraph, and each paragraph should deal with one main topic. Most essays need several paragraphs. Dividing an essay up into sections like this makes it much easier and clearer to read than it would be if all the ideas were run together so that you could not tell where one ended and another began.

Famous essayists include Francis Bacon and Joseph Addison (see separate articles) and Addison's Irish friend Richard Steele (1672–1729). Some of Addison's and Steele's essays were about a delightful character they invented, the kindly country squire Sir Roger de Coverley. Later on, in the 19th century, Charles Lamb wrote his essays, which are among the best loved of all English ones, under the pen-name of "Elia". His friend William Hazlitt also wrote essays, one of which describes an exciting prize-fight he went to see between two champions of the day. Other interesting essay writers, who also wrote books of other kinds, were Robert Louis Stevenson, G. K. Chesterton and Max Beerbohm.

**ESSEX** is a county on the eastern side of England. It is bounded north by Cambridgeshire and Suffolk, east by the North Sea and south by the River Thames, which divides it from Kent. To the southwest is London and to the west Hertfordshire. The River Lea, which forms part of the western boundary, flows into the Thames, as does the Roding a little to the east. The River Stour, forming most of the northern boundary, and the Crouch, Blackwater and Colne flow into the North Sea.

The coastline has many marshy creeks, or inlets, and many islands such as Canvey on the south and Foulness and Mersea on the east. At some places on the coast, for example Walton-on-the-Naze, there are low, soft cliffs which for hundreds of years have been gradually worn away by the sea. In other parts, ditches, banks and sea walls have been built to prevent flooding, and some of these sea defences have been made stronger since the great floods of 1953.

Inland the county is pleasantly undulating, or rolling, with few hills, and in some parts there are large woods. The old forest of Waltham once covered much of southwest Essex, and parts of this still remain in Epping Forest and Hainault Forest. Epping Forest used to be a favourite hiding place for highwaymen like Dick Turpin. About 1870, some people who lived near the forest tried to have it cut down so that houses and farms could be put there. Others objected to this and after a long argument parliament in 1878 decided that the forest should be kept as a big park for the people of Essex and London. The forest contains fine herds of deer, which are carefully preserved, and the most important trees are oak, ash, beech and hornbeam. The oak, which grows well on the heavy clay soil covering most of Essex, sometimes reaches a great size.

Along the coast, birds such as gulls, geese and divers can be seen and the county is visited by most of the migrant birds which fly across the North Sea in the spring and autumn.

Essex has always been mainly a farming county. In the middle ages and later sheep were pastured on the coastal marshes and were valued for the cheeses made from their milk. Dairy farming is now carried on in the Ongar and Epping districts, but most of Essex is too dry to provide good grass for pasturage. Wheat and barley are the main crops in the centre and north of Essex, while potatoes and sugar beet are also grown in some areas. Fruit growing is important around Tiptree and other places in the northeast of the county.

Before 1800 the most important towns were Colchester, Chelmsford, Saffron Walden, Maldon and Harwich. Colchester had been an important centre of the cloth industry from the 15th to the 17th century, and it was also famous for its oysters. Chelmsford was, and still is, the county town. Saffron Walden, an ancient market town, took the first part of its name from the saffron which was grown there. (See CROCUS.) Harwich, the principal port of Essex, had a shipyard which supplied many ships for the Royal Navy in the 17th and 18th centuries, and Maldon was a small port and market town.

During the 19th century the Essex villages nearest to London—West Ham, East Ham, Leyton and Walthamstow—grew into large towns with industries of many kinds. The railway works at Stratford (in West Ham) and the new docks along the Thames provided work for thousands of men. After about 1900 other places in south Essex became towns. However, in 1965 West Ham, East Ham, Chingford, Walthamstow, Leyton, Wanstead and Woodford, together

with Romford, Hornchurch, Dagenham and Barking, all became part of Greater London. This was because the London Government Act 1963 altered the boundaries so that London took in the southwest corner of Essex. The two new towns built in Essex under the New Towns Act of 1946 are Harlow and Basildon.

Since 1800 some of the older towns have also grown much bigger, especially those on the main railway lines. Chelmsford and Colchester now have large engineering works and Braintree is important for its silk factories. There is a nuclear power station at Bradwell-on-Sea.

The seaside resorts have grown up mainly since about 1880, although Southend-on-Sea, which is the oldest and largest in Essex, had begun to grow by 1800. (See SOUTHEND-ON-SEA.) Southend, Clacton on Sea, Walton-on-the-Naze and Frinton provide many amusements for children, while others like Burnham-on-Crouch are more popular with grown-up people, especially the yachtsmen whose boats can often be seen in the river mouths. Although Essex has a long indented coastline the sea is in most places too shallow for big ships. The only important port is Tilbury on the River Thames, which has a very large passenger and cargo traffic. Southend-on-Sea has a busy airport and two places in Essex—Stansted in the west and Foulness Island in the east—were proposed as possible sites for London's third airport.

The road from London to Chelmsford and Colchester was probably made first of all by the Romans. The main railway line, which was built about 1840, runs near to this road and has an important branch from Colchester to Harwich, from which passengers travel by sea to the Netherlands, Denmark and Norway.

### Essex History

In Roman times Colchester was called Camulodunum and was one of the chief towns in Britain. In the year A.D. 60 it was destroyed by Queen Boadicea when she revolted against the Romans, but it was rebuilt and had a forum, or market place, a temple and a theatre. Parts of the Roman walls can still be seen, and also the Balkerne Gate. The Saxons began to settle in Essex about the year 400 and the name of the county actually means "the land of the East Saxons". Their earliest settlements are shown by the names of places ending in *-ing, -ham* and *-ton*. Some of these were near the coast, like Tendring, Tillingham and Frinton. Others, like Patching, Hedingham and Loughton, were inland in the river valleys or near the Roman roads. A few Saxon churches are still standing. St. Peter's-on-the-Wall, at Bradwell-on-Sea, was built about 654 by St. Cedd, and Greensted Church, near Ongar, has wooden walls almost a thousand years old.

In Anglo-Saxon times, Essex was often raided by the Danes, or Northmen, who defeated the Anglo-Saxons at the Battle of Maldon in 991. Many of them settled in Essex and some village names, such as Thorpe-le-Soken and Kirby-le-Soken, are of Danish origin.

The Normans added surnames to many villages, such as Stondon Massey, Tolleshunt D'Arcy and Theydon Garnon. They built the great castles which can still be seen at Colchester and Hedingham, as well as many monasteries such as Waltham Abbey in the west and Prittlewell Priory near Southend. The last abbot of St. John's Abbey, Colchester, was executed by Henry VIII for opposing the break-up of the monasteries in the 16th century.

Robert Fitzwalter, lord of Dunmow, was the leader of the barons who forced King John to agree to Magna Carta in 1215, and four of his principal supporters came from Essex. (At about this time there started the custom of the Dunmow Flitch, described in the article BACON.)

In the Civil War in the 17th century Essex supported parliament, but the royalists took Colchester and held it through a long siege in 1648, when food became so scarce that the defenders had to eat dog-flesh.

During the Napoleonic Wars in the early 19th century the Essex coasts were fortified with Martello towers, some of which can still be seen at Clacton and other places. (See MARTELLO TOWERS.)

It was in the Colchester district that the worst earthquake in Britain occurred on April 22, 1884. It was especially severe in the villages south of the town and in the little port of Wivenhoe, and more than 1,200 buildings were damaged. The Lord Mayor of London raised a special fund to help pay for the repairs.

Essex does not have many very large buildings because there is no local building stone, but there are splendid churches at Thaxted, Saffron Walden and Castle Hedingham. At Willingale there are two churches standing in one churchyard. They were built by two landowners who were rivals. The county has many timber-framed houses of the 13th, 14th and 15th centuries, some plastered and others with brick panels.

Audley End, at Saffron Walden, is the finest house in Essex. It was built about 1604 by Thomas Howard, Earl of Suffolk, and later became one of the palaces of Charles II. New Hall, Boreham, which was built by Henry VIII, was the home of his daughter Mary when she was still a princess and later belonged to Oliver Cromwell for a short time.

William Harvey, who lived at Hempstead, near Saffron Walden, and died there in 1657, made the great discovery of how the blood circulates in the human body.

**ESTONIA** is a small country that has become part of the U.S.S.R. It is not much larger than the highlands of Scotland and about as far north. On the west of Estonia is the Baltic Sea, on the north is the Gulf of Finland and it is bounded by Latvia on the south and the rest of the U.S.S.R. on the east. It is a flat land, all fields and pastures, marshes and lakes, with dark evergreen forests. The winter is long and very cold, but when the summer comes suddenly late

*Keystone*

Above: An Estonian girl weaving at a hand loom. Right: The market place at Kuresaar, a town on the island of Saaremaa. This large island, 45 miles long, lies across the mouth of the Gulf of Riga. The people live mainly by farming and fishing.

in May, the country springs alive with lilac and apple blossom and for two months it is as warm as England.

Most of the Estonians work on the land, growing flax and raising cattle and poultry on their collective farms where all the workers co-operate or work together. They produce more milk, butter and meat than they need, and these are exported. Oil and gas for fuel are obtained from shale (a kind of slaty stone) and gas from shale is supplied by pipeline to Leningrad. The chief Estonian industries are engineering, shipbuilding and the production of cotton and linen textiles. One of the largest cotton-mills in Europe is at Narva on the Narva River, which provides the hydro-electric power. Timber from the forests is used for making furniture, matches and wood-pulp.

The people speak a language that is unlike any other except that of the Finns, who are related to them. They are livelier than the Finns, gayer and more talkative, but they have much in common with them. They are good farmers, good workmen and good athletes.

The capital and chief port of Estonia is Tallinn, on the Gulf of Finland, with a population of about 330,000. It is a quaint town and grew up around a castle, which still stands, along with the walls that enclosed the ancient city. Like all Estonian towns it is clean and well kept. Tartu (Dorpat) is the old university town. The university was founded by Gustavus Adolphus of Sweden in 1632.

Estonian children go to school until they are 15 or 16. As well as the university there are academies of science and agriculture and several technical colleges and schools of art and music.

## History

Throughout their troubled history the Estonians have had a struggle to keep their independence. In the 13th century the Danes made several attempts to subdue them and Tallinn was founded by Danish crusaders in 1219. In 1346, after a series of revolts against the Danes, most of the country was sold to a German crusading order known as the Teutonic Knights, who made the people into slaves. The descendants of these crusaders, known as the Baltic Barons, remained the Estonians' masters until the 20th century, although the country was ruled by the kings of Sweden for a time in the 16th and 17th centuries and by the tsars of Russia from 1721 till 1917.

World War I gave the Estonians the opportunity they had been waiting for. Both the German and the Russian empires fell and the Estonians were able to achieve their independence. They set up a democratic republic (one where the government is by the people), dividing the land into small farms and devoting great attention to education. In 1939, after the signing of the German-Soviet pact of non-aggression, Estonia was forced to give the U.S.S.R. certain naval and air bases. Russian troops occupied the whole country in 1940, but in 1941 it was invaded by the Germans. In 1944 the Russians returned to the attack and drove out the Germans. Since then Estonia has been one of the republics of the Union of Soviet Socialist Republics (U.S.S.R.).

Estonia has a population of about 1,300,000.

**ETCHING.** When you see the kind of picture that is called an etching you may think that it looks rather like a drawing made with pen and ink, for the background of an etching is usually white and the objects shown against this background are black. Some of the black may be solid, but other parts are made up of lines of different thicknesses. In fact, an etching is not simply a drawing in the ordinary sense of the word, but is also a picture made by a process of printing.

The word etching comes from the Dutch word *etzen,* which means "to eat", and an etching is made by drawing lines on a piece of metal and then putting the metal into an acid which "eats into" the lines and makes them deep. When this has been done, ink is put into the lines on the metal plate and a piece of paper is pressed down on it. This makes a picture come out on the paper, with black lines printed from the inked lines in the metal, and the rest white. This is called a "print", and many prints can be made from one metal plate.

Several famous artists included fine etchings in their work; the greatest of them was the Dutch painter Rembrandt, about whom there is a separate article.

The best pictures for etching are those that have plenty of contrast of light and shade, and interesting details which will show up well in the finished print. A good subject, for example, might be a windmill, the sails looking dark against a bank of light clouds, the door and window lying in shadow and the base of the windmill partly hidden by dark bushes.

The metal plates for etching are usually made of zinc or copper, highly polished and free from scratches. For copper plates, the acid used to eat into the lines is nitric acid or a mixture of acids including nitric acid.

If the copper plate were put into the acid just as it is, it would get eaten away all over, but for an etching the only parts to be eaten away are the lines of the picture. In order to keep the acid from working on the plate all over, the whole surface of the metal is covered with a special substance before the drawing is made on it. This substance is called a "ground" and is made chiefly of wax. The metal plate is warmed slowly and then the wax mixture is spread evenly all over the surface; it hardens as it cools, and makes a golden brown skin over the metal.

The drawings may not show very clearly on this, however, and so many artists cover it with a layer of soot, by holding the plate just over the flame of a lighted taper. They can then trace their designs on to the sooty surface through red or yellow carbon paper.

Now comes the stage of drawing, or "needling", on to the plate. Some artists use special etching needles for this, but any strong rigid needle does perfectly well. For etching the needle should not be sharp, for it must not dig into or scratch the actual metal of the plate but simply go through the wax ground. The artist goes over his traced design with the needle just heavily enough to remove the ground, so that when he has finished the lines of the design are free from wax. This means that the acid can "eat away" the metal in these lines, while the rest of the surface is protected. The back of the plate is usually painted with a varnish which is not affected by acid, known as a "stopping out" varnish.

## Biting, Inking and Printing

The action of the acid in eating away the metal is called "biting". The process of biting all the lines of the design as the artist wants them is the most complicated part of etching. In his finished picture he does not want all the lines to be the same thickness and blackness, and the differences are made not by drawing some lines wider or deeper on the metal—for, of course, the needle has not been allowed to dig into the

An etching by Rembrandt, the greatest master of the art.

metal itself at all—but by letting the acid work on some lines longer than on others. The longer the metal is left in the acid, the deeper the lines become; and when the biting is finished, the deeper the line, the more ink can be pressed into it and the blacker the mark on the paper.

The plate is lowered carefully into the dish or "bath" of acid which at once begins to work on the lines that have been drawn with the needle. After a few minutes the plate is taken out, and already the acid has bitten grooves wherever the copper has been exposed. If the artist thinks that the lines of the light parts of the drawing are deep enough he paints those parts with the stopping-out varnish so that the acid cannot get at them any more. Then the plate goes into the acid a second time, until the lines of the "medium" parts of the design are deep enough. These are then painted over with varnish in their turn and the plate is put back into the acid until the lines of the darkest parts are deeper still.

When the biting is finished, the plate is cleaned with methylated spirits and turpentine to get rid of all the ground and varnish, and it is then ready for printing. Special thick printing ink is used, put on to the plate with a dabber or felt roller; a screwing movement of the hand makes sure that the ink is forced well down into the deepest lines. When all the lines are well filled with ink, the surface of the plate is quickly and lightly rubbed over with a clean rag so that the ink is left only in the lines.

The press that is used for printing etchings is simply a flat piece or "bed" of metal which is made to pass between two heavy rollers turned by handles. The clean copper plate is placed in the middle of the "bed"; a piece of paper that has been thoroughly damped is laid over the plate, and then a thick blanket is put on top. When the handles of the press are turned, the whole arrangement slides smoothly between the rollers. The weight of the rollers forces the damped paper into the etching lines so that when the paper is lifted off the plate the lines on it are raised up a little, or "in relief".

In the kind of etching called *aquatint*, a special sort of ground is used which makes it possible for an artist to produce particularly delicate tones and shading in his prints.

**ETHER** is a clear liquid with a strong but rather sickly smell. As it boils at 35 degrees Centigrade—which is a little below blood heat—it very easily turns into a heavy gas or vapour. It was one of the earliest substances used to make the patient unconscious during a surgical operation, and was first used for this by the American doctor Crawford Long in 1842. Its vapour catches fire so easily that it has now been replaced by safer anaesthetics such as nitrous oxide (see ANAESTHETIC).

**ETHIOPIA,** or Abyssinia as it used to be called, is a country in East Africa. It is about twice the size of France and is bordered by the Red Sea, the Sudan, Kenya, the Somali Republic and the French Territory of Afars and Issas (formerly French Somaliland). Ethiopia is now better known than in the past, when it was hard to reach. From the bordering deserts, swamps and scorching plains to the west and south, there

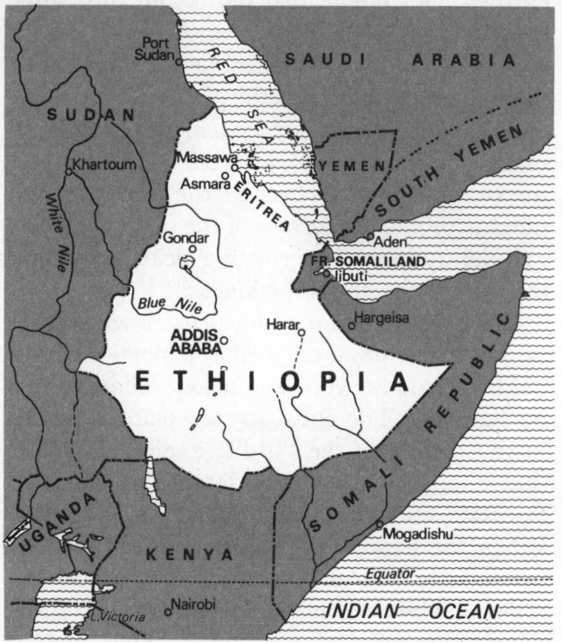


rises the great plateau, or tableland, which covers the western half of the country. This plateau, lying between 5,000 and 8,000 feet above sea level, is crossed by many mountain ranges of fantastic shapes. Some of these mountains reach 15,000 feet, but they are never snow covered. There are tremendous gorges down which flow three of the main rivers feeding the Nile—the Atbara, the Abbai or Blue Nile and the Sobat. Every year, between May and September, the rain falls very heavily and the flooded rivers carry away some of the rich Ethiopian soil, taking it westwards to the Nile and so to the fertile Nile delta in Egypt. The main river flowing east, the Awash, also becomes very full during the rains and overflows its banks, and yet becomes lost in marshes and salt lakes in the desert, never reaching the Red Sea. In the great Rift Valley there is a line of beautiful lakes, while to the northwest is the larger lake Tana.

The eastern half of the country is not so high as the west, although a range of mountains does stretch eastwards to the Somali Republic. In the north the mountains come steeply to an end and then the land slopes rapidly down to the strip of very hot, low desert along the shores of the Red Sea. In the southeast the country slopes down more gradually to hot, semi-desert lands.

Large forests, containing more than a hundred different kinds of trees, still exist both in the highlands and in the lowlands. The desert lands bear mainly scrub, but after rain vegetation suitable for grazing springs up for several weeks.

Lions are found in the east, and leopards, both black and spotted, are found over most of the country. Except in the well-populated areas, there is an abundance of wild life, including zebras, ostriches, monkeys, elephants, and many kinds of antelope. In many of the rivers and lakes there are hippopotamuses and crocodiles.

The name Ethiopia means the "land of the people with the burnt faces". However, the brown-skinned Amhara, who are the true Ethiopians, inhabit only the north. There, Christianity came from Egypt as long ago as the 4th century. Ethiopia has many races and religions. In the centre of the country the Galla peoples are numerous and have much darker skins. In the west are Negro tribes. In the east are Somalis and Afars (Danakils) who have Arab blood.

The official and most common religion in Ethiopia is Christianity, but along the Red Sea coast, in the deserts of the southeast and on the western borders there are numerous Moslems (see ISLAM), while in parts of the south and southwest there are numbers of pagans. There is still one small tribe which remains faithful to Judaism (the religion of the Jews).

The national language is Amharic. Originally, this was spoken only in the north, but it is now spreading to other parts because all government business is done in it and the children learn to read and write it in the many schools which are being built all over the country. The main language in the extreme north is similar to Amharic

## FACTS ABOUT ETHIOPIA

AREA: 471,776 square miles.
POPULATION (estimated in 1967): 23,457,000.
CAPITAL: Addis Ababa.
KIND OF COUNTRY: Self-governing empire.
CHIEF EXPORTS: Coffee, hides and skins, cereals and pulses, oilseeds.
IMPORTANT TOWNS: Addis Ababa, Asmara, Dase, Harar, Diredawa.
EDUCATION: School attendance is not compulsory.

and is known as Tigrinya. Arabic is spoken in the coastal and border areas, but there are many other languages used, notably Galla and Somali. Geez, an ancient language which is the father of Amharic and Tigrinya, is now only used by the priests in the Ethiopian church services.

Farming and stock raising are the main occupations of the people in the settled areas on the high plateau and it is there, where there is plenty of rain and the weather is never very hot or very cold, that the best crops are grown. There the people, usually using simple home-made tools, grow millet and barley, some maize and wheat, pulse and oil seeds. The chief crop is coffee, which first grew in Ethiopia and which is still mostly picked from wild plants. Not much fruit is grown on the plateau and it mostly comes from the lower levels. On the northern pasture lands, large numbers of cattle are kept, as well as flocks of fat-tailed sheep, which store fat on either side of their tails. In the desert areas, where the population are mostly nomads (wanderers), the camel is the most important animal, but sheep and cattle are also raised. Goats exist all over the country. Most of the hides and skins are sold abroad, but some are taken by tanneries which supply leather and footwear for the local people.

*Paul Popper*

The fertile Ethiopian highlands have a healthy climate.

There are few industries in Ethiopia. A railway links Addis Ababa, the capital, with Jibuti in the French Territory of Afars and Issas, and another in Eritrea links Massawa with Asmara. Since the Italian colony of Eritrea (in the northeast) was included in the Ethiopian Empire in 1952, the country has had two ports of its own, Massawa and Assab. Most of the overseas trade passes through Jibuti or Assab. The capital (see ADDIS ABABA) is now linked by air with Khartoum in the Sudan, Cairo in Egypt, Aden on the Red Sea, Nairobi in Kenya, and with Europe. Spreading outwards from the capital to the provinces there is a system of roads which is being constantly extended. Even so, during the heavy rains many areas cannot be reached from the capital by motor transport because the roads are impassable.

## Ethiopian History

The origins of Ethiopia go far back into history. It is believed to have existed as an independent kingdom in one form or another, except for a short period when it was ruled by Italy, since about 1100 B.C. It is said that Menelik, the first king of what is known as the Solomonic line, was the son of Solomon and the Queen of Sheba. That is why the Emperor of Ethiopia has the title of "Lion of Judah", for Solomon was a member of the royal family of Judah, one of the Biblical Twelve Tribes. When the armies of Islam swept through Africa in the 7th century A.D. Ethiopia was left as "an island of Christianity in a Moslem sea". This explains the legend of the great Christian kingdom of Prester John in Ethiopia which grew up in Europe in the middle ages, when people were confused about the various stories which reached them from both Africa and the East. (See PRESTER JOHN.) The country did not really become known to Europeans until the early 16th century, when the Portuguese, having discovered the route to India round the Cape of Good Hope, sent a mission to Ethiopia. They later helped the Ethiopians to defeat the invading Arab armies which had plundered most of the country.

When the Suez Canal was opened in 1869,

Europeans could reach Ethiopia quite easily from the Mediterranean. In 1885 the Italians occupied Massawa and by 1898 they governed the whole of Eritrea. The Ethiopians had thoroughly defeated them when they advanced to Aduwa in 1896, but in 1935 the Italians again attacked in great force and this time occupied the whole of Ethiopia, driving the Emperor Haile Selassie into exile. However, during World War II British Commonwealth forces from the Sudan and Kenya defeated the Italians and in 1941 the Emperor returned. In 1952 Eritrea again became part of the Ethiopian Empire. Since 1941 the Emperor has established a system of government on modern lines and the country is ruled by him through ministers in Addis Ababa and the governors-general of the 14 provinces. In 1962 Eritrea voted to become part of Ethiopia.

**ETIQUETTE** is the name given to the rules which tell people how to behave when they meet one another, especially when they meet on a formal or ceremonial occasion such as a dinner-party or a wedding. Customs and habits change very quickly and people do not think about etiquette nearly as much nowadays as they did in the early part of the 20th century, but there are still occasions when it is useful to know the correct way to dress and behave. The remainder of this article explains some of the rules of etiquette, past and present.

Like most human habits, etiquette varies in different countries, so that what is polite for one nation is not always so for another, and it also changes from time to time, so that the rules of one century are not the same as those of another. In Stuart times, for instance, it was quite correct for men to wear their hats at meals, whereas today it is generally considered impolite for a man to keep his hat on in the house at all. Or again, at the beginning of this century no girl ever danced more than two or three times with the same man at a ball, unless she was engaged to him, and she was not permitted to go out in the evening unless accompanied by her mother or by a chaperon, a married or elderly woman whose job was to take charge of her. In most Western countries ideas on these things have changed and etiquette has changed with them, but in Italy and Spain, for example, young women are still much less free to move about unaccompanied than they are in Great Britain or the United States.

It is polite for a boy to open the door for a girl.

Many social customs are so simple and obvious that they would occur to any thoughtful person without the need of rules. At home or when at someone else's house, a man would normally open a door for a woman or an aged person. He would not sit down when a woman was standing or push into a room in front of her. He would not let her carry a heavy burden if he could do it himself. (You should not, however, jump to the conclusion that wherever women are treated differently the men must be rude. Manners grow out of a people's whole way of life and religion, and where these are different from ours so will their manners be different.) A well-mannered person would not talk all the time himself, giving others no chance to put their point of view; neither would he interrupt a meeting or a service by talking and whispering.

Equally, he would try to be punctual for an appointment, since other people's time is quite as valuable as his own, and to be kept waiting is annoying and inconvenient. There is an idea among some people that women can be unpunctual, without impoliteness, when meeting a man, but this is not so. Punctuality has been called the politeness of kings and should be shown by both sexes. To be late for a meal is bad manners, for it may mean that the meal is spoilt for everyone else; and to break an appointment without due notice and apology shows lack of consideration for others.

Courtesies of this sort need no explanation, for they are simply the result of taking thought for others. There are, however, some rules of etiquette whose origin is not so obvious and

A boy takes off his right glove in order to shake hands.

which are really survivals from an earlier age. It is usual for a man to remove his glove when shaking hands and this is not done, as might be supposed, for fear that the glove may be dirty. It is a very ancient habit that goes back to more dangerous and violent times, when the glove was removed to prove that there was no dagger hidden in it. Again, when a man and woman are walking together in the street, he usually takes the outside of the pavement. Some people think that the origin of this custom was to give the man more freedom of movement in case he had to use his sword. Perhaps a better explanation is that, in olden days when roads were narrow and muddy, the person on the outside of the pavement was likely to be in danger from passing vehicles and be splashed by mud. Today the outside of the pavement is still the more dangerous.

Another survival is that when a man drinks from the loving-cup—a large bowl, often in silver, from which everyone drinks in turn—at any London livery company's banquet, his neighbours on either side rise and remain standing until he has finished. They did so, originally, in case they had to defend him from attack while he was drinking from the heavy cup and unable to defend himself. (See Livery Companies.)

## Calling and At Home Days

In England when a new family settled in a district, they were not formally accepted into its social life until the people who had lived there for a long time had called upon them and left visiting cards; that is, small white cards with the owner's name printed on them. It was for the old inhabitants to decide whether they wanted to know the new people, and the first move was with them. In France, however, the newcomers called upon their neighbours first.

Before World Wars I and II, which altered many old habits, calling played a great part in social life, and there were rules about the leaving of cards and the time to be spent in each house. Many women had regular At Home days, once a month or oftener, when they were at home between certain hours and ready to entertain any acquaintance who chose to call. The time and day was printed on their visiting cards so that everyone knew when the At Home day was.

Nowadays, when most people are much busier than formerly, this custom has fallen into disuse and visits (other than those to intimate friends) are more likely to be the result of a direct invitation. But the old At Home day had many advantages, for the caller was quite certain that his visit was convenient and the hostess was usually sure of seeing all her friends in turn without the trouble of sending out invitations. To be "at home" in the social sense means to be "ready to receive visitors". Therefore, it was quite correct—and not untruthful—to say that a person was "not at home", even though he or she was in the house at the time.

A boy walks on the kerb side of the pavement.

## Letters and Invitations

Etiquette also teaches one how to write and address letters correctly. Letters must be suited to the people who are going to receive them, since one that is suitable for a close friend is unsuitable for a slight acquaintance, and a business letter should not be worded in the same friendly manner as a letter to one's aunt. A letter which has a formal beginning should also have a formal ending, such as "Yours faithfully" or "Yours truly". (See Letter Writing.)

The address on the envelope is also important

and care should be taken to see that it is correct. Most people would take trouble if they were writing to a duke or to an archbishop because these people have definite titles, the first because he has inherited it and the second because it shows his position in the church. Carelessness is often shown, however, over the form of address for people with less obvious titles and over the use of the word "Esquire".

For some occasions a formally worded card is sent.

This word comes from the days of chivalry and originally meant "shield-bearer". In later years it was used for a gentleman of established position who had no other title. It is now used far more freely but people do not always realize that it is a title in itself and must never be joined to any other. Thus, when writing to someone called Henry Martin, it is correct to put "Henry Martin, Esq.," on the envelope, whereas "Mr. Henry Martin, Esq.," is too much. If in the course of time Henry Martin becomes a clergyman or a captain, he is no longer addressed as "Esquire" but by the titles appropriate to clergymen and captains. (See ADDRESS, FORMS OF.)

Sending and replying to invitations is also a matter of rule and custom. For a friendly gathering, a pleasant letter or a telephone call is enough, but for ceremonial occasions a formally worded card is sent and a formal reply expected.

## Dress

Good manners demand that dress should if possible be suited to the occasions on which it is worn. To wear elaborate clothes when simple ones are called for is as wrong as to appear in everyday clothes at a dinner or dance. Etiquette teaches men that they are expected to wear a special kind of tail-coat, trousers and white tie for a ball, and a dinner-jacket and black tie for a formal dinner. When they receive an invitation to a daytime function the invitation card may state that "morning dress" is to be worn, and they know that they must wear another sort of tail-coat with special trousers, waistcoat and tie. Etiquette also lays down the full-dress attire of peers of the realm or Knights of the Garter and the occasions on which it is worn. (The article DRESS describes different types of dress throughout the ages.)

## Rank and Precedence

In Great Britain the law treats everybody as equals, but socially there are many differences. The sovereign and the royal family, dukes, marquesses, earls, viscounts and barons, privy councillors, members of the government, ambassadors, dignitaries of the church, baronets, knights, mayors, sheriffs, judges and many others all have their special place in society, and titles appropriate to their rank. What are known as the rules of precedence tell us where these places are in relation to each other. Without definite rules it would be very difficult for the ordinary person to know how each of the people mentioned earlier should be addressed, either in speech or by letter, or in what order he should sit at table or enter a room at ceremonial dinners or gatherings. It is neither snobbish nor cringing to be careful of such matters, for the rules merely provide an orderly way of doing things and are intended to avoid awkwardness.

Introducing a young man to an older one.

The rules of precedence do not apply only to occasions when very important guests are being entertained. People should still follow them when, for example, they are arranging a meeting or a dinner at which the mayor of the town, the vicar of the parish and an important visiting speaker are all present together. Even a simple dinner party may need some knowledge of these rules, for the host is expected to take the most important lady guest into the dining room; and when introducing two strangers he should present the less to the more important of the two, if they are both of the same sex.

### Professional Etiquette

Finally, there is what is known as professional etiquette, a code of rules for the conduct of doctors, lawyers and other professional men. This code is drawn up by the councils which govern each profession and is not part of the law of the land. A man who broke it could not be summoned before a court of law—unless he was thought to have broken the law as well—but the council of his profession could withdraw his right to practise his profession any more. A doctor never advertises, for it would be considered very improper for him to do so. He would not normally accept as a patient a man who was on another doctor's list, nor would he attend such a person unless he had been called in as a consultant. If he makes any new discovery in medicine he does not keep it for his own use but makes it freely available to all, so that the knowledge of healing may be advanced. Above all, he never reveals or discusses with outsiders the ailments and secrets of his patients.

In the same way, bankers and lawyers are expected to preserve silence about the affairs of their clients and to uphold by their daily behaviour the dignity of their profession. Professional etiquette is based upon a sense of honour and the desire to serve the community and is of great importance to everybody.

**ETNA, MOUNT.** One of the most famous of all volcanoes (see VOLCANO) is Mount Etna in the northeast of the Mediterranean island of Sicily. It is the highest volcano in Europe, reaching nearly 11,000 feet above the sea. A plume of smoke may usually be seen drifting from the summit of its huge, rounded cone and many smaller cones on its slopes also give off steam and fumes from time to time. A whitish crust of sulphur forms round some of these and, being very useful in industry, is gathered by the people who live on the mountain slopes. (See SULPHUR.)

Etna seldom bursts into a violent explosive eruption, though at times lava (about which there is a separate article) pours out from its crater. The oval-shaped base of the mountain is about 90 miles round and nearly the whole of this great mass has been built up from these lava streams. The molten rock or lava fills up the hollow crater and overflows its edge to flow in streams down the sides towards the lower part of the mountain. Fortunately the lava usually flows slowly. When it does overflow the people living in villages in its path generally have time to remove their goods, but their homes are sometimes destroyed and their crops burned.

More violent eruptions do take place at long intervals. The nearby city of Catania has been destroyed several times, and so have many villages and smaller towns. Great damage and loss of life were caused by eruptions in 1381, 1669 and 1928. The village of Mascoli was buried by the 1928 eruption. The eruptions in 1950 and 1951 were probably the most violent for 200 years. During these violent eruptions, great clouds of ashes are thrown out and spread more widely than the lava streams. In time ashes and

*Aerofilms Library from Ewing Galloway*

**Mount Etna erupting, with snow on the upper slopes.**

lava are turned into very rich soil. It is this which draws the peasants to the mountain slopes to cultivate vineyards and orchards.

The ancient Greeks thought of Mount Etna as the chimney of Hephaestus' forge. (Hephaestus was the Greek god of fire.) During the middle ages and in early modern times people looked upon it as a chimney of hell.

**ETON WALL GAME.** The Wall game is one of two special kinds of football that are played only at Eton College. (The other one is called the Field game.) The wall which gives the game its name is a high brick one along one side of a playing field. Five yards from the wall is a furrow which runs parallel to it along all its length. The long, narrow strip of ground between the wall and the furrow is the pitch. The ball is round and about the size of a human head.

Play begins roughly at the middle of the wall and each team of ten players tries to drive back its opponents and the ball to the far end of the wall, which is where scoring can take place. Some of the players form a kind of scrum, called a "bully", against the wall. They can make progress towards the far end either by pushing their opponents back (the bully-players often have the ball between their knees while this is going on) or by kicking the ball outside the furrow towards the end they want to reach. When this happens, the next bully is formed against the wall opposite the place where the ball was stopped by one of the other side's players. If the ball is kicked inside the pitch the "behinds" (defence players) of the other side have a chance of kicking it back.

*Radio Times Hulton Picture Library*
Forming a scrum or "bully" in the Wall game at Eton.

The scoring area at each end of the Wall is known as "calx", and the scores that can be made from it are one point for a "shy" (that is, touching the ball up against the wall), and 10 points for a goal. The goal at one end of the pitch is a door, and at the other end a tree.

When the Wall game was invented, probably in the 18th century, the wall, the door and the tree were standing as they are today. The game was made to fit these things, and therefore it cannot be played anywhere else.

**ETYMOLOGY** is the name for the science which finds out where the words in a language came from and when they were first used. The language people speak and write—whether it is English or any other—is always growing and changing. New words are made or borrowed from other languages, and old words can change their meaning or their spelling. A person who studies the etymology of a language is in fact studying all the different ways in which the language has grown up. The English language is made up of words that come from many other languages as well as from the earliest kind of English called Old English, or Anglo-Saxon. Many come from Latin and French, some from ancient Greek, some even from Persian, Indian and Chinese languages.

An etymological dictionary shows not only a word's meaning but also where it first came from, when it is first recorded in writing and the various ways it has been used. (See ENGLISH LANGUAGE; WORDS.)

**EUCALYPTUS,** the strong-scented oil often used to clear colds in the head, comes from an Australian tree which is also known as the gum tree. It is one of the largest trees in the world and belongs to the myrtle family. With its tall, straight trunk and shiny, leathery, smooth-edged leaves, it is unusually striking in appearance. The saplings, or young trees, sometimes grow as much as 13 feet in one year, and many of them reach a height of over 300 feet. The flowers are small and white or yellow and sometimes the stamens inside are richly coloured. Later the flowers are replaced by woody, cup-shaped fruits which are filled with tiny seeds.

Although a native of Australia, the eucalyptus has been introduced into Europe, India, South America, the southern United States and parts of Africa, including Algeria, Egypt and Natal in South Africa. There are about 500 kinds of eucalyptus, among them being the blue gum, the stringy bark and the jarrah tree. The name gum tree was given to the eucalyptus because gum oozes out of its trunk.

Eucalyptus trees grow in thick forests in Australia. Because they need a great deal of moisture they are often planted in wet regions where the malaria-carrying mosquitoes breed, as the trees help to draw the water out of the fever-infested swamps.

The oil comes from the pores, or holes, with which the leaves are dotted. It is straw coloured and smells rather like camphor, and is sometimes used as an antiseptic, as well as for colds. The wood of many kinds of eucalyptus is tough and hard and is valuable for building docks and ships. It is also used for furniture making, as it polishes well. In Australia the wood is burnt for fuel and the outer bark is used in tanning, while a fibre used in making cord and paper is taken from the inner bark. Bee-keepers value these trees for the quantity of nectar they provide.

**EUCLID** was a famous teacher of mathematics and particularly of geometry. He lived about 300 B.C. and was asked by King Ptolemy I of Egypt to set up a school in the city of Alexandria, then the most important centre of learning in the world. He is thought to have been Greek.

Before Euclid's time quite a lot was known about geometry but most of the knowledge was no more than a set of bare facts or statements without any links between them. Euclid went to work to collect and rearrange all the known facts about geometry in step-by-step order and added some new propositions and proofs which he had thought of himself. This great collection was written out in 13 rolls of parchment or "books" which together were called the *Elements,* and translations of it into other languages were used for teaching geometry for more than 2,000 years. The modern textbooks used in schools are based on the same ideas but are set out rather differently. (See GEOMETRY.)

Euclid's "school" at Alexandria was probably more like what we should call a university because the pupils were expected to have a fairly good knowledge of mathematics. We can picture them gathered round their teacher as he spread a layer of sand on the floor and drew figures in it with the point of a stick to show them the problems and answers.

Boys and girls at school who find geometry difficult may like to know that King Ptolemy asked if there were no quicker way of learning it than studying the *Elements.* Euclid answered "There is no royal road to geometry"—meaning that there are some subjects that even kings must work hard to understand.

**EUPHRATES RIVER.** Rising in the mountains of Armenia, the River Euphrates flows for 2,200 miles to the Persian Gulf.

In its upper course the river crosses the high bleak plateau, or tableland, of Anatolia in Turkey. It then flows southeastwards across a wide strip of steppe country inhabited by wandering shepherds (see STEPPES). At one point it appears to be about to join the River Tigris at Baghdad but turns southwards instead. From here to the sea it flows over a perfectly flat plain which is really the combined delta of the two rivers. (See DELTA.)

When the snow in the Armenian mountains melts in spring, great floods pass down the Euphrates, carrying with them enormous quantities of mud. The current is slowed down by the gentle slope and begins to deposit or drop the mud in the river channel. This causes the main river to break up into many branches and the flood waters spread widely over the flat country.

In the 1960s the Keban Dam was built across the Euphrates in central Anatolia to provide hydro-electric power, and work on the Al Tabqa Dam in Syria was started for power and irrigation. (See IRRIGATION.)

**EUREKA STOCKADE.** When Australians talk about the Eureka Stockade they are referring to the goldminers' revolt in the old colony of Victoria in 1854, during which the miners built a large stockade, or fortification, across the streets of Ballarat. The miners, or "diggers" as they were called, had for a long time been angry about the way the Ballarat Goldfields were run, and they were particularly annoyed at having to pay for a licence to dig for gold and show this to the police when asked. Then in the middle of 1854 the Governor tightened up the regulations still further.

On October 6 a hotel-keeper named Bentley killed a miner, and when the magistrates let him off on a charge of murder the angry miners rioted and burnt Bentley's hotel. For this, three of them were arrested and sent to prison, and on November 11 the others met together and started the Ballarat Reform League. They demanded among other things, that in future all adults in Victoria should be allowed to help in choosing all the members of their own parliament, that miners' licences should be done away with and that the three imprisoned diggers should be freed.

The Governor, however, refused to release the men and sent more troops to Ballarat, so on November 29 the miners decided to burn all their licences and hoist a republican flag, meaning that they no longer accepted Queen Victoria as their rightful ruler. Next day, the police made a raid in which they asked to see all licences, and several diggers were arrested and some wounded. About 200 miners then built and manned the Eureka Stockade which, at dawn on December 3, was attacked by almost the same number of troops and policemen. The miners soon lost the battle and at least 20 of them were killed, together with five soldiers and policemen.

In 1855, partly as a result of this affair, the British government allowed the colony to elect its own two houses of parliament and largely to govern itself. The miners' leaders were found not guilty of treason and two of them, Peter Lalor and John Humffray, later became Cabinet ministers in Victoria. Besides this, diggers were no longer made to buy a licence, but merely to keep a paper called a Miner's Right, which showed that they had a claim on

The diggers who manned the stockade were untrained and short of ammunition. In about 15 minutes it was all over.

a certain piece of land. This could not be asked for by the police, so the miners had in fact obtained many of their demands.

**EURIPIDES** (*c.* 484–407 B.C.). This Athenian playwright was one of the three great writers of tragedy in ancient Greece. Tragic plays in those days were always written about characters and happenings that were already well known in stories or legends, and so a playwright did not invent the plots for his plays as writers do today. Euripides, however, in spite of taking these well known stories, several of which had been used already by other playwrights, made his plays seem very new and different. Instead of showing heroes acting out their great and terrible stories as if they were superhuman, or "larger than life", he made them seem true and natural with the weaknesses and feelings that human beings really have. This makes an audience sympathize very much with the characters on the stage.

Euripides' plays were written in great and beautiful poetry. He is known to have written very many, though only 18 still exist today, and he was famous in all Greece during his life.

He was said to have been born on the island of Salamis, and he died at the court of Archilaus, King of Macedonia. As an old man, according to a story, he lived in a cave with two openings and a beautiful sea view, and there people could see him "all day long, thinking to himself and writing, for he simply despised anything that was not great and high".

**EUROPE.** Although more history has been made in Europe than in any other continent, it is the smallest continent except Australia, and is less than a quarter the size of Asia. It is sometimes said that Europe is not a continent at all but just a part of Asia, and the two together are sometimes called "Eurasia". Certainly Europe differs from other continents by having fewer well-marked boundaries. Its boundary with Asia follows the eastern slope of the Ural Mountains and the north coast of the Caspian Sea, and runs north of the Caucasus Mountains to cross the Black Sea between the Kerch Strait and the Bosporus in Turkey. Thus all the Urals are in Europe and all the Caucasus in Asia.

No other continent has so many advantages for mankind. It has scarcely any desert land and a greater proportion of it can be farmed than in any other continent, though it still has wide forests from which useful timber can be cut. It is rich in coal and iron so that factories of all kinds can be set up. Its climate is generally mild, seldom in any part too hot or too cold for people to work out of doors. Its mountain ranges are not often barriers between regions.

The coastline of Europe, nearly 50,000 miles long, is so irregular that deep inlets reach far inland, with the result that no place is more than 500 miles from a port. This has encouraged fishing and provided a cheap and easy way of carrying goods from one part to another. Western civilization made its beginning in the Mediterranean lands of Europe and has been carried all over the world by European peoples. These facts, and Europe's dense population, show how well the continent has been provided with the things needed by man.

A glance at the map shows that Europe is almost equally divided into two very different parts. The eastern part, shut away from the oceans, is wide open towards Asia. From its earliest history it was overrun by Asiatic horsemen and the result has been a Russian empire stretching far into Asia. The western part, on the other hand, is bordered by the ocean and lapped by great seas, so that its people have been inclined to look westwards and to spread their settlements and trade overseas.

Again, eastern Europe stretches into an unbroken plain from the Arctic Ocean in the north to the Black Sea in the south, and the conditions in it such as the climate and the kind of country change very gradually from one district to another. In the west, however, the conditions may change very rapidly from lowland plains to great mountain ranges and deep valleys, or wide stretches of high moorland, so that within a short distance the kind of life led by the people greatly alters. Thus the shepherd and the miner, the ploughman and the factory worker, the fisherman and the craftsman, live almost side by side and learn from each other. The climate in the west is milder and damper than in the east.

## Mountains, Rivers and Plains

Most of the southern shores of Europe are washed by the Mediterranean Sea, immediately north of which rise the ranges of the Alpine mountain system, sometimes with low plains among them. Along the northern edge of these mountain ranges lie plateaus, or tablelands, and between the plateaus and the North Sea and Baltic Sea is the western part of the great North European Plain. Beyond those two seas are the plateau lands of Scandinavia (Norway and Sweden).

Europe is well supplied with rivers and ships can sail up many of them. One group in the west, including the Rhône, Rhine, Danube and Po rivers, flows out of the Alps. These rivers get much of their water from the melting of the snow on the mountains in spring and summer. Another group in the east includes the much longer Russian rivers such as the Volga, Don, Dnieper, Dniester and Dvina. However, they are of less use than the big western rivers because they freeze over in the winter and do not flow out into the great trading seas. The Scandinavian rivers are too short and rapid for ships to use them, but they are made to give water power for supplying electricity.

About half of Europe is taken up by plains, which seldom rise to more than 1,000 feet above sea level and for the most part slope gently to the coasts. They form the chief farming lands. The vast North European Plain is the whole width of the continent in Russia, but narrows as it stretches west through Poland, northern Germany, the Netherlands, Belgium and northern France. It continues in the English lowlands across the shallow North Sea. Smaller lowlands are enclosed by some of the mountain ranges, among them being the Plain of Hungary, the Lombardy Plain in Italy and the Andalusian Plain in the south of Spain.

Some parts of the European plain are marshy. The great Pripet Marshes lie across the borderlands of Russia and Poland. The North Sea coasts of Germany and the Netherlands have coastal marshes rather like the English fens. The biggest European lakes, Ladoga and Onega, are in Russia on the northern edge of the plain. Many other lakes are found along the highlands of Scandinavia, Scotland, Switzerland and northern Italy, though the largest in central and western Europe is Balaton in Hungary.

## Climate, Vegetation and Crops

Even the southernmost parts of Europe lie well north of the tropics and only a fairly small part is within the Arctic Circle; the continent is therefore nearly all in the cool temperate zone. Its winds blow mainly from the Atlantic, bringing nearly all the rain, which therefore falls mostly in the west, becoming less towards the east. The winds also bring warm air in winter, making it less cold than in any other lands in the same latitudes. As might be expected, Europe gets warmer to the south, although the mountain and high plateau lands are colder and have more rain and snow than the lowlands near them. Three main kinds of climate can be found in the continent:

1. The Russian lands and those near them have a *continental* climate which goes to extremes—with little rain (most of it falling in the hot summers) and bitterly cold winters. Crops and plants will grow for only about seven months of the year even in the south.

2. The western lands, from Norway to Portugal—including the British Isles—have rain in abundance, falling in every month of the year. Their summers are warm rather than hot, their winters cool rather than cold.

---

### FACTS ABOUT EUROPE

AREA: About 3,992,000 square miles (including 2,080,000 square miles in the European part of the U.S.S.R.). Europe contains only 7% of the world's land surface.

POPULATION (estimated in 1966): 534,400,000 (including 176,800,000 in European part of the U.S.S.R.).

RESOURCES: Wheat, barley, oats, root-crops, potatoes, fruit; livestock; timber; coal, iron ore.

FEATURES OF SPECIAL INTEREST: The highest peak in Europe is Mont Blanc (French Alps) which rises 15,771 feet above sea level. The largest lake, Ladoga (Russia), covers about 7,000 square miles. The longest rivers are: Volga (2,300 miles), Danube (1,725 miles), Dnieper (1,400 miles) and Don (1,100 miles). The second and third longest ship canals in the world are in Europe: the Albert Canal in Belgium and the Moscow–Volga Canal in Russia—both 80 miles long.

---

3. The lands round the Mediterranean have hot summers almost without rain. They get their rain in the winter months, when the weather is often warm and seldom gets really cold except in the mountains.

In the course of centuries the farmers have changed the vegetation of Europe by cultivation so much that it is in many places hard to say what it was like originally. The changes have been least in places where the climate was too cold or dry or the country too steep or marshy to be farmed at all.

Much of the land north of the Arctic Circle is covered with tundra—no trees except a few dwarf willows and birches; just moss, lichen and heather. (See TUNDRA PLAINS.) Just south come forests of pine, spruce, fir and larch reaching to Moscow, Stockholm and Oslo and providing valuable timber. The summers are too short for most crops except barley, oats, potatoes, and hay for cattle feed.

Most of Europe was formerly covered with a mixed forest including both evergreen trees such as pine, spruce and fir, and broad-leaved trees that shed their leaves in autumn such as oak, beech and chestnut. This forest has been largely destroyed to make way for farming.

Grain crops are of great importance. Rye is grown mainly in the north and east, wheat in the south and west and barley and oats everywhere. Sugar beet and potatoes are the chief root crops, and in the wetter regions to the west is rich grassy pasture for dairy cattle.

The summers of the Mediterranean countries are too dry for broad-leaved trees or pasture grass, and wide areas are covered with low woody bushes and shrubs and heaths, where only sheep and goats can feed. Wheat and barley grow during the winter and ripen in early summer. Fruits provide the chief crops, being either native kinds such as grapes and olives, or fruits introduced from other lands such as oranges, lemons and peaches.

Across southeastern Europe—mainly in southern Russia—stretch the *steppes,* which are treeless plains ranging from good grain-growing country to what are almost deserts near the Caspian Sea. Wheat, sugar beet, barley, oats and rye are the chief crops. (See STEPPES.)

Although Europe is the greatest food-producing continent, it cannot raise enough to feed its vast population and must import (bring in) both meat and grain. The rich fisheries of its western and northern seas help to make up for its insufficient farm produce.

## Southern Europe

The lands of southern Europe are part of the Mediterranean region. They are mountainous, near the sea and have the kind of climate and vegetation already described. Farming in these conditions is not easy, for the slopes must be terraced in steps to make the soil deep enough for vines and fruit trees, and the long dry summer calls for much watering of gardens and orchards. Both terracing and watering mean a lot of heavy hand work and this is typical of Mediterranean farming, where the spade and the pruning hook take the place of the plough and reaper of most European farms.

Although the Mediterranean is not rich in fish, the land is so poor and the coast in most places so well suited to small craft that both fishing and trading by sea have long been important ways of life. The Mediterranean was one of the busiest trading areas in the world in ancient times and has again become one of the busiest shipping routes since the opening of the Suez Canal in 1869. Some of the ports of southern Europe such as Genoa, Naples, Marseilles and Barcelona have again become important.

The lands round the Mediterranean have always played a large part in world history. Civilization as we know it began in Egypt and Mesopotamia and then spread westwards. By the 14th century Italian cities such as Venice and Florence were rich and powerful but once the difficulty of making long sea voyages had been overcome Portugal, Spain, France and England became the chief trading nations and the Mediterranean became less important.

Southern Europe consists of three great peninsulas—the Iberian Peninsula (Spain and Portugal), Italy and the Balkan Peninsula—all lying south of the main Alpine mountain ranges. The gaps in these ranges, making passages between the Mediterranean lands and the rest of Europe, have always been important highways. First

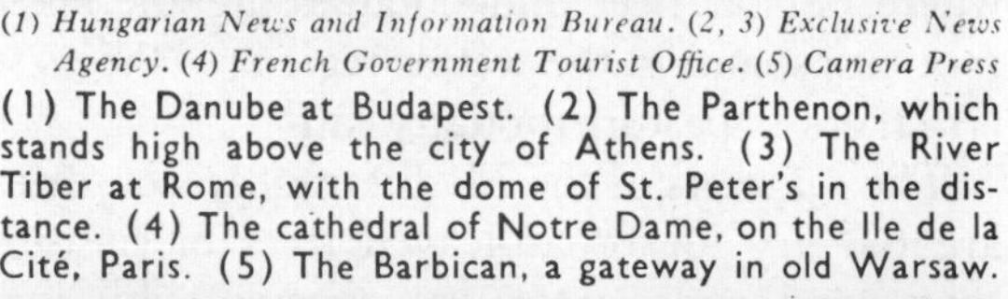

*(1) Hungarian News and Information Bureau. (2, 3) Exclusive News Agency. (4) French Government Tourist Office. (5) Camera Press*

(1) The Danube at Budapest. (2) The Parthenon, which stands high above the city of Athens. (3) The River Tiber at Rome, with the dome of St. Peter's in the distance. (4) The cathedral of Notre Dame, on the Ile de la Cité, Paris. (5) The Barbican, a gateway in old Warsaw.

among them is the Rhône valley, through which the Romans entered France and passed to Britain, the Low Countries and Germany. Since it was founded as a Greek settlement in about 60 B.C. Marseilles has been the gateway to this route. There are less easy routes from the Adriatic Sea near Venice and Trieste and from the Aegean Sea near Salonika to the Danube plains.

The Mediterranean countries are among the poorest in Europe, for while their farms and fisheries are not rich they also lack the sources of power and the raw materials needed for factories, having little coal or oil. The dry summer cuts down the output of water power, though a few large power stations have been built where the melting snows of the Pyrenees and Alps make up for the lack of rain. Iron and chromium ores (that is, the rocks and earth containing the metals) are found, but because coal is lacking they have to be sent abroad for the metals to be got out of the ores. Wool, silk and cotton are obtained, but not in large quantities. The chief manufacturing area is along the northern edge of the Lombardy Plain in northern Italy, where Milan, Turin and a number of smaller towns use water power from the Alpine streams to provide electricity for factories making machinery, motor cars and textiles.

The Mediterranean lands therefore depend to a large extent on farming, and though the farmers are hard working and skilful not one of the countries can raise all the food its peoples need, even though they are accustomed to rather poor living conditions. Therefore many of the people emigrate (go abroad to settle) to other continents, and others live by working in richer countries as labourers, farm workers and sailors, while some depend on the money brought in by tourists to help out the scanty resources of their native land.

The Iberian Peninsula consists of Portugal and Spain. Portugal is an Atlantic rather than a Mediterranean land, and important air and sea routes run from its chief city, Lisbon, to South America. Much of Spain is a dry and barren plateau. Iron ore and some coal are found in its northern mountains and from Roman times copper has been mined in the south. The plain of Andalusia around Seville is its most fertile region and with the land near the Mediterranean coastline produces wine, olive oil, oranges and nuts.

The French Mediterranean shores, the three great islands of Corsica, Sardinia and Sicily and the part of Italy that is a peninsula all present the same picture of blue and often calm seas with wide bays and rocky headlands. Behind, but quite close, lie the hills cut in terraces for growing vines, olives, oranges and lemons, or covered with thin woods. Farther inland the land is dry and scrubby and of little value except as poor pastures for sheep. Where the patches of lowland are large enough towns have grown, such as Palermo in Sicily and Rome, Naples and Leghorn in Italy. In northern Italy the Plain of Lombardy, watered by the tributaries of the River Po, is rich farming country. Wheat, maize, rice and much dairy produce are grown in this plain.

Greece is a country of rugged mountains and scattered islands whose poverty has for centuries driven her people to seek their living on the sea. Less than a twentieth of the land can be used for growing crops. The Turkish empire in Europe, which was once great, has shrunk to a small area around Istanbul. The countries in the northern part of the Balkan peninsula belong rather to central than to southern Europe, so they are described in a later section of this article.

## Eastern Europe

Eastern Europe is about half the whole continent, running nearly 2,000 miles from the Arctic Ocean to the Black Sea and the Caucasus Mountains, and 1,500 miles east and west between the Ural and Carpathian Mountains. Not a single mountain range breaks the almost level surface of this vast area and it is one of the biggest lowlands in the world. It differs from all other parts of the continent by altering so little throughout its extent. The wide, shallow river basins are separated by low, wide uplands which are so alike that it is difficult to tell one from another. The climate in the south is different from that in the far north, but the change takes place very gradually, as do the differences of soil between one region and the next. These differences in climate and soil have caused differences in natural vegetation, and these in turn have brought about differences in the way the people make their living and the kind of crops they grow.

The U.S.S.R. is a snowy land, a little like Canada except that it has no great chain of mountains like the Canadian Rocky Mountains. The snow is not usually very deep, but it lies on the ground for a long time. Even the warmest part, along the shores of the Black Sea, is usually snow-covered for some six weeks of the year, while towards the Arctic Ocean the snow lies for seven months of the year.

In the extreme northeast of Europe and north of the Arctic Circle lie the rich coalfields of Vorkuta, from which coal is taken to factories in Leningrad near the northwestern frontier of the U.S.S.R. Otherwise only a few thousand people dwell in the tundra region along the Arctic shores, depending on their reindeer and on fishing and hunting for a living. From the White Sea to Leningrad and much farther south along the Ural Mountains stretch huge forests of larch, fir and spruce, which provide large quantities of timber for building, sent abroad through Archangel. The summers are too short for farming to be possible.

South of the northern forests there is a wedge of mixed forests; that is, of trees like oaks that shed their leaves in autumn together with trees like firs. This covers the country from the Baltic Sea to the Carpathian Mountains in the west and gets narrower as it goes towards the southern end of the Urals. Here is the real heart of Russia from which the great state of the U.S.S.R. has grown, for the forests provided timber for building houses and when cleared gave good farming land. Moscow stands in the middle of this region, and near by are the Valdai Hills, where several of the great rivers of eastern Europe rise and flow in all directions, making useful trade routes. One of the great Russian coalfields lies on the south edge of the forest and supplies many of the factories in Moscow and the towns in the region. Moscow and the two earlier capital cities, Kiev and Leningrad, lie one at each corner of this big triangular wedge of mixed forest.

The south and southeastern parts of European Russia are areas of grasslands. At first there are many woodlands, especially along the rivers,

*Exclusive News Agency*

**For 80 miles the Rhine flows through a narrow gorge. This great river is one of the main traffic routes in Europe.**

with rich prairies between. Next comes the true steppe, with very few trees but a rich dark soil. This, the "black earth" region, is the part of the U.S.S.R. where most grain is grown. Wheat, rye, barley and oats are raised on very large farms employing thousands of workers. The largest Russian coalfield, the Donbas, and rich deposits of iron ore are found in this area, the Ukraine, so that it has become one of the most important manufacturing regions in the U.S.S.R.

Around the Caspian Sea there is little rain, so crops can be grown only where water can be drawn from the rivers, but the country to the west of the Caspian north of the Caucasus Mountains has the richest oilfield in Europe.

## Central Europe

Central Europe includes those parts of the continent lying between the Baltic Sea and the Mediterranean lands. Slanting south across it runs the great River Danube, and it contains the German and Polish part of the North European Plain, the plateau land of south Germany and Bohemia, the highest parts of the Alpine mountain system, and the wide Hungarian plains of the middle Danube. Its scenery is thus much more varied than that of eastern Europe.

The fact that central Europe is broken up into wide valleys and basins has in the past given rise to many small states, some of which have succeeded in growing into empires only to fall apart again—examples are the Turkish empire in Europe and the Austrian empire.

The northern plain, separated from the Russian lowlands by the Pripet Marshes, is divided between Poland and Germany. Three broad slow rivers—the Elbe, Oder and Vistula—run through it from south to north. In olden times it was covered by mixed forest, and it still is in places where the soils are sandy and poor, as in much of Poland. The wide river valleys with their rich clay soils, however, have been cleared of trees and are rich farm lands, for the meadows make good pastures and give abundant crops of hay. Elsewhere the best soils are used for growing wheat and sugar beet, and the poorer ones for rye and potatoes. The rivers, flowing into seas which are rarely closed by ice except for short periods, carry the produce of the valley farm lands to ports such as Hamburg, Szczecin (Stettin) and Gdansk (Danzig).

Along the southern edge of the northern plain lie the most important coalfields of central Europe, those of the Ruhr, Saxony and Silesia.

*Paul Popper*

St. Moritz, a famous holiday resort in the Swiss Alps.

The ores of metals from the plateau lands and the wool from their sheep gave rise to metal working and the manufacture of cloth and glass as long ago as the middle ages. The great factory centres are in Czechoslovakia, southern Germany and southern Poland. The sheltered river valleys in the southern part of the northern plain are often rich farming lands where warm weather crops such as grapes and tobacco are grown alongside grain and root crops. The valley of the upper Rhine is an example of this type of land.

The mountain ranges of the Alps sweep across Switzerland and fall away as they approach the Danube, on the other side of which the Carpathian mountains form a curve enclosing the

Plain of Hungary. From western Austria another set of mountain ranges runs down into the Balkan Peninsula. The ranges divide into a western line following the shores of the Adriatic Sea into Greece and an eastern line passing across Yugoslavia and Bulgaria to the Black Sea. These mountain ranges are serious barriers to traffic and communications. The main gaps in them are near Vienna, where the Danube cuts through the mountains; near Ljubljana in Yugoslavia, where the River Sava makes a way inland from Trieste on the Adriatic coast; and that made by the rivers that flow from near Belgrade to the sea near Salonika in Greece. Tunnels for railways have been cut through the high central Alps. The Danube, from Vienna to the gorge in Rumania called the Iron Gate, flows across a wide lowland surrounded by the Alpine and Carpathian mountain systems. This lowland, known as the Hungarian Plain or *Alföld*, is a grassland like that of southern Russia, and grows large quantities of wheat and maize as well as pasturing pigs, cattle and horses. After the Danube has passed the Iron Gate it flows into the Black Sea through another large plain of the same kind in Rumania. There are oilfields in the northern part of this plain.

## Northwestern Europe

In Norway, Sweden and Finland there are wide stretches of almost useless land where no one lives because the ground is not fit for cultivation. Finland has large areas of rocky country almost completely without soil. The three countries together, though four times the size of the British Isles, have only a quarter as many people. Most of their land falls within the belt of forest growing pine, spruce and birch, which supplies useful timber but when cleared is not very good for farming. None of the three has any coal worth mentioning, although Sweden has large deposits of very good iron ore, most of which is sent abroad.

Norway is in a good position to share in the northern fisheries for cod and herring. Its sailors trade in every sea and many of the people have gone out to Canada and the United States to make a better living than they could at home. Sweden has been able to set up factories by using the water power from streams and mineral ores from mines, but Finland has few resources beyond timber. Both Swedish and Finnish ports are hampered by ice in winter. Iceland is mostly barren volcanic mountains, but sheep and cattle are raised on its grasslands and the sea around it is very rich in fish.

## The North Sea Lands and France

The North European plain sinks gently below sea level in the west to form the bed of the North Sea, beyond which it rises just as gently to become the British Isles. The sea is therefore a shallow basin almost surrounded by lands which are seldom more than hilly.

In ancient days the lands of the Mediterranean played the largest part in European history, but in the last two or three centuries the North Sea lands have been the most important. It was here that men first learned about steam and electricity and how to use them, and on these lands were raised the best kind of sheep and cattle which now graze in the other continents. Here, too, farmers first worked out the best way of growing crops and of breeding and fattening animals. Young students from other parts of the world come to the schools and universities, the factories, offices and banks of these countries and then return home to practise what they have learned.

Outdoor work is nearly always possible and it is rarely too hot for strenuous work in forge and factory. The great manufacturing centres of Great Britain, northern France and Belgium depend on the abundance of good coal found in places where it is easily mined and easily carried by rail, river and sea. Raw materials for the factories are brought across the seas to the west European coastlands—cotton to Lancashire and northern France, wool to Yorkshire and Belgium, ores of iron, copper, zinc, lead and tin to south Wales and Belgium.

The changeable and generally mild and damp climate of Britain, Belgium, the Netherlands and Denmark helps them to grow heavy crops of many types of foodstuffs, and is especially favourable to the growth of rich pasture grasses for feeding dairy and beef cattle and raising sheep, pigs and poultry. The North Sea and the neighbouring parts of the Atlantic and Arctic Oceans provide some of the richest fishing grounds in the world, and Hull, Grimsby and Great Yarmouth, Ijmuiden, Esbjerg and Bergen all share in this rich harvest.

In spite of favourable conditions and the skill of their farmers, the United Kingdom and the German Federal Republic (Western Germany) cannot feed their millions of factory workers and town dwellers. They must obtain food, as well as raw materials, from distant lands. The Americas and Australia supply them with meat, grain and fruit, as well as wool, cotton and the ores of metals. Thus the prosperity of western Europe depends on ocean trade—the exchange of factory-made goods for food and raw materials from overseas. That is why so many of the world's greatest ports are found in this part of Europe. Such ports include London, Liverpool, Glasgow and Southampton in Great Britain, Antwerp in Belgium and Rotterdam in the Netherlands, Hamburg on the North Sea coast of Germany, Copenhagen in Denmark, Gothenburg in Sweden and Bergen in Norway.

France is the only country in Europe except the U.S.S.R. which stretches across the continent from north to south. Its Mediterranean shores give it a share in southern Europe. In the southeast and the Pyrenees it includes some of the highest mountains of the Alpine system. Its central plateau is in many ways like the plateau lands of southern Germany and its northern and western coasts really belong to the North Sea lands. Thus in France are to be found on a small scale many of the features found in Europe as a whole.

France lies between the two great highways of ocean trade along the English Channel and the Mediterranean, and its main ports—Marseilles in the south and Le Havre, Rouen and Dunkirk in the north—are on those routes. France is on the one hand a rich farming country raising a great variety of crops and animals, and on the other hand an important producer of steel and of manufactured goods calling for skill and artistic sense, such as clothes and furniture. Its capital, Paris, is a very important railway centre.

## European Peoples

During the Ice Age, which lasted about a million years and ended some 10,000 years ago, Europe had very few people, but as the ice sheets finally melted men made their way from North

*Above: Paul Popper. Right: J. Allan Cash*

Above: Windmills have been used for centuries to pump water from the low-lying parts of Holland. Right: A tree-lined road in the rich farming country of Normandy in northern France.

*Paul Popper*

Springtime in Hardanger Fiord, Norway. The fiord, a deep, narrow arm of the sea, stretches inland for 105 miles.

Africa, through Spain, to France and Britain and later to Norway and Sweden, which had been the centre of a great ice sheet. These people lived by hunting and by gathering berries and fruits, so their numbers were small. The population of Britain at that time was a few hundreds.

In about 3000 B.C. people who had learnt to cultivate grain spread to Europe from southwest Asia. No useful plant that could be grown for food had been found in Europe except a poor kind of grain in the southeast. These cultivators, who had no metal axes for cutting down trees but who had boats, spread to those parts of eastern and central Europe that were not covered with thick forests.

From ancient burial places it is known that most of these early peoples, whether hunters or cultivators, were long-headed and generally not very big. It is thought that they had dark hair and eyes but fair skins, for dark skin is chiefly useful in protecting man against the strongest rays of the hot sun in the tropics, and so is not needed in Europe. This helps to explain why so many people in countries like Scotland, Norway and Sweden (where it is never really hot) have little or none of this protecting brown colour in their hair and eyes. Indeed, they are sometimes fair-haired and blue-eyed.

In some regions of Britain, such as parts of south Wales and Cornwall where there are many descendants of the early peoples, there live many people with dark hair and brown or grey-blue eyes. They are not so dark as most Italians and not so fair as most Norwegians.

Besides the long-headed people mentioned earlier, there are signs of broad-headed people from the end of the Ice Age onwards. These broad-headed people have increased in numbers and now form the greater part of the population of what may be called middle Europe—that is, from France to Denmark in the west and from the Black Sea to Finland in the east of the continent. Most of them have brown but not black hair and some brown in their eyes, and the usual pale skin of Europeans.

Because of these facts about head shape and colouring the peoples of Europe are divided into different "races". The main ones are *Mediterranean* with long heads, dark hair and eyes and sometimes some brown in their skin; *Alpine* or central European with broad heads and medium brown hair and some brown in their eyes; *Nordic* with long heads and fair hair and blue eyes; *Dinaric* with round heads and dark colouring; *East Baltic* with rather broad heads, very fair hair and blue or grey eyes; and *Armenoid* with round heads, sloping foreheads and large noses. Today these are all very intermixed, and there are no "pure" races in Europe, despite the ignorant beliefs of such people as Adolf Hitler. Some of these races are also found outside Europe. For example the *Mediterraneans* not only include people like the Greeks but also the Arabs of North Africa.

In Rumania most of the people have broad heads with medium brown hair, but in the Carpathian Mountains are also to be found some dark-haired, long-headed people like those who first lived in the region. Although every European population shows a mingling of types, the mingling does not make them all more or less alike. They often inherit a particular quality such as hair colour or head shape through one line of ancestors. (See Heredity.)

Along the coastlands of the Arctic Ocean there are to be found Lapps and Samoyeds. These are *nomads* (wanderers) whose ancestors came from Asia and who move from pasture to pasture according to the season. They are usually short, broad-headed people with rather brown skins and with straight dark hair like that of the people of central Asia. Probably their forefathers were pushed northwards from central Asia down the Yenisei valley and had to change from herding horses and cattle to herding reindeer as they went north. Their brown skin protects them from the sun's rays reflected from the snow during the long summer days.

Other nomads from northwest Asia have come through the cold northern forests and settled to become the main peoples of Finland and parts of north Russia. The coastal Finns, however, are mostly of Swedish descent and are tall, athletic and fair-haired. Farther south, swarms of fierce warrior horsemen from the steppes of western Asia have over the centuries driven east and west to make themselves lords of parts of China and Europe. They included among them Attila and the Huns who reached as far as France in the 5th century, the Bulgars whose descendants gave Bulgaria its name, the Magyars who became the military nobles of Hungary, and finally Jenghiz Khan who in the 13th century ruled from the Pacific to the Carpathians. (See Attila; Jenghiz Khan.) Some of these warrior horsemen became soldier-farmers and were given lands around the lower Don and Volga valleys on condition that they fought for the tsars (emperors) of Russia. They were known as the Cossacks.

When the Jews were driven out of Palestine by the Romans they spread over the Roman Empire and especially to Spain and Portugal, where they married with the people there, so that Spanish Jews often look like Spaniards with some Jewish features, such as the nose. They were driven out of Spain in the 15th century and many of them settled at Salonika in Greece, while others found a refuge in the Netherlands. Many settled in Roman times in the trading cities on the Rhine and spread eastward as cities grew in Germany, Poland and Russia. They spoke a language called Yiddish, founded on old German and Hebrew, and they are called Ashkenazim, whereas the Spanish and Portuguese Jews are known as Sephardim.

## European Languages

Between about 1500 B.C. and 100 B.C., the invaders from south Russia brought what is called an Indo-European or Aryan language into Europe, and as different peoples learned it this changed into several tongues—among them Celtic, Italic, Greek, the Teutonic-Gothic languages and the Slavonic ones. Celtic, first spoken in what is now south Germany and in some other places, is now found only in Brittany (northwest France), Wales, the Scottish highlands and parts of Ireland. From Italic came Latin and thence Italian, French, Spanish and Portuguese. The Teutonic-Gothic languages

*Courtesy, Portuguese State Office*

The Tower of Belem, near Lisbon. Built in the 15th century, it still stands guard at the mouth of the River Tagus.

turned into Scandinavian, German, Dutch, Flemish and English, and the Slavonic languages gave Czech, Slovak, Polish, Ukrainian, Russian, Bulgarian and some other tongues.

Rumanian is a mixture of the Latin spoken by Roman soldiers with Celtic and Slavonic. Albanian and Lithuanian are survivals of ancient Aryan languages. Finnish, Magyar, Turkish and the languages spoken by the Lapps and Samoyeds are Asiatic. The Romany spoken by a few gipsies is an Aryan language rather like those of India, and Basque, still spoken at the western end of the Pyrenees, is the only survivor of languages older than those of the Aryan family. (See LANGUAGE.)

## One Europe

No continent has such a closely packed variety of peoples, nations and ideas as Europe. This has often led to war, and in the past 500 years most big wars have been fought in Europe. Even now, a man calls himself a Swede, an Italian or an Englishman rather than a European.

After World War II, however, many people saw that western Europe must oppose Communism. In 1949, most of the western European nations joined with the United States and Canada in a military alliance formed as the North Atlantic Treaty Organization (Nato).

In 1951, Belgium, France, the German Federal Republic, Italy, Luxembourg and the Netherlands agreed to pool their coal, iron ore and steel. In 1957, these same countries formed the European Economic Community (EEC, or Common Market). They aimed at a common policy in industry and farming, at reducing customs duties and at a common trading policy with other countries. Their final aim was to unite not only in industry and trade but in politics—to create, in fact, a united Europe. Great Britain supported the aims of the EEC but did not join it, largely because of the strong ties with other Commonwealth countries. However, Britain in 1959 joined the European Free Trade Association (EFTA) with Austria, Denmark, Norway, Portugal, Sweden and Switzerland. This was an organization for trade and industry, not for political union. In 1961 and again in 1967 Britain sought to join the EEC, but was kept out by France. (See COMMON MARKET.)

# Nations and States of Europe

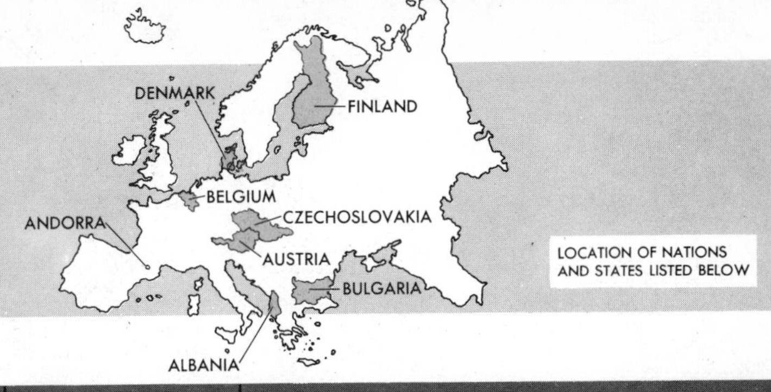


| NAME, AREA, AND POPULATION | EDUCATION, LANGUAGE, AND RELIGION | GOVERNMENT | ECONOMY |
|---|---|---|---|
| **ALBANIA**<br>**Area:** 11,100 sq. mi.<br>**Population:** 1,965,000 | **Schools:** 2,770<br>**Students:** 417,060<br>**Language:** Albanian<br>**Religions:** Moslem; Eastern Orthodox; Roman Catholic | **Political Status:** People's Republic (Communist)<br>**Capital:** Tirana<br>**UN:** Admitted Dec. 14, 1955 | **Products:** Chrome ore, nickel ore; goats, sheep; tobacco, maize<br>**Imports:** Oil and mining machinery; coke; paper; motor vehicles; electric motors<br>**Exports:** Chrome ore; tobacco; petroleum; copper; asphalt products |
| **ANDORRA**<br>**Area:** 175 sq. mi.<br>**Population:** 15,000 | **Schools:** 17<br>**Students:** 1,724<br>**Language:** Catalan<br>**Religion:** Roman Catholic | **Political Status:** Principality<br>**Capital:** Andorra<br>**UN:** Non-member | **Products:** Sheep; grain, vegetables, potatoes, tobacco; timber; tourist services<br>**Imports:** Manufactured goods<br>**Exports:** Cigarettes |
| **AUSTRIA**<br>**Area:** 32,374 sq. mi.<br>**Population** 7,323,000 | **Schools:** 7,487<br>**Students:** 1,118,224<br>**Language:** German<br>**Religion:** Roman Catholic | **Political Status:** Federal Republic<br>**Capital:** Vienna<br>**UN:** Admitted Dec. 14, 1955 | **Products:** Graphite, iron ore; aluminium, steel; potatoes, barley, rye, wheat<br>**Imports:** Machinery and electrical appliances; motor vehicles; coal; iron and steel<br>**Exports:** Base metals; wood, timber; cork; machinery; textiles; paper products |
| **BELGIUM**<br>**Area:** 11,781 sq. mi.<br>**Population:** 9,581,000 | **Schools:** 12,556<br>**Students:** 1,815,625<br>**Languages:** Flemish; French<br>**Religion:** Roman Catholic | **Political Status:** Constitutional monarchy<br>**Capital:** Brussels<br>**UN:** Admitted Dec. 27, 1945 | **Products:** Coal; steel, zinc, glass, machinery, textiles; flax, sugar beet<br>**Imports*:** Motor vehicles; copper; coal and coke; gems; petroleum<br>**Exports*:** Iron and steel; copper; gems; textile yarn and thread; electrical machinery and appliances |
| **BULGARIA**<br>**Area:** 42,823 sq. mi.<br>**Population:** 8,309,000 | **Schools:** 6,212<br>**Students:** 1,556,067<br>**Languages:** Bulgarian; Turkish<br>**Religions:** Eastern Orthodox; Moslem | **Political Status:** People's Republic (Communist)<br>**Capital:** Sofia<br>**UN:** Admitted Dec. 14, 1955 | **Products:** Lead ore, zinc ore; tobacco, sunflower seed; sheep; clothing<br>**Imports:** Iron and steel; cotton textiles; cotton; chemical products; rolled metals<br>**Exports:** Clothing, tomato products; transport equipment; cigarettes; grapes |
| **CZECHOSLOVAKIA**<br>**Area:** 49,371 sq. mi.<br>**Population:** 14,305,000 | **Schools:** 20,125<br>**Students:** 2,842,352<br>**Languages:** Czech; Slovak<br>**Religions:** Roman Catholic; Protestant | **Political Status:** Socialist Federal Republic (Communist)<br>**Capital:** Prague<br>**UN:** Admitted Oct. 14, 1945 | **Products:** Sugar beet, barley, hops, flax, potatoes; pigs; lignite; steel, aluminium, machinery<br>**Imports:** Machinery; petroleum; coal; iron ore; wheat<br>**Exports:** Machinery; coal; motor cycles and bicycles; cotton fabrics; food |
| **DENMARK** †<br>**Area:** 16,614 sq. mi.<br>**Population:** 4,839,000 | **Schools:** 3,672<br>**Students:** 877,631<br>**Language:** Danish<br>**Religion:** Protestant | **Political Status:** Constitutional monarchy<br>**Capital:** Copenhagen<br>**UN:** Admitted Oct. 24, 1945 | **Products:** Barley; dairy products; pigs, chickens; fish; machinery<br>**Imports:** Machinery; petroleum products; iron and steel; motor vehicles; textiles<br>**Exports:** Meat; machinery; butter; livestock; ships |
| **FINLAND**<br>**Area:** 130,119 sq .mi.<br>**Population:** 4,664,000 | **Schools:** 8,057<br>**Students:** 937,924<br>**Languages:** Finnish; Swedish<br>**Religion:** Protestant | **Political Status:** Republic<br>**Capital:** Helsinki<br>**UN:** Admitted Dec. 14, 1955 | **Products:** Timber; paper; vanadium ore, nickel ore, zinc ore<br>**Imports:** Machinery and electrical appliances; motor vehicles; petroleum products<br>**Exports:** Paper products; timber; wood pulp; ships and boats |

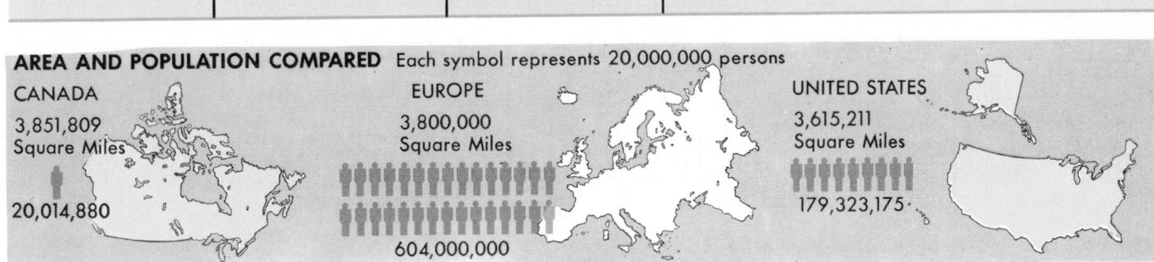


* Includes Luxembourg. † Excludes Faeroe Islands.

# Nations and States of Europe—continued

LOCATION OF NATIONS AND STATES LISTED ON THESE TWO PAGES

| NAME, AREA, AND POPULATION | EDUCATION, LANGUAGE, AND RELIGION | GOVERNMENT | ECONOMY |
|---|---|---|---|
| **FRANCE**<br>**Area:** 212,973 sq. mi.<br>**Population:** 49,890,000 | **Schools:** 88,818<br>**Students:** 9,153,866<br>**Language:** French<br>**Religion:** Roman Catholic | **Political Status:** Republic<br>**Capital:** Paris<br>**UN:** Admitted Oct. 24, 1945 | **Products:** Iron ore, bauxite, gypsum, sulphur; steel, aluminium, motor cars; cereals, sugar beets, fruit; cattle<br>**Imports:** Petroleum; machinery; textile fibres; iron and steel; coal and coke<br>**Exports:** Iron and steel; motor vehicles; machinery; petroleum products; textiles |
| **GERMANY, EAST**<br>(incl. E. Berlin)<br>**Area:** 41,816 sq. mi.<br>**Population:** 17,082,000 | **Schools:** 11,246<br>**Students:** 2,923,370<br>**Language:** German<br>**Religions:** Protestant; Roman Catholic | **Political Status:** Democratic Republic (Communist)<br>**Capital:** East Berlin<br>**UN:** Non-member | **Products:** Lignite, potash, salt; aluminium, steel, chemicals, machinery; potatoes, rye, sugar beet; pigs<br>**Imports:** Coal; coke; petroleum; wheat; motor cycles<br>**Exports:** Electric motors and transformers; petrol engines; tyres; bricks; lignite |
| **GERMANY, WEST**<br>(incl. W. Berlin)<br>**Area:** 95,957 sq. mi.<br>**Population:** 59,872,000 | **Schools:** 41,032<br>**Students:** 8,893,044<br>**Language:** German<br>**Religions:** Protestant; Roman Catholic | **Political Status:** Federal Republic<br>**Capital:** Bonn<br>**UN:** Non-member | **Products:** Steel, cement, motor cars, chemicals, copper; potash, coal; pigs, cattle; rye, potatoes, sugar beet, hops<br>**Imports:** Metals; fruits and vegetables; textiles; petroleum<br>**Exports:** Machinery; transport equipment; metals; coal and coke; chemicals |
| **GREAT BRITAIN †**<br>**Area:** 94,213 sq. mi.<br>**Population:** 55,068,000 | **Schools:** 48,881<br>**Students:** 11,623,261<br>**Languages:** English; Welsh; Gaelic<br>**Religions:** Protestant; Roman Catholic | **Political Status:** Constitutional monarchy<br>**Capital:** London<br>**UN:** Admitted Oct. 24, 1945 | **Products:** Coal, iron ore, gypsum; steel, cement, ships, motor cars, machinery, textiles, paper; sheep, cattle<br>**Imports:** Petroleum; fresh meat; timber; copper; tea<br>**Exports:** Motor vehicles; machinery; iron and steel; tractors; electrical equipment; textiles and clothing |
| **GREECE**<br>**Area:** 50,944 sq. mi.<br>**Population:** 8,716,000 | **Schools:** 11,719<br>**Students:** 1,445,666<br>**Language:** Greek<br>**Religion:** Eastern Orthodox | **Political Status:** Monarchy under military rule<br>**Capital:** Athens<br>**UN:** Admitted Oct. 24, 1945 | **Products:** Tobacco, olives; sheep, goats; bauxite<br>**Imports:** Ships and boats; iron and steel; petroleum; electrical machinery and appliances; wool<br>**Exports:** Tobacco; fruit and spice products; cotton; metal ores; hides and skins |
| **HUNGARY**<br>**Area:** 35,919 sq. mi.<br>**Population:** 10,212,000 | **Schools:** 6,755<br>**Students:** 1,930,819<br>**Language:** Hungarian<br>**Religions:** Roman Catholic; Protestant | **Political Status:** People's Republic (Communist)<br>**Capital:** Budapest<br>**UN:** Admitted Dec. 14, 1955 | **Products:** Manganese ore, bauxite; aluminium, machinery; maize, hemp; pigs<br>**Imports:** Petroleum; coal and lignite; iron ore; coke; motor vehicles<br>**Exports:** Machinery; bauxite; livestock; motor cycles; shoes |
| **ICELAND**<br>**Area:** 39,702 sq. mi.<br>**Population:** 200,000 | **Schools:** 354<br>**Students:** 41,231<br>**Language:** Icelandic<br>**Religion:** Protestant | **Political Status:** Republic<br>**Capital:** Reykjavik<br>**UN:** Admitted Nov. 19, 1946 | **Products:** Fish; sheep<br>**Imports:** Ships and boats; fuel oil; cordage; electrical machines; motor vehicles<br>**Exports:** Fish; oils and fats; fodder; fresh meat; hides and skins |
| **IRELAND**<br>**Area:** 27,136 sq. mi.<br>**Population:** 2,889,000 | **Schools:** 5,996<br>**Students:** 669,274<br>**Languages:** English; Gaelic<br>**Religion:** Roman Catholic | **Political Status:** Republic<br>**Capital:** Dublin<br>**UN:** Admitted Dec. 14, 1955 | **Products:** Peat; sheep, cattle; oats<br>**Imports:** Machinery; motor vehicles; textile yarn and fabrics; petroleum; fresh fruit<br>**Exports:** Cattle; meat; stout; chocolate; wool; whisky |
| **ITALY**<br>**Area:** 116,305 sq. mi.<br>**Population:** 52,334,000 | **Schools:** 55,300<br>**Students:** 7,662,588<br>**Language:** Italian<br>**Religion:** Roman Catholic | **Political Status:** Republic<br>**Capital:** Rome<br>**UN:** Admitted Dec. 14, 1955 | **Products:** Asbestos, mercury, zinc ore, sulphur; steel, motor cars; grapes, olives, tobacco, wheat, tomatoes<br>**Imports:** Petroleum; iron and steel; wool; coal<br>**Exports:** Motor vehicles; machinery; fresh fruits and nuts; fabrics |
| **LIECHTENSTEIN**<br>**Area:** 62 sq. mi.<br>**Population:** 19,500 | **Schools:** 29<br>**Students:** 3,129<br>**Language:** German<br>**Religion:** Roman Catholic | **Political Status:** Principality<br>**Capital:** Vaduz<br>**UN:** Non-member | **Products:** Cattle; fruit; postage stamps; textiles; precision instruments<br>**Imports:** Manufactured goods<br>**Exports:** Cattle; manufactured goods |

† United Kingdom of Great Britain and Northern Ireland.

## IMPORTANT MOUNTAIN PEAKS IN EUROPE

MULHACEN — SIERRA NEVADA (SPAIN)
MATTERHORN — ALPS (SWITZERLAND)
GROSS GLOCKNER — ALPS (AUSTRIA)
GERLACHOVKA — CARPATHIANS (CZECHOSLOVAKIA)
EL'BRUS — CAUCASUS MTS. (RUSSIA)
BLANC — ALPS (FRANCE)
CORNO — APENNINES (ITALY)
OLYMPUS — PINDUS MTS. (GREECE)
KAZBEK — CAUCASUS MTS. (RUSSIA)
PICO DE ANETO — PYRENEES (SPAIN)
GLITTERTIND — JOTUNHEIMEN (NORWAY)
VESUVIUS — APENNINES (ITALY)
MUSALA — RHODOPES (BULGARIA)
BEN NEVIS — GRAMPIANS (SCOTLAND)
ROMAN-KOSH — CRIMEAN MTS. (RUSSIA)
ETNA — (ITALY)
NEGOIUL — TRANSYLVANIAN ALPS (RUMANIA)
NARODNAYA — URALS (RUSSIA)

20,000 FT. · 18,000 FT. · 16,000 FT. · 14,000 FT. · 12,000 FT. · 10,000 FT. · 8,000 FT. · 6,000 FT. · 4,000 FT. · 2,000 FT. · SEA LEVEL · ATLANTIC OCEAN

*Steepness of mountain slopes is exaggerated*

| NAME, AREA, AND POPULATION | EDUCATION, LANGUAGE, AND RELIGION | GOVERNMENT | ECONOMY |
|---|---|---|---|
| **LUXEMBOURG**<br>**Area:** 999 sq. mi.<br>**Population:** 335,000 | **Schools:** 462<br>**Students:** 48,268<br>**Language:** French<br>**Religion:** Roman Catholic | **Political Status:** Constitutional monarchy<br>**Capital:** Luxembourg<br>**UN:** Admitted Oct. 24, 1945 | **Products:** Iron and steel; iron ore; timber; cattle; wheat, oats, potatoes, grapes<br>**Imports and Exports:** (*see* Belgium on earlier page) |
| **MALTA**<br>**Area:** 122 sq. mi.<br>**Population:** 319,000 | **Schools:** 212<br>**Students:** 56,982<br>**Languages:** Maltese; English<br>**Religion:** Roman Catholic | **Political Status:** Constitutional monarchy<br>**Capital:** Valletta<br>**UN:** Non-member | **Products:** Goats; potatoes, fruits, vegetables<br>**Imports:** Metals; wheat; motor vehicles; meat<br>**Exports:** Scrap metal; potatoes; textiles |
| **MONACO**<br>**Area:** 1 sq. mi.<br>**Population:** 23,700 | **Schools:** 19<br>**Students:** 3,187<br>**Language:** French<br>**Religion:** Roman Catholic | **Political Status:** Principality<br>**Capital:** Monaco<br>**UN:** Non-member | **Products:** Tourist services; postage stamps<br>**Imports:** Manufactured goods<br>**Exports:** Postage stamps; souvenirs |
| **NETHERLANDS**<br>**Area:** 13,967 sq. mi.<br>**Population:** 12,597,000 | **Schools:** 11,698<br>**Students:** 2,611,555<br>**Language:** Dutch<br>**Religions:** Roman Catholic; Protestant | **Political Status:** Constitutional monarchy<br>**Capital:** Amsterdam<br>**UN:** Admitted Dec. 10, 1945 | **Products:** Sugar beet, potatoes; dairy products; flax; coal; ships, machinery<br>**Imports:** Petroleum and petroleum products; iron and steel; electrical machinery; motor vehicles<br>**Exports:** Petroleum products; electrical machinery; iron and steel; vegetables; ships and boats |
| **NORWAY***<br>**Area:** 125,181 sq. mi.<br>**Population:** 3,784,000 | **Schools:** 5,822<br>**Students:** 592,987<br>**Language:** Norwegian<br>**Religion:** Protestant | **Political Status:** Constitutional monarchy<br>**Capital:** Oslo<br>**UN:** Admitted Nov. 27, 1945 | **Products:** Magnesium, titanium ore, mica, sulphur; aluminium, paper products; fish; potatoes, barley<br>**Imports:** Ships and boats; petroleum products; iron and steel; electrical machinery; nickel<br>**Exports:** Paper products; fish, wood pulp; iron and steel; aluminium |
| **POLAND**<br>**Area:** 120,359 sq. mi.<br>**Population:** 31,944,000 | **Schools:** 31,446<br>**Students:** 7,100,817<br>**Language:** Polish<br>**Religion:** Roman Catholic | **Political Status:** People's Republic (Communist)<br>**Capital:** Warsaw<br>**UN:** Admitted Oct. 24, 1945 | **Products:** Zinc ore, coal; steel, ships; rye, potatoes, flax, oats, sugar beets, tobacco; pigs, cattle, chickens<br>**Imports:** Wheat, cotton; rolled-metal products; iron ore; petroleum products<br>**Exports:** Coal; rolled-metal products; ships and boats; meat; coke |
| **PORTUGAL**†<br>**Area:** 35,510 sq. mi.<br>**Population:** 9,440,000 | **Schools:** 19,486<br>**Students:** 1,236,580<br>**Language:** Portuguese<br>**Religion:** Roman Catholic | **Political Status:** Republic<br>**Capital:** Lisbon<br>**UN:** Admitted Dec. 14, 1955 | **Products:** Tungsten, sulphur; cork; olives, grapes, potatoes, wheat, maize; sheep; fish<br>**Imports:** Iron and steel; machinery; cotton; motor vehicles; petroleum<br>**Exports:** Fish products; wine; cork and cork products; cotton fabrics |
| **RUMANIA**<br>**Area:** 91,699 sq. mi.<br>**Population:** 19,287,000 | **Schools:** 16,486<br>**Students:** 3,708,051<br>**Languages:** Rumanian; Hungarian<br>**Religions:** Eastern Orthodox; Protestant | **Political Status:** Socialist Republic (Communist)<br>**Capital:** Bucharest<br>**UN:** Admitted Dec. 14, 1955 | **Products:** Petroleum, manganese; maize, wheat, plums, hemp, sunflower seed; sheep<br>**Imports:** Iron ore; coal; coke; motor cycles; machinery<br>**Exports:** Veneer sheets; petroleum products; grain; tractors |
| **RUSSIA** (U.S.S.R. in Europe)<br>**Area:** 2,110,600 sq. mi.<br>**Population:** 176,800,000 | **Schools:** 200,559§<br>**Students:** 47,870,000§<br>**Languages:** Russian; Ukrainian<br>**Religion:** Eastern Orthodox | **Political Status:** Union of Republics (Communist)<br>**Capital:** Moscow<br>**UN:** Admitted Oct. 24, 1945 | **Products:** Wheat, barley, rye, sugar beet, potatoes; sheep, cattle, pigs; coal, petroleum, natural gas, iron and steel, aluminium, timber, machinery, textiles<br>**Imports:** Machinery; raw materials and metals, transport equipment, clothing<br>**Exports:** Machinery, iron and steel, petroleum products |
| **SAN MARINO**<br>**Area:** 24 sq. mi.<br>**Population:** 17,500 | **Schools:** 21<br>**Students:** 1,754<br>**Language:** Italian<br>**Religion:** Roman Catholic | **Political Status:** Republic<br>**Capital:** San Marino<br>**UN:** Non-member | **Products:** Wheat, grapes; hides; woollen goods; ceramics; building stone<br>**Imports:** Manufactured goods<br>**Exports:** Wine; woollen goods; hides; ceramics; building stone; postage stamps |

* Excludes Svalbard. † Excludes Azores, Cape Verde Islands, Madeira. § Includes Russia in Asia.

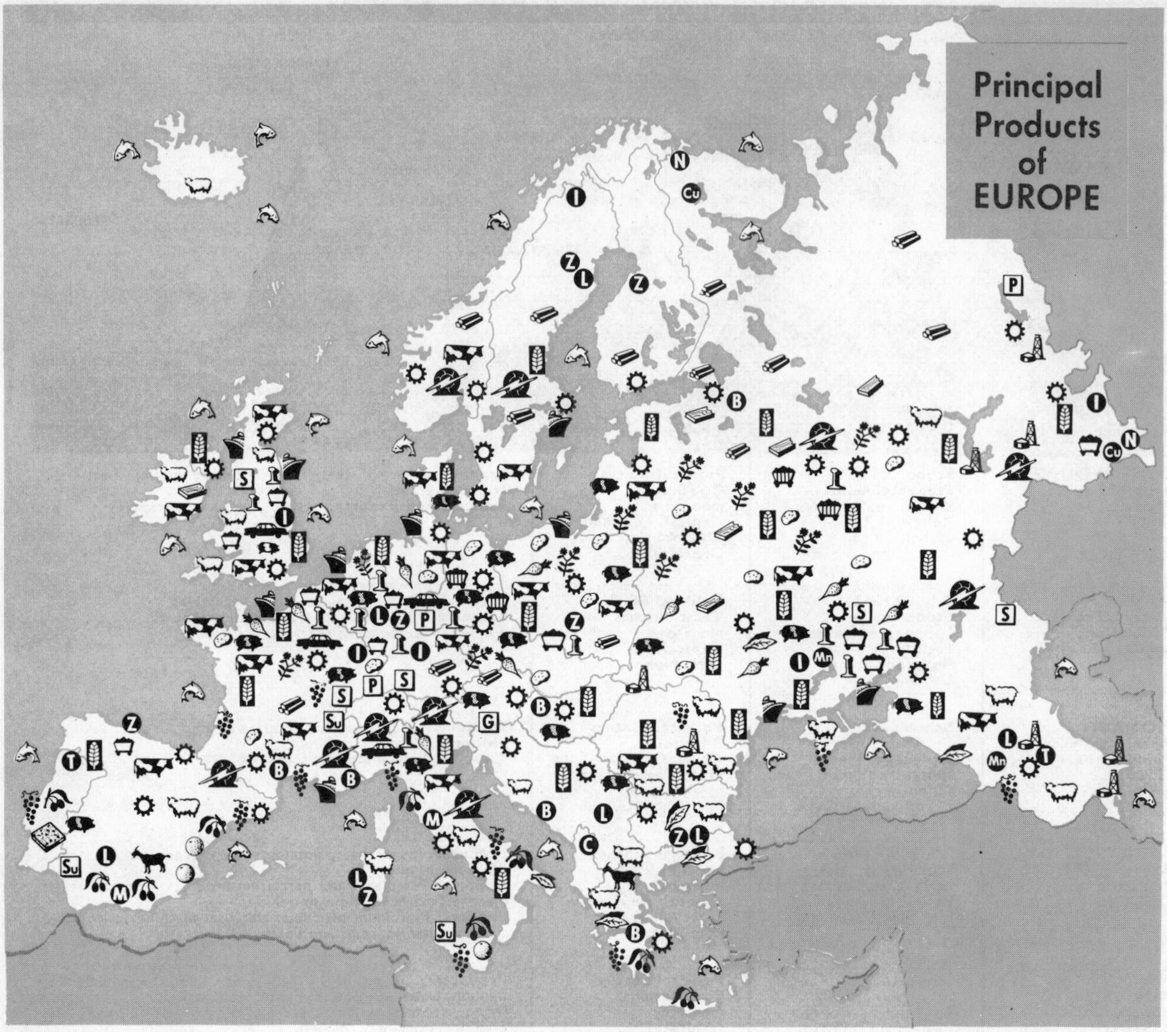

# Principal Products of EUROPE

## Metallic Mineral Ores

- bauxite
- chromite
- copper
- iron
- lead
- manganese
- mercury
- nickel
- tungsten
- zinc

## Mineral Fuels

- coal
- lignite
- peat
- petroleum

## Other Minerals

- graphite
- potash
- salt

## Manufactures

- motor cars
- iron and steel
- ships
- other manufactures

## Livestock

- cattle
- goats
- pigs
- sheep

## Crops

- cereals
- flax
- grapes
- olives
- oranges
- potatoes
- sugar beet
- tobacco

## Forest Products

- cork

- wood

## Other Products

- fish

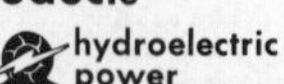

- hydroelectric power

## LAND USE (excluding Russia)

CROPS 31%

PASTURE 16%

FOREST 28%

OTHER* 25%

*Urban, wasteland, unused

# Nations and States of Europe—continued

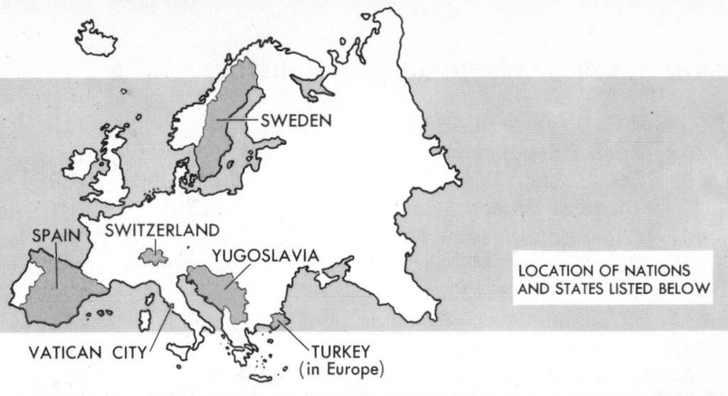


| NAME, AREA, AND POPULATION | EDUCATION, LANGUAGE, AND RELIGION | GOVERNMENT | ECONOMY |
|---|---|---|---|
| **SPAIN*** **Area:** 194,833 sq. mi. **Population:** 32,140,000 | **Schools:** 103,000 **Students:** 4,944,549 **Languages:** Spanish, Basque **Religion:** Roman Catholic | **Political Status:** Nominal monarchy **Capital:** Madrid **UN:** Admitted Dec. 14, 1955 | **Products:** Mercury, sulphur, gypsum, lead ore, zinc ore; oranges, olives, onions, grapes, wheat; sheep, goats **Imports:** Petroleum; cotton; synthetic fertilizer; vegetable oils; iron and steel **Exports:** Citrus fruits; fuel oil; wine; nuts; olive oil |
| **SWEDEN** **Area:** 173,665 sq. mi. **Population:** 7,869,000 | **Schools:** 7,998 **Students:** 1,340,386 **Language:** Swedish **Religion:** Protestant | **Political Status:** Constitutional monarchy **Capital:** Stockholm **UN:** Admitted Nov. 19, 1946 | **Products:** Timber, paper, aluminium, ships, machinery; gold, iron ore, lead ore, zinc ore; oats **Imports:** Petroleum products; iron and steel; machinery; motor vehicles **Exports:** Wood pulp; timber; machinery; paper products; ships and boats |
| **SWITZERLAND** **Area:** 15,941 sq. mi. **Population:** 6,050,000 | **Schools:** 3,160 **Students:** 771,311 **Languages:** German; French; Italian **Religions:** Protestant; Roman Catholic | **Political Status:** Federal Republic **Capital:** Berne **UN:** Non-member | **Products:** Textiles, chemicals, machinery, watches; dairy products, wheat, potatoes; banking services **Imports:** Iron and steel; motor vehicles; petroleum products; machinery; chemicals **Exports:** Watches; machinery; medicines; synthetic dyestuffs |
| **TURKEY** (in Europe) **Area:** 9,158 sq. mi. **Population:** 2,284,625 | **Schools:** 22,824 † **Students:** 4,804,966† **Language:** Turkish **Religion:** Moslem | **Political Status:** Republic **Capital:** Ankara (in Asia) **UN:** Admitted Oct. 24, 1945 | **Products†:** Wheat, barley, cotton, tobacco, olives, fruit, nuts, coal, iron, chrome and copper ores **Imports†:** Machinery, iron and steel, wheat, petroleum **Exports†:** Cotton, tobacco, fruit, nuts, wool, olive oil |
| **VATICAN CITY** **Area:** 1/6 sq. mi. **Population:** 1,000 | **Schools:** None **Students:** None **Language:** Italian **Religion:** Roman Catholic | **Political Status:** Papal State **UN:** Non-member | **Products:** Souvenirs; publications **Imports:** Manufactured goods **Exports:** Souvenirs; publications; postage stamps |
| **YUGOSLAVIA** **Area:** 98,766 sq. mi. **Population:** 19,958,000 | **Schools:** 15,914 **Students:** 3,705,919 **Languages:** Serbo-Croatian; Slovene **Religions:** E. Orthodox; R. Catholic; Moslem | **Political Status:** Socialist Federal Republic (Communist) **Capital:** Belgrade **UN:** Admitted Oct. 24, 1945 | **Products:** Lead ore, chrome ore, mercury, bauxite; machinery; maize, hops, fruit, hemp; sheep **Imports:** Machinery; iron and steel; cotton; motor vehicles **Exports:** Iron and steel; fresh meat; maize; timber; electrical machinery |

## PRODUCTION COMPARED European production as percent of world total

| PRODUCT | EUROPE* | REST OF WORLD | LEADING EUROPEAN PRODUCERS |
|---|---|---|---|
| OLIVES | 80% | 20% | Spain, Italy, Greece, Portugal |
| GRAPES | 60% | 40% | Italy, France |
| POTASH | 60% | 40% | West Germany, France, East Germany |
| POTATOES | 50% | 50% | Poland, West Germany, France, East Germany |
| RYE | 50% | 50% | Poland, West Germany |
| SUGAR BEETS | 50% | 50% | France, West Germany, Italy, Poland |
| AUTOMOBILES | 40% | 60% | West Germany, Great Britain, France, Italy |
| COAL AND LIGNITE | 40% | 60% | West Germany, East Germany, Great Britain, Poland |
| HEMP | 35% | 65% | Yugoslavia, Hungary, Rumania |
| STEEL | 35% | 65% | West Germany, Great Britain, France, Italy |
| BARLEY | 30% | 70% | France, Great Britain, West Germany, Denmark |
| FLAX | 30% | 70% | Poland, France, Belgium, Netherlands |
| IRON ORE | 30% | 70% | France, Sweden, West Germany, Great Britain |
| WHEAT | 20% | 80% | France, Italy, West Germany |
| PETROLEUM | 3% | 97% | Rumania, West Germany |

*Excluding Russia and Turkey

* Includes Balearics; excludes Canaries, Ceuta, Melilla. † Includes Turkey in Asia.

## SIGNIFICANT DATES IN EUROPEAN HISTORY

700–600 B. C.—Rise of Athens in Greece.
509—Roman Republic founded.
499–479—Persian Wars (battles of Marathon, 490; Thermopylae and Salamis, 480; Plataea, 479).
431–404—Peloponnesian War; Athens defeated.
359–323—Rise of Macedon (Alexander the Great's conquests, 336–323).
264–146—Punic Wars—Rome destroys Carthage.
146—Rome completes conquest of Greece.
60–44—Rise of Caesar (conquers Gaul, 58–51).
31—Roman Empire founded under Augustus.
A. D. 311—Christianity made legal.
395—Roman Empire divided into Western Empire and Eastern (Byzantine) Empire.
476—Germanic leader Odoacer conquers Rome.
481–511—Clovis founds Kingdom of Franks in Gaul.
711—Moors conquer Spain.
732—Charles Martel defeats Moors at Tours (France).
768–814—Charlemagne rules Frankish Empire; crowned Holy Roman emperor, 800.
843—Frankish Empire divided into France and Germany.
862—Russian Kingdom founded by Rurik.
962—Otto I of Germany revives Holy Roman Empire.
1066—Battle of Hastings—Normans conquer England.
1096–1270—The Crusades.
1215—King John of England grants Magna Carta.
1237–40—Tatars (Mongols) conquer Russia.
1300–1500—Italian Renaissance.
1337–1453—Hundred Years' War.
1420–98—Height of the Inquisition in Spain.
1492—Spain expels Moors; Columbus discovers America.
1494–1555—Spain becomes dominant European power.
1517—Luther launches Protestant Reformation.
1588—English fleet destroys Spanish Armada.
1618–48—Thirty Years' War.
1642–60—English Civil War and Commonwealth.
1701–13—War of the Spanish Succession.
1707—England and Scotland united as Great Britain.
1740–49—War of the Austrian Succession.
1756–63—Seven Years' War.
1789–95—French Revolution.
1796–1815—Napoleonic wars (battles of Trafalgar and Austerlitz, 1805; Russia, 1812; Waterloo, 1815).
1814–15—Congress of Vienna.
1854–56—Crimean War.
1867—Dual monarchy of Austria-Hungary founded.
1870–71—Franco-Prussian War; German Empire proclaimed.
1914–18—World War I; defeat of Central Powers; end of Austro-Hungarian and German empires.
1917—Bolshevik Revolution in Russia.
1919—Treaty of Versailles.
1933—Hitler rises to power in Germany.
1936–39—Spanish Civil War.
1938—Munich Pact.
1939–45—World War II (battles of Stalingrad, 1943; Normandy, 1944); Nazi Germany crushed.
1945–48—Communist states set up in Eastern Europe.
1949—North Atlantic Treaty Organization formed.
1958—European Common Market begins operating.
1963 and 1967—Britain attempts entry into Common Market.

## MEMBERSHIP IN PRINCIPAL EUROPEAN ORGANIZATIONS*

| NATION | ORGANIZATIONS | | | | | | |
|---|---|---|---|---|---|---|---|
| Albania | | | | | | | WTO‡ |
| Austria | CE | | EFTA | | | OECD | |
| Belgium | CE | EEC | | NATO | | OECD | |
| Bulgaria | | | | | | | WTO |
| Czechoslovakia | | | | | | | WTO |
| Denmark | CE | | EFTA | NATO | NC | OECD | |
| Finland | | | EFTA† | | NC | OECD‡ | |
| France | CE | EEC | | NATO‡ | | OECD | |
| Germany, East | | | | | | | WTO |
| Germany, West | CE | EEC | | NATO | | OECD | |
| Great Britain | CE | | EFTA | NATO | | OECD | |
| Greece | CE | EEC† | | NATO | | OECD | |
| Hungary | | | | | | | WTO |
| Iceland | CE | | | NATO | NC | OECD | |
| Ireland | CE | | | | | OECD | |
| Italy | CE | EEC | | NATO | | OECD | |
| Luxemburg | CE | EEC | | NATO | | OECD | |
| Malta | CE | | | | | | |
| Netherlands | CE | EEC | | NATO | | OECD | |
| Norway | CE | | EFTA | NATO | NC | OECD | |
| Poland | | | | | | | WTO |
| Portugal | | | EFTA | NATO | | OECD | |
| Rumania | | | | | | | WTO |
| Russia | | | | | | | WTO |
| Spain | | | | | | OECD | |
| Sweden | CE | | EFTA | | NC | OECD | |
| Switzerland | CE | | EFTA | | | OECD | |
| Turkey | CE | EEC† | | NATO | | OECD | |
| Yugoslavia | | | | | | OECD‡ | |

KEY

CE—Council of Europe

EEC—European Economic Community (Common Market)

EFTA—European Free Trade Association

NATO—North Atlantic Treaty Organization

NC—Nordic Council

OECD—Organization for Economic Cooperation and Development

WTO—Warsaw Treaty Organization

**Only European members are listed*

*†Associate member*

*‡Special status*

## EVAPORATION.

**EVAPORATION.** Wet clothes are hung out to dry, puddles on the pavement after rain soon disappear and garden soil dries up in a drought. In these and similar cases the water *evaporates*.

A liquid as it evaporates changes into an invisible vapour or gas. The little particles called molecules of which all matter is made up (see MOLECULE) are in a liquid continually moving about, being held together because attracted to each other by a force called *cohesion*. Some of the molecules of a liquid open to the air escape from this cohesion and jump from the surface into the air to form vapour.

The rate at which evaporation takes place depends mainly on the temperature; the hotter the liquid the faster its molecules are moving and the more readily they escape as vapour. The amount of surface open to the air also affects the rate; thus if a saucepan and a wide frying pan each holding a pint of water are put outside, the water in the frying pan will evaporate more quickly. The sea is continually evaporating, and its water vapour is blown over the land to fall as rain (see CLOUD; RAIN).

Liquids such as petrol and methylated spirits evaporate quickly because the cohesion between their molecules is much less than that in water, and are called highly *volatile* liquids. ("Volatile" comes from a Latin word meaning to fly, and the molecules of such liquids *fly off* as vapour very readily.)

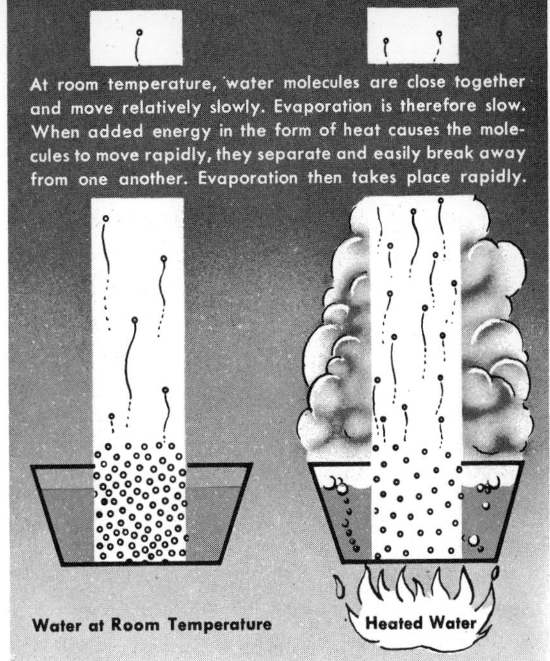

At room temperature, water molecules are close together and move relatively slowly. Evaporation is therefore slow. When added energy in the form of heat causes the molecules to move rapidly, they separate and easily break away from one another. Evaporation then takes place rapidly.

Evaporation has a cooling effect. Suck your finger and blow on it and it feels cold; stand about in a wet swimming suit and you feel cold all over. This is because the molecules escaping as vapour take heat with them from the liquid that remains. In the hot countries of the East drinking water is often carried in porous earthenware pots. As it reaches the outer surface of the pot the water is evaporated and takes heat away from the water left behind, which is thus kept cool. The cooling effect of evaporation is used in refrigeration (see REFRIGERATOR).

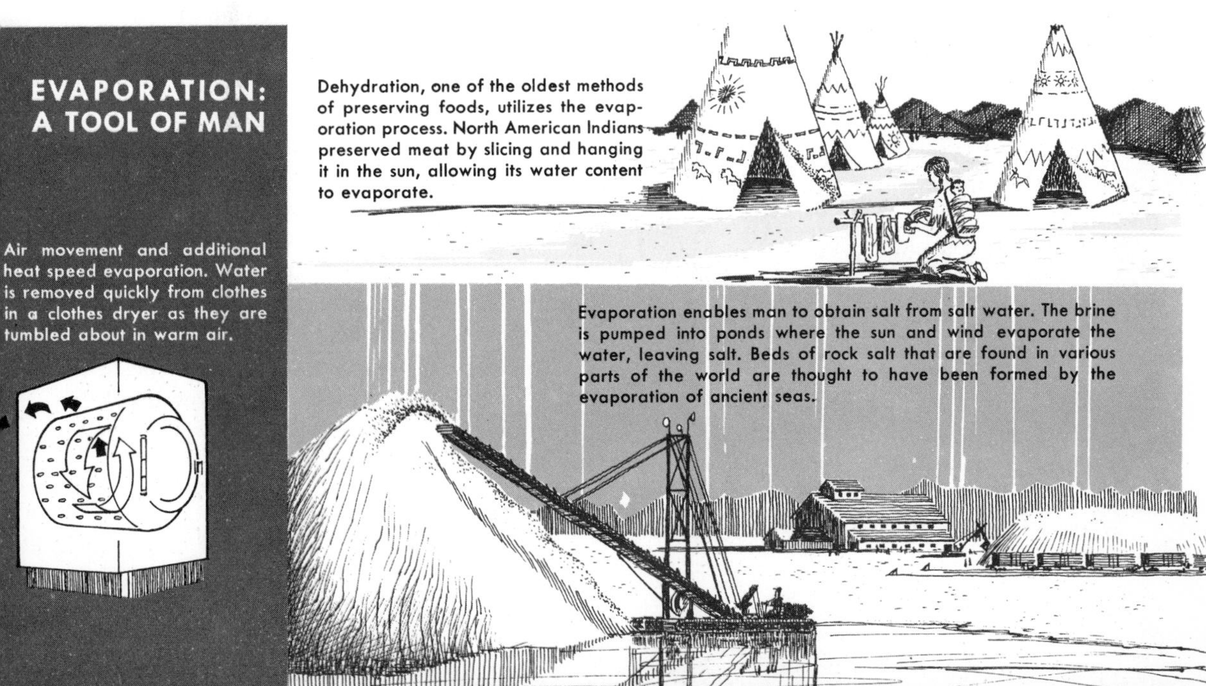

**EVAPORATION: A TOOL OF MAN**

Dehydration, one of the oldest methods of preserving foods, utilizes the evaporation process. North American Indians preserved meat by slicing and hanging it in the sun, allowing its water content to evaporate.

Air movement and additional heat speed evaporation. Water is removed quickly from clothes in a clothes dryer as they are tumbled about in warm air.

Evaporation enables man to obtain salt from salt water. The brine is pumped into ponds where the sun and wind evaporate the water, leaving salt. Beds of rock salt that are found in various parts of the world are thought to have been formed by the evaporation of ancient seas.

**EVEREST, MOUNT.** Towards the eastern end of the great mountain range known as the Himalayas, on the frontier between Nepal and Tibet, stands Mount Everest. Very few travellers are to be seen in this remote part of the world and this is one reason why Mount Everest was not discovered and its height measured until about 1850. At that time the British surveyors who were making maps in the north of India sighted a tiny white pyramid far away to the north and when they had measured it by means of a special sort of mathematics called trigonometry they discovered that it was the highest mountain in the world, rising to 29,002 feet. (Recently, more accurate measurements have shown that it is 29,028 feet high.) In 1858 it was given the name of Mount Everest in honour of Sir George Everest who was the Surveyor General in India at the time of its discovery.

*The Times, London*

Tenzing, photographed by Hillary on the summit of Mount Everest. The flags of Nepal, the United Nations and India fly from his ice-axe, together with the Union Jack.

Because the people of Nepal and Tibet kept very much to themselves and did not like visitors from the outside world, very little was known of the mountain for a great many years. During the second half of the 19th century, however, mountaineers began to explore the remote and unknown country of the Himalayas. By the beginning of the 20th century the possibility of forming an expedition to climb Mount Everest was being discussed by British mountaineers but it was not until the end of World War I that serious plans were made.

The first difficulty was to obtain permission to approach the mountain, and in 1920 the Tibetan government granted permission for a British expedition to enter their country and explore and draw maps of Mount Everest. Their ruler, the Dalai Lama, promised to give the explorers every help.

The second problem was to find out how men could climb at great heights and what clothing, food and equipment they would need to take with them. During the winter months a very cold wind blows southwards across Tibet and mountaineers had found earlier that it was not possible to climb very high whilst this wind was blowing. During the summer a very warm, wet wind, called the monsoon, blows up from the Bay of Bengal across India, bringing with it heavy rain. When this wind reaches the great mountain ranges to the north of the plains of India the rain turns to snow and at great heights it becomes both difficult and dangerous to climb, for large quantities of fresh snow are lying on the mountainsides and tend to form avalanches. (There is a separate article AVALANCHE.) It is extremely difficult to climb through soft snow, because every time a climber takes a step he may sink in up to his knees or even deeper and will have to make a great effort to pull himself out for the next step. So it was decided that the best time of year would probably be in the spring, when there would be a short break between the cold winter wind and the summer snows brought by the monsoon.

Another difficulty was the effect of great heights on the human body. As one gets higher above sea level, the amount of oxygen in the atmosphere becomes less and, since oxygen is necessary for life, the higher one goes the less lively one becomes. Fortunately, however, the human body becomes used to these conditions after a certain time and up to a certain height, which is generally agreed to be about 18,000 feet. Between 18,000 feet and 24,000 feet it is much harder for the body to get used to the height. Above 24,000 feet or so, it is now generally thought that the human body cannot become acclimatized, or used to the conditions, any further and the longer a man stays above this height the weaker he becomes. It may take quite a long time for a man to become acclimatized even below this height and climbers who have been to these great heights agree that they feel much weaker and less inclined to do any hard work than at more normal heights.

The expedition which first reached the summit in 1953 was the eighth to make the attempt.

## The First Expedition

On May 18, 1921, the first Mount Everest expedition left Darjeeling, near the northern frontier of India. Its leader was C. K. Howard-Bury and its object was to explore the mountain thoroughly and to choose the most likely route by which it could be climbed. In this wild country there are no roads and all the stores, tents and climbing equipment were carried on the backs of mules. Later, when the expedition crossed the high mountain passes into Tibet, the mules were replaced by ponies and yaks. (See Yak.)

When the expedition had climbed to a considerable height it was no longer possible for the yaks to accompany them. The loads had then to be carried on the backs of men and for this purpose the best were found to be the Sherpas, a race of men who came originally from the Nepalese valleys south of Everest. These tough men, who are often only about five feet tall, can carry heavy loads of 60–80 pounds for a whole day and nearly always remain cheerful.

The expedition made its way into Tibet and then turned westwards along the north side of Everest. After several weeks' travel the climbers agreed that Mount Everest could be climbed, but there was only one reasonable route. It was necessary to reach a saddle on a ridge known as the North Col, at a height of 23,500 feet and then to climb up to the great northeast ridge of the mountain. It was thought that this ridge, once reached, would offer no great climbing difficulties. The expedition returned to England full of optimism and in the following year the second Mount Everest expedition of 12 people under the leadership of General C. G. Bruce set out. On this expedition it was decided to carry cylinders of oxygen which the climbers could use above the North Col.

Three of the climbers, G. L. Mallory, E. F. Norton and T. H. Somervell, reached a height of about 27,000 feet without the use of oxygen, and G. I. Finch and J. G. Bruce, carrying oxygen, got up to 27,300 feet a few days later. Both parties were forced to turn back by exhaustion and intense cold. The expedition suffered a disastrous setback when seven porters were killed in an avalanche on the slopes below the North Col and as the monsoon arrived at about this time further attempts on the mountain were given up.

## The Expeditions of 1924 and 1933

In the expedition of 1924 two camps were established above the North Col, Camps V and VI. The northeast ridge had been found to have two short steep sections on it, which were known

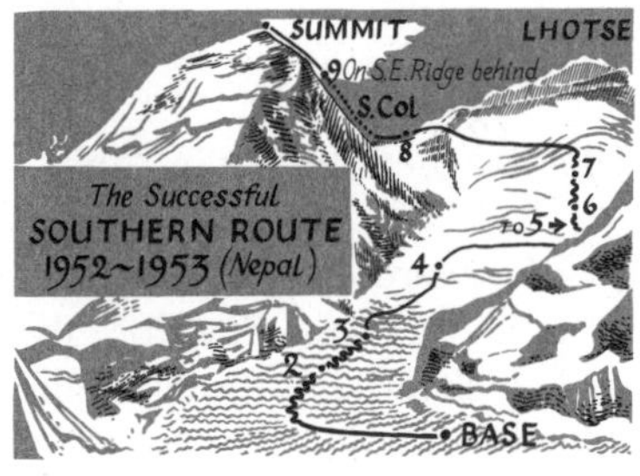


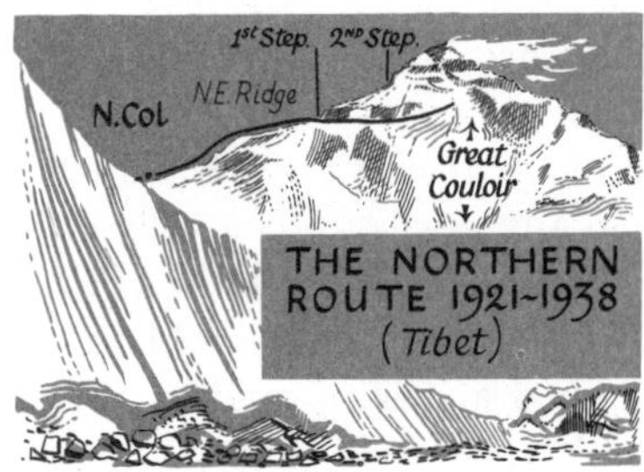


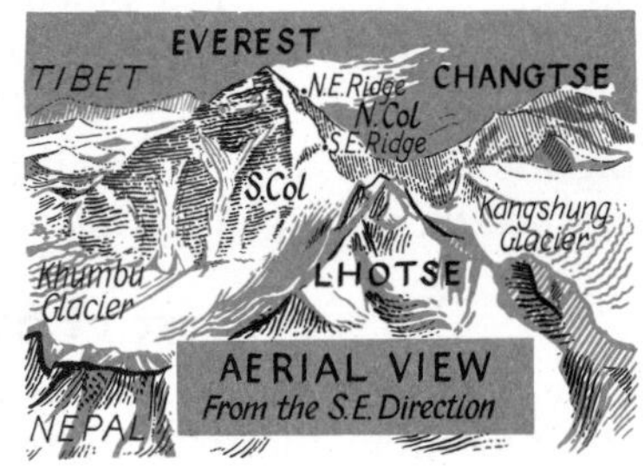

as the first step and the second step. In order to avoid these, Norton and Somervell, in their attempt on the summit, crossed the north face of the mountain, gaining height as they went. Somervell finally felt ill and unable to go any farther, and Norton went on alone to a height of about 28,000 feet; that is, about 1,000 feet from the summit. This was the highest point so far reached. Here he had to give up.

Four days later two other climbers, Mallory and A. C. Irvine, set out from Camp VI for their attempt on the summit. Mallory was an experienced climber and had taken part in both the earlier expeditions. He was known to favour the route along the ridge. A third climber, N. E. Odell, followed them up to Camp VI and through a break in the clouds saw two tiny figures making their way up towards the pyramid-like summit. That was the last to be seen of Mallory and Irvine. They never returned and it seems unlikely that they reached the summit.

Nine years passed before another expedition set out, under the leadership of Hugh Ruttledge. On this occasion Camp VI was established at 27,400 feet, the highest camp ever set up, and two attempts were made to climb the summit. P. Wyn Harris and L. R. Wager started first with the idea of following the ridge and, if possible, of climbing the first and second step. On the way they found an ice-axe which had belonged to Mallory. The two climbers got up to the second step and decided that it was impossible to climb it and so crossed the mountain face as far as the Great Couloir, or gully, which runs down the middle of the face from below the summit. They too had to give up the attempt as they had to get back to camp by nightfall.

Two days later F. S. Smythe and E. E. Shipton followed Norton's path across the mountain face but very soon Shipton found he could not go on. Smythe reached much the same point as Wyn Harris and Wager but was turned back, largely by the difficulty of the climbing in crossing the Great Couloir. The three of them had reached the same place as Norton in 1924.

## The Conquest of Everest

In 1953 Mount Everest was climbed at last, this time from the south through Nepal. On May 29 of this year E. P. Hillary and the Nepalese Tenzing Norgay reached the summit.

The expedition was led by Colonel John Hunt. In early May Hunt decided that the two climbers T. D. Bourdillon and R. C. Evans should make the first attempt from the South Col, and that Hillary and Tenzing should follow from a higher camp. On May 17 a camp was pitched on that part of Everest called the Lhotse face, at a height of 24,000 feet. The route on the upper part of the Lhotse face was first made by C. W. F. Noyce and a Sherpa on May 21. On the next day 13 Sherpas led by Major C. G. Wylie, with Hilary and Tenzing ahead of them, reached the South Col and placed stores there. On May 23 the first party, supported by Hunt and two Sherpas, reached the Col. On the 26th Evans and Bourdillon climbed to the south summit of Everest at a height of 28,700 feet, but it was too late to go farther. Meanwhile, Hunt and his Sherpa left supplies for the ridge camp at 27,350 feet.

On May 28 a camp was set up at 27,900 feet by W. G. Lowe, A. Gregory and a Sherpa. Hillary and Tenzing passed the night there and next day reached the south summit at 9 a.m. Two and a half hours later they had crossed the final ridge and stood on the summit of Everest. Hillary and Hunt were later knighted for their great achievement. (See HILLARY, SIR EDMUND.)

Four members of a Swiss expedition reached the top of Everest in May 1956. Four climbers of a Chinese expedition claimed to have done so on May 25, 1960, and on the same day a party of Indian climbers, approaching from the other side, were turned back by the weather within 700 feet of the summit. In 1962 another Indian attempt failed, but in 1963 a large American expedition sent three parties to the top, one by way of the supposedly unclimbable West ridge. This effort was related to the United States space programme and was particularly concerned to study the effects of lack of oxygen on men under stress. An Indian expedition reached the top in 1965.

**EVOLUTION.** The word evolution means "unfolding" and it is used to describe the gradual process by which all the forms of life today have evolved, or "unfolded", from earlier

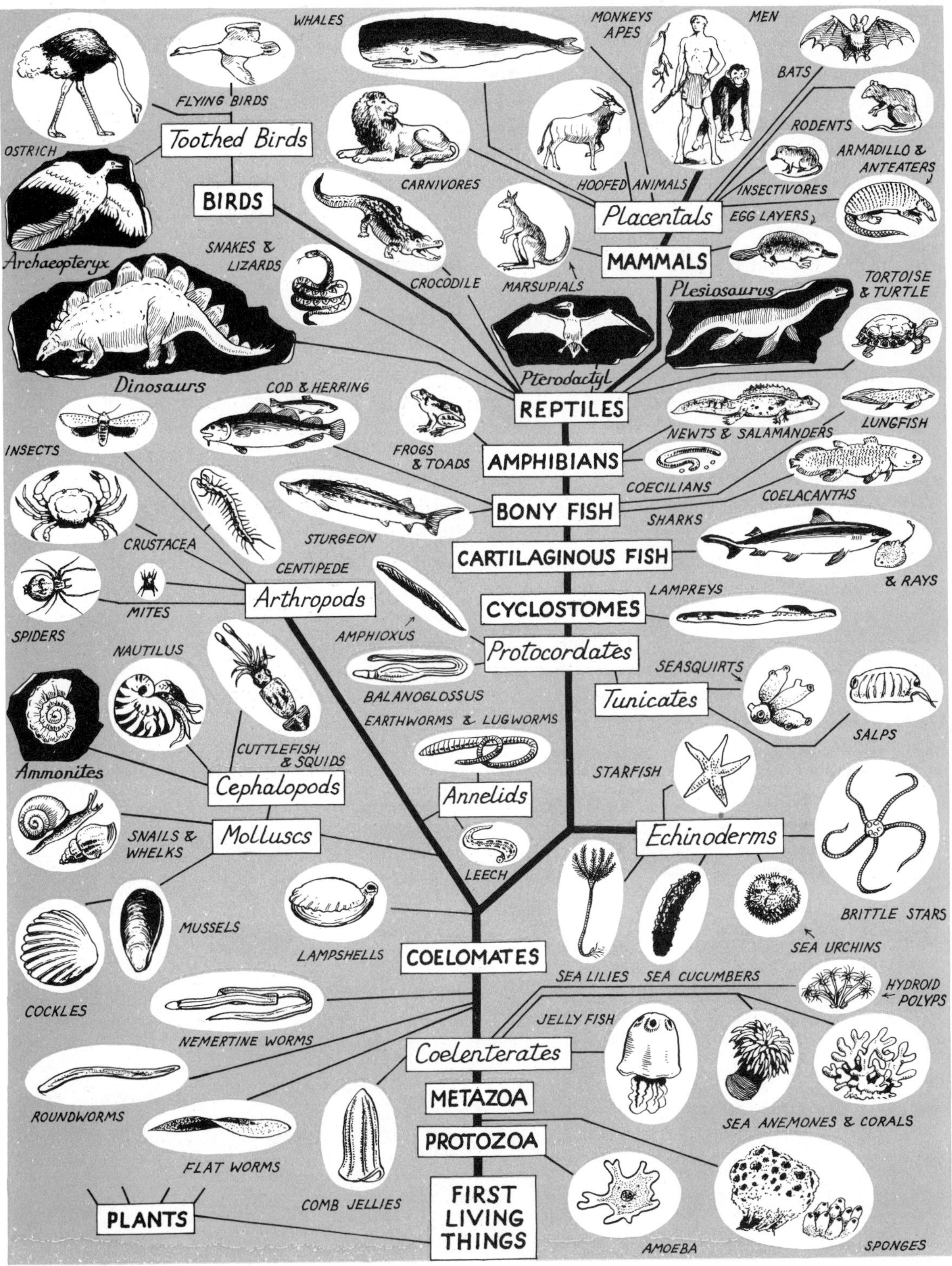


This "tree" shows how the different kinds of animal have developed from the first simple living things on earth. (Animals that have died out are shown here on a dark background.) The evolution of plants happened in a similar way.

forms which were on Earth in the distant past.

All living things can be classified into groups. The animals or plants within each group differ in detail and yet have certain main things in common. Scientists believe that this resemblance within a group of living things is really a family resemblance, arising from the fact that they are descended from the same ancestors. Thus the first birds, about 150,000,000 years ago, had wings and feathers and certain other features that are found in all birds nowadays. Their descendants gradually branched out in many different directions through the ages, until there are all the thousands of different kinds of birds in the world of today.

As with birds, so it is with other animals and plants. The living things we know now have not always existed but are believed to be descended from others which resembled them in some ways but were often simpler. Some creatures very like the ancestral forms still exist, but most died out millions of years ago and have been replaced entirely by modern forms.

Among the proofs that evolution has really happened are traces of earlier forms of life hidden away in the rocks beneath the soil. Most of the rocks near the surface of the Earth were formed by fine particles of mud or sand settling on the bottom of seas or lakes. As more and more settled, the layers underneath became packed tightly together and gradually turned into rock. Sometimes the mud contained dead bodies of animals or plants living at that time, and often the shell, bones or other hard parts remained when the mud became rock. Sometimes the hard parts of land animals or land plants were preserved in the same way, by falling into the water, being covered by blown sand or by sinking into the swamps on land.

These remains of animals or plants that lived many years ago are called fossils. (See FOSSIL.) In the course of time the sea bottom has often been raised up, very gradually, and become dry land. Thus rocks that were formed under the sea can now be studied in chalk pits, railway cuttings, cliffs or mountains, and in the rocks there are often fossil remains of animals or plants that lived and died millions of years ago. Geologists can tell the order in which the various rocks were formed and so they can tell which fossils came earlier and which came later in the history of the Earth. It is even possible to tell, roughly, the age (in millions of years) of a particular rock and so of the fossils it contains.

Shown below is the evolution of vertebrates (animals with backbones) from a simple to a more complicated form. This development is not a matter of steps. These changes are caused by changes in nature. For example, the glacier which covered much of Europe one million years ago made it necessary for animals to change in order to stay alive. The animals on the right are a few of the thousands of vertebrates that have at one time lived on the Earth.

ASTRASPIS: a small fish with the front of its body enclosed in plates of armour.

EUSTHENOPTERON: could paddle its way out of the water. It had jaws and fins which in later animals developed into bones.

ICHTHYOSTEGALIAN: the first four-legged vertebrate, resembled a lizard. It spent most of its time in water.

SEYMOURIA: amphibian reptile. It had a better brain, ribs for breathing, and a device for hearing on land, a simple slit in the skin.

Very old rocks contain only the traces of simple creatures, representing some of the first steps in the story of life; a full range of creatures resembling closely those now living is only found in rocks formed nearer the present time. This is a proof that evolution has taken place. The oldest rocks contain no clear traces of living things. Then come traces of jellyfish and worms. Then later a variety of creatures without backbones. Then the first fishes are found. In later rocks still, a growing variety of land plants and land creatures is found, until, in the more recent rocks, there are many forms which closely resemble the plants and animals of today.

## The Vertebrates

The first vertebrates (backboned animals) were fish-like creatures of which the earliest traces are found in rocks about 400,000,000 years old. They had no proper jaws and were covered with scaly armour. Some of their descendants evolved, or developed, proper jaws and became the first true fishes. Many of these early fishes lived in lakes, and about 280,000,000 years ago the climate became very dry and many of the lakes dried up. Some of these early fishes began gulping air at the surface and storing it in a pair of pouches at the back of the throat.

In some of the fishes these pouches became the first lungs, gradually replacing the gills by

CENOZOIC ERA

70 million years ago to the present

DRYOPITHECUS: a primitive early ape-like animal.

PARAPITHECUS showed development of teeth. It had many ape-like characteristics and was a tree-living beast.

ANCESTRAL LEMUROID, the ancestor of the present-day wild animal, the lemur, was a tree-living beast.

CYNOGNATHUS: a dog-jawed reptile, had limbs under its body instead of at the side.

ICTIDOSAURIAN: a reptile which had many features of the mammal (animal that feeds its young with milk and is warm-blooded). The first ear had developed.

AMPHITHERIUM: the first mammal.

which fishes normally breathe. Fishes that had lungs stood a better chance of surviving in the shallow, stagnant pools of that time. Some of them went even farther. Their fins gradually became adapted for scrambling about on land, so that if one pool dried up altogether the creature could find its way to another. These adapted fins were the first legs, soon with five toes to get a grip on the ground; now these creatures were fishes no longer but the first amphibians—the ancestors of the newts, frogs and toads of today.

For millions of years the amphibians flourished and some of them grew very big, but meanwhile some were taking a further step on to dry land. They began laying eggs with shells, which could survive even the scorching sun. Their legs got stronger, lifting their bodies off the ground. Their skins got thicker and drier, and so they became proper land creatures—the first reptiles.

The reptiles were the lords of the land for millions of years. Some were small, like the lizards of today. Others, like the dinosaurs, were as big as double-decker buses. The dinosaurs died out, but the ancient reptiles gave rise to the reptiles of today (crocodiles, lizards, snakes, tortoises) and also to two other great groups of animals, the birds and mammals.

The birds continued to lay eggs like those of the reptiles, but developed wings and feathers and warm blood. The mammals found a different way of keeping their eggs safe. They kept them inside their own bodies until the young mammal was ready to be born.

The first mammals appeared at least 150,000,000 years ago, but the evolution of the main kinds found today has chiefly happened in the last 70,000,000 years. Some of the early mammals, rather like the tarsiers of the East Indies today, are believed to have lived in trees and so became good at using their hands and eyes, and their brains developed rapidly. Some became the first monkeys. Others, perhaps, evolved directly into the first apes, creatures with large brains, keen eyes and skilful hands. Now fossils are being found which seem to link these first apes with the most primitive human fossils, the "near-men" who lived less than 1,000,000 years ago. Human beings are certainly not descended from apes such as the chimpanzee or gorilla, but scientists believe that these apes and people had ancestors in common, which would be described as apes if they still existed. (See MAN.)

## How Evolution Happens

That evolution has happened is something few scientists can doubt. *How* it has happened is something that is still discussed. Most biologists now believe that Charles Darwin (see DARWIN, CHARLES ROBERT) got very near the truth in his theory of evolution by natural selection. He pointed out that living things vary. They differ in speed, in strength, in all sorts of small ways, and many of these differences are inherited; that is, they are passed on to later generations. He also pointed out that an intense struggle for existence is always going on. In this struggle it is the fittest that survive and the fittest are those that are best adapted to the life they lead. So creatures which possess variations that favour survival live and reproduce their kind and those which do not have these variations die out. In this way the favourable variations will, according to Darwin, gradually appear in all those animals.

Darwin first thought of his theory in about 1840, but he went on collecting evidence patiently for nearly 20 years before he published it. Then, in 1858, A. R. Wallace (1823–1913) sent Darwin an article to criticize which contained just the same idea. Wallace's article and a summary of Darwin's work were published together. In the following year Darwin published his great book *The Origin of Species.*

**EXAMINATIONS.** "It's exams this week!" Probably every one who reads this has said that at some time or another, for nearly all schools have examinations. Mostly they are held at the end of term and are set and marked by the children's own teachers. These are known as internal examinations: the other type, known as external, or public examinations, are set and marked by people who have had nothing to do with teaching the candidates who sit for them. Most children at primary schools in England and

Wales have personal knowledge of one external examination—that which helps to decide what kind of education is most suitable for them after the age of 11. They will probably also have done intelligence tests—a modern form of examination—which are not intended to test their knowledge in any particular subject, but to show how much they are capable of learning.

Many people dislike examinations but no one has yet discovered a satisfactory alternative to them, although this is not for want of trying. Examinations have taken many forms since the Chinese first used them 3,000 years ago to choose officers for their government services.

The Chinese required candidates to repeat from memory extremely long passages from the works of their great religious teachers. For many centuries this was the favourite method of examining in the East. In Europe examinations began when the universities were started in the 12th and 13th centuries, and they took the even more difficult form of "disputations". Each candidate for a degree was given a statement which he had to prove true or false by arguing about it with a group of professors. These "disputations" were often open to the public, and usually went on for hours if not for days. This practice still survives in Norway and Sweden.

Written examinations became common in England in the 19th century when many examining bodies were set up. (An examining body is a group of people who have been given the right to set and mark external examinations. For example, the universities and professional institutions such as the Institution of Electrical Engineers are examining bodies.) The questions schoolboys often had to answer in those days seem unreasonable now. How would you like to have to answer the following question?

> When the adjective occurs in the accusative after a verb, it is a tertiary predicate. Is this the whole truth?

Between 1862 and 1895 teachers in English public elementary schools were paid according to how well their pupils did in examinations in reading, writing and arithmetic (the "three Rs"), conducted every year by government inspectors. Also, part of the money paid by the government for the upkeep of a school was withheld if pupils failed. These things had very bad effects on the children's education, for teachers often spent the whole year only on the subjects in which their class would be examined. All that is done away with now.

Examinations are set for one of two purposes: to show whether candidates have reached a certain standard or to select the best candidate out of many who may be good. The General Certificate of Education is an example of the first: the open scholarship examinations at Oxford and Cambridge, and the Civil Service examinations are examples of the second. In either case the examination may consist of questions to be answered in writing; spoken, or oral, questions to be answered orally; practical tests; or a combination of two or more of these methods.

Intelligence tests are rather different. Their purpose is to discover how much intelligence one has—which is not the same thing as how much one knows. A person may be highly intelligent but at the same time know very little, because he has never been taught. The results of intelligence tests done by children are sometimes shown in terms of "mental age"; if, for example, a child of six gets a result that is normal for a child of eight, he is said to have a mental age of eight. To make sure that they will work properly, all intelligence tests are tried out first on very large numbers of children before being used. (See INTELLIGENCE TESTS.)

There are, besides, aptitude tests. These show what type of work a person will do best if he himself does not really know.

**EXCAVATION** means making a hole in the ground, from the Latin word meaning "to hollow". The word is normally used to describe the methods employed by archaeologists when they dig up ancient sites in order to discover their story.

Throughout history there have been people who have collected ancient objects for their beauty or for their value. In the 19th century wealthy persons and museums sent out expeditions to dig up these objects in the ancient cities of Mesopotamia, Egypt and Mexico. As time went on more people began to be interested in

*Radio Times Hulton Picture Library*

**Left: Excavating a Roman wall which has been discovered under the great Norman bank in Castle Park, Colchester. Right: An archaeologist at work. His young assistant notes the exact position in which objects are found.**

seriously studying the lives of those who had lived long ago. Excavators began to take more care in digging to find out the kind of house that was lived in, how the town was built, or in what kind of tomb a man was buried, rather than simply to find ancient objects which might prove valuable.

To understand how modern excavation is done let us look first at what happens in the history of a house. When the builder had cleared the ground, he first dug trenches in which to build the foundations on which the walls stood. Then he levelled the ground and raised the floor before he laid down the concrete or the mosaic, which is made up of hundreds of tiny pieces of coloured stone or glass joined together by cement to form pictures. During this time a careless workman may have dropped a coin from his pocket into the foundation trench, or broken his dinner bowl and thrown it away in the earth beneath the floor. Thus thousands of years later, perhaps, things belonging to the time when the house was being built are found. These things had been covered up by parts of its construction.

When the house walls were built and the roof put on, the owners came to live in it. Gradually things got lost in the house, coins rolled in dark corners, broken pottery was left behind, and so things belonging to people living in the house collected to form what is called by archaeologists the "occupation" period.

Lastly, perhaps there was a war; the occupants were chased away or killed and the house burned down or abandoned. In time the roof fell in, the doors and windows rotted and the walls fell down. Finally, the whole place became overgrown with weeds and bushes.

Now the archaeologist's task is to unravel this story by working backwards into the past and to find out about the events that have just been described by studying the remains which are found. For this he needs to find the "plan" showing how many rooms there were and so forth; he also requires a diagram to show from bottom to top the foundations and floors, the rubbish the occupants left behind and how the roof fell in and the walls collapsed. This is called a "section".

The archaeologist can find out the plan by clearing all the earth and bricks from the house, but this will not give him a section. Therefore an excavation is usually begun by digging a trench, from the side of which the section may be drawn in the diagram.

The first job is to mark out the trenches to a certain size (not more than ten feet) with pegs and string so that the sides may be kept straight for the drawing and because all excavations must be kept tidy. Each trench must be given a number and a page in a notebook, after which digging can begin.

One thing about earths and soils that has been discovered by excavators is that, once disturbed, the sign of the disturbance will always be seen in the ground. The excavator's aim, therefore, is to dig up the soil so carefully that it will be possible to see all the disturbances described above. Each different soil is called a "layer" and, in digging, the purpose is to take each one out separately, and the objects from each layer are kept and labelled.

The first trench will be dug down through all the layers till natural or virgin soil is reached, when the section, or diagram, of one face is drawn. This shows how the layers are combined and which of them belong to the floors, the occupation and the destruction that have just been described in the story of the house.

At this point the pottery and the objects are examined. All those from under the original floor are collected together; those from the occupation and the destruction are in two other groups. The first thing to find out is when the house was built, then how long it was occupied and lastly when it was destroyed. Below the floor the latest or newest piece of pottery or coin found will give the date *after* which the floor was made. How long after can be told from the objects of the occupation; the next newest object found in that layer will belong to the time when the occupation began, the latest object again giving the date *after* which the destruction occurred. The objects from the destruction layer can be considered in the same way. Thus the history of the site is told.

In the second place, the excavator wants to know as much as possible about how the house was built, how the people lived and how it was destroyed. He does this by digging a number of trenches or squares until the original plan of the house is uncovered, measured and drawn on a diagram. He digs several trenches below the floors and foundations, which show up clearly how they were built. In other parts the whole room is cleared and the things found in it show whether it was the kitchen or store-room, for example. If bones and corn are found they show what the people ate; when the pottery is mended it shows what kind of jugs and pots they used; a lost ear-ring shows what the jewellery was like and a fragment of leather or cloth of what the clothes were made.

Finally, there may be a deep black layer over the occupation, showing that the house was burnt, or just decayed wood and earth showing that it was no longer lived in and collapsed.

How to excavate a house has been discussed very briefly but excavation is often a very complicated and skilful job. More than one building may be erected on the same site at different times, as in London or Troy. In that case the method of excavation, called "stratification", where the archaeologist must find out from the layers the order in which the buildings were erected, becomes complicated. It can only really be learnt by experience. (See ARCHAEOLOGY.)

**EXHIBITIONS.** Shows and displays of all kinds are called exhibitions, and thus an exhibition may be a display of paintings or photographs or of animals, such as horses and cattle.

A great many exhibitions are like huge market places for the sale of goods, and these are often called trade fairs. This is because, although fairs are generally places of entertainment nowadays (see FAIRS), in the middle ages a fair was a special market, held usually once a year, where the people of the district gathered to buy and sell as well as to have a good time.

In Europe some of these fairs were very large and lasted for two or even three weeks. From them developed many great international trade shows and exhibitions, and a famous example was the Nijni-Novgorod fair in Russia. In fact, Nijni-Novgorod had three fairs—a timber fair in January, a horse fair in July, and in August and September the great St. Peter and St. Paul fair which attracted crowds from all over Europe. (Nijni-Novgorod is now called Gorki.)

Great Britain still has some traditional fairs such as the St. Giles' fair in Oxford and the Stratford-upon-Avon "mop" fair, but trade fairs are more important as they attract overseas buyers and help trade. Many are held each year in Britain. The *Daily Mail* Ideal Home Exhibi-

*Radio Times Hulton Picture Library*

Inside the Crystal Palace, the huge "glasshouse" built in Hyde Park for the Great Exhibition of 1851.

tion displays the newest furniture, ways of designing houses, processing food and equipping the home. It is held each year at Olympia in London. Other great exhibitions held in London are the Motor Show, the international Boat Show, Cruft's Dog Show and Chelsea Flower Show. The Royal Agricultural Show was formerly held in a different place each year, but now has a permanent site in Warwickshire.

International exhibitions, in which many countries take part, are usually very large. In 1851 the exhibition known as the Great Exhibition of the Works of Industry of All Nations was held in London, and exhibits (more than 19,000 of them) from all over the world were shown in the Crystal Palace, a building of glass and iron like a monster greenhouse which was specially erected in Hyde Park for the Great Exhibition; it was later enlarged and rebuilt in the neighbourhood of Sydenham, to the south-east of London. Many beautiful firework displays were held there until it was burned down in 1936.

In Paris the Eiffel Tower still stands as a reminder of another exhibition, the Paris Exhibition of 1889. This was in memory of the French Revolution, which had broken out 100 years before, and with 32 million visitors it outshone every exhibition yet held. The Chicago Exhibition of 1893, held on the shore of Lake Michigan, was intended to celebrate the 400th anniversary of the discovery of America by Christopher Columbus. It was the first exhibition to be lit by electric light and was attended by 21 million visitors.

The British Empire Exhibition held at Wembley in Middlesex in 1924–1925 had 27 million visitors. Part of the exhibition was Wembley Stadium, where the football cup finals are held. The smaller Festival of Britain Exhibition, held in London in 1951, likewise left a permanent reminder—the Royal Festival Hall, where concerts and ballets are performed.

In 1928 an international meeting took place about the holding of big exhibitions. It made a number of rules. It defined a first-class exhibition as one in which each country taking part builds a national pavilion for its exhibits, and it

*British Travel Association*

An open-air exhibition of sculpture in Battersea Park, London.

laid down intervals of time to prevent such exhibitions from being held too often in any one part of the world. The International Bureau of Exhibitions was therefore formed to control the holding of these big shows.

The last big exhibition before World War II was held at Paris in 1937 and attracted 34 million visitors. The New York World's Fair of 1939–1940 was in honour of George Washington, who became the first president of the United States 150 years before. It had nearly 45 million visitors, at that time a record.

The Brussels Universal Exhibition of 1958 was held mainly to show the progress made in science since the war. Its central point was a huge silvery construction called the Atomium representing the structure of the atom. In much the same fashion, the New York World's Fair of 1964–1965 displayed the Unisphere, an open model of the Earth made in steel. This fair had not been approved by the International Bureau and lost a lot of money, although some 50 million people attended.

The 1967 international exhibition, Expo 67, was part of the celebrations of Canada's 100th birthday. Staged at Montreal, it attracted 50 million visitors and 61 countries built national pavilions. Like most big exhibitions it had a fun-fair, which remained as a permanent feature of Montreal.

The British pavilion at Expo 67, the international exhibition held at Montreal, Canada, in 1967. The cliff-like pavilion with its high tower was designed by Sir Basil Spence, the architect of Coventry Cathedral. Inside, the pavilion was divided into sections showing Britain's history, discoveries and way of life, and an important display of scientific and industrial exhibits.

Most big exhibitions have a considerable influence on architecture. For example, the ornamental *art nouveau* style was encouraged in Europe because there was a lot of it in the buildings of the Paris exhibition of 1900. The Chicago Exhibition of 1893, held in grand pillared buildings with classical fronts, started a fashion in America for pillars and columns that lasted for about 50 years.

A remarkable feature of Expo 67 was a block of 158 flats called Habitat, intended by the Israeli architect Moshe Safdie to show "how people in cities could really live." Made of hollow concrete boxes, with the roof of one flat serving as a garden or terrace for the one above, Habitat remained as a permanent feature.

**EXMOOR.** In the western corner of Somerset, and stretching into Devon also, is a high moorland called Exmoor. The highest point is Dunkery Beacon (1,705 feet) which is now looked after by the National Trust. (See NATIONAL TRUST.) In the north, Exmoor borders the Bristol Channel and forms a very beautiful and rugged coastline. Most of the area is wild and uncultivated, but the coarse grass provides food for cattle and also for flocks of horned sheep, which are found only in a few other places in England. Many of the attractive wild ponies are rounded up each year for the October Pony Fair at Bampton. Red deer still run wild on Exmoor and are hunted from time to time, while in the Exe, Barle, Lyn and other streams fishermen can find trout. Crossing the River Barle near Dulverton there is an ancient bridge built of great slabs of stone. If you have read R. D. Blackmore's book *Lorna Doone* you will know that much of the story takes place on Exmoor.

*Mustograph*

A view of Exmoor from the slopes of Dunkery Beacon.

**EXPANSION** is an increase in size or swelling. The opposite is contraction, or shrinking. Nearly every substance expands when heated and contracts when cooled. All gases expand to the same extent but liquids and solids vary. Thus a bar of iron ten feet long expands about one-seventh of an inch when its temperature is increased by 100 degrees Centigrade, whereas a brass bar expands nearly twice as much. Among liquids, alcohol when heated expands nearly seven times as much as mercury.

The expansion of iron when heated was long used by wheelwrights for fixing iron tyres on to the wheels of carts and wagons. The tyre, made as a band just too small to fit round the rim of the wheel when cold, was expanded by heating over a ring-shaped fire and then forced on to the rim. On cooling it contracted to grip the rim firmly. The steel tyres on railway-carriage wheels are fixed in the same way. The differing expansion of metals is used in the thermostat, which is a device for regulating temperature found in electric irons, refrigerators and heating systems. It contains a *bimetallic strip*, or strip of two different metals welded together. When heated the strip curls and when cool it straightens. This movement is used to switch the current on or off in an electric iron or refrigerator, or to work a shutter controlling the draught through a heating boiler.

The expansion of liquids when heated is made use of in thermometers (see THERMOMETER).

**EXPLORERS.** In all countries and in all ages men have left their homes and ventured into strange lands. Very different reasons have led them to do this. Some hoped to become wealthy by trade or by finding new supplies of valuable silks and spices, gold, precious stones and oil. Some sought fame; others went for the love of adventure, to prove an idea right or wrong, to win lands for their governments or to convert people to their own religion. But whatever their reason was for going, those who discovered lands that had been unknown before were explorers.

Explorers include not only the people described below, who added to what Europeans knew of the world's geography, but also the explorers belonging to other peoples. The Phoenicians sailed the Indian Ocean and the Arabs crossed the great deserts of Africa and Asia long before these were known in Europe. People of the South Sea Islands still sing of their great men who sailed to South America centuries before the white man reached either of these regions. It is well to remember that almost all the places said to have been "discovered" by white men have in fact already had people living in them, the main exceptions being Iceland and the Antarctic.

However, it was a European people, the Greeks, who were the first to build up any great knowledge of geography. They collected the records of journeys made by merchants and travellers in all the surrounding lands, together with accounts of war campaigns such as those of Alexander the Great. Later, the Romans continued to collect similar accounts. From them we can tell that, by about A.D. 150, the shores of the Mediterranean and Black Seas were well known and that the lands of western Europe as far north as the Baltic had also been visited. The coasts of India had been explored by a few adventurous sailors and some merchants had reached China by land. However, although men had gone through the Red Sea and Persian Gulf, even the most northerly parts of Africa were still practically unexplored.

Between about A.D. 500 and 1000 all this knowledge was lost. It is true that the Norsemen discovered Iceland and Greenland and even reached America, but for the most part Europeans were content to hear fanciful tales of lands where people had dogs' heads or no heads at all, and of other people with only one eye or one foot which they used to shade their faces from the sun. At this time sailors kept near the shores and seldom dared to make long voyages, for when they were out of sight of land it was difficult to be sure that they were travelling in the right direction. However, about

1300 or earlier, European mariners began to use the magnetic compass, which helped them to make longer journeys and more accurate maps. (See COMPASS.)

## Routes to the East

During the 13th century the Tatar chiefs of Mongolia had built up a great empire over the grasslands of central Asia, and their armies had begun to overrun southeastern and then central Europe. The Pope sent envoys to the Tatar rulers and some made their way far to the east. Merchants also set out to trade with the Tatars, and much the most famous of these merchant travellers was Marco Polo. He reached the court of Kublai Khan, near Peking, in 1275 and was employed by that great Tatar ruler for nearly 20 years. After his return to Italy his story of life in Asian lands was written down, and this was the first good account of Cathay (China) and the way to get there. (There are articles KUBLAI KHAN and POLO, MARCO and other articles on many of the great explorers mentioned in this article.)

During the middle ages the wars of the crusades helped to increase Europeans' knowledge of the world they lived in. (See CRUSADES TO THE HOLY LAND.) The wars brought them into touch with the Arabs, who told them what they had learned of North Africa, southwest Asia and the Indian Ocean. The western knights fighting in the Holy Land became familiar with fine cloths of silk, calico and muslin, with the spices used in eastern cookery and the medicines used by Saracen doctors. They learned how all these things came by caravan across the deserts (that is, on the backs of camels or horses owned by merchants), but at this time the enmity between the Christians and the Moslems of Asia Minor made it impossible for European traders to reach the eastern lands themselves.

In this period the people of southern and western Europe were almost like prisoners within their own lands. To the north were dark forests and frozen seas, to the east the Tatars, to the southeast and south the Saracens and the deserts, and to the west the wide Atlantic. (Both Tatars and Saracens were Moslems.)

Between the Mediterranean and the islands of the east where spices come from (the Indies, or East Indies as they were later called) lay the double barrier of the desert and the Saracens. The Portuguese were at the western end of the barrier, and they were the first to realize that a way round it might be found by sea. About 1418, Prince Henry of Portugal began to gather information and train navigators to make the attempt. (There is an article NAVIGATION as well as one called HENRY THE NAVIGATOR.) He sent out many expeditions along the west coast of Africa, and before his death they had reached the Cape Verde Islands.

His work was continued. A Portuguese explorer reached Egypt through the Mediterranean and went through the Red Sea and on by sea to India, making a report which further encouraged those who searched for a route round Africa. Bartholomew Diaz had rounded the Cape of Good Hope in 1488 and Vasco da Gama went farther by completing the first sea voyage to India and back in 1499.

On a second voyage the ships of the expedition sailed so much farther to the west than they intended that the leader, Pedro Cabral, landed on the shores of Brazil in 1500. He had learned the lesson just taught by Christopher Columbus —that the wide ocean need no longer be a barrier. It could be safely crossed. (See COLUMBUS, CHRISTOPHER.)

In those days people believed the distance round the Earth to be much smaller than it really is. Since the distance to the East Indies by way of the Red Sea was known to be considerable, Columbus was led to believe that these islands could not be very far to the west of Spain. He therefore proposed to reach them by sailing westwards. The Spanish rulers, King Ferdinand and Queen Isabella, provided ships and Columbus set off in 1492. The journey was longer than he expected, but he reached land aften ten weeks and thought that it was part of the Indies. Actually, of course, he had reached one of the islands now known as the West Indies.

Later, Columbus and other Spanish expeditions discovered the coasts of Central America and the lands near by. His greatest successor, Ferdinand Magellan, followed the South

American coast southwards from Brazil and in 1520 found a way to the Pacific through what is now called Magellan Strait lying between the mainland and the island of Tierra del Fuego. Crossing the Pacific he actually reached the spice islands (the East Indies), and although he was killed there some of his ships returned by the Cape of Good Hope, so completing the first voyage round the world. One of the most important results of this expedition was the discovery of the great stretch of water lying between America and Asia. It was Magellan who named it the Pacific Ocean.

Magellan's success in sailing to the south of America encouraged other people to try to reach the East Indies by sailing to the north of the continent. John Cabot, an Englishman, had already discovered the Newfoundland fishing grounds in 1497 during an attempt to reach Asia by sailing westwards, and both the English and the French kept on trying from the 16th century onwards. In 1534 Jacques Cartier sailed into the Gulf of St. Lawrence, Canada, hoping that it would lead into the Pacific. Modern maps make it easy to see how mistaken he was. However, his successor Samuel de Champlain followed the St. Lawrence River and started the French colony of Canada. Meanwhile, Martin Frobisher and John Davis had found the channels between Greenland and Labrador (part of the Canadian mainland) and in 1610 Henry Hudson reached the bay which now bears his name. In later years many people, including John Franklin, tried to find this north-western route to the Pacific, but no one succeeded in following it the whole way until 1905. (The article Polar Exploration tells more about this in the section on the North-West Passage; there is another section on the North-East Passage which tells how in 1879 a Swedish expedition eventually reached the Pacific by sailing to the north of Asia.)

## Exploration in America

By the early years of the 17th century the Spaniards were settled in Mexico, Central America and the West Indies, the Portuguese in Brazil, the French along the St. Lawrence and the English in Virginia and New England (both on the east coast of what is now the United States) and on the shores of Hudson Bay. All these were starting points for the further exploration of America.

In 1513 Vasco de Balboa, a Spaniard, had crossed the isthmus of Panama (the narrow neck of land between North and South America), and six years later one of his countrymen, Hernan Cortes, began the conquest of Mexico. Before his death Cortes and other Spaniards had explored Central America from Panama to California and made known the rich silver mines of Mexico. Francisco Pizarro, with 180 men, sailed along the Pacific coast and conquered Peru for the King of Spain, and it is said that the ruler of Peru, in an attempt to save his own life, paid gold bars enough to fill a room 22 feet by 16 feet, as high as a man could reach.

Some of Pizarro's companions conquered the western lands of South America as far as Chile, and others reached the streams that fed the Amazon. One of them, Francisco de Orellana, followed this great river to its mouth on the Atlantic in 1541. The Portuguese added little to what was known of South America until 1638, when Pedro Teixeira explored the main course of the Amazon. By 1800 all the main regions of South America were known.

In North America the Spaniards explored the lands north of Mexico and started settlements in New Mexico and California which were later seized by the United States. Traders and settlers from Virginia pushed westwards, slowly at first because of the mountains and forests in their path. Further north, Robert La Salle and other Frenchmen pushed inland more rapidly, for they had the waterways of the St. Lawrence and the Great Lakes to help them. Going southwards from Lake Michigan in 1681, La Salle claimed the whole valley of the Mississippi River for France.

Following the capture of Quebec from the French in 1759, Canada and all the lands east of the Mississippi became British. After the United States became independent in 1783, expeditions went west of the Mississippi. Between 1804 and 1806 Meriwether Lewis and William Clark went up the Missouri River and reached the mouth of the Columbia River on the Pacific.

Fur traders and gold seekers made known the Rocky Mountains and Pacific coast lands.

In 1670 the Hudson's Bay Company began its work, and its men gradually established trading posts along the rivers of the forest country in the west. In 1789 one of these men, Alexander Mackenzie, traced to the Arctic the river which now bears his name. Four years later he followed one of the smaller rivers that joined this Mackenzie River, going right into the Rockies and on to the Pacific. He was thus the first man to cross the North American continent.

Other traders made known most of the rivers of this region in the 19th century, but parts of Canada are still known only from the air.

## Australia and the Pacific

From the days of the ancient Greeks it was believed that a great continent lay to the south of Asia. Magellan had crossed the Pacific without finding it, but there was still room enough for a vast land between his route and Africa. The land now known as Australia was probably first seen by both Dutch and Spanish explorers in 1606, and its western shores were certainly known to Dutch captains by 1630. Abel Tasman was sent in 1642 to find out the size of this new land. He passed south of it, called at Tasmania, sighted the shores of New Zealand and called at New Guinea on his way back to the Dutch colony of Java. In 1699 William Dampier, who had been a buccaneer in his early days, sailed along the northern coast of Australia and the northern coast of New Guinea.

However, in the early 18th century there were still three main problems in the Pacific—the size of Australia and the nature of the coasts of northeast and northwest America. One man, James Cook, solved all three problems. Rounding Cape Horn he discovered many islands in the South Pacific in 1769 and 1770, drew maps of the coasts of New Zealand and eastern Australia, and eventually returned by the Cape of Good Hope to England. On a second voyage Cook sailed round the world, far to the south of Australia, without finding any continent there. On his third expedition he passed from the Pacific through the Bering Strait, between America and Asia, and mapped the coasts of both continents in this area.

Another great name in the history of Australian exploration is that of Matthew Flinders, who was the first to sail right round the continent, keeping close to the coast, at the beginning of the 19th century. However, as in

America, much of the exploration of the interior of Australia was done by unknown pioneers who pushed inland looking for pasture for their animals or else in search of gold. Between 1828 and 1836 Charles Sturt and Thomas Mitchell traced the courses of the Murray River and the smaller ones that joined it. Famous journeys inland across the desert and semi-desert country were made by Sturt in 1845, A. C. Gregory in 1856 and 1858, Robert Burke and W. J. Wills in 1860 and J. M. Stuart in 1861. There are still parts of the continent which the white man has not visited on foot.

## The Opening-up of Africa

The interior of Africa remained unknown to Europeans long after its coasts had been mapped. Its main secrets were revealed during the exploration of the courses of its four great rivers—the Niger, the Nile, the Zambezi and the Congo. All were finally traced from their upper courses to the sea by explorers of British birth. Mungo Park in 1796 and 1805 traced much of the Niger, but he was killed by natives before reaching its mouth. The lower course of the river was not traced until 1830, for in that year it was explored by Richard and John Lander. David Livingstone, who was the greatest of African explorers, discovered and mapped the Zambezi and crossed the continent from the Atlantic to the Indian Ocean, but he failed in the main task he set himself, which was to discover where the River Nile began. When nothing had been heard of him for some years he was found, as most people know, by H. M. Stanley.

Livingstone died while following the River Lualaba, which he believed to be the upper part of the Nile, but Stanley proved that the Lualaba joined the Congo, and then in 1876 and 1877 he followed this great river westwards to its mouth. He had thus made the second journey across Africa. The mystery of the sources of the Nile was solved by J. H. Speke and J. A. Grant in 1863 when, having followed the river which flowed northwards from Lake Victoria, they met Samuel Baker who had travelled up the Nile from Cairo in Egypt.

These great journeys led to the division of Africa between the European nations, and this in turn led to more detailed exploration, especially by the French in the Sahara and the Sudan.

## Modern Exploration

Little by little the blank parts on the map of the world have been filled in—by people like Bertram Thomas and H. St. John Philby in Arabia, by Sven Hedin (a Swede) in central Asia, by British officers in India, Russians in northern Asia and missionaries and traders of many nationalities in China.

In recent years the most exciting journeys have been those to reach the North and South Poles. The attempts to find the North-West Passage from the Atlantic to the Pacific went on all through the 19th century, and these provided the knowledge needed for attempts to reach the North Pole, which began in 1875. The most thrilling attempt was that made by Fridtjof Nansen between 1893 and 1896, but the Pole (or a point near it) was finally reached by Robert Peary, an American, in 1909.

Few people tried to explore in the Antarctic for a long time after Cook's voyage, although the seamen who hunted whales and seals found out a great deal about the area. Important discoveries were also made in 1840–1843 by James Ross, in 1902 and 1912 by Robert Falcon Scott, and in 1908 by Ernest Shackleton. In the race to reach the South Pole in 1911, Scott was just beaten by Roald Amundsen. Scott's last expedition had the first motor-drawn sledges, but they soon broke down. No explorers then had the efficient motor sledges and aircraft used by expeditions such as the Commonwealth Trans-Antarctic Expedition of 1955–1958. (See POLAR EXPLORATION.)

As man has explored the remaining unknown parts of the land and sea, so his thoughts have turned to what lies beneath them, as well as to the upper air and finally outer space. The article POT-HOLING AND CAVING tells how the deep caves below the earth are being explored, and UNDERWATER EXPLORATION tells of the great descents made beneath the sea. For a description of man's discoveries in outer space you must turn to the article SPACE EXPLORATION.

**EXPLOSIVE.** Any substance set on fire gives off a quantity of hot gas as it burns, which is one reason why a fireplace has a chimney. An explosive is a substance that gives off so much hot gas so quickly that it will burst open and even shatter anything surrounding it, and does this with great noise and violence.

*Radio Times Hulton Picture Library*

Blasting in a Yorkshire quarry. Nearly five tons of explosive, skilfully placed, brings down many thousands of tons of limestone from the quarry wall.

## Kinds of Explosives

The oldest explosive, and one still used in fireworks, is *gunpowder,* which may have been known to the ancient Chinese thousands of years ago but was first described by an English friar, Roger Bacon, some time before 1249. It was used for firing guns by the middle of the 14th century but not until 1660 were ways found to use it for blasting rock in quarries or other peaceful purposes.

Gunpowder is a mixture of potassium nitrate (saltpetre), charcoal and sulphur, and when burnt it gives off about 4,000 times its own volume of gas. The charcoal and sulphur burn in the oxygen given off by the saltpetre, and the action is very rapid.

A more powerful explosive discovered in 1846 by the German chemist Christian Schönbein was *guncotton,* made by treating cotton fibre with strong nitric and sulphuric acids. (See Nitric Acid; Sulphuric Acid.) A piece of fibre treated in this way would burn quietly but very quickly if set alight, but if struck sharply it would explode with great violence. The modern explosive of this kind is made by using the acids to treat paper or wood shavings instead of cotton and is called *nitro-cellulose.*

In 1847 the Italian Ascanio Sobrero discovered *nitro-glycerine,* made by dripping glycerine slowly into strong nitric and sulphuric acids. (See Glycerine.) This is an extremely powerful explosive, giving off 12,000 times its own volume of gas when exploded; but for some years it was too dangerous to use as it can be set off much too easily by rough handling or shaking. Then in 1866 the great Swedish chemist Alfred Nobel found by accident that if nitro-glycerine were mixed with a kind of sandy earth called kieselguhr it became a solid cheesy substance which although still a powerful explosive could be handled safely, and this he called *dynamite.* He also discovered that guncotton mixed with nitro-glycerine formed a stiff jelly, and this *blasting gelatine* is much used for quarrying.

By reducing the amount of nitro-glycerine and increasing that of the guncotton in the mixture Nobel made a horny substance which he called *ballistite*; the difference between it and blasting gelatine or dynamite was that it went off much more gently and gave a pushing action instead of a shattering action. It could therefore be used for pushing the bullet or shell out of a gun, whereas dynamite if used would burst the gun. (See Gun.) Alfred Nobel made a fortune from explosives and with some of the money he set up a fund to give prizes to writers and scientists whose work helped mankind. (See Nobel Prizes.)

Explosives are usually divided into *propellents,* which have this pushing action, and *high explosives,* which are used where a shattering or blasting effect is wanted. Modern propellents such as *cordite* are made by mixing nitro-glycerine and nitro-cellulose and are used in cartridges for all kinds of guns and sometimes for starting aero engines and diesel engines. They are also used for propelling—or pushing along—guided weapons and rockets (on which there are separate articles).

The high explosive most used in the two world wars was trinitrotoluene (T.N.T.). Others have long names like cyclotrimethylene-trinitramine (cyclonite) and pentaerythritol-tetranitrate (P.E.T.N.), but nearly all high explosives are made by treating some substance containing carbon with nitric acid. (See also the article NUCLEAR ENERGY.)

## Setting off Explosives

Gunpowder could be touched off from a spark or flame but modern explosives are less easily set off. Propellents are set off by a flame coming either from a small quantity of lively explosive held in a cap which explodes when struck, as when the trigger of a pistol or gun is pulled; or from a gunpowder igniter which is lit by sending an electric current through a thin wire embedded in the powder; the current makes the wire white hot just as it would in a torch bulb (see TORCH).

High explosives have to be set off by a very violent shock as a flame will not explode them; indeed some high explosives when set alight will merely burn fiercely but without violence. This shock is given by exploding a small amount of violent explosive like tetryl or cyclonite in a tube called a *detonator* which is carried inside the high explosive to be set off. The detonator is exploded either by striking a cap fixed to it, or electrically as already described, or sometimes by lighting a small pinch of guncotton dust in the detonator by means of what is called *safety fuse*. This fuse looks like rather stiff cord and has a central core of very slow-burning gunpowder, so that if some yards of fuse are connected to the detonator a man can light the other end and have time to get to safety.

Explosives are as important in peacetime as in war. Huge quantities are used for blasting in mines and quarries all over the world to ob-

The swift current of the Saguenay River in Canada made it impossible to construct a dam in the water. (1) The dam was built standing on end on one bank of the river. Engineers measured the position they wanted the dam to occupy. (2) Dynamite was placed to blow away the supports holding the dam upright. At the explosion the dam fell. (3) Five seconds later the dam was in place.

*Courtesy, Du Pont Company*

tain coal, building stone, chemicals and metals (see MINING and QUARRYING), and also for making tunnels and cuttings for roads and railways, and canals and harbours. The high explosive used for these purposes is usually wrapped in paper packets about the size of sausages and these are pushed into holes drilled in the face of the rock or earth.

It is extremely dangerous for anyone who is not an expert to try to make or use explosives.

**EXPRESSIONS, ORIGIN OF.** The language we speak is always changing. Words and expressions that our forefathers used may seem unusual to us because they have dropped out of use, while on the other hand our forefathers would be unable to understand many words and expressions which we use today.

Words, phrases and expressions with a story behind them have always found a place in all languages. Many explain themselves, like the phrase "at last he has met his Waterloo", from the battle in which the French leader Napoleon was finally defeated after his many victories. There are doubts about how others started, however, such as the expression "to send somebody to Coventry". One idea is that in the Civil War the Roundheads had a specially strong camp at Coventry for prisoners of war to which the most difficult of their Royalist captives were sent; another is that at some vague time in the past the citizens of Coventry had such a dislike for soldiers that if one of their womenfolk was seen talking to one she was ignored (that is, sent to Coventry!) by everybody else.

The story behind most of the phrases of this kind can in fact be traced quite clearly. "Hobson's choice", for example, has been used for 300 years; it comes from the unusual business methods of Hobson, a carrier in Cambridge in the 17th century, who owned a number of excellent horses which he let out on hire. When a customer approached him he would take him to the stable and invite him to "choose" his mount —but he would insist on his choosing the first horse in the stable. Therefore, if a person today says that something was "Hobson's choice" he means that he really had no choice in the matter at all. An Australian expression with much the same meaning is "Buckley's chance", which is a pun on the name of the Melbourne business firm of Buckley and Nunn ("none").

Language is made by ordinary people in the words they use, not by scholars laying down rules and drawing up lists of words and phrases. For this reason many expressions with a story behind them have a Biblical origin, because for centuries the Bible was almost the only reading-matter for most people; even if they could not read they knew it through hearing it read in church. For instance, one expression comes from the Book of Exodus, which tells how Pharaoh said that the Israelites were to make their supply of bricks but in future no straw would be issued with which to make them. (These were a kind of brick used in many hot countries, made from clay mixed with straw to bind them.) Thus the phrase "making bricks without straw" means a hopeless task.

Although many expressions have their origin in a particular story or incident, there are more general ones reaching far back into history. Most of them spring from the main interests of the people—farming, war, recreation and, in an island like Britain, the sea. From the sea we have "to rest on one's oars", "to weather the storm" and many more. From war we have "to steal a march on somebody", "to return to the charge", "to come off with flying colours", "to throw down the gauntlet" (meaning to challenge), perhaps "shoulder to shoulder" and many other phrases which have lost their military importance as the art of war has changed. Some expressions last only a few years, like "napoo" which in World War I was used for something finished and done for. It came from the French *il n'y en a plus* ("there is no more of it").

"To cut the Gordian knot", meaning to solve a difficulty at one stroke, is a much older expression. Alexander the Great was told that whoever untied the Gordian knot would conquer Asia. He solved the difficulty by cutting the knot with his sword. "To climb on the bandwagon", which means to join in with a popular movement, is an American expression. In the late 19th century political and other public meetings in the United States were advertised by a band that went through the town seated on a wagon. The expression "according to Cocker", which people



☐ Read about WORDS AND MEANINGS in the blue pages of volume 6 sometimes use to mean exactly according to the rules, is a memory of an arithmetic book once much used in schools and written by Edward Cocker (1631–1675).

Some expressions are almost international. Thus the saying "he'll never set the Thames on fire", which means that the person concerned will never make a great name for himself or become an important figure, was used with slight variations by the Romans about the Tiber River, and is used by the French about the Seine and the Germans about the Rhine. The expression "it will all come out in the wash" means everything will turn out well in the end. It was used early in the 17th century by the Spanish writer Cervantes in his famous book *Don Quixote*. "As plain as a pikestaff" is used for something quite unmistakable, but originally the word was "pack-staff". This was the staff on which a pedlar, or travelling salesman, carried his pack and the staff became worn smooth and plain.

From sport and games there are expressions from archery ("to score a bull's-eye", "drawing the long bow" meaning to tell a tall story); from hunting and riding ("swapping horses in midstream", "to give somebody a leg-up"), and dozens of expressions from card games, like "turning up trumps", "sweeping the board" and "the game is not worth the candle"—a phrase which obviously dates from the days when games were played by candle light.

It is probably to farming and the land, however, more than to any other single source that English owes its colourful expressions—"ploughing a lonely furrow", "a long row to hoe", "sowing seeds of discontent", "a bitter harvest" and many others.

Other expressions connected with farming or the household include "to save one's bacon", which means to escape injury or loss, and "to kick the bucket", meaning to die. Both are connected with the English country custom whereby the cottager kept a pig, whose bacon fed him and his family for many a day. Great care was taken to hang the bacon from the ceiling where the dogs could not reach it—hence "saving one's bacon". The bucket was the name given in East Anglia to the beam from which the newly killed pig was hung.

When a statesman tells us we must all "put our shoulders to the wheel" he no longer sees in his mind's eye the heavy wagon that has slipped into the muddy ditch, the straining horses and the heaving, slithering men and boys all bent low for the last desperate heave. The expression has travelled far beyond its homely origins and has become a part of the language.

**EXTRUSION** is a method of shaping metals or plastics into rods, strips or tubes. The principle is that of squeezing tooth-paste from a tube. A "slug" (lump) of the metal is put in a strong steel cylinder in one end of which fits a ram. The ram is forced down by pressure and the metal is squeezed out of a hole called a die in the other end of the cylinder. The shape of the extruded strip depends on the shape of the die; thus flat strip can be produced or round, triangular or hexagonal (six-sided) bar. Extrusion can be done with brass, copper, bronze, aluminium and lead. With the harder metals the slug is heated before extrusion, but this is not necessary with lead. Extrusion is used for sheathing electric cables with lead. The extrusion of protein plastics is described in the article PLASTICS.

**EYCK, Jan van** (?1385–1441). In the late middle ages in the lands of the dukes of Burgundy, which are now part of Belgium, there was a famous family of painters by the name of Van Eyck. Most of their work was done in or near Ghent for rich patrons such as the Church, the counts of Holland or the dukes of Burgundy. The most famous painter of this family was Jan van Eyck who was born about the year 1385. Nothing is known of his early years or training as an artist until he became painter to the count of Holland in 1422. Three years later he became painter to the powerful duke of Burgundy, Philip the Good, for whom he travelled to Portugal to ask for Isabella of Portugal as a wife for the duke. The marriage was arranged, partly because the duke was impressed by a portrait of the princess, painted by Van Eyck. On his return he settled in Bruges where he painted portraits, religious pictures and altar pieces until his death. Among these paintings was the completion of the famous altar piece at St. Donat's Cathedral in

*Courtesy, Trustees of the National Gallery*

**"Man in a Turban", painted by Jan van Eyck in 1433.**

Bruges, begun by his brother Hubert who had died in 1426.

Although Van Eyck did not invent oil painting, he was the first great artist to use oil widely in painting. In the article PAINTERS AND PAINTINGS there is a reproduction of his famous painting "The Marriage of Giovanni Arnolfini". This is an oil painting and shows many great differences from painting in the middle ages. For one thing the subject is not religious, but is of a very prosperous citizen of the day and his wife. Secondly, the picture is not "flat". There is a sense of perspective—the room behind the two people really gives the impression of depth. Thirdly, the painter has created the effect of light; from the window on the left a soft light comes in, casting shadows and lighting up the faces. The colours are also more natural, bright colours, red and green, but set against greys and browns. But the most startling difference is the artist's eye for detail—the odd objects that are found by accident in the room such as the dog, the two pairs of cast off shoes and the fruit on the window sill. This shows Van Eyck as one of the earliest great portrait painters and at the beginning of that great line of Flemish and Dutch painters of local scenes. Later Hobbema, Vermeer and de Hooch went much further with this new way of seeing things.

**EYE.** The human eye is a form of camera. It has an adjustable opening to admit light, a lens which makes the light waves come together to form an image, and a sensitive film on which the image is recorded.

The eye is connected to the brain by a nerve called the optic nerve which serves as a highway along which nerve impulses travel from the eye to the brain. These nerve impulses are caused by the image on the "film" at the back of the eye camera and when they reach the brain we sort them out and "see" a man, a dog or whatever it is that we are looking at.

Except for a bulge where the light enters, the eye is round. Its outer membrane, or skin, called the sclera (of which the "white" of the eye is a part) is very tough and strong; it is opaque, or milky, except where it covers the bulge of the eye—where it changes its character and becomes transparent, or clear. This outer layer of the

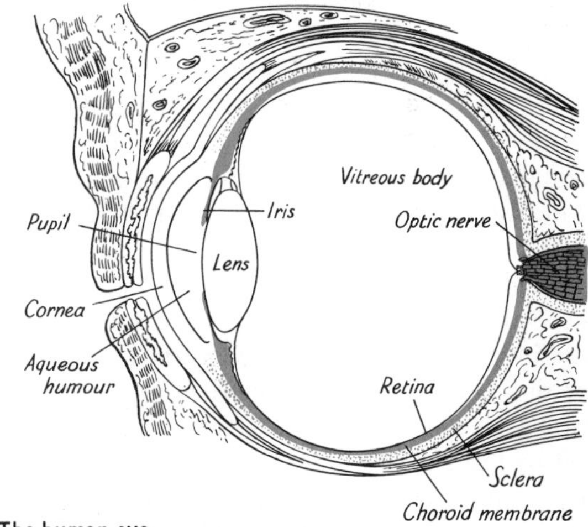


The human eye.

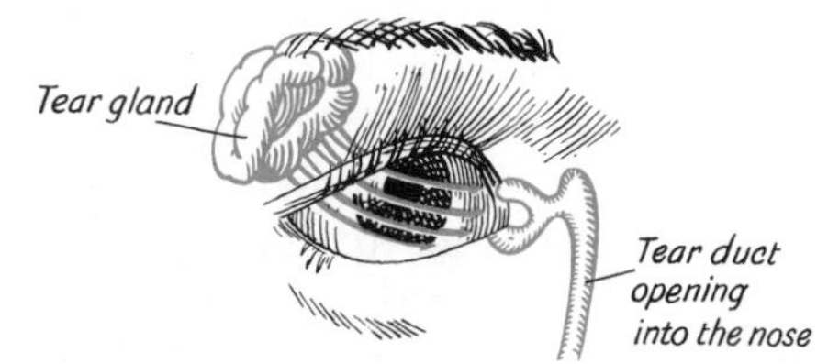

front part of the eye, called the cornea, has very important duties: it helps to bend the light rays as they enter the eye, it must remain clear, so that light will pass through it undimmed, and since it guards the opening into the eye it must be very sensitive, so that any dust or dirt that settles on it may be quickly felt and removed.

Close inside the outer skin and going round the back and sides of the eye is the choroid membrane, which supplies the eye with life-giving blood and, like a lining within this, is found the all-important retina. The retina is the camera film of the eye, on which pictures are recorded. It is made up of ten exceedingly thin layers of cells, the ninth being the real vision layer. Where the optic nerve joins the retina in the middle of the eye, at the back, there is a blind spot which is useless for vision. Close to the blind spot is the yellow spot, a point where the cells (see CELL) are so arranged that vision is at its keenest. The inside of the eye is filled with a substance called vitreous, or glassy, humour, which is really nothing more than a very weak salt jelly. It is the duty of the vitreous humour to keep the eye round and shapely.

The front of the eye contains the iris and pupil—the circle of colour and the black dot in its centre—and it is their job to let light into the eye. The pupil actually lets the light in and the iris controls the amount let in by controlling the size of the pupil. They can therefore be compared to the opening and shutter of a camera. The iris contains tiny muscles which close the pupil to a pinhole in bright light when less is needed, and open it in dull light when more is needed. The pupil is black because it opens into the interior of the eye, which is dark. Directly behind the iris and the pupil lies the lens, so called because it is transparent and curves outwards just like the lens of a magnifying glass. It is much more delicate, however, than any artificial lens for it is elastic and its muscles adjust it according to whether an object is near at hand or far away. It is the lens that bends the rays of light so that they will all be focused on the retina and thus produce an image of the object which the eye is looking at. The spaces between the lens and the iris, and between the iris and the cornea, are filled with a liquid called the aqueous, or watery, humour, which is a salt solution similar to the vitreous humour. The eyes of all the higher forms of animal life are fairly similar in construction to the human eye.

The eye is so delicate that it needs the greatest possible protection; it is housed in a soft-cushioned bony socket and protected still further by the eyelids and lashes. If, in spite of this protection, dust falls on the eyeball, tears are provided to wash it away; they come from the tear glands, one to each eye, which lie at the upper and outer part of the socket. Little tubes called tear ducts clear the tears away and are found on the inner side of the socket near the nose; there are two of them for each eye, one on the upper and one on the lower lid. Thus tears leave the glands and flow across the eye, some of them flowing into the ducts and down into the nose.

Like any other part of the body the eye sometimes becomes diseased and needs the care of an oculist, or eye specialist. Cataract, or milkiness of the lens (which ought to be clear and transparent), is one very common eye disease, and in former days always caused blindness. Now it can be removed by an operation. However, disease is responsible for only a few eye troubles; most of them are due to a fault in the shape of the eye and can usually be corrected by wearing glasses. If the cornea does not curve evenly, light does not enter the retina in a point, as it should, and round objects look as though they were oval. This condition is known as astigmatism. If the eyeball is unusually long from back to front, people cannot see very far and are called near-sighted; if it is unusually short, they see distant things better than near ones and are called long-sighted. Sometimes the muscles that move the eye are too short or tight and then the eyes may be crossed, but this can usually be corrected by operation, glasses or exercise. (There is a separate article BLINDNESS.)

**EYESIGHT.** Your eyes show you light and colour, tell you the size and shape of objects, find them for you—both in space and in relation to each other—and guide thousands of your movements. All these things seem so natural that people seldom realize how valuable their eyes are until they cease to work properly. (See EYE.)

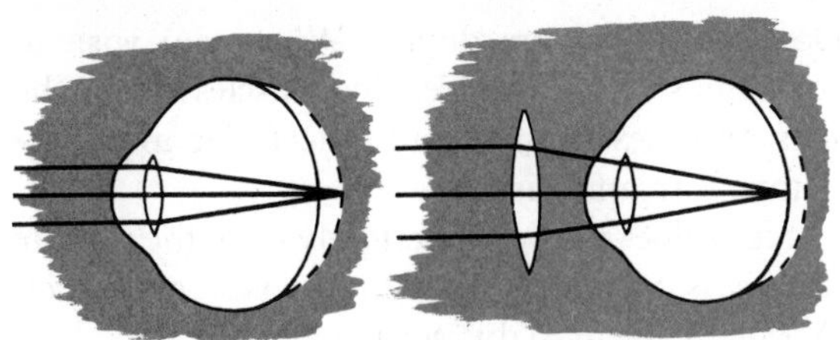

A long-sighted person does not see nearby objects clearly. The rays of light are focused so that they would come to a point behind the retina, on the broken line in the diagram. A glass lens bends the light rays and helps the eye to focus them properly on the retina.

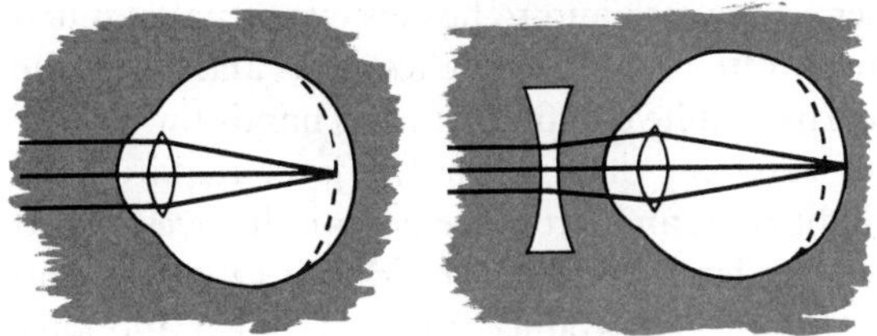

A short-sighted person needs spectacle lenses of a different shape. This is because the light rays from distant objects come to a point in front of the retina.

Suppose you could not see properly and were suffering from one of the commoner forms of visual defect. *Short-sighted* people see everything blurred and indistinct. Their world is out of focus, like a poorly adjusted lantern slide. Some people have only *tunnel vision*; for them, seeing is like looking through a tunnel, for they can see nothing with the sides of their eyes but only what is directly in front of them.

If you were an albino—that is, a person or animal whose skin, hair and eyes lack the normal amount of colour pigment—your eyes would not work properly because too much light would be constantly let into the retina. You can imagine what the world looks like to albinos, and why they squint, if you remember how difficult it is to see when you go suddenly from a dark room into one that is brilliantly lit. Suppose you were colour blind. If you had the most common type of colour blindness you would not see much difference in colour between bright red strawberries and the green dish on which they were heaped. You could not be trusted to drive a car because you would be unable to distinguish the colours of the traffic lights. (See Colour.)

At night you cannot see at all until your eyes have become used to the darkness, and then a second visual apparatus comes into operation and you see by using the sides, and not the centre, of your retinas. This is why you may see a star disappear when you look directly at it, and find it reappear when you turn your head to look somewhere else. Seeing at night becomes especially important in war time and soldiers, sailors and airmen are taught how to make the best use of their night vision. They may wear special goggles or spend half an hour in the dark before going to their stations. When trained and accustomed to the dark they can see even a lighted match for great distances. Night eyesight responds quickly to any moving objects, especially when they differ from their background in shape and brightness.

In seeing, as in taking photographs, you must have enough light but not too much. In the camera you have an aperture, or opening, which can be widened or narrowed to admit as much light as you need. In your eye this aperture is the black pupil and it is regulated by the coloured part, or iris; this contains tiny muscles which squeeze the pupil down to a pin-point when the light is strong and open it up wide when the light is weak. To see your iris in operation, hold up a mirror and look into your eyes in a weak light. You will see a wide-open pupil.

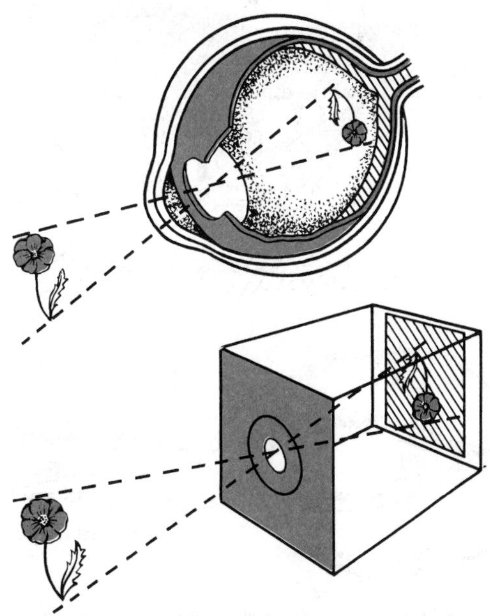

The eye receives an image of the flower in much the same way as a camera takes a picture of it.

Then turn on an electric light so that it shines into your eyes, and you will see the iris squeeze the pupil down to a tiny circle that quivers. In the camera you have a sensitive film upon which the picture is taken; in your eye the sensitive surface is the retina. However, clear and distinct pictures can be obtained only when the rays of light are focused, or brought to a point, by a lens. In the camera the lens must be moved out or in according to the distance of the object. In the eye the lens is focused by the muscles round it; they do not move it out or in but change its shape. In all close work such as reading and and drawing, these muscles about the lens have to be contracted, or tightened, and this gradually tires the eyes. To relax and rest them you should occasionally look up and away from any close work you are doing. When you wish to see things at a distance, the muscles relax, the lens becomes thinner and objects far away become clear and distinct.

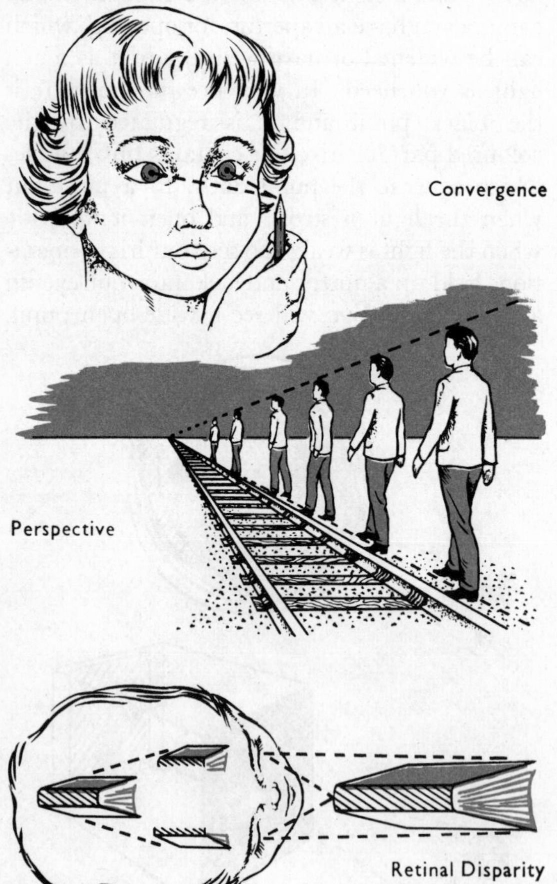


These are three of the ways the brain judges the distance and shape of things seen. "Convergence", "perspective" and "retinal disparity" are explained in the article.

Sight does not work perfectly from the minute a baby is born, even though his eyes are perfect. A one-year-old baby staring at you may look wise as an owl, but he sees little. Soon after birth the baby's iris responds to light. Somewhat later his eyes will follow a light moving before his face. After some weeks the focus of his lens begins to work and so he gets clear images much more often. As he reaches here and there, he learns that he can find with his hands the objects he can see, that narrow objects require only slight right and left movements of his eyes, broad objects lead to extensive sideways motions and high objects produce up and down motions, which are a little more difficult.

Building upon this he will go on to the much harder process of three-dimensional vision; that is, seeing the height, breadth and thickness of things. This will help him to judge distances, for when the size of the object is known, its distance can be judged.

Perspective helps you. If you look down a straight stretch of the railway the lines seem to come together in the distance. As you know that the width between them is always the same, its apparent narrowing becomes an indication of their distance. Hazy objects appear to be farther away. Shadows help you to tell hills from hollows. Nearer objects often cover up parts of things that are farther away, so you can tell that one distant tree or house is nearer than another by seeing which one is partly cut off. Moving the head will help you to decide whether a tree or a pole is farther away. Close one eye and move your head, or take a few steps sideways while you watch them. The object farther away will seem to move with you, while the nearer objects go the other way. Even focusing the eyes helps you to judge the distance of objects near you, for you are conscious of more strain as you fix your eyes on near than on far objects.

Through the combined action of both eyes working together, two further indications are given you. These are called convergence and retinal disparity. Hold up a pencil about 18 inches in front of your eyes. Move it towards your nose, looking at the point as long as you can. Soon you will feel definite strain because the muscles on the sides of your eyes nearer to your nose are contracting strongly and making your eyes converge or "toe-in". This strain of convergence becomes an indication of distance, a greater strain indicating a closer object.

By retinal disparity is meant the differences in the images in the two eyes, which never give quite the same picture. Hold up a book with its back edge towards you and about six inches away. Look at it first with one eye and then with the other. With the right eye you will see the back edge and the right-hand cover; with the left eye you will see the back edge and the left-hand cover. When you look with both eyes the back edge is the same to both, but the differences given by the two eyes act as indications for distance and you see a solid object stretching away from you. Hold up a finger about 18 inches in front of your nose and look beyond it at the wall and at various objects in the room. If you fix your gaze on the wall you will see two fingers; if you fix your gaze on your finger you may see two door knobs or two lamps where you know there is only one. This doubling of objects and the minor differences in the pictures given by the two eyes are of the first importance to your judgment of where objects are. If you use a stereoscopic camera, that is, a camera with two lenses set two and a half inches apart (about the distance between the centres of the two eyes), take twin pictures and then look at your pictures in a machine known as a stereoscope, which presents the right-hand view to the right eye and the left-hand view to the left eye, you get an impression of distance and depth which is missing from the ordinary flat picture. Trees and shrubs seem to stand out from their backgrounds and roads seem to go off quite naturally into the distance. Two eyes are far better than one!

**EZEKIEL.** In 597 B.C. Judah was conquered by the Babylonians and many of the Jews were carried away into captivity. Among them was Ezekiel who, some few years later, was called by God to be a prophet; that is, to interpret or explain God's will to men. As the Jews were in exile in a foreign land their religion was in danger of being lost, and it was largely because of Ezekiel's teaching that it survived.

He taught that God had allowed them to be captured as a punishment for their worship of false gods, and to prove to the people that He was the only true God of Israel, but that if they repented He would restore them to their own country.

After the Babylonians had completely destroyed Jerusalem, including the Temple, in 586 B.C. Ezekiel's many visions prophesied the return of the Jews to Jerusalem, and the rebuilding of the Temple. In his vision of the valley full of dry bones, he describes how God brought the bones to life so that they "stood upon their feet, an exceeding great army". This represented the return of the Jews to their own land, and the rebirth of the Jewish nation.

**EZRA.** After King Cyrus of Persia conquered Babylonia in 539 B.C. he allowed the Jews in that country to return to their own land, Judah, and helped them to rebuild the Temple at Jerusalem, which had been burned when the city was destroyed by the Babylonians in 586 B.C. (The Jews were in Babylonia because they had been carried off from Judah, as prisoners, by the Babylonians.) Ezra, a priest and learned man, was a Jewish leader who arrived in Jerusalem some time after the first Jews had returned; it may well have been three or four generations later.

He found that the Jews had fallen into bad habits in their religion and had mixed their worship with the non-Jewish worship of the peoples amongst whom they had lived. He therefore reminded them that they were God's chosen people and must keep themselves separate from other peoples. He forced them to divorce their foreign wives and said they were to marry women of their own people only. Daily, for seven days, he read to them the laws and commandments that had been given to Moses by God, and the people agreed to obey them. An account of Ezra's work can be found in the Bible in the Books of Ezra and Nehemiah, and in the Apocrypha in 1 Esdras.



☐ Read about OPTICAL ILLUSIONS in the blue pages of this volume

*Courtesy, Trustees of the British Museum*

Left: The wolf in sheep's clothing devoured many of the flock before he was discovered by the shepherd who saw through the disguise. Right: The ass eating thistles was content with his humble fare although he carried many rich foods on his back. Both these illustrations appeared in an edition of Aesop's Fables published in 1640.

**FABLE.** A fable is a short story which is generally told to teach a useful lesson. The story is usually about animals which behave and talk as if they were human beings. This enables the story-teller to show up the many foolish things which human beings do, and he hopes people will heed his advice because it is given through an amusing and interesting story. To make quite sure that the lesson is understood it is usually set out clearly at the end of the story and is called the moral.

An example of a fable is the story of two cocks who had a fight. One was beaten and slunk away out of sight. The other was so pleased at his victory that he flew up to the roof and began boasting loudly. An eagle saw him and swooped down and carried him off. The moral of this story is: "It is foolish to boast".

This is one of the many fables told by Aesop (see AESOP'S FABLES). Many collections of fables by various story-tellers were made, both in Greece and India. The Indian fables were usually told to explain some fact in nature, rather than to point a moral.

Though fables are often very old, many of them, like *The Fox and the Cock, The Fox and the Grapes, The Ant and the Grasshopper, The Town Mouse and the Country Mouse, The Wolf in Sheep's Clothing,* are still among the first stories which children hear and they are told in many different languages.

The Greek and Indian fables were retold in Latin and later translated into many European languages. The English poet Geoffrey Chaucer retold the story of the Fox and the Cock in his *Canterbury Tales.* The most famous modern writer of fables was a Frenchman of the 17th century, Jean de la Fontaine. He told his stories in verse, poking sly but friendly fun at the people of his day. (See LA FONTAINE.)

**FACTORY.** A factory is usually thought of as a large, somewhat ugly building with high chimneys pouring out black smoke. Inside, workmen dressed in greasy overalls work at large, complicated and noisy machines to produce enormous articles made of iron or steel. Many factories in industrial towns do fit this description, but there are also factories that have pleasant, airy buildings. For example, along the Great West Road out of London are many factories making things like cosmetics, biscuits and stockings—these are known as light industry factories.

In British law the word factory applies to many kinds of places. Any place is a factory if it employs workpeople to make, repair or alter some article, but the article may vary from a large aeroplane to a small drawing-pin, or even an invisible chemical. The word also covers the construction, repair and breaking up of ships and buildings, harbours, sewers and pipelines, and the loading and unloading of ships.

The number of workers may vary from several thousands to one. There may be machines as big as a house or none at all. The work may be carried out in buildings covering acres or in one room or even in the open air with no shelter. It is therefore impossible to describe any one kind of factory as typical.

Nearly all factories have the same basic idea, however. They take in raw materials or partly finished goods, work on them in one way or another and send out either a finished article, such as shoes, or a semi-finished product, such as a motor body, to another factory to have more work done on it or to be used as part of a larger article.

A factory making motor bodies has very large buildings covering many acres. First in the manufacturing process (after the drawing office where designs of the parts are made) is the raw material store where flat steel sheets are delivered from other factories. Then come the cutting shop where these sheets are cut into the right shapes, the press shop where the various pieces are bent by enormously powerful machines into the various curved parts needed for a motor body, the welding shop where the parts are joined together, the paint shop where the finished bodies are dipped in paint or sprayed with it, and so on. Finally the beautiful shiny bodies are sent away to another factory to have engines and wheels fitted to make complete motor cars.

The different materials and parts are moved by trolleys or by conveyor belts, which are rather like escalators, moving all the time. They are in the roof and the parts are hung from them by hooks.

As a rule, factories are divided into two sections—the works, where the goods are actually made, and the offices, where the affairs of the factory are managed. Sometimes these are called productive and non-productive sides. The offices deal with such matters as paying the workers, buying the raw materials, advertising and selling the goods, drawing up the plans of what is to be made and what each machine is to do each day.

Then there are the parts of the factory that

*Aerofilms*

A big factory from the air. Can you pick out the offices, the foundry (with its chimneys) and the railway sidings?

look after the workers themselves. In a large factory there is a canteen for them to eat their meals in, and also a medical department, where any injuries or illnesses are treated.

In early factories the power, which is the energy that does much of the work, came from water wheels driven by streams or even, like windmills for flour-making, from wind. However, the need to have factories in places where there was no water supply brought about the use of steam as well.

During the 19th century most factories had their machinery driven by steam engines, but by the end of the century these began to be replaced by electric motors and today the steam engine is seldom used except in some textile factories in the north. Often nowadays each machine can be driven by its own separate electric motor, thus doing away with the dangerous shafts, belts and gears which used to take the power from the engine to the machines. Other kinds of engines, of course, have been and still are in use, the main ones being the gas engine and the diesel or oil engine.

**FACTORY ACTS.** People in factories often work under difficult conditions or have to do jobs that put a severe strain on them. It has therefore been found necessary to have laws making sure that they do not come to any harm because of their work.

The early laws of the 19th century were made at a time when children still worked in factories, and they limited the number of hours that children were allowed to work. The man who did most to bring in these laws was the 7th Earl of Shaftesbury (about whom there is a separate article) who was shocked by the way in which women and children had to work in factories.

Today the laws cover all questions of safety, health and welfare, as well as working hours, and they are contained in the Factories Acts of 1937 and 1948. As England was the country where the system first grew up of producing goods in factories instead of in craftsmen's cottages, it was also England that first brought in factory laws.

In general, the factory acts make employers responsible for seeing that their factories are clean and properly heated, lighted and ventilated. They must protect their workers by fencing dangerous machinery and by preventing dust and fumes from getting into the air of the workshop. Places for washing and first aid must be provided and hours must be reasonable.

When some very early laws about factories were passed by parliament, it was soon discovered that it was necessary to have inspectors to visit factories to see that the rules were obeyed. So in 1833 the first government inspectors were appointed with powers to inspect the factories and to prosecute factory owners if they disobeyed the law. This act of 1833, since it was the first one to be properly enforced by the inspectors, is usually taken as the real beginning of factory legislation, or law-giving, in Great Britain.

During the first half of the 19th century, a large number of British people thought that the government should not interfere in industry, but that employers and workers should be left alone to make what arrangements they liked about work in factories. In spite of this, the factory acts, which took away some of the power of the employers in order to protect the younger and weaker workers, were extended bit by bit.

The Act of 1833 applied only to mills where cotton, wool and other textiles were spun and woven, for these were the factories of importance at that time. As late as about 1860, small children were working for as many hours in the pottery and lace industries as they had done in the textile factories before 1833. However, an act called the Factory Acts Extension Act was passed in 1867, and it made the laws that already existed apply to new trades and also to any factory that employed more than 50 people. Places that manufactured goods with less than 50 people were then called workshops, and another act extended some rules to them.

The Act of 1833 stopped young persons from working for more than 12 hours a day or for more than 69 hours a week, and no child less than nine years old could work in a factory. Factory children had to attend school for two hours a day on six days a week. Gradually the ages were raised and the number of working hours reduced, until today the earliest age at which anyone may work in a factory is 15. A 15-year-old is allowed to work for 44 hours a week, while women and young persons of 16–18 may work for 48 hours a week. The hours of women had been controlled quite early on, as they too were being overworked, and they, as well as boys and girls of 15–18, are still called "protected persons" today. Men, on the other hand, except in potteries and chemical works, have never had their working hours controlled. The average actually worked by men in factories is about 47½ hours a week, while the average for youths and boys is 43½ hours and for women working full time 40 hours.

In the early days before parents had to register their children's births, it was difficult to prove the real age of a child and a certificate had to be obtained from a doctor stating that the child appeared to be over the age at which he was allowed to work in a factory. Today, this special doctor, known as the "Appointed Factory Doctor", has also to certify that anyone under 18 entering a factory is fit for that particular job and he has to examine him again each year until he is 18.

Another law, the Factory Act of 1844, was made to look after the safety of factory workers. Some dangerous parts of machinery had to have guards put round them so that no one could be killed or hurt by them, and certain accidents had to be reported to the local factory doctor. Today, accidents which cause anyone to be away from work for more than three days have to be reported to the inspectors. The inspectors investigate the accidents to see whether any laws were disobeyed and if anything can be done to save someone else being hurt in the same way.

Since 1891 there have also been rules to reduce the risk of illnesses caused by factory work, for some kinds of work are known to be dangerous and unhealthy. Lead poisoning was one of the diseases that used quite often to be got by working in factories, but now, owing to medical care and good working conditions, this is unusual.

**FAEROE ISLANDS.** Almost halfway between the Shetland Islands and Iceland, 21 small islands called the Faeroe Islands or the Faeroes rise steeply out of the wild North Atlantic. They are swept by storms and heavy rain, and thin grass grows on poor soil. Clouds of seabirds nest on the surfaces of the towering cliffs, while between the islands the sea swirls in swift and dangerous currents.

These bleak islands were first inhabited by Irish hermits in the 7th century, but Norsemen settled there about 200 years later and the

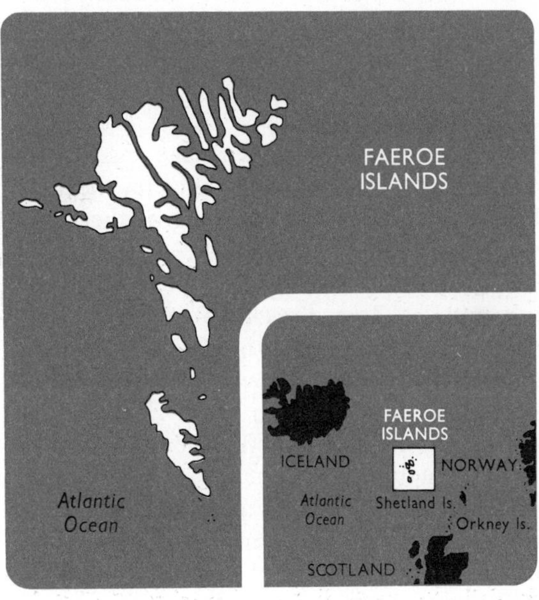


present-day islanders are descended from them. In 1966 there were about 37,000 of them, most of the men working as fishermen and going to Bear Island in the Arctic and to west Greenland, where they have their own special harbour. Some sheep farming is carried on in the Faeroes.

The islanders, who speak Faeroese, a language rather like Icelandic, are hard-working people. They are very proud of their independence, for, although the Faeroes belong to Denmark, they have a local parliament in Thorshavn, the capital, and their own flag. Indeed, when the Danish government wanted to dismiss a doctor in the Faeroes in 1955, the islanders banded together and attacked several Danish officials.

At certain times of year schools of "caaing whales" appear. (These are pilot whales, of the dolphin family.) The people drive them into a shallow bay with boats and kill them with lances for their meat and fat. The Faeroese word for these whales is "Grind", and everyone gets tremendously excited on "Grind" day, as it means plenty of extra meat for the home.

**FAGS.** To "fag" means "to toil painfully", and that is why junior boys who have to do various jobs for prefects and senior boys at some boarding schools are called "fags"! The tasks which the junior boys had to perform, and still do at some schools, were to run errands and make tea for the senior boys, sweep and tidy their studies and act as ball-boys at the cricket nets and on the tennis courts. Many years ago fags also had to clean boots and cook breakfast for the senior boys, and had to work as long as the seniors wanted them.

Once fagging was closely linked with bullying and, as *Tom Brown's Schooldays* shows, there was plenty of both when Dr. Thomas Arnold, a famous headmaster of Rugby School, started his work there in 1828. Many people hoped that he and the other headmasters who were trying to improve the public schools would stop fagging. "Flogging and Fagging", an article written in a newspaper at that time, told of the terrible bullying of the younger boys by the older ones.

Dr. Arnold, however, did not stop fagging. His reply to the article was that bullying and fagging were not at all the same thing. Bullying was wrong and must be stopped, but fagging properly controlled was good and necessary. It was good because it taught young boys to be helpful; it was necessary because servants could not do all the domestic work of a boarding school. So he organized a proper system of fagging which did not permit bullying. There is one great comfort—the fag of today grows into the fagmaster (senior boy entitled to have a fag) of tomorrow: or as a school song puts it, Jerry "a poor little fag, carrying kettle and tray", becomes in due course

> a Monitor bold
> Champion at Rackets and Fives
> ........................................
> Verily Jerry is now
> Monarch of all he surveys.

**FAIRIES.** People all over the world have believed in fairies from very early times. They have thought of them as supernatural beings, able to interfere magically for good or evil with human people. Nowadays we think of them either with silver wings and wands, like the fairy queen in pantomime, as the sprites and elves often illustrated in picture books, or as the fairy Tinkerbell in J. M. Barrie's play *Peter Pan*. Yet the word fairy comes from the Latin *fatum,* meaning fate or destiny, something of great and mysterious power, and the idea of fairies has changed through the ages.

Some fairy beliefs may have origins in history. One idea about this, which cannot be proved, is that some of the earliest inhabitants of Europe were smallish dark people who lived more or less underground and fled to the swamps, woods and hills when the taller invaders occupied their land. The little people, as they were called (see LITTLE PEOPLE), were thought to have magical powers and as they had their own cattle they probably were skilled in doctoring animals, as well as in poisoning people they did not like. Their little flint arrowheads, still found today, are called elf-arrows. They were said to come down into the villages sometimes and steal babies, leaving their own instead. Thus began the belief in fairy changelings. From memories of them and their evil powers developed the idea of witches. They also account for many of the stories of elves and brownies or house spirits (called "boggarts" in the north of England), full of mischief, but able to help their friends. There may also have been real local heroes who slew tyrants and freed their peoples and became the originals of such stories as that of Jack the Giant Killer.

Many fairy stories and beliefs are just more modern forms of the myths of the ancient Greeks and Romans. They believed that all sorts of things and places had their own special spirits. There were fauns, spirits of the countryside, and naiads or water-nymphs, and also spirits of the woods and hills. These beliefs were brought to England by the Roman invaders. Long after people had forgotten the Roman occupation, they remembered the legends connected with particular places, but now they thought of the

water-sprites and the rest as fairy people. (See MYTHS.)

As the myths were forgotten, writers and story-tellers did not bother to keep closely to them and invented bits of their own, or copied them from the legends of other peoples. For instance, *The Arabian Nights*, including such stories as that of Sindbad the Sailor, came to Europe from India by way of Persia. The stories of the Persian flying "peris" and of djinns and other spirits were told and retold and altered by the countries through which they passed until they became mixed with other stories.

In Great Britain the popular idea of fairies was greatly influenced by the writings of poets and playwrights and particularly of William Shakespeare. In *A Midsummer Night's Dream* Shakespeare described Oberon and Titania, king and queen of the fairies, and Puck, or Robin Goodfellow, and the fairy court. All his fairies were unseen by mortals unless they chose to show themselves. Gradually a new idea of fairies grew up and they were described as wearing red pointed hats, mantles of green cloth, inlaid with wild flowers, green pantaloons buttoned with bobs of silk, and silver shoes. A play written in 1633 mentions:

> Fairies small, two feet tall,
> With caps red on their head
> Dance a round on the ground.

This poetical idea almost took the place of the earlier idea of fairies being the same size as ordinary people, or only a little smaller. The little people were called pixies in the west of England, trolls, or hill people, in Scandinavia and kobolds in Germany.

The idea of a people midway between humanity and the unknown, half-human and half-angels or devils, has always fascinated people. Poets and storytellers still write fairy stories which pass on some of man's earliest fears and beliefs. The brothers Grimm (see GRIMM, THE BROTHERS), writing in Germany in the 19th century, collected hundreds of folk stories and published them as *Grimm's Fairy Tales.* They are still among the first stories heard by many children. The Dane Hans Andersen (see ANDERSEN, HANS CHRISTIAN) wrote beautiful fairy stories, some sad, some happy. Two well-known examples are *The Ugly Duckling* and *The Red Shoes.*

Among other writers and collectors of fairy stories the best known is probably Andrew Lang, who wrote the *Blue Fairy Tale Book* in 1889 and followed it with the *Red*, the *Green* and the *Yellow* fairy books.

**FAIRS.** All over the world a fair is among the most exciting events of the year. This is especially true in villages in Great Britain where,

just before the appointed day, the showman's gear comes thundering through the street and draws into the fair ground. Everything is quickly unloaded and soon the quiet meadow is transformed into a gaudy collection of caravans, swings, roundabouts (without which no fair would be complete), coconut shies, shooting galleries and stalls with every kind of attraction.

The lights are lit at dusk. Nowadays they are electric, but once they were smoky flares of naphtha oil. The mechanical music plays a tune or two by way of attracting people's attention, although it is not until much later that the fair really gets going. Then the music grows louder and the lights brighter as the crowd of villagers wander round the stalls, trying their skill at hooplas or coconut shies and spending their money on fairings (gifts they have bought at the fair).

For a few hours they live as if in another world where all is gay and full of light, colour, music and laughter. Later still, they straggle home through the dark lanes, fairings bulging from their pockets and tired children crying in their arms. Next day there will be nothing to show for it all in the meadow where everything was so bright and noisy but litter on the grass. The showman will already be on his way to the next place of call.

In the countries of the East it was the custom long ago for merchants driving their heavily laden camels from one remote town to another to arrive on the day that a local festival was being held. The people would then be in holiday mood, which was good for trade. This is probably the origin of the fairs that have ever since been held all over the world.

In fact, the first purpose of fairs has always been trade of one sort or another, although what are known as trade fairs are more like exhibitions, as they are for showing off goods. (See EXHIBITIONS.) The amusements were a popular addition by fun-making people such as clowns, players, prize-fighters, performing animals, and so on, thus making the fairs (which came at regular intervals) occasions for excitement and pleasure.

In Britain the great fair of the year was the Stourbridge fair which used to be held in Cambridge and was started at the beginning of the 13th century. It lasted for three weeks every year, and traders came to it from Europe as well as all parts of England. Farmers from East Anglia and Yorkshire rubbed shoulders with wealthy merchants from Italy and the Netherlands. Streets of booths (stalls) were set up for business, chief among the goods for sale being cloth and wool, corn and hops and salt fish. In addition, of course, there were many stalls where housewives could buy their stores, and there were amusements for everybody. Stourbridge was said to be the fair upon which John Bunyan based his description of Vanity Fair in *Pilgrim's Progress*. If so, he must have found it wicked as well as gay, for it was at Vanity Fair that Faithful was burnt at the stake. (See BUNYAN, JOHN, and PILGRIM'S PROGRESS, THE.)

Other outstanding fairs in Britain were St. Bartholomew's fair in London, St. Faith's fair in Norwich, where for a fortnight animals that had been driven into the town from all over the shires were bought and sold, and the great St. Giles's fair in Winchester, Hampshire. This fair was begun by William the Conqueror, and was later given over to the local bishop, whose officers were given the power to take a toll, or tax, of all goods sold during fair time.

Most medieval fairs were named after a saint because they were held on the local saint's day, which was a holiday. They were also held within the grounds of the principal church of the town.

Perhaps the oddest of all British fairs was the Frost Fair, as it came to be called, which was held in February 1814, when the River Thames between Blackfriars and London Bridge was frozen to such an extent that amusement booths were set up on the ice. There were swings, skittles and dancing, a whole sheep was roasted, verses about the event were printed on the spot, and enormous crowds gathered under a full moon.

Some fairs in Britain, besides being places of trade and amusement, were also labour exchanges. This means that at such fairs, which were known as "mops" in the West Country, farmhands and servants who wanted to change their jobs hung about the streets and pavements while farmers and their wives looked them over. Shepherds wore a wisp of wool in their hats, carters a piece of whipcord, milkmaids had a strand of cow hair and servants carried a mop. After a discussion and agreement upon terms, the matter was settled by paying a shilling, or a "fastening penny", and then the workers went to the amusement section of the fair to make merry on one of the few holidays they got in the year.

Mops like these were held until the end of the 19th century, and although some fairs are still called mops, they are now ordinary amusement fairs. In many towns they are still held in the middle of the main street, just as they were in the days when it mattered less that they held up the traffic.

**FAKIR** comes from the Arabic word *faqir* which means "poor" or "a poor man". From this it is easy to see why it came to be used for a holy man of the Moslem faith (see ISLAM) who lived by begging and led a very strict and simple life without possessions of any kind. A fakir of this type can be compared to the Christian friars of the middle ages who wandered from place to place, begging their way. Since the time when Moslem people conquered India the word "fakir" has been used for holy men of the Hindu faith as well (see HINDUS AND HINDUISM).

The fakirs very often have a great influence over people because they are holy men, and because they are thought to have miraculous powers of healing the sick. Some fakirs have not been genuine holy men, and instead of begging merely for food and shelter have used their special position to make people give them far more than that. Although some live a very strict life, others go round with performing animals, selling powders supposed to produce magical effects or claiming to be able to turn silver and other metals into gold. Some of them have attracted great attention because of the extraordinary things they can do, such as sitting on a bed of nails or walking on red-hot coals.

There are people called Dervishes, who belong to the Moslem faith, and who are rather like the fakirs. Their name comes from the Persian language, and the article DERVISH describes them.

**FALCONRY** is the art of catching birds and beasts by sending trained falcons and hawks after them. It is a very old sport indeed; it was known to the Chinese in 2000 B.C. and was a favourite pastime of the Saxon kings of England. Today, however, it is rarely seen because it is so very much easier to kill game birds (birds hunted for sport) and rabbits with a gun.

Many special words are used in falconry; thus to tame a falcon is to *man* it, after which it must be trained to catch its particular prey—whether starlings, rooks, grouse, partridges or rabbits. The female falcon is sometimes preferred to the male because it is larger and stronger, but the training is always a long and difficult task. When the bird is taken out to hunt she perches on her owner's gloved left fist and wears a leather hood which keeps her quiet and calm. When the owner sees the prey—say, a rook—he unhoods the falcon and casts her off by throwing his arm forward; she then dashes after the rook and when at last she has risen above it she *stoops* to it or pounces, killing the

Casting off
Luring a Falcon
A Falcon Hooded

rook with a fierce blow from one of her talons or rear claws.

This method would not do for hunting fast-flying birds like grouse and partridges, as the falcon cast off from the fist could never catch them. This kind of quarry needs a falcon that has been trained to *wait on* or hover overhead until the grouse or partridges have been "flushed" (made to fly up) with the help of a dog such as a setter or pointer.

In order to call back a falcon a *lure* is used, this being a bunch of feathers tied together so as to look like the quarry and fastened to a long string. The falconer swings this round above his head and whistles until his falcon returns and seizes the lure. She can then be caught, hooded and put on his fist again.

The birds most used for falconry in Great Britain are the peregrine falcon, merlin and sparrowhawk; the kestrel is too slow and lazy. (See Hawk and Falcon.) Falconry is practised most in Persia, Arabia, India, China, and in central Asia where eagles are trained to attack large game such as antelopes and wolves.

**FALKLAND ISLANDS.** The bleak and windswept Falkland Islands lie in the South Atlantic Ocean, nearly 500 miles northeast of Cape Horn at the tip of South America. About 2,100 people, nearly all of British descent, live there. Sheep-farming is their main occupation.

There are two main islands, East and West Falkland, divided by a channel of the sea called Falkland Sound. Both islands have ragged coastlines and a fringe of smaller islands. The only town, Stanley, where half the population lives, is on East Falkland, and the rest of the territory is known as "the Camp". Besides many sea birds, there are also sea lions and elephant seals in the Falklands.

The Falkland Islands are in the same latitude in the south as London is in the north, so the climates are much alike, but the wind blows almost without stopping in the Falklands. The landscape is nearly treeless. The people eat a great deal of mutton and vegetables, and most families have their own vegetable gardens, and get their fuel by peat-cutting.

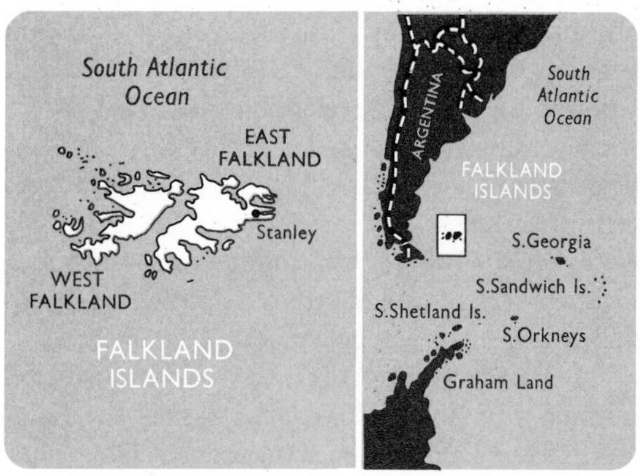


Wool, sheepskins and tallow (a substance obtained from fat and used for making candles and soap) are exported. On the ranches, or large farms, some of which are as much as 400,000 acres in size, it is a hard and lonely life. The people still go from place to place, chiefly by horseback or boat, though since 1948 an air service has linked Stanley with outlying points.

The Falkland Islands were discovered in 1592 by the English navigator John Davis in the ship "Desire". They were named after Viscount Falkland, the treasurer of the navy in 1690. No settlements were made until nearly 200 years after their discovery. For some time France, Spain and Great Britain quarrelled about who should own the Falklands, but in 1832 Britain took them over and from then onwards remained in possession. During World War I the Falklands were the scene of a British naval victory, the Battle of the Falklands in 1914. The islands are claimed by Argentina, where they are called the Islas Malvinas.

The Falkland Islands government also administers, or manages, the affairs of some scattered islands still farther south, which are called

### FACTS ABOUT FALKLAND ISLANDS

AREA (excluding dependencies): 4,700 square miles.
POPULATION (estimated in 1966): 2,079, with a few more in the dependencies.
KIND OF COUNTRY: British colony.
CAPITAL: Stanley.
CHIEF EXPORTS: Wool, tallow and whale oil.
EDUCATION: Children must attend school between the ages of 5 and 14. A number are unable to do so and depend on travelling teachers.

Falkland Islands Dependencies. These islands are South Georgia and the South Sandwich Islands, which were discovered in 1775 by Captain Cook. Grytviken on South Georgia is an important whaling base in summer (see WHALES AND WHALING). The Antarctic explorer, Sir Ernest Shackleton, died and was buried there in 1922. The South Sandwich group consists of uninhabited volcanic islands. The Falkland Islands Dependencies have a population of about 1,000 in the whaling season and less than 500 in winter. They are looked after by an organization called the Falkland Islands Dependencies Survey (F.I.D.S.).

To the south of the dependencies lie the South Orkney and South Shetland islands, the Weddell Sea and the wedge-shaped piece of the Antarctic continent stretching from Graham Land to the South Pole. These were part of the Falkland Island Dependencies until 1962, when they became a separate colony known as the British Antarctic Territory.

**FAMILY.** In most parts of the world a family is made up of a man, his wife and their children. Sometimes grandparents, uncles and aunts and even cousins are also included. However, not all peoples of the world believe that a man must have only one wife, or that a woman must have only one husband. In some countries a man has several wives at the same time; this is called polygamy, which means "many women". Sometimes, though this does not happen so often, a woman has several husbands at the same time, and the name for this is polyandry, meaning "many men".

From the very beginning people have lived in the group called a family; and they have done this almost always so that the children can be properly looked after and brought up in safety. Animals, too, live in families while the young ones are too little to look after themselves; but human children need looking after for much longer than young animals do, therefore human families stay together longer than most animal families. From very early times people have wanted to make marriage that will last, so that everyone can be contented and cared for.

The father and mother have different parts to play in the family life. With us, the father usually works and earns a living, while the mother looks after the home and brings up the children. Among primitive peoples, the work is sometimes shared differently, for the father often has to defend his wife and children. In many parts of Africa this means that a man must hold his spear ready in case of danger, so his wife or daughter usually carries the burdens. If he had a burden on his back it would make it difficult for him to fight. The man usually does the heavy work of digging the land ready for planting, and often does this with other men so that they can defend themselves if attacked. The woman does the weeding and sometimes harvests the crops. Men build the huts, plant trees, hunt and fish, and sometimes build boats. The women bring up the young children, but the men train the boys when they are old enough and the women train the girls. Women do the cooking and make the clothes; and one very important job for them is to keep the fire burning. (See FIREMAKING.)

Among tribes where a man has several wives the family is arranged differently. In parts of Africa it is usually the chief or some other important man who has more than one wife. Each wife probably has a separate hut in the village for herself and her children; this means that there are several families sharing one man. In countries such as Arabia, where the religion is Islam (this religion was taught by the prophet Mohammed), a man can have up to four wives, though this is not done as much now as it was in the past. Here all the wives and children live together in what is called a compound family. (The group of buildings the family live in is known as the compound.)

In the old days in China an important man was allowed to have several women belonging to him, but only one was called a wife. She might be the first one he married, but if she had no sons then one of the others who had sons would become the chief woman of the compound family. They often all lived together as one household, as this was part of the Chinese custom of showing great respect to the family. The eldest son learnt to perform the family ceremonies, and was supposed to see that his father

*Radio Times Hulton Picture Library*

Though it has changed in many ways through the ages, the family is the oldest and most lasting human group.

behaved well enough to be worthy of honour after his death.

In India, China and some other countries where many farming people live close together, the land has been divided up so much that it is difficult to share out a small farm when the sons marry. So they and their wives and children often live in their father's house, and all work on the farm together. The father, and after him the eldest son, is the master; but the eldest woman who has sons is usually the most important person in the house. She sees that all the old customs are properly kept up.

In some primitive villages (in Indian jungles, for instance, and in southeast Asia) the huts are too small for large families. So when the boys are old enough, they sleep in a special boys' hut. Sometimes there is a girls' hut too, but often the girls sleep in the huts of widows whose children have grown up and started families of their own.

Many peoples like these had by tradition no law courts where people who had done wrong could be given punishment. So if a man harmed another person in some way, that person could not ask a court to punish the offender. He appealed instead to the other members of his family to help him. The whole family, even the distant relations, joined together against the wrongdoer.

Suppose a member of family A killed a member of family B. Family B would avenge their relative by killing one of family A. They might be so angry that they killed more than one; then family A would be angry and want revenge in their turn. So the quarrel would go on, perhaps with much killing, for many years.

Gradually people came to realize what a bad thing all this was; they worked out schemes where the wrongdoer would try to make it up to the family of the man he had wronged in some other way—for instance, by paying them a sum of money. This is called compensation. The old system of family vengeance lasted in parts of the Scottish highlands until 200 years ago, and in Corsica until about 100 years ago. (A feud like this is often called a vendetta, which is a Corsican word.) It still exists in a few parts of the world.

Men are usually the masters of the family, even though the women may often have a great influence inside it. When the head of a family dies he is succeeded by a new head. In some societies he is succeeded by his son, or perhaps by his brother; in this case inheritance and succession are through men. But in other societies they are through women; here a man has control over his sister, but his successor is the child of his sister, his nephew, and not his own son. In these societies the position of women is very high, and the older women may be the most important people of the tribe. Here also women may often marry more than one husband. A woman may marry several brothers, who come to live in her house and are very much under her control. People who do this are found in Tibet and parts of southern India.

Where men may marry more than one wife, they have to be very careful not to make them jealous and to share everything equally between them. In the Zulu and other tribes of southern Africa wives are ranked, and one is the "Great Wife" and controls the others; also her son is the chief heir. Here it is common for a widow to marry the brother of her dead husband; this is called the Levirate, and was practised by the ancient Hebrews. It means that when a man dies his family does not die out but continues with his own brother in his place.

**FAMINE.** When all the people in an area have hardly anything to eat they are suffering from famine, and if these conditions last for long many die of starvation. The main causes of famine are lack of water for crops; war; plant diseases and insect pests; earthquakes; and floods.

India receives the whole year's rain during a period of a few months (see MONSOON) and if it fails to come then it does not come at all. Without rain there are no crops, and if the rain is scanty so are the crops. In recent years great dams have been built to store water during the rains so that it can be used in time of drought (see DAM and IRRIGATION). While these have helped to produce more food the danger of famine from drought is by no means over.

Famine often accompanies war. Because of its position in the fighting, a city may be cut off from its food supply. War may make the transport of food impossible—in World War II many people died of starvation in Amsterdam, Rotterdam and Utrecht (Netherlands) during the winter of 1944–1945 because the Germans had taken all the railway wagons and food could not be sent into the towns from the country. Fighting may destroy crops or prevent their being sown or reaped.

A dreadful famine occurred in Ireland in the winter of 1846 and in 1847 because the potato crops were ruined by a disease known as potato blight. Many of the people lived almost entirely on potatoes, and when these failed they died of starvation (see BLACK FORTY-SEVEN OR POTATO FAMINE). In Africa and the Middle East great swarms of locusts sometimes eat up every crop in their path, and famine is only prevented by destroying the swarms and their breeding grounds.

In 1950 earthquakes in Assam, India, destroyed roads and railways, caused landslides and made rivers burst their banks, drowning crops and cattle (see EARTHQUAKE). The Yellow River of China is known as "China's Sorrow" because it so frequently floods the lands and brings famine (see YELLOW RIVER).

If famine cannot be prevented, the roads, railways and aeroplanes of modern times usually make it easier to help its victims, as food can be sent to them from more fortunate places. At the end of World War II the United Nations sent great quantities of grain to Europe and saved millions of people from starvation. When famine is due to earthquakes and floods, however, it is very difficult to get food into the area because roads and railways may be destroyed, and it is not easy to feed people by air.

The Freedom from Hunger campaign launched in 1960 by the Food and Agriculture Organization (F.A.O.) of the United Nations works to overcome the problems of famine.

**FAN.** From the earliest times people have used fans to keep themselves cool in hot weather, holding them in their hands and waving them to and fro to make a draught of cool air blow on their faces. Long ago fans were also used for making draughts to keep fires alight and for winnowing grain; that is, separating the chaff or worthless part from the good grain. In ancient Egypt women cooled themselves with date-palm leaves and priests fanned the flames of fires used in religious ceremonies. The office

of fan-bearer to the king was a much prized honour, and the fans used by the bearers were made of feathers arranged in a half circle and fixed on to a long handle.

There are all kinds of legends about how the fan came about. The Chinese believed that it was invented by the daughter of a mandarin, or public official, who took off the mask she was wearing at a summer feast and fanned her face with it. In Japan it was thought of as standing for life itself, which widens out as the fan widens out from its handle. It was used there until modern times by everyone on every occasion: even the condemned man marched to the scaffold fan in hand and the executioner held a fan as he cut off the victim's head. It was the Japanese who, in about A.D. 670, invented the folding or pleated fan, which when shut up looks like a little bundle of sticks one above another.

In ancient Greece men and women kept themselves cool and brushed away flies with fans made of peacock feathers, and the smart young gentlemen of Rome used to carry fans made of precious wood or finely carved ivory for their ladies. The oldest fan in existence, which is preserved in the cathedral of Monza in Italy, is said to have belonged to Theolinda, queen of the Lombards of north Italy in the 7th century.

Until the end of the 16th century, fans were made of feathers or tufts. Fans with plumes were fashionable in England during Henry VIII's reign when "even young gentlemen carried fans of feathers in their hands". In 1556 Mary Tudor was given seven fans to keep off the heat of the fire. When the Portuguese sailors came back from trading with China, they brought with them the pleated fan, which became popular in England about 1590. There is a portrait of Queen Elizabeth I, who loved gloves and fans, holding one of these. A special code of signalling with fans developed, and court ladies could convey loving messages to their admirers simply by the way in which they handled their fans.

When the Portuguese princess Catharine of Braganza married Charles II she introduced large green fans to shade the complexion from the sun. The carved sticks then came from India and the coverings, or mounts, from Italy, but the English fan-making industry was started by some of the French Protestants who had fled to England from their own country in 1685. In the 18th century the fashion for fans, many of them very beautifully painted, was at its height. A fan was an essential part of woman's dress. The sticks of fans were made of ivory or mother-of-pearl, encrusted with gold, silver, enamel and jewels, and the mounts were made of such materials as kidskin, silk, lace or parchment.

During the 19th century women still used fans, especially with evening dress, but fans became less beautiful in design. Large ostrich feather and lace fans were popular at the end of the 19th and beginning of the 20th centuries. Today they are no longer much used in Europe, but fans are still seen in the Far East.

**FANFARE.** A fanfare is a short piece of loud and stirring music, played on trumpets or bugles. It is usually performed at important occasions, such as coronations, when the king's or queen's heralds wear a special costume and have the royal standard attached to their instruments. A fanfare may also be played before the curtain rises at a theatre, on sporting occasions and at musical festivals.

**FARADAY, Michael** (1791–1867). This great English scientist was the son of a Yorkshire blacksmith who had moved to London. He was largely self-taught, for at the age of ten he became an errand boy at a bookseller's shop where he was later apprenticed as a bookbinder. He became interested in the books about chemistry and electricity that came to him for binding, and in 1812 he went to some public lectures given by the chemist Sir Humphry Davy, on whom there is a separate article. He copied out the notes he had taken of these lectures and bound them up as a book which he sent to Sir Humphry with a letter asking if he could be given a job. Davy then made him a laboratory assistant at the Royal Institution, and soon afterwards took him as manservant and secretary on a tour of Europe in which they met many famous scientists.

Faraday's work in chemistry was of itself quite important, for he discovered the substance benzene, made a special study of the gas chlorine, succeeded in changing several gases into liquids and invented new kinds of glass for optical instruments such as microscopes. Nevertheless it was his work on electricity and magnetism that made him famous. The Danish scientist Hans C. Oersted had in 1820 shown that electricity would produce magnetism, and Faraday thought about this and made experiments to find out more. Then he had the idea that magnetism might produce electricity, and in 1831 he proved that it could by moving a magnet near a wire. Although somebody was bound to find this out sooner or later, it was a discovery of the first importance because it opened the way for the making of electric current on a large scale (see DYNAMO).

Faraday then received many honours, but he remained a simple and modest man; he never bothered his head about the money that he might have made from his inventions and several times refused offers of employment from manufacturers.

For 30 years he was the adviser to Trinity House as to the best kind of lamps for use in lighthouses (see TRINITY HOUSE), though of course he went on with his experiments in the laboratory. He did important work on electrolysis (on which there is a separate article) and also on the effect that magnetism has on rays of some kinds of light.

He was very fond of children though he had none of his own and he would sometimes take his nephews and nieces into the laboratory and show them exciting experiments. It was he who started the lectures for young people which are still held in the Christmas season at the Royal Institution.

*Radio Times Hulton Picture Library*

Michael Faraday at work in the laboratory of the Royal Institution, where many of his discoveries were made.

**FARMING** is the most important industry in the world because it produces food, without which no one can keep alive to work in any other industry. Food, shelter and warmth are all necessary to man, and food is the most necessary of the three because he cannot build a shelter or search for fuel if he is starving to death. For thousands of years men have grown food and raised animals because they could not live off wild fruits, wild grain and wild animals. This article deals mostly with the type of farming carried on in Great Britain. The article AGRICULTURE, HISTORY OF, describes the history of farming, and the article on each separate country describes its own particular kind of farming.

Men have learnt a great deal about the best ways of growing crops and raising animals. They know that soil and climate are most important, because different sorts of crops need different kinds of soil and climate if they are to grow properly. Farming therefore varies from country to country, and even from area to area in a country that has several different kinds of climate. Consider, for example, England, a small country with the Pennine chain of hills running down the middle of the northern part of it like a backbone. West winds coming from the great Atlantic Ocean are full of moisture, and when they meet these hills they drop the

Animals now tend to be kept in larger herds. Mechanized feeding reduces the amount of labour needed to look after them, and animals are often wintered under cover.

moisture on the west side of England in the form of rain or snow. The hilly areas in Wales and Scotland and on the Pennine Hills are much colder as well as wetter, whereas in the east and south of England it is drier and warmer. These differences in climate result in great differences in the types of farming. For example, in the wetter areas in the west grass is the crop that grows best and there is a lot of dairy farming. On the hills and mountains, the grass is not good enough for dairy cows, so beef cattle and sheep are kept. Growing crops in these hilly areas is difficult because the ground is steep, the soil is poor and stony and the rainfall is high. If the soil is wet in the spring the farmer cannot easily prepare a seedbed for sowing his crops; also, it is difficult to harvest any crop in the rain.

So it is in the warmer and drier areas to the east of the Pennines that crops grow best. This is where most of the cereal crops such as wheat and barley are grown, and also the root crops such as sugar beet, potatoes and carrots. (There are separate articles on most of the crops mentioned.)

Apart from the climate, the kind of soil is the next most important thing that decides what crops the farmer should grow. Heavy clay soils need large tractors if he is to get them ploughed properly ready for sowing. If he cannot afford this expensive machinery he may find it easier to leave the fields as grass. A light and sandy soil is easy to plough and cultivate but it may get so dry during the summer that the crop suffers from drought. If the land is very poor it may be of no use for farming and may be left as a heath with gorse and bracken growing on it, or it can be used for growing trees for timber. The kind of soil (see SOIL) that a farmer likes best for growing crops is called a loam. This has just the right mixture of sand and clay to make it easy for ploughing and sowing and it has also enough moisture and plant foods. It gives high crop yields. So on each farm the crops grown and the animals kept depend mainly on the climate and the soil.

## Farming in Britain

From about 1850 to 1950 farmers in Britain believed that it was best to have what is called "mixed farming". This meant that they grew grass and many different crops, and that they kept all the different kinds of animals—cows, sheep, pigs and chickens. If in one year the price was very low for pigs or potatoes, the farmers hoped to make up for it by having other things to sell at a good price, such as barley, or sheep for mutton. Another reason for mixed farming was that all the fields got a change from growing only one crop. After growing grass for two to three years, each field was changed to some other crop such as wheat, potatoes or barley. This helped to keep the soil free from diseases and pests that attack crops and spoil their yield. (Temporary grassland is called a "ley"; see GRASSLAND.)

But since about 1950 farmers have learnt a lot more about the best way to grow their crops. They know how much plant food each crop needs and can add the right amount of fertilizer to the soil to give high yields. (See FERTILIZER.) Nowadays the farmer can use sprays on nearly all his crops to kill weeds and prevent them from choking the crops. Moreover, scientists have provided the farmer with new kinds of seeds which are less liable to get attacked by diseases and pests.

Nowadays, therefore, instead of having mixed farms we find each farmer trying to grow those few crops that suit his climate and soil best. If he decides to grow a lot of wheat and barley he can then get all the right machinery such as sowing drills and combine harvesters, which will help him to get the work done quickly. If he prefers a lot of root crops, such as potatoes or carrots, he will buy the special machines that dig the potatoes or carrots out of the ground. This saves him from having to employ a lot of men to help with the harvest who would not have much work to do for the rest of the year. (See FARM MACHINERY.)

If you visit a crop-growing farm that carries few animals you will find that the buildings at the farmyard are used for keeping tractors, harrows, drills and combines, and that some special buildings are used for storing wheat, barley and potatoes until they are sold. The fields on a crop farm are large so that the tractors can get on with their work quickly. There are hardly any hedges between the fields, as there are no sheep

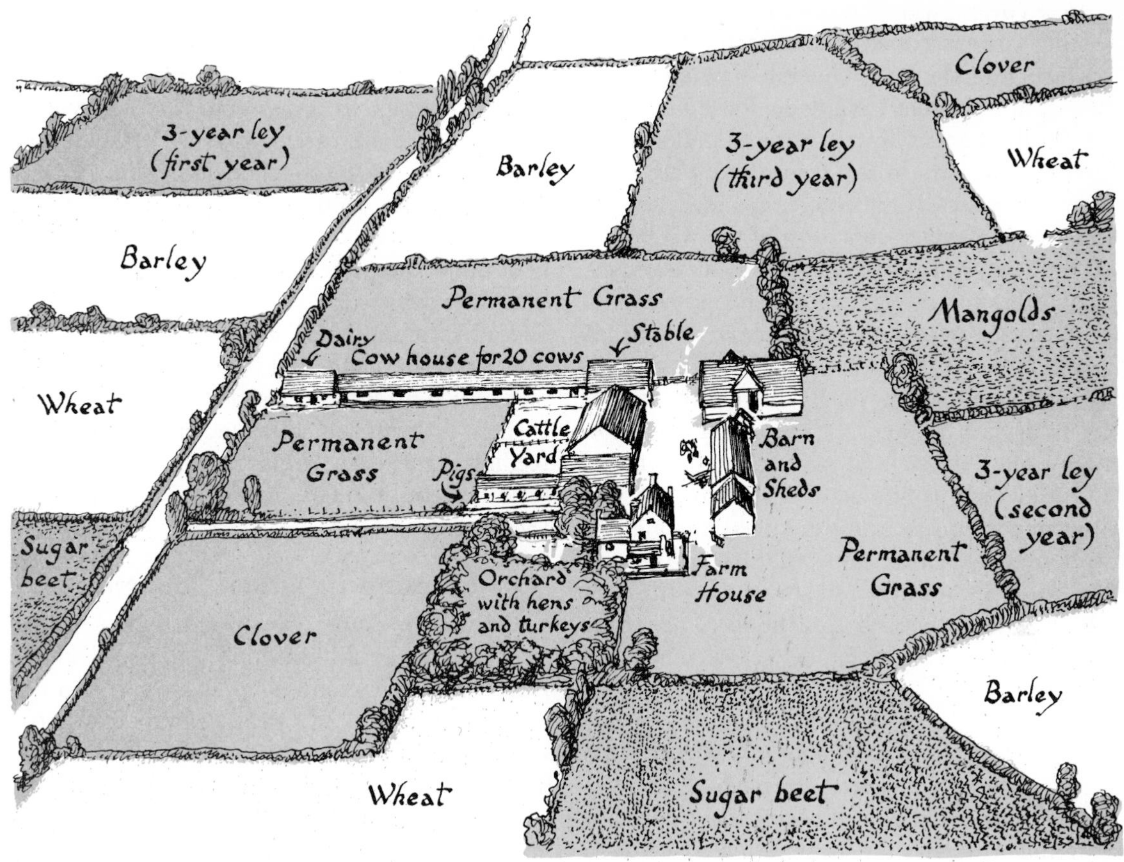


or cows to stray, so it is easy to see which crops are being grown. Because it is so important for crops to be sown and harvested at the right time, farmers are very busy indeed at these periods. You will see the tractors and combines busy working until dark, and sometimes they may even use headlights and carry on all night long.

Where the conditions are suitable, some farmers concentrate on growing crops. However, there are still many farms where crops are grown for several years in each field, and it is then planted to grass for feeding cattle and sheep. (See SHEEP FARMING.)

If the farmer keeps a herd of dairy cows to produce milk, the cows get nearly all the food they need during the summer by grazing the grass pastures. Some of the grass is made into hay (see HAYMAKING) or silage to provide the cows with food during the winter, when it is too cold for the grass to grow. (Silage is explained later in this article.) The cows are then kept indoors in a large yard with a covered roof. Straw is used for bedding and when this becomes cow manure it is carted out into the fields that are to grow root crops. Thus the waste products of the farm help to raise the yield of crops. (See DAIRY FARMING.)

Herds of pigs and flocks of hens are not nowadays kept in the open so much as they used to be. Farmers keep them indoors all the year round so that they are out of the cold and draughts. The pigs then get fat quicker and the hens lay more eggs.

The illustration shows an imaginary mixed farm. When looking at it, remember that next year each field will be growing a different crop to the one shown, except the first-year and second-year leys and the fields given over to permanent grass. Although the drawing shows a farm with square fields grouped round the house, many farms have fields of irregular shapes scattered over a wider area, with fields belonging to other farmers dotted among them. However, this farm is imaginary. The public road running through it is another advantage, for it allows lorries to collect and deliver goods and milk churns. Mixed farms vary in size from small ones of 50 acres to large ones of 300 acres or more. On the smallest, the farmer does most of the work himself and employs outside help only occasionally. On the big farms eight or ten people are employed and a great deal of machinery is used. A farm of about 150 acres is a useful size, for it is big enough to make it worth while for the farmer to buy machinery, and not so big that he has to employ more than about two men to help him.

Outside help is needed at certain times, such as when hoeing root crops in late spring and for harvesting sugar beet and potatoes in autumn. The farmer ought to be able to manage the corn harvest without extra help if he has a combine harvester, for this machine saves time and labour.

Autumn is a busy time on a farm. The fields are ploughed, harrowed and made ready for winter wheat which is sown in October and begins to come up in November. Wheat does not grow much during the winter but is ready to begin again in the spring. Alongside this work goes the harvesting of sugar beet. A machine is often used to lift the crop out of the ground, but the beet then has to be carted to large heaps by the roadside from which lorries take it to the factory where the sugar is extracted (see SUGAR). Then, when the frost makes most other work on the land impossible, hedging, ditching and general tidying up are done (see HEDGING AND DITCHING).

After the frost has gone there is more ploughing and harrowing in readiness for the sowing of the spring root crops and barley. When the root crops come up they must be hoed; that is, the seedlings have to be thinned out by a man with a hoe so that each plant has enough room to grow properly, and the spaces between the rows must be hoed to kill the weeds. Modern farmers try to save this hoeing work by sowing the seeds of the root crop more evenly and by using sprays to kill the weeds. Then comes haymaking, and if bad weather has delayed the hoeing the two jobs may have to be done at the same time.

Instead of making hay the farmer may make silage, for which the grass is cut while still young, juicy and full of proteins. It is not left to dry but is gathered in almost immediately and pressed down hard (to keep out the air) in a container called a silo. A silo usually consists of a concrete floor under a barn which has wooden or concrete sides into which the fresh grass can be pressed down by a tractor running over it. The absence of air and the slight heat from the grass form an acid which preserves the proteins in the grass. It is these proteins which make silage a far better feeding stuff than ordinary hay, for animals need proteins to build muscle and to make milk. (See PROTEIN.)

## Farming in Other Countries

Farming in some other countries is very different from British farming. Parts of North America have much colder winters and much hotter summers than Great Britain. Until 100 years ago much of the land had never been farmed before, and was therefore fairly fertile. The first farmers grew wheat only and did not realize that the soil would be ruined if they went on growing the same crop year after year. This happened both in Canada and the United States, and even now, though the farmers in these countries look after their soil more carefully, they do not produce, *per acre*, half as much wheat as British farmers produce. (The *total* amount they produce is naturally very much greater as they have much more land.) Some of the American and Canadian wheat farmers leave their farms in the autumn and go to the cities to find other work or to have a long holiday. They return to their farms for the spring sowing and stay there only until the wheat has been harvested. In Canada this happens in the provinces of Saskatchewan, Manitoba and in large parts of Alberta and Ontario, and it happens because the winters come early and the farmers cannot sow their grain in the autumn, nor can they plough their frozen, snow-covered land during the winter. In areas like south Ontario, Quebec and New Brunswick, where the winter is not so severe, other crops besides spring wheat are grown and the farmers stay on their farms all the year round. They grow some winter wheat, along with oats, barley and apples, and keep cattle and pigs. The animals can scarcely ever graze out of doors during the winter because, even in these areas, the climate is too cold.

Over in the west, in British Columbia, there are still other types of farming. West winds blow in from the Pacific Ocean and drop their moisture as they rise over the great Rocky Mountains, which run from north to south. This means that British Columbia and the western part of the British Isles have very similar weather. They both have rain, and as they lie in the same latitudes (see LATITUDE AND LONGITUDE), have the same sort of temperature. In southern British Columbia a great amount of fruit is grown, especially apples. In the middle part wheat is grown and cattle are kept, while in the north there is forestry (see FORESTRY).

Australia produces a great variety of food because it is a large country and thus has several different types of climate. In northeastern Queensland, which is hot and wet, fruits such as pineapples and bananas are grown, while in the drier parts of Queensland and in the Northern Territory great numbers of cattle are kept. Oranges, peaches, apricots, plums and several other types of fruit grow well in the southeastern areas. The state of New South Wales is famous for its sheep and its wheat.

New Zealand has a mild climate rather like that of the British Isles. The farmers there have covered more than a quarter of its land area with excellent pasture of sown grasses and clovers. There are also huge areas of rough tussock grass. Sheep are reared for wool and meat on the higher ground, while in the lower, sheltered districts Jersey cattle are kept on small, family farms for dairy produce. Many of the crops grown are fed to livestock.

**FARM MACHINERY.** Farming is an old occupation, but most of the machines which a modern farmer uses to help him till the soil are completely different from those of the past. Until the 19th century the plough was pulled by oxen or horses. Then, as the steam engine (see

Plough.

STEAM ENGINE) had been invented, people realized that it could be used to pull a plough. One method employed a single engine with an arrangement of anchor pulleys, but later two engines—one at each end of the field—were used to pull the plough back and forth between them. But the machinery was cumbersome and costly, so most ploughing continued to be done by horses.

In the 20th century, however, the motor-driven tractor (see TRACTOR) has taken the place of both horses and steam engines for ploughing, and is used for much work besides ploughing.

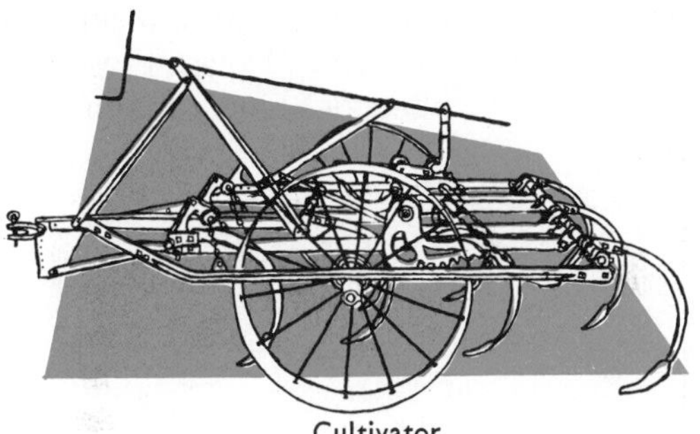

Cultivator.

Since much of the hard work on a farm is now done by machines, we say that farming is *mechanized*. Some of the most common machines are described in this article and are put in groups according to the work they do.

## Preparing the Ground

Before each year's new crop can be planted, the ground must be properly prepared, and different implements are used at different stages of the preparation. First is the plough, which turns a layer of earth over and exposes to the sun and air the part that had been deepest in the earth. At the same time weeds and the remains of the old crop are buried to rot away and enrich the soil. The plough cuts into the earth as it goes along, making a groove, or furrow. The cutting is done by the pointed steel share and by the coulter, which makes a cut above and in front of the share. Behind the share is the mouldboard, a large curved piece of metal which turns the cut earth over and leaves it in the furrow that we always associate with ploughed fields. (See PLOUGH AND PLOUGHING.)

The weather has a good effect on the upturned earth and helps to break it up, but before the seed can be sown the soil must be worked still more—to break up the clods and to make its surface even again. This process is called preparing a tilth, and several implements are used for it.

Cultivators are generally used first. They are strong, heavy implements with metal teeth which point downwards. These teeth can be lowered so that they dig deep into the soil or raised so that they go through the surface layers only. As the cultivator is pulled along, the teeth drag through the soil and break up the clods.

Harrows are used for many jobs, including the preparation of the tilth. They are usually lighter than the cultivator, but work in the same way, with metal teeth pointing downwards. The teeth are much shorter and therefore do not go so deep into the soil, but as there are more of them they work it into finer particles. There are various types of harrow, each one for a special purpose. They are used for covering seed after sowing, working weeds out of the soil, breaking up a hard soil surface and for improving grassland by dragging out the old dead grass and moss.

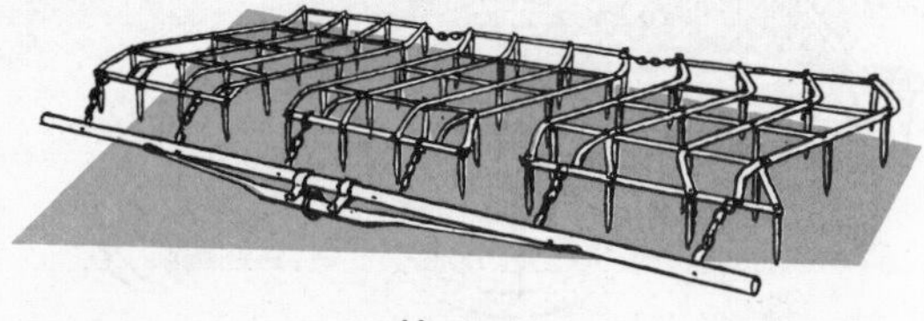

Harrow.

Rolls are also used to prepare a tilth. After the land has been ploughed, cultivated and harrowed the soil sometimes needs to be pressed to make it firm before the seeds are sown. Rolls are used for this work. They have a series of metal rings like solid wheels which go over the soil and press the particles down. They are also sometimes used on fields of young corn in spring to press the soil firmly round the roots of the plants.

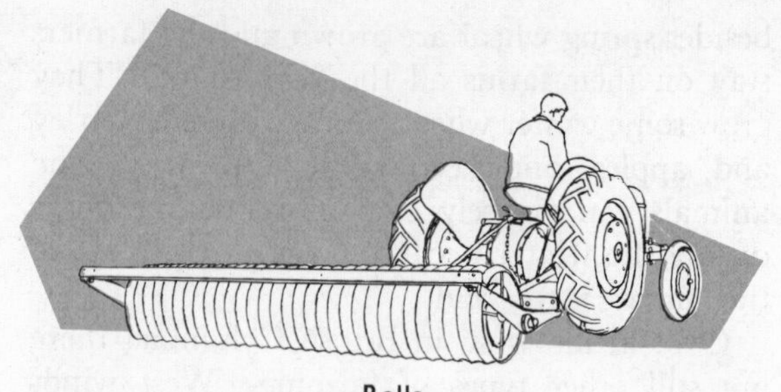

Rolls.

## Fertilizers and Manure

Before the seed is sown, manure and fertilizer (see FERTILIZER) are often added to the seed bed so that when the seedlings begin to grow they will have plenty of the right kinds of plant food. Fertilizer is spread from a machine called a distributor, which is a long box between two wheels. Fertilizer is put into the box and as the machine goes along the fertilizer falls out on to the ground through holes in the bottom of the box. It is then either worked into the ground by cultivation or left on the surface to be washed in by rain.

Farmyard manure is thick and heavy, so it needs a different type of machine to spread it. The floor of the wagon on which the manure is loaded has a moving part which carries the manure to the end of the wagon, where another piece of machinery breaks it up and throws it evenly over the ground. Quite often, however, the manure is spread by men with forks, from little heaps dropped from a wagon in neat rows across a field.

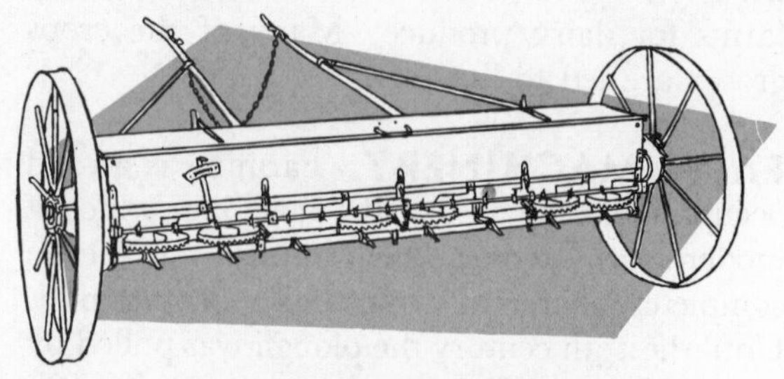

Distributor for fertilizer.

## Sowing the Seed

Grain and root crops are usually sown in rows by a process known as "drilling". Small seeds such as grasses are sometimes drilled and sometimes "broadcast", or scattered by hand. The seed drill looks very like a fertilizer distributor, as it also consists of a long, narrow box between two wheels. In the bottom of the box there are evenly spaced openings, with a metal spout under each. The seed falls through these openings, down the spouts and into grooves in the soil, made for it by metal blades in front of the spouts. It is then covered over by harrowing.

Seed drill.

Special equipment is needed to plant potatoes because they are fairly big and because they are usually planted on ridged land. The ridges are made by a ridging plough which is like an ordinary plough but has two mouldboards, one each side of the share. These throw up the earth on both sides, leaving a central furrow in which the potatoes are set, either by hand or by machine. The ridging plough is then taken down the centre of the ridges, splitting them so that the soil falls over the potatoes in the furrow.

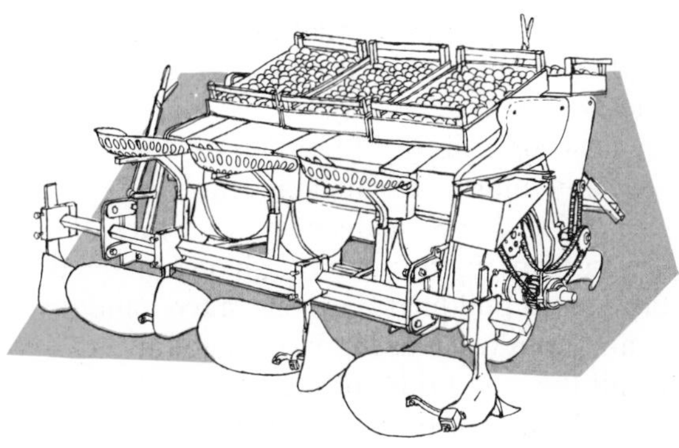

Potato planter.

One machine, known as the potato planter, can do all this work in a single operation, taking three rows at a time. Three men sit on the machine and drop potatoes into slots from which they fall into the furrow at evenly spaced intervals. The machine has two ridging ploughs, one in front of the slots to make the furrow, and one behind them to close it.

## Destroying Weeds and Pests

While a crop is growing it must be kept free from weeds, which would steal the food and light it needs for healthy growth. Much can be done to prevent weeds by proper cultivation before the crop is sown, but as they grow very quickly it is often necessary to kill them while the crop is growing. As the rows of cereal crops (wheat, barley, oats and rye) are only about six inches apart it is impossible to cultivate between them so, where necessary, these crops are sprayed with liquid weed-killer.

In crops planted with rows farther apart, such as sugar beet and vegetables, there is room for hoeing. The hand hoe is often used for hoeing between plants in the same row, and for thinning out a crop; that is, removing some of the plants in order to let the others grow well. Hoeing between rows is usually done by hoes pulled by horses or tractors. These implements can work several rows at a time, and have a light frame with teeth pointing downwards; the position of the teeth can be changed for use with different crops, so that they do not damage the plants. Plants may be attacked by insects or

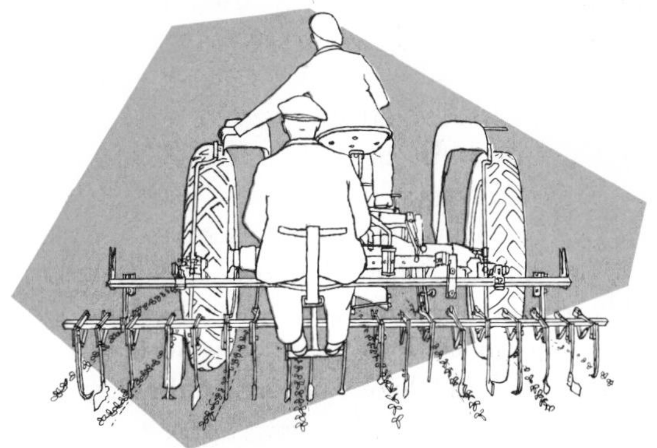

Mechanical hoe.

pests which will cause them to die or develop diseases. Spraying machines are used to spray liquids or powders on to the crops to prevent such attacks.

### Harvesting and Grading

The first crop of the year to be harvested is usually grass, and it is cut by the mower. This machine, pulled by tractor, has a row of sharp triangular knives close to the ground. When it moves, these knives cut a strip of grass from three to six feet wide, called a swath. A few days after being cut this swath is turned over, to dry the under side, by a machine called a swath turner. Then comes the baler. This gathers up the hay and presses it into bales, ties them up and throws them out on the ground. The farmer may decide not to bale the hay, but to make a haystack instead. He then uses a sweep to carry the loose hay to the stack. A sweep is an implement with long, straight "fingers", which is fixed to the front of a tractor. As the tractor is driven along, the fingers of the sweep slide under the hay and gather it up. When no more hay can be held on the sweep the tractor driver drives to the stack and drops his load at the foot of it. The hay is lifted to whatever height the stack has already reached by an elevator. This is a machine rather like a moving staircase, which stands by the side of the stack; the hay travels up the middle of it on an endless belt. (See HAYMAKING.)

The reaper-binder is seen at work in late July and in August, when the corn crops are ripe. This machine cuts corn in much the same way that the mower cuts grass, but it is a more complicated machine and binds the cut crop into bundles, called sheaves. These are left to dry out in the field, standing in little groups or "stooks" and then built into stacks. In the winter the thresher will be used to thresh the corn out of the ears. It is a large machine, worked by a tractor, which beats out the grain from the ear, delivers it by chute into waiting sacks and separates the chaff from the straw, or husks. Many farmers now use a combine harvester which cuts and threshes the corn in one operation as it moves round the field at harvest time. (See REAPING AND THRESHING.)

If a combine harvester has been used, grain may need to be dried, cleaned and graded before it leaves the farm. Cleaning and grading is often done by one machine which removes weed seed, dirt and dust from the grain and separates good grain from undersized and damaged grain.

The harvesting of root crops follows the corn harvest. There are potato harvesters which lift the crop, separate the tops and clean the potatoes. There are other simpler and less expensive machines that lift the potatoes out of the ridge and scatter them on the surface of the soil, where they are picked up by hand.

Sugar beet is harvested in much the same way as potatoes though it grows much deeper in the soil. Some farmers cut off the tops of the sugar beet before they are lifted and feed the leaves to cattle or sheep.

During the winter the potato sorter is used to separate potatoes into three sizes. It consists of riddles, or wire trays with holes in them, each tray having holes of a different size. The riddles are one above the other and shake backwards and forwards when the machine is working. The large potatoes, called "ware", are too big to fall through the holes in the top riddle and so are carried to sacks at the end if it. The smaller ones fall through the second riddle and are collected in other sacks and later used as seed. The smallest potatoes fall through still smaller holes and are used as pig food.

**FASHION.** The word "fashion" is usually applied to clothes, especially to women's clothes. People speak of some shape of hat or of dress as being "in fashion" or "out of fashion". "In fashion" simply means that these are the kind of clothes which people like to wear at that time; and "out of fashion" is used to describe clothes which people liked a few years ago but do not like any more. Fashion, in fact, enters into everything that is made, not just clothes. There are fashions in furniture, fashions in pictures, fashions in buildings, fashions in food and drink —and even fashions in places to go for holidays. In all the many sides of life people have a feeling of liking certain things at one time, and then getting tired of them and wanting something

*Right: Camera Press. Remainder: Radio Times Hulton Picture Library*

All these clothes were the height of fashion at the time when the photographs were taken. From left to right: spectators at Cowes Week in 1911; Ascot in 1927; Ascot again in 1939; Longchamp (a race-meeting near Paris) in 1949.

new and different. It is this natural feeling that makes fashions in everything.

Why do people like certain clothes at a certain time? Why do they then get tired of them and want something different? And why do they all want to dress in the same way?

People like certain clothes at a certain time because they suit the feeling of that time and often because they are a complete change from what has gone before. The "New Look" that became fashionable in 1947, when women began to wear clothes with tight waists, soft rounded shoulders and long full skirts, came in as a complete contrast to the clothes of the war years 1939–1945. Then, when everyone was working for the war effort and material was scarce, no trimmings or extra cloth were allowed to be used and women's clothes were plain and business-like. During the 1920s dresses were short and straight and women wore their hair cut short; this was because they had turned away from the elaborate clothes and hairdressing that had been fashionable before, and it was also an outward sign that women no longer felt that their place was only in the home and were going out into the world to work independently. Skirts reaching the ground were no good for a modern woman.

People get tired of a fashion and want something different either because it no longer expresses their feelings or because it is simply human nature to enjoy change. There is something in human nature too that makes most people like to do what everyone else is doing and especially to look the way everyone else looks. On the other hand, they also get bored eventually with doing the same things or with looking the same way, and they are very ready to follow anyone who proposes something exciting and new—as long as there is something about it that they like!

Leading people in the dress business are able, because of their talent and their experience, to foresee the changes that people will be ready to welcome. Just as the farmer or the sailor can look at the clouds and feel the wind and know what kind of weather is coming, so fashion changes are "in the air" and some people can all "feel" them at the same time. This is because alterations in dress fashions are of two main kinds—either developments of what is fashionable already or complete changes from it.

Designers who spend their whole lives studying fashion are able to understand whether there are still interesting developments to be made in the existing fashions or whether the thing to do is to start all over again with something quite different. It is as if some children were to play a game; from time to time one or another of them suggests some variation, and then suddenly they all get tired of it and decide to play something quite different.

Paris has been the centre of fashion for women for a long time, for the French are an artistic people who take the whole business of dressing women very seriously indeed: the design of the fabrics used, the clothes, the hats, the "accessories" (the things that go with the main outfit, such as shoes, gloves, hats and handbags) and the jewellery. When the Paris designers show their clothes in what are called their "Collections" each spring and autumn, journalists who write about fashions in newspapers and magazines, designers of ready-to-wear clothes and people whose job is to buy the clothes which will eventually be sold to the public in the shops go from all over the world to see them.

Many Paris dress designers, by a feeling of what is "in the air", show clothes of a similar kind, and journalists, ready-to-wear designers and store buyers with their trained fashion sense, by instinct choose similar lines and colours to show in their magazines, to copy in their factories or to buy for their stores. So it happens that the fashion papers and the shop windows are filled with similar styles and women see them everywhere and begin to think that they would like them. The designers have to be clever enough to design (and the journalists and buyers clever enough to choose) clothes which women who see them will want to possess, for if they guess wrong they will soon be out of business.

The fashion industries in much of Europe and in North America have grown enormously during the present century, because many more ready-to-wear clothes, mass produced in factories, are sold in shops at all sorts of prices to suit people of different incomes.

To be "in fashion" is only part of good dressing. It is also necessary for a woman to dress suitably for her age, for her type of figure and colouring and for the occasion. Elaborate clothes can be smart if they are well designed and made and worn by the right person at the right time; but simple clothes are always right, at any age, for any type and for any occasion.

**FASTING** really means doing without food and drink completely, and in some parts of the world people do fast in this way, sometimes for religious reasons. However, these days the word more often means that someone is eating and drinking very little. People may do this in order to lose weight or perhaps, even, to earn money in a fair-ground. Or they may feel that fasting is the only way of drawing attention to something they think is wrong or to something that they think ought to be done. The suffragettes (women who were agitating in the early 1900s for women's right to the vote) often fasted when they were imprisoned for creating disturbances. (See SUFFRAGETTES.) The Indian leader Mahatma Gandhi used fasting as a way of influencing political events (see GANDHI, MOHANDAS KARAMCHAND). People fasting all take water or mineral waters or some other drink, and many of them take vitamin tablets as well.

Complete fasting was often ordered by doctors in the old days but few now advise it, though they often order their patients to go on special diets which avoid certain types of food.

People often fast for religious reasons, the best known Christian fast being the 40 days of Lent (see LENT). Moslems, Hindus and Jews keep very strict fasts in preparation for religious ceremonies and before going on pilgrimages. The Moslems also have a special month of fasting each year, during which no food or drink may be taken between sunrise and sunset.

**FATES, THE.** By the side of Pluto, King of the Underworld, according to Greek tales, sat three old women called the three Fates in whose hands lay the destiny of man. They were the daughters of the god Zeus and were called Clotho, Lachesis and Atropos. Clotho held a distaff on which the thread of a man's life was wound. Lachesis spun it out and Atropos cut the thread with a pair of scissors. When the thread was cut the man died and not even the gods could save him. The Fates were not always thought of as being old: sometimes Clotho was young, Lachesis was middle-aged and only Atropos was old.

Their names in Roman mythology were Nona, Decuma and Morta.

**FATHER CHRISTMAS** is known in many lands and his habits vary according to the country he is in. The articles NICHOLAS, SAINT and CHRISTMAS CUSTOMS explain his history and what he does in some of the countries he visits.

**FATS** are substances found in animals and plants; they may be solid or liquid, though most animal fats are solid. Liquid fats are commonly called oils, or more exactly fat oils, but not all oils are fats. (See OIL.) Common fats are dripping and the white solid known as "cooking fat", also butter and margarine. No fats will dissolve in water, which will not even wet them but if poured on will collect in tiny droplets. Oils and fats float on the surface of water because they are lighter than water.

All fats are made up of the three elements carbon, hydrogen and oxygen, and when set on fire they burn with a black sooty flame which shows the presence of carbon. A fat can always be split by chemical action into two substances, which are glycerine (see GLYCERINE) and a *fatty acid*. The kind of fatty acid depends on the fat, thus the chemical splitting of butter gives butyric acid, tallow gives stearic acid and olive oil oleic acid.

Fats can be dissolved in liquids such as ether, chloroform, benzene and carbon tetrachloride, and liquids of this kind are often sold for taking grease spots out of clothes. When a fat is boiled with an alkali such as caustic soda (see ALKALI) it is split into glycerine and a soap. Hence the soap making industry uses large quantities of fats (see SOAP AND SOAP MAKING.)

Fats are one of the three main kinds of foods for people, the other two being carbohydrates and proteins, on which there are separate articles. Fat can also be formed in the body by other foods and forms a useful reserve store of energy. Much of it is stored under the skin so that it also helps to keep us warm by acting as a kind of blanket.

**FAUST,** or Faustus, is the name of a magician of the 16th century, famous in legends and in literature. Many legends grew up about his strange powers and the agreement he made with the Devil, although most of the learned men of his time considered that Magister Georgius Sabellicus Faustus Junior, as he called himself, was nothing but a swindler who made money by pretending to have supernatural knowledge and powers. Gradually, however, some religious and learned men began to believe that Faustus really did have these powers, and that they were given him by the Devil.

More and more details were added, and soon the Faust story was complete. It was that Doctor Faustus, a learned doctor who longed to have knowledge of everything and power over everything, promised his soul to the Devil when he died on condition that the Devil would give him during his lifetime all the magical power that he craved. Thus Faustus turned away from God to get knowledge and power for himself. His punishment came when, at the end of his life, the Devil claimed his soul and bore him off to eternal damnation.

Many Faust stories, ballads and plays have been written. The most famous are Christopher Marlowe's play *The Tragicall History of Dr. Faustus*, published in 1604, and the play *Faust* by the German writer Johann Wolfgang von Goethe (1749–1832). The composer Charles Gounod wrote an opera based on Goethe's work.

**FAWKES, Guy** (1570–1606). The man who has given English children an excuse for fireworks and bonfires on November 5 for so many years was born in York in 1570 and was the son of a lawyer, Edward Fawkes, and his wife Edith.

Fawkes went to school in York and was brought up as a Protestant, but after his father died he became a Roman Catholic. In 1593, at the age of 23, he left England and joined the Spanish army in Flanders. (Flanders consisted of part of what is now northeastern France and

Belgium, and the Spanish army was there because Spain ruled over Flanders at this time.) As a soldier he impressed people by his good qualities.

In 1603 Elizabeth I died and James I inherited the throne. For some time in England there had been struggles between Roman Catholics and Protestants, some people wanting a

Guy Fawkes laying a trail of gunpowder to act as a fuse.

Roman Catholic sovereign on the throne and others a Protestant. When it became clear that the new king intended to keep to Protestantism, some Roman Catholic gentlemen plotted together to blow him up, along with members of both the House of Lords and the House of Commons, when he opened Parliament on November 5, 1605. They hoped to take over the government of the country and appeal to Spain, a Roman Catholic country, for help.

The leaders of this plot, Robert Catesby, Thomas Percy and several others, asked Guy Fawkes to help them. Being both a fearless man and a fanatical Roman Catholic he agreed, and crossed to England in 1604. For the plotters, Percy rented the house next to the building where parliament met and Fawkes was installed there, pretending to be Percy's servant and calling himself Johnson. The plotters intended to dig a tunnel under the parliament building, but later managed to rent a cellar that was immediately beneath the House of Lords. Fawkes arranged the barrels of gunpowder in it (they contained more than a ton and a half) and covered them up with firewood and coal. He was to be responsible for firing the gunpowder and had arranged to use a method that would give him time to escape before the explosion took place.

At the last moment, however, one of the plotters, most probably Francis Tresham, wrote to Lord Mounteagle, who was his brother-in-law, warning him not to be present at the opening of parliament, saying that, "though there be no appearance of any stir, yet I say they shall receive a terrible blow, the Parliament, and yet they shall not see who hurts them". Mounteagle showed the letter to members of the government and the cellar was searched on November 4. Fawkes was discovered and in his pockets were the special "slow" matches with which he was going to light the fuse.

He was arrested, imprisoned in the Tower and tortured to make him betray the others. He was very brave, however, and did not tell the names of his fellow conspirators until after they had already made themselves known by trying to start an armed rebellion. Fawkes and seven others were tried and sentenced to death. On January 31, 1606, he was taken from the Tower to Westminster and executed opposite the building that he had attempted to blow up.

(For an account of the searching of the cellars of the Houses of Parliament each year since 1605 see PARLIAMENT.)

**FEATHER.** Only birds have feathers and no bird is without them, not even the penguins which are at home in the water and never fly, although some of their feathers look almost like fish scales. Originally, feathers were evolved, or developed, as a covering to protect the body, just as hair grew to protect the mammals, and it was only later in the evolution of birds that feathers became important in helping them to fly. (See EVOLUTION.)

The main protection which feathers give a bird is to keep it warm, and anyone who has handled a bird and put his hands through the feathers will probably have noticed how very warm its body is. This heat would quickly be lost into the surrounding air if it were not for the feathers.

Many birds are protected in another important way by their plumage, for its colour and pattern often fit in with the surroundings. This natural camouflage is found particularly in many ground birds, such as pheasants and partridges, and in birds which live in open places like the edge of a desert, where the only way of escaping from an enemy is to sit still and try to look like part of the scenery.

Baby birds have only soft, fluffy feathers known as down feathers, and some adult birds also have these as an under covering. However, if you look at the ordinary kind of feather covering a bird's body you will see that it has a fairly thick quill hollow at the base, tapering off higher up into a narrower shaft, on either side of which is a vane, or web. The vanes are made of many thread-like fibres called barbs and these barbs are "glued" together by rows of smaller hooked fibres known as barbules. Vanes, in fact, are made rather like a silk stocking. They are not completely airtight, but they divide the air up into tiny pockets so that it cannot pass easily from one side to the other. It is this which keeps the warm air in and the cold air out, and when birds fluff out their feathers in cold weather, this provides more air pockets for protection.

It is particularly important that the vanes of the main wing feathers should be closely woven, for they have to form a fairly solid surface when the bird flaps its wings downwards in the air. You have probably noticed that one vane of a feather is not so wide as the other. This allows the narrow vane of one feather to overlap the broad vane of the next, so that on the down stroke the feathers are pressed together—rather like a venetian blind when the slats are closed—but on the up-stroke the feathers open

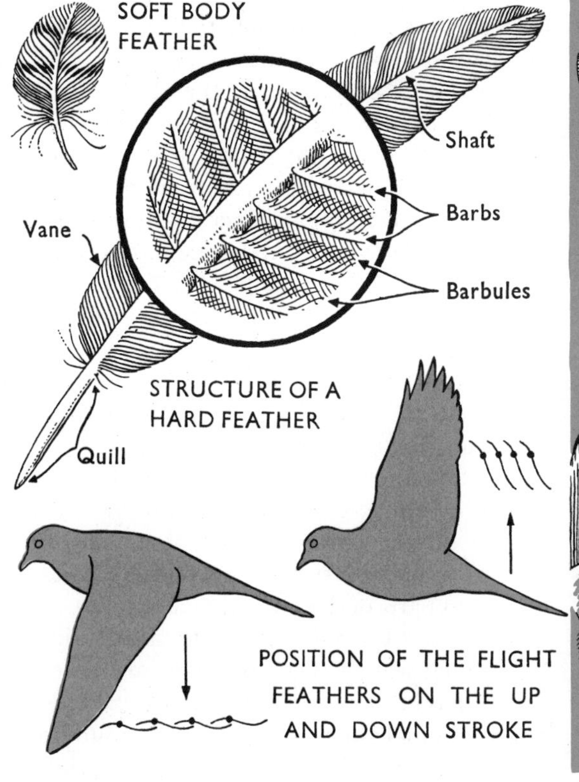


POSITION OF THE FLIGHT FEATHERS ON THE UP AND DOWN STROKE

a little so that the wing passes through the air more easily.

Many male birds use their feathers for display, or showing off to the females, as well as for protection and flight. The magnificent tails of the peacock and the extraordinary plumes of the birds of paradise are striking examples of display feathers, but these are lost when the birds moult at the end of the breeding season and regrown in time for the next season. Man has always been attracted by the beauty of feathers and has made use of those he could obtain. Feathers have been used to decorate kings and chieftains in many parts of the world, and they have also been important in the decoration of ladies' hats for centuries. In South Africa the ostrich is kept and bred for the sake of its plumage.

People have long used feathers in other ways, too. From the 6th century to the early part of the 19th century writers depended entirely on quill pens, particularly goose quills. There is still a great demand for feathers for stuffing bedding and cushions. An eiderdown quilt is made from the down feathers of the eider duck, and the feathers of swans and geese make very soft pillows. Specially selected feathers are used for such things as badminton shuttlecocks (see BADMINTON), artists' brushes and the imitation flies with which anglers tempt fish.

## FEDERAL BUREAU OF INVESTIGATION

**FEDERAL BUREAU OF INVESTIGATION** is the full name of the American institution that is usually known as the F.B.I. Its job is to identify and find persons who have committed crimes which break the federal laws (these are the laws that apply to everyone in the United States) and to gather facts which show that these people have broken the law. Each of the 50 states runs most of its own affairs, but there are certain laws, the federal laws, all persons in the 50 states must obey. The headquarters of the F.B.I. are in Washington and it has 57 branches in the United States and Puerto Rico. It was founded in 1908.

Only citizens of the United States can join the F.B.I. and they must first pass examinations and be investigated so that the F.B.I. will know they have always led honest lives and have no connection with anything or anyone working against the United States government. Many of the special agents—that is, the men who do the F.B.I.'s investigation work—have had a complete legal training and have been called to the Bar (see BAR, THE) or have been to an accounting school and had three years' experience in that

*Radio Times Hulton Picture Library*

Special agents of the F.B.I. escorting a car. They are alert for the slightest suspicious movement in the crowd.

kind of work. Some of the others are scientists or have other special talents.

Part of the F.B.I. is the Identification Division, to which fingerprints are sent by all city, county, state and federal law authorities. When a person is arrested and his fingerprints sent to the F.B.I., it can generally be discovered within a few minutes whether he has previously been found guilty of a crime. The F.B.I. laboratory is fitted with the most modern equipment, and the scientists there work every day examining documents, blood, hair, soil, or any other clues that may help to prove a criminal's guilt and bring him to justice.

In 1935 the F.B.I. National Academy was set up to train police officers from all over the country in the latest methods of making sure the law is obeyed and to run police schools in their own parts of the United States.

When the F.B.I. was first founded it dealt with much less than it does now. During the years it has been in existence, it has helped to put down criminal gangs, to trace spies and to bring kidnappers to justice.

**FELT** is a very closely matted cloth, usually made of wool or fur. The material, which may or may not be woven first, is wetted and then squeezed together so that the little scales on the fibres hitch together. This process is called "felting" and it sometimes happens to a pair of woollen socks that have been washed in water that is too hot, making them matted and uncomfortable to wear.

Proper felt has many uses. Very fine, smooth kinds are used for the lining of gloves, for hats and for the green covering on billiard tables; these are made in the Yorkshire woollen towns. Much thicker, coarser kinds may be put beneath carpets to prevent them from wearing out so quickly, or perhaps soaked in tar and used in the roof to keep the house warm and dry. Very thick kinds are used as shock absorbers under typewriters and even large machines.

**FENCING,** or the sport of sword-play, can be said to have grown from the old habit whereby men settled quarrels or avenged insults by duelling or fighting with swords. The modern sport is carried on with three distinct weapons—foil, épée and sabre. With all of them the fencer tries to hit his opponent without being hit, and the winner of a bout is the one who first scores five hits.

The fencers have to wear wire mesh masks, strong sailcloth jackets and padded gloves so that they do not get hurt. The *assault* (as a bout is called) takes place on a long strip six feet wide called the *piste*.

The foil is a thin, yard-long weapon tipped with a button and with a small bell-shaped guard. It is the weapon with which all fencing should be learned. In order to score, hits must be made with the point on the trunk of the body—those landing on the arms, legs or head do not count. The fencer moves forward or backward by short, quick steps. In making an attack he thrusts at his opponent with an extension of the arm, body and legs called the *lunge*. A thrust is warded off or *parried* by swiftly moving the foil into one of eight positions, which defend every part of the target, or by retreating out of distance. After an attack has been parried a hit can be scored on the attacker. This is called the *riposte*. Direct thrusts are easily parried and therefore the attacker tries to confuse his opponent by false attacks called feints, hoping to make him parry too soon and so leave himself open to the real attack.

The épée is a stiffer, heavier weapon than the foil with a larger bell-shaped guard. It has a triangular blade whose tip carries three short prongs to catch in the clothing to show when a hit is scored. The épée is the duelling sword. Hits may be scored anywhere on the opponent's body, head or limbs and a bout is made as like a real duel as possible.

The sabre is used both as a thrusting and as a cutting weapon. It has a flattened blade and a half-rounded guard. Hits may be scored with point or edge anywhere on the opponent above the waist.

Fencing makes a person swift and supple and helps mind and body to work together. Quick thinking and movements are more important than strength and therefore the sport can be enjoyed by women and children as well as men.

Left: Courtesy, Gwynnes Pumps Ltd. Above: The Times

Left: One of the diesel pumping stations which drain the Fens. Above: Making reed mattresses as foundations for sea walls.

**FENS.** For many hundreds of years a large low-lying area of eastern England was almost entirely marshy and unusable. This fen country, as it was called, stretched to the south and west of the shallow arm of the sea named the Wash, and covered large parts of what are now Lincolnshire, Huntingdonshire, Cambridgeshire and Norfolk.

All this area is in fact a shallow basin, through which the Rivers Ouse, Nene, Welland and Witham now flow to the Wash. It is not yet known for certain whether the area became marshy simply because the rivers became choked up and overflowed their banks, or because nobody knew how to continue the drainage of the land after the Romans had left Britain. It may have been for both reasons. (The Romans had built the big ditch called Carr Dyke, which links the Witham near Sleaford with the Nene near Peterborough, and they had also built a great bank along the coast to help to keep the sea out.)

Whatever the reasons, by Anglo-Saxon times the fens had been formed, with great beds of reeds growing out of the stagnant waters, and the remaining inhabitants had collected on the islands of higher ground. It was on the Isle of Ely that Hereward the Wake gathered his English supporters together for their last great stand against William the Conqueror. (See HEREWARD THE WAKE.) Monks settled on the islands to build their abbeys and they made important attempts to drain the fens—efforts which were well worth while for they made it possible to grow good crops on the low-lying land that was drained.

In the 15th century Bishop Morton made the dyke called Morton's Leam which cuts off a big corner of the River Nene and so makes the water flow more quickly towards the sea. However, it was not until the 17th century that a really big attempt was made to drain the fens and so reclaim the land for farming. The man who started this great scheme was the 4th Earl of Bedford, who was followed in turn by the 5th Earl, and the names Old and New Bedford Rivers remind people today that these two great drainage channels were dug on their orders. So much hard work had to be done that it took 20 years—interrupted it is true by the Civil War—to clear a great part of the southern fens, later known as the Bedford level. However, by 1652 more than 600 square miles of fens—an area about four-and-a-half times the size of the Isle of Wight—had been made fit for farming. The man in charge of the work was the great Dutch engineer Sir Cornelius Vermuyden, and many of those who toiled at the job were also Dutchmen, skilled in the art of draining land. (The article NETHERLANDS describes the Dutch system of dykes and canals.)

Some people objected because Vermuyden did not simply employ local men to do the work. Others came out of the fens to complain that their livelihood depended on fishing and snaring wild fowl and that if the fens were drained neither fish nor fowl would remain. Some went so far as to attack the workmen and break down the embankments that were being built, but in the end the job was done.

Crops like wheat, oats, turnips, beans and flax

were soon being sown on the Bedford level, part of which had probably never been ploughed before, but it was soon obvious that all was not well. The trouble was that the peaty land shrank as it dried and the surface level fell, so that the drainage channels were higher than the land they were supposed to drain. For a time it looked as if a great deal of work had been wasted, but fortunately a way was found to save the situation. By the early 18th century there were many windmills to be seen working pumps for pumping water to the level needed, so that it could be drained away. Even so, floods were frequent and damaging, and it was not until the early 19th century, when steam pumps were used instead of windmills, that the land was saved for farming once again. Where necessary the land was then "clayed", or marled, meaning that the clay soil below the peat (see PEAT) was dug up and spread on top. This helped to grow better crops and also different ones such as potatoes, vegetables, fruit and flowers, particularly bulbs.

Nowadays the pumps are worked by diesel engine (see DIESEL ENGINE). There are many small ones and also some of the largest in the world. At St. Germans, near Kings Lynn, there are four huge pumps, each of which can deal with 1,000 tons of water a minute. The visitor to the fen district does not always realize the wonderful drainage system which makes it possible to grow such fine crops today, but if he scrambles up one of the great embankments, high above the roadway and even higher above the fields, he can see the enormous amount of water that is being safely carried away, especially after winter rains. Some of the rivers and other channels have sluices, or special gateways which can be used to let the flood waters flow through to the sea and yet prevent the sea water flooding inland at high tide.

Drainage of the fens has made them smaller, chiefly by shrinking the peat. The Holme Post, an iron standard which in 1851 was buried upright with its head level with the ground in Holme Fen, Huntingdonshire, now stands 13 feet above the surface.

Because of the drainage of the fens, the great copper butterfly and other insects died out completely during the 19th century, and many water birds such as the bittern had to find other breeding places. Now there are special nature reserves at places like Wicken Fen, in Cambridgeshire, where typical water birds, insects and fen plants, such as alder, willow, buckthorn, reeds and sedges, are preserved. Other places are used for skating races in the winter.

**FERDINAND** (1452–1516) **AND ISABELLA** (1451–1504) started their reign as King and Queen of Aragon and Castile, but are famous for uniting the whole of Spain under one ruling family and for helping to make it a powerful country feared by many others.

For centuries before this Spain had been divided into several separate kingdoms, each with its own ruler. By the 1400s there were three main ones—Aragon, Castile and Granada. In 1469 Ferdinand of Aragon married Isabella of Castile, and as he later became King of Aragon and she Queen of Castile the two kingdoms were united under their joint rule. This was the first step.

King Ferdinand and Queen Isabella were strong rulers and succeeded in controlling their powerful and rebellious nobles who, for years, had refused to obey the kings and had pleased themselves. Ferdinand and Isabella defeated them in several battles and destroyed many of their castles. Determined to keep the nobles under control, they stopped giving them government posts and started, instead, to use paid civil servants to help in the government of the country.

Ferdinand set out to conquer the kingdom of Granada—the last remaining Moorish part of Spain—and it surrendered to him in 1492. (See MOORS.)

Ferdinand and Isabella tried to make all people become Christians and were harsh to those of other faiths. In 1492 the Jews were given the choice of either becoming Christians or of being expelled from Spain, and many chose the latter. Some years later the Moors (who were Mohammedans, see ISLAM) were forced to become Christians but had no real chance of leaving the country.

By this time there had been set up the Spanish Inquisition, which was a court of law that sentenced to torture and death people who refused to obey the teaching of the Roman Catholic Church. (See INQUISITION.) Naturally, the Moorish and Jewish converts were hardest hit, and after a time the expulsions and persecutions weakened Spain because the Moors and Jews were gifted and hard-working.

It was at this time that Spain began to build up a great empire in the New World. In 1492 Christopher Columbus discovered the continent of America; as he had sailed from Spain with the help of Ferdinand and Isabella he returned there and Spain became the first European country to hold territory in the New World. (See COLUMBUS, CHRISTOPHER.)

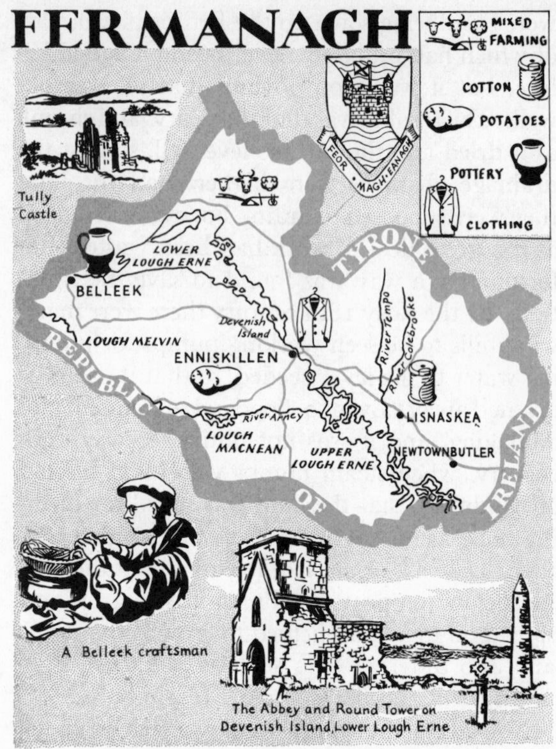

A Belleek craftsman

The Abbey and Round Tower on Devenish Island, Lower Lough Erne

**FERMANAGH** is an inland county of Northern Ireland. It is bounded on the northeast by County Tyrone and on the west, south and east by the frontier of the Republic of Ireland. The River Erne, which widens into two loughs, or lakes, called Upper and Lower Lough Erne, runs from the southeast to the northwest, dividing the county in half. The southern frontier passes through Lough Melvin and Lough Macnean Upper, and there are other lakes, but in many places it is hard to find water on the surface. This is because so much of the county is made of limestone, which drains water away into deep unexplored caverns and underground rivers. There is much high ground and hilly country on either side of the Erne, the highest point being Cuilcagh (2,188 feet) in the south.

The main occupation in Fermanagh is farming and particularly cattle rearing. The main crop is potatoes. However, nylon stockings and clothing are made at Enniskillen, the county town, which has a beautiful position between the two Loughs Erne, while pottery is made at Belleek and cotton thread at Lisnaskea.

In ancient times Fermanagh was the country of the Maguires, who took their name from Magh-uire, or "the country of the waters". The county has many monuments left by the ancient Irish, particularly on the beautiful wooded islands in the lakes. On Devenish Island, in Lower Lough Erne, there are many ruins from the 6th century, including an abbey with a round tower 81 feet high. British settlers began to come to Fermanagh in the reign of James I in the 17th century. After the Enniskillen men had defeated at Newtownbutler a stronger force sent against them by James II in 1689, a new regiment called the Royal Inniskilling Fusiliers was set up in the British Army.

**FERMENTATION.** If sweet fruit or vegetable juices are left standing they are partly turned into alcohol, and this is one kind of fermentation. What actually happens is that tiny specks of living matter, mostly yeast, which are contained in the juice, form a substance called an *enzyme* which turns the sugar in the juice into alcohol and the gas carbon dioxide. The kind of fermentation that takes place depends on the kind of enzyme present.

At one time it was thought that sugar fermented, meat decayed and wine went sour by themselves. Then in 1680 a Dutchman named Anthony Van Leeuwenhoek who was interested in studying things under his microscope, found that sugar mixtures that became alcoholic after standing contained yeast. Over a century later the famous French scientist Louis Pasteur discovered how yeast caused fermentation. (See PASTEUR, LOUIS.) Since then many enzymes have been examined by scientists.

Examples of fermentation are the changing of grape juice into wine and of wine into vinegar, the digestion of food in the stomach and the decaying of meat. All these are the work of enzymes produced by tiny living things which may be bacteria (see BACTERIA), yeasts or moulds. Fermentation is important to man in a number of ways. Alcoholic drinks such as wine, cider and beer are made by fermenting fruit and vegetable juices, and if they are bottled at the right stage the bubbles of carbon dioxide gas given off in fermentation are trapped in the drink and make it fizzy. It is the bubbles of the same gas caused by the yeast acting on flour that puff out bread and make it rise. It is fermentation that rots down leaves and dead vegetable matter into substances that help to make new soil for growing fresh plants and crops.

Fermentation takes place more readily under warm conditions than cold, though it will not work at all under very hot conditions as the enzymes are then destroyed. Hence food is prevented from going bad by keeping it in a cool place or in refrigerators which check the growth of the tiny living things that make the enzymes. Food can be preserved by heating it to kill off the bacteria and enzymes and then sealing it in tins or jars. (See PRESERVATIVES.)

**FERN.** Ferns can be distinguished from other plants by the fact that they have no proper flowers and also by their leaves, which are usually feathery in appearance. Each of these feathery leaves has a stalk from which a number of branches spring out, and each branch bears little green leaflets. The best example of this kind of fern in Great Britain is the bracken, which can be found spreading over large areas of moorland, heath and common and in oakwoods. (See BRACKEN.) A few ferns have leaves all in one piece and among these is the hart's tongue fern, with spear-shaped leaves.

Ferns are very ancient in origin. They first appeared on the earth during what is called the Devonian period, more than 300 million years ago, long before any animals lived on land. In

The plants in the picture are (from left to right) maidenhair fern, black spleenwort, adder's tongue fern, lady fern, royal fern, male fern, hart's tongue fern, spear-shaped spleenwort and horsetail with a spore-bearing growth.

the Carboniferous period, about 250 million years ago, dense fern forests covered the swampy regions of the earth, before flowering plants or trees grew. The coalfields of the world almost certainly come from these fern forests of prehistoric times. We know these particular ferns only by the fossils they have left in rocks, but their descendants can still be found living in many parts of the world, though some large groups are entirely lost.

Wherever there is sufficient moisture and protection from the direct rays of the sun, ferns can be found. They range in size from tiny moss-like plants to the tree ferns of the tropics, some of which reach a height of more than 80 feet. A few ferns can grow in the far north and on the tops of mountains, but on the whole they are most plentiful in warm and moist climates. They are most dense in damp tropical forests, where they form a green carpet over the forest floor and on the trunks and branches of the trees. In Great Britain they are plants of woodlands, heaths and waste places.

Ferns are vascular plants, which means that their stems, roots and leaves contain ducts along which water and food pass. The stem is often short or creeping so that the leaves appear to grow straight out of the ground. In the tree ferns there is a stout, erect stem with a cluster of leaves on the top, while in the bracken the stem creeps along under the ground.

One of the commonest sights to be seen during a walk in an oakwood or over a common in early spring is young bracken plants with their leaves tightly rolled up so that each plant looks like a shepherd's crook. As the plant grows, the leaves gradually unroll and spread out. Most fern leaves die down in winter and a new set grows up the following year.

In the autumn strips or groups of little powdery brown dots can be seen on the underside of a fully grown fern leaf. These are called sori, and when they are examined through a magnifying glass round structures called sporangia are seen. Each sporangium contains several hundreds of a certain kind of cell called a spore, and if the weather is dry it is sometimes possible to see the sporangia burst and scatter the spores into the air. The spores are extremely small and light and are carried long distances from the fern by the slightest breeze.

These spores are not the same as ordinary seeds, for they do not grow into young ferns. After settling on damp ground, each spore develops into a collection of cells called a prothallus, and this in its turn produces male and female organs, from which the young fern develops. At first it is like a small version of the large fern, with a small root growing down into the soil and a young leaf growing into the air. It may take several years before the fern is fully grown and able to produce spores. After that it will shed spores in great numbers every autumn.

A few ferns are able to reproduce themselves without the prothallus. For example, the walking fern forms buds at the end of the leaves where they touch the ground. Each bud grows roots and thus a new fern is produced, in much the same way as a gardener grows new plants from strawberry runners.

It is quite easy to grow spores on a piece of damp material, for example, peat. They should be dusted from the underside of a fern frond on to the surface of the peat and a glass bell jar placed over it. The jar and peat should then be put into a shady position, and after several weeks the tiny green prothalli appear. The peat must be kept moist all the time or else the spores cannot develop.

## Kinds of Fern

Besides the bracken, two other large ferns grow in the woods and moist shady places of Great Britain. These are called the male fern and the lady fern, and they both have a handsome crown of leaves. The largest fern in Great Britain is the royal fern, which is a fine plant with grey-green leaves and plumes of brown spore cases. It may grow to a height of ten feet in the west of England. One of the smallest British ferns is the adder's tongue, only two or three inches high, with one tongue-like leaf. A rare and pretty fern is the delicate maidenhair, and the spleenworts and the rusty back, which grow on stone walls, are also attractive. Ferns are often grown in gardens and greenhouses, the best way of growing them out of doors being on a rock garden shaded by trees so that the sun does not beat down on them. They can also be grown in pots inside houses, where it is necessary to keep them out of strong draughts, to water them once a day, making sure the water does not stagnate, and to supply them with rich soil containing plenty of leaf mould or peat.

No ferns provide human food, but some kinds, particularly bracken, are cut for bedding or fodder for animals, and the male fern provides an oil used in medicine. Ferns have also been a great help to botanists in the study of how the present-day land plants have developed from their ancestors.

### Relatives of Ferns

The large group of plants (called Pteridophyta) to which ferns belong also includes the horsetails, sometimes called the scouring rushes, and the club mosses, both of which are found in tropical and temperate, or mild, regions of the world. They are both unlike ferns in appearance but they are part of the same group because they reproduce in the same way as ferns. They were both much commoner in prehistoric times than they are now, and today all that remain are a few scattered species, although these grow in fairly large numbers.

The horsetail is a common plant of hedges, waste ground and marshes. It has whip-like branches and joints which are easily pulled apart. In the spring and summer small brown cone-like structures can often be found at the top of the stems and it is these that produce the spores.

The club mosses are common in mountain pastures and tropical forests. They have many tiny leaves arranged closely round the stem and look rather like moss, but in the upper leaves are tiny sporangia which produce countless spores.

**FERRET.** For over 2,000 years the ferret has been kept by man and trained to kill rats and mice and to help in catching rabbits. It is a member of the weasel family and has descended from one of the wild polecats; certainly it has the long, low shape of a polecat. Its body is about 14 inches long with a 5-inch tail, and it usually has cream-coloured fur and pink eyes.

The ferret can be a very vicious animal and should always be handled with care. When it is taken out to hunt rabbits it is muzzled—that is, a net is tied over its mouth—so that it cannot kill the rabbits and eat them in the burrow. It is then placed in a rabbit warren (a place where

Ferrets usually have cream-coloured fur and pink eyes.

many rabbits live) where it runs along the underground passages, chasing the rabbits and driving them to the surface. These can then either be caught in nets or shot. While being trained for this kind of work, ferrets should be fed twice a day on bread and milk with a little raw meat and kept in hutches that are clean and well aired. It is unfortunate if they escape, for their natural prey is all kinds of poultry; they love blood and suck it from the animals they kill.

The ancient Romans used ferrets not only to kill rabbits but also as mousers, and even today farmers use them for clearing rats out of barns.

**FERTILIZER.** A fertilizer is a chemical substance which contains plant foods. Plants take about 12 different foods from the soil, but they often need more nitrogen, phosphorus and potassium than it supplies, so these substances are given in fertilizers. (See Nitrogen; Phosphorus; and Potassium.) Some fertilizers are prepared from natural substances found in the earth's surface and mined for this purpose, some are made in fertilizer factories and some are the waste products, or by-products, of the manufacture of other articles. (See BY-PRODUCTS.)

Although plants need nitrogen they do not take it from the soil as pure nitrogen. They take what are known as nitrogen compounds; that is, nitrogen combined with other substances. Therefore all nitrogenous fertilizers are compounds such as calcium nitrate, nitrate of soda, ammonium nitrate and sulphate of ammonia. Nitrate of soda comes from great mines in Chile, South America. Sulphate of ammonia is the most widely used of these fertilizers, and it supplies nitrogen in a most interesting way. It is ammonia that is put into the soil, but the bacteria in the soil (see BACTERIA and SOIL) change this into nitrate—which is the substance that the plants need. This change takes only a few days, and sulphate of ammonia sown at the same time as the seed is changed into nitrate by the time the seed has become a young plant. Some of this fertilizer is a by-product at the gas works, but most of it is made in factories.

Different amounts of these nitrogenous fertilizers are applied to different crops—about one or two hundredweight an acre for cereal crops (wheat, oats, rye and barley), two to four or more hundredweight for potatoes and kale and rather less for mangolds and sugar beet. To get a good crop of grass two or more hundredweight might be used for each acre.

Phosphorus is also taken in as a compound. The most common phosphatic fertilizer is superphosphate, which is prepared from the calcium phosphate that is mined in North Africa, the United States and the U.S.S.R. In Great Britain it is used mainly for swedes, sugar beet and potatoes. In Australia even small amounts of it have greatly increased the yield of wheat, and both in that country and New Zealand the pastures have been much improved by it. Another phosphatic fertilizer comes from the manufacture of steel. This is called basic slag and is much used in Great Britain and north-west Europe for grassland and for encouraging clover to grow in it. In earlier days ground bones were the only form of phosphatic fertilizer and they are still used by some farmers.

Potassium, the third important material for fertilizer, is mined in Germany and Alsace. It is also obtained from the Dead Sea and from some dried-up lakes in the western United States. Two main types of this fertilizer are made—sulphate of potash and chloride or muriate of potash. The first is more usual for gardens, and the second, being cheaper, for farms. Potassic fertilizers are needed most in dairy farming and for growing fruit, potatoes and sugar beet. They help the leaves to make more sugar (see PLANT), and by making plants stronger, enable them to stand up well to disease and drought.

People often ask which is better for crops—fertilizers or farmyard manure. Both are needed. Manure helps to keep the soil in good condition and supplies plant foods which, however, have to be worked on by the bacteria in the soil before plants can use them. (See SOIL and FARMING.) Fertilizers supply plant food in a form that plants can use immediately.

Besides the three elements so far described several others, called "trace elements", are needed in small, even minute, quantities. If they are lacking they must be supplied. Thousands of acres of land that were once waste have thus been made productive.

**FESTIVALS, MUSICAL.** In the 17th century the custom grew up in England of having special gatherings of musicians giving performances at fixed times, and this gradually developed into the large festivals of today, many of which are heard over the wireless by millions of people. There are two kinds of musical festivals. One is a large gathering where special or little-known works of music are played; the other is a competition between musicians.

In the early days musical festivals were mostly for church organists and singers, and the oldest in England, the Festival of the Sons of the Clergy, was held every year in St. Paul's Cathedral. This still goes on, but it is now more of a church service than a musical festival. However, the second oldest festival, the Three Choirs Festival, which was founded in 1715, still goes on as it used to. The choirs of Gloucester, Worcester and Hereford cathedrals join once a year for a week's music in one of the three cathedrals, which are visited in turn.

Every year more and more festivals are held all over Europe. In Britain, festivals are held every year at Aldeburgh, Bath, Cheltenham, Edinburgh and many other places. For example, Dorking in Surrey has the Leith Hill Musical Festival founded by Ralph Vaughan Williams. In western Germany Bonn holds a Beethoven festival, as the composer was born there, while at Bayreuth, also in Germany, there is the celebrated Wagner Festival.

The oldest known musical competition is the famous Welsh Eisteddfod which goes back to the 7th century and perhaps earlier. Other competitions began with the musical tournaments, or contests, of the middle ages (examples of these appear in Wagner's operas *Tannhäuser* and *The Mastersingers*), and the pipers' contests which form part of the Highland Games. (There are separate articles EISTEDDFOD and HIGHLAND GAMES.)

Many competition festivals are held in Britain for young people and are organized with the help of the British Federation of Music Festivals. There are also contests between choirs and orchestras, while special festivals for brass bands are held in Manchester and London.

**FEUDALISM.** The Roman Empire in the west ended about 1,500 years ago, and modern times are thought of as beginning about 500 years ago. The period of about 1,000 years which lies between the two is called the middle ages. The first half of the middle ages was a time of much fighting and turmoil for the European peoples and it is sometimes called "the dark ages". Gradually, however, people began to find ways of protecting themselves by attaching themselves to a more powerful person and thus began to build up a way of life that has come to be known as feudalism.

Before feudalism can be explained it is first necessary to look back to Roman times. The Romans had a strong government that collected taxes and used the money to pay men (who would now be called civil servants) to carry out its orders, police to protect people from criminals, and sailors and soldiers to protect them against enemies from outside. Because they could thus live in safety the Roman people (this means the people of the whole of Italy; see ROMANS) had the chance to become highly civilized and to build up a great empire. However, as the Roman Empire became weaker in the 4th and 5th centuries A.D. life became far less secure and far less civilized. The government could not always collect its taxes and therefore could not pay its civil servants, police and armed forces as regularly as it had done earlier. Soon there were not many soldiers and officials who could be relied upon to do their duty properly. Criminals went unpunished and foreign enemies invaded the Empire with no fear of the Roman soldiers who had once been so strong.

Naturally, it was the people living near the frontiers of the Empire who suffered most from invasions, and their crops were often burned and their cattle stolen. Those living on the coast suffered from pirates. Inside the Empire the cities became short of food, for even if the farmers had food to sell, they hardly dared to take it into the cities because the roads were infested with robbers. Great cities decayed and finally all the western part of the Roman Empire was conquered by invading tribes. In many places there was no proper government and each man had to protect himself.

In order to do this it was natural to turn to the most powerful man of the district, and to ask him, for example, to get rid of the robbers. In the same way people expected such a man to lead them when they had to fight against invaders. This local strong man was nearly always the person who owned more land in the district than anyone else. Thus, as time went on, the big landowners began to carry out the work that in Roman times had been carried out by the government, and they began to be called "lord" by the people they protected.

Something very like this had also been happening in Germany, the country from which some of the invaders came. The various German tribes were fighting one another, and people were banding themselves round a lord for protection. Thus, when some of the German tribes invaded the Roman Empire they already had the sort of organization which the people whom they invaded had to adopt in order to

protect themselves. Invaders and invaded therefore had a similar way of life.

When a lord agreed to help the smaller landowners in his area he naturally expected them to help him in return. The lord promised to protect them and their land, while they promised to give him "service", and became known as his "vassals". They had to help him with "counsel", or advice, and to sit as members of his court when he was carrying out the duties of judge and chief of police. Above all, they had to be ready to fight in his army and to protect his castles. When a man became the vassal of a lord he handed over his land to the lord, who let him continue to use it in return for his promise of service. When a new lord took over after his father's death a most important ceremony took place. The vassal knelt before the new lord, gave him his lands and swore to become his man.

So far we have explained lords and vassals. However, by far the biggest class of people were the peasants, who were called "villeins" or "serfs", and all of whom served a master. Usually the land of a village was divided into strips (see Manor). The serfs had strips for their own use but had to work so many days a week on the strips of the lord of the manor, who had far more. The ancestors of many serfs had once been free peasants; that is, they had served no lord and owned their own small farms. Just as the owners of medium-sized estates had given their land to a lord in return for protection (and had become his vassals), the free peasants had given their tiny farms to a lord and had become his serfs.

This organization of people and land is what we mean by feudalism, or a feudal system. It soon became much more complicated than the system described above, for the smaller lords did not feel safe enough on their own and, in their turn, became the vassals of a greater lord, behaving to him just as their own vassals did to them. Thus, in time, western Europe came to be governed by the great feudal lords, each one at the head of his estate. Although some of their estates were very big they were far smaller than the countries of the old Roman Empire, and instead of one government there were hundreds.

It was not such an efficient system, but it was much better than no government at all, even though the feudal lords quite often used their armies against each other, not merely against invaders from outside.

The dukes of Normandy, in France, were extremely powerful lords and it was one of them, William, who conquered England in 1066 and is known as William the Conqueror. Between 950 and 1050 the various dukes were energetic men who had organized their territory in a very efficient manner. Feudalism elsewhere was often rather a muddled, inefficient system. In England there were lords, vassals and serfs before the Normans came, but the system was not nearly so well organized as that in Normandy.

## The Normans in England

William and his followers brought the Norman system to England, and from the time of the conquest everything was much more highly organized than it had been before. As soon as William had conquered England he began to share out its lands among his followers. This enabled him to have Norman soldiers all over England, ready to defeat the English if they rebelled. At the same time, the lands he handed to his followers were a reward for their support in his invasion.

In 1085 William ordered his officials to make a great survey of his new kingdom, and the facts they collected were written down in what became known as the Domesday Book. (See DOMESDAY BOOK.) As it still exists (in the Public Record Office in London) we can see what England was like at that time. Apart from the king there were no longer any landowners, although there were many men with large estates, called land*holders*. This is because, under the feudal system, men did not own land; they held it from their lord in return for the services they had to do for him. As William was the lord of all, every acre of land belonged to him. Even the greatest lords were his vassals and held their land from him. They were called tenants-in-chief because they held lands directly from the king himself (the French word *tenir* and the Latin word *tenere* mean "to hold"). Lesser men were called sub-tenants because they did not hold directly from the king, but from some lord more important than themselves. There were sometimes several men between the king and the tenant who actually used the land, but in the end everything belonged to the king.

By the time of the Norman conquest the services that a vassal rendered to his lord in return for lands and protection had become very varied. Domesday Book shows what they were. Military service was still the most common and lands held in this way were said to be held in "military tenure". For example, a great vassal, or tenant-in-chief, held his lands in return for supplying a certain number of knights, or mounted men, whenever the king summoned his army. Even the church held some of its lands in this way—the Archbishop of Canterbury and the Bishop of Winchester, for instance, each had to supply 60 knights when called upon to do so.

The tenants-in-chief, therefore, had to be sure of having knights ready for service, and they did this by handing over parts of their lands to lesser men who, in return, had to come with their horse and armour whenever called. In Domesday Book there are examples of many small estates held in this way, which was called "knight service".

Sometimes men held land in return for some duty less stern than that of fighting. This kind of land-holding was called "tenure in sergeanty". (The English word "sergeant" comes from the Latin word *servire* which means "to serve".) Often a man who had held land in this way was a servant of the king or of some great lord, his butler, for example. Some "sergeants" had to supply so many horses or so many arrows each year. One small estate in Kent was held by a man whose duty was to hold the king's head whenever he crossed the English Channel! (As he was also Duke of Normandy he often crossed to France.) A king might give an old servant a pension by letting him have a small estate in return for a rose to be presented each year on June 1.

Feudalism, as we have seen, grew up in times of violence and trouble. Over the centuries it succeeded in bringing safety, and as life became safer people began to buy and sell things much more, both inside their own countries and between different countries. This meant that they used money much more than they had done. As money became more common the kings found that they could have more efficient armies by paying men to serve in them full-time, rather than by relying on their vassals to bring men who were really only part-time soldiers. Therefore they began to accept money from their vassals, instead of requiring military or other services from them. In their turn, the lords did the same thing and accepted money instead of services from their vassals. Thus, people began to pay money, or rent, for their lands instead of paying for it by service. In some cases the serfs, also, began to pay rent for a plot of land. This meant that they no longer had to work on the lord's land and therefore became much more independent. As time went on the kings became stronger and the lords weaker, for the kings were no longer dependent on them for their armies. Instead of having each part of his kingdom governed by a great lord, a king began to govern his kingdom himself. Thus one government, that of the king, began to do what a great number of lords had done in the past. Because of these changes the system was beginning to be very different by 1300 from what it had been in the previous four centuries. The military side of it—whereby vassals held land in return for military service—gradually disappeared everywhere. In other ways there was a difference between what happened in England and what happened in other European countries.

In England by 1500 most serfs had become completely free from duties to the lord of the manor, and were able to live where they liked and to earn their living in whatever way they chose. This had begun to happen in several other European countries, but the change did not continue in those countries and was in fact stopped. By 1500 some of the serfs who had gained their freedom were becoming serfs once more. This happened particularly in Germany and to a lesser extent in France and the countries we now call the Netherlands and Belgium.

In France the peasants continued to owe certain duties to the big landowners for several hundred years longer, and it was not until the French Revolution that they became completely free (see FRENCH REVOLUTION). In Germany they mostly became free in the early part of the 19th century, but in central Europe the great landowners kept their privileges and the peasants remained serfs until the middle of the 19th century.

**FIBRES.** A fibre is a kind of thread which is obtained from animals, plants and from one kind of mineral, asbestos. Artificial raw materials for paper, felt and textiles are also called fibres. Because they are hundreds of times longer than they are thick, fibres can be twisted together to make strong, useful materials.

Sheep's wool is the most important animal fibre, and it varies according to the kind of sheep from which it comes. Goats, alpacas and llamas have hairs which are woven into special cloths, including mohair, cashmere and alpaca.

Fibres are also made from the hairs of the cow and the camel, and from rabbit fur, which is used for making felt. Silk is the only important fibre obtained from an insect. Until rayon was invented, silk was the only fibre that could be obtained in extremely long lengths, as it is spun like that by the silkworm. Rayon was for some time known as artificial silk.

There are more vegetable than animal fibres. The stringy parts of stalks and leaves are used in making linen, ramie (a fibre obtained from a Chinese nettle-like plant), jute, sisal and hemps. Cotton is the hair surrounding the seeds of the cotton plant. Wood, grass and other short fibres are used to make paper.

Man-made fibres are of two kinds. Some start with a complicated natural chemical, such as wood-pulp or milk. Rayon is one of these. Synthetic fibres are entirely man-made from simple chemicals. Among these fibres are glass, nylon and Terylene. (See NYLON.)

**FIELD NAMES.** Often the only way of discovering field names is to ask the local people, as these names very rarely appear on maps. Because of this and because the names are full of interest, collecting them is an enjoyable thing to do during a country holiday.

Some names describe the field itself, and some

give an idea of the people who cultivated or used it. A rich pasture might be known as Butter Field, while one that was useless might be called Bare Bones. Barber's Furlong was once cultivated by the barber and Constable's Field by the village policeman. Almost every county has several fields called Butts, where the villagers used to practise archery. (The butt is the archer's name for his target.)

In Nottinghamshire a field named Candle Rush Car was where they grew rushes for rush lights. Some names appear to be nonsense, but they are worth puzzling over. In Buckinghamshire is a field with the curious name Therthe-oxylaydede, which marked the spot where "the ox lay dead".

**FIELD OF CLOTH OF GOLD** is the name given to the place just south of Calais, in France, where Henry VIII of England and Francis I of France met in June 1520 to show that they intended to be friends.

At this time the English king still had territory in France, and the meeting took place between the English castle of Guînes and the French castle of Ardres. Vast preparations were made—Henry had a temporary palace erected that was richly furnished and decorated with gold ornaments, and for less important people 2,800 tents were put up.

The two kings held their great meeting on June 7 and the scene was so magnificent that the place became known as the Field of Cloth of Gold. For three weeks after this there were banquets, tournaments and wrestling, and the knights and ladies who attended were gorgeously dressed (see TOURNAMENT).

Although all Europe was impressed by the splendour of these occasions no difference was made to relations between England and France, for the two countries soon quarrelled again.

**FIFE.** This county of central Scotland is a peninsula, for it is surrounded on three sides by the sea—on the east by the North Sea itself and on the north and south by two of its arms, the Firth of Tay and the wider Firth of Forth. (See FORTH RIVER.) The inland border is formed by the counties of Perth, Kinross and Clackmannan. Much of the county is hilly and in the west the Lomond Hills reach a height of 1,713 feet above sea level. Not far from here the River Eden enters the county and winds eastwards through the valley called Stratheden. This widens out into the broad flat fertile area known as the Howe of Fife and then the river turns farther to the north past Cupar, the county town, to the sea. The area near the mouth of the Eden has been made by nature and is increasing in size every year by the wind blowing sand off the sea. This area is known as Tents Muir and has been planted with trees by the

The splendour of the Field of Cloth of Gold is shown in this 16th-century painting, now at Hampton Court Palace.

Forestry Commission. In the southwest there are some small lochs, or lakes, such as Loch Fitty on the stream called Fitty Burn, which joins the River Ore and then the Leven.

Lying off the coast at the mouth of the Firth of Forth is the Isle of May, with its ruined chapel of St. Adrian. This island is a danger to ships and therefore a lighthouse was erected in 1636. The first one was lit by coal in a brazier, or pan, 40 feet from the ground. There is a bird observatory on the Isle of May where records are made of the birds which use the island as a resting place during the spring and autumn as they travel. Records are also made of the many varieties of sea birds which nest on the island. Some of these migrating birds are caught and ringed. (See MIGRATION.)

As Fife is a peninsula it has always been difficult to reach some of the counties near by. In the past, the town of Dundee to the north could be reached only by ferry or else by going inland to the bridge at Perth and then back along the other side of the Firth of Tay, but now there is a railway bridge across the firth and lying just east of it, the Tay road bridge opened in 1966. Similarly, Edinburgh to the south could only be reached by going west to Stirling and returning on the other side of the Firth of Forth, but now the firth is crossed at Queensferry by one of the most famous railway bridges in the world. It took several thousand men seven years to build, and there is so much steel to paint that a squad of men has to be employed all the time, starting again at one end as soon as they have finished at the other. Half a mile upstream is the Forth road bridge, opened in 1964. It is the longest suspension bridge in Britain, with a span of 3,300 feet. The river here is more than 200 feet deep.

Fife can be divided into two distinct parts, for the farms are mostly in the east and the mines and factories in the west. The whole of the eastern part is in fact one of the richest farming areas of Scotland, but it was not always so. In the 16th century, James VI of Scotland (afterwards James I of England) described Fife as "a beggar's mantle with a fringe of gold", meaning that it was a very poor county except for the farms and fishing near the coast. Nowadays, however, there are many fields of oats, hay, wheat and barley. Swedes, turnips and sugar beet are also important crops, and Fife is well known for its seed potatoes. Cattle are kept for beef and milk, and sheep are grazed in many places.

Near the eastern tip of the county, called the East Neuk, are the fishing ports of St. Monance, Pittenweem, Anstruther and Crail. During the middle ages merchants from the continent of Europe brought silks and wines to these ports and took back potatoes and other produce from the county. The fishing fleet is smaller than in the past, but fishing boats are still built at St. Monance and Anstruther, while at Inverkeithing many famous old liners are broken up in a yard which people call the ships' graveyard.

The ancient burgh, or town, of St. Andrews is famous for its university and also as the "home of golf". Golf clubs are made there and sent to many parts of the world. (See ST. ANDREWS.) However, one must turn farther to the west for most of the factories and mines of Fife.

Coal has been worked in west Fife since the 13th century, but the coalfields here and over the border of Clackmannanshire still have more coal to the acre than anywhere else in Scotland. The richest fields of all are between Kirkcaldy and Leven on the shores of the Firth of Forth. New mines and shafts have been sunk and, in time, Fife is expected to produce one-third of all the coal mined in Scotland.

However, coal is not the only industry in Fife. In the past it was well known for the skill of its craftsmen, such as the village folk who wove cloth on handlooms and the smiths of Culross who were until 1725 the only people allowed to makes girdles. (A girdle is a round iron plate hung over a fire for toasting cakes.) Nowadays there are many modern industries in the villages and smaller towns as well as in the big ones. Cupar has a sugar-beet factory and Markinch a distillery where whisky is made, while the Howe of Fife is well known for malting (turning barley or other grain into malt for brewing beer). Two of the largest linoleum firms in Great Britain have their factories at Kirkcaldy and there are smaller firms making the same product in Newburgh and Falkland. Paper making is also an important industry. Linen is made in

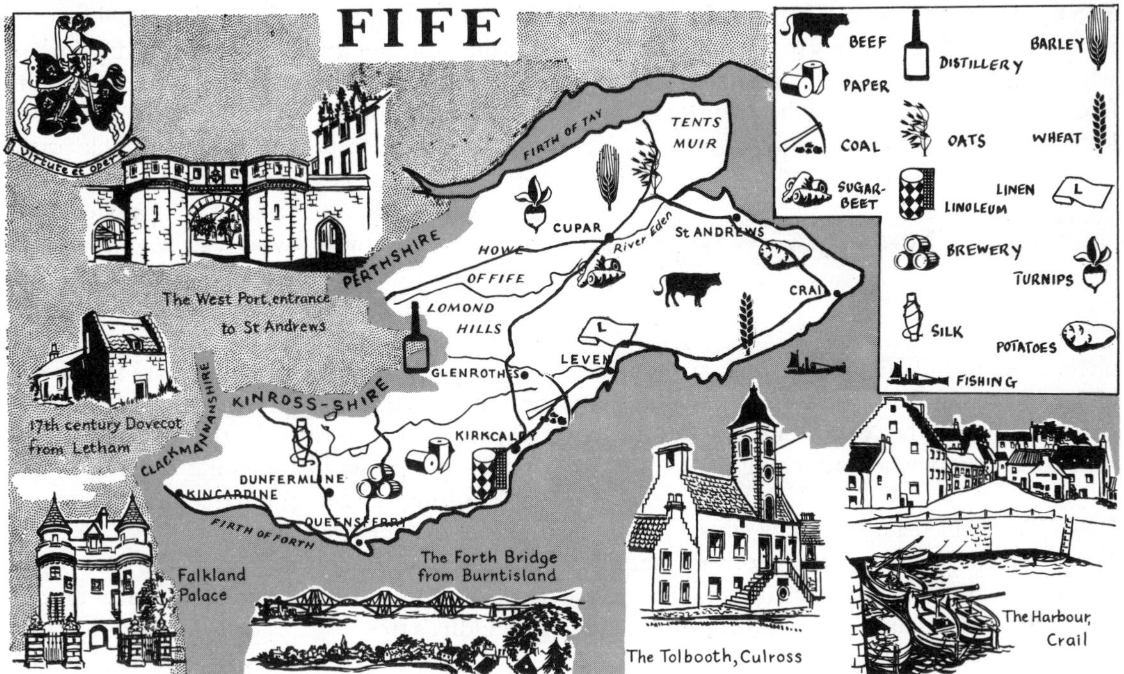


The West Port, entrance to St Andrews

17th century Dovecot from Letham

Falkland Palace

The Forth Bridge from Burntisland

The Tolbooth, Culross

The Harbour, Crail

Falkland, Cupar, Leven and other smaller towns as well as in the large towns of Kirkcaldy and Dunfermline. The silk for the wedding dress of Princess Elizabeth (later Queen Elizabeth II) was woven in Dunfermline.

To encourage the spread of industry in central Scotland the new town of Glenrothes was established in the middle of Fife in 1948. Glenrothes has four industrial estates with a wide range of manufactures, and is expected to benefit from the improved communications provided by the Forth and Tay road bridges.

The people of Fife are still proud to talk of the Kingdom of Fife, for in this part of Scotland the early Pictish people had a kingdom of their own known as Pictavia until as late as the 8th century. Fife has also been called the Royal County of Scotland because of the great interest taken in it through the ages by Scottish kings.

Dunfermline was the first capital city of Scotland and it was here that Malcolm Canmore (Malcolm III) lived with Margaret (queen and saint) in the 11th century. King Robert Bruce was buried in Dunfermline Abbey in 1329. King Charles I was born in the Royal Palace near by and the last king to reside in the palace was Charles II.

The county still has a great many ancient castles, palaces and country houses, many of which have played an important part in history, one of the best known being Falkland Palace. In a charter James II in 1459 gave it the title of palace. James V was kept prisoner at Falkland by the Earl of Angus until 1528 when, at the age of 17, he escaped to Stirling in disguise. Later in the 16th century Queen Mary stayed on many occasions at the palace, practised archery in the grounds and hunted in Falkland forest with her court.

In the 18th century Fife was notable for having about 360 beautifully designed "doo-cots" (dove-cots), but fewer than 100 of them can still be seen. They were built for the pigeons of the lairds, or landowners.

Well-known people who were born in Fife include Adam Smith the economist and Andrew Carnegie the philanthropist, on whom there are separate articles.

Daniel Defoe took the idea for his book *Robinson Crusoe* from the true story of Alexander Selkirk, whose birthplace was at Lower Largo, on the shores of the Firth of Forth. On the wall of the cottage where Selkirk was born stands a statue of Robinson Crusoe.

**FIFE.** The fife is a small, high-pitched musical instrument held crosswise like the ordinary flute when being played. It was brought to England from Switzerland in the 16th century and was known then as the Swiss pipe. There are six finger holes in the fife today, which are covered by keys. The fife has always been a military instrument, and today drum and fife bands are used by the army when marching.

A modern fife.

**FIG.** This fruit belongs to the genus, or group, *Ficus*, which is part of the mulberry family. When growing on the tree, the fig is rather pear-shaped, and the many varieties turn several different colours when ripe, being green, yellow, purple or black.

The fig has been grown for food in warm countries from very early days and was one of the fruits most often eaten by the ancient Greeks and Romans. Today it is still an important crop in Turkey, Greece, Italy, Algeria, Spain and Portugal, and it is also grown in America, South Africa and parts of Asia. In Great Britain figs are sometimes grown in sheltered positions, and the fruit was probably first brought into the country in about the 12th century, although it seems to have died out for a time during the middle ages.

The fig tree is not very tall, being the size of a large bush or a small tree. It prefers a dry, semi-tropical climate with hot summers and short cold winters, but it will grow on many different kinds of soil.

The dried figs bought from the grocer in boxes are full of seeds, which were originally tiny flowers. In order that the fruit can develop, these flowers must be pollinated so that they will later become seeds. (Pollination is explained in the article FRUIT.) The fig flowers, being inside the fruit, cannot of course be pollinated by wind or bees, as other flowers are. The only approach to them is through a hole at the top of the fruit, and through this crawls a tiny wasp called *Blastophaga,* carrying pollen from the wild, uneatable Capri fig. Figs are eaten fresh, dried or tinned. Syrup, jam, paste, alcohol, a coffee substitute and also a dye can be made from their juice.

Among relations of the fig tree are the peepul or bo tree, the banyan and the india-rubber tree, which is described in the article RUBBER. The bo tree grows in India and Ceylon. It was while sitting under a bo tree that Gautama Buddha reached Enlightenment (see BUDDHA AND BUDDHISM), and a bo tree still growing in Ceylon is said to have sprouted from a branch of Buddha's tree.

By the fig leaves worn by Adam and Eve after the Fall, the Bible possibly means the leaves of the great banyan tree. John Milton, in *Paradise Lost,* makes this plain by saying "The fig tree, not that kind for fruit renowned" in the passage describing how Adam and Eve chose leaves to cover themselves.

**FIGHTING FISH.** Many fishes, like other animals, fight each other at some time, particularly during the breeding season, but a small fish found in Siam (Thailand) is so remarkable for its fighting habits that public contests have become a national sport in that country.

If two males are put in the same tank they will fight savagely until one is killed. The Siamese have bred these fish for centuries and have produced champions which fight for as long as ten hours, although a fish taken straight from the wild state seldom lasts an hour. These contests are arranged in much the same way as cock-fighting, and the people who arrange them bet on them.

However, Siamese fighting fishes are favourite fishes for aquariums in Europe and America, and their owners breed them for their fine appearance and not for their fighting qualities. Aquarium-bred males have much larger fins and more brilliant colours than the wild fish and are much less fierce. Nevertheless two males should not be put together and it is usual to separate them by putting a glass partition in the tank. If this is done the fish can see each other and will want to fight. They will thus show off their beautiful colours and spread their fins.

The Siamese fighting fish and the fishes related to it have a special breathing organ above the gills. With this the fish breathes the air that it takes in mouthfuls at the surface. If not able to breathe in this way, it sickens or even dies, as its gills are less well made for taking oxygen from the water than are those of other fishes.

Two male fighting fish, a female and the nest of bubbles.

It is the male Siamese fighting fish who looks after the eggs and young fishes, and he does this by blowing bubbles at the surface of the water so that they stick together to form a kind of raft. He then courts the female, who lays her eggs among the bubbles, and if any fall out the male catches them in his mouth and blows them in again. He guards the nest of bubbles carefully, keeping it in repair and driving away any other fish that comes near—even his wife. When the eggs hatch out he takes care of the babies until they are old enough to look after themselves.

**FIGURES OF SPEECH.** A language can be used for a number of different purposes. One of them is to describe things that happen and to put forward ideas in such a striking way that other people will pay attention to them. A person may also use language to call attention to his own feelings about something or to rouse feelings in other people. When he feels deeply about something he will try to choose words that are more vivid and colourful and emphatic than usual, and in doing so he will probably use some *figures of speech.*

A figure of speech is a special way of speaking (or writing) which says a thing more vividly than the ordinary words do. In William Shakespeare's play *Henry IV,* Lady Hotspur says to her husband:

Out, you mad-headed ape!
A weasel hath not such a deal of spleen, [bad temper]
As you are toss'd with.

This leaves us in no doubt as to how she feels about him at that moment. When she calls her husband an ape, Lady Hotspur is using a figure of speech to express her feelings—she does not mean it to be understood that he really *is* an ape.

There are many different figures of speech, which students of language worked out and gave names to long ago. Here are some of them.

One of the best ways to describe things vividly is to use a comparison of some kind, a simple example being the common phrase "as busy as a bee". When the Pied Piper stepped out into the street to call the rats, the poet says:

And green and blue his sharp eyes twinkled,
*Like a candle flame where salt is sprinkled,*
And ere three shrill notes the pipe uttered
You heard *as if an army muttered.*

This kind of comparison is called a *simile* and it is one of the commonest figures of speech.

Often the "like" or "as" or "as if" is left out and the two things being compared are spoken of as if they were actually the same thing. For example, "the knight was a *lion* in battle", "Friendship is a *sheltering tree*", "life's but *a walking shadow*", or "up *leaped* of a sudden the sun" (the sun did not really leap, but it looked *as if* it did). This figure of speech is called a *metaphor.* (Lady Hotspur was using a metaphor.) A special kind of metaphor is when a thing is spoken of as if it were a living person.

Thus a ship is referred to as "she", a country may be called "Britannia" or the moon .addressed as "queen and huntress".

A simple way of expressing feelings in words is to use exclamations. The effect is often made stronger by repeating words as well. In the Bible, King David shows his grief at the death of his son in these words: "O my son Absalom, my son, my son Absalom! would God I had died for thee, O Absalom, my son, my son!"

Another way of emphasizing is to exaggerate, as when people say "a thousand apologies". Sometimes the very opposite of exaggeration—understatement, or saying less than you mean—can also be used for emphasis, as when someone says "Not half!" or "Rather!" meaning "very much".

In one group of figures of speech a thing is called not by its usual name but by the name of some part of it or of something closely connected with it. Thus sailors are called "hands" and "the crown" is used for the monarchy.

Another group of figures of speech deals with contrasts and opposites. For instance, in the figure called *sarcasm,* people say the opposite of what they have in mind and show their real meaning by their tone of voice or the arrangement of words: a person may say "That was a clever thing to do", meaning quite the opposite.

Sometimes words are used playfully. A common form of playing with words is the *pun,* when a word is used to have a double meaning or to sound the same as another word with a different meaning. The answer to the riddle "When is a door not a door?" is a pun: "When it's *ajar.*"

A person sometimes tries to use language vividly but chooses the wrong word. In Richard Brinsley Sheridan's play *The Rivals* a character called Mrs. Malaprop is always making this kind of mistake. For example, "He is the very *pineapple* (instead of pinnacle) of politeness", or "Comparisons are *odorous*" (instead of odious). This is known as a *malapropism.*

**FIJI.** The Fiji archipelago, or group of islands, forms an important British colony in the Pacific Ocean, lying to the east of Australia and north of New Zealand. These islands have the lovely coral reefs (see CORAL) and the coconut palms which people expect to find in the Pacific, but it is their wonderful mountain scenery which first attracts attention. The eastern slopes of the mountains are covered to their summits with thick tropical vegetation, and below them there are grassy hills with many flowers and ferns. Fields of sugar cane grow in the rich soil of the coastal plains, and the islands are ringed with palm-fringed beaches and reefs on which the waves continually thunder.

The capital and chief port, Suva, is on the largest island which is called Viti Levu. Fiji's other main island is Vanua Levu, and between them they make up more than nine-tenths of the colony's area. These two islands are about 40 miles apart, but some of the others lie much farther away. The most distant is Rotuma, 400 miles northward. Altogether there are about 300 islands, of which about 100 are inhabited.

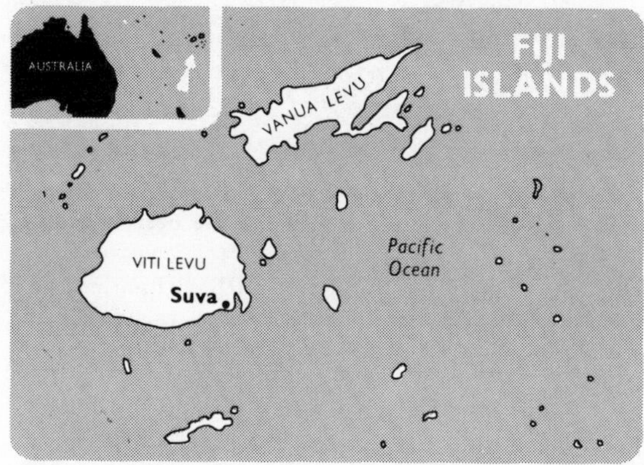


The climate is warm and pleasant. Most of the rain falls in the hot season between December and March, when hurricanes are liable to blow. (See HURRICANE.) Fiji has no large wild animals and few birds of interest. The island of Taveuni off the coast of Vanua Levu is a national park.

Nine people out of every ten are either Fijians or Indians, the rest being Europeans or people with European blood, Chinese and others. Fijians were the original inhabitants, but in 1879 Indians were brought to the islands to work on the sugar plantations and most of them stayed. As most Fijians have fewer children than the Indians, the Indians outnumber them.

*Courtesy, Public Relations Office, Suva*

Above: The Fijians are a fine looking people. Above, right: A fish-drive on the outer reef of an island. The fish are forced into a large pocket net. Right: A village on the outlying island of Yaqeta. The houses are built with a timber framework and thatched walls and roof. Kitchens are built separately near by.

The people make their living chiefly by growing foodstuffs for themselves, together with sugar, coconuts and bananas to send to other countries. Sugar is by far the most important export. Gold is mined in Viti Levu. Factories process copra and produce cigarettes, but industry is hampered by a lack of cheap power.

Until they had accepted Christianity, the Fijians were cannibals, usually eating the flesh of Fijians captured from other tribes. Certain white men—seamen who had run away from their ships, escaped convicts and the like—used to offer their services to the chiefs who offered the biggest reward. There was continued warfare as one chief after another tried to gain control over the entire people, and their quarrelling made peaceful living impossible. It was really not until 1874, when the British government agreed to look after Fiji at the request of the Fijian chiefs themselves, that the people were able to settle down to the peaceful improvement of their lives.

The Fijians are a fine looking people and the men look splendid with their mass of frizzy hair and their peculiar skirts called "sulus". They are skilled farmers and fishermen and are still very clever at building thatched wooden houses and making brilliantly decorated cloth from the bark of trees. Their pleasures are simple ones, such as dancing, story-telling and feasting.

### FACTS ABOUT FIJI

**AREA:** 7,055 square miles.
**POPULATION** (estimated in 1967): 490,000.
**KIND OF COUNTRY:** British colony.
**CAPITAL:** Suva, on Viti Levu.
**CHIEF EXPORTS:** Sugar, gold and copra.
**EDUCATION:** School attendance is not compulsory.

**FILM-MAKING.** A great book is the work of one writer, a great painting is the work of one artist, but the making of a film is the work of a whole team of people—writers, actors, painters, musicians, cameramen and many more. The head of the film-making team, the producer, begins his work long before the first scene of the film is photographed and gathers together all the people who are going to work with him.

The first essential in making a film is to have a subject. It may be an idea for a story or it may be the theme, or general subject, for a documentary film, which is one showing real life and ordinary people in their own setting. Whatever it is the film cannot exist without it. In the case of a story film, the subject may be one that has been fully worked out in a book or a play already, or it may have been published in a magazine as a short story. When a film producer notices it and thinks it will make a good film he buys, from the author or publisher, the rights to make a film version of it. On the other hand, the subject for a film may be a story written specially for the screen, and the producer decides on this after it has been shown to him in the form of a synopsis, or summary of the story.

## The Producer and his First Helpers

The producer is like the captain of a ship. His are the final orders which must be obeyed. He chooses the story or theme. He finds the money to make the film and gives a promise to the people who provide the money that the film will not cost more than the amount for which he plans. He makes sure in advance that the finished film will be shown in cinemas or to the audience for which it is intended. He chooses the technicians — the skilled workers like cameramen and electricians—who will do the work for him and he supervises the film from beginning to end. A producer usually works with a particular film studio and so he can make use of all its equipment and its trained staff.

The first member of the team the producer chooses to join him is the screen writer. His job is to rewrite the story (which is still in its first form as a novel or play or synopsis) to make it completely suitable for a film. Some changes may be made, because a story is told in a film in a very different way from the way a novelist or playwright tells it. This rewritten version made by the screen writer is known as a "treatment".

After the first treatment has been finished a full treatment, or "master-scene script", is written, probably by the same writer. Perhaps the producer will bring in another writer to work with him : a specialist in writing dialogue, for instance, or if the film is a comedy someone who can invent jokes and funny situations.

## The Director and the Shooting-Script

At this early stage of the film the director is chosen. He is the senior craftsman of the producer's team and ranks next to him in authority. The finished film will owe more to him—to his artistic skill and judgment—than to anyone else. The producer chooses the director according to what kind of film he directs best. Directors who can make films that make people laugh may not be able to make films that thrill them. Sometimes the director makes suggestions for the full treatment, which may be written several times before everyone is satisfied. Screen writers are used to this and learn to accept suggestions as part of the team-work of film-making.

Next the technical "shooting-script" is written. This is the script from which everyone engaged on the film will work. It not only contains every word of what the actors will say but also all the details of every scene, including instructions to the cameramen such as *long shot* (a scene photographed from a distance), *close-up, tracking* (moving the camera in closer or pulling it back) and *panning,* which means following the action round with the camera to give the effect of a wide unbroken view of the scene. The work of preparing the shooting-script is done by a writer who knows the whole craft of film-making inside out and how to get the best effect from each scene on the screen. This is very skilled work. Sometimes the director writes the shooting-script himself or he may like to work together with the writer while it is being made.

## Cameraman and Lighting

The next member of the team to be chosen is the cameraman. He is brought into the production while the script is being written and comes to script conferences with the producer, director and writers. The chief cameraman on big pictures is called the lighting director. He is responsible for arranging the electric lamps in the studio to give each scene exactly the atmosphere and effect that the director wants. During the making of the film he himself scarcely touches the camera, which is worked by his chief assistant, the camera operator.

The film camera needs a great deal of light to take good pictures; much more for colour pictures than for black-and-white. The most powerful light of all is the sun's light, but it is difficult to make complicated films out of doors. The weather is not certain; time may be wasted waiting for the sun to come out; there are too many sounds outside which the sound-camera (the machine that "takes" the sounds just as the ordinary camera takes the pictures) may pick up, for it is so sensitive that it records even the slightest little noise; and it is difficult to move the camera about without all the equipment, such as camera cranes, which is used in the studio. Most of a "story" film, therefore, is made indoors in the big halls or rooms of a studio, called stages. These are soundproofed so that no sound from outside can be heard inside them and they are equipped with wiring that can carry a big supply of electricity. Very strong artificial light is thrown on to the scenes being photographed by means of high-powered lamps.

The lighting director arranges these lights in different ways for different scenes. Every time there is a different set-up (that is to say, when the camera position is changed, even slightly, to get a new shot) the lights have to be changed and the scene relit. Lighting can set or alter the whole mood of a scene, giving it terrifying shadows or the bright clear light of day or a soft glow suitable for a love scene. All this the chief cameraman—the lighting director—plans in his mind's eye as he goes through the script with the director.

## The Work of the Art Director

The next specialist to be called in to the film-making team is the art director. His job is to design the settings for the scenes. These are called the sets. The characters in the film story, if they are to seem real and natural, must appear in settings that are completely suitable to them. For instance, some may be historical characters and then every detail of their background, designed by the art director, must be exactly as it would have been in the times when the characters lived. The art director may have a historical expert to help him in this, but he himself must know the natural backgrounds of all kinds of people, whether in the past or in the present. If a whole street with houses and shops is needed he has to use his knowledge of models and painted backgrounds. Although all the sets built in the studio are made of light wood, canvas and plaster, the art director must see that they look quite real on the screen. He must be able to draw and paint well enough to make sketches of the sets, and these have to be coloured if the film is to be in colour.

He must know a great deal about film-making too, for the sets he designs must be practical and easy for the camera to move about in. The camera is mounted on a truck with wheels, called a velocilator or dollie, and it is always moving about the set and hardly ever used from a fixed position. It follows the characters as they walk up and down, or comes in close to one of them at an exciting moment, or draws back to show the whole room and everyone in it. If a shot has to be taken from above the camera is fixed on to a crane which needs plenty of space. Tracks rather like railway lines are laid down on the floor of the stage when the camera has to move slowly and steadily. On these lines the wheels of the dollie can run so smoothly that the camera, which is upset by the slightest jerkiness, can take a perfect picture. A good art director must be able to make his sets fit in with all these requirements.

For example, suppose a scene is to take place in the living room of a small modern house. If the art director designed a set and had it built with all four walls and ceiling fixed exactly like an actual room, the cameras could not move about in it and there would be no room for the big lamps or for the microphone "arm" of the sound-camera. Therefore, the art director finds out beforehand what parts of the room are the most important in the scene to be photographed and designs them to be built by his assistants on the studio floor. The other less important walls of the room are designed so that they can be pushed into place easily and quickly and then "floated" away when necessary.

The art director has his own department and assistants. He works closely too with the dress designer and the property department, who buy the objects to be used on the sets.

## Cast and Sound

Before the script is finished the producer will have been thinking about casting the film; that is, choosing which actors and actresses he would like to use, particularly for the main parts. The small parts and the crowd parts can be decided upon later, but the success of a film often depends on which stars are in it and how popular they are and so the producer is anxious to obtain the ones he wants as soon as possible. Film stars are usually under contract to a particular studio (that is, they have signed an agreement, called a contract, to appear in films made by the studio) and stories often have to be chosen to suit them. However, film companies can usually "borrow" stars from each other so that producers can normally have the actors they know will play the parts best in the films they are planning. The director and the producer choose the cast together.

When the script is written and the producer, director, lighting director, art director and the cast of actors and actresses are all ready to start work, other important people are still needed. The film is a sound film, so another senior helper to join the team is the sound supervisor. He and his staff are responsible for everything you hear on the screen, they must record all the dialogue, sound effects and music. On the set the sound is "photographed" by the sound camera, worked by the same electric motor as the picture camera. This is in order that sound and picture will be synchronized; that is, will fit together exactly. It would never do to see someone's mouth moving and hear the words they are speaking a few seconds afterwards. Music and sound effects, such as thunder or the sound of rustling leaves, are recorded separately from the dialogue (the words spoken) and the different recordings, called sound tracks, are kept separate until a later stage of the film work.

## The Team is Completed

The director has several assistants to help him. The first assistant director is responsible for organizing the photographing, or "shooting", of scenes both inside the studio and out of doors. He makes detailed lists of all the scenes which take place on a certain set—in the living room of a house, for instance—so that they can be photographed together. All the scenes which take place in the living room are "shot" at the same time, whether they come at the beginning or the end of the film. This is because building and pulling down sets takes time, and with so many people present and on the job film-making is very expensive and studio time costs a great deal of money. The assistant director's work of arranging the scenes in the order in which they will be shot is called breaking down the script. Details concerning the actors needed for each scene and the properties required for them (everything in a scene except the actor's clothes is called a property or "prop") are also noted in the "break-down", and everyone working on the film is given a copy of it. From the break-down a timetable of the work to be done, called a shooting schedule, is worked out.

The fact that a film is not shot straight through from beginning to end but often in completely the wrong order means that someone has to keep a careful note to make sure that all the details of various scenes fit together smoothly. (The proper name for this is *continuity*.) Details of the actors' clothes and hairstyles, for instance, must be precisely the same in two scenes which will be joined together and seen next to each other, even though one may have been shot weeks before the other. The person who sees that there are no mistakes is the "continuity girl" or floor secretary. She works with the assistant director when he is making the break-down and while the film is being shot she sits at the edge of the set with her typewriter and records a full description of every shot: where the scene is set, what properties there are in it, what the actors do and say, what they wear, how their hair is arranged, the type of make-up used, and so on. Each scene is numbered and so everything can be matched up exactly when the next scene is being shot in some weeks' time.

Lastly, the man who actually sees that the pieces of film are joined together with all the scenes in the right order is the editor. His job is not as simple as it sounds, however, and his work in cutting and joining the pieces of film is extremely important to the finished picture.

For instance, if a dramatic scene does not seem fast and exciting enough as it has been filmed, the editor may be able to improve it by cutting out some action that is not really important. This action may take up a few feet of actual film and when it has been cut out the editor joins the film up again. He must be very skilful and experienced to do this without making the picture look jerky on the screen. He cuts and joins up the filmed dialogue and sound to match.

## 8.30 On the Set

The evening before a film "goes on the floor" for the first pictures to be taken, the assistant director sends out a sheet of instructions for the next day's work, after discussing it with the director. This call-sheet, to give it its proper name, states clearly what time shooting will begin in the morning, what scenes are to be shot and which actors are required for them. Carpenters, plasterers and painters will already have built the sets for the scenes according to the instructions of the art director. The electricians will have put the lamps into the positions wanted by the lighting director and arranged all the electric cables and other apparatus ready for the morning.

The call is for "8.30 on the set", which means that everyone, perhaps as many as 100 people, is ready for the first scene to be shot at exactly 8.30 a.m. next day. Before they are ready for the camera to turn, however, there will be two or more hours' preparation for many of the technical staff. The camera assistants, who have cleaned and oiled all the cameras they need the night before, now check them over carefully. There must be nothing to spoil the perfect working of the most important piece of equipment in the whole process—the camera. They will make sure that there is enough film ready; the reels of celluloid (usually 1,000 feet on each reel) fit into the camera and unwind as the camera shoots. The sound assistants must also have their delicate instruments and tools ready to run absolutely smoothly. The electricians, called "sparks" by the studio staff, arrive an hour before shooting is timed to begin. They too have to check all their equipment.

Actors and actresses are no exception to the rule of having to arrive early. They may have to get to the studio several hours beforehand to be made up and dressed, and this means that make-up experts, hairdressers, wardrobe assistants and dressers must be there too. The sets must be "dressed" by the property men. They arrange the flowers, place the ornaments and cushions in position, straighten the pictures, sweep the carpet and generally make the set look like an actual room. At last with everything ready, the whole team of people whose skill and hard work will produce the finished film are ready to begin work on the first scene at 8.30 a.m. sharp.

## The First Take

From this moment the work goes according to a fixed plan. The actors rehearse their parts with the director. When he is satisfied, the electricians light the lamps and the camera operator watches the scene through the eye of the camera to make sure that there are no ugly shadows, that the action is taking place within the range of the camera and that the actors are not moving too quickly for a smooth picture to be taken. When the camera department is satisfied, there is another rehearsal for the sound recordist. He fixes the microphone so that it picks up the speech of the actors clearly. Other "mikes" may be needed if sound has to be recorded at several points on the set.

When everyone is satisfied, the great moment for a "take" has arrived. The red light goes on inside and outside the stage to warn the studio people that no one must come in or out of the sound-proof hall or the shot will be spoiled.

"Stand by for a take!" announces the assistant director. The property man sweeps the floor; a lick of paint may be added by a painter if it has been knocked off during rehearsal; the make-up man dusts the star's face with powder; the hairdresser makes sure there is not a hair out of place. Sound and picture cameras start up and the sound recordist announces, "Camera running". The camera operator replies, "Speed up". The assistant director says, "Mark it", and a board with a number on it is held for a moment in front of the cameras, to mark the scene number so that the editor will know where the shot is to go in the finished film.

The director gives the word for action and the actors start playing the scene exactly as rehearsed. Everyone except the actors is quite still and silent, hardly daring to breathe because the sound camera will pick up and magnify the slightest sound and this would spoil the shot. As it is, the scene may have to be taken several times before everyone is satisfied, the director satisfied with the action, the lighting director and the camera operator with the picture and the sound recordist with the sound. Each take is numbered—take 1, 2 or 3—and the director decides which are the best and worth printing and which "n.g.", no good.

## After the Take

At the end of the day the negative film of all that has been photographed, both pictures and sound, goes off to the film laboratory to be developed and printed into positives. (The article PHOTOGRAPHY gives information about the process of developing and printing photographs.) Next day these printed scenes and dialogue, called "rushes", are projected. That is to say, they are shown on the screen in the private theatre of the studio for the producer and director and other chief members of the production team to see and hear and criticize. These "rushed" positive prints, with the negative, are sent to the editor in his cutting rooms.

Here the negative reels of picture and sound are cut into their separate scenes by the negative cutters. They are then rolled up, marked with their special numbers on paper labels held in place by rubber bands and put away in tins. The editor cuts and joins the positive film with the scenes in the right order. Editors and their assistants work with machines called movieolas, which can project the picture and the sound track at the same time. When the editor decides where he wants to cut the film—at the beginning or end or even in the middle of a scene—he marks the place on the celluloid strip with a yellow pencil. He cuts the strip with a pair of scissors and then places it next to another scene so as to obtain the best effect of suspense or movement.

To join two pieces of positive film together, the cut ends of the celluloid are finely scraped and brushed over with a substance called acetate which makes them soft. The soft end of one piece is laid over the soft end of the other, the two strips are clamped together for a few seconds and the two ends become joined together making one continuous strip. Exactly the same method is used for cutting and joining the sound track.

After the editor has finished his work on the film of the action, the work of fitting the complete sound track to the action still remains to be done. When the music for the picture has been composed and recorded, all the sound tracks have to be "mixed together" by the sound recordist. In his studio he plays recordings of all the tracks at the same time and re-records them together on one new track which carries all the sound for the film—music, words and sound effects.

Finally, the complete negatives of pictures and sound are sent to the laboratory and printed together on one piece of film, called a married print. Very many more prints can then be made to be sent out to the cinemas. Now, at last, the film is ready for the public to see.

## Cartoon Films

Instead of being photographs of live actors in real settings, cartoon films are made up of hundreds of drawings. These drawings are made on transparent sheets of celluloid called cels, placed on top of a painted background and photographed one by one. Each drawing is slightly different from the one before, and this is what makes the figures seem to be moving in a cartoon film. The separate photographs follow one another so quickly on the screen that the eye is not quick enough to see the change from one to another. For instance, if the scene is of an elephant lifting its trunk to reach a banana on a tree, in each cel the drawing of the trunk will show it a fraction higher until in the last one it reaches the banana; but on the screen the elephant will seem to lift its trunk in a continuous action.

The background artists draw and paint the background to the scenes—grass, trees, a house. This is done on a piece of stiff board with holes at the sides so that it can be pegged down. Then each celluloid sheet in turn can be pegged on to it without fear of slipping even a fraction out of place and so spoiling the picture. The key artist or animator draws the figures which will seem to move. (He is called the animator because he brings the figures to life.)

When all the cels for one scene are complete they are taken with the background drawing to be photographed by the animation camera. The background is fixed flat under the lens of the camera (the pictures are taken from above) and the first cel is pegged to it. The camera takes a picture and then stops automatically. The cameraman takes out the first cel and replaces it with the second—the elephant's trunk slightly higher—and shoots another picture, and so on until all the cels have been shot and the scene is complete.

**FILMS.** The first public film show in Great Britain was given at a hall in Regent Street in London, called the Polytechnic, on February 20, 1896. The machine used had been invented in France the year before by two brothers, Auguste and Louis Lumière. It was called the Cinematograph, which means simply "moving picture". Although the Cinematograph was the first really successful machine for showing moving photographs, various other inventions had been tried before. Some were simple working toys, with names like the Phenacistiscope and the Zoetrope, for showing pictures very quickly one after another so that the figures in them appeared to move. Others were much more complicated, like Thomas Edison's Kinetoscope which used lengths of celluloid film exactly the same as the film generally used today. (Thomas Edison and his work are described in a separate article.)

William Friese-Greene (also described in a separate article) was one of the English inventors of these early machines, and another was Robert Paul, who later became an important early film producer. Robert Paul gave a private demonstration of his machine, called the Bioscope (later rechristened the Theatrograph and, after that, the Animatograph), on the same day that the Lumière cinematograph show was taking place at the Regent Street Polytechnic.

The Lumière brothers were not only inventors, but also made the films shown by their machine. Their films were very short because the Cinematograph, which was both a camera for taking the pictures and a projector for throwing them on to a screen, could hold only 50 feet of film. This meant that each film lasted about three-quarters of a minute.

Included in the programme at the historic performance of 1896 were *Workers leaving a Factory*, a film which had been made during one lunch-hour at the Lumière photographic factory at Lyons, and *Train Entering a Station,* which is said to have terrified some members of the audience who watched a train rushing towards them on the screen for the first time. The most famous of these early Lumière films, however, was *Watering the Gardener.* In this, a gardener's boy stepped on the hose and took his foot off as the gardener peered down the nozzle. This was the first film to tell a story and the first screen comedy.

The home of the film was, to begin with, the music hall. In Great Britain the Empire Theatre in Leicester Square, London, included moving pictures as a 20-minute turn in a variety programme in 1896. Soon music halls all over the country followed suit. Most of the films shown were simple pictures of real things called "actualities", such as street scenes, boats in harbour, foreign scenery, and so on. Occasionally an acrobat or comedian would be filmed and news films, like Robert Paul's *The Derby 1896,* were often presented. People were not particular about what they saw; they went merely for the new excitement of seeing photographs which moved. In time the excitement wore off and the craze for moving pictures seemed to be over. Music hall audiences had grown so tired of films that they were put on at the end of the programme to clear the hall quickly; as a result they earned the nickname of chasers.

The cinema was saved by the fairground showmen, who began to take films into the country districts. The fairground cinema was a tent with a screen hanging on the kingpole and the audience seated on the grass. Some of the film showmen grew rich and by about 1906 many of their cinemas were very smart with gilded entrances, electric organs and plush seats for as many as 500 people.

The first permanent cinemas sprang up in the towns. Usually they were just shops turned into cinemas that were often very makeshift. A typical shop cinema in Birmingham was described in a report to the chief constable in 1909 as follows:

> The shop is 14 feet wide by 70 feet long. A woman sat in a chair by the door taking the money—one penny each—about 60 persons being admitted each time; seating, boards on ginger-beer boxes, etc., the windows being obscured with brown paper, and the wall of the shop being white-washed forming the screen.

By 1914 the shop cinema was being replaced by the "picture palace". Admission to the cheapest seats was usually still a penny and the front rows were often wooden benches, but at least the audience no longer sat on ginger-beer boxes. Except in the very latest cinemas, the showing of the film was often bad and the operators kept a slide which said, "One moment, please: the performance will be resumed shortly", ready to use when there was a hitch. The actual celluloid of the film was often so badly scratched that every scene looked as if it were taking place in pouring rain. Pictures sometimes flickered badly and this earned films another nickname—"the flicks".

## America takes the Lead

As early as 1901 a French conjurer named Georges Méliès made story films lasting 20 minutes, but it was not until about 1905 that films lasting 10 to 15 minutes became usual. These were known as one-reelers, because they were on one reel holding 1,000 feet of film.

The most famous early British story film was probably *Rescued by Rover* (1904), about a kidnapped baby discovered by a dog. It was made at a cost of £7 13*s*. 9*d*. by Cecil Hepworth. In America in 1903 Edwin S. Porter, one of Edison's film workers, made *The Great Train Robbery,* which is usually considered the first American story film. It was also the first "western".

The one-reeler was the usual film length until about 1912. A typical programme (all silent, of course) might consist of a couple of ten-minute "dramas" (usually ending in a chase), one or two comedies of the rough knockabout kind called "slapstick", a trick film where photography was used to give odd and surprising effects, a news film, a travel film and perhaps a nature study or other scientific film.

The actors in the one-reelers were generally unknown and their performances very bad; because the films were silent, actors made up for lack of speech by frantic and unnatural gestures and movements. A new and better style of acting came from America, where a young actress called Mary Pickford showed that a simple, natural style was more effective on the screen than dramatic arm-waving and chest-thumping. She quickly became a world-famous "star".

A great film comedian arose in America at about the same time, the one film actor whose greatness is agreed upon by everyone. His name was Charles Spencer Chaplin. The kind of character he created—the awkward little man with a bowler hat, big feet and little black moustache, a sad figure at the same time as being a funny one—became and has remained more famous than any other character in films so far. Other American film actors who were world famous included Harold Lloyd, Buster Keaton and Harry Langdon, who made comedies, and Douglas Fairbanks, who appeared in historical and "costume" films—films with exciting stories set in historical times.

The United States gained the lead over the rest of the world in film production during World War I. This was partly because there was plenty of money in America for making films, partly because of the popular stars appearing in American films and partly because of the genius of a man named David Wark Griffith, the first great film director. In 1915 Griffith made *The Birth of a Nation,* a film of the time of the American Civil War, and in 1916 *Intolerance.* These were three-hour films, America's answer to the spectacular Italian films such as *Quo Vadis* and *Dante's Inferno* (both made in 1912) which had earlier astonished the world. For *Intolerance* Griffith had a set built, of an ancient Babylonian city,

*(1, 3, 4) National Film Archive. (2) Radio Times Hulton Picture Library. (5) Courtesy, M.G.M.*

(1) *Rescued by Rover,* one of the first British films to tell a story. It was made in 1904 at a cost of £7 13s. 9d. (2) Charlie Chaplin and Jackie Coogan in *The Kid,* made in 1920. (3) Charles Laughton in *The Private Life of Henry VIII,* made by Sir Alexander Korda in 1933. (4) *The Secret Game* (1952), a French film directed by René Clément. (5) The chariot race in *Ben-Hur* (1959). This American spectacular film was directed by William Wyler.

which was over a mile long and he photographed it from a balloon. Griffith was a genius, not just because he knew how to show huge and thrilling scenes on the screen but because he realized and showed that a film could be a work of art.

## The Art of the Film

Making a film is a very complicated business (see FILM-MAKING) but some of the most important things about the art of films are very simple. One of these is that the camera, unlike the spectator in a theatre, is free to move about and so can show a scene from different viewpoints and different distances. The film director can choose exactly what he wants his audience to see and can emphasize any details that he feels are important by showing a close-up picture of them. There is a good example of this in *The Birth of a Nation*. At one point, Griffith put his camera high up on a hillside to photograph a battle raging in the valley below; he then moved it slightly to the left and brought into the picture a weeping woman, quite close to the camera, in order to emphasize the sadness of the scene.

Another important fact about film-making is that since a film story is told on strips of celluloid, the director, after his film is photographed or "shot", can join these strips together in one of many different ways. He can put the shots in any order he likes and he can cut each shot to any length he pleases. This process is called editing. D. W. Griffith was the first great editor and his "last-minute rescue" scenes are famous. For example, in *The Birth of a Nation* there are rapidly changing shots of a family trapped in their log cabin by attacking Negroes, then of the masked riders galloping to the rescue—back to the cabin—the riders again—the attacking Negroes—the riders—and so on. The effect of film editing is most clearly shown in an exciting sequence such as this, but it is equally important in quieter scenes.

When films began to be produced in Europe again after World War I, Germany took the lead. The weird *Cabinet of Dr. Caligari,* made in 1919, was the first of a series of remarkable films, often gloomy or sinister, but full of fine lighting effects, camera work and sets, and with magnificent screen actors such as Conrad Veidt and Emil Jannings.

Among the best silent films of all were the Russian propaganda films of 1925–1927. Sergei Eisenstein and V. I. Pudovkin, the leading directors, were great admirers of Griffith, particularly of his methods of editing. Their own films are brilliantly edited and stand alongside those of Griffith and Chaplin as the highest achievements of the silent cinema. Eisenstein's films *The Battleship Potemkin* and *October* (the story of the Russian Revolution of 1917) are two of the masterpieces of the cinema.

In France many interesting films were made in the 1920s and it became clear in 1927 that France had at least one brilliant film director; in that year René Clair made *The Italian Straw Hat,* a comedy second only to the best work of Chaplin.

Great Britain's most important silent film was perhaps John Grierson's *Drifters* (1929), the first of a long line of documentary films about real people and places. These have been Britain's most important contribution to the cinema. A documentary that became very famous had been made earlier in 1922 by an American director named Robert Flaherty. This was *Nanook of the North,* showing the life of Eskimoes.

## The Coming of Sound

The method of "recording" sound on film which is used in film-making today had been invented in 1906, but it was not until 1927 that the public saw the first sound film. The singer Al Jolson starred in *The Jazz Singer* in 1927 and *The Singing Fool* in 1928, and these films marked the end of the silent cinema. Within a few years the production of silent films had almost ceased.

At first the "talkies", as they were called, talked far too much. All but a few directors forgot the art of telling a story in pictures, and the outstanding films of the early sound period were those in which sound was used, not to take the place of the pictures, but to add to their effect—G. W. Pabst's mining film *Kameradschaft,* René Clair's *Le Million,* King Vidor's all-Negro film *Hallelujah* and some fine British documentaries such as *Night Mail,* by Basil Wright and Harry Watt, about how the mail is carried by the night mail trains.

Great Britain's leading film directors in the 1930s were Anthony Asquith and Alfred Hitchcock, a master of films of suspense. In 1933 Sir Alexander Korda produced an historical film called *The Private Life of Henry VIII,* with Charles Laughton, and followed it with other films of good quality. Not many British films of the years before the outbreak of World War II were as good as the best ones being made in France, however. There, very fine directors such as Jean Renoir made films starring brilliant actors and actresses.

The stars of the films being made in Hollywood became known in every corner of the world. Among them were James Cagney and Clark Gable, Marlene Dietrich, who had first appeared in films in Germany, the Swedish Greta Garbo, perhaps the finest of all screen actresses, and the young Shirley Temple. Some of the most famous of all were Mickey Mouse and other characters of Walt Disney's cartoons.

## World War II and After

In Britain during the war a number of films were made about the lives of the British people, films which were in some ways like documentaries, recording people's lives as they were really lived. Among the directors who became well known for these films were Sir Carol Reed, Michael Powell, Frank Launder and Sidney Gilliatt, David Lean and Thorold Dickinson. One film of this kind was *The First of the Few,* about the designer of the Spitfire aircraft which fought in the Battle of Britain. Others were *This Happy Breed* and *Brief Encounter.*

After the war Sir Carol Reed became internationally famous for his films *Odd Man Out* and *The Third Man,* which was set in the war-damaged city of Vienna. Other British films praised both at home and abroad were Sir Laurence Olivier's films of Shakespeare's *Henry V* (made in 1944) and *Hamlet,* and the film of Charles Dickens's novel *Great Expectations,* directed by David Lean. Comedies included several from the Ealing film studios, such as *Kind Hearts and Coronets* and *Passport to Pimlico.* A large number of films about the war were made, both in Britain (where the most successful was *The Dam Busters,* directed by Michael Anderson) and the United States.

The most remarkable films after the war, however, came from Italy. The director Roberto Rossellini made two fine films called *Open City* and *Paisa,* which gave a picture of life in Italy at the end of the war. Another Italian film which became very famous was *Bicycle Thieves,* by Vittorio de Sica; although it told a story of poverty and unemployment it was one of the loveliest films ever made. From France, too, have come excellent films both funny and serious. Among the comedies were two starring the actor Jacques Tati: *Jour de Fête,* which showed the hilarious adventures of a village postman on fair day, and *Monsieur Hulot's Holiday.* Serious films included *Beauty and the Beast* by Jean Cocteau, *The Secret Game* by René Clément and *The Wages of Fear,* a story about the perilous journey of lorries loaded with high explosive.

In 1950 a Japanese film, *Rashomon,* was shown in Europe and America and won such high praise from film critics that other Japanese films were brought to Western countries. Among the best were *The Seven Samurai,* a fierce tale of medieval warriors, and *Throne of Blood,* a Japanese version of Shakespeare's play *Macbeth.*

During the war and afterwards all sorts of films of high quality continued to be made in the United States. They included Charles Chaplin's *Limelight,* the fine "western" *Shane,* a drama of the New York docks called *On the Waterfront* and many high-spirited "musicals" of which *On the Town* was one of the best. A new development was the making of films from plays written for television. One of these, *Marty,* although cheaply made with almost unknown actors, won several prizes at international film festivals.

Television became a rival to the cinema and from 1950 onwards film audiences began to dwindle, first in the United States and later in Britain, as more and more people bought television sets. To attract people back into the cinemas new inventions were brought into use. Three-dimensional (3-D) films, for which the audience had to wear special glasses, were tried, but were not popular. About the same time the first "wide screens" were fitted in cinemas and CinemaScope films, in which the picture is about 2½ times as wide as it is high, began to appear. These were soon followed by Vista-Vision films, with a picture about 1¾ times as wide as it is high. The invention called Cinerama is much more elaborate, using three projectors at once to give a huge picture. A double-width colour film is used to give an extra sharp and life-like picture. This invention was first used to help in training gunners of the United States armed forces during the war. Cinerama gives the audience the sensation of actually being part of the scene shown on the screen and is very exciting.

Experiments are also being made to give more natural and exciting sound in films. Instead of a single loudspeaker behind the screen eight or ten speakers are set round the hall and in the roof. Thus the sound comes to the audience from different directions, giving what is called stereophonic sound. The word stereophonic means "solid sound".

**FINCH.** The finches form one of the largest families of birds in the world, one kind or another being found in almost every country. Finches are small birds with stout, short bills which help them in crushing the seeds they eat, although many also feed on insects.

The best-known British finch is the chaffinch, which is about the same size as the house sparrow and is even more common. The male is brightly coloured with a rosy breast, blue-grey head and a noticeable white patch on the shoulder. The female is duller but has a similar white shoulder patch. The chaffinch has a cheerful rattling song and a double call note, "pink pink", which is frequently heard. From April onwards its beautiful mossy nest can be found in hedges or small trees, with four or five brownish eggs spotted and streaked with darker purplish brown. In winter these birds form large flocks, often mixing with other finches and sparrows. A bird sometimes seen with them at this time is the brambling, or bramble finch, which is distinguished from the chaffinch by an orange shoulder patch and a white rump, or hinder part. This bird, which is very fond of beech mast (the fruit of the beech tree), nests in northern Europe and Asia. Chaffinches are found all over Europe, in North Africa and also in western Asia; they have been introduced into New Zealand and South Africa.

The rather smaller goldfinch is the most beautiful British finch and has a very pretty song. The male and female are alike with crimson faces, white at the sides, and with black colouring on their heads and tails. The wings are also black but with broad patches of brilliant gold. In either May or June the female builds an even more beautiful nest than the chaffinch. Often she places it in a fruit tree, using spiders' webs to bind together the moss, grass and wool, and lining it with hair and vegetable down. The three or four eggs are whitish with a few brown spots. The young birds do not at first have the same red, white and black pattern on their heads as the older birds. Goldfinches go about in flocks and are particularly fond of the seeds of thistles. Though scarce in the north, they are found over most of the British Isles and Europe as well as in parts of Asia and were introduced into New Zealand.

The bullfinch is a plump, sturdy bird with a piping note. The male has a beautiful rosy red breast and grey back, with black on the head, wings and tail, but the female is duller with a pinkish grey breast. Both sexes have a noticeable white rump and white lines on the wings. The first eggs, greenish blue with a few dark spots, are usually laid early in May in a nest of twigs and moss lined with roots, placed in a hedge or an evergreen tree. A second clutch of eggs is laid later. Bullfinches prefer to keep under cover of bushes and trees and seldom form flocks in the autumn.

The greenfinch is olive green with yellow on the wings and near the tail, the female being duller than the male. The call, a long-drawn-out "breeze", is one of those heard most frequently during the summer, and the birds also have a twittering song. The nest is solidly built in a hedge, bush or small tree. It is made of

Finches are small birds with stout bills. The six shown here are (from left to right) a bullfinch, a greenfinch, a chaffinch, a hawfinch, a goldfinch and a brambling.

moss on a foundation of twigs and is lined with hair or a few feathers. The first eggs are laid towards the end of April and are white or pale greenish, with a few reddish brown spots. Greenfinches are common in most parts of the British Isles and are found all over Europe; they have been introduced into New Zealand.

The hawfinch is unmistakable when seen, for it has a very large, thick bill which can crack cherry stones. However, it is a shy woodland bird and is not found at all in some districts in Britain. Its presence is often discovered only from its calls, one a whistle and the other a clicking note.

Other British members of the finch family are the linnet, siskin, redpoll, twite and crossbill. The linnet is rather a dull brown bird, but in spring the cock has crimson on his head and breast and a very pretty song. This bird is common all over the British Isles and is frequently found among gorse bushes. The twite is only found on moorland in the north. The siskin and redpoll are best known as winter visitors; they are fond of alder trees. The crossbill is rather a rare bird which nests in pine trees. Its bill is crossed at the tip and this helps it to take the seeds out of pine cones.

The many Canadian finches include the purple finch, which is one of the best songsters of that country. This bird is really purplish rose in colour and the male has a rosy coloured head. It is found in wooded country in most parts of Canada and travels south through the prairies in the autumn. The common rosy finch is mainly brown in colouring with a rosy tinge on back, underparts and wings. It spends the summer in high mountains, but comes to the lowlands and near towns in winter.

There are no native finches in New Zealand but, as already mentioned, several British kinds have been successfully introduced round the towns. Australian "finches" are all really in the weaver-bird family to which the sparrows belong. There are many beautiful kinds which are popular in Britain in aviaries; among the most striking are the Gouldian finch and the painted finch.

About 20 finches occur in South Africa, mostly relatives of the canary or buntings. (See Canary and Bunting.) The bully seed-eater is like a big greenish canary with a strong beak.

**FINGERPRINTS.** The skin covering the tips of the fingers and thumbs is crossed by many tiny ridges and furrows which are arranged in distinct patterns. No one in the world has fingertip patterns exactly like anyone else's in every detail. Even the fingerprints of identical twins are not exactly the same. Sir William Herschel and Sir Francis Galton, the noted scientist, discovered that the patterns never change throughout life, although the skin may become wrinkled and cracked with old age. There are also creases on the palms of the hands and the soles of the feet, which are there when a baby is born, and they are as distinctive as those on the fingers.

Because each person has his or her own fingerprints, they are obviously an excellent method of identifying people. A man who has committed a crime, for instance, may have held a bottle or placed his hand on some other object with a smooth surface in such a way that an impression of his fingertips is left on the object, and these marks are called fingerprints. Detectives searching the scene of a crime look for fingerprints and if they find any they have a most important clue as to the identity of the criminal.

In Great Britain fingerprints are only used in criminal proceedings, and records of them are kept at New Scotland Yard, which now has about 1,500,000 sets of prints. Very occasionally, when fingerprints are found on an object at the scene of a crime, the fingerprints of every grown-up person living near by are taken for comparison. Printer's ink is used on the fingertips to make sure the prints are very clear, and then they are pressed on to a sheet of paper.

Arch

Loop

Whorl

Composite

Every fingerprint belongs to one of these four groups, but no two prints have the same ridge characteristics.

The Federal Bureau of Investigation in Washington, United States, has an enormous collection of fingerprints, for besides the prints of criminals it includes those of the armed forces and people working for the government. Also many ordinary people have had them taken in case they lose their memories or other people try to cheat them by using their names. (See Federal Bureau of Investigation.)

It has been claimed that the Chinese knew about the importance of fingerprints and used some kind of fingerprint system thousands of years ago, but no one knows whether this was really so. Almost certainly the science of fingerprint identification practised today is quite new. An Englishman called Sir Edward Henry found, after many years of work, a method of classifying fingerprints so that each set of them can now be filed away and easily found when required. This system is used in one form or another throughout most of the world today. It was adopted at New Scotland Yard in 1901, when Henry was an assistant commissioner of the Metropolitan Police Force. It would take too long to explain just how Henry's system works, but here are a few interesting facts about it.

## The Four Main Types

Henry, realizing that all fingerprints could be divided into four main types—namely the arch, the loop, the whorl and the composite (these can be seen in the picture)—then worked out a way of dividing a collection of fingerprints into 1,024 groups. By making use of detail in the patterns, these 1,024 groups are further divided into thousands of smaller groups, which means that any particular set of prints can be found in a few minutes.

All fingerprints are either in the arch, loop, whorl or composite groups, but the print of each separate finger is different from all the others. This is because of what are known as *ridge characteristics*. The ridges on the fingertips vary; some end more abruptly than others, some fork and here and there are formations looking like the drawings of small islands and lakes found in maps. These details are the ridge characteristics. They occur in every fingerprint, but they never exist in the same order in prints taken from different fingers. It is the order of them that makes each fingerprint quite different from any others.

If the ridges on the fingertips are examined through a magnifying glass, it can be seen that each ridge is studded with small holes. These holes are the openings from which the sweat escapes from the glands situated below the surface of the skin. When a finger is pressed on some smooth object the small deposits of sweat join together and a picture of the ridges in sweat is left behind. These sweat prints are called latent prints, latent being a word that means hidden, because the prints are often difficult to see. To overcome this difficulty when prints are found at the scene of a crime, certain powders are applied to them with brushes and they become visible and easy to photograph. After latent prints have been photographed they can be classified almost in the same way as inked prints, and many criminals have been found by this method.

So safe is the fingerprint system that not a single case has occurred of a person who has been fingerprinted being mistaken for someone else.

**FINLAND.** The republic of Finland in northeast Europe is bordered by Norway on the north, Sweden and the Gulf of Bothnia on the west, the Gulf of Finland on the south, and the U.S.S.R. on the east. Although Finland is nearly one-and-a-half times the size of Great

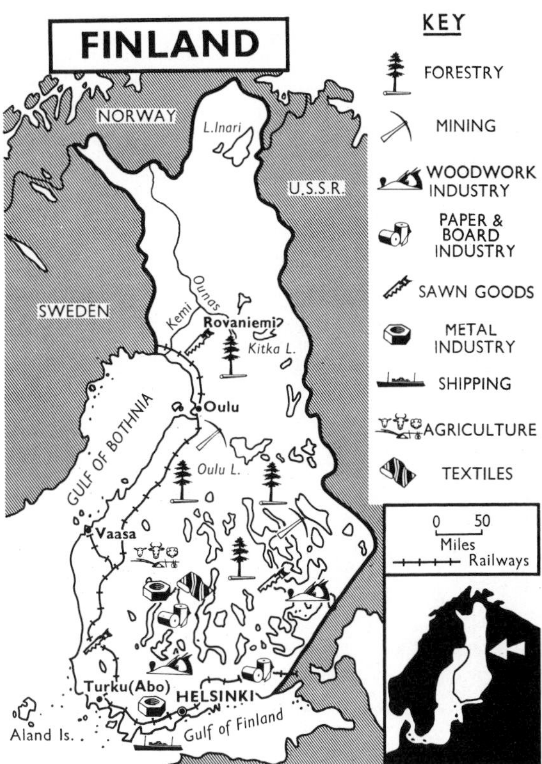


Britain, it has only about one-twelfth the number of people living in it.

Only a small part of the country can be cultivated. Great forests of pine, spruce and birch cover nearly three-quarters of its area. In south and central Finland there are more than 60,000 lakes, and in the north much of the land is swampy or boggy. The coastline is broken by many bays and tens of thousands of islands.

The climate can be very hard. In some years snow begins to fall in October or November and may not melt away completely until May. North of the Arctic Circle, in Finnish Lapland, the sun never appears for 51 days in midwinter, but in summer there are seven weeks of continuous daylight. In the south, daylight lasts 5 or 6 hours in midwinter and more than 20 hours in midsummer.

In the forests and wastes of Finnish Lapland live bears, wolves and herds of reindeer. The rivers hold salmon and trout, and many seals are found in the Gulf of Bothnia.

The Finns are a people of varied looks. Some are very fair, some are rather dark. Their ancestors crossed over from the southern shores of

### FACTS ABOUT FINLAND

**AREA:** 130,119 square miles.
**POPULATION** (estimated in 1967): 4,664,000.
**KIND OF COUNTRY:** Self-governing republic.
**CAPITAL:** Helsinki.
**GEOGRAPHICAL FEATURES:** Seven-tenths of the country is covered by forests, one-tenth consists of lakes, and less than one-tenth of the total area is cultivated land.
**CHIEF EXPORTS:** Timber and timber products, wood pulp, cardboard and paper.
**IMPORTANT TOWNS:** Helsinki, Tampere (Tammerfors), Turku (Abo), Lahti.
**EDUCATION:** Children must attend school between the ages of 7 and 15.

*Courtesy, Finnish Tourist Association*

Above: A lake steamer passing the castle of Olavinlinna in south-east Finland. Right: Schoolboys running at a Helsinki sports ground.

the Gulf of Finland in about A.D. 100 and are thought to be of the same race as the Magyars of Hungary. Among their ancient customs is that of the *sauna* or steam bath. The first thing a Finn builds when he moves to a new place in the country is a bath-house, a little wooden hut with a high wooden platform and a stove with cobbles on top. Steam comes from water thrown on the hot cobbles, and the Finn lies on the platform and beats his naked body with leafy birch twigs. In a temperature of about 200 degrees Fahrenheit the sweat begins to run; then he goes out to bathe in the lake or roll in the snow.

A striking thing about Finland is that ancient and modern ways of living go on side by side, for the Finn is just as much at home in his new centrally heated and electrically fitted flat in the town as he is in his wooden house in the country. Finland is very up to date in many ways, and there is less difference between rich and poor than practically anywhere else. The Finns have made their country known all over the world for athletics and the arts—especially architecture, sculpture and music. Jean Sibelius, the composer, was a Finn.

Finnish is a beautiful and complicated language which is extremely difficult to learn, but not difficult to speak, because every word is pronounced exactly as it is spelt. About one in ten of the people are Swedish-speaking, and therefore Swedish is used as a second language. Many of the towns, for instance, have a Swedish as well as a Finnish name. The Finns are very well educated, thanks to their excellent schools and universities. Most of the people belong to the Lutheran (Protestant) religion.

Helsinki (in Swedish, Helsingfors) is the capital city, and stands on a splendid harbour. In the old days it was built of wood, and there were many fires before granite began to be used during the 19th century. It is a modern city with some very fine buildings and wide streets lined with trees; and it has no slums. The industrial centre of Finland is the city of Tampere (or Tammerfors), which is built on a strip of land between two long lakes. It is a clean, well-planned and lively city. Turku (Abo) was once the capital, and is the oldest city in Finland, with a 13th-century cathedral and an old castle. It is a very important port, because a channel to its harbour can be kept ice-free all through the winter, when the other ports are all frozen over.

The huge forests of Finland provide work for many people and most of the wealth of the country. Many of the Finns are farmers who own a stretch of forest as well as their fields, or go to work in winter in the forests owned by the state or the great timber companies. Then there is plenty of work, felling and stripping trees and carting them to the water's edge. When the thaw comes, the logs are floated through a network of lakes, rivers and canals to the sawmills and the ports. Much of the timber is sent abroad in the form of pit props, planks and beams, and every summer it can be seen as deck cargo piled high on ships sailing to Great Britain. The Finns also make their timber into plywood, prefabricated houses, furniture (some of the best modern furniture comes from Finland), and into cardboard, and every sort of paper, including newsprint, coarse wrapping paper and the finest air-mail writing-paper.

About four logs out of every ten are used inside the country, for there is no coal in Finland, and wood must be used in the stoves of the houses and in the railway engines (except in the new diesel-electric locomotives). The Finns have always made great use of wood. In the country they used to eat with wooden spoons from wooden bowls, wear wooden shoes and carry birch-bark baskets. In times of famine they had to mix bark with flour to make bread, and even today some people drink alcohol made from wood pulp.

There is enough dairy farming in Finland to keep the people well supplied with milk, butter and cheese and to have some over to send abroad, and fish from river, lakes and the sea is plentiful. The short summer makes it difficult to raise large crops, but grain, potatoes and root crops are all grown, and in southern Finland some green vegetables and fruit can be grown.

There were few factories in Finland before 1944 other than those connected with timber and woodworking. Since that date, however, many more have been built, and Finland has produced a large number of ships and a good deal of machinery and metal goods. Several splendid new hydro-electric plants have been set up to harness the water-power of the many rapids on the rivers, and these supply electricity for the factories.

The inland waterways of Finland, formed by lakes joined by rivers and canals, carry a certain number of passengers and goods in summer, and provide cheap transport for the timber that is floated down. The Finns have always been good sailors, and they have a fairly large fleet of sea-going merchant vessels. Finnish air lines connect Helsinki with other important points in Finland, and with Norway, Sweden, Denmark, Germany, the Netherlands, France, Great Britain and the U.S.S.R.

## History

The history of Finland before the 20th century is largely a tale of wars between Sweden and Russia. During the 12th and 13th centuries, Sweden gradually got control of Finland, which became, in the 14th century, a Swedish province. Finland remained part of the Swedish kingdom until 1809, when it was taken by Russia. The Swedes treated the Finns well, allowing them much liberty and bringing them Christianity, education and the law, but Finland suffered terribly in the Swedish wars with Russia. Thousands of Finns were killed fighting for Sweden, and famine and disease spread through the country.

The Russians tried in many ways during the 19th century to take away the Finns' freedom. In the end, in 1905, the Finns went on strike and demanded their rights and liberties. They wanted to manage their own affairs, and they forced the Russians to let them set up a new parliament, whose members were elected by the votes of all the people over 21. Thus Finland was the first country in Europe to give votes to women.

The Russians, however, continued to interfere, while the Finns wanted above all to have their own country, and to be free from the rule of Russians or Swedes or anyone else. They took their opportunity when the Russian empire collapsed in 1917, and they declared that Finland was an independent country. In 1919, the Republic of Finland, with a President at its head, was set up.

In the autumn of 1939 the government of the U.S.S.R. suddenly demanded valuable stretches of land from Finland. When the Finns refused to give them up, the Russians attacked them. The Finns resisted bravely and at first successfully, but after a hundred days' fighting they were defeated, and the Russians took southern Karelia, Finland's richest province. In 1941, when the Germans invaded the U.S.S.R., the Finns took up arms again, this time on the same side as the Germans, to try to win back their lost province. However, the defeat of the Germans meant the defeat of the Finns, and in 1944 the U.S.S.R. made them accept harsh armistice terms. Finland had to give up not only southern Karelia, but also its only port on the Arctic, Petsamo. It had also to agree to manufacture huge quantities of wood products, ships and machinery for the U.S.S.R. in the next eight years, by way of compensation.

Most people expected Finland to fail in this. After the losses and upheavals of two wars, and with the problem of finding new homes and work for the 500,000 Finns from Karelia who had left their homeland rather than live under Russian rule, it seemed that Finland might well find the burden too heavy to bear. But by hard work and steady determination the Finns succeeded in overcoming all obstacles. They held on to their independence and remained as free and as highly civilized as any country in western Europe.

**FIR.** The word fir is sometimes used for any conifer, or cone-bearing tree. It was the Scandinavian name for the Scots pine, but is now used for silver firs and other trees in the *Abies* group of the pine family. There are about 40 species of the true firs, widely distributed in the northern hemisphere.

Silver firs may reach a height of 200 feet. They are quite like pines and spruces, but their needles—the narrow leaves—grow in single rows along the twig, whereas pine needles grow in groups. (See Pine.) Fir needles are also shorter and flatter. Their under surface has two white stripes which give the tree a silvery appearance because the needles tend to curl upwards. Firs can be distinguished from spruces by their cones, for those of the spruces hang down but fir cones stand up. (See Spruce.) Fir cones have many overlapping scales each bearing two winged seeds. These cones ripen and break up in a year, whereas pine cones take two or three years.

Silver firs grow in forests in cool mountainous regions. They are common in the Alps, the United States, Canada and the U.S.S.R., and have grown in Britain since the 17th century. They produce turpentine, which forms in blisters on their trunks in summer. (See Turpentine.) The balsam fir of North America is a widely branching tree up to 70 feet tall. The turpentine obtained from it is called Canada balsam and is used when mounting specimens for the microscope because its optical properties are like those of glass.

Among the biggest firs are those of western North America, including the white fir up to 250 feet tall; the grand fir,

*Paul Popper*

A sawmill near the head of the Gulf of Bothnia in northern Finland. The logs have been floated down from the forests and are now waiting to go into the mill.

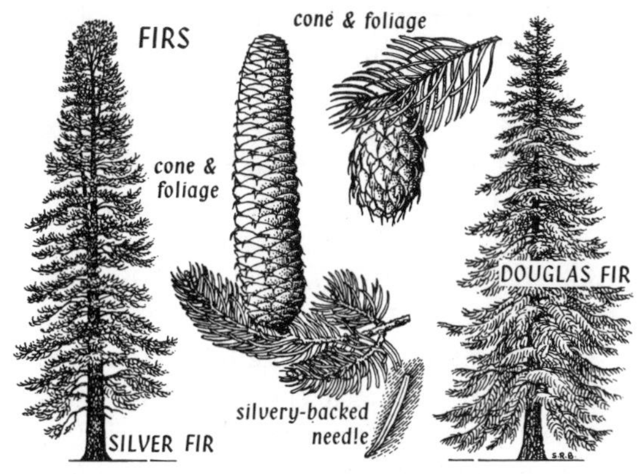


sometimes reaching 300 feet; the Pacific silver fir and the noble fir. Most fir wood is inferior to that of pine or spruce, but some is used as timber and a great deal is used as wood pulp for making paper. The Douglas fir, also called the Oregon pine, is the most important timber tree of North America. Several other kinds of fir are grown for ornamental purposes in Europe and North America. Among these are the Spanish fir, the Greek fir and Algerian and Japanese firs.

**FIRE.** Because outbreaks of fire are always dreaded great care is taken in cities everywhere to prevent them from occurring, and there are many ways of extinguishing them. In spite of all precautions, however, serious fires still occur several times each year in every country of the world, causing great damage to property and sometimes loss of life.

Here are some examples of such fires. In 1948 a tailor in Castries, the capital of St. Lucia, in the Windward Islands, shut up his shop one June night and went home. A little later two passers-by heard a noise that sounded like the bursting of an electric light bulb and soon afterwards the shop was seen to be on fire. The flames quickly spread to adjoining buildings and before morning almost the whole of the business and government centre of Castries had been burnt to the ground. No lives were lost, but thousands of people became homeless.

In August 1956 a wagon fell into the ventilating shaft of a large coal mine at Marcinelle in Belgium and cut an electric cable. This caused a short circuit of electricity and started a fire which burned for 71 days. More than 280 miners working there were killed.

In a factory in the north of England certain parts of fast-moving machinery had to be kept oiled. Each of the two men responsible believed that the other had done the job. The bearings of the machinery became overheated and a fire followed. When it was at last extinguished little of the factory remained standing.

An Essex farmer, in too much of a hurry to get his hay in, stacked most of it before it was properly dried. The hay heated up, smouldered and burst into flames. Three of his barns were burnt down.

In many instances, fire breaks out because of the carelessness of people. The fire in the factory was caused by the misunderstanding that led to each of the two workers to take it for granted that the other had oiled the machinery. The barn fire was caused by the impatience of the farmer to get his hay stacked. The fire in the Belgian mine was caused by the failure to keep the wagon running on its proper track. There are many other ways in which fires are caused. A heath or forest fire often begins by a lighted cigarette being thrown away and falling on a clump of grass or a dry twig. The poles supporting power lines have sometimes been allowed to become so rotten that they fall. Many chemical explosions have occurred, causing terrible flames to shoot up. Fire often breaks out when two cars or trains crash.

There are, however, many fires which flare up in spite of precautions or where the cause is never discovered. The 1948 fire at Castries is an example of this. Sometimes fires break out on ships in spite of every care being taken. The rays of the sun can make flames leap up in dry grass, and lightning may set fire to places where lightning conductors cannot be set up. Great blazes may occur for no apparent reason in oil-tanks, in heavily stocked warehouses, in mills and in factories. Church fires may be started by rats or mice nibbling away the insulation, or outer covering, of electric wires and causing a short circuit. Fires have even begun in such unlikely places as swimming baths and aquariums. Fire frequently follows earthquakes, particularly in Japan, where the houses are built of wood, paper and thatch, and any small fires, such as those in stoves, instantly spread when the surface of the earth trembles, and the houses burn very quickly.

### Insuring against Fire

The ways in which fires are put out are described in the article FIRE-FIGHTING. Even when a fire is successfully put out, however, it has often done so much damage that a great deal of money has to be spent on repairing it. In time, therefore, people decided that it would be a good idea to provide beforehand for the cost of replacing what fire destroys. This was first decided on shortly after the Great Fire, and in 1720 charters were granted to two assurance corporations and the foundations of fire insurance had been laid (see INSURANCE). In 1771 the merchants and other businessmen who met at the famous coffee-house of Lloyd's in Lombard Street decided to form a group to protect the business interests they all had in common. (See LLOYDS.)

In fire insurance, money contributions, known as premiums, are charged according to the risk of fire. As there is more danger of fire in a timberyard than in a house, the timber merchant pays a higher premium—that is, gives more money to the insurance company—than the owner of a house. In the same way, the owner of a mill where wood is ground down to make sawdust must pay a higher premium than a garage proprietor. This principle is simple, but the way it works is very complicated, particularly as fire insurance is now carried on in all parts of the world. At one time it was feared that if people were allowed to insure their property against fire they would be tempted to burn it in order to get the insurance money. There have been attempts to do so, but the crime is usually discovered without much delay and the punishment is severe.

In fact, fire insurance has proved useful in making people more careful. Whenever it is found that the risk of fire anywhere has become less the premiums are reduced, and when the risk has increased they go up; so, in order to save money, it is obviously best to make everything as secure against fire as possible.

**FIRE-FIGHTING.** When a fire breaks out and the firemen are called to deal with it, the first thing they have to do is to make sure no one is trapped or in danger. The next thing is to find out exactly where the fire is, which is often more difficult than one might imagine, for the building is full of smoke. The firemen then try to put out the fire as quickly as possible without causing too much damage to the building.

If the fire is in a house or factory, the firemen try to prevent it from spreading beyond the room or place where it started. Failing that, they make sure that the fire is surrounded, not only on every side, but also above and beneath. If the whole building is burning then firemen must surround the fire so that it does not spread to other buildings. At the same time other men are doing salvage work; that is, rescuing property from the fire or covering it up against damage by water from the hosepipes.

The first vehicle to leave the fire station is always a motor pump carrying a fire escape, in case anyone is in danger. The escape consists of a number of extending ladders mounted on wheels; as soon as it reaches the fire it is dropped to the ground and wheeled to the burning building. The firemen then turn a handle which raises the ladders one above the other to about 50 feet from the ground. When a wheeled escape cannot be moved to where it is needed, a fireman may use a ladder which can be hooked on to the window sills, so that he can climb straight up the face of the building. For very tall buildings firemen use a turntable ladder mounted on its own vehicle, which has the power to raise the ladder to the correct angle, turn it round in any direction and extend it to a length of 100 feet. A turntable ladder can be used to bring the end of a hose above the fire as well as to save life. The firemen of Great Britain rescue about 450 people a year from fires and other dangers.

Most fires are put out with water. Fire engines usually carry some in a tank to deal with small fires, but for bigger ones the fireman uses water from the ordinary water mains (the large pipes that supply all the houses with water). He does this by connecting his hose to a hydrant, which is an opening in the water main with a valve to turn the water on and off. Hydrants usually lie in pits under the pavement or the road, covered by an iron plate and marked on a nearby wall by a tablet marked with a capital H. The water comes out of the hydrant with some force behind it, but the fireman usually needs water with even greater force to put a fire out, so he uses a pump driven by an engine to increase the pressure. Thus the water flows through a length of hose from the hydrant to the motor pump and out again through more hose at higher pressure to the fire. If the fire is in the country and there are no water mains, the firemen may be able to take water from a pond or river near by, but sometimes they have to take it along with them in a special vehicle called a water tender.

The firemen also carry to the fire all sorts of equipment which they may need. When one of them goes into the burning building to find the fire, he usually takes with him one or two of the red cylinders called fire extinguishers, because the jet of water produced by one of these may be enough to put the fire out by itself. There is breathing apparatus to supply the men with oxygen, in case the smoke is too thick to breathe or there is poisonous gas about, and many other things such as axes and crowbars and tools to break into locked buildings which are on fire.

There are some fires which the firemen cannot reach by land because the buildings are in harbours or on the banks of rivers. Some fire brigades therefore have fast boats which can fight fires from the water, pumping this straight through a water-gun called a monitor.

By a clever engineering device, it is now possible to make a fire put itself out before it becomes too big. This is done in the following way. Pipes filled with water pass through a building, and at regular intervals there are sprinkler heads to scatter the water widely. Each head is kept closed by a plug which melts and falls away when the temperature of the building is raised by an outbreak of fire, and in this way a powerful shower of water is released. Each of these heads can spray a floor area of about 100 square feet, besides throwing jets up to the ceiling. Immediately the water begins to flow through the pipes it causes an alarm bell to ring outside the building. The device is known as the sprinkler system.

Firemen use water to put out fires because the force of the jet knocks the fire out and its wetness prevents the flames from spreading. Water cannot always be used, however, for if it is put on certain burning materials it will only make the fire worse. It is useless to send a jet of water into an oil fire, for example, because burning oil will float on top of the water. Then it can turn the water underneath it into steam, which will blow the burning oil right out of the tank. In this kind of situation, the fireman tries to cut off the supply of oxygen from the air by covering the burning substances with foam or gas. (No fire can keep going without oxygen.)

In the case of an oil fire he mixes chemicals with water to make foam, which looks very like thick soap suds. The foam is then dropped or slid on to the burning oil until the surface is covered and the fire dies from lack of oxygen. Oil fires are some of the most dangerous a fireman has to tackle. Sometimes, as for example when the engine of a motor car catches fire, the fireman uses an extinguisher filled with a chemical called carbon tetrachloride, because it does not conduct electricity as water does. When this liquid is forced out it becomes a gas which surrounds the fire, so that oxygen cannot reach the flames.

## History and Organization

It was a long time before men began to find effective ways of putting out unwanted fires. There were forms of fire extinguishers in use as far back as the 1st century A.D., and throughout the middle ages it was the rule to extinguish the house fires when the curfew bell rang at 8 or 9 o'clock (see CURFEW), but at the time of the Great Fire of London in 1666 (see FIRES OF LONDON), the only kind of fire engine in use had to be operated by hand, and the water could not be squirted for more than a short distance. The engine often had to be taken so close to the flames that it caught fire itself.

After the Great Fire a number of insurance companies were formed, as explained at the end of the previous article, and in order to reduce the amount of money they had to pay out for fire damage these companies set up proper fire brigades. However, it was not until the second half of the 19th century that steam engines were used to work the pumps. Even then the fire engines were still pulled to the scene of the fire by men or by horses, for motor fire engines did not come into use until the 20th century. By then, many towns and villages had their own fire brigades. During the great incendiary (fire bomb) raids in World War II, the many local brigades had to start working more closely together, and now, instead of about 1,500 small ones, there are roughly 150 large brigades in Great Britain as a whole. Each has a number of fire stations scattered throughout its town or county.

The most important part of a brigade's main fire station is the room where the engines stand behind their folding doors, ready to be put into action at a moment's notice. Next to this is the watchroom, where the man or woman on duty receives fire calls, usually by telephone or by direct wire from a street fire alarm box. As soon as a fire call is received at the station the alarm bells are sounded and the firemen run to their vehicles (called appliances), on which their fire-fighting clothes are waiting. A few seconds after the call the first vehicle leaves, followed by others, all ringing their bells on the way to the fire although not on the way back.

The greater the danger to life and property in the area of the fire, the more fire engines are sent. Later, if the fire is a big one, engines may have to be sent from other fire stations in the area or even from other fire brigades. In the country, where the fire engines are manned by people who do other jobs for part of their time, these people can be called quickly into the station by sounding a siren or, at night, by electric bells in their homes.

The officer in charge of the firemen at a fire must be able to get in touch at once with his headquarters in case he needs more equipment or anything else. He may be able to use the telephone, but nowadays he sometimes keeps in touch by wireless. If the fire is a big one, some of the firemen may have what are known as "walkie-talkie" wireless sets (small battery sets strapped on their backs), so that the officer in charge can keep in touch with the firefighters on all sides of the fire.

A person who wishes to be a fireman must above all be fit and strong enough to fight fires. If he passes the doctor's examination and also a

*Courtesy, London Fire Brigade*

Above: These firemen are wearing breathing apparatus. Left: Sliding down the polished pole that leads from the firemen's quarters. The men's fire-fighting clothes and equipment are on the fire engine. A motor pump carrying a fire escape is the first vehicle to leave the station in answer to a fire call.

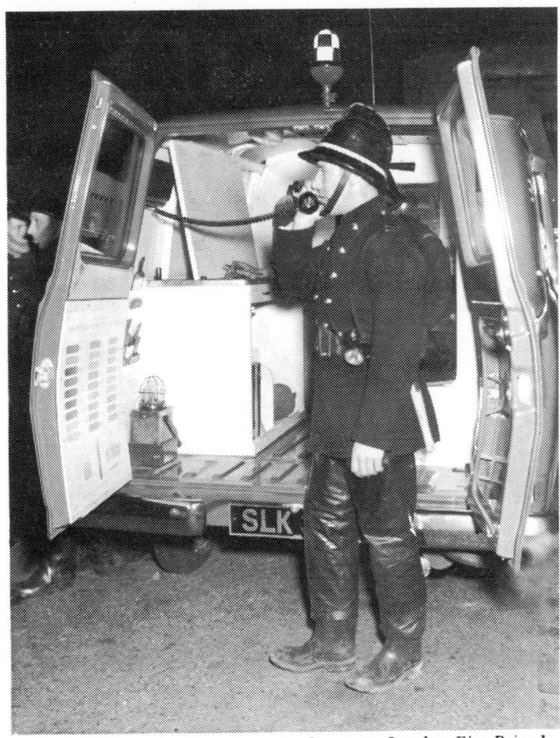

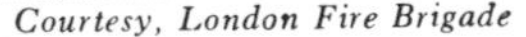

*Courtesy, London Fire Brigade*

Above: Using radio to summon reinforcements. Right: Fire in a city street. Wheeled escape ladders allow firemen to enter the burning building while 100-foot turntable ladders are used to direct hoses on to the heart of the fire.

test in ordinary school subjects, he then goes to a training school. However, he can only learn his job properly by doing it with his brigade, and indeed a fireman is always learning, because no two fires are the same. A full-time fireman spends many hours a week just cleaning his station and the vehicles and practising fire drill, but every so often the fire bells ring and he has to drop what he is doing, or perhaps run in a few seconds from his dinner or his bed to one of the appliances going to the fire. Then, if it is a real fire and not a false alarm, he must work in smoke and heat, until at last, tired and wet, he goes back to the fire station to rest, or maybe soon to answer another call.

**FIREFLY AND GLOW-WORM.** In spite of their names, fireflies and glow-worms are neither flies nor worms, but beetles. What is so remarkable about them is that they can produce either a flashing light or a steady glow. The light usually comes from little rounded patches on the sides or underneath of the beetle, and there is little doubt that it helps the male and female to find each other. They are also helped in this by having unusually large eyes. In the glow-worm of northern Europe it is the grub-like wingless female that shines most brightly, although the winged male and even the grub and the egg may be faintly luminous; that is, they give off a faint light. In the firefly of

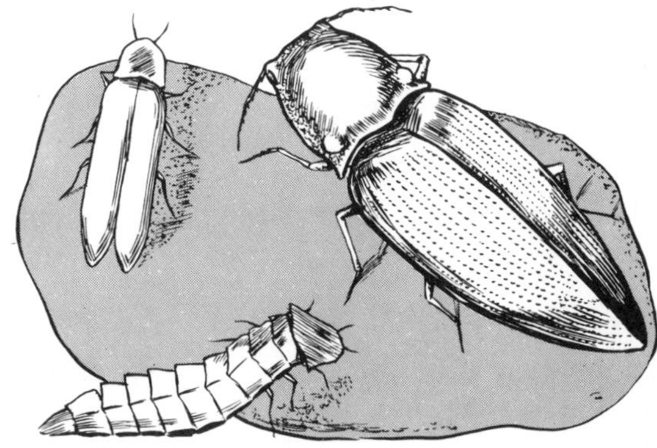

The wingless female glow-worm (lower left) shines much more brightly than the winged male (upper left). In the case of the firefly (right) it is the male that shines.

Three ways to make fire: by striking sparks from flints; by rubbing dry sticks together; and by spinning a pointed fire drill in a hole in a piece of wood.

southern Europe, however, it is the male that produces the light.

Fireflies are to be found in nearly all the tropical countries. Generally they have a greenish light, but in South America there is one kind that has both red and green lights and for that reason is known as the railway beetle.

The insects seem to be quite able to control the light they give out, whether this is a glow or a flash. In the flashing kind the beetle usually flies along giving his signal at fairly regular intervals, but some kinds will occasionally all flash together while on the wing at night and this is a wonderful sight to see. Many of the grubs, which are also often luminous, feed on snails and are most helpful in keeping down the numbers of these garden pests.

Scientists do not yet know exactly how the beetles' lighting system works, but it seems to be a matter of chemistry; in other words, it is caused by the effect which two or three chemical substances have on each other. However it is done, the insects have a rather better way of making light than man has yet discovered, for they do not waste any of their energy in the form of heat, as an electric light bulb does. Many other insects give off light in some way, but none seems able to control it like the firefly.

**FIREMAKING.** Before matches were invented men had to find some way of making fire. At first they had to depend on fires caused by the sun's rays falling on dry leaves, which burst into flame when they were hot enough. (The Greek legend of how Prometheus brought fire down to men from heaven comes from this. The story is told in the article PROMETHEUS.) Gradually, however, all sorts of other ways of making fire were found, so that men could make it when they wanted to. It is said that some primitive peoples, such as the Andaman islanders of the Bay of Bengal, still cannot make it for themselves, but have to get it from some other tribe and then keep it going.

Many ways of making fire have been used among the various peoples of the world. All of them were aimed at making a spark which would set light to dry sticks, leaves or grass. Some people got sparks by striking pieces of flint together and sparks are still sometimes made by striking a piece of flint against steel, in places where it is too damp for matches. The best kind of flint for striking sparks has some iron in it.

Another more common way of making fire was by rubbing sticks together until they were so hot that a spark came from them. The people of the Pacific islands rubbed a stick quickly up and down a groove in a piece of wood, and a people in Burma used to fix a bamboo cane so that it did not move, and then rub another cane along it. The Balkan people, in southern Europe, used to rub two dry sticks quickly against one another. It often takes a long time to make a spark by these methods, and it is not always easy to get the fuel of wood or leaves alight with it.

Another way to start a fire is by making the sun's rays gather together on one spot which gets so hot that it starts to burn. This is done by reflecting the rays in a mirror or letting them shine through a magnifying glass.

The most common way of making fire has been with a fire drill. In this a hole is made in a solid piece of wood which lies on the ground. A sharp-pointed stick is fitted into this hole and then spun round as fast as possible. Sometimes people do this by rubbing the stick backwards and forwards between the palms of their hands; sometimes they wind a cord round the stick and then unwind it very quickly so that the stick spins round. The sparks that fly out as the stick spins set fire to the fuel that has been put near by. Boy Scouts still sometimes learn to make fire this way, using a bow in the manner shown in the illustration.

Fire is so important to men that many ancient peoples thought it was sacred, as some still do. The sticks used to make sparks are often specially sacred, and are kept by the chief of the tribe. Some peoples have thought that fire is like a man's life. Fire is born and has to be fed (with fuel) and dies, like a human being; a man has two parents, and so does fire (the board and the twirling stick).

Sometimes it is the custom for a woman to hold the board while a man twirls the stick in the hole, as if they were parents of the fire.

There are often ceremonies for keeping the fire alight. Some African tribes have a sacred fire in the hut of the chief's most important wife, and all new fires are lit from this. The early Israelites kept a fire burning in the most holy place in the temple. The sacred fire was never allowed to go out. In ancient Rome there was a temple of Vesta, the goddess of the hearth, where a sacred fire was kept going by specially chosen women called the Vestal Virgins who were whipped if they let the fire go out. Among some people the sacred fire is put out on solemn feast days, and a new one is lit with special ceremonies and sacrifices.

**FIREPLACE.** From very early times men have made fires to cook their food or warm themselves, and for centuries the hearth or fireplace has been thought of as the centre of family life. The round stone huts of the early Britons on Dartmoor had a hearthstone on the mud floor. These huts had no chimneys and the smoke escaped through the door or through the roof made of boughs and turf.

Fireplaces like this, with no chimneys, were sometimes used even in the great houses of the middle ages, such as Penshurst in Kent. At Penshurst the fireplace is just a raised stone slab in the middle of the hall, with a turret in the roof far above to draw off the smoke. However, most fireplaces were made against a wall, with a hole or flue sloping up to the outside of the wall to carry away the smoke. The smoke was gathered into this flue by a great hood over the fireplace. This hood was wide at the bottom and narrow at the top and stuck out perhaps five feet into the room. It was shaped like a lady's mantle (cloak), and that is how the word "mantelpiece" began. If the hood was made of stone, it was usually held up at the sides on pillars, and this made an opening with room for several people to stand.

Sometimes wooden hoods were used instead of stone, and these were hung on the wall when

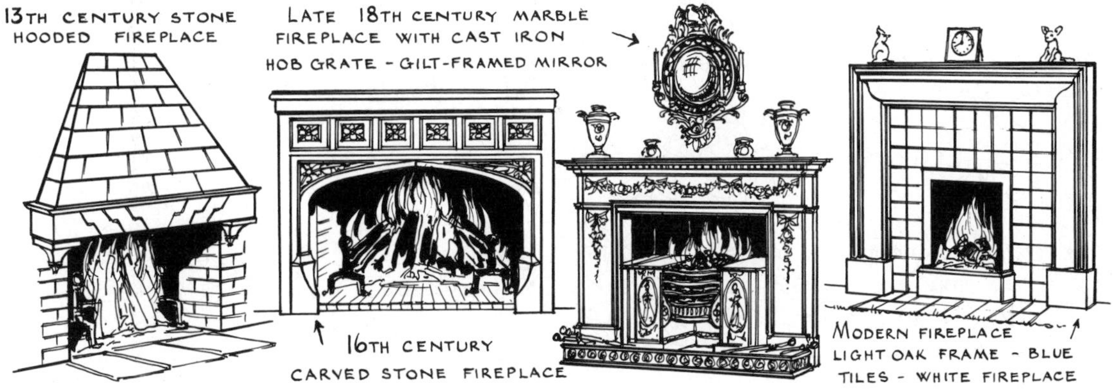

the family went away. In smaller houses, hoods were of wickerwork plastered over, or covered with cloth or brown paper. The fire was made with wood laid on iron supports called dogs.

When chimneys came to be made instead of holes in the wall, hoods were no longer needed because the smoke rose more quickly of its own accord. The fireplace was set back in the wall and the opening was made lower. Fireplaces in Tudor times usually had a wide opening about four feet high, with an arch over it, flat against the wall. The mantelpiece became a very important part of the room, with a complicated stone design that often reached to the ceiling and included the family coat of arms. At the back of the fireplace was a richly decorated iron "fireback" to stop the fire burning the wall.

Till about the year 1700, wood was generally burnt in fires and so fireplaces still had to be made wide and deep enough to hold logs. When coal began to be used, however, the design of fireplaces changed and iron grates, pokers and fenders came into use. The coal was placed in an open grate on legs, called a basket. Because the coal was lifted off the hearth in this way, there was a strong draught under it which made the coal burn quickly, and meant also that a lot of heat was wasted up the chimney. Near the end of the 18th century fireplaces were made smaller to stop waste of this kind, but grates were still raised well above the hearth until the 20th century when lower grates were introduced to save fuel and warm the room better.

The designs of fireplaces have changed through the ages from the richly carved mantelpieces of Tudor times to the plain shelf of today. In the 18th century, many very beautiful fireplaces were designed by the architect Robert Adam, who is described in a separate article.

**FIRES OF LONDON.** When people talk about the Fire of London they mean the Great Fire of 1666. This was not the first time that large parts of London had been destroyed by fire, for that happened in 798, 982 and 1212. Nor was it the last time, for there were fires in the 1800s and again in World Wars I and II.

The Great Fire was discovered at 2 a.m. on September 2, 1666, in a wooden house in Pudding Lane that belonged to the King's baker, John Farynor. Pudding Lane was a narrow street of crowded houses near London Bridge. The fire spread only slowly at first, and many people at the time blamed the Lord Mayor, Sir Thomas Bludworth, for not putting it out before it had a chance to spread. It seems, however, that the people themselves did little to stop it. In his diary Sir John Evelyn said, "they hardly stirred to quench it . . . without at all attempting to save even their goods". Samuel Pepys, another famous diarist, also gives an account of the Fire (see PEPYS, SAMUEL). By eight o'clock the flames were racing onwards through the crowded wooden houses, helped by a strong wind from the northeast. London Bridge and the houses on it (bridges often had houses built on them in those days) were blazing, and that night Londoners saw their city being burned. The next day Lombard Street and Cornhill were destroyed, and on the third day, the Royal Exchange (the business centre), Guildhall (the "town hall" of London), the Custom House and St. Paul's were wholly or partly burned down. By this time the King and his brother, the Duke of York, had taken charge of the fire-fighting operations (which consisted largely of blowing up houses to stop the progress of the flames), and mercifully the wind died down, so by the fourth day the fire was almost out.

At the end of the Great Fire most of the older part of London had been wiped out. In addition to the buildings already mentioned, the following were destroyed: 13,200 houses, 89 churches, 52 halls belonging to guilds (see GUILD), such as the Merchant Taylors' Hall, 4 bridges, 4 prisons and 400 streets. Strangely enough, only 6 people were killed, so far as we know. To commemorate the Great Fire a monument (now called "The Monument") was built close to the place in Pudding Lane where it started. The Monument is a pillar 202 feet high with golden "flames" coming out of a bowl at the top.

Though this fire caused so much loss it was in some ways a good thing, for the old city was dirty and overcrowded, and in these unhealthy conditions the Great Plague (see LONDON) of the

*Radio Times Hulton Picture Library*

Londoners escaping from the Great Fire of 1666. It raged for four days, destroying most of the older part of London.

year before still lingered on. Apart from that, the streets of the old city were too narrow for the coaches of the 17th century, and when they were destroyed it gave a chance for wider ones to be made. Fine new buildings replaced the old ones, many of them designed by Sir Christopher Wren, who is most famous for his rebuilding of St. Paul's Cathedral (see WREN, SIR CHRISTOPHER).

In the 19th century there were several big fires in London, but they were nothing like the Great Fire. In 1834 the Houses of Parliament were burned down. In 1838 the Royal Exchange (which had been rebuilt after the Great Fire and was opened in 1670) was destroyed. In 1861 a fire in the docks round Bermondsey destroyed wharves, boats, barges and shops. In 1866 the Crystal Palace (see EXHIBITIONS) caught fire for the first time—and was damaged by fire in 1923 and 1936 before the last building was destroyed by fire in 1950. Paper in a printer's warehouse in the City of London went up in flames in 1893 and started a fire that destroyed an immense block of warehouses and offices. It lasted all day and many of the fire engines of London went to fight the flames.

In World War I the Germans sent Zeppelins (see AIRSHIP) to raid London and in the second of these raids, in 1915, 29 fires were started. In World War II the Germans made their first big air attack on London on September 7, 1940, hitting the dock areas and causing great fires. On the night of December 29–30 the whole district round St. Paul's was set alight by fire bombs. St. Paul's, in the middle of it all, escaped the flames thanks largely to the efforts of the firewatchers on duty there. (Later, arrangements were made for firewatchers to be on duty in other City buildings.) On April 16 and 17, 1941, there were more great fires caused in the same way. The House of Commons was destroyed by fire on May 10 of that year. As many of these attacks hit the City of London they destroyed a great number of the churches and other buildings put up after the Great Fire in 1666.

**FIRE WALKING.** There seems to be no doubt that after some kind of religious preparation people have walked over hot embers or ashes with bare feet and not been burned. No one has really explained how this is possible, except to say that it must be something to do with the state of mind of the fire walkers.

Fire walking is done either as part of the worship of a god or as a proof of innocence. When people suspected of crime were made to fire walk, it was believed that they were innocent if they were not burned at all. In some cases, where priests walked over embers or even through flames, it was done in order that the harvest that year should be good.

Fire walking still goes on in India, the Fiji Islands, Tahiti, Japan, Bulgaria and Trinidad.

**FIREWORKS.** A firework consists of a "case", generally of paper and in the form of a tube, filled with firework (or "pyrotechnic") mixture. Such mixtures are so made that they are able to burn without the aid of oxygen from the air. A candle burning in an enclosed space will go out as soon as the oxygen in the air surrounding it is used up; not so a firework mixture. Although a firework case may be entirely filled with a mixture so that no air whatever is present, the contents will burn until they are entirely consumed. The reason for this is that

*Fox Photos*

A fireworks display lighting up the River Thames during Coronation Night, 1953.

one of the substances in the mixture holds a supply of oxygen which it readily gives up.

For many centuries the chemical used for this was *saltpetre*, potassium nitrate. This salt is found throughout the East and it was there that firework mixtures of saltpetre, sulphur and charcoal first appeared. Although gunpowder is made with those same substances it was not until guns were invented in Europe at the beginning of the 14th century that a particular mixture of them came to be known as gunpowder. (See EXPLOSIVE.) Meanwhile such mixtures were used in China in making fireworks, both for war and for fun.

Knowledge of fireworks spread to Europe during the 13th century and developed rapidly, first in Italy, then in France and other countries. Displays were first given in connection with religious festivals, but later came to be a feature of most public national rejoicings. These firework displays were usually carried out by military engineers called "fireworkers". During the 18th century, a growing number of civilian "pyrotechnists" or firework makers provided one of the main attractions at the public pleasure gardens which had sprung up round most European cities. Such displays grew more and more elaborate; those at Vauxhall Gardens, London, remained outstanding until surpassed by the famous Crystal Palace displays staged by C. T. Brock. Beginning in 1865, they continued until the destruction of the building in 1936.

Until the beginning of the 19th century, the only colours known in fireworks were those of ordinary flame; then the introduction of the chemical potassium chlorate in the 18th century made real colours possible. A mixture containing it burns with sufficient heat to turn a metal to gas, so tinting the resulting flame. (See FLAME.) Barium salts give green, strontium red, sodium yellow, and copper, in the presence of chlorine gas given off by the burning potassium chlorate, blue.

Fireworks are of two main types, those producing flame and those giving force and sparks. The ones that produce flame have thin cases, which burn away as the mixture they contain is consumed. This class includes coloured lights of all kinds and the stars which are thrown out by rockets, shells and roman candles.

The cases of the second type are sufficiently thick and strong to remain unburnt. The pressure set up by the gases resulting from the mixture burning inside the case throws out a jet of partly consumed particles, or sparks, to give the well-known golden rain and similar effects. Such ingredients as iron or steel filings, lamp-black or an excess of charcoal give varying results. It is this internal pressure in a strong, specially designed case, that provides the motive power of the rocket. (See ROCKET.)

**FIRST AID** is the branch of medical science in which treatment is given to people suffering from accidents or from sudden illness. It is called first aid because the treatment must be given at once, and, as it is usually not possible to get a doctor or a nurse to the patient immediately, the first aid may be given by a person who has learned a few simple rules about looking after injured or sick people, but who is not a doctor. First aid is usually not enough to make the patient recover completely, but is given to prevent him from getting any worse while waiting for a doctor to come or for a hospital ambulance to arrive.

A very important point is that the person giving first aid must always remain as calm as possible, or else the patient will grow frightened and the treatment may be unsuccessful. Unless the injury or illness is so serious that the patient is in danger of dying, the treatment should always be given slowly and carefully, or it may not be successful.

Another important point when an accident has taken place is to consider whether there is any danger of the patient being further injured. If a man has been knocked down by a car he should either be lifted on to the pavement or bystanders should signal to other traffic either to go another way or to stop. While the person is being moved, any injured parts, such as broken limbs, should be supported carefully. If, after a bad accident, there is likely to be delay before a doctor comes, the patient should be taken care of in some sheltered place; a house, for instance.

After an accident, get help without delay.

In every case needing first aid the patient should be put in a comfortable position, usually flat on his back, and (unless he is unconscious) warned not to move in case he hurts himself. Anything that may cause death, such as asphyxia, or stoppage of breathing, or severe bleeding should be attended to first. These are the two worst conditions and must always be treated at once.

The patient ought to be kept warm while he is being treated, and tight clothing round the neck, chest and waist should be undone. If he is unconscious, his head should be turned to one side and his false teeth, if he has any, taken out. This is because they may become loose and choke him.

*Shock*. This is a dangerous condition that follows many accidents and sometimes occurs in sudden illness. The patient looks as if he has fainted. His face is pale and his lips and cheeks may be blue. His skin is cold and clammy while the pulse is quick and feeble. He does not always lose consciousness, but instead is nervous and frightened and complains of thirst.

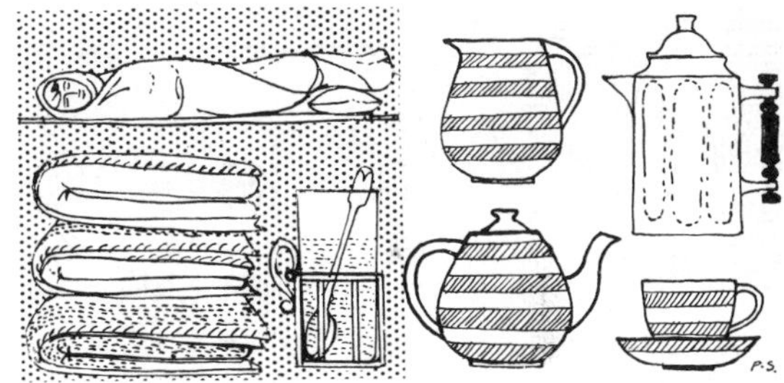

Treatment for shock.

After a bad accident, treatment for shock should be started at once, even before its signs appear, since it is often delayed. The patient must be kept warm by being wrapped in blankets. The legs must be raised and supported while the head and shoulders are kept low. Small quantities of liquids given frequently are helpful; suitable drinks include hot tea and coffee with plenty of sugar, meat extracts and salt and water—half a teaspoonful of salt to each pint of water.

*Wounds*. Whenever the skin is broken, even

by a scratch, germs can enter. The wound becomes painful, looks unhealthy and may discharge a sticky whitish substance known as pus. Occasionally the germs enter the bloodstream and cause septicaemia, or blood poisoning, so no wound, however small, should be neglected.

The germs which cause poisoning may come from the cause of the accident, such as the metal of a car, the air, dust, the patient's skin, or from the hands or breath of the person giving first aid, who must therefore wash his hands thoroughly or bathe his fingers with an antiseptic before he treats the wound. He must also handle dressings—bandages and so on—as little as possible and avoid sneezing and coughing near the wound.

Cleansing to remove germs which have already entered should only be undertaken for wounds that are so small that the patient will not have to go to a doctor. Small pads of cotton wool soaked in an antiseptic should be dabbed over the wound and squeezed so that the lotion penetrates it. After it has been cleansed, the wound and surrounding skin should be mopped over with surgical spirit.

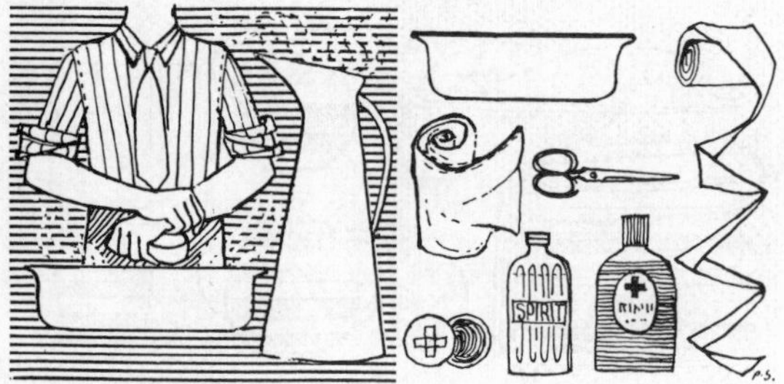


Things to remember when dressing a wound.

Every wound should be covered with a dressing, and the best ways of doing this are described in the article BANDAGE. Ready-made or "standard" dressings and bandages should be used whenever possible since they are sterile, or free from living germs.

A dangerous wound is the puncture kind caused by a stab, bullet or dog-bite. This wound is small but it is often deep. A way of dealing with a puncture wound in the chest before the doctor comes is by covering it immediately with an airtight dressing; for example, a thick layer of petroleum jelly may be spread between two pieces of lint and then strapped firmly in position over the wound with adhesive plaster.

*Bleeding.* Serious bleeding must be stopped in a very short time. First the wound should be firmly pressed with the thumbs, fingers or palm of the hand. If possible, the wound should be covered with a piece of sterile material before pressing. When there is something in the wound, such as a piece of glass, the thumbs should be pressed on the sides of the wound so that the patient is not hurt too much.

After this pressure, a dressing which includes a thick pad of cotton-wool should be placed over the wound and bandaged tightly. If blood oozes through the dressing, it must be left on and another pad placed on top and bandaged even more firmly.

If the bleeding still continues in spite of this treatment, the blood supply to the wound must be stopped for a short time, and this is done in one or other of the following ways. A bandage of rubber or soft material is bound tightly round the limb between the wound and the heart; it is known as a "constrictive bandage". Otherwise, the main blood vessel leading to the wound must be pressed at the pressure point—any place in the body at which an artery can be pressed against the bone. As the arteries, or main blood vessels, come straight from the heart, a cut in one of them causes the blood to gush out in spurts in time with the beating of the heart.

Whichever of these two methods is used, the pressure must be released every 15 minutes, or else, as no blood is going to the limb, it may develop the dangerous condition known as gangrene. A constrictive bandage is applied only in the last resort to stop bleeding.

Some people are likely to lose a lot of blood from the nose. When a nose bleed occurs, it is sometimes safe to let it go on for a minute or two. If, however, it shows no sign of stopping, then the patient should sit (not lie) down. He must be told not to swallow blood nor to blow his nose and to breathe through his mouth. Generally the bleeding is in one nostril only, and so a finger should be pressed against the side of the nose to compress the blood vessel that is causing the bleeding. Sometimes it helps to put cold compresses, which are pads of material soaked in ice-cold water, on the bridge of the nose. If a nose bleed is still going on, a doctor should be called in.

When a person has had a tooth out and blood is flowing from the socket, the raw area should be covered with a small pad of lint or cotton-wool with a hard object, such as a cork, placed on top of it. The patient must then bite on the cork. Neither nose bleeding nor bleeding from a tooth socket is often serious.

*Asphyxia.* A person who cannot breathe is in danger of asphyxia, or suffocation, and this comes about from many different causes. The person may be choking with a lump of food stuck in his windpipe, or he may have breathed in a poisonous gas, such as coal gas. A common cause of asphyxia is drowning, when, even after the person has been taken out of the water, he is still in danger from the water he has breathed into his lungs.

First-aid medical treatment cannot be started on a patient suffering from asphyxia, except in the case of choking, until he has been rescued from whatever is causing the asphyxia and has been moved into fresh air. Artificial respiration, which is described in the article LIFE SAVING, should then be applied. When the patient has recovered he must be told to lie down for a time and keep quiet.

A person who is choking must have the lump in his throat removed as soon as possible, and this can be done by leaning him forward and thumping him smartly on the back between the shoulder blades while he coughs in order to bring up the lump. If this does not move the lump, then his mouth should be opened and the person giving first aid should pass his forefinger down his throat, hook it round the lump and draw it up into the mouth.

When it is a small child who is choking, he should be held upside down, as this is sometimes enough to bring the lump into his mouth. If not, he should be thumped between the shoulders.

*Electric Shocks.* In the case of a person suffering from an electric shock, the electric current must be switched off quickly. Sometimes, however, this cannot be done, and so the patient must be pushed away from the electricity. In order to prevent the current from passing through the patient to the person giving first aid, he should only be touched with something that does not conduct electricity. (See ELECTRICITY.) A good example of this is a dry wooden pole. Another way of protection is for

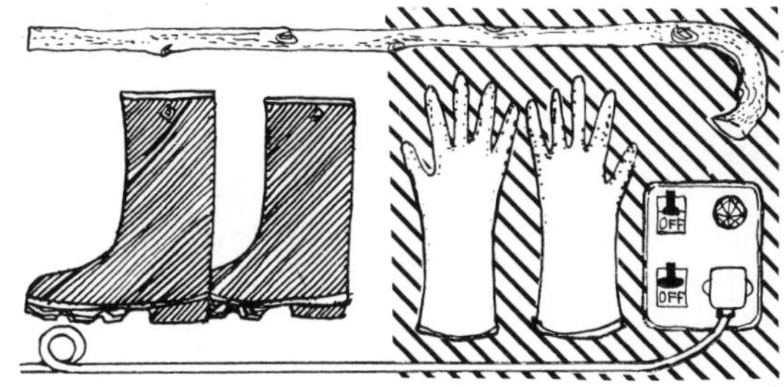


In a case of electric shock, switch off the current if possible. Otherwise, push the patient away from the electric point with a stick, or wear rubber boots and gloves when touching him.

the first aider to stand on a thick rubber mat or to wear rubber boots or thick rubber gloves.

*Burns and Scalds.* These are dangerous if much of the skin is affected. They are particularly dangerous to children or old people. In such cases the patient must be treated for shock and taken to hospital without delay. An absolutely clean dressing—sheet or handkerchief—should be used to cover the area. The injury itself should not be treated by the first aider.

When the burn or scald is only a small one, it should be covered with a clean, dry dressing and firmly bandaged (unless there are blisters, in which case it should be lightly bandaged). The patient should be given large quantities of warm liquids—preferably weak tea sweetened with sugar—but on no account should any lotions be applied to the burn or scald.

If a person's clothes are on fire he should be laid on the ground and the flames smothered by a rug or mat. Any water near at hand should be thrown on to the flames. Then the treatment for dangerous cases must be applied.

*Fractures.* A fracture is a broken bone, and there are several kinds of fracture, the most important being simple and compound. In a simple fracture there is no wound or injury to a nerve or vital organ; in a compound fracture there is a wound as well as a fracture and germs may enter and cause blood poisoning. Sometimes the wound is caused by sharp, jagged ends of the broken bone piercing through the flesh and skin, and this will happen if the patient does not lie still after his accident or if the first aider handles him carelessly. The wound of a compound fracture must be covered at once with a dressing.

Pain and shock are signs of fracture. The injured limb often swells, looks out of shape and

Do not attempt to set a fracture. Cover the wound if there is one and give treatment for shock.

hurts if touched. This is known as tenderness, and it is a rule that if an area of tenderness is discovered a fracture should be suspected, even if there are no other signs of one. A doctor should be called in and no attempt should be made to set the fracture.

*Dislocations.* A dislocation is the injury that occurs by the bones of a joint moving out of place. The symptoms and signs are very like those of a fracture, except that the injured joint becomes locked and cannot be moved by the patient or the first aider. It is difficult to discover a dislocation without X-raying the injury, and in first aid it is usually treated like a fracture. Pain can be eased by cold compresses.

*Sprains and Strains.* A sprain occurs when a joint is wrenched or twisted and the ligaments, which are tough bands holding the bones together, are torn. The treatment is to cover the joint with cotton-wool and to bandage it firmly, supporting the limb in a raised position.

A strain is caused by the stretching or tearing of a muscle, often in the back, the forearm or the calf of the leg. A person with a strained muscle feels intense pain, almost as though he had been struck by a whip, and swelling and bruising follow. The strained part should be kept warm by either a hot-water bottle or hot compresses.

*Fainting and Fits.* People faint, or lose consciousness, for several reasons, among which are heat, fright or the sight of blood. Because it is caused by a short stoppage of blood to the brain, a person may sometimes be prevented from fainting if he is seated in a chair and his head is bent down to his knees, in order to bring the blood back again. However, when a patient actually does faint, he should be laid flat and treated like a case of shock.

Besides fainting, unconsciousness is also caused by fits. Epileptics, who are people suffering from the disease called epilepsy, fall down in fits every now and then, losing consciousness, becoming stiff all over and then jerking violently. Epileptic fits are not dangerous and they pass off in a few minutes. The only first aid that need be given is to support the patient's head and put some suitable object, such as a pencil, between his teeth to prevent him from biting his tongue.

*Eye Injuries.* Tiny objects, such as pieces of grit or flies, often get into the eye and cause pain. They should be removed quickly, and the patient must not be allowed to rub or poke his eye at all, or else the object (or foreign body, as it is usually called) may damage the eye.

The first thing to do is to find the exact position of the foreign body in the eye, if it cannot already be seen. The patient should be told to sit down and to put his head back. First the lower eyelid should be turned down so that the inner surface can be seen. If the foreign body is still invisible, the patient should be told to relax and look downwards. Then the first aider must grasp the eyelashes of the upper lid and turn the lid upwards until its inner surface can be seen. (There is a special knack of doing this and no untrained person should attempt it.) As soon as the foreign body is found, it must be removed with the corner of a clean handkerchief or with a damp wisp of cotton-wool.

If, however, the foreign body is stuck to the cornea, which is the transparent front of the eye, the first aider must not attempt to remove it, but should simply put in a few drops of castor oil and cover the eye with a pad and a bandage before taking the patient to a doctor.

*Other Injuries.* Young children sometimes push small hard objects such as beans or marbles up their noses or into their ears. It is best to leave these alone and take the child to a doctor, for a first aider often simply manages to push the foreign body in a little farther. The child must not, of course, be allowed to touch the affected part at all.

Great care must be taken when splinters of wood or glass are being removed from the skin. If the forceps (an instrument that looks something like pliers) do not grip the splinter firmly, the end may break off and leave the other half still embedded in the skin. A splinter under the nail is even harder to get rid of, and it is best to take the patient straight to a doctor for this.

*Poison*. A person may be poisoned in many ways besides getting infected wounds or breathing in dangerous gas. He may eat food that has gone bad or take an overdose of medicine, such as sleeping pills. Children sometimes eat poisonous berries, about the commonest being those of the deadly nightshade plant, and toadstools and other poisonous fungi are sometimes cooked and eaten in mistake for mushrooms. When a case of poisoning is discovered, first aid must be given immediately, after sending for a doctor.

Except in the case of corrosives, or burning poisons, such as ammonia, caustic soda, many acids and some disinfectants, the poison must be removed from the stomach by making the patient sick. This is done by giving what is known as an emetic. A simple emetic is two

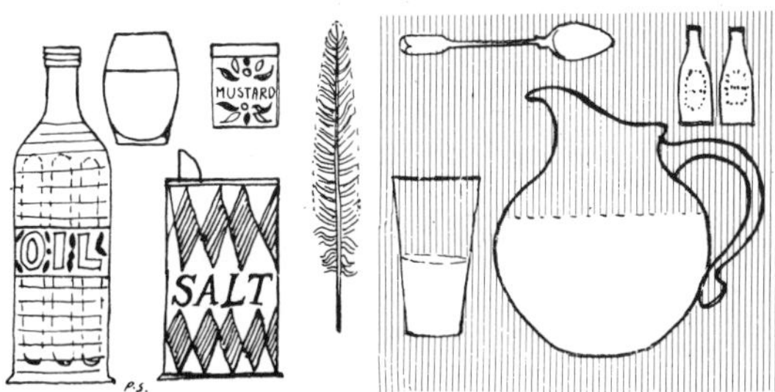


First aid for poisoning.

tablespoonfuls of salt, or one tablespoonful of mustard, in a glass of lukewarm water. Next, large drinks of lukewarm water should be given, and other methods of making the patient sick should be tried. One that seldom fails is tickling the back of the throat (inside!) with a straw or a feather. If the patient has not been sick at the end of ten minutes, another emetic should be given.

When the patient has been sick he should be given an antidote. This is a substance which fights the poison and generally turns it into something harmless. (A list of antidotes is given in the article POISONS.) If a corrosive poison has been swallowed, the antidote should be given immediately without any attempt to make the patient sick.

All cases of poisoning should be treated for shock, and soothing drinks or mixtures, such as milk, barley water, salad or olive oil, gruel or a paste of flour and water, should be given to protect the lining of the digestive system.

Many of the treatments suggested in this article should if possible be carried out only by a qualified first aider. First aid training is of course very valuable for everybody and people should try to take the opportunity of receiving some instruction in it.

**FISH** are cold-blooded animals with a backbone and a jaw. They have fins instead of limbs and, with a few exceptions, spend all their lives in water.

As can be seen from the diagram, the body of a fish is quite different from that of a land animal. The fins are of two kinds, paired and unpaired. The paired fins are the pectorals and the pelvics, and one of each is on either side of the body. The pelvic fins are usually situated nearer the tail than the pectoral fins. The unpaired fins are the dorsals on the back and the ventrals or anals on the underside, and the fish may have only one of each. The caudal or tail fin is usually the main means of propelling the fish through the water, although the pectoral fins may sometimes be used for this purpose. The fins are supported by rays and it is often possible to distinguish between closely related types of fishes by counting the fin rays.

There is a great variation in the size, shape and use of the fins. The pectoral fins are generally used for steering or propulsion, but sometimes they have other uses. For example, some of the rays of these fins may be very long and used as feelers, as in the thread-fins. In the so-called flying fish the long pectoral fins almost reach the tail. These fish do not fly by flapping their fins, but merely glide. However, the hatchet fishes of South America can flap their pectoral fins as if they were wings, and the tropical fish called the mud-skipper has strong pectoral fins which it uses almost like limbs for walking on mud banks.

The pelvic fins are mainly used to keep the fish steady. In many fishes, however, they form a sucker, and in others they have long rays which serve as feelers. The position of the pelvics varies in different fishes. In some they may be in the middle of the underside or else below—or even in front of—the pectorals. Others have very small pelvics, and some, such as the eels, have none at all.

The dorsal fin may extend along the whole length of the body and may join the tail fin. Sometimes the front dorsal fin rays are spiny, like those of the John Dory, or like a streamer, as in the oar fish. In the remora the dorsal fin has become a powerful sucker situated on the head. In the angler fishes the first ray of the dorsal fin is long and is used to attract the attention of other fishes.

The shape of the body of fishes is quite as varied as that of the fins described above, and this is because the shape is usually suited to the habits of the fish. Fast moving fishes are streamlined, while fishes living on the bottom are usually flattened.

## Breathing, Blood and Internal Organs

Fish breathe by means of gills, and these are always found between the mouth and the beginning of the gut, or food tract. This region of the body is called the pharynx. In sharks the walls of the pharynx have a series of narrow slits in them which open from the pharynx to the outside water. Thus water can be taken in through the mouth and passed out over the gills. In the bony fishes, which are the most common, these gill slits are covered by a moveable bony plate called the operculum, or gill cover, so they cannot be seen until the operculum is raised away from the body of the fish. The gills are sausage-shaped structures which are supported by a special part of the skeleton called gill arches.

Only a few fishes can breathe in air as mammals do. (See BREATHING.) Most kinds must have water passing over their gills, and it is from this water that the fish gets its supply of oxygen, which passes through the thin wall of the gills into the blood. Carbon dioxide is passed from the blood through the gills and into the water. When a fish breathes it takes water into its mouth, then closes its mouth, and the pharynx

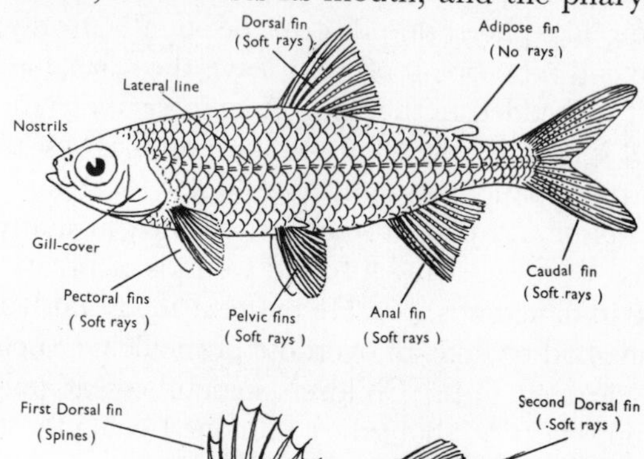


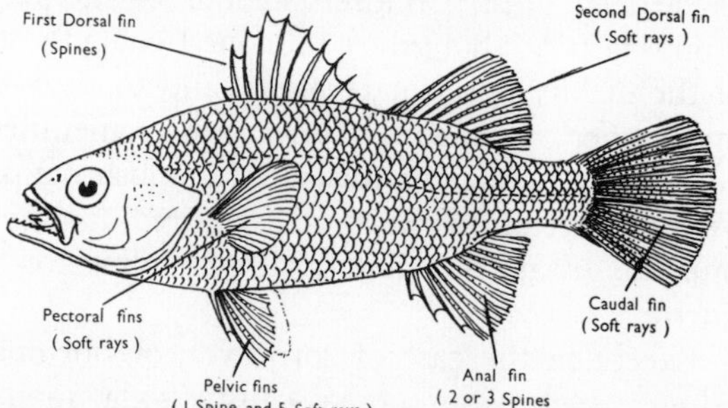


becomes compressed, or smaller, so the water is pushed out over the gills.

Fishes have a well-developed blood system. The heart pumps the blood to the gills, and from there it is carried by blood vessels (arteries) all over the body. Eventually it is carried back to the heart by the veins. Fish are cold-blooded, which means that the temperature of their blood is only very slightly higher than that of the water in which they live. Therefore fish are very sensitive to changes of water temperature. When the water is too cold they become sluggish and eat very little, but on the other hand many fish become sick and die if the water becomes much warmer than it is normally.

The alimentary, or food, canal is rather like that in mammals. Food, which may be animals or plants or both, is taken in at the mouth, but is not digested (broken up) until it reaches the stomach, which is usually U-shaped. There a digestive juice acts on the food, which then passes into the intestine, or gut—a long, coiled tube.

There the partly digested food is mixed up with more digestive juices which are formed in the liver and pancreas. It is then taken up by the blood and carried to various parts of the body where it is used to supply energy. Some of the food may be stored as fat around the gut and in the muscle, and it is because of this store of fat and oils that salmon and herring are such excellent food.

Also to be found in the body cavity of fish are the kidneys, which are generally long, thin, dark red organs alongside the backbone. There are also the gonads, which in the female fish are called ovaries and produce eggs (hard roe), and in the male fish are called testes and produce the sperm or milt (soft roe).

## Other Organs

Many fishes have an organ called the air bladder just below the kidneys. This may be used as a lung, a float or to produce sound. In primitive fishes the air bladder may be connected to the gut. When it is used as a float the air bladder enables the fish to adjust itself to different pressures of water. In the air bladder are small areas supplied with blood vessels, from which gases can be passed into the bladder. In other areas gas is absorbed from the bladder. However, this is a slow process and a fish caught in deep water and pulled very quickly to the surface will swell because the air in the bladder has expanded as the pressure on the fish has been reduced too quickly. Normally the fish can protect itself against changes in pressure by absorbing some of the air from the bladder into the blood stream.

Fishes can be taught to remember such things as smell and even colour, as they have quite well-developed nervous systems. The nostrils open into little sacs into which water enters, and the sense of smell is good. Many fishes hunt by smell, and some, like the salmon, use their sense of smell when migrating, or travelling from place to place.

The eyes of fish are suited to seeing under water, but most kinds are not able to focus both eyes on one object at the same time. One curious fish from Central America has eyes which stick out and each eye is divided in two, the upper half being focused for seeing in air and the lower half for seeing under water.

It is doubtful whether fishes hear as people do, but they are very sensitive to vibrations in the water. The ear of a fish is entirely under the skin. In many fishes some of the water vibrations may be picked up and magnified by the air bladder and carried to the ear by three little bones at the front of the air bladder. As in human beings, the ear of a fish is also concerned with balance. In the inner ear are three canals which are lined with a sensitive tissue and filled with a fluid. These canals contain the otoliths, or ear-bones, which are produced from a substance given out by the walls of the canals and increase in size as the fish grows, so they can be used for telling the age of a fish. At the end of each canal is a swelling and there the lining is very sensitive. When a fish turns on its side the otoliths roll and touch the sensitive tissue. A message is sent to the brain along a nerve and the fish then knows that it is not upright.

## The Lateral Line and Sense of Touch

Another sense organ found in fishes but not in higher animals is called the lateral-line system. This consists of a line of little tubes which end

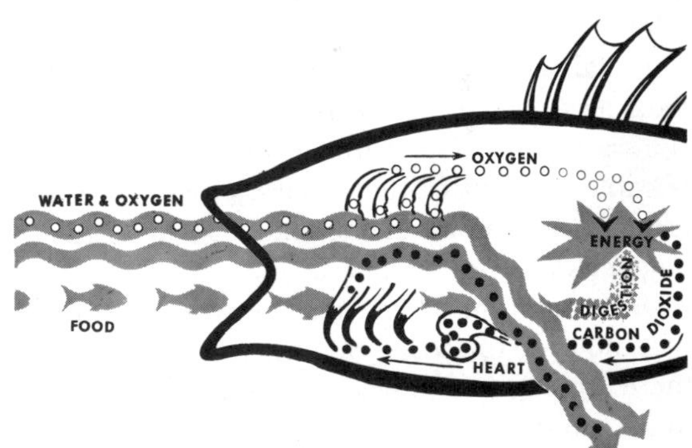


in pores, or openings, along each side of the body and also on the head. Each tube has nerves at its base, and these nerves join together and run to the brain. Complicated experiments have shown that it is more than likely that this lateral-line sense organ can be compared to radar. When a fish swims near a rock the vibrations produced as it swims hit the rock and are reflected and picked up by the lateral-line canals.

That is why fishes can swim quickly in between rocks without hitting them.

Fishes have a keen sense of touch. Spread over the body are tiny buds connected with nerves, and these are most numerous in the barbels, or feelers, around the mouth. Little is known about the sense of taste. Most fishes gobble their food, and many have no tongue, which is where the human taste-sense lies. However, taste buds are scattered over the surface of a fish's body, widely in some kinds, around the mouth in others.

## Scales and Colours

The bodies of most fishes are covered with scales, which vary from the teeth-like scales of sharks to the flat, plate-like scales of the salmon. In the bony fishes the scales can be used to find out the age of the fish. Some fish, such as the sturgeon and the stickleback, have no scales and instead large bony plates are found on parts of the body. In other fishes, such as the armoured cat fish, the sea horse and the pogge, or armed bullhead, nearly all the body is covered in a bony armour. Such fishes are very slow-moving and the armour helps to protect them from their enemies. Other fishes have spines instead of scales. The spines of the puffer fishes stand erect when the fish puffs out its body with air. They are excellent protection against enemies.

Usually the scales of the bony fishes have a fixed arrangement on the body, and by counting the scales on various parts of the body it is often possible to identify the species, or kind, of the fish. For example, in salmon there are 120 to 125 scales along the lateral line, and 10 to 13 scales in a slanting line from the adipose (fat-fin with no rays) to the lateral line, whereas in trout there are 115 to 130 scales along the lateral line and 13 to 16 scales in a slanting line.

Many fishes have vivid colours and striking markings. It is very likely that some colour markings may help fish to recognize their own kind, and in others bright colours may, when displayed quickly, be used to frighten away enemies. In some cases the markings act as camouflage. Perch have bars down the body which help to hide the fish while it swims amongst the weeds. The pipe-fishes look remarkably like the seaweed amongst which they live, and the slender file-fish, which feed by standing on their snouts, look in that position so much like leaves of weed that they are very hard to see. A most peculiar fish, the sea dragon, has spines sticking out of its body, and the skin is drawn out into filaments, or threads, which closely resemble weed. Deep-sea fish, which live where there is little or no light, are usually brown, black or violet-black in colour, and have no spots, bands or other easily noticeable markings.

Fishes can change colour to suit their backgrounds. The colour change may be slow, as in trout and plaice, but some tropical fishes can change almost immediately from black to white, from yellow to scarlet, or from red to a dull green or dark brown. Even though flatfish take a fairly long time to change colour, the result is so successful that they are almost invisible against their surroundings.

In some fishes remarkable changes take place after they are dead; for example, mackerel look brightest a few hours after death. The Romans used to bring living red mullet on to their banqueting tables and watch the vivid colour changes as the fish died.

## Migration and Breeding Habits

The distribution of fishes over the world is an interesting but vast subject. Each species, or kind, of fish has a definite area in which it exists. Even so, fishes may undertake long journeys from one place to another within their area. These journeys (migrations) are carried out for spawning or feeding purposes, and are therefore called spawning or feeding migrations. Eels and salmon carry out spawning migrations and pilchards carry out feeding migrations, during which they come to the coasts of Cornwall from July to October.

At the breeding season, many bony fishes gather together in shoals and the females lay eggs while the males pass out milt, or sperm, which fertilizes the eggs. (See Reproduction.) The fish that spawn in this manner usually produce vast numbers of eggs. A ling was found to have over 28,000,000 eggs in her ovaries (egg-producing organs), a turbot over 9,000,000, and so on. Some fishes have eggs which float at or near the surface of the water and others, for

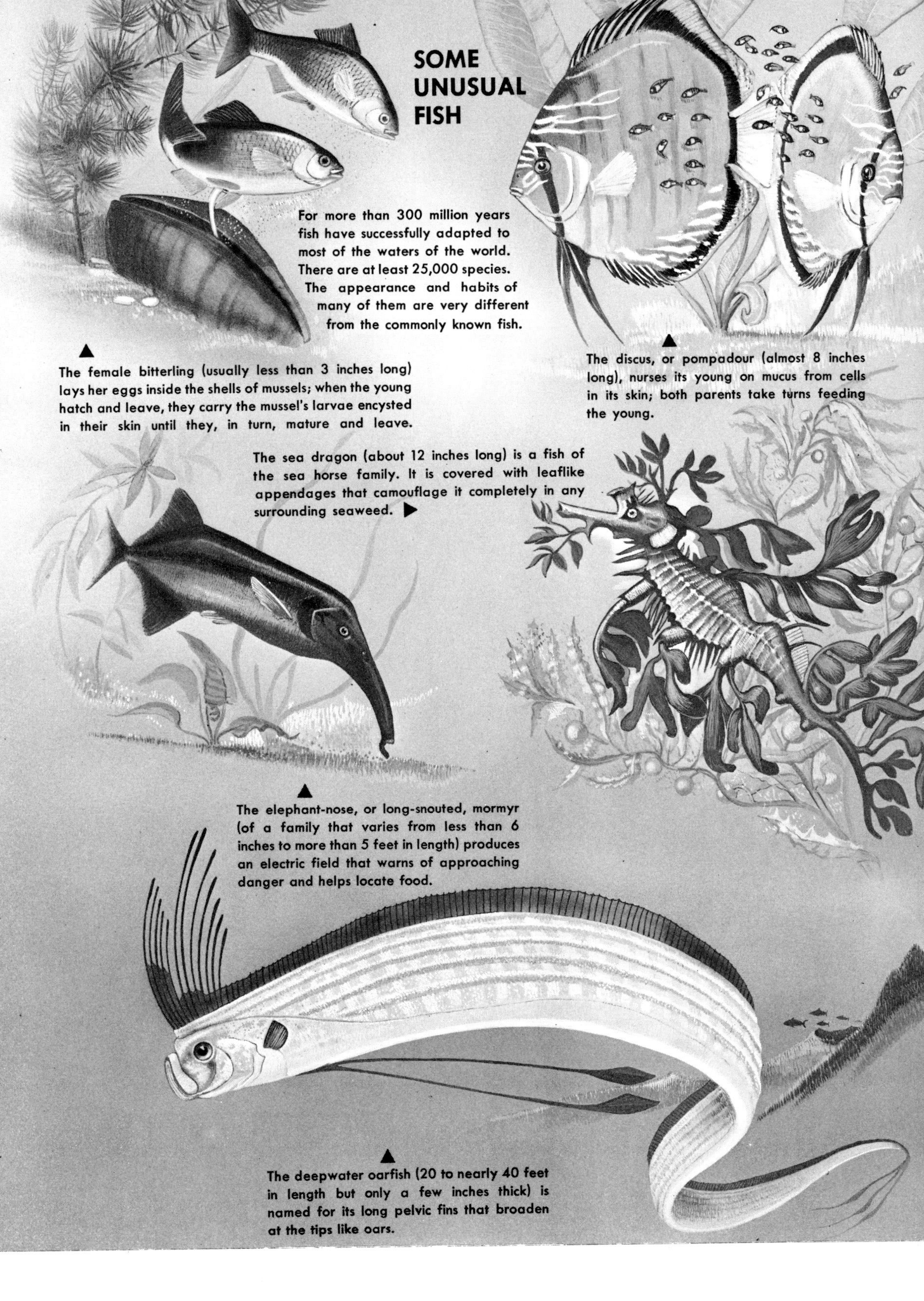

# SOME UNUSUAL FISH

For more than 300 million years fish have successfully adapted to most of the waters of the world. There are at least 25,000 species. The appearance and habits of many of them are very different from the commonly known fish.

▲ The female bitterling (usually less than 3 inches long) lays her eggs inside the shells of mussels; when the young hatch and leave, they carry the mussel's larvae encysted in their skin until they, in turn, mature and leave.

▲ The discus, or pompadour (almost 8 inches long), nurses its young on mucus from cells in its skin; both parents take turns feeding the young.

The sea dragon (about 12 inches long) is a fish of the sea horse family. It is covered with leaflike appendages that camouflage it completely in any surrounding seaweed. ▶

▲ The elephant-nose, or long-snouted, mormyr (of a family that varies from less than 6 inches to more than 5 feet in length) produces an electric field that warns of approaching danger and helps locate food.

▲ The deepwater oarfish (20 to nearly 40 feet in length but only a few inches thick) is named for its long pelvic fins that broaden at the tips like oars.

Chub; 12–24 in. England; Europe to Asia Minor

Barbel; 12–30 in. England, France and Germany to the Danube

Salmon; 20–48 in. North Atlantic coastal regions south to New England and France

Perch; 6–12 in. England, Europe and northern Asia

Pike; 16–40 in. Cool and cold waters of Europe, Asia and North America

Brown trout; 6–12 in. Europe and Asia Minor; introduced into North and South America, Africa, India and New Zealand

Arctic char; 10–16 in. Regions around the pole, south to the Alps, Japan and North America

Roach; 6–12 in. Europe, north of the Alps and Pyrenees

Grayling; 10–20 in. All of Europe except Spain, southern France and Italy

Bleak; 4–8 in. England and Europe, north of the Alps

Tropical two-winged flying fish; 6 in. All tropical oceans

Burrfish; 10 in. Southern coasts of U.S., West Indies

Mud skipper; 8 in. East Indies

Four-eyed fish; 12 in. Rivers of eastern South America

Sea horse; 6 in.
Tropical and temperate oceans

Batfish; 4 in. Tropical and temperate Atlantic

Shrimp fish; 6 in.
East Indies

Cowfish; 15 in. Western tropical Atlantic, Carolinas to Brazil

Sargassum fish; 5 in.
Tropical Atlantic

FISH. These examples of temperate and tropical fish give some idea of the enormously varied shapes and colours which abound in the oceans and rivers of the world. Such variations are the results of millions of years of adaptation to local surroundings.

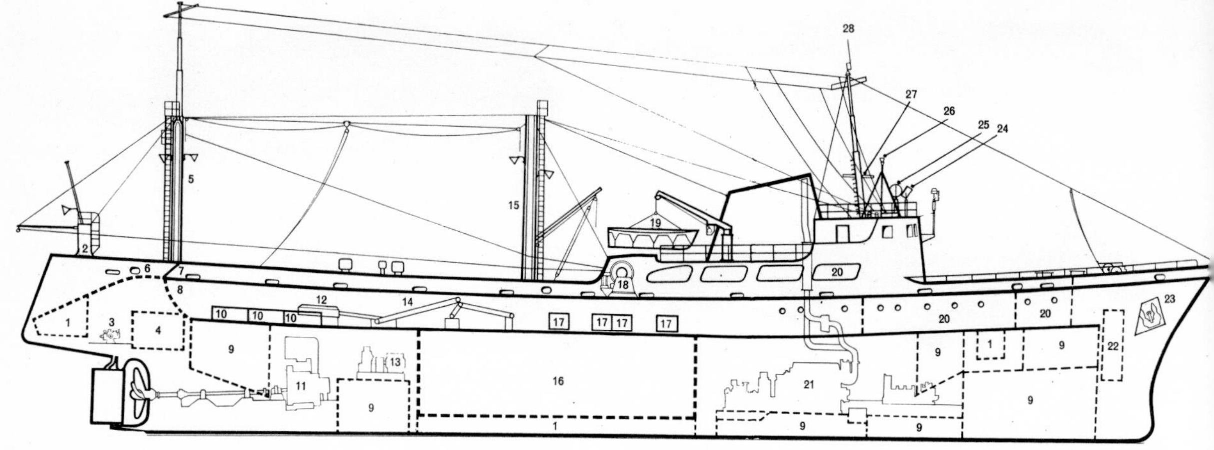

## THE "JUNELLA"

1 Fresh water tank
2 After gantry
3 Steering gear
4 Cod liver oil tanks
5 After bipod mast
6 Stern ramp over which the trawl is hauled
7 Trap-door on main deck
8 Chute from main deck to fish pounds
9 Oil fuel tanks
10 Fish pounds
11 Propulsion motor
12 Fish washing machine
13 Refrigeration compressor
14 Conveyor belts from washer to freezing compartments
15 Forward bipod mast
16 Cold store
17 Freezing cabinets
18 Trawl winch
19 Ship's lifeboat
20 Crew accommodation
21 Diesel engines and electricity generating plant
22 Chain locker
23 Anchor
24 Searchlight
25 Direction finder
26 Fishing lights
27 Radar scanner
28 Mast

*Courtesy, J. Marr and Son Ltd.*

FISHERIES. The "Junella" of Hull, a modern trawler designed for distant-water fishing—which may mean a return voyage of up to 5,000 miles. The trawl is shot and hauled over a ramp at the stern, and the entire catch is frozen directly it has been sorted and cleaned, so that it can be kept in perfect condition in the large cold store amidships. Diesel engines drive electric generators for propelling the trawler and for operating the freezers.

example those of the herring, are heavier than sea water and are deposited in sticky clumps on stony parts of the sea bed. Many fishes migrate into shallow water, where they may place the eggs in carefully prepared nests. Others, such as the American catfishes, protect their eggs by carrying them in their mouths.

In pipe-fishes and sea horses, the male carries the fertilized eggs in pouches on his belly. The eggs hatch there, and afterwards the baby fishes hide in the pouch of the male fish when danger threatens.

A peculiar nest is produced by the fishes called bubble nest builders. The male makes it by blowing bubbles of air and slime to form a floating mass of foam. In the kinds whose eggs are heavier than water the male catches the eggs in his mouth as they fall from the female and places them in the foam, afterwards guarding the nest. Another kind has eggs lighter than water which float up to the foam raft.

## Different Groups of Fishes

More than 30,000 different kinds of fishes are known. Many fossil fishes have been discovered and by studying them we can see how some fishes have changed since they first existed. (See EVOLUTION.) In 1938, a fish called the coelacanth which was thought to have died out some 60 million years ago was caught off the east coast of South Africa. This was truly a "living fossil". Several coelacanths have since been caught and scientists have learnt much about these primitive fish which have hardly changed over the ages. Fishes with features in common are classified, or grouped together. The classification is complicated, but some of the groupings are :

*Sharks and Skates.* These fish, together with some others, have a skeleton of cartilage, or gristle, and their bodies are covered with scales which are rather like human teeth in structure. They have no operculum (cover) over the gills. Some sharks grow to a length of 35 feet or more, but others, the dogfishes, are quite small. They are all fast swimmers. The large basking shark strains its food (which is made up of small animals) out of the water by means of special comb-like structures on its gills. The man-eating shark has fierce-looking teeth. Some extinct forms of this type grew to a length of 90 feet.

The skates and rays have become flattened for living on the sea floor in shallow waters. Their pectoral fins are wide at the base and are used to propel the fish through the water. Some, the sawfishes, have their snout drawn out into a long saw-like structure, and the electric ray has an organ which gives off powerful electric shocks.

*Polypterus.* This fish, the bichir of some African rivers, is—like the coelacanth—another "living fossil", being the only living representative of a group that was quite common many millions of years ago. It has thick scales on its body and a long dorsal fin divided into a dozen smaller fins.

*Sturgeons.* These fish are also relics of another group of fishes which lived a long time ago. They have a gristly skeleton and very weak jaws. The American sturgeons are called paddle fish because they have a long snout which is rounded and wide at its front end.

*Lungfishes.* The lungfishes are also primitive forms which are nowadays found only in Africa, South America and Australia.

*Bony Fishes.* These are the most numerous and advanced fishes. They include salmon, carp, roach, perch, eels, cod, angler fish and mackerel.

There are separate articles on many of the fishes mentioned in this article.

**FISH-BREEDING.** For many centuries men have kept fish in special ponds so that they have them at hand to catch and eat while they are still perfectly fresh, and today there are large farms for breeding fish in Europe and the United States. Great Britain, which is surrounded by shallow seas that are rich in fish, does not need to breed much fish for food. However, fishes such as trout are bred to replace those caught by anglers, who fish for sport.

As early as 3000 B.C. grey mullet were being bred in brackish (rather salt) pools in China, where the large population often suffered from hunger. Fish-breeding was an important industry there, with fishing instructors and inspectors appointed by the emperor. The Chinese soon found that when the fish ponds were cleaned out the mud at the bottom was valuable in helping their rice and mulberry trees to grow. The

*Sport and General*

Trout are reared in thousands at this commercial trout farm near Nailsworth, Gloucestershire. With good feeding and freedom from natural enemies, the fish grow rapidly in size. Yearling trout are being sorted in the upper picture at the left, and the fish in the lower picture is between three and five years old. These trout are bred for sport—they will be put into lakes and streams to take the place of fish caught by anglers.

mulberry trees provided food for silkworms, while both rice and the pupa (chrysalis) of the silkworm, which is not wanted after the cocoon has been removed for silk, were used to feed the fishes.

In Europe, the ancient Romans built great ponds and aquariums close to the villas where they lived. They bred mullet and carp, but preferred to eat sea fish, and one noble is said to have had a tunnel cut through a mountain in order to bring sea water to his pools.

After the fall of the Roman Empire the true art of fish-breeding was lost, although in the middle ages monks in abbeys and monasteries had "stew ponds" in which carp and other fish were kept as food. The monks did not, however, breed fish by taking the eggs of fishes and hatching them by artificial means, thus rearing the young fish away from their natural enemies. This was not done again in Europe until about the middle of the 19th century, when an artificial "hatchery" was set up by the French government. Fish farms were soon after established in other countries of Europe.

The fish bred on fish farms can be divided into three main classes: fish for food, fish for aquariums and fish for sport. Fish for food include carp and bass, while those for aquariums are chiefly goldfish.

In a typical carp farm there are ponds of different kinds and sizes. The spawning ponds are kept dry during the winter and filled in May. Because they are shallow, the water has become warm by June, when adult fish are put in them. Round the edges are bundles of branches of willows and other trees, and it is here that the adult fish lay their eggs. After spawning, as the egg-laying is called, the parent fish are caught in nets and taken away so that they do not eat the young. The eggs hatch in a few days if the water is warm enough.

For a few days after they are hatched the fish feed on their own supply of food which is carried in a yolk-sac attached to the belly of the fish. This supply is used up in a few days, after which the fish are fed with finely ground food. After about ten days the fish, which are now called fry, are carefully netted and placed in fry ponds, each of which holds about 3,000 fish.

The ponds have been prepared so that they

contain plenty of natural food for the young fish. Here the fish grow rapidly and by the end of the summer are transferred to the growing ponds. Each of these ponds contains about 2,000 fish and has also been prepared with natural food. In late autumn the fishes are placed in the deep winter ponds which do not freeze; therefore the fishes are not in danger of being frozen. In many fish farms the fish are fed on such artificial food as minced offal and fish.

Each time they are moved, fewer fishes are placed in each pond, for if they are overcrowded they will not grow to their full size. At the end of their third year they will weigh about two-and-a-half pounds each and from then on they can be sold.

Large numbers of salmon and trout eggs are hatched every year in hatcheries. The adult fish are caught in traps or nets, and kept until they are ripe; that is, until the eggs and milt can be squeezed out by pressure on the sides of the fish, without hurting it.

The eggs and sperm are mixed together, and after about ten minutes the surplus sperm is washed off. The eggs are then placed in special troughs in hatcheries. About two gallons a minute of cold, clean water passes through each trough, which has a cover on to prevent the eggs being damaged by sunshine. Some of the eggs may be taken from the hatchery when they are eyed; that is, when the eyes of the little fish can be seen through the egg wall. Eggs cannot be handled without damage until this eyed stage is reached. The eyed eggs are placed, or "planted", in small streams in which there is plenty of food. They must not be planted in streams where there is already a large fish population. Nowadays, as a great deal of the spawning grounds of salmon and trout are destroyed by hydro-electric and other power schemes, hatcheries are used to hatch and sometimes rear the fish in the hope that the population of salmon, especially, will not die out. (See TROUT and SALMON.)

**FISHERIES.** Fishes are found in all but the very deepest water and in the Dead Sea, where it is too salty for them to live, but they are most abundant in the surface of the seas and near the great land masses of the continents. Because men have valued fish for food since very early days, they have found out which parts of the sea are best for fishing. "Fisheries" means the catching of fish on these fishing-grounds.

Countries with long coastlines and good harbours are usually also those that have the largest and most important fisheries. In places where meat is scarce, much fish is eaten, but fisheries are not usually very important when cattle-rearing and meat production is easy, because meat can then be sold more cheaply than fish.

The most important fishing country in the world is Peru, which catches about one-seventh of all the fishes caught each year. The U.S.S.R. comes next to Peru, followed by Japan, the United States, Norway and Spain. The United Kingdom and China also have important fisheries. In 1965 the world's fisheries caught about 51,800,000 tons of fish and sea creatures such as molluscs and crustaceans.

Several hundreds of kinds of fishes and other sea creatures are taken by fishermen, but the greater part of the total catch is made up of herring, pilchard, cod, haddock, hake, salmon, mackerel, tuna, flatfish such as plaice and halibut and shellfish such as crabs and oysters.

Crabs and lobsters are caught by being trapped. They are enticed by bait into wicker-work or netting pots with openings so shaped that it is easy for the creatures to get in but hard for them to get out. In South Africa, crawfish are attracted by bait on to netting stretched across hoops which, when hauled up, take the crawfish with them. Their tails, either frozen or canned, are exported to many countries. Molluscs such as oysters and clams are usually caught in dredges dragged along the sea bed by motor boats.

Compared with the sea fisheries, the fresh-water fisheries are not very important, except for those in the U.S.S.R., the African lakes and the pond and paddy-field fisheries of China, Japan, Indonesia, India, Malaysia and some other hot countries. In tropical countries where there is no refrigeration, the transport of fish over great distances without its going bad is very difficult, but the problem is largely overcome by fish-farming in small inland ponds.

There are two classes of marine (sea) fish: pelagic fish and demersal fish. The word pelagic comes from *pelagos,* the Greek for sea, and pelagic fishes are those which live near the surface, such as herring, pilchard, sprat, tuna and mackerel. The word demersal comes from the Latin *demergere,* to sink, and demersal fishes are those that live on or near the sea bed, such as cod, haddock, hake and the flatfish family.

## Demersal Fishing

Most demersal fishes are caught by trawling. The special ship for this is called a trawler, and it drags a net along the sea bed to collect the fishes in its path. The trawl net is like an enormous, somewhat flattened, cone-shaped bag, and its mouth, which may be as much as 100 feet across, is kept open by two special boards, one on each side. These are attached to the steel towing cables from the trawler. While fishing is going on, the trawl net is towed for one-and-a-half to three hours and is then hauled up by a special machine called a winch, emptied and sent down again to catch more fish. The fishes are gutted (opened and their insides taken out) and washed and packed away in ice in the trawler's hold to keep them fresh.

Some big modern trawlers have refrigerated fish rooms in which the catch is frozen as soon as it has been cleaned. These "all-freeze" trawlers can hold up to 500 tons of fish and stay at sea for six or seven weeks.

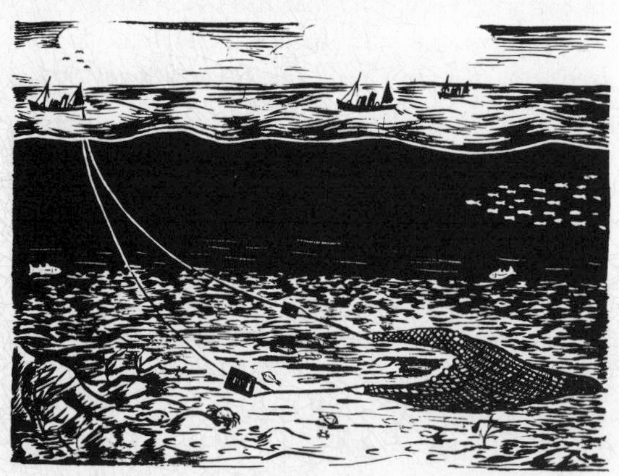

Trawling.

Lining is another way of catching demersal fishes, especially halibut and cod. Several miles of lines with baited hooks at intervals are laid out on the sea bed and their position marked with buoys. The lines are lifted once every 24 hours for the fishes to be removed from the hooks and new bait to be put on.

## Pelagic Fishing

The two main methods of catching pelagic fish are drifting and purse-seining. The word *seine* is French for net and a purse-seine is a kind of fishing net which closes round the fish.

In drifting, a string of many fine nets, perhaps a mile long, is put out with floats attached so that it hangs like a curtain in the water. The ship then rests attached to one end of the line of nets and drifts with the tide and wind for several hours during the night. Shoals of fish swim into the netting and are held by their gills in the meshes. When the nets are hauled the fish are shaken out into the drifter's hold.

Drifting.

In purse-seining, the ship first finds a shoal of fish and then surrounds it with a curtain of netting through which the fishes cannot escape. The net is then closed by pulling on lines which act like purse strings in gathering together the bottom edges of the net, so that the fishes are completely trapped and can be scooped out of the water into the ship's hold. Purse-seines are used by the fishermen of North America, Norway, Japan, Australia and Iceland.

Tunny, the other kinds of tuna, and mackerel will snap up any shiny object that glistens in the water like a small fish, so they are caught on hooks with shiny metal pieces attached to

Purse-seining.

them. Tuna may also be caught by scattering small, sardine-like fish as bait and then catching them on rods and lines.

## British Fisheries

Great Britain has one of the largest fleets of deep-sea fishing vessels in the world, and its fisheries produce about 1,000,000 tons of fish each year, of which two-fifths is cod. English fishermen went to Newfoundland to fish immediately after it had been discovered in the 15th century, and they were also pioneers of fishing round Iceland and in the Arctic Ocean. They developed deep-sea trawling and brought in steam trawling at the end of the 19th century.

Almost every port or harbour round the coasts of England, Scotland and Wales is used by fishing vessels, but the chief fishing ports in England and Wales are Hull, Grimsby, Fleetwood, Milford Haven and Lowestoft, and in Scotland, Aberdeen, Granton and Fraserburgh. Grimsby and Hull together deal with nearly half of all the fish landed in Great Britain.

British trawlers fish all the year round in waters as far afield as the Arctic Ocean and off West Africa. The large trawlers from Grimsby and Hull that fish regularly in the Arctic land a quarter of Britain's fish. They catch vast quantities of cod and much haddock in depths of 100 fathoms and more (1 fathom = 6 feet). During the winter months the trawlers work in almost perpetual darkness, often with severe gales blowing or with the sea spray freezing and covering the ships, fishermen and fish with ice. Cod and halibut are caught on the Newfoundland banks and also, together with haddock and plaice, off Iceland and round the Faeroe Islands. Hake is caught chiefly to the west of the British Isles and sometimes off West Africa.

The North Sea has very rich fishing grounds which provide a great variety of demersal fish. From the northern part come haddock, cod, skate, whiting and ling, and in the southern part and the rich fishing grounds of the Dogger Bank are caught plaice, turbot, soles, brill, cod and haddock. The Irish Sea, Bristol Channel and English Channel yield plaice, turbot, sole, whiting, skate and cod.

Herrings are caught in great numbers off the coasts of the British Isles. The shoals are fished off the northwest of Scotland early in the year, off northeast Scotland in the spring and summer, off northeast England in the summer and off East Anglia and in the English Channel in the autumn and winter. The Scottish ports of Stornoway, Lerwick, Peterhead, Fraserburgh and Aberdeen, and the English fishing ports of Yarmouth and Lowestoft deal with much of the herring fishery. Drifters fish for pilchard and mackerel off Cornwall.

## Commonwealth Fisheries

The fisheries of Canada are one of its chief industries. Besides the cod and haddock of Newfoundland, large quantities of cod are caught off other parts of the Atlantic coast, although there the lobster and herring fisheries are the most valuable; about 30,000,000 lobsters are caught each year.

On the Pacific coast the salmon fishery in the estuaries of the rivers in British Columbia is the most important and the richest fishery in Canada. The fishes are caught by gill-netting, which is similar to drift-netting, and in purse-seines. There are also fisheries of halibut, which are caught by lining, and of herring and pilchard, which are caught by purse-seines. The fisheries of the Great Lakes yield chiefly white-fish, pike, lake trout and lake herring.

The fisheries of South Africa, Australia and New Zealand are still fairly small, though those of South Africa are growing rapidly. Stockfish, pilchards and crawfish are mostly caught.

*Left: B. Milns. Above: J. H. Dobson*

Above: "Boston Halifax" of Lowestoft, a modern trawler, designed for fishing-grounds around the British Isles. Left: A trawl full of cod has just been hauled and emptied.

Australian fisheries are chiefly on the east coast, near the areas where people live. A few trawlers work there, but they are hindered by water too deep to fish in and by coral reefs on which their nets get ripped. Tuna, pilchard and mackerel are sought after by purse-seine fishermen, and aircraft help them to find shoals. Off northern Australia diving goes on for oysters with mother-of-pearl or (occasionally) pearls inside their shells. (There is a separate article PEARLS AND PEARL FISHING.)

## Fishery Problems and Uses of Fish

One of the greatest threats to the British fishing industry is overfishing, which means that some kinds of fish are being taken out of the sea faster than the fishes can breed and grow. This is particularly the case with the trawl fisheries in the North Sea and the hake fishery in the Atlantic. Where there is overfishing it becomes unprofitable for trawlers to work and some have to be laid up. A method of overcoming this problem is to have meshes in nets large enough for baby fishes that are caught to escape and grow to a more useful size.

In the pelagic fisheries, scientists have found a sure way of discovering shoals. This is by means of echo-sounders, which measure the depth of water beneath a ship by sending out a sound and receiving its echo back from the sea bed. Such echoes are also returned from shoals of fish. In very clear waters such as the Pacific, shoals swimming near the surface can be spotted from an aircraft even better than from the crow's nest of a fishing vessel.

Fish is used in many different ways. When fishing vessels return to port, their catches are unloaded into boxes to be sold by auction in the quayside markets. The fresh fish for fishmongers' shops is sent, packed in ice, from the ports by rail or road. In the United States and Canada a great deal of fish, especially pilchard and salmon, is canned, but in Great Britain only fairly small quantities of herring, pilchard and sprats are canned. Some fish is frozen hard and kept in refrigerated stores for sale later when supplies may be scarce.

Some fishes are also put through certain processes and sold under other names, the best example of this being the herring. By being split and hung on racks over smouldering oak shavings and sawdust, herrings become kippers, and after being salted and slightly smoked they are called bloaters.

Fish oil is used in the manufacture of margarine, ice-cream, soap and paint, and fish meal, which is made by grinding cooked fish into powder, is valuable for pig food and artificial manure. Fish scales are used in making imitation pearls and imitation mother-of-pearl plastics for buttons, umbrella handles and the backs of hair brushes and hand mirrors.

The skins of sharks and cod can be made into glue or turned into excellent leather for shoes, bags and gloves. From the livers of cod and halibut come two valuable oils, much used in medicine. Fish-sounds, or air-bladders, are made into isinglass, a form of gelatin which is used in cooking and for purifying alcoholic liquors.

**FISHING.** The sport of fishing with a rod, or *angling* as it is often called, can be done in rivers, lakes, canals and ponds, and in the sea. The rod gives the angler a longer reach and also allows him to *cast* or throw out the bait or fly. Moreover, as it is springy, it bends under the sudden snatch of a fish and thus saves the line from being broken.

Rods are made of cane (because it is springy), steel tube, or glass fibre, and are usually divided into jointed lengths so that they can be taken to pieces for carrying. From the handle or *butt* where the reel is attached the rod tapers down to a thin tip, and rings fixed along the rod guide the line to the reel, which may hold 30 yards or more of line.

## Freshwater Fishing

Before 1800 most freshwater anglers used no reel but fixed the line to the tip of the rod, which made it very hard to land a big fish. It is easier with the reel because if the fish puts up a fierce struggle more line can be paid out to ease the strain, after which the line can be wound in as the fish tires. Much of the skill of angling lies in *playing* the fish—that is, knowing when to give line and when to reel in and in judging how much strain the line will stand against the pull of a strong fish in a rapid current. When the fish is tired it can be drawn in so that it can be lifted out of the water with a landing net or a pronged hook called a *gaff*.

Hooks can be of all sizes depending on the kind of fish it is hoped to catch, but the point of the hook is always formed with a *barb* so that it cannot draw out of the fish's mouth. Most hooks have a ring or eye at the end of the shank, to which is fixed a *cast* or *trace* made of gut, nylon or wire which connects the hook to the line. All the angling gear described makes up the fisherman's *tackle*, and it should be as fine and light as possible because a shy fish will be scared away by a thick line and cast.

On the hook is the *bait* with which the angler hopes to tempt the appetite or greed of the fish. This may be the natural food of the fish such as insects, grubs, worms, small frogs or fish and some kinds of weed, or it may be something which is known to attract the fish by its shape or taste or colour. Baits of this kind are bread paste, gentles (maggots), boiled wheat, hemp seed and even cheese. Some fish can be attracted to a moving bait which the angler draws through the water; this may either be a small fish or an artificial one such as a sham minnow or a *spoon*—a piece of curved bright metal that twists and flashes.

The art of the angler lies in putting the bait in the place and at the level where the fish are looking for food. The fly-fisher puts the artificial fly on or just under the surface in places where trout and grayling generally look for insects. Many "coarse" fish, a term which covers all freshwater fish except salmon and trout, feed on or near the bottom. It is therefore often worth while in coarse fishing to put down *ground bait*—food like that on the hook laid on the bottom to attract fish to the spot.

*Fly fishing* is usually for salmon, salmon trout, trout and grayling and can be used for catching chub, dace and rudd. The fly may have to be cast some distance, sometimes against the wind, so the rod needs to be whippy and the line fairly heavy and tapering. To the line is fixed a gut or nylon cast two or three yards long the end of which is knotted to the fly, which is made of scraps of feather, fur, silk or tinsel tied to the shank of the hook.

The *dry fly* generally used for trout is meant to float on the surface and it and the cast are oiled to help it do so. It is made either to look like a real insect or may depend on some attractive feature such as tinsel or bright colour.

The *wet fly* used for salmon and sea trout is allowed to sink a few inches as the angler draws it in. It is not made to look like a real insect (because these fishes do not usually feed on insects) but acts as a lure to excite curiosity. The tackle for salmon and sea trout must be fairly stout as they are powerful fighters and must often be played in swiftly flowing rivers. The actual casting of the fly is a trick that cannot be mastered except by practice, though it can be practised on a lawn.

*Dibbing* or shade fishing is done by putting a natural fly, beetle, or grasshopper on the hook and lowering it on to the surface of the water where trees overhang. Trout, carp, and chub can be taken like this but it can be done only on calm days with clear water, as the angler needs to see the fish to put the bait in its path.

*Dapping* or blow-line fishing is used for catching Irish lough trout, using a long, light rod and a mayfly or daddy-long-legs as bait on the end of a fine, floss-silk line. A fair breeze is needed to blow out the line over the water and the tip of the rod is lowered to put the bait on the surface near a fish.

*Float fishing*. Most people start by angling for roach, perch, or bream in this way. Fine tackle is used and the line, greased to float, is fastened to a gut cast having a fairly small hook baited with paste, a worm or gentles. One or more pieces of split shot are bitten on to the gut (with the teeth) so as to sink the bait and make the float "cock" or stand upright in the water with about an inch showing. The float is a porcupine or goose quill which can be slid up or down the line; its position is set so that the bait is the correct distance from the bottom. This distance can be found only by trial. In a river the float and bait are allowed to drift down with the current past the angler, care being taken to pay out line in order to prevent them dragging. When they have drifted 20 yards or so they are drawn back, cast upstream again, and the process is repeated. The area of water thus covered is known as the "swim", and it is usual to ground bait the swim the day before. Chopped worms or worms in a clay ball, brewer's grains, or bran and blood can be used for ground bait. A sudden check in the movement of the float or its dipping or bobbing tells the angler that a fish has taken the bait, and at the right moment he must *strike* or drive the hook into the fish's mouth by lifting the point of the rod with a movement of the wrist which must be sharp but not violent. In this kind of fishing it is important to make as little noise and movement as possible so as not to frighten away the fish, which are quite easily scared.

In freshwater fishing there are *close seasons* fixed by law in which fish may not be taken because they are breeding. Often the people who own the rights of fishing make rules about the size and number of fish that may be taken. At most places in Great Britain where there is fishing to be had there is an angling club which the beginner will find it helpful to join.

*Spinning* is a method in which the bait, which is usually a spoon or artificial minnow, is cast a long way through the air and then reeled in, spinning round and wobbling as it goes through the water. A special kind of reel is needed for spinning, which is used for salmon, pike, and trout.

*Trolling* is sometimes used in lakes for catching trout and pike. Either a natural bait such as a live perch or other small fish, or a spoon, is trailed by means of a strong rod at the stern of a rowing boat; often two rods are used, one each side. Not a great deal of skill is needed as success depends chiefly on trolling in the right places and on getting the bait to the proper depth by rowing the boat at the right speed.

## Sea Fishing

Sea fishing nowadays means more than dangling a hand line off the end of a pier. As a sport it uses tackle much the same as that described for freshwater fishing, though generally stronger and with heavier weights and bigger hooks. Flatfishes such as dabs and plaice, also whiting, cod and haddock, can be caught by fishing on (or near) the sea bed, using shrimps, mussels or lugworms for bait. Mackerel and pollack are caught by *whiffling*, which is a form of trolling using a spoon or a natural bait. Fly fishing with a fly rod can be used for bass, pollack and sometimes mackerel, though of course the "fly" is an imitation of a small fish

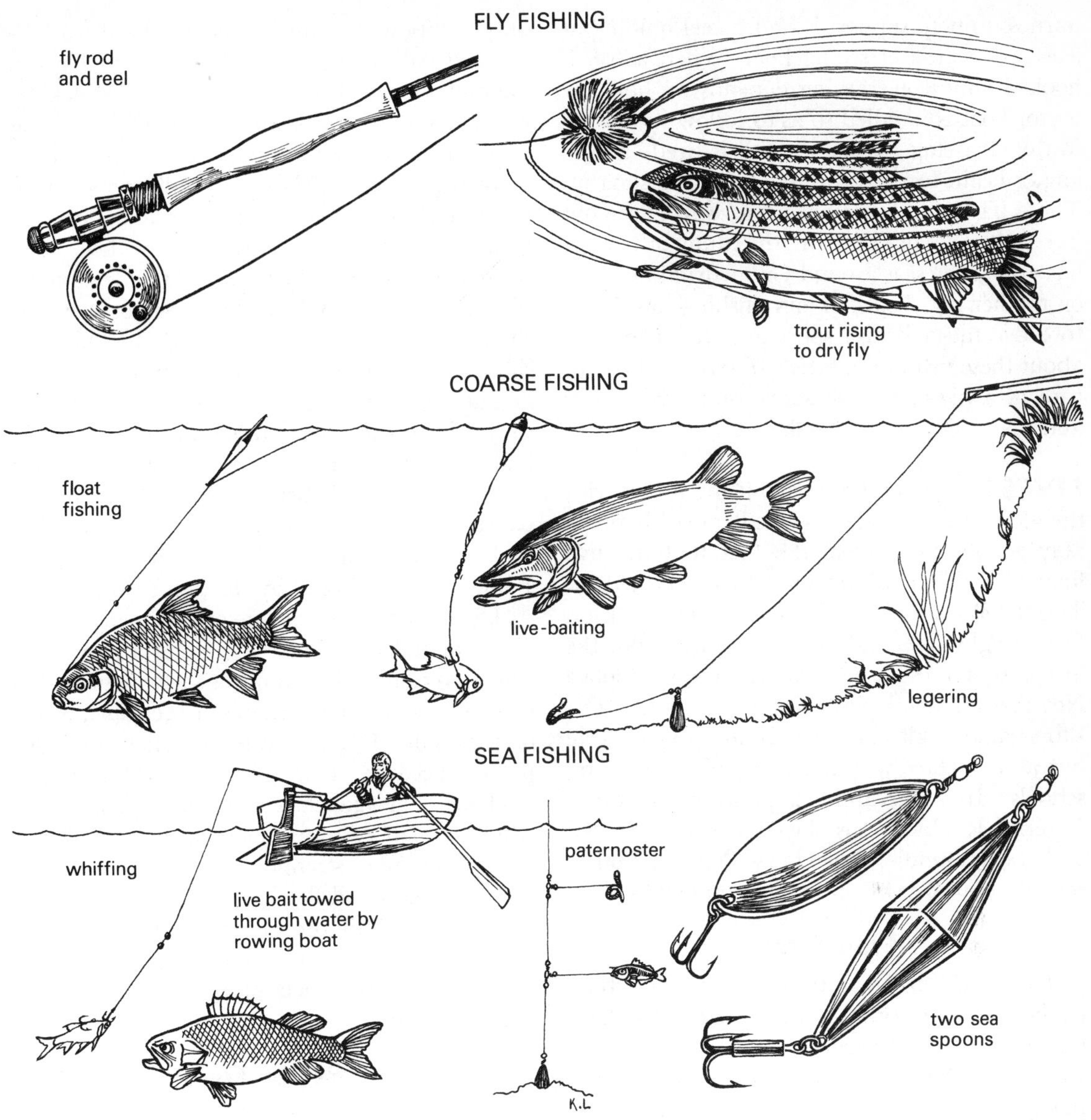


instead of an insect. It is cast from a boat or from the rocks at low tide.

A method often used for sea angling is that of *paternostering*. A lead weight or plummet is fixed to the end of the cast and at intervals up the cast are fixed lengths of brass wire which stand out; to these are fastened short lengths of gut having baited hooks. In this way the fishes are offered several baits or kinds of bait. The line is kept as taut as possible between the plummet and the rod, so that the angler can strike without delay when a bite is felt or signalled by a small bell clipped on the end of the rod.

*Big-game fishing*. The big-game fish of the sea are swordfish, sailfish (or marlin), mako sharks, tarpon and tunny, and some of them may reach half a ton in weight. Fishing for them is a popular sport off the coasts of California and Florida (United States), and Australia and the North Island of New Zealand. It is usually done by a form of trolling from a motor boat, using a short stout rod with a special harness to help support it and a reel holding at least 400 yards of strong line. When a fish is hooked almost everything depends on how the motor boat is handled so as to follow it, as only in the later stages when the fish is tired can the angler begin to put pressure on it by reeling in. These big-game fishes belong to warm seas but in recent years one of them, the tunny or bonito, has visited the seas around Great Britain to feed on the herring shoals. Tunny fishing has therefore become a British sport and you can read about these fish in the article TUNNY. The capture of a big-game fish sometimes takes hours and may last most of the day.

**FIVES** is a game played by hitting a ball with the gloved hand inside a walled court. It probably got its name from the fact that the five fingers of the hand are used together in play. The three main kinds of game played are Eton fives, Rugby fives and Winchester fives, but the first two of these are by far the most popular. Not many schools play Winchester fives. The Eton game is played not only at Eton College but also at Harrow and several other boarding schools. It is also quite popular in Northern Nigeria. Rugby fives is played at Rugby School and also at Oundle, Haileybury, Fettes and other schools, as well as by universities and clubs.

## Eton Fives

The game of Eton fives began some time in the 19th century when the boys of Eton College found that a particular part of the north wall of the chapel made a natural court. It was partly enclosed by two large buttresses and contained several ledges and steps. There was also a small buttress, at the foot of which was a drain, projecting from the left-hand wall into the court. In 1840 most of the peculiar features of this natural court were copied when the school built four separate courts. Unfortunately the measurements of the various features were not the same in the new courts. This probably explains why, as the game became more popular and more courts were built in different parts of Great Britain, each court seems to be slightly different from the others.

The game is played between two pairs, the only equipment required being a hard leather-covered ball about two inches in diameter and padded gloves (because the ball is struck by hand). A game starts when the player standing on the top step (see diagram) serves the ball by throwing it first on the front wall and so on to the right-hand side wall so that it bounces in front of one of the opposing pair who makes what is called the "first cut". He does this by hitting the ball back on to the side wall and thence on to the front wall above the "line" (a sloping ledge running across the front wall at a height of four feet six inches). After the first cut a player from each pair takes it in turn to hit the ball. The rally ends when one of the players either hits the ball below the "line" or out of court. A game consists of 12 points and matches are generally the best of five games. Points are scored only by the pair serving.

The laws of the game are quickly learnt when one is actually playing. The better a player becomes, the more he enjoys a game which, because of the unusual features of the court, is one of real skill. It is a game at which an older player, because of his greater experience, can hold his own against a younger opponent and which he can continue playing when he is too old for the more strenuous court games such as squash rackets and Rugby fives.

In Great Britain there are two important Eton fives competitions—the Public Schools competition and the open championship for the Kinnaird Cup.

## Rugby Fives

Rugby fives is less complicated than the Eton game, being played in a court enclosed by four walls and having a flat floor and no steps or buttresses. On the front wall is a board about two feet six inches from the ground, and the ball must hit the wall above this board to remain in play. The court also has right and left side walls and a back wall. Padded gloves are worn as in Eton fives but the ball is a little lighter and smaller.

The game can be played by two or four players. After a short preliminary rally, the game begins by either the *server* or his opponent, who is called the *receiver*, throwing the ball so that it bounces from the front wall to the

The first Eton fives court.

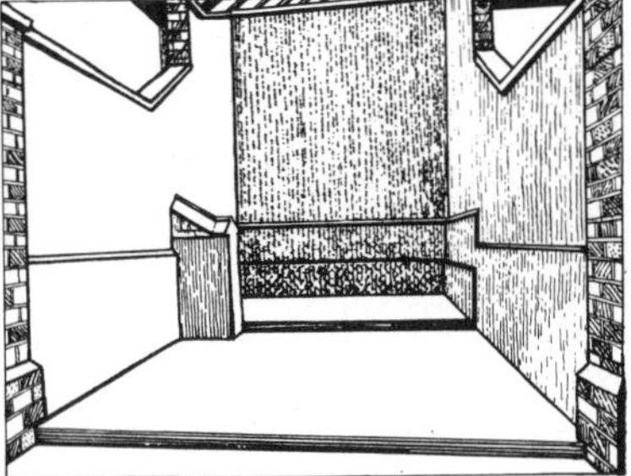

Eton fives court.

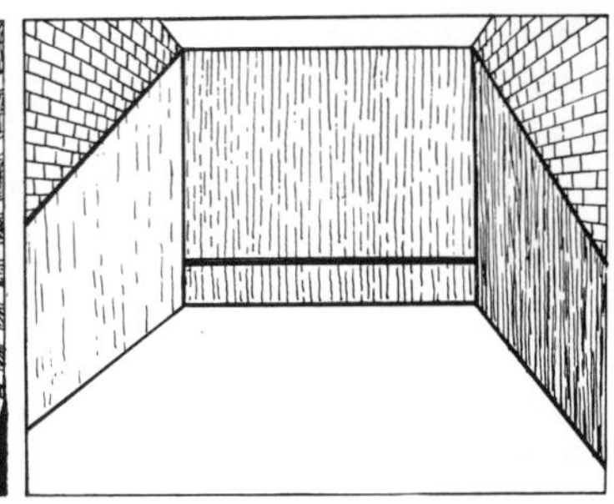

Rugby fives court.

nearest side wall. If the server is satisfied with the way in which the ball is thrown up, he returns the ball by striking it so that it hits the side wall off which the service came and then the front wall above the board. After that, the two players strike the ball in turn before its second bounce so that it hits the front wall above the board, either direct or after bouncing off one of the other walls. The rally, or exchange of strokes, continues until one of the players misses the ball, strikes it so that it hits below the board or goes out of the court, or lets it bounce more than once before striking it.

If the receiver wins the rally he wins a point; if the server wins the rally he becomes the receiver, and, if he wins the *next* rally, wins a point. As in Eton fives, only the player serving can score points. In the doubles game, when the server's side loses a rally the service passes to his partner. If the server's side loses another rally, the service passes to the other side. The game is won by the player (or side) first scoring 15 points. If both players (or sides) reach 14 points, the first to score two points wins the game.

A good player can hit just as well with either hand. He strikes the ball with the palm rather than the fingers and tries to keep it only just above the line on the front wall. A high shot gives the opponent the chance to volley, or hit the ball back before it bounces. The ball's flight can be varied by using the side walls and sometimes an angled shot across the court is used to draw the opponent to the front of the court, where he will not be able to reach a hard drive.

Besides being a fast game needing great activity and energy, Rugby fives demands quickness of thought. To reach and strike the ball requires much bending and stretching as well as agility, so the game is one of the few to exercise every part of the body.

Winchester fives is like the Rugby game except that there is a buttress built in the left-hand side wall.

**FIVESTONES** is a children's game that in the old days was played with knucklebones (sheep's trotters), but nowadays stone or metal knobs shaped like dice and called *gobs* are used. There are several ways of playing, but the general idea is that the players start together and have to get through a fixed set of throws; the one to finish first is the winner. For instance, one way is to toss one stone—the *jackstone*—into the air and before it falls to gather up one or more stones from the table. There are different ways of throwing and picking up, such as *chucks, dibs, peas in the pod, donkeys, creeps* and *horses in the stable*; the stones may have to be caught on the back of the hand, knocked on the ground or against the mouth, or picked up in twos and threes.

Both boys and girls are often very clever at this game and sometimes use a large marble that will bounce called a *bonser* instead of a jackstone. The bonser is thrown up and after it has bounced once the gobs must be picked up and the bonser caught before it hits the ground a second time.

The game was certainly played by the ancient Greeks and Romans. Other names for it are *knucklebones, hucklebones, dibs, jackstones* and *chuckstones.*

**FLAG.** Flags are so old that nobody knows who invented them, although the Bible mentions them and all the ancient peoples used them. They may have begun as ornamental streamers on images, and then have been used instead of the images. Many of them were used as signs of power by kings and other rulers.

In the dust and confusion of battle the commander's flag heartened his followers by showing that he was still there to lead them, but if it fell they feared that he had surrendered or been killed or captured, and they gave up the fight. What lost the Battle of Hastings may not have been the death of King Harold but the fall of the Saxon banner. (See HASTINGS, BATTLE OF.)

The Roman Eagles—images which the legions (divisions of soldiers) used as emblems—were sacred, and the soldiers would face any peril rather than let them be captured. Napoleon I followed the Roman example by displaying the eagle on the standards of his regiments, and for long the "French eagles" were unbeatable. Several modern countries, including the United States, still use the eagle as a national emblem.

During the middle ages there were several types of flags. The *gonfalon* hung downwards from a cross-bar and the *standard* was long and tapering. The *banner* was square or rectangular and its size showed its owner's rank. A knight's *pennon* ended in swallow-tails, and to honour him for courage in battle the king might cut away the swallow-tails, making the flag into a small banner and the knight into a "banneret" (now called a "baronet"). The squire's *pennoncel* tapered to a point.

## Flags of the British Commonwealth

The modern standard is rectangular, and is mostly used as the official flag of the ruler of a nation. It should never be flown except to show where the ruler is. The British Royal Standard has had many changes before coming into its present form. The three lions, gold on red, have been an emblem of the Kings of England since Richard the Lion-heart, who reigned from 1189 to 1199. The rampant lion, red on gold, within its ornamental frame, became the banner of the King of the Scots during the reign of William the Lion (1165–1214), and although it is really a royal emblem many Scotsmen fly it as a sign of loyalty. The harp, gold on blue, was chosen to represent Ireland by Henry VIII. Each member of the British royal family has his or her Personal Standard.

For centuries flags have represented not only leaders but nations. The dragon banner used by the Roman auxiliary troops became the flag of the Saxons of Wessex, and the Red Dragon still appears on the national flag of Wales. Another Saxon emblem was the white horse, and the Vikings had their raven flag.

During the Crusades, St. George became the patron saint of England, and his cross, blood-red on white, became the English emblem. At sea it is the flag of an admiral, and nobody else may fly it, but on land it may be flown by any patriotic Englishman. It is often flown over churches, though it should then have the arms of the diocese in the upper quarter nearest the flag-staff. With the sword that beheaded St. Paul displayed in the same position it forms the flag of the City of London.

The patron saint of Scotland is St. Andrew, and his emblem, a white diagonal cross on blue, forms the country's national flag and is much flown by patriotic Scotsmen. When in the 17th century James VI of Scotland became James I of England he ordered the two crosses to be combined, forming the first Union flag of "Greater Britain".

St. Patrick is the patron saint of Ireland, and when the United Kingdom of Great Britain and Ireland was formed in 1801 he was represented on the Union Flag by a red diagonal cross on white. Thus was formed the modern Union Flag, the emblem not only of the United Kingdom but of the British Commonwealth. It may be used *on land* by any British subject—but people who use it should take care to fly it the right way up, with the broad white stripe uppermost nearest the flagstaff.

At sea the Union Flag may be worn, as seamen say, only by ships of the Royal Navy. Flown at the masthead it either shows that the sovereign is on board or forms the command flag of an admiral of the fleet. Flown at the jackstaff in the bows of the ship it becomes the *Union Jack*.

Ships of the Royal Navy wear the White Ensign, which is also the flag of the Royal Yacht

Squadron (a St. George's Cross with the Union in the upper quarter nearest the mast) at the stern, and the long tapering commission pendant at the masthead. A warship returning to port at the end of her commission hoists the paying-off pendant, which is sometimes so long that its end may be supported by a bladder floating in the sea.

In the British Army most regiments have their own Colours, some of which began as the personal flags of their colonel. Cavalry regiments have either a rectangular *standard*, a *guidon* with its ends slit and the corners rounded, or embroidered *drum banners*. Infantry regiments have two *colours*, the King's or Queen's and the Regimental: one consists of the Union Flag with special badges, the design of the other differs for the various regiments. It is impossible to take flags into land battles in modern warfare, so nowadays they are carried only on ceremonial parades.

The Blue Ensign is the flag of the Royal Naval Reserve, and also, sometimes with a distinguishing badge, of government vessels and of some yacht clubs. The Red Ensign, sometimes called the "Red Duster", is the flag of the Merchant Navy. This includes not only cargo vessels but fishing craft and passenger liners and pleasure yachts, though some yacht clubs use it with a special badge.

In modern times two new ensigns have come into use, both showing the Union Flag on sky blue. The Royal Air Force Ensign displays the well-known "target" of red, white and dark blue. The Civil Air Ensign bears a large dark blue cross, edged with white.

The overseas Commonwealth countries have their own flags. The Canadian flag displays a red maple leaf on a white ground between two vertical red stripes. The national flags of Australia and New Zealand are Blue Ensigns with stars representing the Southern Cross; Australia adds a large "Commonwealth Star". India's flag has horizontal stripes of saffron (yellow), white and green, with the wheel of Asoka (the Buddhist ruler of the 3rd century B.C.) in blue on the white stripe. The green and white flag of Pakistan bears the Moslem crescent and star. Ceylon's national flag displays a lion holding a sword—an ancient royal emblem. Ghana has a flag with red, white and green horizontal stripes and a black star on the white stripe.

## Other National Flags

In the United States the President's Standard is blue and displays the American eagle and the national motto, which means "One out of many". The national flag, the Stars and Stripes (also called "Old Glory"), has 13 red and white stripes to represent the original states of the Union and 50 stars, white on blue, to represent the states of today. The flag originally showed the first British Union Flag, but when the Americans decided on complete independence they replaced this by 13 white stars, another star being added whenever a new state was admitted

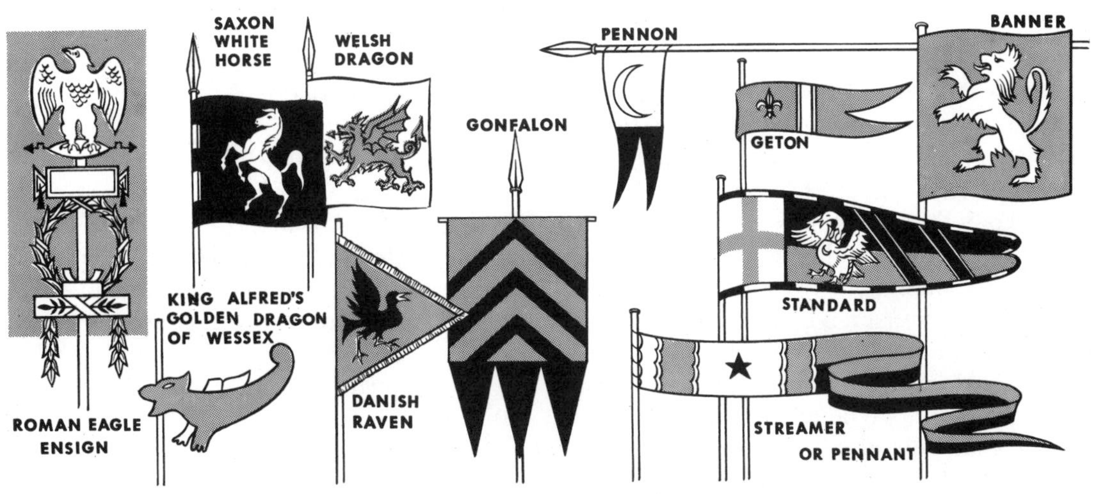

to the Union. Two were added in recent times when Alaska and Hawaii became states.

The flags of the Scandinavian countries bear crosses resembling that of St. George, although their colours are different. The Danish National Flag, the *Danebrog*, is the oldest flag still in use. Switzerland and Greece use crosses with arms all of equal length.

For many years the *tricolour* (a flag with three stripes) has been the sign of a successful revolution. It was first used by the Netherlands in the 16th century, though its original colours, orange, white and blue (those of its leader, the Prince of Orange), have been changed to red, white and blue. When France became a republic it chose the same colours but arranged them vertically instead of horizontally, blue, white and red. The same patterns, but with different colours and sometimes with a distinctive badge, are used by many other countries in Europe and in South America, including the Republic of Ireland. Flags of countries under the influence of the U.S.S.R. display either a red star or a gold star on red, with their own national emblems.

## Signal Flags

Until recently, flags formed the chief method of signalling at sea. At first they were rather crude, so that only a few simple messages could be sent, but by Horatio Nelson's time improvements made more complicated messages possible, such as his famous signal at Trafalgar. Later the system was adapted for merchant ships by the well-known naval writer Captain Frederick Marryat.

Even in these days of radio, signal flags are still used, the warships having their own secret signal codes and the International Code of Signals being used the world over. The "Blue Peter" shows that a ship is preparing to put to sea. A red swallow-tail flag means that the ship is carrying explosives, a red flag with a white circle at its centre that it is carrying oil. A yellow flag means that the ship has not yet been visited by the port doctor to make sure it is free from infectious disease. A blue and white swallow-tail means "Get out of my way, I'm on a speed-trial!" A flag halved red and white means that a pilot is on board.

Signal flags are also used as decoration to "dress" a ship on occasions of national rejoicing or at regattas (yacht races) and other festivities. Such flags do not then spell out messages but simply make an attractive display.

## Rules for Flying Flags

Everybody who flies a flag should keep to the rules. It should be hoisted briskly and lowered slowly. It is flown at the top of the mast except when half-masted as a sign of mourning, and then it should be fully hoisted first and at once lowered slightly. One national flag should never be flown above another, for that would insult the lower flag. The two should be flown at the same height side by side.

A flag flown upside-down is a signal of distress; to "strike" the flag (lower it) in battle is a sign of surrender. Flags are usually hoisted, perhaps with some ceremony, in the morning, and are lowered at sunset. Only for special reasons are they flown day and night, like the Admiralty Flag in London and the Stars and Stripes over the Capitol at Washington.

A ship visiting a foreign port may hoist as a courtesy the flag of the country being visited. This is at the foremast, with the ship's own ensign at the stern. At the mainmast the "house" flag shows the shipping company to which the ship belongs.

The national flag is sometimes used to cover the coffin at a funeral. Even then, however, it should not be allowed to touch the ground. Flags of the Commonwealth may touch the ground only when they are lowered ceremonially as at a royal inspection.

## International Flags

Except in some countries such as Turkey and Persia, the Red Cross flag is an international emblem hoisted over such places as hospitals to ask protection for the sick and wounded. Its colours, the red cross on white, are the reverse of those of Switzerland, the country where the flag was adopted.

When the United Nations Organization was formed (see UNITED NATIONS) it chose a new flag. This shows, in white on light blue, two olive branches, the ancient symbol of peace, on each side of a map of the world centred on the North Pole.

**FLAME.** When gases combine (join together) so as to give off both light and heat there is said to be a flame. Coal gas burning on the gas ring or cooker, the lighted candle and the flickering blue and yellow flames of a coal fire are all examples of this. In each of these there is so much heat produced by the gases as they combine that they become *incandescent* or glow brightly. With every flame there is one gas burning and another which is needed to *support combustion*, or keep the flame going. For instance, in the case of the gas ring it is hydrogen and methane—the chief gases making up coal gas—that combine with the gas oxygen contained in the air, while in the candle flame it is the paraffin wax changed into vapour which combines with the oxygen of the air. (See Oxygen.) Sometimes it is hard to say which of the two gases it is that is burning. Diagram (1) shows a glass bulb with two tubes entering at the bottom and one coming out of the top; inside the bulb air is burning in gas but outside the gas is burning in air!

The gas ring or oven burner usually has a number of small jets from each of which a mixture of gas and air comes out to burn in a very hot flame. This kind of jet is really a form of one called the Bunsen burner which is said to have been invented by the German chemist Robert von Bunsen and is used in nearly all laboratories. Diagram (2) shows how the gas rushing towards the burner draws in air to burn with it; the gas ring is simply a cluster of such burners. A flame of this kind has a blue spike in the middle and this part is actually cold unburnt gas and air. If a stick is held for a second or two in the flame, as shown in diagram (3), two small charred bars appear on the wood at the sides but the part in the blue spike is unchanged, showing that the centre of the flame is not hot.

The flame of a candle also has near the wick a small colourless part which is unburnt vapour from the wax, but the rest of the flame is yellow chiefly because of carbon particles from the wax which get white hot without burning. A cold plate held over a candle flame quickly becomes black with soot showing that there is much carbon in the flame. (See Carbon.)

Some substances when vaporized, or changed into gas, in a hot flame will make it coloured; thus copper compounds give a green flame and those of sodium (such as washing soda) a vivid yellow one, while calcium and strontium give red flames. The colours from fireworks are obtained in this way. (See Fireworks.)

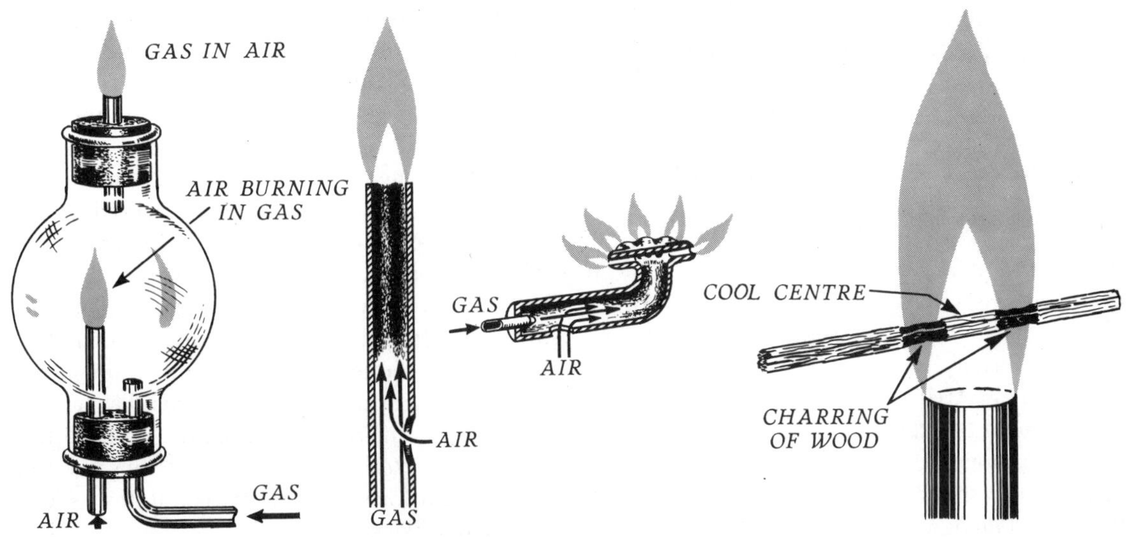


(1) Air can burn in gas. (2) Bunsen burner and gas ring. (3) The cool centre of a Bunsen flame.

**FLAMINGO.** The flamingo is a lovely bird but strange to look at, with long neck and legs and a heavy bill, curving downwards in a curious shape. Its colouring is a beautiful rosy white, with scarlet and black feathers in the wings. The bill is pink with a black tip and the legs are also pink. In flight it stretches out its neck and legs, making itself look about six feet long, and one can see the full beauty of the scarlet and black wings. A flock of thousands of these splendid birds is a wonderful sight and makes a babbling sound like a flock of geese.

These flamingos are found in one or two places in Spain, southern France and other countries round the Mediterranean and also in Africa and Asia; occasionally they have even been seen in Great Britain. There are other kinds in both North and South America, one of which is bright rose-pink all over with black wings, and in Africa and India.

*Planet News*
A flamingo breeding "village" beside a lake in Florida.

Flamingos breed in colonies, or groups, which are often known as "villages", in or on the edge of lakes and shallow lagoons (salty lakes beside the sea). The nest is usually a low heap of mud with a hollow scooped out in the middle for the one or two white eggs. When first hatched, the young birds are covered in silvery white and grey silky down (baby feathers), but they already have pink beaks. The flamingo feeds by bending its long neck nearly double and with its head upside down, raking in the mud with its peculiar beak to find plants and small creatures.

In ancient Rome flamingos' tongues were eaten as a rare delicacy.

**FLATFISH.** One of the best known flatfishes is the plaice. Examination shows that both its eyes are on one side of its head, and that its flat body and head are coloured on the eye side and white on the other. It is important to remember that these are the *sides* of the fish. Other flatfish—also good to eat—include the flounder, dab, sole, turbot, halibut and brill.

Flatfishes often lie on the bottom with their coloured side uppermost, covered with sand so that only the eyes show. The upper side, which has the eyes, can change colour to match the sand or shingle. This colour depends on light, and if a fish is kept in a glass-bottomed tank with a light underneath, colour appears on the white side too. Experiments made with flatfishes have shown that the fish must be able to see the ground on which it lies in order to imitate it successfully. Certain kinds lack this power of camouflage and many albino or colourless varieties have been found.

Flatfishes are descended from perch-like fishes, probably deep-bodied and flat-sided, that swam the right way up. Over millions of years the flattening increased until the fish became unbalanced and fell on its side. Then one eye moved to the new top surface. As a result of this eye movement the head becomes twisted as the fish develops. The tropical fish *Psettodes* has the head less twisted, with one eye on top of it. It is not certain on which side this fish will lie, and some are left and some right-sided. Other flatfishes are definitely either left or right-sided, and it is very rare to find specimens that lie differently from the rest of their kind. Unlike other flatfishes, *Psettodes* has spines in its fins like the perches, and forms a link between flatfishes and their perch-like ancestors.

The development of a flatfish from an egg to

*Courtesy, National Geographic Society*

FLAG. International Code flags and pennants. The two-letter signal R Y flying from the masthead signifies "Crew have mutinied". The other two-letter groups on the halyards hoisted to the yardarm have the following meanings: N C—"I am in distress and require immediate assistance"; K A—"My vessel is very seriously damaged"; K T—"Have you a line-throwing apparatus?"; I X—"I have received serious damage in collision"; C G—"You should alight as near to me as possible"; A D—"I must abandon my vessel".

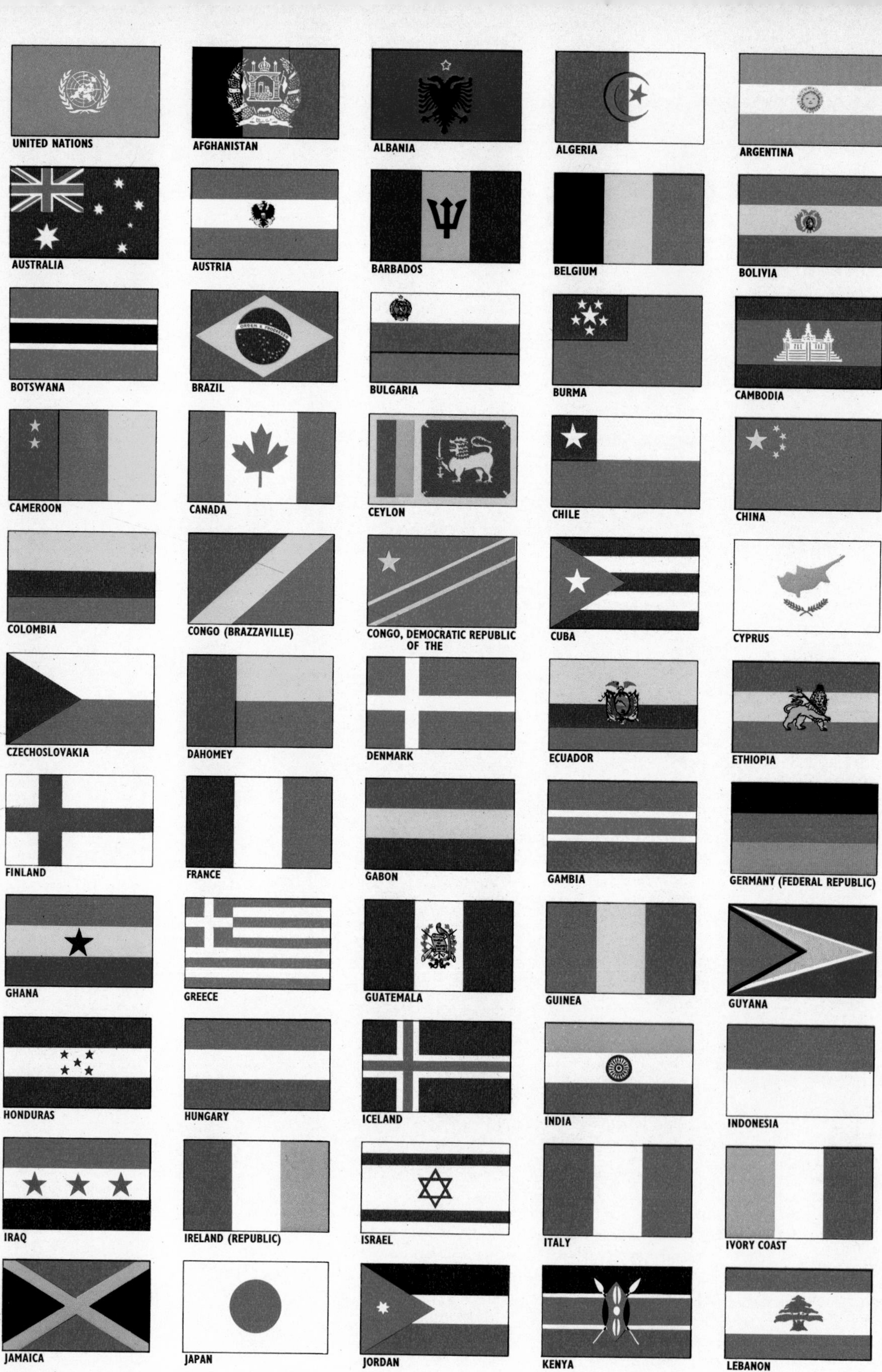
UNITED NATIONS
AFGHANISTAN
ALBANIA
ALGERIA
ARGENTINA
AUSTRALIA
AUSTRIA
BARBADOS
BELGIUM
BOLIVIA
BOTSWANA
BRAZIL
BULGARIA
BURMA
CAMBODIA
CAMEROON
CANADA
CEYLON
CHILE
CHINA
COLOMBIA
CONGO (BRAZZAVILLE)
CONGO, DEMOCRATIC REPUBLIC OF THE
CUBA
CYPRUS
CZECHOSLOVAKIA
DAHOMEY
DENMARK
ECUADOR
ETHIOPIA
FINLAND
FRANCE
GABON
GAMBIA
GERMANY (FEDERAL REPUBLIC)
GHANA
GREECE
GUATEMALA
GUINEA
GUYANA
HONDURAS
HUNGARY
ICELAND
INDIA
INDONESIA
IRAQ
IRELAND (REPUBLIC)
ISRAEL
ITALY
IVORY COAST
JAMAICA
JAPAN
JORDAN
KENYA
LEBANON

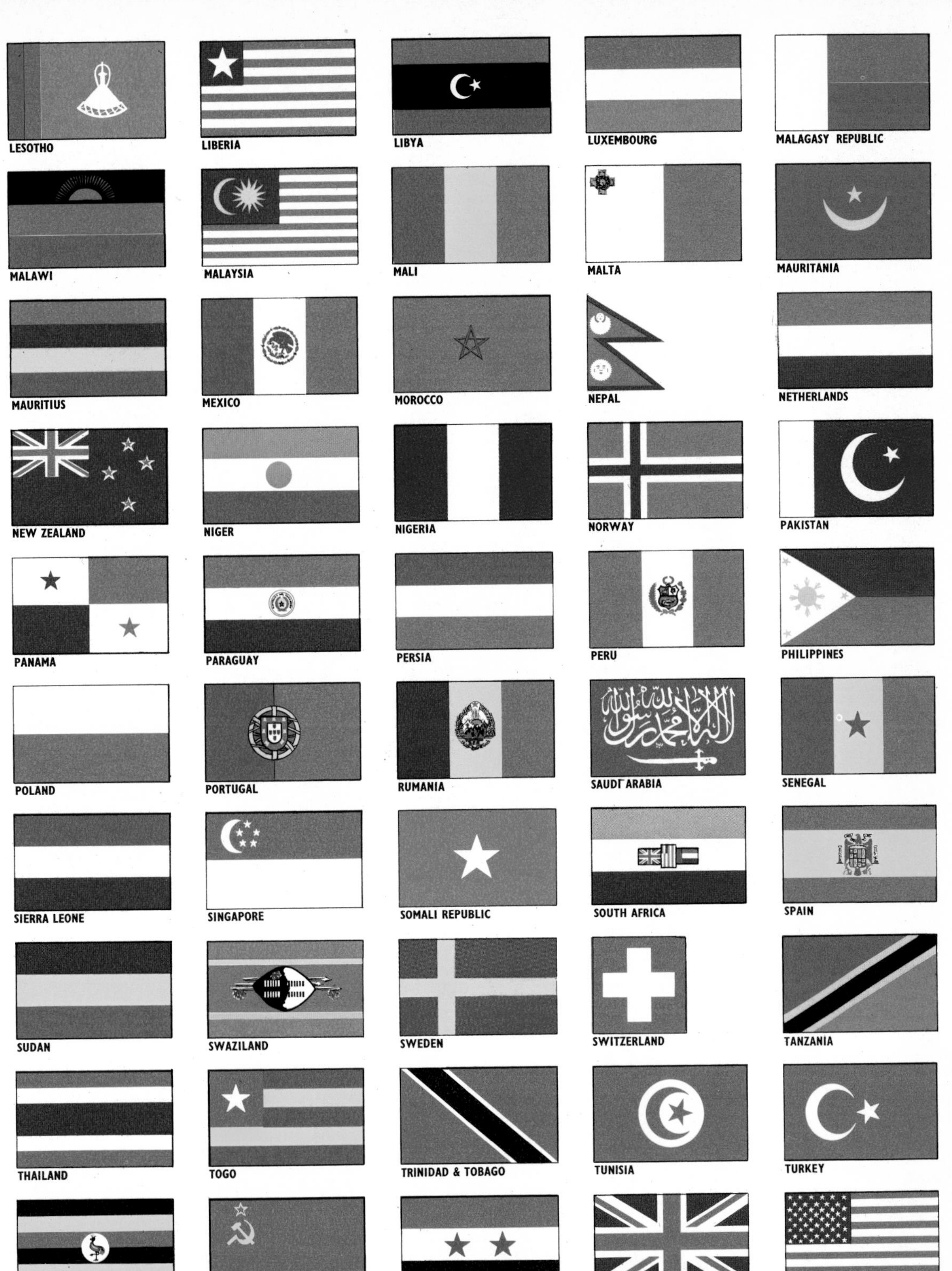
LESOTHO
LIBERIA
LIBYA
LUXEMBOURG
MALAGASY REPUBLIC
MALAWI
MALAYSIA
MALI
MALTA
MAURITANIA
MAURITIUS
MEXICO
MOROCCO
NEPAL
NETHERLANDS
NEW ZEALAND
NIGER
NIGERIA
NORWAY
PAKISTAN
PANAMA
PARAGUAY
PERSIA
PERU
PHILIPPINES
POLAND
PORTUGAL
RUMANIA
SAUDI ARABIA
SENEGAL
SIERRA LEONE
SINGAPORE
SOMALI REPUBLIC
SOUTH AFRICA
SPAIN
SUDAN
SWAZILAND
SWEDEN
SWITZERLAND
TANZANIA
THAILAND
TOGO
TRINIDAD & TOBAGO
TUNISIA
TURKEY
UGANDA
UNION OF SOVIET SOCIALIST REPUBLICS (U.S.S.R.)
UNITED ARAB REPUBLIC
UNITED KINGDOM
UNITED STATES OF AMERICA
URUGUAY
VENEZUELA
YEMEN
YUGOSLAVIA
ZAMBIA

FLAGS USED BY LIEUTENANT PASCO, H.M.S. VICTORY, FOR LORD NELSON'S SIGNALS AT TRAFALGAR

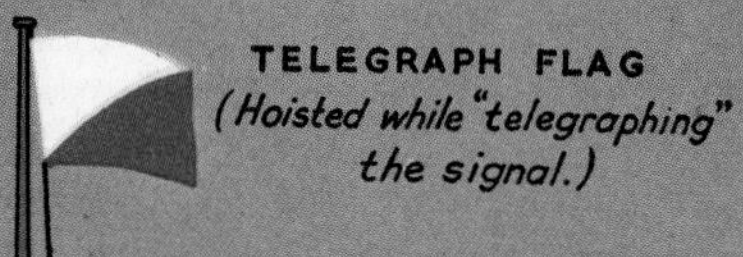


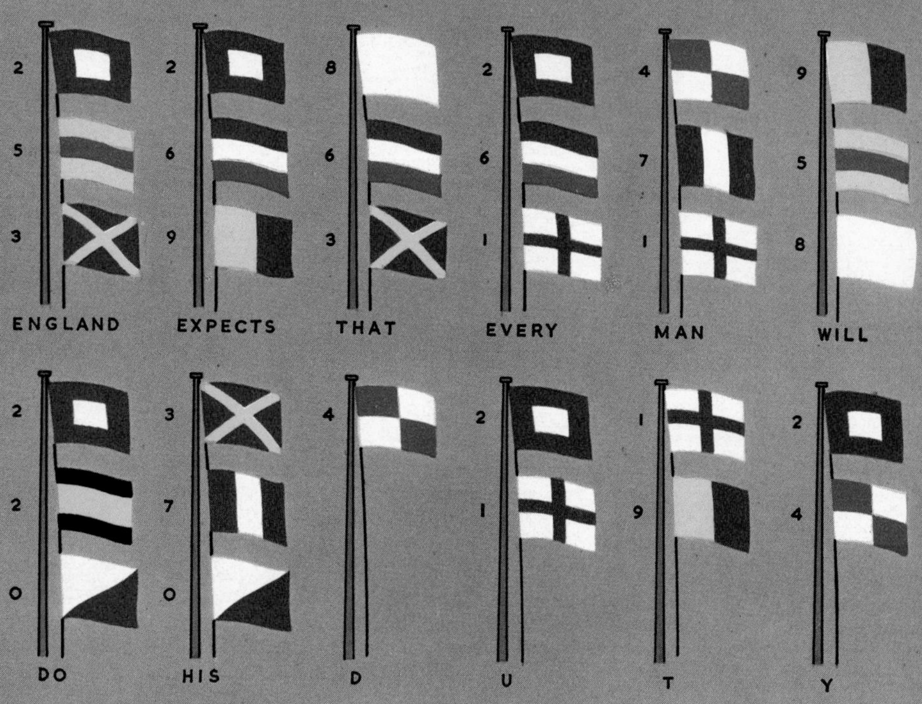


1
6

ENGAGE THE ENEMY MORE CLOSELY

*Hoisted and kept flying when the preceding signal had been completed*

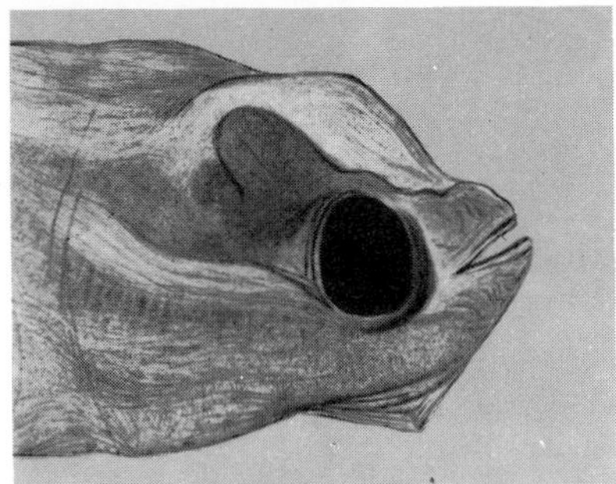

The flatfish starts life swimming upright, with an eye on each side of its head. This is a baby flounder.

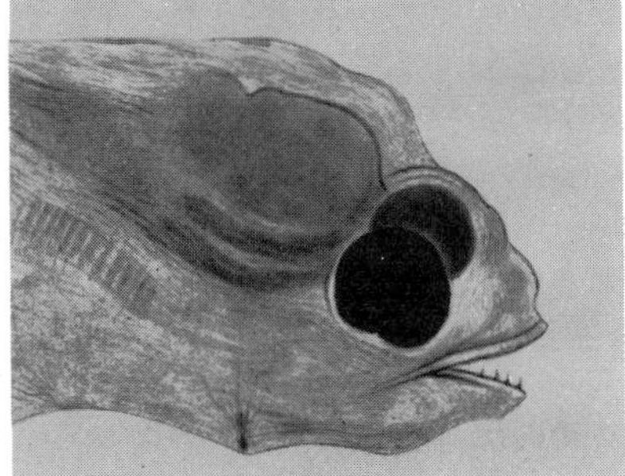

When the fish is about half an inch long, one eye begins to "travel" and the fish swims on its side.

FLATFISH. A flounder, like many other kinds of flatfish, has the power to change its pattern and colour to resemble the ground on which it lies. Experiments have shown that the fish has to see the ground in order to imitate it.

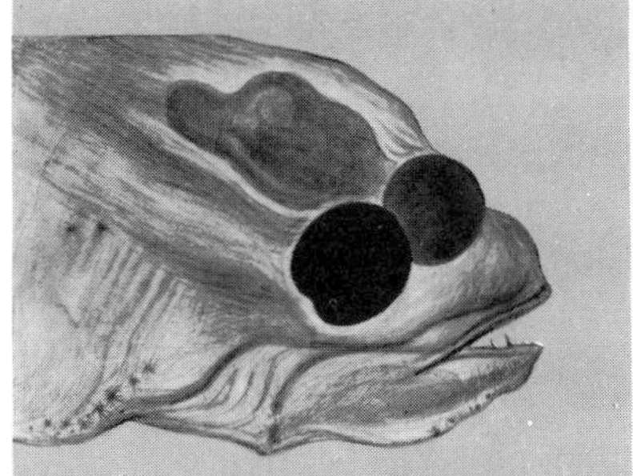

The "travelling eye" has reached the upper edge of the head and the skull and jaw are becoming twisted.

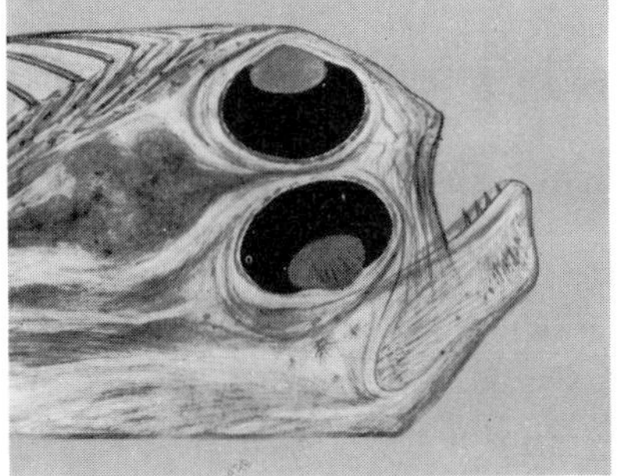

Both eyes are now on the upper side. They stand out from the head and can look in different directions.

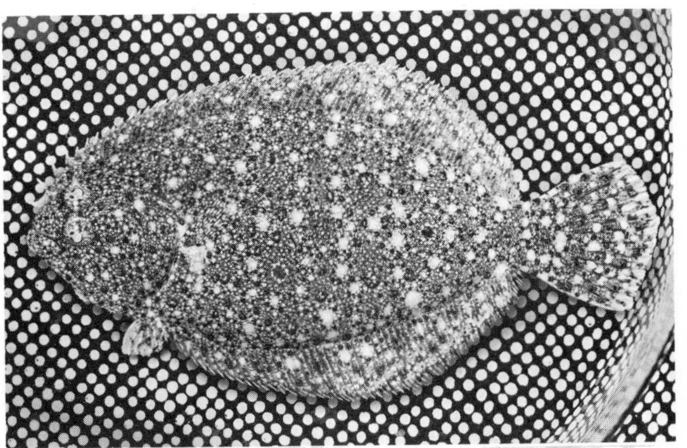

*Courtesy, U.S. Department of the Interior, Fish and Wildlife Service*

an adult shows clearly that flatfishes have evolved, or developed, from upright fishes. The baby flatfish is very like any other young fish. It has an eye on each side and swims upright. When it has grown nearly half an inch long, the eye on one side begins to move. It travels up and over the top of the head until it is beside the other eye. This takes about six weeks. Meanwhile the skull becomes twisted and eventually the fish loses its balance, leans over gradually on the eyeless side and falls slowly to the bottom of the sea.

A flatfish swims with its coloured side uppermost. It swims by means of the wave-like movements passing along the anal and dorsal fins which extend along the sides of the body. Sometimes it happens that the eye of a flatfish does not complete its journey over the head, so that the fish swims more normally, and then some colour appears on the blind side as well. Such cases are very rare, but they help us to understand the strangeness of the usual ones.

A pair of plaice (swimming) and a sole on the sea floor.

The twisting of the head means that the mouth is more on the blind, underneath side, and often the teeth are also more developed on that side. This is because flatfishes feed mainly on animals that live on the seabed, such as molluscs, small sea urchins, sea worms and similar creatures, though a few can chase and catch fishes or crabs. The eyes of flatfishes usually stick out and are protected by thick, fleshy lids and one can be moved without the other, so that they look in all directions for food or enemies while the fish lies hidden in the sand.

## Kinds of Flatfish

Flatfishes live in nearly all the seas; there are about 600 species, or kinds. Many of them are of great importance to man as food, particularly the plaice, which can be recognized at once by the red or orange spots on the upper side. It is caught in trawl nets, mainly at night when it is feeding above the sand.

The dab is rather like the plaice, but is usually smaller and without the spots. It is often caught by people fishing off the end of a pier. A near relative, the flounder, is interesting because it often leaves the sea and travels a long way up rivers. Freshwater flatfishes are known in some parts of the world.

All the flatfish described so far are right-sided species, and so is the giant of the family, the halibut, which is said to reach 10 feet in length and 600 pounds in weight. It is caught by long-line or trawl in northern seas and its flesh is of fine quality. A useful oil is also obtained from its liver and used in medicine.

The soles are also right-sided, but, unlike the plaice family, they have a small mouth with a curiously overhanging upper lip. The common sole is among the most prized of food fishes because of its delicate flavour. The so-called "lemon sole" sold in shops is really a fish called the smear dab and is not a true sole.

Of the left-sided flatfishes, the turbot, which has warty growths on its skin, and the smooth-sided brill are the two largest found in British waters. Both are popular as food.

**FLAX** was grown in what is now called Switzerland by the people who lived in wooden houses built on posts over the lakes, long before history was written. It is one of the oldest cultivated plants and is thought to have come from western Asia where it grew wild. The mummies of ancient Egypt (see MUMMY) were wrapped in cloth woven from the fibres of its stems. We call this cloth "linen"—a word that comes from *linum*, the Latin name for flax. "Linseed", the seed of this plant from which oil is obtained, also comes from the same Latin word.

The flax usually grown today is an annual, living only for one year, and grows between 12 and 40 inches high. It is a slender plant with narrow leaves growing alternately up the stem and small blue or white flowers with five petals, which grow at the end of the branching stems. Each seed capsule, or bag, normally contains ten smooth, oval, brown seeds.

When a farmer grows flax he must decide whether he wants to produce fibre for spinning or seed that will contain a lot of oil, for he must follow different methods according to the type of flax he decides to grow. When grown for its fibre, special varieties are chosen that grow tall and do not branch out much. In order to help it to grow tall and unbranched it is sown thickly —as much as 160 or 170 pounds of seed to the acre. When the plants are fully grown, they are pulled, either by hand or machine; they are pulled instead of being cut in order to obtain fibres as long as possible. The seeds are threshed out even though some of them will still be unripe and then the plants are *retted*, or partly rotted, which loosens the inner fibres from the rest of the stem. Two common methods of retting are known as water and dew retting. In water retting, which provides better fibre, bundles of flax stems are weighted down under water by stones or sods of earth for 10 to 20 days. In dew retting the plants are spread out on the ground for several weeks to be moistened by dew or rain. Retting by chemicals is possible but is very expensive.

After retting, the flax is dried. It is then passed through rollers to break up the hard core of the stem and some of the outer parts which have no value. The valuable fibres are then freed from the unwanted parts by beating with paddles. This process, known as *scutching*, is performed either by hand or by a machine with revolving blades. The fibres are hackled, which means that they are put through machines with steel combs which separate the coarse, brittle fibres called tow from the finer and more elastic strands. The cleaned fibres are then bundled and made ready for spinning (see Spinning), and finally the spun fibre goes for weaving (see Weaving). If the fibre is fine and delicate, beautiful linen is woven; if it is rough and coarse, thread and rope are made.

The U.S.S.R. grows as much flax for fibre as all the other countries of the world combined. Other great flax fibre producing countries are Poland, France, Belgium and the Netherlands.

When flax is grown mainly for seed, special varieties are sown that have many branches and therefore many seeds. More space is allowed for each plant, only 70 to 100 pounds of seed being sown per acre, and the crop is not cut until the seeds are ripe. The seeds are threshed out, and contain between 31% and 39% of oil. To extract the oil they are first heated and crushed, after which they may either be pressed, put through expellers—machines like big mincing machines—or have the oil dissolved out of them by hot petrol. The oil thus obtained is the linseed oil which is used in making paints, varnish, printer's ink, linoleum, oilcloth and imitation leather.

What is left after the oil has been extracted is valuable food for cattle. There are the rippled linseed cakes from the presses, the small chips from the expellers and the meal from the petrol extraction plants. These contain more food value than hay or straw, and are used to improve the diet of milk cows so that they will give more and better milk. The United States, the U.S.S.R., Argentina, Canada and India are the greatest producers of linseed.

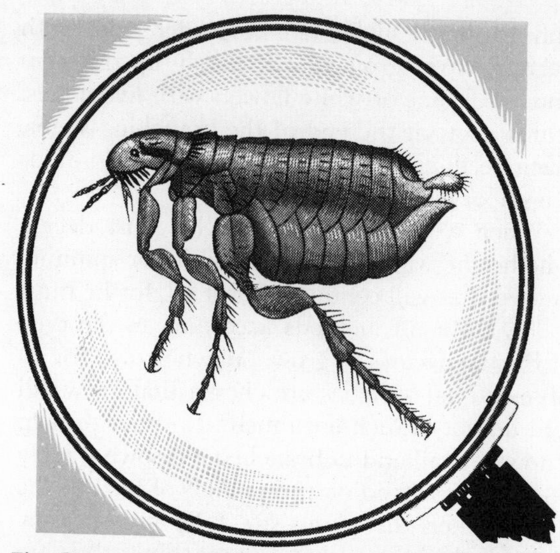

The flea has three pairs of strong legs which help it to jump as much as 100 times the length of its own body. In this picture it is seen through a magnifying glass.

**FLEA.** The flea is a tiny, wingless, dark brown insect, with three pairs of strong legs that help it to jump a great distance—even as much as 100 times the length of its own body. It has a small, rounded head and mouth parts with which it can pierce the skin of the animal it lives on and suck the blood. Its body is very much flattened from side to side and is made up of a number of segments, or jointed parts. Behind the head and also on the segments of the body are rows of stiff bristles. The flat shape of the flea allows it to move forward very quickly among the hairs or feathers of the animal on which it lives. The bristles prevent it from slipping backwards again.

Female fleas lay their eggs in the hair of animals, in nests or in cracks and crannies full of dirt and rubbish, where the grubs can find plenty to eat when they hatch out. The grubs are very like small white caterpillars, and when they are full fed they, too, spin cocoons and turn into pupae, just as a caterpillar turns into a chrysalis. It is only when they break out of the cocoons as full grown fleas that they become parasites, living on the blood of other creatures.

The animal or bird on which the flea lives is called its host, and most kinds prefer one particular kind of host. For example, the common European flea, whose Latin name (*Pulex irritans*) means "the irritating flea", much prefers man. However, fleas will often move from one host to another, and flesh-eating animals often get fleas from the animals they prey on.

Because they move so freely from host to host and because of their blood-sucking habits, fleas are dangerous insects, often carrying germs from sick to healthy animals. During the middle ages millions of people died in outbreaks of bubonic plague, and it is now known that this terrible disease was carried into houses by rats, whose fleas bit people and gave them the bubonic germs. (See Black Death.) Because the number of rats is kept down, bubonic plague is rare nowadays, and fortunately few of the 1,000 other kinds of fleas are really dangerous. Some, however, such as the "stick-tight" fleas, and particularly the jiggers or chigoes found in tropical countries, burrow through the skin and cause very troublesome sores.

**FLEMING, Sir Alexander** (1881–1955). Like Louis Pasteur and Joseph Lister, Alexander Fleming did much to overcome the germs that cause disease. He discovered penicillin, which is a powerful killer of germs and has saved many people's lives.

Fleming was a Scotsman and the son of a farmer. He did not at first think of being a doctor, but worked for a London shipping company which paid him ten shillings a week. Later, however, he took up medicine and studied at St. Mary's Hospital Medical School in the University of London. He became a doctor in 1906, and in the same year he met Sir Almroth Wright, who was an expert in the study of the germs known as bacteria. Fleming also became interested in bacteria and antiseptics. (See ANTISEPTIC.)

In 1928 he was examining a special plate called a culture plate containing jelly on which some germs called staphylococci were being

*Central Press*

Sir Alexander Fleming discovered penicillin, the first of the antibiotic drugs which have saved countless lives.

grown. He noticed that a speck of mould was growing on the jelly and that around it the jelly was free of germs. When he saw this he realized that the mould had power to kill germs.

He made further experiments and named this germ-killing mould penicillin. It was the first of the antibiotics, which kill germs in the body without harming the cells of the body. (See ANTIBIOTICS.)

Although Fleming understood that he had made a very important discovery, two other scientists, Howard Florey and Ernst Chain, developed and purified penicillin in 1938, and then it was found to kill other kinds of germs as well as staphylococci. Florey and Chain, as well as Fleming, were awarded the Nobel Prize for medicine in 1945.

Fleming received many other honours, and was made a knight in 1944. Yet although he knew that penicillin was being used by doctors and in hospitals all over the world for all kinds of infections, and that his name had become a household word, he still continued quietly with his medical research work.

**FLEMINGS.** The name of Flemings is given to the inhabitants of northern Belgium who speak the Flemish language. Written Flemish is very much like Dutch, but there are many *patois*, or local dialects. Thus the language spoken in Antwerp, for instance, is different from that spoken in Bruges or in Ghent. (These are the three principal towns of the Flemish provinces.) About half the people of Belgium speak Flemish and about one-third speak French. The remainder are bilingual; that is, they can speak both languages. The Flemish-speaking parts are the northern provinces of Antwerp, Limburg and east and west Flanders, and the northern half of the central province of Brabant. In southern Brabant and in Brussels, the capital, both French and Flemish are spoken.

Most Flemings work on the land, but since the beginning of the 20th century industry has made great progress, not only in the towns but also in the countryside of Limburg, where new coalfields have been opened. The prosperity of northern Belgium still depends largely on farming, and on the port of Antwerp which has played such an important part in the trade of Europe since the 16th century.

In the middle ages the country of Flanders included French Flanders as far south as the River Somme. It was the richest country in northern Europe, both for its trade and its cloth industry. Flanders was also a great artistic centre and Flemish painters, such as Hubert and Jan Van Eyck in the 14th and 15th centuries, and Peter Paul Rubens and Anthony Van Dyck in the

17th, were famous in France, England, Germany and Italy.

From the end of the 19th century the Flemings pressed for their language to be recognized and used in schools and by the government. Gradually this was done and now Flemish is used in the schools of the Flemish provinces and at Ghent university, and together with French is an official language, being used both by the government and the army.

Most Flemings are Roman Catholics and are separated by their religion from the Protestant Dutch and the Belgian non-Christians of the industrial south. For the same reason, Belgium is divided politically between the Social Christian party (mostly Flemish) and the Socialist party (mostly Walloon). (See WALLOONS; BELGIUM.)

## FLEUR - DE - LIS.

This graceful pattern is usually thought to represent three flowers of the white lily, the middle one erect and the outer ones curving downwards. The phrase is French and means "lily flower". Nobody is certain, however, that the pattern has anything to do with lilies, even though it looks like them.

It is a very old pattern and was used as a decoration in ancient times in countries as far apart as India, Egypt and Italy. In the 12th century in Europe people began to use it on their coats of arms (see HERALDRY). At that time the kings of France began to use it and on their shields and banners had several gold fleurs-de-lis on a blue background. Later they reduced them to three, to stand for the Trinity (see TRINITY, THE). When Edward III of England (1312–1377) claimed the throne of France, he placed the French fleurs-de-lis on his shield beside the three lions of England. They remained in the English royal arms until 1800, and are still part of the decoration of the royal crown. The fleur-de-lis became a popular emblem in English and French heraldry and was adopted by many families not connected with royalty. In religious pictures the fleur-de-lis, like the ordinary lily, is an emblem of the Virgin Mary.

## FLINDERS, Matthew (1774–1814).

One of the great explorers of the Australian coast was the Englishman Matthew Flinders. It was he who insisted on calling the continent Australia, after it had been named New Holland by the Dutch and New South Wales by Captain Cook. Flinders was a surveyor employed by the Royal Navy and while he was stationed at Sydney between 1795 and 1799 he and another young officer named George Bass made a map of the eastern coast as far south as Tasmania, using, to begin with, a boat of only eight-foot keel, the "Tom Thumb". They were the first to discover the strip of water between Tasmania and the mainland now called Bass Strait.

Flinders was sent out to Australia again in 1801, this time with a properly equipped expedition, and within two years he had mapped the whole of the south and east coasts and most of the north and gone on to complete the first very difficult voyage right round the continent. On his way home he was wrecked on a coral reef and later imprisoned by the French for over six years.

## FLIGHT, NATURAL.

There are two kinds of bird flight: flapping flight and gliding. In flapping flight the bird moves its wings up and down. This keeps the bird in the air and propels it along. It is a useful method of flying for small birds that live near their nests and make frequent landings. Usually, the smaller the bird, the faster it flaps its wings. For instance, humming birds flap their wings 50 times in a second whereas the heron beats its wings twice a second.

Of the gliding birds, there are the low gliders such as the albatrosses and shearwaters, and the high soarers such as the vultures and eagles. The gliding birds make use of upward air currents, which are often caused by the wind meeting an obstruction and being deflected upwards. For example, gulls use air currents along the edge of cliffs and swifts glide on current along the eaves of buildings. Gulls and other sea birds use variations in the wind above the sea for flying. Other

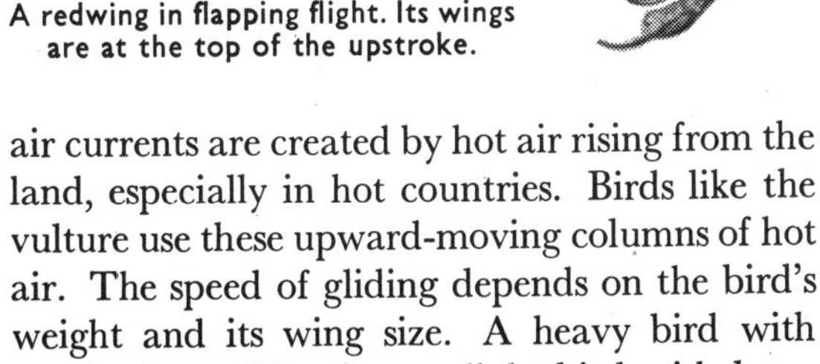

*Eric Hosking*

A redwing in flapping flight. Its wings are at the top of the upstroke.

air currents are created by hot air rising from the land, especially in hot countries. Birds like the vulture use these upward-moving columns of hot air. The speed of gliding depends on the bird's weight and its wing size. A heavy bird with small wings glides fast; a light bird with large wings glides slowly.

Birds are able to fly because their wings produce "lift" as air currents pass over and under them. The faster the air moves along a surface, the less the air pressure on it. (You can see this if you blow along the upper surface of a piece of paper. The greater pressure underneath pushes the paper upward.) The wing of a bird is shaped so that air currents flowing over it have to travel farther and faster than the air moving across the bottom surface—and this effect is increased as the wing is tilted slightly upwards. As a result the pressure below the wing is greater, and the air currents tend to move upwards in eddies towards the lower pressure region above the wing. The wing tends to rise in the air and keep the bird aloft.

Some birds have on the first digit, which corresponds to the human thumb, a small extra, or bastard, wing which is separated from the rest of the wing by a gap. The high pressure from beneath the wing can pass through this gap towards the lower pressure of the upper surface, lessening the risk of stalling. Stalling occurs when the wings cease to produce enough lift to support the bird in the air.

When birds are about to take off they must produce enough forward momentum to give the lift required. For small birds a jump is enough, but larger ones have to run or swim fast to be able to take off. Coming in to land is a difficult task for a bird especially if it is going to perch on a small surface such as the branch of a tree. First

*Eric Hosking*

A whinchat coming in to land. Its wings are extended, and its tail is spread out and lowered to brake it.

it lowers its tail and spreads it out to act as a brake, and then it lowers its feet. The bird often gives one more beat of its wings so that it lands on the branch.

Birds must have very powerful muscles to be able to fly. As these are large and heavy, they have to be situated below the wing for reasons of balance, but as they must pull on the upper surface of the wing they are attached to this by a kind of pulley system.

Differently shaped wings are suitable for different kinds of flight. For a bird to fly fast the wings should be long and narrow. However, this kind of wing stalls easily below a certain speed, making it more difficult for the bird to land. As a result, the birds that have this sort of wing are those that glide constantly or fly very fast. Small birds, living near their nests and having to manoeuvre constantly, have short, fat wings. They cannot fly so fast but they do not stall.

The passerine birds which include the wrens and birds of paradise, mostly fly at 15 to 25 miles an hour, while ducks fly at 45 to 60 miles an hour and the common loon reaches 90 miles an hour. However, one of the fastest of all birds is the swift, which is now thought to fly at well over 100 miles an hour.

Not only do migrating birds fly great distances, but geese, for instance, have been photographed flying at a height of 29,000 feet.

**FLINTSHIRE** is the smallest but by no means the least important county of Wales, and lies in the northeast of the country. When Edward I formed the county in 1284 he did not have the whole of the area in his own hands as Wales had been conquered piece by piece and much of the land belonged to the great barons. This explains why Flintshire is in three separate parts. The largest is bounded by Denbighshire on the southwest and the English county of Cheshire on the east, while its northern coastline is formed by the Irish Sea and the estuary, or tidal part, of the River Dee. Around the mouths of the Dee in the east and the Clwyd in the northwest the land is low, but inland there are broad hills with some moorland rising to about 1,800 feet on the Clwydian ridge. The second largest portion of Flintshire, called Maelor, lies further inland, being mostly surrounded by Cheshire and another English county, Shropshire. The smallest portion lies between the other two parts and is entirely surrounded by Denbighshire.

Both the smaller parts of the county have good farming land but few towns. The Clwyd Valley is well known for its farming, and many cattle are raised both here and near the mouth of the Dee. Some of the land is ploughed up for wheat and oats and other crops, while on the hills sheep are reared.

The strip of coast along the estuary of the Dee, from the Point of Air in the north to Sandycroft in the east, is one of the wealthiest and most crowded industrial districts of Wales. Here, thousands of people earn their living by mining coal or by helping to produce iron, sheet steel, chemicals, paper and rayon (an artificial clothing material). Woollen textiles, bricks and cement are also made. Many of the people who work in the factories live in places such as Connah's Quay, which is visited only by small craft now that the Dee estuary has become so shallow, and Flint, which used to be the county town.

Mold is the present county town and has a busy market, but the largest town in the county is the seaside resort of Rhyl, which is popular in summer with people who work in the factories of Lancashire. Many holidaymakers visit Prestatyn, which is a quieter place than Rhyl and has pleasant sand dunes as well as a beach. Holywell has for centuries been a place of pilgrimage for cripples and other invalids wishing to bathe in the well of St. Winifred. According to an ancient legend, the spring of the well burst from the ground exactly where the saint's head was struck off by a prince whom she refused to marry. This is easier to believe than the story of how her uncle replaced her head and brought her back to life. Another local saint was St. Asaph, who lived in the 6th century, and the city named after him has a population of only about 2,000 and has the smallest cathedral in Wales.

Every field in Flintshire has a story to tell from history. The people of the Bronze Age left many burial mounds, in some of which important discoveries of golden objects have been made. In the Clwydian Hills there are remains of hill forts of the Iron Age which may have been occupied in the Roman period also. On the plateau called Halkyn Mountain and elsewhere the Romans mined lead. For a thousand years Flintshire was a battlefield between the peoples of England and Wales. The Anglo-Saxons marked out the boundary of the Kingdom of Mercia by digging dykes (ditches with banks of earth beside them) known as Offa's Dyke and Wat's Dyke. Later in the middle ages castles were built at Rhuddlan, Flint, Ewloe, Mold, Hawarden and other places, some of which have seen more than 100 battles. Hawarden is also famous as the home of W. E. Gladstone, one of the great British prime ministers of the 19th century.

**FLODDEN, BATTLE OF.** On September 9, 1513, at Flodden, in Northumberland, the English won a great victory over the Scots who had invaded England under their King, James IV. James put his army in a good position on Flodden Edge, about six miles south of Coldstream, with his back to Scotland and his face to England. The Earl of Surrey, who led the English army, marched round the Scots and drew his army up behind them, forcing them to turn round in order to fight, and making it impossible for many of them to escape into Scotland if they were defeated. It was a daring thing to do because if he was defeated he could retreat only into Scotland, the enemy country.

The Scots moved their army to Branxton Hill, still with their backs to England. The battle began at 4 p.m. and continued into the night. Surrey's archers and cannon soon gained the upper hand; then the Scots' left wing drove some of the English back. The English were gradually winning, however, and it was only in the Scottish centre, where the King fought, that the Scots held out. The circle of spearmen round the King grew less and less and soon he and all his nobles died fighting.

The English did not follow up their victory by invading Scotland, and peace was made. The Scots lost 10,000 men and among them were all the leading men of their country. There is a famous Scottish lament, or song of mourning, for the nobles killed at Flodden called "The Flowers of the Forest".

**FLOOD.** The histories of most ancient peoples tell of some disastrous flood, and the story is usually much the same—everyone was swept away and drowned except a few who lived to tell the tale. Best known is the Old Testament story of Noah and his ark, though similar tales are told in China, India and Egypt. In the early days people liked to settle in river valleys because the soil there was easily farmed and grew rich crops. Flooding of the valley meant the loss of homes, crops, animals and all too often of human lives, and it is small wonder that in such countries people made sacrifices to the river gods to turn away their wrath. However, this article shows floods can be helpful as well as harmful.

*Mirrorpic*

Flooded countryside around Tonbridge, Kent.

The three rivers whose flooding is most often heard about are the Nile, the Yellow River and the Mississippi. The Nile in Egypt makes a strip of fertile country in the midst of a great desert, for each year its flood water brings down a load of rich mud which it spreads over the land as fertile soil. Its floods, which seldom do damage, are caused chiefly by the heavy summer rains on the mountains of Ethiopia where two of its main tributaries, or branches, rise.

The Yellow River or Hwang Ho in northern China and the Mississippi in the United States are rivers which have brought down so much mud in the past that they have raised their beds above the level of the country through which they flow. This means that the banks have had to be raised in turn by the people in the valleys, who must build up high embankments, or *levees*. Sections of the banks of the Mississippi have been raised 22 feet in this way since 1882. In spite of this, a river when in flood is always liable to rise above or break down these man-made banks. Not for nothing was the Yellow River known to the people as "China's Sorrow", for in 1887 its floods caused 900,000 deaths, while in 1935 they drove 4,000,000 from their homes. At intervals this river has completely changed its course and now flows into the sea 200 miles from where it did a century ago. The floods of the Mississippi and its tributary the Ohio in 1936 and 1937 did damage to property amounting to hundreds of millions of pounds.

## The Causes of Floods

Floods happen when the ordinary channel of a river cannot carry away all the water entering it. This may be because the channel is blocked, but it is more often caused by too much water.

In cold lands the rivers often freeze over in winter, and sometimes their upper courses thaw before those near the mouth, so that ice jammed in the lower river blocks the channel and the water cannot escape to the sea. Floods are caused thus every year along the rivers of northern Canada and northern Russia, and sometimes along the Rhine and Danube. In 1824 the River Neva flooded in this way and drowned 10,000 people in what is now Leningrad (Russia). A river mouth may also be blocked if it is allowed to become choked with mud and not cleared out by dredging. (See DREDGING.)

Too much water can be caused by heavy rainfall or the melting of snow or by both together. During winter much snow collects on high mountains like the Alps and the Himalayas. In the spring this thaws and fills every stream with rushing water, so that the level of the main river rises. If the thaw is sudden the rise may be enough to cause damaging floods, especially if there is heavy rain immediately following the thaw. Even in England, where there is not usually a great deal of snow, quite serious flooding can be caused in this way, as happened in March 1947.

In some parts of the world the year can be divided into a wet season and a dry one, and where this is so the rivers are fuller during the wet season and may overflow somewhat. However, so long as the time of the rains and the amount of rainfall are regular, more good than harm is done. The farmer builds his home out of reach of the floods and plans his crops to suit the rise and fall of the river. The Nile, Indus and Ganges are examples of this.

The sea can cause flooding at the times of spring tides (see TIDES AND CURRENTS), especially when the sea level has been raised by very high winds. The high tides are then called "storm tides", and one of these which flooded the coasts of England and the Netherlands in 1099 caused 100,000 deaths. Again in February 1953 the level of the North Sea was raised by gales from the north, and storm tides flooded parts of East Anglia, the Netherlands and Belgium and drowned nearly 2,000 people. Tidal waves in the sea made by earthquakes can also cause floods, as happened in 1755 at Lisbon.

## Controlling Floods

Some rivers, like the St. Lawrence in Canada which flows from the Great Lakes, seldom overflow their banks. Melted snow and rain bring plenty of water into the lakes, but these have such a large area that their level does not rise very much. Therefore one way to check flooding is to make artificial lakes or reservoirs along the river, so as to be able to store up water at times of flood and then let it go slowly later on. This can be done by building dams across the valley, with sluice gates that can be opened or closed to control the flow of water (see DAM). Examples of flood-control reservoirs are to be found on the River Euphrates (Iraq), the River Tennessee (United States) and at the Aswan Dam on the Nile, but it is often too expensive to build such dams unless they can also be used for irrigation, water power, or water supply. (See IRRIGATION; WATER POWER; WATER SUPPLY.)

A river that meanders (twists and turns) can sometimes be prevented from flooding by digging new and straighter channels for it. These make it slope more steeply and so run faster and therefore there is less tendency for the mud to settle on its bed, as the more rapid flow of the water has a scouring or clearing action. Flooding from the sea can be prevented by building dikes, on which there is a separate article. (See also the article COAST PROTECTION.)

**FLOOD, THE.** Stories of a great flood covering the whole earth are found in the traditions of several ancient peoples.

In Chapters 6–9 of the Book of Genesis the Hebrews tell their story of the Flood—and they tell two slightly different versions of it. One of these says that the Lord told Noah to take two of every animal and living thing into the ark, and that the Flood lasted 150 days. The other says that the Lord told him to take seven of all the birds and of all the animals used for sacrifices (two of all other things), and that the Flood lasted 40 days.

The ancient Babylonians told a similar story of a great flood, for a clay tablet at least 2,500 years old has been found with the story written on it. The Greeks had several versions of a myth in which a king and his wife escape from a great flood by floating in a chest that finally lands on the top of a mountain. An Indian myth from the 6th century B.C. tells how the hero Manu was advised by a fish to build a ship as a means of escape from the coming flood. When it came, the fish towed the ship to a mountain top. Similar stories come from southern Asia, the South Sea Islands and all parts of the continent of America, but they are very rare in Africa and Europe (apart from the Greek myths).

Although the details of the Flood story given in Genesis may be imaginary, there is good reason to believe that some such happening did take place about 3000 B.C. The excavations at Ur by Sir Leonard Woolley in 1929 are generally agreed to have confirmed this ancient belief of many nations.

**FLORENCE,** or Firenze, as it is called by the Italians, is a large city in Italy, with a population of about 450,000, and lies in the pleasant valley of the River Arno, about 150 miles north-west of Rome, with high hills to the north and south. The many beautiful flowers to be seen

*Mansell Collection*

The Duomo in Florence and Giotto's bell-tower. These buildings are covered with beautiful coloured marble.

in and around Florence have earned it the name of "The City of the Flower".

Florence is one of the greatest artistic centres of the world, and has been ever since the 14th century, at the beginning of the great revival of learning and art called the Renaissance. Florence was the city of the architect Brunelleschi who invented the idea of perspective (see DRAWING), of the sculptor Donatello, the painters Giotto, Masaccio and Fra Filippo Lippi and his pupil Botticelli, and of those artists of tremendous genius Leonardo da Vinci and Michelangelo. In Florence also lived Dante, one of the world's greatest writers, and his childhood sweetheart Beatrice; Savonarola, the monk who tried to reform the church; and the great astronomer Galileo.

For many years Florence was ruled by the Medici family, bankers and merchants who helped the city to become rich and important and encouraged artists to work for them. The Florentine artists did not work at one art only; Andrea del Verrocchio, for instance, was a goldsmith, painter and sculptor, and Michelangelo was painter, sculptor, architect and poet.

In the middle of Florence stands the black and white marble baptistery, and opposite is the Duomo (House of God), or cathedral, with its magnificent dome designed by Brunelleschi. Beside the cathedral is the great campanile (bell tower) built in red, white and green marble by Giotto who painted, among many other pictures, the portrait of his fellow-citizen Dante. Outside the church of Or San Michele stands Donatello's statue of St. Michael and in the open colonnade called the Loggia dei Lanzi are Benvenuto Cellini's "Perseus" and other statues. On the front of the Foundling Hospital are little round medallions by Della Robbia of babies wrapped in swaddling clothes.

Inside the buildings the painters covered whole walls of churches, monasteries and palaces with pictures. Fra Angelico painted a picture in every cell of his monastery of San Marco, so that each monk had something beautiful to look at when he studied and prayed. On the walls of the Medici palace chapel, Benozzo Gozzoli painted the procession of the Magi (the three wise men from the East) winding down the hills outside Florence, and in the procession he painted portraits of all the great people then in Florence, among them Lorenzo de Medici, the Magnificent. The Church of San Lorenzo contains Michelangelo's finest sculptures and that of Santa Croce has splendid paintings by Giotto.

The bridges across the river are in their way as fine as the buildings of the city. Among them are the Ponte Vecchio, or Old Bridge, lined with little workshops and houses, just as London Bridge once was, and the rebuilt Ponte Santa Trinita. The skill of the Florentine craftsmen still survives and the shops are full of beautiful things. The art galleries are among the finest in the world and include the Uffizi, the Pitti Palace and the Bargello museum of sculpture.

On November 4, 1966, the Arno overflowed its banks in the worst flood ever recorded in Florentine history, and 39 people in the district were drowned. The flood waters, mixed with escaped oil from fuel tanks, did enormous damage to the city's art treasures. Many countries, including Britain, collected money and sent experts to help in the giant task of restoration.

(See BOTTICELLI; DANTE; DONATELLO; LEONARDO DA VINCI; MEDICI FAMILY; MICHELANGELO.)

**FLORIDA,** the most southerly state of the United States, was discovered by the Spaniards in 1513 and given its name in honour of "Pascua Florida"—the feast of flowers or Easter Day, when it was first seen. The Spaniards used Florida chiefly as a place from which to defend their rich colonies in Cuba and Mexico, and built forts such as that of St. Augustine, which is the oldest European settlement in the United States. In 1763 Florida became a British colony, but 20 years later was returned to Spain and in 1821 became part of the United States. It was made a state in 1845, with its capital at Tallahassee, and in the Civil War fought on the side of the South.

Most of Florida forms a peninsula between the Atlantic and the Gulf of Mexico; it is the size of England and Wales and has a population of about 5,000,000, of whom one-fifth are Negroes. Its chief products are oranges, grapefruit, vegetables, maize, peanuts, tobacco, sugar cane, cotton, timber, paper, fish, pigs, cattle, phosphates for fertilizers and limestone. Every year some 3,000,000 holiday makers come to Florida and the money they spend makes it prosperous. Most of them come in the winter, because it is then warm and sunny in Florida, and enjoy themselves on the wonderful bathing beaches or camping, fishing and hunting among the pine forests and many lakes.

In the wide grasslands of northern Florida there are big cattle ranches and cowboys ride the range much as they used to in the "Wild West". There are a very few Seminole Indians but they live peacefully in a "reserve" or tract of country set apart for them. In the south is the flat, marshy area known as the Everglades.

Many of the wild parts of Florida are very beautiful, the trees draped in Spanish moss which hangs from the branches like a row of grey beards, and the forest and marshes bright with flowers, including orchids, and rare butterflies. Pelicans, egrets and spoonbills can be seen, and in the swamps lives the deadly water moccasin.

*Courtesy, United States Information Service*

A silver-scaled tarpon, one of the huge game fishes that are caught by rod and line off the coasts of Florida.

Miami is the starting point for air lines to the countries of Central and South America. Other important cities are Jacksonville and Tampa.

**FLOUR.** In Great Britain, the United States and many Commonwealth countries, flour is made by milling, or grinding, grains of wheat. Flour is also milled from rye, barley, maize and rice, while oatmeal and oatflakes for porridge are made by grinding oats. All these grains are cereals; that is, they are the fruits of various kinds of grasses. (See Cereal.)

This article describes wheat flour and how it is milled, for wheat is the most important of the cereals. If you look at a grain of wheat you will find that it has three main parts. There is a brown coat called the bran. Inside is the white part called the endosperm and at one end of this is the yellow germ which becomes the new plant when the grain is sown in the ground. The endosperm feeds the young plant before it has roots and leaves, while the bran protects both germ and endosperm.

The part used for making flour is the endosperm. If it is gently crushed it gives a mixture of large and small particles. The small particles are flour and the larger ones are called semolina. A little of the semolina is used for making semolina puddings but most of it is crushed down to tiny particles, or in other words, to flour.

The endosperm contains starch, which is an important food providing energy, and also a substance called gluten, which is a body-building protein. (See Starch and Protein.) When flour is mixed with water to form dough, the gluten becomes rubbery and can be stretched. This allows the dough to expand in the baker's oven to make a large, light loaf. Other cereals contain both starch and nourishing proteins, but only wheat has the protein called gluten.

The bran is firmly fixed to the endosperm but is of little use in making bread, so the miller normally separates the two when he is grinding wheat into flour. Some of the bran is used as a breakfast cereal but most is fed to farm animals, which can digest it properly. The germ of the wheat is a valuable food, for it contains oil and vitamins (see Vitamin), but flour keeps better

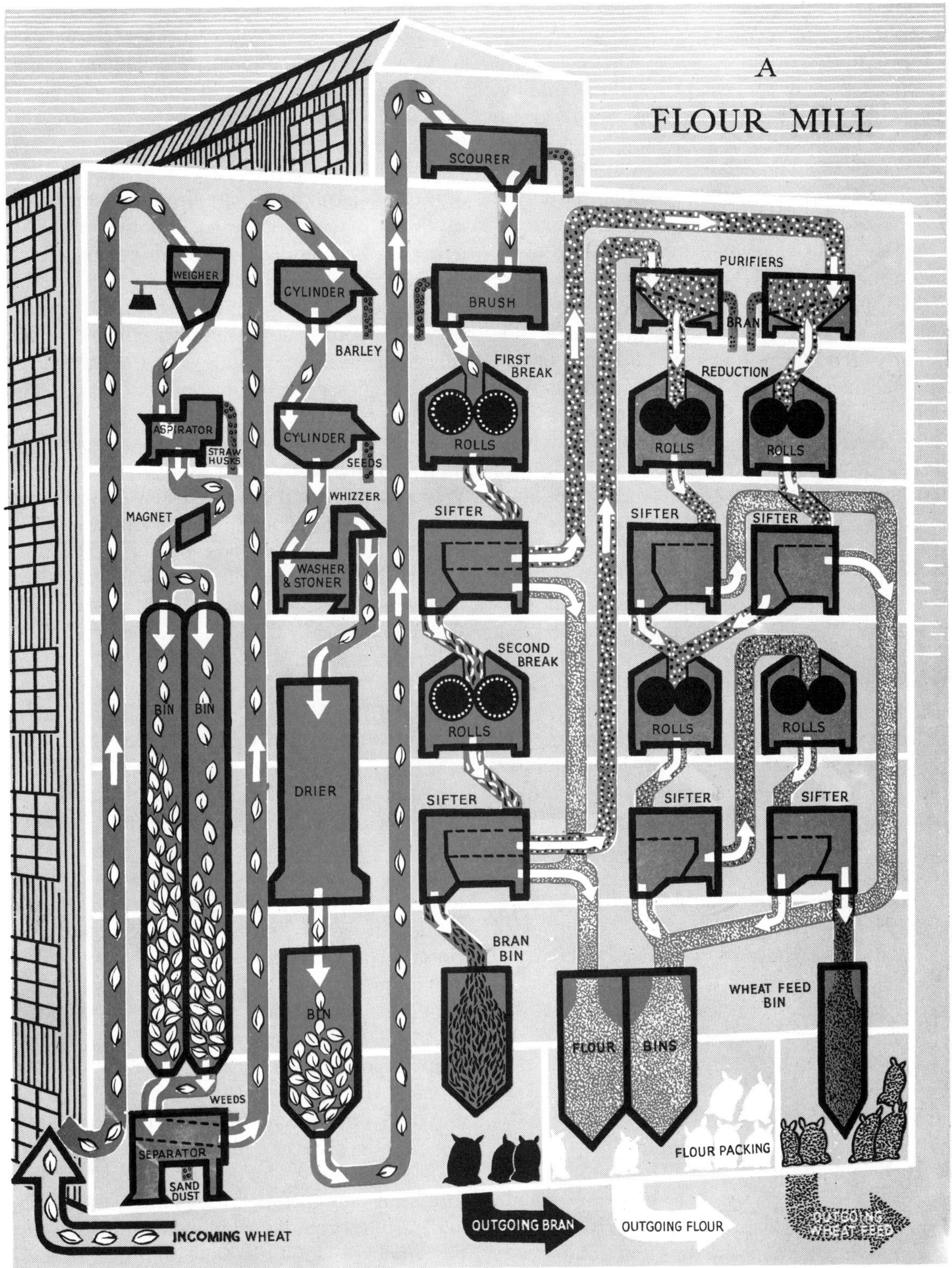


The diagram shows what happens to wheat as it is made into flour. The grains are broken down gradually and stripped of their bran. Each grind gives a mixture of flour and larger particles which go on to the next set of rollers.

when most of the germ is removed, as normally happens during milling.

Wheat is always cleaned before milling. Sieves with large holes let the wheat grains through but hold back sticks and straw, other sieves with small holes being used to let grit and small seeds through while holding back the wheat. Magnets are used to remove any metal fragments, and chaff and dust are blown away by currents of air. Weed seeds of the same size as the wheat grains will still be left among the wheat, but as the weed seeds are shaped differently from the wheat they can be removed by machinery which has pockets of various shapes. The wheat is then washed with water, strained off and dried by warm air. Any loose shreds of the bran are removed by a brush machine and the wheat is then ready for milling.

### Flour Milling

During milling the wheat is broken down gradually in about 18 grinds. Each grind gives a mixture of small and large particles. The small particles (the flour) are sifted away from the large particles (the semolina and bran coats) which go to another grind. The wheat is not crushed in one very heavy grind because the bran would be powdered down and would go into the flour. Grinding gently and gradually helps to keep the bran in large pieces so that the fine particles of flour can be sifted away from it.

The first few grinds are designed to separate the endosperm from the bran coats. First of all the grain is torn open by passing it between two long steel rollers which have sharp cuts or grooves along their length. These rollers, which turn at different speeds, also start to scrape the endosperm from the bran and this scraping process is finished in the next three or four grinds in which similar grooved rollers are used. A little flour is sifted away each time, but the large particles of endosperm (the semolina) have to be crushed in further grinds between smooth rollers, each of which turns at nearly the same speed as the one opposite it. Flour continues to be sifted away after each grind.

The flour obtained in this way is creamy coloured. It becomes whiter and makes better bread after it has been stored for three or four months, but small amounts of chemicals can be added to bleach it (make it white) and make it ready for baking more quickly. Brown and wholemeal loaves are made of flour containing most or all of the bran as well as all the germ and endosperm, and there are also some kinds of flour to which an extra amount of wheat germ has been added. Self-raising flour, which is used for cakes and puddings, is made by adding small amounts of two chemicals, bicarbonate of soda and calcium phosphate. When this flour is mixed with water the chemicals form the gas carbon dioxide, which raises the dough in the oven.

Bread is made wholly or at least partly of flour milled from a hard kind of wheat. (See WHEAT and also the article BREAD, which says something, too, about the history of flour milling.) The article MACARONI tells how macaroni, spaghetti and vermicelli are made from semolina which has been milled from a very hard Canadian wheat. Biscuits, however, need flour from a softer grain. (See BISCUIT.)

**FLOWER.** A person who thinks that flowers are simply the brightly coloured parts of a plant is wrong. The purpose of a flower is to produce seeds that will develop into new plants like the one on which it grows, and this must always be kept in mind when studying flowers. Some blossoms, such as those of the poinsettia, are not true flowers, but brilliant red leaves that surround the small flowers at the centre of the cluster. In the arum lilies, which are used so much for Easter decoration, the great white sheath is not a single flower but a special bract, or leaf, surrounding and protecting a club-shaped mass on which many small flowers are tightly crowded together.

To a botanist, a flower is a structure containing all those parts of a plant that are closely concerned with producing seeds. It follows, therefore, that only seed-bearing plants have flowers and, in fact, the plant kingdom is divided into two great groups—the flowering and the non-flowering plants. Among the non-flowering plants are lichens, fungi, liverworts, mosses, club-mosses, horsetails and ferns. (See PLANT.)

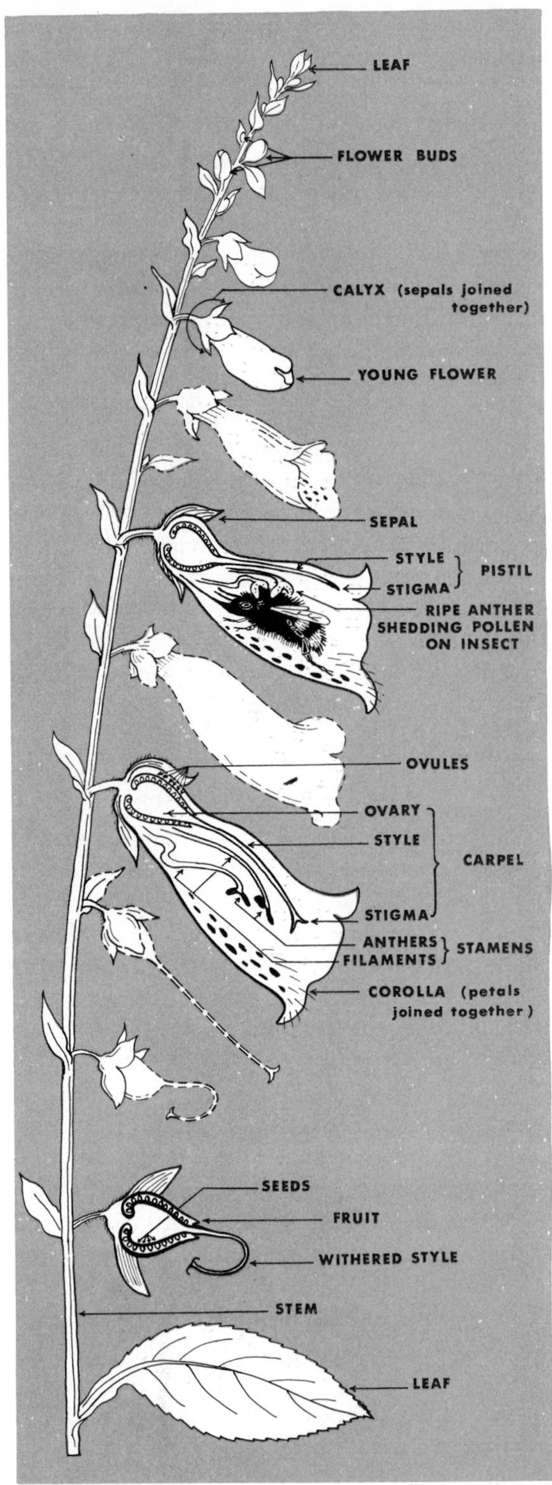


The flowers on this foxglove stem are at different stages of their life, from bud to fruit. The bumble-bee in one of them will carry away some pollen on its body and in this way it may pollinate the next flower it visits.

## The Parts of a Flower

Most flowers are made up of four different kinds of parts arranged in circles one inside the other. These parts are called the calyx, the corolla, the stamens and the carpels. Some flowers have no corolla; in others the calyx and corolla are exactly alike, as in the tulip; some may have no stamens and others no carpels—in other words flowers vary in a great many ways. In a typical flower, however, such as the buttercup or the foxglove, the four rings of parts are present. The outer one is the calyx and is made up of sepals. These are usually green in colour, and when the flower is in bud the petals are folded away inside them and they form a protective covering. The sepals may be joined together as in the foxglove, or separate as in the buttercup. (See the illustration in the article PLANT.)

Inside the corolla are the stamens, and they may vary in number from two to several hundred. They produce the pollen and they are made up of filaments, or stalks, with an anther, or pollen sac, at the top of each.

In the centre of the flower are the carpels, each made up of a stigma at the top, generally a style or stalk, and an ovary at the bottom containing ovules. The stigma and style together are known as the pistil, and it is by means of the pistil that the pollen grains from the anthers reach the ovary. The stigma, when ripe, has a sticky surface from which pollen grains cannot be blown away or fall off. This is very important because it is in the ovary, at the lower end of the style, that the cells in the pollen join the cells in the ovules. It is only after this that the ovules become the seeds from which new plants grow. The transfer of pollen is called pollination.

## How Pollination takes place

The pollen escapes when the anthers are ripe. They open by slits or tiny holes, releasing the pollen as fine yellow dust. Sometimes the pollen simply falls on the stigma of the same flower and stays there, and this is called self-pollination. More often, however, the pollen has to be carried from the stamens of one plant to the stigma of another, and this is usually done by the wind or by insects. Among the plants that are pollinated by wind are the grasses, not only the grasses of the meadows but also wheat and other grains. The stamens of these plants have long slender filaments so that the anthers wave in the slightest breeze and their pollen escapes. The stigmas of most grasses are like tiny plumes, which catch large quantities of pollen. Many trees are wind-pollinated, examples being the birch and the oak. The flowers of wind-pollinated plants are not brightly coloured, and in fact they often have no corolla. They are not sweet-smelling.

Insect-pollinated flowers, on the other hand, generally have brightly coloured petals and often a sweet scent. The scent comes from certain substances known as volatile or essential oils in the flowers. The colour and scent seem to attract bees, small flies and other insects. Bees visit the flowers for the nectar, which is the sweet fluid that they make into honey, and for the pollen, which they eat. As an insect collects pollen from a flower (there is always more pollen than the plant needs), some of it comes off on its body; then, when it goes to the next flower, some of the pollen is rubbed on to the stigma. Thus the insect helps the plant while it is helping itself. This transfer of pollen from one flower to another is called cross-pollination.

Some flowers can be pollinated only by certain kinds of insects because of the shape of the corolla. The larkspur, snapdragon and orchids have "landing stages" on which heavy insects can alight; in the snapdragon only a heavy bee can part the lips of the corolla to reach the nectar within. Many flowers, such as the larkspur, nasturtium and honeysuckle, have their nectar concealed in such long tubes that only insects with long sucking mouthparts, such as hawk moths or butterflies, can reach it.

Although many flowers are pollinated by wind or insects, some are pollinated by birds that feed on nectar. This happens most often in hot countries where humming-birds and honey eaters live, but the garden fuchsia and scarlet sage are often bird-pollinated. Some flowers are pollinated by fruit-eating bats such as the "flying fox" of southeast Asia, and the small Australian marsupials called honey mice pollinate trees. Even snails have been observed to pollinate plants.

When the pollen has settled on the stigma it begins to grow, and each grain develops a tube which extends down the style to the ovules. Inside each pollen tube are two cells which by the growth of the tube are carried to an ovule. When a pollen tube reaches an ovule it grows into it, then the tube breaks and the cells are released. One unites, or joins, with the egg cell in the ovule and from this a new plant later grows. The other cell unites with another cell in the ovule, and from this union a food supply for the new plant develops. This process is called fertilization. Thus each seed as it matures, or ripens, contains a new plant and some food, and round these there is a protective seed coat, which may become rather papery, as in the bean, or very hard, as in the Brazil nut.

An important point to remember about pollination is that if pollen from one kind of plant is carried to the stigma of another kind it will not generally develop a pollen tube and so no seed is produced. For instance, pollen from a grass plant blown on to the stigma of an apple flower would not produce an apple.

## The Uses of Flowers

It is by the flowers that botanists classify plants, or arrange them in scientific groups. It has been found that if several plants of one species, or kind, are grown under very different conditions the leaves and stems may be different but the parts of the flowers will always be arranged in the same way and the flowers will look much the same as the normal ones.

The details of floral structure—the way in which the different parts of the flower are arranged in different plants—are most important to anyone who is grouping plants into families, and then dividing the families into genera and species. (See BIOLOGY.) Colour and size are not very important because they vary according to climate, soil and other things. The botanist looks most closely at the number and arrangement of the sepals, petals, stamens and carpels, because these details will be the most helpful in his work of classification.

The arrangement of flowers on their stalks is also important in classifying plants, and there are a great many different arrangements. Some —the violet and the daffodil, for instance—have one blossom at the end of each stem. Others, such as the apple and the cowslip, grow in loose clusters at the end of the stem. The flowers of some plants hang from short stalks attached along the main stem, as in the foxglove and the Solomon's seal. In some plants, such as wheat, the flowers are densely placed around a central stem in a cluster called a spike. In other plants, such as the white cow parsley, the flowers form a flat-topped, umbrella-shaped head. This umbrella-shaped head is called an umbel.

Apple blossom.

One of the most closely packed clusters is found in the large Compositae family, which includes daisies, asters, thistles, zinnias and dandelions. In these, and in the other plants of the same family, what looks like a single flower is really a whole crowd of tiny flowers, not all alike, which are arranged in a special way and stand upright on a flat disc. When you "pull petals off a daisy" you are really pulling apart a bunch of tiny flowers. This tight packing is a good way of making sure of pollination. A bee or a fly can hardly walk across a daisy in full bloom without pollinating many of the little flowers.

Flowers are still used in the manufacture of perfumes, although products made in factories generally take their place nowadays. The oils of lavender, thyme and rosemary are three perfume oils which come partly from flowers, and the sweet-smelling and costly attar of roses is still made from roses. The drugs arnica and opium both come from the flowering heads of plants, arnica coming from a plant of the same name and opium coming from the poppy. The nectar of flowers is used by bees for the manufacture of honey. The chief value of flowers to man, however, is their beauty—in the garden, in the house and in the woods and fields. And of course if there were no flowers there would be no fruits. (There is a separate article WILD FLOWERS in which hundreds of different flowers are described.)

**FLUORESCENCE.** The strip lighting often seen inside shops, offices and factories comes from tubular lamps which give off light because of fluorescence, and the brightness of a television screen is caused in the same way. The insides of the lamp tube and of the screen are coated with substances which glow brightly when certain kinds of invisible rays fall upon them. In the case of the fluorescent lamp these rays are *ultra violet* and in the television set they are *cathode* rays.

A fluorescent lamp contains a small amount of mercury vapour or gas, and when the electric current is switched on it passes through this vapour and creates ultra violet rays which, although they cannot be seen, behave just like light rays. These rays hit the coating on the inside of the lamp and make it glow brightly. Light of a different colour can be obtained by using a coating of another substance, and some lamps of this kind are made to give off light that is an almost exact copy of daylight and can thus be used for matching colours. The advantage of fluorescent lamps is that they use only a fraction of the current of ordinary lamps.

The cathode rays which cause fluorescence on a television screen are explained in the article ELECTRONICS. Ultra violet rays can serve other purposes besides lighting, and are also used to tell apart drugs, ores of metals, fungi and germs by means of the different colours of fluorescence given off. The screens used for X-rays—as in hospitals and the machines used by dentists for examining teeth—are coated with a substance that gives a greenish glow when the X-rays fall on it. (See X-RAY.)

The coloured strip lighting outside shops and cinemas is usually not the fluorescent kind, but is obtained by passing electric current through special gases. These *discharge lamps* as they are called are sometimes used for street lighting,

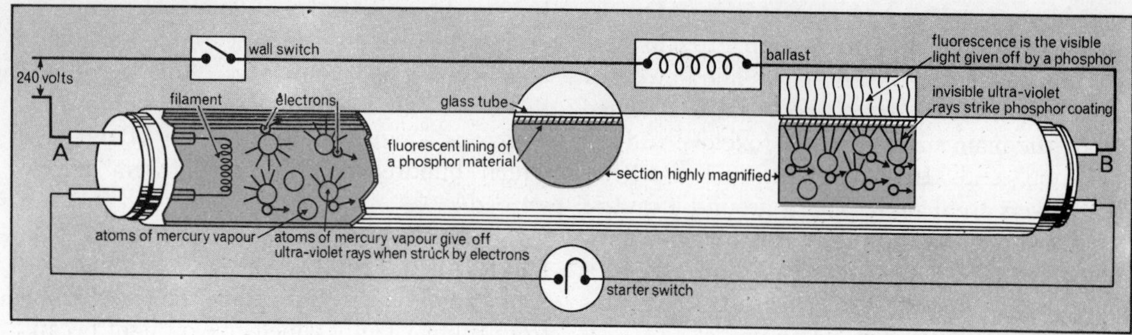


**How a fluorescent lamp works. When the wall switch is closed, or on, the 240-volt current flows through the entire lamp circuit. The path is through the ballast (which controls the amount of electricity), the filaments inside the tube at each end, and the starter switch. The electricity heats the filaments, which then give off large numbers of electrons. The starter switch also is heated, opens, and breaks that part of the circuit. The electric current in the form of free electrons flows through the tube from A to B. The tube also contains small drops of mercury, which produce some mercury vapour. As the electrons strike the atoms of mercury, invisible ultraviolet rays are produced, which make the phosphor lining of the tube glow with light. The light we see is from the glowing phosphors.**

such as, for example, the kind using sodium gas, which gives a yellow light.

The hands and figures of a luminous watch glow at night because of phosphorescence, but this differs from fluorescence, which ceases directly the electric current causing the rays is turned off.

**FLUTE FAMILY.** The flute, one of the most ancient of all musical instruments, has the form of a tube of wood or metal (usually silver, but sometimes gold or platinum) pierced with holes over which are pieces of metal called keys. Unlike all other woodwind instruments, the flute has no reed and the flute-player, or flautist, blows *across* a small oval-shaped hole called the embouchure near one end of the tube. This end is stopped by a plug.

*Courtesy, Rumanian Minister of Education and Culture*
**A young Rumanian boy playing the flute.**

In the time of Bach (the early 18th century) the flute had only six finger-holes and one key. The flute of today is sometimes called the transverse flute (connected with the word "traverse", to cross) because it is held across the player's lips. It has about 16 finger-holes and was invented in the 19th century by a German jeweller called Theodore Boehm. It is therefore also known as the Boehm flute or the German flute. In the orchestra it can play softly and sweetly, and also very rapidly and brilliantly so that it can be easily recognized, even against the background of a full orchestra.

Other members of the flute family are the piccolo and the fife, about which there are separate articles. The recorder is another kind of flute known also as the whistle flute. This is held straight in front of the face and is played with a whistle mouthpiece. (You can read more about this instrument in the article RECORDER FAMILY.)

**FLY.** Already over 75,000 different kinds of flies are known to scientists and new ones are being discovered every day. In fact flies form one of the largest groups of insects in the world.

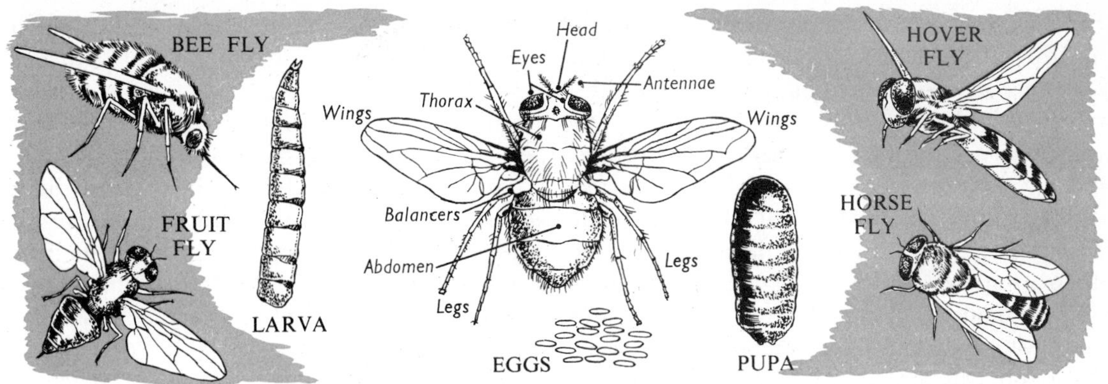


It is easy to tell them apart from the many other tiny flying insects, such as aphids and small beetles and wasps, because flies have only one pair of wings. (Butterflies, dragonflies, mayflies and caddis flies are not true flies.) Behind the one pair of wings—where a second pair would be on a wasp, for example—the true fly has two small knobs known as balancers. If the fly loses these it cannot steer properly. Indeed it can hardly fly at all, for it seems to need them as a balance against the strains in its body caused by the very rapid movement of the wings. Flies that have no wings have no balancers either, and such flies are usually parasites (living on other creatures) or else live in places where, if they flew, they might be blown away by high winds.

The smallest gnats and midges (see GNAT and MIDGE) fly only very feebly or hardly at all, but other kinds of flies fly as strongly as any hawk moth or humming bird. Nevertheless, even the fastest hardly ever fly at more than 30 miles an hour, and the tale often told about the American bot fly reaching 600 or 700 miles an hour is simply nonsense.

In most flies the middle part of the body, known as the thorax, is stout, because it needs strong muscles to work the legs and wings. The most noticeable parts of the head are the large compound eyes made up of hundreds of tiny lenses. The antennae, or "feelers", are really used for smelling, not feeling. In some flies, such as the mosquito and daddy-longlegs, the antennae are fairly long, while in others, such as the house-fly and bluebottle, they are quite short. (There are articles on each of these four common flies.) In all flies the mouth is shaped for either sucking or licking, and although many flies are said to bite they cannot actually do so, for they have no jaws. They prick the skin with a kind of dagger and then suck the blood through a narrow tube.

Some of the tiniest flies have bodies barely half a millimetre long, whereas the largest may be nearly two inches long and even more across the wing. This range of size may not seem very great; actually it is, in proportion, about the same as that between a mouse and an elephant.

## Life History

Flies have the same kind of life history as butterflies, beetles and bees. They start as an egg, hatching into a legless larva, or grub. This feeds and grows, but stops when it becomes a pupa (like a chrysalis). From the pupa comes the fully grown fly.

The eggs are laid where the grub will be able to find food, and they may be any shape—round, oval, flat, even, in one case, shaped like a horseshoe. Sometimes they are laid singly and sometimes in masses. The eggs of some of the mosquitoes have floats to keep them on the surface of the water, in which the grubs will live when they hatch out. Other eggs can remain dried up for months and yet hatch as soon as they are wetted by the rain. The larva often has an "egg-tooth" on the back of its head which helps it to cut a way out of the shell, just as a young chick uses the egg tooth on its beak.

The best-known fly grubs are probably the maggots of the flesh flies, known to fishermen as gentles. Another common kind is the leather-jacket, which is the grub of the daddy-longlegs.

(See Leatherjacket.) Dirty drains often contain the rat-tail maggot of a big hover-fly, the tail being in fact a breathing tube, while the wriggling "blood-worms" so often found in water tubs are the grubs of a small gnat. Some of the grubs that feed on growing plants, such as the European frit-fly and the American Hessian fly, do enormous damage to oats and other grain crops. Fly maggots, frequently prettily coloured orange, pink or red, cause the knobbly growths called galls on bushes and trees. There is hardly any situation in which fly grubs of one kind or another do not live, either on land or in water, and some are even found in the sea. Perhaps the strangest of all is the Californian fly grub, which lives in thick pools of crude oil, breathing by means of a tube pushed above the surface and feeding on other insects that fall in.

A great many fly grubs live by feeding on other insects. For instance, those of many hover-flies feed on harmful aphids (see Aphid) and are most valuable helpers to the gardener. They are flattened, greenish grubs which move around actively, swinging their heads about in search of prey. Many fly grubs are parasites, too. The butterfly collector is occasionally disappointed to see a large hairy fly, rather like a house fly, hatching out from his treasured chrysalis instead of the moth he was expecting. The simple explanation is that a fly has laid an egg on the living caterpillar, and the grub which hatched burrowed into the caterpillar and grew up inside it without killing it, turning into a pupa at the same time as the caterpillar.

Much more troublesome are the warbles and bots which live inside the bodies of cattle and sheep, giving them immense discomfort and often making them useless for man as well, because the damage they do to the skins spoils them for use as leather.

Whereas a caterpillar always sheds its last skin when it turns into a chrysalis, many fly grubs turn into pupae inside this skin, which then swells up and hardens, forming a protection for the pupa. When such a fly hatches from its pupa, its head opens and out comes a kind of balloon which the fly "blows up" until it forces a cap off its stiff outer case, so providing a way out. As soon as the fly has escaped from its case and, if it was below ground, has pushed its way up through the soil, the balloon goes down again and is drawn back inside the fly's head, leaving only a scar to show where it has been.

Adult flies may not have quite so many different habits as their grubs, but they are just as interesting. There is one tiny gnat which, being fond of blood, obtains it by "biting" mosquitoes that have drunk their fill from some unfortunate animal. There are other gnats that travel about attached to the wings—not the bodies—of dragonflies. A rather larger one uses bees as a means of transport and will even persuade the bee to provide it with honey when it is hungry, while quite a number have learnt to steal food from ants, even from the fierce driver ants.

Another group of flies lives amongst the hair and feathers of animals and birds, sucking their blood. Some of these fly short distances but many are quite wingless, having specially strong claws for clinging to their living food supply. Another peculiarity of these parasites is that they do not lay eggs. Instead, the grubs develop inside the body of the mother fly and then, almost as soon as they are born, turn into pupae.

Flies which live on the blood of other creatures also include the horse-flies (see Horse-Fly) which are found in Great Britain, and which often give human beings quite a painful "bite", and the black flies of the plains of Hungary, which swarm in such countless numbers that their "bites" have been known to cause the death of cattle. One way that flies carry diseases from man to man (or from animal to man) is by biting them in this manner. (See Tsetse Fly, for example.) They also spread disease by carrying germs on their hairy legs, feet and mouth parts after they have been feeding on filth. This is why they must be kept off food.

Fortunately, not all flies have merely odd or unattractive habits. It is fascinating to watch the dancing swarms of midges during their mating flights—sometimes so closely packed in the air as to look like a cloud of smoke—or to admire the perfection of the hover-fly, poised motionless in mid-air, or the bee flies, looking just like bees in flight and settling to suck nectar (the honey fluid) peacefully from the flowers.

**FLYCATCHER.** The flycatchers are a family of small perching birds found in Europe, Africa, Asia and Australia. They are so named because of their habit of darting out from a look-out post or tree to catch flies and other insects in the air. The birds called tyrant flycatchers in America have similar habits but belong to a different family.

The spotted flycatcher is common throughout the British Isles. It is a neat, slim-looking bird, nearly six inches long, greyish brown above and whitish below, with faint streaks on its head and breast. Its scratchy call-note, "tzee", may be heard in large gardens, parks and open woodlands from the middle of May, for it is one of the last of the summer visitors to arrive from abroad. The nest of moss, hair and wool is bound together with cobwebs and built against a wall or tree, often supported by creepers; the birds will also use an open nesting box. The four or five greenish grey eggs with reddish blotches are laid from the end of May. The birds winter in Africa and southwest Asia.

Pied and spotted flycatchers. They are often seen perched on a twig, watching for insects. One of the spotted flycatchers in the picture is in hot pursuit of a fly.

The scarcer pied flycatcher arrives earlier and breeds here and there in Devon, through Wales and northern England to central Scotland. The male is black above, with white lines on the wing, white forehead and white underparts, and looks very striking in spring. The female is brown where he is black, with less white. The call note is a sharp "whit" or "whit-tic" and the male has a simple, pleasing song. The nest is built in a hole, usually in a tree, and four or five pale blue eggs are laid.

One of the Australian flycatchers is known as the scarlet robin because of its bright breast, while others, with the habit of flicking open their long tails, are called fantails.

**FLYING.** Learning to fly an aeroplane is not much harder than learning to drive a car. Most pupils are allowed to "go solo" (on their own) after only a few hours' dual instruction in a light training aeroplane. In dual instruction an instructor goes up with the pupil to tell him what to do and show him how to do it. A special aeroplane is used which has two sets of interconnected controls, one set of controls for the pupil and one for the instructor so that he can take over and put things right if the pupil gets into difficulties. No pilot ever forgets his first solo, however many thousands of hours he has flown since. (Flying time is always counted in hours, and some experienced airline pilots have flown more than 15,000 hours.)

Although it is easy for most people to learn how to take off, fly and land a light aeroplane in good weather conditions, it is only long experience that enables a pilot to fly any kind of aeroplane in all sorts of weather. Indeed, the most experienced pilots say that they never cease learning.

### How an Aeroplane is Controlled

You will see from the diagram shown below that the pilot has only two controls with which to guide him in flight, the *control column* (often called the "stick") which he holds in one hand and the *rudder bar* which he operates with

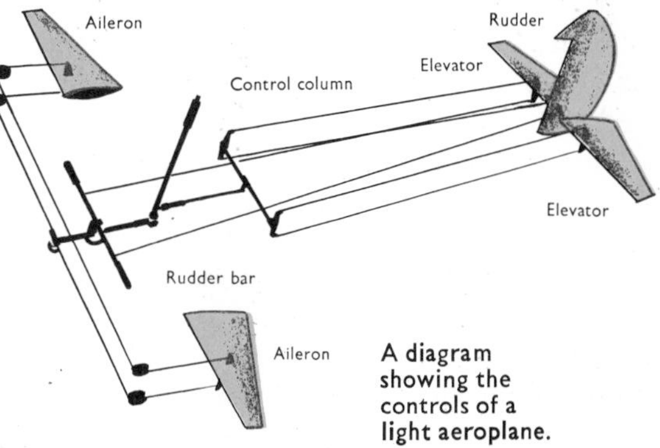


A diagram showing the controls of a light aeroplane.

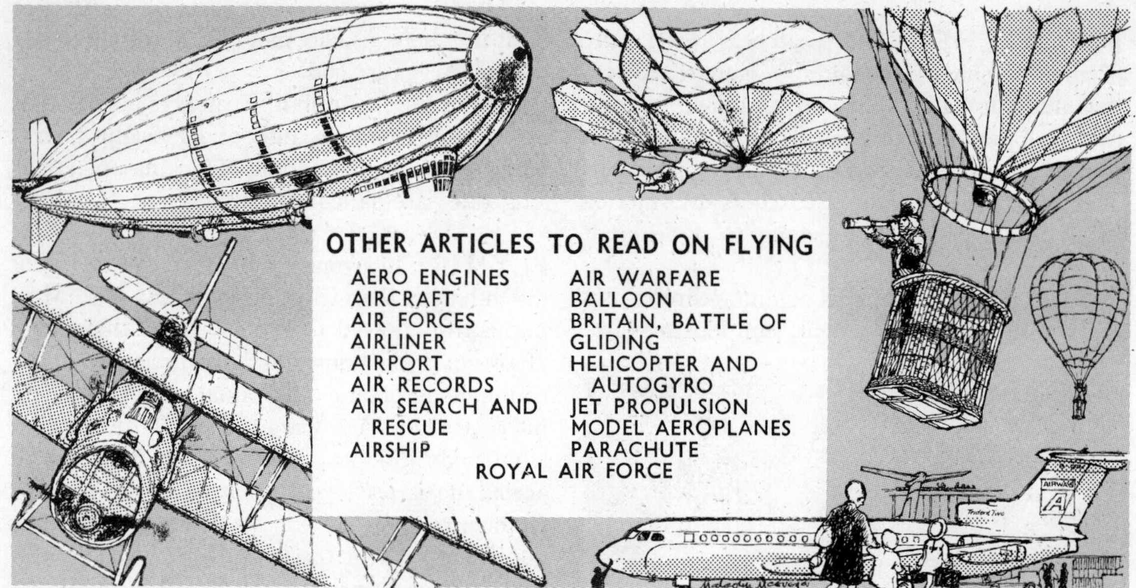


his feet. The control column works the two *ailerons* and the *elevator*. The ailerons are separate, movable pieces at the back of the wings, which are fixed to the wings by hinges. When the "stick" is moved to one side the aileron on that side moves upwards and that on the other side moves downwards. The aeroplane tilts over in the direction of the one that is upwards, so that if the right aileron is lifted the plane will bank, or dip, towards the right. The elevator is another horizontal hinged part, which is fixed to the tail of the aeroplane. By moving the "stick" forwards the pilot lowers the elevator and makes the plane dive. It dives because the air presses against the lowered elevator and therefore pushes the tail upwards. When the "stick" is pulled backwards the opposite happens and the aeroplane climbs. The rudder also belongs to the tail, but to the vertical part of it. This part consists of two sections, one that is fixed and one behind it, hinged to it, that moves. This rear movable section is the rudder, and the pilot moves it to the right or left (by means of the rudder bar) when he wants to change the direction in which he is flying. The aeroplane turns in the direction to which the rudder is pointing. (The ailerons also are used in turning.)

Most flying schools use light, two-seater aircraft for the first stages of training. Usually, training aeroplanes are monoplanes, or aircraft with only one wing on each side of the body; examples are the De Havilland Chipmunk and Piper Cherokee. Biplanes (with two wings on each side) are seldom used as trainers nowadays. As even training aeroplanes fly at 90 miles an hour people flying in them must be well wrapped up in helmet, goggles and a wind-proof jacket if the aeroplane has an open *cockpit*, as the pilot's compartment is called.

The aeroplane has a single engine of 100 to 200 horse power, and its speed is controlled by a *throttle lever*. This is pushed forward to increase the speed at which the engine revolves (when the pilot wants more power) and pulled back to reduce it. The only other engine controls in a small trainer are the two *switches* to switch the two *magnetos* on and off. (The magnetos make the spark which ignites the petrol.) Aero engine switches are "off" when down and "on" when up.

The pilot sits with the control column between his legs. It is a straight stick, usually with a loop at the top so that he can grip it. His feet rest on the rudder bar. The throttle lever is at one side of the cockpit, and on the other side there may be a wheel to "trim", or alter, the angle of the tail plane (the part of the horizontal tail in front of the elevator). Trimming is particularly useful at take-off and on landing.

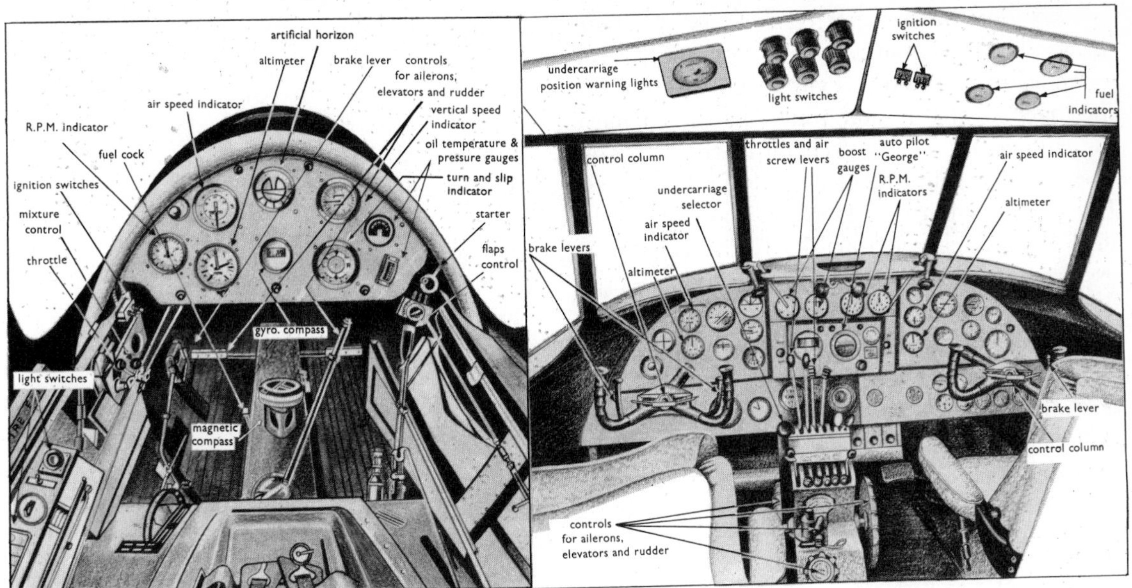


The cockpit of a light aeroplane. The cockpit of a commercial airliner.

In front of him is the *dashboard* with the dials which give him information all the time. One of the most important is the *air speed indicator* which shows the speed of the aeroplane through the air. Then there is the *altimeter* which shows height above the ground. The altimeter is generally set at zero at the home aerodrome. If the pilot is going to land at another aerodrome he is careful to find out its height above sea level and to compare it with that of his own.

Next there will be the *revolution counter*, showing the speed at which the engine is running. Full power is needed to leave the ground, but once at a safe height, the engine is "throttled down" to a lower speed, or cruising speed, in order to save strain on it. The *oil pressure* and *temperature gauges* show whether the oil is circulating properly and whether the engine is getting too hot. Finally, there will probably be a *turn and bank* indicator to show whether the aeroplane is turning correctly. This is especially important in darkness or cloud.

## First Lessons

Suppose that you have decided to learn to fly and are going up on your first flight. You have already put on the harness of your parachute and buckled it round you. As soon as you have sat down in the aeroplane fasten the safety belt round your body. This is made of canvas straps fixed on either side of your seat and clipped together in front of you, holding you firmly at such bumpy times as take-off and landing. The simple trainer in which you are about to fly has dual control and the instructor will be able to speak to you through a speaking-tube. You will of course have already studied the controls and instruments and will be ready for the take-off.

You must give yourself as long a run across the aerodrome as possible and must take off into the wind. (The direction of the wind is shown by a "wind sleeve", a piece of material like the sleeve of a coat, which is hung from a mast on the airfield. As full engine power is needed for take-off, push the throttle lever forwards. Push the control column forwards also to put the elevator down and lift the tail of the aeroplane. The pilot wants the tail lifted because that puts the wings in the best position for getting up speed quickly and so for gaining the greatest "lift" as soon as possible. When you feel you are going fast enough for the wings to lift the aeroplane off the ground pull the column gently back and the machine will take to the air and begin to climb. When you have risen to, say, 2,000 feet, stop climbing—push the control column to the central position—and watch the altimeter so that you stay at 2,000 feet.

After you have mastered how to do these things the instructor will probably tell you to make a turn. To do this you both turn and tilt the machine at the same time. To turn it push the rudder bar in the direction of the turn you wish to make and tilt it by moving the ailerons. If you used only the rudder, the machine would slip outwards away from the turn, and if you used only the ailerons it would slip inwards without turning. Only by using both can you make the aeroplane turn perfectly on to its new course. Slight use of rudder and ailerons gives a slow, gentle turn; full rudder and sharp tilt give very quick turns. It is possible to turn while climbing with full engine power in use or while gliding with the engine fully throttled down.

Your next task is to return to earth. As an aeroplane must take off into the wind, so it must land into the wind. It must also land as close to the near edge of the aerodrome as possible, so as to be able to run its whole length, if necessary. It is important to choose the right moment to throttle down the engine and begin to glide. If you do this correctly, the aeroplane will cross the aerodrome boundary at a low height and at a speed of about 65 miles an hour. As it nears the ground ease back the control column to reduce speed until, at a few inches above the ground, the aeroplane loses flying speed. It then sinks gently to the ground, the main wheels and tail wheel touching ground at the same time in a good landing.

Your first flight is over and you "taxi" into the hangar. *Taxying*, or driving an aircraft on the ground, is done by careful adjustment of the engine and the controls and it is not as easy as it looks.

You will be surprised at how quickly you get the "feel" of the air and are able to handle your machine properly. Soon you will go off on your first solo, and then you will have more dual instruction in between solo flights, so that the instructor can make sure that you are not developing bad flying habits. He will also teach you aerobatics in order to make you really the master of the aeroplane and to give you confidence. First, he will teach you how to recover from a *spin*.

If an aeroplane stalls in the air it is likely to go into a spin; that is, to fall in a very steep spiral. This is frightening, but it is quite easy to get out of a spin. If the machine is spinning, say, to the left, move the rudder as far to the right as it will go and push the control column slightly forwards. These actions stop the spin. When the aircraft has stopped spinning, move the column slightly backwards to stop your dive and open the throttle to increase power.

## Aerobatics

Aerobatics might be called acrobatics in the air. The simplest one is the *loop*, which consists of making the aeroplane turn a somersault in the air and then continue on its original course. Speed is gained by putting the aeroplane into a dive with the throttle open. Then the "stick" is pulled back (to make the aeroplane climb) and is held in position until the machine goes over the top of the loop, upside down. The throttle is then closed and the aeroplane dives to

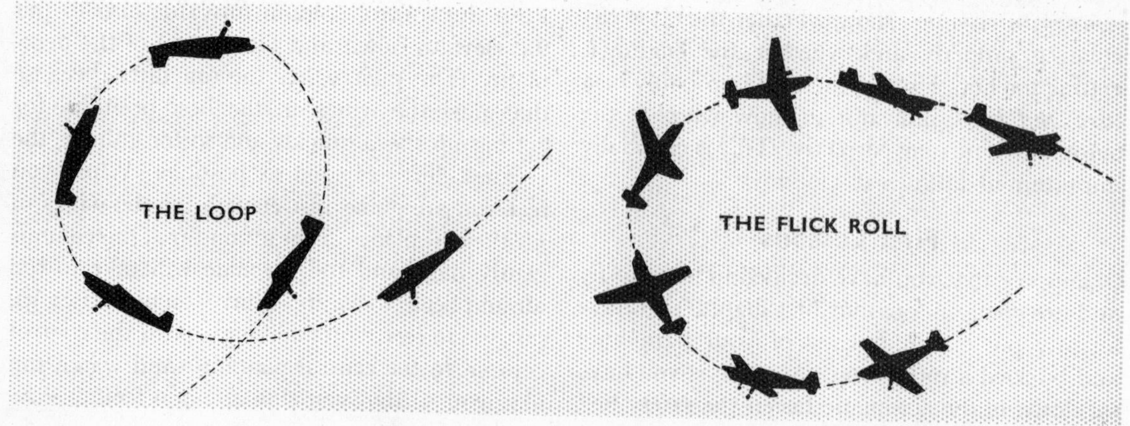

complete the loop. The throttle is opened and, if the loop has been perfect, the aeroplane continues in the same direction and at the same height as before.

The *roll* is begun by a slight dive. The "stick" is then moved in the direction in which the roll is to be made, in order to work the ailerons. At the same time the rudder bar is used to move the rudder into the direction of the roll. The machine tilts so that one of its wings points down to the earth and the other up into the sky, and it then turns right over on to its back. At this point the engine is throttled down and the pilot prevents the machine from going into a dive by careful use of the ailerons and rudder. The circular movement continues and the aeroplane comes back to its normal position. Ailerons and rudder are brought back to the straight flying position and the throttle opened.

The *half roll and dive-out* is a means of changing direction and losing height. The aeroplane is rolled on to its back and then the pilot does the second half of a loop. He has thus turned round and lost height far more quickly than by a normal turn and dive.

*The half roll off the top of a loop* is a means of changing direction and gaining height. It starts as for a loop; at the top of the loop the pilot uses the ailerons to bank his machine to right or left and does a half roll, thus facing in the opposite direction at the end of it.

Then there is flying upside down. In order to turn an aeroplane on to its back the first half of a roll is made; then the ailerons and rudder and "stick" are used to keep the machine level. To return to normal flight the roll is merely completed. For flying upside down a pilot must wear a special harness to prevent him from falling out of the aeroplane.

There are several other aerobatic manoeuvres —*flick rolls, hesitation rolls, inverted spins* and others—all based on those already described.

## Advanced Flying

As the pupil passes on to more complicated aeroplanes he has many more gadgets to handle. These may include two or more engines, each with its separate controls; devices to help in take off and landing; wheel-brakes for use on the ground; an undercarriage (see AIRCRAFT), drawn up after take off and let down for landing; a gadget known as an automatic pilot (often nicknamed "George"), which can be switched on if the human pilot wishes to stay on the same course for a long time. As its name suggests, it keeps the aeroplane on its course and is able to make the adjustments necessary for this. In big aeroplanes there are instruments of all sorts to help with navigation (see NAVIGATION), such as radio compasses and various radar devices (see RADAR) to show the course in bad weather when the navigator cannot check it by looking at objects on the ground. There is deicing equipment to prevent ice from forming on the wings and pressurization to make breathing possible at great heights. (See ATMOSPHERE.)

All this equipment must be watched and handled and the pilot in a big aeroplane has a whole crew to help him—navigator, flight engineer, radio operator, as well as a second pilot to share the flying with him. However, he must never forget the simple rules which he learnt in his first flying lessons, for if his instruments fail, his life and the lives of his passengers depend on these simple rules.

(For an explanation of training and flying with the Royal Air Force see ROYAL AIR FORCE.)

**FLYING DUTCHMAN.** Superstitious sailors believe that on stormy nights a phantom ship called "The Flying Dutchman" may be seen beating its way against the wind near the Cape of Good Hope at the tip of South Africa. They think it is a bad omen to see this ship.

One of the legends about "The Flying Dutchman" says that the captain, Vanderdecken, swore he would sail round the Cape if it took until Judgement Day. For this vain boast he was doomed to sail for ever near the Cape without ever rounding it.

Another legend says that the captain is condemned to sail for ever in a ship without helm or steersman, playing at dice for his soul with the devil.

The German composer Richard Wagner wrote an opera round the story called *The Flying Dutchman.* The legend was also used by Captain Marryat in *The Phantom Ship.*

Large fins help the flying fish to glide through the air.

**FLYING FISH** is the name given to the kind of fish that can raise itself above the surface of the water in which it lives and "fly" through the air. Flying fishes are often seen gliding over the surface of warm seas. They are rather like herrings, but all species have long pectoral fins just behind the head and some, the so-called four-winged kinds, have large pelvic fins under the body as well. When alarmed by the approach of enemies, they move so fast through the water that they shoot through the surface, and as they do so they raise first the pectoral and then the pelvic fins, so that all except the lower part of the tail fin is above the water. Then they lash the tail from side to side, zigzagging along the surface until they can rise into the air. They glide, rather than fly, for they never flap their "wings", and the distance they can glide depends a good deal on breezes and other air currents.

Flying fishes make a kind of nest by binding floating weed together with sticky threads, and their eggs, which are heavier than water, are thus kept near the surface of the ocean and warmed by the sun.

Some little freshwater fishes of South America, called hatchet fishes, have strong muscles with which they can flap their pectoral fins like the wings of a bird. In this way they can skim along the surface of the water at a great speed and even, it is said, rise into the air for a short distance.

**FOG.** When damp air is cooled sufficiently, that is, below its dew-point (see Dew), some of the moisture in it condenses to form tiny visible droplets. If the cooling takes place immediately above the earth or the sea, these water droplets will form a fog or mist. So a fog is likely to form if the air is damp and the earth becomes very cold at night, or if warm damp air comes over a cold sea current or over land that is already cold.

Inland, a clear still night allows the earth to give off its warmth and a low mist may form. If there is no wind, cold air tends to roll down into the valleys and it is there that the early morning mist may often be seen. Sometimes from the top of a hill one can look down on the fog over all the lower land around. Clouds help to keep the earth warm at night and so fog is less likely to form on a cloudy night. Wind

Warm, moist air moving over cool land or water forms banks of fog as the moisture cools and condenses.

Another kind of fog is formed when cool air comes down on warm water or moist land.

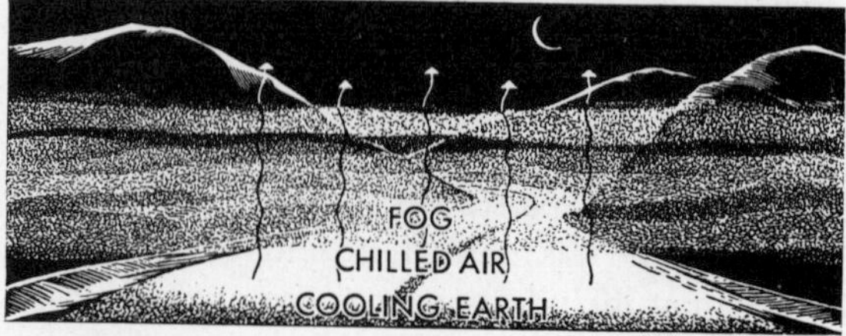


Radiation fog forms in low places as the earth's heat escapes upward, leaving the lower air cool enough for fog.

*Courtesy, Hawker Siddeley*

**A Trident airliner making an automatic landing in fog. Normally an airport would be closed in fog as dense as this.**

soon sweeps fog away and generally the windiest places have the least fog.

In and around great cities like London and in areas where there are many factories, fogs are usually dark, not white as they are over the sea. Londoners used to talk about a "pea-souper", though "smog" is the word more often used. The tiny water droplets of the fog quickly collect particles of smoke and dust which make the fog darker and much more unpleasant and unhealthy than a Scotch mist or a sea fog. A big city fog is specially harmful to anyone suffering from any chest trouble.

Fogs, whether on land or at sea, make travel dangerous and slow. Every ship has its fog horn and special devices are needed to keep railways running. Road services are often stopped altogether and aircraft grounded.

The experts who study weather do not think of fog and mist as different things. If the visibility (how far you can see) is very bad, then they speak of fog; if it is not quite so bad, they speak of mist. "Haze", however, is different, for it is dry, being caused by dust or smoke, while fog and mist are wet.

**FOG SIGNALS.** Fog greatly delays road and rail traffic and also aircraft and ships, because drivers and navigators and pilots cannot then see clearly ahead nor see the lights and signals provided to guide them.

Fog signals are not needed on railways where there is colour-light signalling, for then each train as it goes past alters bright lights which show the driver of the next train whether he can go on or not. However, if this system (or another one called "automatic train control") is not fitted, the signalman calls out the fogmen who go to their places alongside the line. When the arm of the distant signal is at "danger" the fogman places a *detonator*—a metal disc with explosive in it—on the rail. The detonator goes off with a bang when the leading wheel runs over it and warns the driver of the train to stop. The fogman also has a lamp and flags for signalling the driver when to go on again. In some places the detonators are put on the rail by machinery connected with the levers that work the signals, and so special fogmen are not needed.

At sea, the danger due to fog has been reduced for modern ships fitted with radar, which shows the position of the shore and other ships on a screen (see Radar). Nevertheless, lighthouses and lightships have to make sound signals when it is foggy, these being horns or sirens which are arranged to give a certain number of blasts at definite intervals. Such signals are made by machinery because the fog may last for hours and the exact timing and length of the blasts are important. If the timing and length of the blasts were not exact the navigator of the ship could not tell which lighthouse or lightship was making the signal. The ships themselves have to make fog signals on their whistles or sirens every minute or two. Thus a steamer sounds a long blast every two minutes whilst moving ahead and two long blasts whilst stopped. When at anchor it rings a bell for five seconds every minute. There are other fog signals for ships towing others or being towed, for sailing vessels, vessels aground and vessels engaged in fishing. Buoys which are used to mark channels and shoals (shallow areas) sometimes carry a bell which rings as they rock on the waves.

Ships can also be navigated with the aid of signals sent out by radio beacons carried in lighthouses and lightships. These signals, which are a great help in fog, tell the navigator of the ship in which direction the beacon lies. (See Navigation.)

Aircraft can be steered by radio course-marker beacons on the ground. If the aircraft is on its correct course there is a steady humming note in the navigator's earphones, but if it wanders off that course the note changes to either a dot-dash or a dash-dot signal, depending on whether the aircraft has strayed to the left or right. Other methods of radio navigation such as Loran and the Decca navigator have been developed which actually tell the aircraft's navigator where he is (instead of merely telling him he is to the right or left of his course) and all he has to do is to read off the dials on an instrument and then refer to a special chart, or map.

Efforts have been made to clear fog away by several methods. The British FIDO (Fog Investigation Dispersal Operations) equipment of World War II burnt oil in jets arranged round the airfield, but was very expensive to set up and use. The heat of jet-engine exhausts has been tried, as also has a beam of rapidly vibrating sound which makes the droplets in fog cling together. But aircraft using airfields in thick weather rely chiefly on radio, radar, powerful lights and automatic landing systems.

**FOLK DANCING** is the name used to describe certain types of dancing performed by country folk since early times. Some folk dances are performed on one particular day of the year. Others are performed at any time and are danced for fun or on social occasions, such as parties. These are known as country dances. Well-known English country dances danced in school today include the Brighton Camp, Calopede, Durham Reel and Cumberland Square.

The term national dances is often applied to folk dances performed in peasant costume and when a folk dance of a particular country is singled out as being typical of that country—say a Russian dance or an Irish dance. But of course there are many types of "national" dance, and a "national" costume is nearly always a type of regional peasant dress.

Another kind of folk dance is the ceremonial dance. These dances are probably the oldest, although both the social and ceremonial folk dance date from before the days of Christianity. In pagan times religious ceremonies were held to mark the different seasons, in connection with the coming of spring, or with the sowing or the reaping of the harvest. Dances took place at these festivals and forms of them have survived in certain places today. Among them are the Furry or Floral Dance at Helston in Cornwall, which is described in the article Customs, Old. This is a spring festival; other such festivals are the hobby-horse processions at Padstow, in Cornwall, and Minehead, in Somerset, and the Whitsuntide morris dancers in many parts of England. The most famous May Day dances, of course, are those which include the choosing and crowning of a May queen. A very familiar May Day figure used to be the Jack-in-the-Green, or Green Man, hidden in a wicker framework covered with leaves and flowers. He was still dancing in the streets of London at the beginning of the 20th century. The social folk dance, or country dance, probably developed from the May Day processions and the great ring dances round the maypoles which were set up in every English village in the middle ages. (See May Day.)

Besides the hobby-horse dances there are other dances in which people dress up as animals. In Derbyshire they once disguised themselves as rams and in Staffordshire they still disguise themselves as deer. In the north of England there are groups of people known as plough stots. (Stot is an old English word meaning a young ox.) These plough stots dance the sword-dance on Plough Monday, which is the first Monday after Epiphany (January 6) and also act a play showing the battle between life and death. The English sword-dance is performed by a group of men, and the swords are either blunt and wooden or are strips of steel with a handle at each end. Each man holds his own sword in one hand and that of his neighbour in the other. The dance is very active and includes leaping over the swords and going under them. The English sword-dance is performed in Durham, Yorkshire and Northumberland and in Shetland. In the Scottish sword-dance the dancers step over the swords, which are laid on the ground.

Country dances were once danced to the music of a wind instrument called the hornpipe. The dances themselves became known as hornpipes, and today the word refers to a lively dance usually done by one person. (See HORNPIPE.)

Country dances began to be popular at the English court in the 16th century, when Henry VIII, who was fond of music and dancing, introduced them in a court masque, or play. Music was written for them by the composer Henry Purcell and they were first collected into a book in 1650 by a printer of music called John Playford. This handbook of country dancing continued to be published by the Playford family for nearly 100 years and then others carried it on. Printed collections of country dances have been bought and sold ever since, but the real source of the English folk dances has been the country people themselves.

Folk dances are now encouraged and have been revived in nearly every country in the world. In England the man who has done most to collect and preserve them is Cecil J. Sharp, who founded the English Folk Dance and Song Society. As a result of his efforts, more is known about the details and origins of English folk dances than about the folk dances of any other country.

There is more about morris dancing in the article called MORRIS DANCING. More about how country dancing developed will be found in the article DANCING.

*Left: Western Morning News. Right: T. Holte*

Left: Children dressed in white, dancing in the streets on Furry Day at Helston, Cornwall. This ancient festival is held on May 8 every year and celebrates the coming of spring. Right: Warwickshire boys performing a morris dance.

**FOLKLORE** really means "things that people know". Nowadays we find out many of the things we know from books; but in the days when very few people could read, they had to learn from the stories other people told them. The knowledge handed on in this way, without ever being written down, is called folklore. It has always been strongest in country districts, where old customs and ideas usually last longer than in towns. Myths and legends of heroes, fairy stories and nursery rhymes, as well as knowledge of, for instance, plants which can be used to cure diseases, are all part of folklore.

Writers of history books are usually careful not to put anything in them which cannot be proved true, but the folk tales of things that happened in the past are full of fancies, and every story-teller probably added something from his own imagination to make the story better. In this way many tales have grown up about the deeds of famous heroes, like King Arthur and Robin Hood. Often stories which are not at all like history may have in them a true memory of something that happened long ago. Newcomers to ancient Britain may have found, living on the moorlands, a much older people who had not learnt to make stone houses. When they saw the strangers approaching, they probably disappeared into what must have looked like holes in the ground, for they lived in low huts covered with turf. The newcomer would tell stories about these people, and soon they would be described as fairies living under the ground. A race of small people might tell stories of huge giants, though all they had really seen was men much taller than they were. The more times a story was told, the more strange it became.

People used to tell stories about the things they saw round them, like trees and rivers and mountains. In early times they often thought that these things were alive in the same way that human beings are—that a tree or river was really a living being, sometimes called a nymph. Later on, nymphs were thought of as supernatural beings who *lived in* rivers and trees, and not as if they actually *were* the rivers and trees. You will find more about this kind of story in the article MYTHS.

One of the interesting things about folklore is that slightly different versions of the same story can be found in different countries all over the world. For instance, the story of the great flood, which we know from the story of Noah and the ark in the Bible, is also found in ancient Greek folklore. In the Greek legend it was Deucalion and his wife Pyrrha who were the two people left alive on the Earth after the flood had gone down. People as far apart as Red Indians and South Sea Islanders have their own version of the flood story.

Nearly all fairy stories are folk stories which had been told to children for centuries before they were written down. The brothers Grimm did not make up all the stories in their book of fairy tales. They were very interested in folklore, and collected the tales from the German people themselves. The story of Cinderella, which is one of the best known of all fairy stories, has over 300 versions in different parts of the world.

Though nursery rhymes are often written in books now, they used to be handed down by word of mouth as folklore. They are now told just to amuse small children but there are some things in them which go back hundreds of years, to magic spells, and ceremonies that used to be very important.

**FOOD SUPPLIES.** When people see joints of meat at the butcher's or carrots and apples at the greengrocer's they realize, easily enough, that these things have been grown to feed them. When they see rows of tins, bottles and packs in the supermarket, however, they do not always realize that animals have to be reared and crops grown in the same way to fill those packages.

Although about 1,000,000 different sorts of plants grow on the land and in the water, human beings get their main supplies of food from only about 20 of them. For adequate health, people need 2,000–3,000 kilo-calories of energy and 50 to 80 grammes of protein per day in about 1 kilogramme weight of dry food. (A kilo-calorie is enough heat to raise the temperature of 1 kilogramme of water by 1 degree Centigrade.) Most people in the world eat a lot of food containing cereal grains (see CEREAL). Wheat, maize, rice, millet and sorghum are the most important, followed by rye, oats and barley. If you read the separate articles on these plants you will see that they each need different conditions in order to grow properly. For example, rye and oats can grow in cold, wet places, barley prefers drier conditions, wheat needs a warmer, drier climate and maize a still warmer, wet climate. Rice likes hot, wet places while millet and sorghum grow well in hot, dry climates.

Plants that grow tubers (short, thick underground stems) supply another main human food. In this group the potato is the most important (see POTATO), but other tuberous plants are the artichoke and the sweet potato. The potato needs a fairly cool climate, whereas the sweet potato grows well in hot climates and is particularly suited to them as its underground tubers are safe from locusts. (See LOCUST.)

Other important foods are meat, milk, butter, cheese and eggs, which all provide high quality protein. These foods are mainly eaten by the people of the rich, industrial countries, however, for they cost more than foods from plants.

Many of the people of Asia have never had enough food and have never been able to buy meat, milk, butter or cheese. Their methods of farming are often poor and they have not the money or the education to use improved varieties of plants and animals, fertilizers to make plants grow well, or machines to cultivate and harvest them. (See FARM MACHINERY and FERTILIZER.)

## Buying and Selling Food

Some countries, for example, Canada, Australia, Denmark and New Zealand, earn their living mostly by producing food to sell to other countries. Others, such as Great Britain, produce manufactured goods which they sell abroad. The British people have to buy from abroad about half of the food they eat, for only half of what the country needs is grown in Great Britain. British farmers produce all the milk, eggs, large vegetables and potatoes needed, about 70% of the meat, 50% of the wheat, 40% of the cheese, only 10% of the butter and, of course, none of the tropical fruit which the people eat. Wheat comes from Canada, Australia, the United States and Argentina; beef from Argentina, Canada and New Zealand; live cattle from the Republic of Ireland; lamb and mutton from New Zealand; butter from New Zealand, Denmark and Australia; and bacon from Denmark and the Republic of Ireland.

Great Britain pays for this food by selling manufactured goods to the food-producing countries. Thus, every car or aeroplane sold to Canada or New Zealand buys so much wheat, or so much butter. Many other industrial countries of northwestern Europe, like Great Britain, produce less food than they need and have to buy food in the same way, although Britain is more dependent on food imports than any other country. (See TRADE.)

**FOOL.** In the middle ages the fool or jester was a well known figure with his "motley" (clothing of at least two colours), tight trousers, closely fitting hood adorned with ears and bells and his bauble. This was a short stick that had a jester's head carved at the top, and sometimes had a bladder tied to it.

Kings, great lords and even city corporations (see CORPORATION AND COMPANY) kept fools who were paid regular wages and treated as members of the household. King Henry VIII had a famous fool called Will Somers. Sir Thomas More (see MORE, SIR THOMAS) had one called Henry Paterson who is said to have mocked his master for refusing to acknowledge Henry VIII's authority over the church. Charles I was the last king to keep a fool in England, but as late as 1728 the Earl of Suffolk had one.

At the French court, Louis XIV's fool L'Angely used to stand behind the king's chair and terrify courtiers with his remarks. Some of them bribed him to keep quiet about them, and when he was dismissed for impertinence he had made his fortune.

Court fools belonged to the time when kings were all-powerful. The fool's business was to amuse his royal master and to drive away, with his jokes, the loneliness of a man set high above all his fellow men. In order to amuse, he was free to mention and make fun of people and topics that nobody else would have dared to mention. Sometimes he even teased the king himself.

Some of the best known fools are found in the plays of William Shakespeare, where they sing songs and often provide much of the fun. Two such men are Feste in *Twelfth Night* and Touchstone in *As You Like It*.

**FOOT AND MOUTH DISEASE.** Nearly all cloven-footed animals (those with divided hooves) such as cattle, sheep, pigs and goats can catch this highly infectious disease. It is possible, but unusual, for human beings to have it.

It is caused by a minute germ called a filtrable virus (see GERMS), which is so small that it cannot be seen even through a microscope. Like the influenza germ which attacks human beings, it spreads rapidly.

Early signs that an animal has the disease are dullness, loss of appetite and a high temperature. Later, the animal becomes lame, has a great amount of saliva in its mouth and smacks its lips constantly. Blisters develop inside its mouth and on its tongue and lips. Its feet blister—especially where the hoof joins the skin—and when these blisters break they release a straw-coloured liquid and leave an angry looking sore. This liquid contains the virus which causes the disease and therefore infects everything it touches. People looking after infected animals may easily carry the virus on their hands and clothing. They must not visit other farms and must wash themselves and their clothes in disinfectant. At the entrance to an infected farm is placed a container with disinfectant in it, through which people must walk to disinfect their boots.

Foot and mouth disease causes great losses in many countries. It used to be common in Great Britain, but since 1892 special measures have been taken against it. Farmers have to report outbreaks immediately they happen, infected animals and other animals that have been in close contact with them have to be slaughtered and the farm buildings thoroughly disinfected.

Britain's worst outbreak of the disease was in 1967–1968, when more than 400,000 animals had to be slaughtered.

**FOOTBALL** of a kind seems to have been played by the ancient Greeks and Romans and the game may have been brought to Britain by the soldiers of the Roman Conquest. In Tudor times matches were sometimes played on public holidays between whole towns and villages using the main street as a "ground"; anyone could join in—even on horseback—and there were no rules, so that it is not surprising that one writer described the game as "nothing but beast-like fury and violence".

Modern football dates from about the middle of the 19th century when it began to be played regularly under proper rules by schools, universities and clubs. The two kinds chiefly played in Great Britain are association football or "soccer" and Rugby football or "rugger". Gaelic football, in which a player may take three steps with the ball in his hands, is a mixture of these two games which is popular in Ireland.

The football chiefly played in the United States and Canada, although it started as "soccer", has since altered so much that it has become a quite distinct American game, in which the players wear heavy padding and the rules are so complicated that three and sometimes five officials beside the referee are needed to control it. Some English schools such as Eton, Harrow and Winchester play their own special kind of football. (See AMERICAN FOOTBALL; ASSOCIATION FOOTBALL; RUGBY FOOTBALL.)

**FORCE.** If a man pushes a lawn mower, or a locomotive pulls a train, or a hook supports a picture, the man, engine and hook are said to exert force. If it were not for these forces the mower and the train would stand still and the picture would fall.

A force known to everyone is that of gravity, which is actually the force on any object caused by the Earth pulling it downwards. (See GRAVITATION.) A brick dropped from the hand falls to the ground with increasing speed or *acceleration* because of the force of gravity acting on it; but if the brick is carried on the palm of the hand, the force of gravity is exactly balanced by the upward push of the hand. When a horse is pulling a barge steadily along a canal by means of a tow-rope, the pull of the rope on the barge is the same as the force of the resistance of the water, and if the horse pulls any harder the barge moves faster. These remarks clear the way for the three important ideas about force set out in 1687 by the great English scientist Sir Isaac Newton, on whom there is a separate article. These three ideas, which are set out below, are often known as the Laws of Motion.

1. Every object remains stopped or goes on moving at a steady rate unless acted upon by another force. (Notice that if a bus stops suddenly the passengers are thrown off their seats because they go on moving at a steady rate.)
2. The amount of force needed to make an object change its speed depends on the weight of the object and the amount of acceleration (alteration of speed) required. (It is much harder to stop a golf ball than a table-tennis ball moving at the same speed, because the golf ball is so much heavier.)
3. To every action there is an equal and opposite reaction. (This is clearly seen with jet-propelled aircraft. The jet aero engine is squirting a huge mass of gas behind it all the time, or forcing the gas backwards; therefore the aircraft is forced forwards.) (See JET PROPULSION.)

When a horse is pulling a barge at a constant speed, the pull of the rope on the barge is the same as the force of the resistance of the water, and if the horse pulls any harder the barge moves faster. The jet-propelled aircraft overhead illustrates another idea about force.

**FORD, Henry** (1863–1947). The first person to discover how to produce cars cheaply and in large numbers was Henry Ford. He was the son of a farmer in Michigan, United States, who had crossed the Atlantic from Bandon in Ireland. However, from the time he was a small boy, Henry was more interested in machinery than in farming and he often earned pocket-money by repairing neighbours' watches. When he was 16 he left the farm and walked nine miles to Detroit and from that time, except for a short period on the farm, he worked his way up from one engineering job to another. He built his first motor engine in his wife's kitchen in 1893 and three years later built his first car in a workshop in the garden. He set up his own business in 1903, which between 1908 and 1927 produced more than 15,000,000 of the famous T-model cars alone.

Ford's method was to make "small profits on enormous sales". In other words he only made a very small profit on every car he made, but because the vehicles were cheap many people bought them and so the small profits mounted up to a great deal of money. He was one of the first people to use mass production methods, in which moving bands brought the parts to the men instead of the men having to waste time moving about when they put the parts together. He paid his workers good wages and used a large part of his profits to build new factories and buy other things like iron and coal mines.

Ford thought that work was better for the community than charity and so he tried to give people work so that they could help themselves. He started, for instance, a school in Detroit where poor boys could be educated and could also earn money by making useful things. When Ford retired in 1945 he was succeeded as president of the company by his grandson Henry Ford II, his only son, Edsel, having died in 1943. The largest part of his money, and that of his son Edsel, was left to be used by the organization called the Ford Foundation, which helps education in various ways. In 1948 it

*Courtesy, Ford Motor Co.*
Henry Ford at the tiller of the first Ford car.

started a new university in the western part of Berlin, for example.

The Ford company's main English factory, which is beside the Thames at Dagenham, is now one of the largest in Europe. The Dagenham factory provides jobs for thousands of people and makes its own types of road vehicles and tractors.

**FOREIGN AND COMMONWEALTH OFFICE.** A modern government has many dealings with the governments of other countries and bodies such as the United Nations. It may have to discuss matters like a proposed treaty in which countries promise not to attack each other; passports (see PASSPORT); or the help to be given to a country which has had a severe earthquake. Such matters are looked after by a government department which, in Great Britain, is the Foreign and Commonwealth Office in London. The head of this government department is the Secretary of State for Foreign and Commonwealth Affairs, usually referred to simply as the foreign secretary, and he is helped by several ministers of state. He is responsible for British dependencies as well as for relations with independent countries of the Commonwealth.

Although the ministers change from time to time (see CABINET, THE), members of the staff of the Foreign and Commonwealth Office continue at their jobs, ready to serve each foreign secretary in turn. The foreign secretary himself sees all important communications from abroad, like telegrams from other governments and reports from his country's ambassadors and high commissioners (see AMBASSADOR), but he turns for advice to his officials, who also deal with less important matters from day to day.

**FOREIGN LEGION.** In the past many countries encouraged foreigners to fight in their armies. The Romans relied mainly on "legions" consisting of their own men, but also formed "cohorts" (regiments) from the people of the lands they conquered. In the British Army the King's German Legion, formed in 1803, made a name for itself in the Peninsular War against France and at the Battle of Waterloo. A "British Legion" fought in the Spanish Civil War of 1835.

The term "Foreign Legion" began in France when, in 1831, King Louise Philippe formed a unit at Toulon called the *Légion Etrangère*, which foreigners could join. In a few years the Legion was nearly 6,000 strong and for more than a century and a quarter it has been one of the most famous forces in the world. It lost more than one quarter of its numbers in the Crimean War, and has since then fought in all the wars in which France has taken part. During World War II soldiers of the Legion served in Norway, North Africa, Italy and in the liberation of southern France. Although it has served in many parts of the world the Legion was for long famed for fighting in the deserts and mountains of North Africa. Its headquarters were at Sidi-bel-Abbès in Algeria until 1962, when they were moved to France.

Men wishing to join can go to any French police headquarters and will then be directed to the nearest recruiting post. A recruit is not asked to produce any papers from his own country and in consequence many men wanted by the police, or who wished to hide their identity, found their way into the Legion.

Normally men are accepted by the Foreign Legion between the ages of 18 and 40. They must be in first-class physical condition and they usually join for three or five years, but can extend their service, and many spend long periods in the legion. For a trained soldier the pay is higher than in the French regular army, and men qualify for a pension after 15 years. As a general rule commissioned officers are Frenchmen, but there are occasional exceptions in the lower officer ranks. Many of the non-commissioned officers are foreigners.

Discipline in the Foreign Legion has always been very strict and the punishments for misbehaviour are severe. It is famous for its long marches and even today, when troops often move in lorries, the Legion still keeps its marching reputation. In spite of the hard life they lead, legionaries (members of the Legion) take a great pride in the Legion's fine record. Although men from many countries enlist, those speaking the same language are usually kept together in the same companies and platoons.

In recent times there have been many instances of men serving under the flag of another country. In the Spanish Civil War of 1936–1939 five International Brigades (about 20,000 men), composed of men from Belgium, Great Britain, Czechoslovakia, France, Germany, Italy and Poland, fought on the side of the Spanish government. (See SPAIN.)

**FOREST.** A large area well covered with trees is a forest, but if the area is small it is called a wood. If the trees are small, and particularly if they are dotted about here and there, it may be called a scrub, bush or waste land. There are many different kinds of forest, and each kind needs a particular sort of climate, soil and place in which to grow.

Although there may be as many as 20,000 different kinds of tree in the world only about 500 are used for timber. These 500 can be divided into two kinds. There are trees with needle-like leaves, such as pines and firs (called coniferous because they bear cones), which are almost all evergreens, dropping old leaves and making new ones all the time; and there are the broad-leaved trees. Most of the broad-leaved trees in cooler countries drop their leaves in the winter; in hot dry countries they drop them in the dry season, whenever that is. In hot wet countries, however, most of them are evergreen. (See TREE.)

The finest forests in the world are the coniferous forests of western North America—where the trees are redwood and Douglas fir—and the eucalyptus, or gum tree, forests of Australia (see EUCALYPTUS). In both these types of forest the trees may be 300 feet or more high and the trunks more than 50 feet round. Some of the most varied and the thickest forests are found in tropical (see TROPICS) areas that are wet; hardly two neighbouring trees are alike, many are big and their giant trunks are festooned with woody climbers, ferns and other plants to such an extent that it is impossible, from the ground, to see their highest parts. However, many of the forests in the tropics are found in drier areas, where there is not enough rain for all this growth, and they do not look very different from the broad-leaved forests of cooler countries. There is a separate article, RAIN FOREST, which describes forests that grow near the equator.

Special types of forest are found where conditions are unusual; for example, at the mouth of big rivers where the ground is flooded at high tide with salt or half-salt water. Only a few kinds of tree can grow in these conditions, such as the mangroves which raise their trunks above the water on tall roots like stilts. There are some forests where the trees always have their roots in swampy ground, and here palm trees are the most common. There are others, called "cloud" forests, where there is a constant mist and the trees are covered in mosses which like the extreme dampness. On the other hand, there are dry areas where the trees are thorny and flat-topped, and are mostly acacias (see ACACIA).

Forests once covered the earth's surface wherever it was not too cold, as on the high mountain tops and towards the North and South Poles, nor too dry, as in the hot deserts. Over the centuries about half of these forests have been cleared to give land for growing food and grazing animals, cut down for timber or destroyed by fire. The chief forest areas now are the vast regions where pines and firs grow in western Canada, northern Europe and Siberia; and the wet tropical parts of South America, Central Africa and southeast Asia. The hot, wet

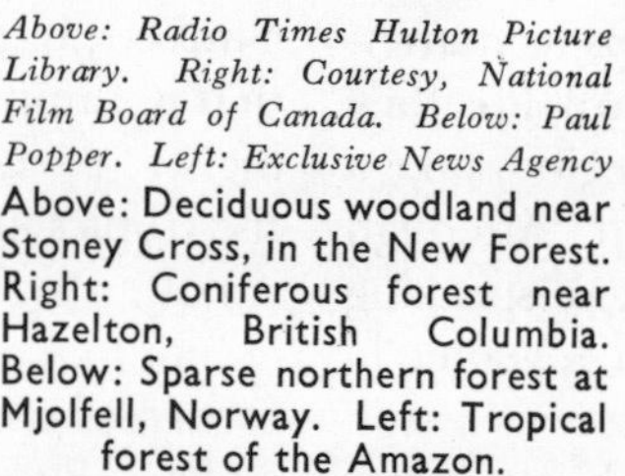

*Above: Radio Times Hulton Picture Library. Right: Courtesy, National Film Board of Canada. Below: Paul Popper. Left: Exclusive News Agency*

Above: Deciduous woodland near Stoney Cross, in the New Forest. Right: Coniferous forest near Hazelton, British Columbia. Below: Sparse northern forest at Mjolfell, Norway. Left: Tropical forest of the Amazon.

forests are so noted for hard and heavy woods that it is sometimes forgotten that they also contain some very light ones. An example of a soft, light wood is balsa, which is only one-fifth of the weight of English oak. It is, however, true that many woods from wet tropical forests are very hard and so heavy that they sink in water. Some such woods are used only in relatively small quantities and for special purposes, greenheart being used for the underwater parts of docks and *Lignum vitae* for bearings and machine parts. On the other hand, wood from pines and firs is used for most ordinary purposes, so that much more of it is needed.

If a forest is cut down in a country that takes care of its forests young trees are planted or those that spring up naturally are helped to grow properly. The area is thus soon under trees again. Elsewhere, especially in the tropics, the natural forests are being cut down and no new trees are being planted. If this continues for much longer there will not be enough timber left for the world's needs. In some countries big new forests are being made on land that had long been treeless or only has small trees on it, like the heath and moorland in Great Britain.

Even if man does not interfere with a natural forest, changes are going on all the time. Trees are constantly growing, and when they become old they die. The gaps left by dead trees are soon filled, either by new trees or by the surrounding trees which grow bigger in the extra space. As soon as a tree has reached a certain age and size it begins to produce seeds, which are scattered in various ways. Some of these seeds grow into seedlings, or young trees, and though most of them do not live for long, enough survive to fill all the gaps, and so the general appearance of the forest is the same.

Many trees have seeds that are easily caught by the wind and carried some distance away from the parent tree; the pines and maples have winged seeds, for example, and the aspen has a very light downy seed. This scattering of the seeds means that a type of tree may begin to grow in some particular part of the forest where it had not grown before without being new to the forest as a whole. Sometimes a forest may be almost entirely killed by a calamity such as a fire, a hurricane or even a shower of dust from a volcano. If the land is left to itself trees begin to grow again, in time, and some trees such as silver birch and Scots pine in Britain or aspen and paper birch in Canada usually appear before any others.

It is only fairly recently that people have realized that forests are good for an area, quite apart from the wood they supply. If they are destroyed, the bare soil becomes dry and sandy, and as it is no longer sheltered by the leaves nor held together by the roots of the trees, it is easily blown away by the wind, and often buries good land elsewhere. It is also washed away by the rain and this fills the rivers with sand and mud which block them and cause floods and great destruction. Reservoirs (see RESERVOIR) may be filled up with soil and be unable to do their job. Often springs and streams dry up. This happens because the sandy soil lets all the rainwater run away as soon as it falls. Good forest soil takes in the rain and lets the water drain away gradually, keeping springs and streams always supplied. Forests have been cut down in the Middle East and elsewhere without being replaced by new trees, and the land there has become very much poorer. The article EROSION describes the way in which trees are used to keep soil fertile. Although it takes only a few years to destroy the soil by cutting down trees, it takes many years to build it up again if it has been washed away down to the bare rock.

The most important product of forests is of course wood, and wood is put to a great many different uses. Where it is plentiful, houses are built almost entirely of wood, and elsewhere it is used in most buildings, especially for roofs, floors and staircases. It is widely used for heating and cooking in many parts of the world.

In the future we shall probably use even more wood than we do at present because wood can be reduced to pulp and treated in various ways to make many things, some of which appear to have no connection with wood. For example, hundreds of acres of forest have to be felled every day to make our daily newspapers and woodpulp is the most important of various materials from which it is possible to make the rayon of a shirt or blouse. Therefore, although many people no longer use wood for heating or cooking and often build houses with less wood in them than those of the past, the forests are as necessary to man as ever they were. They produce wood and they protect the soil.

**FOREST, SUBMERGED.** At Leasowe, on the coast of Cheshire, is what is known as a submerged, or sunken, forest. When the tide is very low the stumps of a great many dead trees can be seen on the shore. At the first glance it seems as though they had floated down some river or been washed along the shore from a neighbouring wood. When they are examined closely, however, it becomes clear that this was not what happened, for the roots are there and are spread through the clayey soil, just like those of living trees.

These trees could not have grown in such wet soil and in salt sea water. It was in fact the sea water that killed them. Long ago, they grew on dry land near the shore, but the land slowly sank till the sea covered it and killed the trees as they stood.

Submerged forests like the one in Cheshire can be found in other places around the shores of England and Wales. When docks have been built along the estuaries, or mouths, of such rivers as the Thames and the Humber, completely buried dead forests have been found. Nuts and cherry stones, the remains of reeds and fern leaves and the decayed wood of fir, oak, birch and alder trees have been found more than 30 feet below the highest point to which

*Crown Copyright*
Tree stumps uncovered at low tide on the Yorkshire coast.

the water rises. Teeth and bones of extinct animals are sometimes discovered, and one of the places where they have been dragged up is the Dogger Bank, the rich fishing ground in the North Sea.

These submerged forests grew when what is now the sea or rivers was dry land, so from them scientists can learn much about the appearance of the earth long ago. They show, too, how coal was laid down, for every bed of coal is really an ancient submerged forest.

**FORESTRY.** When people see a crop of wheat being harvested they realize that the farmer has put a lot of work into producing it. When they see trees being felled in a forest, however, they do not always realize that a great amount of care has also gone into producing them, and that they are crops as well.

In order to look after forests properly people have to be specially trained. Such people are called foresters and their work forestry. It is very varied work, for a forester does not only look after the trees while they are growing ; he is responsible for everything from raising young seedlings to selling the timber after mature, or full-grown, trees have been felled, or cut down.

The first responsibility of the forester—because everything else depends on it—is the care of the land on which the trees are growing. It must be kept fertile and it must be properly drained to prevent it from becoming swampy. Before seeds are planted the ground must be prepared so that they will grow well.

Raising seedlings, or young trees, from seeds is an important part of the forester's work. He must know when and how to get the seed, how it germinates, or sprouts, how quickly it grows, what sort of soil it likes and whether it grows better in one place or another. When the seedlings are big enough they will be planted out, either in places where trees have been felled in an existing forest or on bare ground to make a new forest.

As the trees get bigger some of them have to be cut down from time to time, otherwise there would not be enough room for them all to grow properly. This is known as thinning out. The forester removes the poorer trees and tries to get even spacing of those he leaves standing.

Throughout the year he has to be constantly on the watch for signs of disease among his trees or for harm done by animals, insects and by plants such as fungus. Deer, rabbits, hares and squirrels take the bark from the trunks of young trees and moles and rabbits can sometimes cause damage by burrowing among the roots. The most serious insect pest in Great Britain is the pine weevil, which destroys the bark of young trees. Fungus grows on the trunks and branches and feeds off the tree. The good forester attacks all these things before they have had a chance to become a serious danger.

In dry weather he is also on the look out for forest fires because once started they are very difficult to stop. They can lay waste thousands of acres and do not only burn down the trees but also dry up the soil so that it easily blows away. That is why people walking in forests or having picnics should be very careful with matches and should not light fires there at all.

*Courtesy, Forestry Commission*

Loading a lorry with pulpwood for a pulp and paper mill. The timber is loaded by a hydraulic grab.

The forester must judge when a tree is mature and ready for felling, and how it should be felled. After that the tree is often sawn up into logs which have to be transported to a road so that they can be carried away by lorry. The forester must know what each type of timber is best suited for and where to sell it. He must also know its *value* because the owner of the forest naturally expects to make a profit. The stage at which trees are felled and sold may be anything from 60 to 120 years after they were planted, so you can see that the forester has to wait much longer than the farmer for his crops to mature and be ready for "harvesting". Indeed, the man who planted the trees would be very old by the time they were mature even if they only took 60 years, although he does of course fell a small amount of timber every five or ten years when he thins the trees out.

In Great Britain most forests are plantations; that is, they consist of trees planted by man, usually all at the same time. The opposite of this is a natural forest, where new trees grow either from seeds that fall from the trees already there or from seeds that are sown among them by man. In most other countries the new crops are produced in the existing natural forests. It has been found that in Great Britain the plantation method gives better results.

Sometimes it is possible to have forests with trees of all sizes and ages mixed up together, with new seedlings springing up wherever there is room. Yearly or every few years the older and bigger ones are felled. This type is known as a selection forest, and the type where trees are all of the same age and all mature at about the same time is an even-aged forest.

From time to time foresters count and measure their trees in order to find out whether they are growing as well as is expected. When trees are classed together according to size and the various size classes are counted, this is known as a "cruise". From these counts the forester makes a working plan for the management of the whole forest for a period of years, cutting about the same amount of timber each year.

In Great Britain people did not realize until this century how important it was to have forests and to manage them properly. Then, in 1919, the government set up the Forestry Commission to create and manage state-owned forests. The Commission makes experiments to find which kinds of tree grow best in Britain and how to look after them. It has nurseries for growing young trees and it gives advice to owners of forests. The Forestry Commission has forests all over Britain. Some are old forests which it has taken over, such as the New Forest in Hampshire. Others, such as Kielder Forest, have been created largely on moorland or waste land.

Seven of the Commission's properties are forest parks open to the public and with camping sites. They are Dean Forest Park between Gloucestershire and Monmouthshire; Snowdonia Forest Park in Wales; the Border Forest Park around Kielder; Glen Trool Forest Park in Galloway; the Queen Elizabeth Forest Park east of Loch Lomond; Argyll Forest Park; and Glen More Forest Park in Inverness-shire.

The Forestry Commission has four arboreta, or collections of specimen trees. These are at Bedgebury, Kent (conifers); Westonbirt, Gloucestershire (broad-leaved trees and conifers); Crarae, Argyll (conifers); and Kilmun, Argyll (eucalyptus trees). Northern Ireland has an arboretum (broad-leaved trees and conifers) in Tollymore Forest Park, County Down.

**FORGE.** A forge is a workshop or factory where metal—usually steel or iron—is shaped by hammering while it is hot, or joined together by welding (see WELDING). The trade is a very ancient one and until the early part of the 20th century nearly every village in Britain had its blacksmith who made horseshoes and farm tools.

Nowadays most forgings are made in factories where the blacksmith's strong arms are replaced by powerful machines which in Great Britain turn out more than 300,000 tons every year.

If a bar of iron or steel is cold it takes a great deal of hammering to beat it into a new shape and the bar is liable to crack or split in the process. If, however, the bar is made red-hot or white hot (depending on the kind of iron or steel) in a furnace it becomes soft and almost pasty and can easily be hammered into another shape. The village blacksmith did this with a hammer and other hand tools using an *anvil*, or solid block of steel, as his work table. In 1839 the Scottish engineer James Nasmyth invented the steam hammer and thus opened the way for making very large forgings such as the propeller shafts for ships and crankshafts of big engines.

A forging is tougher and less brittle than a casting which is made by pouring melted metal into a mould (see FOUNDING). When forgings are required in large quantities they are made by a process called "drop forging" in which the hot lumps of steel are one after another shaped between the fixed anvil and a drop hammer called a *tup*. The actual shaping is done by *dies* fixed to the tup and anvil. The dies are like the article to be shaped in the same way that a jelly mould is like a jelly. They are made of hard steel and are very expensive but will last a long time.

Large forgings are often made in the same way but by squeezing instead of hammering. This is done in a *press* which uses oil under pressure to force the ram down. Forgings used in everyday life are the blades of scissors, hammer heads, pliers and many other tools, nuts and bolts and parts of a motor car engine such as the crankshaft and valves. If the finished article has to be of an exact size so as to fit with another part the forging for it is made a little too big and then cut or trimmed to shape by machining (see MACHINE TOOLS).

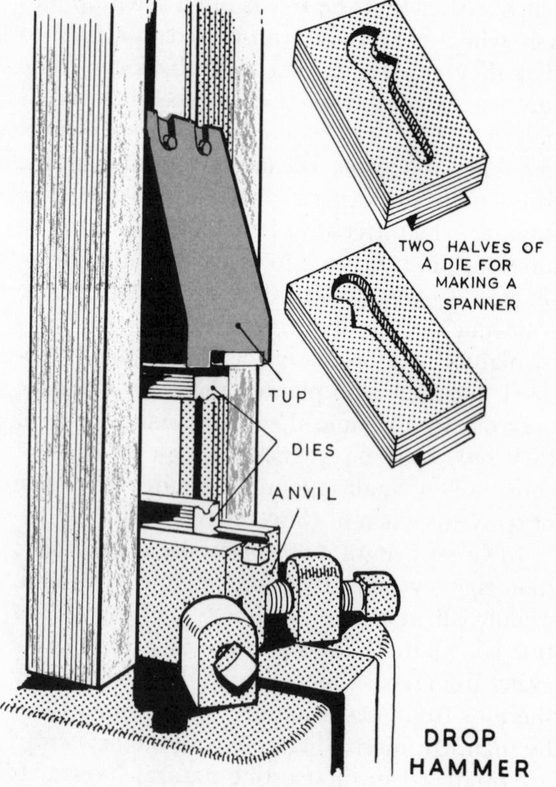

DROP HAMMER

**FORGERY.** The verb "to forge" once meant "to make", and a blacksmith's shop is still called a forge, but by the end of the middle ages it had also come to mean writing something so that it should appear to have been written by someone else. This is a crime, called forgery. The crime lies in making a document or signature appear to be what it is not. Forgery includes printing, engraving and typewriting as well as handwriting. Thus a rail ticket can be forged.

For the making of a false document to be a crime, it must be done with the intention of fraud. (See FRAUD.) Suppose a man makes a will—the document in which he says who shall have his possessions when he dies. One nephew sees the will and finds that he is to be left nothing but that another relative is to get £1,000. So he alters the name of that relative to his own name. This is forgery.

Other ways of forging with fraudulent intent are the making of false bank notes and the filling in of figures on a cheque different from those written in the first place.

Another kind of forgery is coining or making counterfeit, or false, money. Some criminals make a business of this. They use discs of base, or inexpensive, metals and stamp imitations of real coins on them.

In the 17th century forgery was a capital offence and forgers were put to death. In 1913 an act of parliament called the Forgery Act became law, and under this people who obtained money or other valuables by forgery could be imprisoned for 14 years, while the forgery of certain documents such as bank notes and wills was made punishable by imprisonment for life.

One of the most brilliant forgers was the Dutch artist Han van Meegeren (1889–1947), who between 1936 and 1943 painted ten Biblical scenes in the style of the 17th-century master Jan Vermeer (see VERMEER). Six of these were sold as genuine Vermeers for some £700,000, one being bought by the Dutch government.

**FORGET-ME-NOT.** The forget-me-not has many tiny flowerheads growing close together. The buds are pinkish, but when they open, the flower petals are a beautiful bright or pale blue. The forget-me-not belongs to a genus, or group, called *Myosotis*, which is Greek for mouse's ear, and describes the shape of the small leaf.

Forget-me-nots are pretty flowers to grow in garden borders, where they like moist soil. Field, wood, creeping, rock and water forget-me-nots grow wild in Great Britain. They are sometimes called scorpion grasses because their blue flowers are turned back at the top like a scorpion's jointed, stinging tail.

Forget-me-not.

A legend says that when Adam was naming the flowers in the Garden of Eden he at first overlooked one shy little plant, so when he at last saw it he called it forget-me-not. Another legend says that a knight tried to gather the flower for his lady, but as it was growing by water he was drowned in the attempt. According to this legend the flower was given its name from his last words, "Forget me not."

**FORK.** Although special "suckett" forks seem to have been used in England for eating sticky sweets as early as the reign of Henry VIII in the 16th century, when forks were first brought from Italy as a normal tool for eating they were despised as "yet another foreign affectation [fad]". Thomas Coryat in 1611 described how he had been hurt by his friends' scorn when he tried to make them use forks instead of fingers. The haberdashers were against them, too, for they were afraid that fewer new table napkins and cloths would be bought if people started eating with forks. However, there was no doubt that a fork was a great help in carving a joint and this helped to make it popular. People started carrying a set of folding knives, forks and spoons on their travels, but it was not until the reign of Queen Anne that innkeepers and private hosts thought it necessary to provide such things for their guests.

When Sheffield plate was invented—that is, articles made of copper which had been silver-plated in a special way in Sheffield—sets of tableware became much less expensive and more people were able to buy them. By the middle of the 19th century various kinds of forks were being made for dealing with different kinds of food. Nowadays, table forks are mass-produced by stamping the rough shape out of a spade-like bar of metal, and the slots are cut afterwards.

Besides table forks, there are special forks for other purposes—garden forks and pitchforks, for example—while other objects with a similar shape are often called forks. They include the two-pronged tuning forks which are used by piano tuners because they give off a note of a definite pitch when struck.

**FORMOSA,** which means "beautiful", is the name given by the early Portuguese voyagers to the large island of Taiwan which lies some 90 miles from the south China coast. It is about half the size of Ireland and its eastern part is steep mountainous country which slopes gently to a broad fertile plain on the west. The climate is tropical and extremely wet in the mountainous part, which is thickly wooded and contains bears, wild pig and deer.

Formosa is one of the few places where the valuable camphor tree is found and in the western lowlands grow sugar cane, rice, tea, sweet potatoes, fruit and tobacco. In the mountains dwell primitive tribes, but most of the people are descended from settlers who came from the southern Chinese provinces.

The capital is Taipei, a modern city in the north linked by a railway with the ports of Chi-lung and Kao-hsiung, although until 1894 Tainan in the southwest was the capital. The third main port is Hua-lien on the east coast. Most of the people are farmers, but some coal and sulphur are mined and petroleum and natural gas are produced. The north and west parts are well served by a railway along the western plain and there is a narrow-gauge line along part of the east coast. A north–south highway links Taipei with Kao-hsiung and there is a road crossing the island. Hydro-electric power is obtained from the Sun-Moon Lake in the central highlands. Industrial resources are limited. Main agricultural products are rice, sugar, sweet potatoes, tea, peanuts, wheat and fruit.

There were Portuguese and Spanish settlements in Formosa in the 16th century but in 1622 these were taken by the Dutch, who after some 40 years were driven out by a Chinese pirate named Koxinga. He and his family ruled the country until 1680, after which it became part of the Manchu (Chinese) empire. In 1895 Formosa was taken by the Japanese, who for some years had a lot of fighting with the mountain tribes, but at the same time did a great deal to develop the country by building railways, roads, ports and schools during their 50-year rule. At the end of World War II Formosa was handed back to China and in 1949, when the mainland of China became Communist, the Nationalist government, which opposed the Communists, retreated to Formosa.

---

### FACTS ABOUT FORMOSA

AREA (including Pescadores and neighbouring islands): 13,885 square miles.
POPULATION (estimated in 1967): 13,142,000.
KIND OF COUNTRY: Self-governing republic: since 1949 Formosa has been the only territory under the control of the Chinese Nationalist government.
CAPITAL: Taipei.
CHIEF EXPORTS: Sugar, coal, salt, rice, tea and fruits.
EDUCATION: Children must attend school between the ages of 6 and 12.

---

(This is explained more fully in the article CHINA.) By a treaty signed in 1954 the United States agreed to protect Formosa and the nearby Pescadores Islands against attack.

**FORT.** A fort is a stronghold built to defend the men within it from attack, or to guard the country round it, in which case it is usually manned by soldiers. In prehistoric times the walls of a fort were usually made by piling up earth to form a bank, or rampart, with a ditch outside it, but later forts had ramparts and often towers of stone. Forts have been used ever since men living in groups or tribes learned to grow crops and to keep domestic animals and other possessions that needed protection, and to fight with their neighbours. Early man often built earth forts to protect his villages and his crops and cattle from raids by other tribes. These forts were usually built on hill-tops, which made them difficult to attack. Later, in times recorded by history, communities were usually defended by a fort, a fortress or a castle. Forts of this kind were not usually very large, and only a small number of soldiers could live in them. This was because they were intended to guard only the land and property near to them. The fortress, on the other hand, was the main stronghold of a whole region, and it was large enough to hold a legion. In time of war the fortress was generally used as a base behind the front lines. The castle was usually for the protection of a noble family and its servants and retainers. There is a separate article CASTLE.

## Prehistoric Hill Forts

Some hill forts were lived in all the time, and formed actual villages, while others were used only as places of refuge when an enemy threatened to attack. During the Bronze Age, for instance, the population lived in villages on the slopes of the hills, and the forts were often deserted. Earlier, in the Neolithic period, however, the forts were lived in. Remains of some of these, which have been found on the top of the chalk downs of south-eastern England and in France, show that they were a plot of ground either circular or oval in shape, and defended by an earth bank and a ditch, both of which

An Iron Age hill fort as it looks today. The picture below shows the banks and ditches as they were built.

had gaps at frequent intervals. The inhabitants lived in huts in the shelter of the ditch, and the animals could be driven inside the fort.

When iron came to be used to make swords and other hand weapons, the fort builders needed a defence that made it more difficult for the attackers to storm their homes. They still used a bank and ditch to defend their forts, but the bank was high, and the earth was often strengthened with timber or stone walling. There was a ledge (called a berm) between it and the deep ditch outside, and room to walk along a path made in the inner wall of the bank. There were also extra banks in front of the entrances to the fort, or else the ends of the main bank were turned inwards to form a passage way over which could be built a wooden gate-house. The defenders placed their huts inside the shelter of the bank. The bank was usually built round the edge of the flat ground on the hill top and followed the shape of the hill.

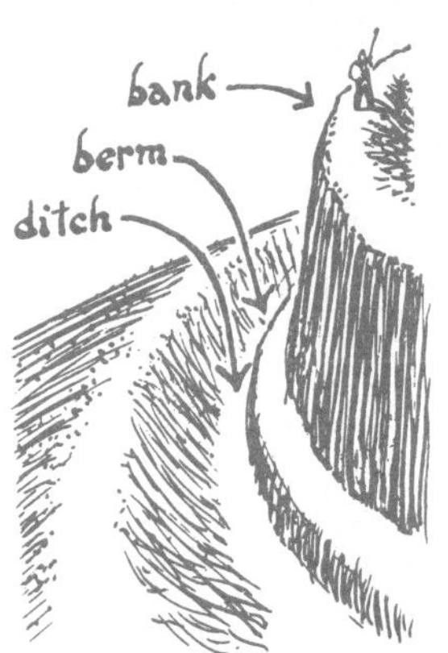


Later in the Iron Age, in France and south-western England, more elaborate forts were built which had two or more banks, making them very much more difficult to capture. One of the finest examples is that of Maiden Castle in

Above: Llanmelin hill fort in Monmouthshire was built early in the Iron Age, that is, before 350 B.C. It is in a strong defensive position on the top of a hill with steep slopes on its north, west and south sides. The builders took advantage of this to save themselves a certain amount of labour. The population for which a fort was built cannot have been large, and building it must have been an all-out effort to cope with some very serious and dangerous emergency. Such an emergency—perhaps the approach of aggressive alien tribes—might well come in the midst of long periods of peace. At Llanmelin, therefore, the builders put their strongest defences on the east side where the natural defences were weak, and they also put an outpost 1,000 feet northeast of the ramparts at this point. The fort is roughly oval and 5½ acres in area. A trackway climbed from the valley to the entrance. Flanking this trackway was a strongly defended box fortification which was joined to the main part of the fort. The earth banks had a revetment, or facing, of dry-stone walling, and the ditch was cut into the rock. The cross-fire from the well-protected wooden fighting platforms would have made it difficult for an attacking force to reach the gateway. *The drawings are by Alan Sorrell.*

Right: Maiden Castle occupies a saddle-backed hill on the chalk downland of Dorset. There was a Neolithic (New Stone Age) settlement on the site as early as 2500 B.C. At that time the East Knoll was probably surrounded by an embankment and ditch, and later the East and West Knolls were connected by a long mound which has never been explained. In the Bronze Age that followed, Maiden Castle was deserted, but it was occupied again and developed as an Iron Age fort. Its defences reached their final grandeur and complexity at the beginning of the 1st century A.D. under the rule of the Belgae, tribes which had come from Gaul and colonized southern Britain from possibly as early as 150 B.C. Maiden Castle, unlike other hill forts, could be called a town, for there is much evidence that it was inhabited continuously. Probably in A.D. 47, the fortress-town was stormed by the Romans commanded by Vespasian, who was later to become Emperor. The fortifications had been designed for defence by slingers—countless sling-stones have been found on the site. But the Roman legionaries advanced under a barrage of iron-shod arrows fired from ballistae, which were like giant crossbows. They demolished the palisades and under cover of the smoke from burning huts broke into the town.

Dorset. The people of this time had to defend themselves against an enemy armed with sling-stones made from beach pebbles. When they stood on the top of their high land, they were able to fire farther downhill than their enemy could uphill. Often attackers would try to burn down forts, and in some places, where remains have been found, the stones have been discovered melted and fused together by the flames. Later, when the Romans attacked native forts, they used battering-rams and large catapults which could fire heavy stones. The Gauls learnt to build walls of stone, wood and earth which could stand up against the battering-ram, and which were difficult to set on fire.

## Later Forts

Roman forts, or *castella,* were rather like the prehistoric forts, but more complicated and often stronger. They were square or rectangular in shape, and surrounded, like the hill forts, by one or more outer ditches which curved round the corners. There were four entrances, one on each side of the fort, and gaps were left in the ditches opposite these. The ramparts were of earth and strengthened by wood which was built up to form a parapet, or low wall, behind which the defenders could shelter and walk round the rampart. If the fort was in use for a long time, stone ramparts were usually built instead.

There were many buildings inside a Roman fort. In the centre stood the headquarters, or *principia,* and the commanding officer's house, the *praetorium.* The soldiers lived in long narrow blocks of barracks. There were also offices, cook-houses, latrines (lavatories) and sometimes, built outside the fort, a large bath house. In addition there might be one or two warehouses, or *horreae,* with raised floors for storing grain away from damp.

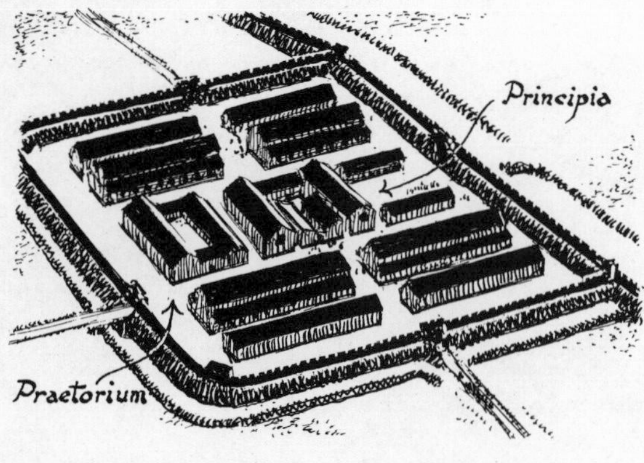


A Roman fort, showing the *principia* (headquarters) and the *praetorium* (the commanding officer's house).

When Saxon raids on Britain grew more frequent the Romans built extra strong forts, known as the Saxon Shore forts, to defend the coast. These had thick, high stone walls, some with projecting platforms called bastions, and narrow entrances. You can see forts like these still standing at Richborough in Kent, at Pevensey in Sussex and at Porchester in Hampshire.

Forts have been built at many periods in history since the time of the Romans, although they are no longer built to defend towns and villages, for they are useless as a protection against modern weapons. The French Foreign Legion, for instance, built forts in North Africa to defend itself against the Arabs, and trading companies in North America built forts to defend their trading posts against attacks from Red Indians.

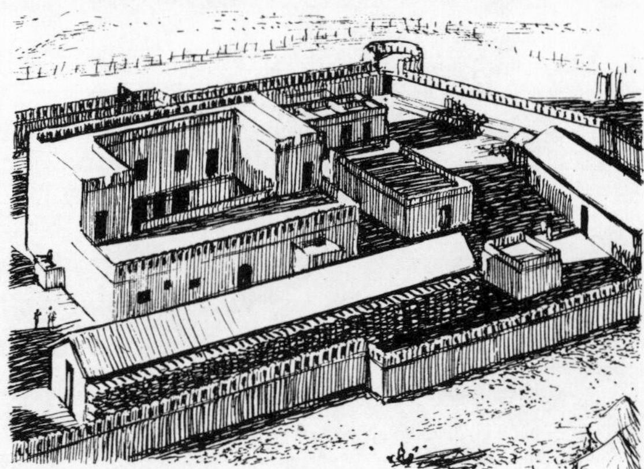

A North African desert fort of our own time.

**FORTH RIVER.** The River Forth starts as two tiny streams near Ben Lomond, a mountain of western Scotland, and ends on the east coast as a great firth, or arm of the sea, which is 17 miles wide at one point. The river forms much of the boundary between Stirlingshire and Perthshire. From Gartmore to Alloa it flows slowly in a very winding course across the flat lowlands of Flanders Moss and the Links of Forth. The full length of the river is thus 66

*Scottish Tourist Board*

The Forth road bridge, completed in 1964. The famous cantilever rail bridge of 1890 can be seen in the distance.

miles, although it travels between two points only 30 miles apart. The firth, beginning at Kincardine, is 48 miles long, making a total of 114 miles. The river is tidal (that is, the rise and fall of the tide can be seen) up to Stirling.

The Firth of Forth is the main gateway from the North Sea into Scotland, and there are ports on both sides of it. On the south are Grangemouth, Bo'ness and Edinburgh's port of Leith, and on the north Methil, Burntisland, Kirkcaldy and the naval base of Rosyth. There are lighthouses on some of the islands in the firth, such as the Isle of May and Bass Rock near the entrance, both of which are of interest to birdwatchers. (See EAST LOTHIAN.) Inchkeith, opposite Edinburgh, has a lighthouse, while on Inchcolm can be seen the remains of the 12th-century abbey.

In early times the Forth was an important barrier between southern Scotland and the rest of the country. In those days the land near the river was mostly marshy and very hard to cross, and the only good road northward passed through Stirling, and over a raised causeway more than a mile long, overlooked and guarded by the castle high on its rock. The Battles of Stirling and of Bannockburn, Sauchieburn and Sheriffmuir near by show how important this route was for the armies of those days.

Until the road bridge was opened at Kincardine in 1936, car and lorries could only cross the Firth of Forth by means of the ferries at Granton and Queensferry, although the great Forth Bridge already carried trains across. In 1964, a road bridge was opened half a mile upstream of the railway bridge and greatly eased the traffic problem. The river is here at its deepest point of 200 feet.

**FORTIFICATIONS** are obstacles or defences built around a place to make it difficult for an enemy to attack it. The verb "to fortify" means "to make strong".

Some fortifications have been built to serve as barriers along the frontiers of countries, examples of these being the very ancient Great Wall of China, Hadrian's Wall built by the Romans across the north of England (there are separate articles on these) and the Maginot Line built between World War I and World War II by the French along their frontier with Germany. This kind of fortification is defended by soldiers in forts built at intervals along the line of defence (see FORT).

Until the middle ages towns were fortified when necessary by having thick stone walls round them. The defending soldiers on top of this wall were sheltered behind *battlements*—a smaller wall having gaps in it through which they could shoot arrows down on the attackers. As, however, the enemy would probably attack in a line with shields in front of them, it was usual to build towers jutting out from the wall so that the defenders could shoot along the enemy line. The towers were higher than the battlements so that if the enemy did succeed in scaling the wall, the defending archers could still fire down on them. The main intention was to build the fortifications so that no part of the walls could be approached by an enemy in safety. Fortifications of this kind, which can still be seen in England at York and Chester, were of little use against cannon balls which could smash down stone walls, and later fortifications were usually built outside the town walls so that an enemy could not bring his guns close enough to attack the town. They were made chiefly as earthworks—low, solid banks of earth called *ramparts* broad enough to mount cannon behind a *parapet* or protecting wall, and having a steep outer face and usually a *moat* or broad ditch round the outside.

As time went on these earthworks became more complicated, for military engineers began to draw plans of fortifications that could not be stormed by an enemy at any point without his being fired on from three sides. This resulted in places which, seen from above, were star-shaped and had every kind of zig-zag outline. Some of them enclosed a second line of fortifications inside the first. Defence works of this kind are usually coupled with the name of the great 17th-century French engineer Sebastian Leprêtre de Vauban who designed many fortifications for King Louis XIV. No place defended by Vauban was ever taken, though he never claimed to have thought of any wonderful scheme, saying "one does not fortify by systems but by common sense". What is sometimes forgotten is that Vauban was as clever in attack as defence, for no place that he attacked was ever held!

The assault of a fortification was best done by digging trenches towards it—preferably at night—in such a way that the trench never pointed in a direction so that the defenders could fire along it. In other words, the trench advanced zig-zag fashion. Cannon would be moved forward along it in darkness, and might, at last, be brought close enough to smash down the ramparts.

A very large fortified place capable of holding an army of men, and sometimes containing a town as well, came to be called a *fortress*; Gibraltar is an example.

In the 19th century guns became very much more powerful, for not only could they shoot farther and with greater destructive power but also they could fire shells that exploded on hitting instead of solid cannon balls. The fact that guns could shoot farther meant that the fortifications of a town had to be situated on the outskirts, and the fact that guns had more destructive power meant that earthworks were not enough—the ramparts must now be of thick concrete and the guns of the fortification must have heavy steel shields. (See Gun.)

Fortification therefore became a very expensive business; moreover, it did not seem to be very successful. In the war between France and Germany (1870–1871) the Germans took all the French fortresses except one, with ease, and in the Russo-Japanese war (1904–1905) the Japanese brought up heavy guns which soon smashed up the fortifications of Port Arthur (now in China, but then in Russia). In World War I, although much had been hoped of the Belgian fortifications, those outside Antwerp were far enough apart for the Germans to advance between them, and the others at Liège and Namur were quickly battered to bits by the German guns.

Yet in one way World War I saw a tremendous use of field fortifications. For most of the war the Allied and German armies on the western front faced one another from an amazing system of trenches running from the English Channel to the Alps, in some places only a few score yards apart. Thick entanglements of barbed wire were laid in front of the trenches and deep shelters called dug-outs were made for use when the enemy fired shells against the trench. Fighting in these *field fortifications* was called "trench warfare" and was very costly in lives. An attack—even one that gained ground—nearly always cost the attacker many more soldiers than the defender. Not until tanks were used in the latter part of that war was a way found of advancing through a trench system.

The idea of permanent fortifications came to life again between the two world wars, when the French built along their frontier with Germany a powerful line of strong points with guns and obstacles called the Maginot Line. In 1940, however, the Germans when they attacked came

through Belgium and thus into France through an area which the Maginot Line had not been lengthened to cover. Also, World War II saw the use of parachute troops which could be dropped from aircraft to land behind defences of this sort, making it unlikely that fortifications in a continuous line can ever be a complete barrier in future.

During World War II the British army in France was at first engaged in extending the Maginot Line defences as far as the Channel coast by the construction of field fortifications. Later it was engaged in the task of strengthening the British coastal defences during the time when the country was threatened by invasion.

Trenches were dug and concrete strongpoints, called "pill boxes" from their shape, were built along the coast so that the defending army could be sheltered from the attackers. Barbed wire entanglements were erected along promenades, on cliffs and on the beaches, on which land mines were laid and iron spikes and stakes were dug in as obstacles to landing craft. All these defences were covered by coastal defence guns and machine guns, whilst inland huge ditches were dug to stop the advance of tanks and vehicles. These were called "tank traps". Mines were laid beneath the surface of fields, roads and paths so as to blow up infantry soldiers who marched over them or to damage tanks that tried to pass.

The British defences were never put to the test, but on the coasts of France, Belgium and the Netherlands the Germans installed a similar defence system, and it was against such obstacles that the Allied forces carried out their successful invasion of France in 1944. They broke through all these obstacles and drove the Germans back from their coastal defences.

**FORTUNE TELLING.** Among the side-shows at a fairground may often be seen a booth in which, according to the advertisement outside, a person may have his or her fortune told for a small sum of money. If you go in, the fortune teller (usually a woman) may either look at the palm of your hand, or gaze into a ball of crystal, or deal out cards in a special way, or use some other method which, like these, is supposed to reveal to her the happenings lying in store for you in the future. These happenings are your "fortune", and the fortune teller will give you an account of them and may also add a warning or a piece of advice.

Many of the people who go to have their fortunes told nowadays do so for fun without seriously believing that the fortune teller or anyone else can foresee future events. Among ancient peoples, however, fortune telling was a much more serious business and in many places it is even now. The idea that some happening of today is a sign or omen of some other happening that is going to occur in the future is a very old one. To ancient peoples the things that happened in the heavens (the movements of the sun, moon and stars) were the most important of all, and they believed that by studying the positions of the stars in the skies they could forecast the fate and future of human beings. (The article ASTROLOGY describes these ancient practices.) The columns in newspapers and magazines today where people's fortunes are told according to what "star" they were born under have in fact come down from those times.

A quite different method of fortune telling is known as palmistry. According to this system a person's fortune can be told by examining the pattern of the lines on the skin of the palm of his hand.

By another system, cards may be dealt out of a pack, all having some special meaning; and even the pattern of tea leaves left in a person's cup may be used to foretell his future. Some fortune tellers gaze into a ball of polished crystal, or a vessel of water or a mirror, in which they claim to see pictures of future events.

**FORUM.** In the middle of most old towns in Great Britain there is a market place. It is much more than just a place where a market is held —there are shops and offices, public gatherings are held there and people stand round it and talk. In much the same way the ancient Romans had a space in the middle of their towns, and the Latin word for this is *forum*.

The forum was a very busy place, used for markets, shopping, political gatherings and as a general meeting place. It was oblong and was surrounded by public buildings such as law courts and temples, which often had tall pillars and imposing entrances which made it a place of great dignity.

The oldest and most famous forum of Rome, the *Forum Romanum*, lay between two of the seven hills on which Rome was built, the Palatine and the Capitoline. It was a large area and in the early days athletic games were held there. There was a special place in one corner for open-air town meetings and, in another place, a platform for public speakers. Round the forum there were important buildings such as the senate chamber (*Curia*), the law courts (*Basilica Aemilia*), and temples to the Roman gods, besides smaller buildings and shops. Great archways led into the forum and there were many statues round it.

As Rome grew bigger one forum was not enough and several others were made. These later ones were either legal and official centres or markets, but not both. There were separate markets for cattle, vegetables and so on.

The remains of many of the Roman fora (this is the plural of the word "forum") and of those of other great cities such as Pompeii have been discovered and partly restored. If you go to Italy you can walk in places where the ancient Romans bought and sold and argued 2,000 years ago. The article ROME: ANCIENT tells you more about them and about Rome itself.

**FOSSIL.** Fossils are the hardened remains of plants or animals or their impressions and are found in rocks. This is because such animals and plants were covered by mud or sand which later changed into rocks, sometimes over a period of millions of years.

Among the rocks that are likely to contain fossils are limestone, shale or clay, and also chalk, which is partly made up of tiny shells which sank to the bottom of the sea. However, fossils are not found in every part of a quarry or cliff. They occur along definite layers, and the best chance of finding them is to split the rock carefully along the "bedding planes", which are the parts of the rock that formed the sea-floor long ago. The bedding planes are

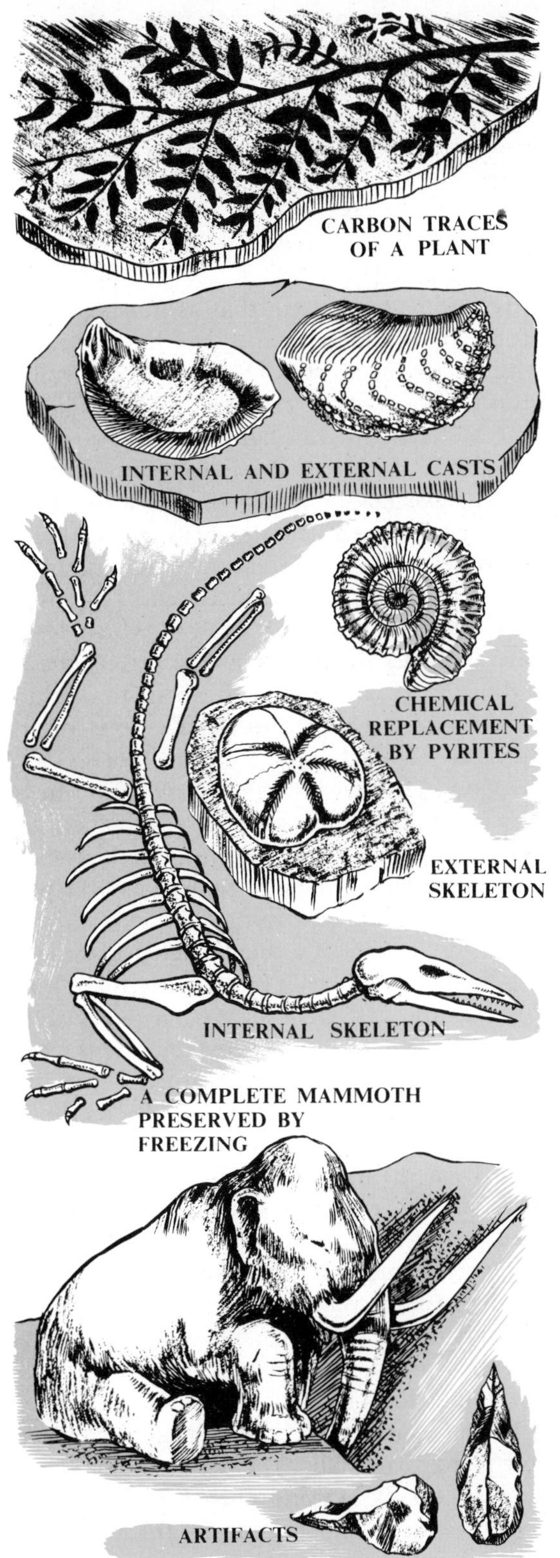


usually found where there is a change in the appearance of the rock.

There are several kinds of fossils. Very occasionally the complete animal, even including its skin and hair, may be preserved, so that people know exactly what that animal looked like. Fossil mammoths, which were long-haired elephants that are now extinct, have been found buried in ice, looking just as they did in life. People tried to eat steaks cut from these mammoths that had been kept in cold storage for thousands of years, but they did not taste at all pleasant.

Not only the great mammoths but also tiny creatures such as ants and beetles have been found kept in perfect shape as fossils. Along the southern shores of the Baltic Sea yellow amber with perfectly preserved insects embedded in it is found in large quantities. Amber is formed from resin, and these tiny insects, which lived millions of years ago, were caught in resin as it oozed from the trees and imprisoned in it when it hardened into amber.

It was much more usual, however, for the soft parts of the animal to decay before it was buried in mud or sand, and so only the bones and shells, which are made of mineral matter, remained.

Fossils are often in the form of petrifactions, a word that comes from the Greek word *petra,* meaning a rock. Water passing slowly through the rocks laid down mineral matter about the shells and bones. If this process occurred slowly enough, all the detail of the shell is preserved even though some of the shelly material may have been replaced. In many clays fossil shells can be found, but instead of the original paper-thin limy shell there is a shining compound of iron or iron pyrites, which is composed of iron and sulphur. These pyritized fossils, as they are called, can easily be found at low tide at East Wear Bay near Folkestone in Kent. They are often beautifully coloured, but this is entirely due to the pyrites and not to the original shell.

In Arizona in the United States there are petrified forests, for the plant substances of the trees have been completely replaced by a mineral called silica, which appears in quartz and sandstone. So complete was this process that original details of the stone trees can be studied through a microscope.

Sometimes water passing through the rocks dissolves away the shells, and if the rock is strong enough hollow spaces are left. These spaces (moulds) can be filled with substances such as plaster of Paris which, when lifted out, has marks on it that show what the inside of the shell looked like. In the stone quarries in Portland, Dorset, there is one bed of limestone where all the fossils have been dissolved, but beautifully clear moulds which show all the detail of the inside of the shells have been left.

One of the most famous fossil beds in the world consists of some shales at Mount Stephen, British Columbia (Canada), which contain traces of soft-bodied creatures like jellyfish and worms that lived about 500,000,000 years ago.

Creatures walking or crawling over the soft mud or sand of the seashore often leave footprints or trails. When this happened long ago and the mud or sand was changed into rock, the marks were sometimes not destroyed. Such marks are called trace fossils. Many plants and certain primitive groups of animals, such as the graptolites, which had horny hard parts, are to be found crushed flat on the faces of rocks as black or greyish marks.

It is something of a miracle that fossils are found at all, especially in the older rocks. The chances of an animal or plant that lived some 100,000,000 or more years ago being found fossilized today are extremely small, for there are all kinds of ways in which it might have been destroyed.

In the first place, the living thing must have been buried quickly after its death, or else it would have decayed altogether. By far the greatest number of fossils are of sea animals and plants, for, as they sank into sand or mud, they were usually buried much more quickly than those that lived on land.

Yet even if the animal or plant was safely and quickly buried and became a fossil, there were still several ways in which it might be destroyed. Water seeping through the rocks might dissolve it away and the rock might not be strong enough to keep open the mould the fossil once occupied. Another reason why many fossils have been destroyed is that rocks containing them were affected by great folding movements of the earth, so that they buckled and changed their shape, destroying the fossils in the process. Also, molten (melted) rock may have been forced into the rocks from below or have flowed over them as lava. When this happened, the heat completely altered the rocks and the fossils were destroyed.

It is thought, indeed, that as much as 99% of all living things of the past have perished without leaving any trace behind. In particular, little is known about creatures with soft bodies that had none of the hard parts usually preserved. It is only in the finest grained muds, which have not been folded or heated at all, that traces of such delicate creatures as jellyfish or worms can be found. Many fossil insects are known from only a single specimen.

If we think of all the ways in which fossils have been destroyed, it is not surprising that it is difficult to find out much about the distant past. Even so, enough fossils have been left for the study of fossil animals (palaeozoology) and the study of fossil plants (palaeobotany) to be very useful in teaching scientists much about the appearance of creatures that lived in the remote past, thus helping them to understand the process of evolution. (See EVOLUTION.)

In 1861 a print of a single feather was found in a kind of limestone in Bavaria, Germany, and this was the first trace of *Archaeopteryx,* the earliest known bird. Later, two more specimens were found of this strange creature, which had teeth in its bill and a tail like that of a reptile.

Then, too, fossil remains of the earliest men have been discovered, usually buried beneath rocks and other rubbish in caves. Much of the history of man, from its beginnings about 1,000,000 years ago to the first written history less than 10,000 years ago, has been worked out by studying the fossil remains of human beings and their artifacts (objects made by men, such as the flint tools in the illustration).

In the article COAL there is an account of how plants over millions of years have sunk into the earth and been transformed into coal.

Generally, the older the rocks, the more difficult it is to find fossils in them and, if some are found, to remove the pieces of rock, known as matrix, sticking to them. Sometimes limestone is removed with a stiff brush or with a knife or needle, but it may be so hard that it has to be removed either by applying certain chemicals or by using a special small type of dental drill or a mechanical hammer.

The fossil skeletons of dinosaurs, the enormous reptiles that lived more than 100,000,000 years ago, have to be put together and often taken from place to place in ships, and this is a real science. Parts of the skeletons are often discovered lying on top of the ground, as the rock in which they were fossilized has been worn away.

When such a find is made, the bones that are still buried are uncovered and painted with something like shellac (a kind of varnish) to harden them. After this, they are covered with a layer of plaster of Paris to protect them. The whole of the rock containing the fossil is shipped in crates to a museum, where the skeleton or bone is carefully separated from the rock by chipping. Then the fossil is hardened with shellac or some other mixture, the pieces are cemented together and models are made to look as much like the missing parts as possible. After a study of the remains and the nearest relatives of the creature still alive, all the parts are fitted together into a full skeleton, as may be seen in the fossil reptile galleries of the British Museum at South Kensington in London.

**FOUNDING,** which comes from the French word meaning "to pour", is the shaping of metals by pouring them when molten (melted) into a mould. Articles made in this way are called *castings* and the workshops where they are made are foundries. There are ornamental castings over 5,000 years old in museums and the Bible tells how the Israelites in about 1490 B.C. melted their ornaments to cast a golden calf. Common examples of castings are the big pipes for gas and water mains, garden rollers, kitchen cookers, manhole covers, the legs of school desks and the cylinder blocks of motor cars. All these are iron castings, and iron is often used unless very great strength is wanted, when steel is used.

If a pencil is pushed into damp sand and carefully pulled out the hole can be filled with melted metal which when it cools will set in the shape of the pencil. This is the general idea of all foundry work. The *mould*, or impression, is usually made by packing stiff damp sand around a wooden *pattern* which has the shape of the article to be cast.

The making of a pattern is highly skilled work. The casting shrinks as it cools and this must be allowed for by making the pattern slightly bigger, though the allowance is different for each sort of metal. Then again, a pattern for a cylindrical casting such as a metal roller could not be *drawn*, or removed from the sand, unless made slightly tapering or given a *draft* by the pattern maker. Lastly, it is clear that a pattern for a ball could not be drawn without breaking up the sand packed round it; this difficulty is overcome by making the pattern out of two half-balls joined together by guide pins as shown in the middle picture.

The mould is made in a frame consisting of two metal moulding boxes without top or bottom

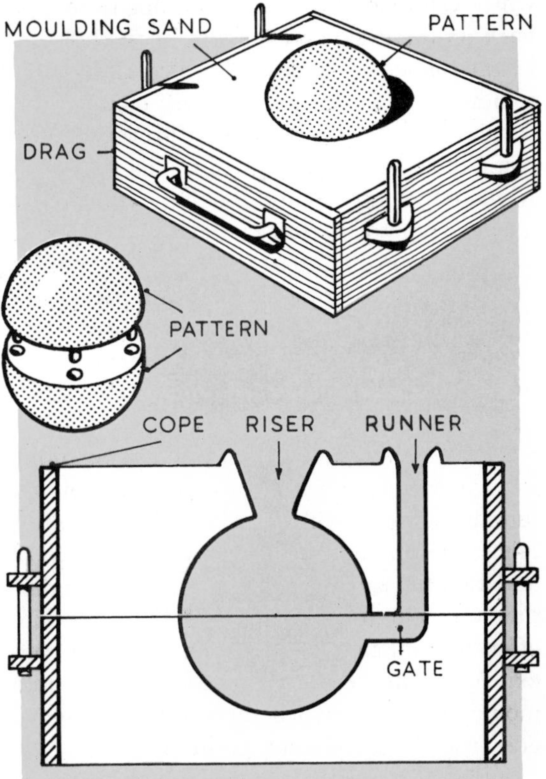


How a sand mould is prepared for casting a solid ball.

fitting one above the other. One half-ball (that is, half of the pattern) is laid on a flat board and the lower moulding box, called the *drag*, is placed over it; the drag is rammed full of moulding sand and then turned over. The second half-ball is now joined to the first as shown in the upper picture, and the upper face of the mould dusted over with dry *parting sand* so that later the two halves of the mould can be separated without sticking. The *cope*, or upper moulding box, is now put on top of the drag, a round peg called a riser peg is supported upright on the top half of the pattern and another called a runner peg a few inches from it. These pegs form channels in the mould for the molten metal to flow through. The cope is rammed full of moulding sand, levelled off and *sleeked* or smoothed, and the two pegs drawn out.

The cope is lifted off and turned over so that the top half of the pattern can be drawn. A channel called a *gate* is cut in the surface of the sand in the drag to connect the hole made by the runner peg to the bottom half of the pattern, which can then be drawn. The cope is then put back on the drag, and the tops of the holes left by the runner peg and the riser peg are enlarged somewhat as shown in the lower picture. The cope is loaded with weights to prevent it from being lifted by the pressure of the molten metal, which is then poured in through the runner until it comes up to the top of the riser. Thus the riser contains that part of the molten metal which went into the mould first; this part is most likely to have dirt and bubbles of air or gas in it. When the casting has cooled the boxes are separated, the sand knocked out and the casting removed for cleaning and trimming.

From this simplified description of moulding with an easy shape of pattern it can be seen that foundry work is complicated and highly skilled. Sometimes moulding machines are used to fill and ram the sand mechanically, and foundries that turn out many castings of the same kind often have metal moulds which, although very expensive, can be used again and again. Metal moulds may be carried on a turntable which goes round to different positions so that the moulds are in turn filled, opened, the casting removed, the mould cleaned and closed again.

Large pipes or hollow cylinders may be cast by pouring the molten metal into a cylindrical or drum-shaped mould which is spun round so that the metal is flung against the inside wall of the mould, where it solidifies. This is called *centrifugal casting*.

*Die casting* is a method of making small parts of a complicated shape by pouring molten metal into a steel die (a kind of mould). The metal is usually forced into the die by pressure and the machine that does the work is automatic. For making small steel castings with a fine finish the *lost wax* process is used. In this the pattern is made of wax—sometimes in a die-casting machine—and then coated with a clay-like substance called *slurry*. A small hole is left in the coating and when it is hard the mould is heated so that the wax pattern melts and runs out; molten steel can then be poured into the mould which is broken away when the casting is cool.

**FOUNDLING HOSPITAL.** Homes which are run specially for foundlings (children abandoned by their parents) are often called foundling hospitals. There were one or two in Italy and France as early as the 7th or 8th centuries, but none in Great Britain until the 18th century. At that time babies and young children were often found deserted in the streets of London and in March 1740 a home was opened for them through the efforts of a kind-hearted sea captain named Thomas Coram. For this home a fine building was put up in Bloomsbury, London, and many people took an interest in this Foundling Hospital. George Frederick Handel, the musician, presented an organ to the chapel, and William Hogarth and other artists gave pictures.

In the 20th century the London Foundling Hospital was moved into the country, and for about 20 years it was situated at Berkhamsted in Hertfordshire. Nowadays, however, many people think it better for foundling children to be looked after in ordinary homes and go to ordinary schools rather than live together in large buildings. The Foundling Hospital at Berkhamsted was finally closed down in 1954, and the organization now known as the Thomas Coram Foundation for Children now arranges for its children to remain with their foster parents instead of going to boarding school, as before. (You can read more about this subject in the article CHILDREN ACT, 1948.)

**FOUNTAIN.** Many of the fountains that people see today were made simply to be beautiful and delightful to look at, but in earlier days —and in some countries still nowadays—fountains were intended for use. When there was no such thing as a water supply laid on in pipes to almost every house, people depended on wells, springs and fountains for their water. The fountain in a village was an important part of everyday life, and so it used often to be thought of as a place with a special meaning.

The ancient Greeks often dedicated their fountains to nymphs and goddesses, and sometimes built a temple or shrine close by. One fountain at the city of Corinth was dedicated to the nymph Pirene, for according to legend the tears she shed for her dead sons formed the spring of water. The Romans also dedicated their fountains and even set aside one day in the year (October 13, the *Fontinalia*) as the festival of fountains, decorating them for the occasion.

*Paul Popper*

A floodlit fountain in the Place de la Concorde, Paris.

In Roman cities water from the reservoirs was taken in pipes not only to baths and large houses but also to many public fountains from which the poorer people could draw their supply. These fountains, usually at street corners, were often decorated with carvings of human or animal heads, the water pouring out of their mouths.

In Italy and other Mediterranean countries fountains are still used to supply water. The fountain usually stands in the chief square of the town or village and is often sculptured. To it the women bring their jars to be filled and it is usually the favourite meeting place of the villagers.

Very different from these useful fountains are the huge, beautifully sculptured ornamental fountains of Versailles in France. They were built by King Louis XIV and are among the most famous in the world. They are particularly beautiful when lit up at night. Other famous ornamental fountains are those in Trafalgar Square, London, and the Trevi fountain in Rome. Near the shore of the Lake of Geneva in Switzerland is a fountain whose jet rises to 425 feet.

There are still small wayside drinking fountains in many cities. They used to have an iron cup chained to them, but now they are often "bubbling" fountains from which the water is drunk straight from the jet without a cup.

**FOX, Charles James** (1749–1806). Charles James Fox, famous as a politician and as a brilliant speaker, was the third son of Lord Holland and was born in 1749. Educated at Eton College and at Oxford University, he became fond of learning, and for the whole of his life enjoyed reading in Greek, Latin, French and Italian as well as in English. His early life was often spoilt, however, by heavy gambling and too much drinking.

Fox entered the House of Commons in 1768, when he was 19, and was a member until he died in 1806. In all this time—38 years—he was an important member of the government on only three occasions, in 1782, 1783 and 1806, and spent most of his time opposing the government. He started his political career as a Tory, following in his father's footsteps, but soon found a section of the Whig party more to his liking—the section led by Lord Rockingham and Edmund Burke—and joined them. (See LIBERAL PARTY and BURKE, EDMUND.) He supported the American colonists in their fight for independence from Great Britain (see AMERICAN WAR OF INDEPENDENCE), and he rejoiced when the French started their revolution (see FRENCH REVOLUTION).

Fox supported these movements because he believed that people ought to be free to govern themselves in the way they wished. For much the same reason he wanted to weaken the power of King George III in Great Britain and to make parliament strong, for parliament, although it still did not fully represent the people, did act as a check on the power of the sovereign. This made him very unpopular with the King. In 1806, while he was Secretary of State in charge of foreign affairs, he successfully put forward a motion to abolish the slave trade (see SLAVERY AND SLAVE TRADE).

Fox was gay, open-hearted and friendly. As a young man he was a great leader of fashion and once wore red heels on his shoes and blue powder on his hair. (This was not so extraordinary as it would be today.) He was clumsy and untidy in later life but was such an exciting speaker that people could not help but listen to him, even if they did not like what he said.

**FOX, George** (1624–1691). George Fox was the founder of the Society of Friends, a religious group that worships God in a very simple, straightforward way. We often call the members of this group Quakers, which was originally a nickname, given to them because Fox bade people "tremble at the word of the Lord" (see QUAKERS). Fox was the son of a weaver who lived at Fenny Drayton in Leicestershire.

He was a serious child, and when he became a young man he left his home and friends to visit preachers in various parts of the country, searching for knowledge about God. In 1647 he started preaching himself and his preaching took him abroad as well as all over the British Isles. In 1671–1672 he visited the West Indies and America, in 1677 Holland and Germany and in 1681 Holland again.

At this time many Protestants followed the teaching of John Calvin, who thought that God chose only certain people to go to heaven and left others to everlasting misery. (See CALVIN, JOHN.) Fox brought a message of joy and hope, for he taught that if men followed Our Lord's teaching and allowed themselves to be guided by the "Inner Light" of the Living Christ they could all go to heaven when they died. He believed that churches were not important (he called them "steeple-houses") and that people could worship God wherever they were. These ideas led him into trouble, and he spent six years in various prisons, at Nottingham, Derby, Carlisle, Launceston, Lancaster, Scarborough and Worcester.

Fox was a big, tall man, with long hair and piercing eyes. He was full of courage and honesty. Although he was not what we should call a learned man he had an extraordinary knowledge of the Bible and could argue about it with the most famous scholars. Three years after his death in 1691 his *Journal,* the most famous of his writings, was published by some of his followers, of whom William Penn was the most outstanding (see PENN, WILLIAM).

**FOX.** One of the cleverest animals is the fox, and hundreds of stories have been told of his cunning. When pursued by hounds, he will wade brooks or leap on the backs of running sheep to break the trail of scent which the dogs are following. Sometimes he will pretend to be dead, even allowing himself to be handled, in the hope of finding an opportunity to escape later. His bright eyes, sharp muzzle (nose and mouth), pointed ears and bushy tail all make him look watchful and lively.

Foxes belong to the dog family and they are all much the same to look at, except in colour,

Many stories have been told of the cunning of the fox.

and have similar habits. Their homes are generally burrows in the ground, called "earths", which they leave at night to hunt birds, rabbits, mice, poultry and frogs. The vixen, or mother fox, has four to six cubs at a time, generally in March or April, and their eyes do not open for about a fortnight.

Foxes are found in more parts of the world than any other animal. They now live in every continent, although they were taken to Australia by man in order to help keep down the rabbits.

The red fox is found in parts of Europe, Asia and North America. It is about three feet long from its nose to the tip of its tail, the tail itself being 12 to 16 inches long. It stands about one foot high. Its back is reddish brown and its face red, while the body is white underneath and the tail a mixture of black and white. The American red fox is slightly larger and has longer hair.

The silver fox of Canada, which is black with white-tipped hairs, is a colour variety of the red fox. The cross fox looks like a mixture between the red and the silver fox, but is just another form of the red fox, with a dark cross on the back and shoulders.

The Arctic fox, which is found in countries round the North Pole, has a shorter and stouter body than the red fox. In summer its fur is brownish on the back but in winter it turns completely white. The blue fox is a colour variety of the Arctic fox and is smoky grey throughout the year.

The raising of silver and blue foxes is a profitable business, for their winter pelt, or coat, is very valuable. The first silver fox farms were started on Prince Edward Island, Canada, and now they are found all over the colder parts of North America as well as in suitable parts of Europe. At first these foxes were allowed to run loose, but it has been found that silver foxes do just as well in pens. Blue foxes are still kept in a semi-wild state on islands near the Alaska coast.

Another interesting kind of fox is the fennec of the Sahara Desert in North Africa, which lives on mice and insects. This is not much more than a foot long, stands about eight inches high and has very large ears. The long-eared fox of South and East Africa feeds mainly on white ants and other insects.

**FOXGLOVE.** The foxglove grows wild in woodlands and rocky places in Great Britain, and is also a garden flower, blooming in July. It is tall, sometimes as much as five feet high, and the flower heads, or bells, hang on a single stem. Wild foxgloves are purplish-pink, but the garden flowers may also be lilac, rose or white. By carefully lifting a foxglove bell and looking into it, hairs and an attractive pattern of deep red or purple spots can be seen on the inside. The bells are made up of four joined petals with irregular edges.

Foxglove.

The name foxglove probably has nothing to do with foxes but may come from "folk's glove", the "folk" being the fairies. In Scotland they are called bloody fingers and dead-men's bells, in Ireland they are known as fairy thimbles and in France they are called *gants de notre dame*—gloves of Our Lady.

The foxglove belongs to the genus, or group, *Digitalis,* a name that comes from digit, meaning a finger. From the seeds of the foxglove and from its large, greyish, downy leaves, collected in the second year of the plant's life, is made a drug, which is also called digitalis.

**FOX HUNTING** is the sport in which people breed a pack of hounds to hunt the fox and then ride after them on horseback to watch them do so. In some very rough countries, however, such as the mountains of north Wales and the Lake District, the huntsman and followers go out on foot. Hounds may be either pure English bred, when their coats are smooth, pure Welsh (there are not many of these) when their coats are very rough, or a cross between English and Welsh, in which case their coats may be either rough or smooth.

The fox replaced the stag as the favourite quarry of the chase during the 18th century and now packs of foxhounds hunt all over Great Britain and Ireland and there are other packs overseas, for example in Canada. Every hunt has a master, who is the most important person and whose decision on all questions is final. Hounds are hunted by the huntsman, who may also be the master. The whippers-in, of whom there may be as many as three, help the huntsman in the kennels and when he is hunting. There is also a secretary and treasurer, while the ordinary members and followers are known as the *field*. A hunting man wears a red coat with a silk hat, a black coat with a silk hat or bowler, or a "rat-catcher outfit" which can be riding clothes of almost any kind. Ladies wear a riding habit with a silk hat and veil when riding side-saddle, or breeches and black coat and bowler when riding astride. A hunting whip is carried and gloves are worn.

*Keystone*

Hounds moving off after a meet at Battle Abbey, Sussex.

Cub-hunting starts when the harvest is in, about September, and the purpose is to break up litters of cubs (young foxes) and teach them that it is safer to run away. The fox-hunting season begins on November 1 and continues until about the end of March.

On the morning of the hunt, hounds arrive at the meet, in charge of the huntsman and whippers-in, just before 11 o'clock. The secretary has already sent out appointment cards, letting members of the hunt know where the meet is to be, often at a cross roads, an inn or a church. Sharp at 11, hounds move off to find their first fox. They are taken to a wood called a *covert*, to a woodland (which is a large wood), or to some such place as a field of kale. In some rough countries foxes lie out on the ground, when they are said to *kennel*.

The huntsman now puts hounds into the covert and throughout the day encourages and instructs them by his horn and his voice. If there is a fox there, the covert is said to *hold* and the fox *breaks covert* when he leaves it. Hounds then follow his scent and if they lose it this is known as a *check*. In this case they either try to find the scent again themselves (which is known as *casting*) or the huntsman casts them. When they find the scent again, they are said to *hit the line*. Sometimes, when the fox appears to be lost, a countryman or a member of the field sees him. He lets the huntsman know by shouting "Tally-ho", if he is near him, or screaming a "holloa" if he is farther away. Should hounds hunt the fox in the direction from which he has come they are said to be *running heel* and when they get so close to him that they rely on their eyes instead of their noses they are then said to be *coursing* the fox.

On the death of the fox, the huntsman shouts "Who-oop", and hounds break it up. The head (mask), tail (brush) and feet (pads), which together are known as the trophies, are cut off and presented to members of the field who were up at the kill.

**FRACTIONS.** At one time or another you have probably bought a quarter of a pound of sweets, or heard people talk about three-quarters of a yard of material or half an hour. You may know, too, that milk is supplied to schools in Great Britain in bottles holding one-third of a

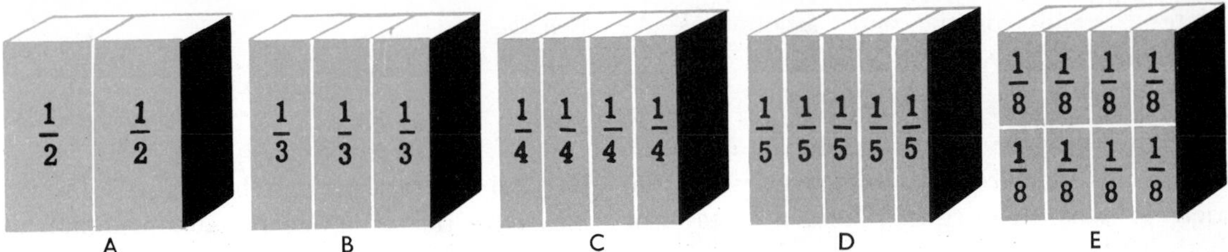


pint. In figures a quarter is written $\frac{1}{4}$, three-quarters as $\frac{3}{4}$, half as $\frac{1}{2}$ and one-third as $\frac{1}{3}$.

The word fraction comes from the Latin *fractio*, meaning "a breaking". The pound of sweets is broken, or divided, into 4 parts so that each part is one-quarter ($\frac{1}{4}$) of a pound. The pint of milk is divided into 3 parts, each part being one-third ($\frac{1}{3}$) of a pint.

Fractions such as $\frac{1}{2}$, $\frac{3}{4}$, $\frac{14}{15}$ are called *vulgar fractions* to distinguish them from the "decimal fractions" explained in the article DECIMALS. The word "vulgar" here means "common", as vulgar fractions are in common use in Britain and some other countries.

The diagrams show five blocks cut into a number of equal parts, each part being a fraction of the whole block. In diagram A the block is divided into two equal parts, each part being one half ($\frac{1}{2}$) of the whole block. In B the block is divided into three equal parts, so each is one-third ($\frac{1}{3}$) of the whole block. In the same way C shows fourths or quarters, D shows fifths and E eighths. Many school rulers show some of the inches divided into ten equal parts, each part being one-tenth ($\frac{1}{10}$) of an inch.

It is also possible to take a fractional part of a *group* of things. Imagine, for example, that 20 biscuits have been divided into 5 equal piles so that there are 4 biscuits in each pile. Now suppose that 3 of the piles are put on a large plate and that the other 2 piles are put on a small plate. The large plate then holds three-fifths ($\frac{3}{5}$) of the biscuits and the small plate holds two-fifths ($\frac{2}{5}$) of them.

A fraction also shows that division is needed. $25 \div 7$ and $7\overline{)25}$ both mean "25 divided by 7"; this can also be written as a fraction $\frac{25}{7}$ and in mathematics it is often more convenient to do so.

In the fraction three-quarters ($\frac{3}{4}$) the 4 is called the *denominator* and shows that the whole is divided into fourths, or quarters. The denominator is always the number below the line. The 3 is called the *numerator* and shows how many parts of the whole have been taken. The numerator is always the number above the line. Thus:

$$\frac{3}{4} = \frac{\text{numerator}}{\text{denominator}} = \frac{\text{number of parts}}{\text{name of parts}}$$

Fractions such as $\frac{2}{3}$, $\frac{3}{4}$, $\frac{3}{5}$, $\frac{14}{15}$ are called *proper* fractions as each is less than a whole "one". You will see that each numerator is less than its denominator. However, fractions such as $\frac{5}{5}$, $\frac{8}{7}$, $\frac{9}{5}$, $\frac{4}{3}$ are called *improper* fractions as they are not less than a whole "one"—the first is equal to it and the others greater. So in all improper fractions the numerator is equal to or greater than the denominator.

Numbers such as $1\frac{1}{2}$, $2\frac{3}{8}$, $6\frac{5}{12}$ are called *mixed* numbers because they are mixtures of whole numbers and proper fractions. Mixed numbers can be changed to improper fractions by multiplying the whole number by the denominator and then adding on the numerator.

*Examples:*

(a) $1\frac{1}{2} = \frac{3}{2}$ (b) $6\frac{5}{12} = \frac{77}{12}$

An improper fraction is changed to a mixed number by dividing the numerator by the denominator.

*Examples:*

(a) $\frac{14}{3} = 4\frac{2}{3}$ (b) $\frac{27}{8} = 3\frac{3}{8}$

## Addition and Subtraction

When the biscuits mentioned earlier were divided between the two plates, the large plate had on it 3 of the 5 piles or $\frac{3}{5}$ of all the biscuits. This represented 12 of the 20 biscuits or $\frac{12}{20}$ of all the biscuits, so the two fractions $\frac{3}{5}$ and $\frac{12}{20}$ must be equal because they each represent the same amount. In the same way, on the small plate $\frac{2}{5}$ stands for the same amount as $\frac{8}{20}$, therefore:

$$\frac{3}{5} = \frac{12}{20} \text{ and } \frac{2}{5} = \frac{8}{20}$$

In each case the fraction on the left of the = sign stands for piles of biscuits and that on the right for separate biscuits. The denominator of both left-hand fractions is 5 and the denominator of both right-hand fractions is 20. The importance of understanding what the denominator stands for is seen when we try to add or subtract fractions. We can add 1 pile to 2 piles making 3 piles ( $\frac{1}{5} + \frac{2}{5} = \frac{3}{5}$ ), and we can add 3 biscuits to 4 biscuits making 7 biscuits ($\frac{3}{20}+\frac{4}{20}=\frac{7}{20}$), but we cannot add together 3 biscuits and 1 pile until we have changed them both to the same kind of thing.

As 1 pile contains 4 biscuits, then

3 biscuits + 1 pile = 3 biscuits + 4 biscuits
= 7 biscuits

or $\frac{3}{20} + \frac{1}{5} = \frac{3}{20} + \frac{4}{20} = \frac{7}{20}$

Subtraction is done in the same way, thus

3 piles − 5 biscuits = 12 biscuits − 5 biscuits
= 7 biscuits

or $\frac{3}{5} - \frac{5}{20} = \frac{12}{20} - \frac{5}{20} = \frac{7}{20}$

You can see, therefore, that if you wish to add or subtract fractions you must change one or more of them so that they all have the same denominator. A fraction can be expressed in another way without its value being changed if you multiply or divide both the numerator and the denominator by the same numbers.

*Examples:*

(a) $\frac{3}{4} = \frac{9}{12}$ (both numerator and denominator have been multiplied by 3)

(b) $\frac{21}{28} = \frac{3}{4}$ (both numerator and denominator have been divided by 7)

When a fraction is written using the smallest possible numbers without changing its value it is said to be written in its *lowest terms*. In example (b) above, the fraction $\frac{21}{28}$ has been changed to its lowest terms $\frac{3}{4}$ by dividing both the numerator and the denominator by 7.

Changing several fractions so that they have the same denominator is called bringing them to a *common denominator*, which must be a number into which the denominators of all the fractions in the sum will divide exactly. The following examples show how this is done.

*Example:*

$$\frac{1}{2} + \frac{2}{3} + \frac{3}{5}$$
$$= \frac{15}{30} + \frac{20}{30} + \frac{18}{30}$$
$$= \frac{53}{30}$$
$$= 1\frac{23}{30}$$

Here all the fractions have been changed so that they have the same denominator (common denominator) 30.

When mixed numbers have to be added the method is the same except that the whole numbers are added together first.

*Example:*

$$2\frac{3}{4} + 3\frac{1}{3} + 4\frac{7}{8}$$
$$= 9\frac{18}{24} + \frac{8}{24} + \frac{21}{24}$$
$$= 9\frac{47}{24}$$

$= 10\frac{23}{24}$ (The improper fraction $\frac{47}{24}$ has been changed to a mixed number $1\frac{23}{24}$ and added to the 9.)

Subtraction of fractions is done using the same method of bringing the fractions to a common denominator.

*Example:*

$$\frac{3}{4} - \frac{2}{3}$$
$$= \frac{9}{12} - \frac{8}{12}$$
$$= \frac{1}{12}$$

Mixed numbers are subtracted by substracting the whole numbers first.

*Example:*

$$4\frac{3}{8} - 2\frac{1}{6}$$
$$= 2\frac{9}{24} - \frac{4}{24}$$
$$= 2\frac{5}{24}$$

When the fraction to be taken away is larger than the first, subtraction can be done in two ways.

*First method:*

$$4\frac{1}{3} - 2\frac{3}{4}$$
$$= 4\frac{4}{12} - 2\frac{9}{12}$$

(Now add $\frac{12}{12}$ to the left-hand number and 1 to the right-hand number)

$$= 4\frac{16}{12} - 3\frac{9}{12}$$
$$= 1\frac{7}{12}$$

*Second method:*

$$4\frac{1}{3} - 2\frac{3}{4}$$
$$= 4\frac{4}{12} - 2\frac{9}{12}$$

(Now change one of the whole "ones" in the left-hand number to $\frac{12}{12}$)

$$= 3\frac{16}{12} - 2\frac{9}{12}$$
$$= 1\frac{7}{12}$$

## Multiplication and Division

It is easy to multiply or divide fractions by whole numbers. Three-fifths multiplied by 3 is nine-fifths, and two-elevenths multiplied by 5 is ten-elevenths.

(a) $\frac{3}{5} \times 3 = \frac{9}{5} = 1\frac{4}{5}$ (b) $\frac{2}{11} \times 5 = \frac{10}{11}$

In the same way nine-elevenths divided by 3 is three-elevenths, and three-fifths divided by 5 is three-twenty-fifths, for each fifth when divided into five equal parts gives twenty-fifths.

(a) $\frac{9}{11} \div 3 = \frac{3}{11}$ (b) $\frac{3}{5} \div 5 = \frac{3}{25}$

When multiplying one fraction by another fraction, simply multiply the two numerators to get the new numerator and the two denominators to get the new denominator, thus :

$$\frac{3}{5} \times \frac{2}{7} = \frac{3 \times 2}{5 \times 7} = \frac{6}{35}$$

The multiplication can sometimes be made easier by what is called *cancelling*, which is done by dividing one of the numerators and one of the denominators by the same number before multiplying, as in the following :

$\frac{3}{4} \times \frac{8}{9}$ First cancel by 3 to give
$\frac{1}{4} \times \frac{8}{3}$ Then cancel by 4, so that
$\frac{1}{1} \times \frac{2}{3}$
$= \frac{2}{3}$

This is usually written as follows :

$$\frac{\overset{1}{\cancel{3}}}{\underset{1}{\cancel{4}}} \times \frac{\overset{2}{\cancel{8}}}{\underset{3}{\cancel{9}}} = \frac{2}{3}$$

To multiply mixed numbers, first change them to improper fractions, then cancel and multiply out.

*Example:*

$$2\tfrac{1}{2} \times \tfrac{3}{10} \times 1\tfrac{5}{9}$$

Change to improper fractions and cancel.

$$= \frac{\overset{1}{\cancel{5}}}{\underset{1}{\cancel{2}}} \times \frac{\overset{1}{\cancel{3}}}{\underset{2}{\cancel{10}}} \times \frac{\overset{7}{\cancel{14}}}{\underset{3}{\cancel{9}}}$$

$$= \tfrac{1}{1} \times \tfrac{1}{2} \times \tfrac{7}{3}$$

Multiply out. $= \frac{7}{6} = 1\frac{1}{6}$

*Example:*

$$2\tfrac{1}{2} \times 3\tfrac{1}{2}$$

Change to improper fractions—no cancelling possible.

$$= \tfrac{5}{2} \times \tfrac{7}{2}$$

Multiply and change to a mixed number.

$$= \tfrac{35}{4} = 8\tfrac{3}{4}$$

## Division by a Fraction

To divide a fraction by another fraction the rule is quite simple—change the division sign $\div$ to a multiplication sign $\times$, invert (turn upside down) the divisor, and then work out exactly like a multiplication sum.

*Example:*

$$\tfrac{3}{4} \div \tfrac{1}{2}$$

Change the sign, invert the divisor and cancel.

$$= \frac{3}{\underset{2}{\cancel{4}}} \times \frac{\overset{1}{\cancel{2}}}{1}$$

Multiply and change the improper fraction to a mixed number.

$$= \tfrac{3}{2} = 1\tfrac{1}{2}$$

When a mixed number is divided by another mixed number, both are changed to improper fractions and the example worked in the same way as that above.

*Example:*

$$3\tfrac{1}{3} \div 1\tfrac{1}{6}$$

Change to improper fractions.

$$= \tfrac{10}{3} \div \tfrac{7}{6}$$

Change the sign, invert the divisor and cancel.

$$= \frac{10}{\underset{1}{\cancel{3}}} \times \frac{\overset{2}{\cancel{6}}}{7}$$

Multiply and change to a mixed number.

$$= \tfrac{20}{7} = 2\tfrac{6}{7}$$

When an example contains a mixture of multiplication and division only the fractions following the division signs are inverted.

*Example:*

$$2\tfrac{2}{3} \times \tfrac{7}{12} \div 2\tfrac{1}{10}$$

Change to improper fractions.

$$= \tfrac{8}{3} \times \tfrac{7}{12} \div \tfrac{21}{10}$$

Change the $\div$ sign, invert the divisor and cancel.

$$= \frac{\overset{2}{\cancel{8}}}{3} \times \frac{\overset{1}{\cancel{7}}}{\underset{3}{\cancel{12}}} \times \frac{10}{\underset{3}{\cancel{21}}}$$

Multiply out. $= \tfrac{20}{27}$

**FRANCE** is the foreign country nearest to Great Britain, and its northern shore can be seen from the Kent coast on a fine day. It is about two-and-a-half times the size of Great Britain and its greatest length from north to south is about 600 miles, which is roughly the same as its greatest breadth from east to west.

The south coast of France is on the Mediterranean, the sea which was the centre of the ancient world. The high wall of the Pyrenees forms a frontier with Spain which can be crossed only at its two ends. The west coast looks on to the Atlantic and the north coast on to the English Channel (in French, *La Manche*). The eastern frontier with Italy and Switzerland runs along the Alps and that with Germany along the Rhine, but the northeastern border stretching from the Rhine to the North Sea has no natural barriers and invading armies have often entered France by this way.

Within these frontiers the land is divided into a high central plateau, or tableland, and the valleys, plains and basins of broad rivers. The Rhône River valley forms a wide corridor between the Alps and the central plateau and is the natural entrance from the Mediterranean. The port of Marseilles at the mouth of the Rhône is the largest port in France and was founded by Greek settlers in about 600 B.C. The western rivers of France are the Garonne, with the Atlantic port of Bordeaux near its mouth, and the winding Loire which has the ports of Nantes and St. Nazaire. The chief northern river is the Seine, which flows through the capital city of Paris to the Channel, with the port of Rouen some way from its mouth.

The climate of France differs very much from one part of the country to another. In the north it is very like that of England while on the south coast it rarely rains in the summer and is usually sunny in winter—the French call it the "sky-blue coast" (*Côte d'Azur*) for that reason. The high mountains of the Alps, which include Mont Blanc, the highest peak in western Europe, are snow-covered all the year. As there are no mountains in the west, the rain clouds from the Atlantic pass well into the country and keep it well watered. Frenchmen sometimes say that they have no need to go abroad for their holidays as they can find any climate and scenery they want in their own country.

About one-fifth of France is covered with woodland. In the Vosges and Jura Mountains there are large forests of pine and fir and on the lower slopes grow beeches, oaks and chestnuts. Olive and fig trees are common near the south coast and in the Pyrenees grow forests of cork oak, ash and beech. Behind the sand dunes on some parts of the west coast, pine trees have been planted to protect the soil.

The wild animals found in France include brown bears in the Pyrenees, a few wolves in the foothills, chamois (a kind of small antelope) on the mountain peaks and wild boar in the forests.

## The French People

Although the people differ somewhat from one part of the country to another, there are some qualities that are to be found in most of them. They are hard working and thrifty, they like to think things out clearly and they are realistic; that is, they face facts. They respect brains and intelligence and they have a more lively sense than most peoples as to what is good and bad in art and literature. The family and the home are the centre of French life, and good cooking and good talk have an important place in it. The people like to sit in the open air cafés to sip drinks or coffee over a newspaper and watch the world go by.

The Bretons, as the people of Brittany are called, are simple hardy folk, mostly farmers and fishermen, who speak a language like Welsh and have kept their old local costume. The Basques, who live at the western end of the

*Courtesy, The French Government Tourist Office*

FRANCE. The Hall of Mirrors in the Palace of Versailles, designed by Jules Mansart in 1678.

*Mansell Collection*

FRANCIS OF ASSISI blessing the birds—a fresco by Giotto in the church of St. Francis at Assisi.

J. Allan Cash

Stalls for second-hand books and prints beside the River Seine in Paris.

Pyrenees, are a separate race who have their own language. In the south of France the people are on the whole darker, livelier and more gay than those in the north, and in Alsace and Lorraine in the east many folk speak German as well as French because both regions have belonged to Germany in the past. More French people belong to the Roman Catholic Church than to any other.

## Towns and Farming

Paris, the capital, is by far the largest city in France, the other chief cities being Marseilles, Lyons (or Lyon), Toulouse, Bordeaux, Nice, Nantes and Strasbourg. (See BORDEAUX; LYONS; MARSEILLES; PARIS; STRASBOURG.) Only Paris, Marseilles and Lyons have populations over 500,000, for France has few very large towns. The country is divided into *départements*, of which there are 94 in mainland France. Each *département* is controlled by a paid official called a *préfet*. The *départements* are grouped into 21 regions with a regional *préfet* over each group. Within *départements* there is a division into *communes*, each under a mayor and numbering about 38,000.

The largest single occupation is that of farming, for over a third of the working people work on the land. Most farms are very small compared with those of Great Britain, the average size being less than 40 acres, and most are farmed by their owners and their families. Since 1946 many more tractors have come into use, even on small farms, and in the north there are some very large and efficient farms.

The chief crop is wheat, since the French eat much bread, but oats for fodder and other grains are also grown. Of root crops, potatoes are the most important and are grown in Brittany and around Strasbourg. Much sugar beet is grown near Paris and some tobacco and hops on the Rhine plain in Alsace. Cattle are raised throughout France, though chiefly in Brittany and Normandy. Bullocks are often used for drawing ploughs and carts, but meat is less important than dairy produce, for although the French do not drink much milk they are famous for their cheeses, such as Gruyère, Camembert and Brie. Roquefort cheese is made from sheep's milk, and many sheep are pastured in the southeast and on the central plateau. Pigs and poultry are bred very widely. Figs, citrus fruit (oranges, lemons and grapefruit), almonds and olives are grown in the Mediterranean coast land as well as flowers for making perfumes. Apples for cider are grown in the northwest, but of all the special products of the soil the most important by far is wine, which is very widely drunk in France, even by young people. Vineyards are to be found all over France except in a belt within 120 miles of the north coast, and usually the wines are named after the district where they are grown and made. Champagne, Burgundy, Graves, Bordeaux and Sauterne are examples. The wines and brandies of France include the finest and most highly valued kinds in the world. (Brandy is made by distilling wine; see DISTILLATION.)

The general arrangement of the forests in France is that pines and firs grow on the higher slopes and trees such as beech, ash, elm and oak lower down. In many places the woods belong to the government or to a nearby town and supply timber, paper, resin and turpentine.

---

### FACTS ABOUT FRANCE

AREA (including Corsica): 212,973 square miles.
POPULATION (estimated in 1967): 49,890,000.
KIND OF COUNTRY: Self-governing republic.
CAPITAL: Paris.
GEOGRAPHICAL FEATURES: The great north European plain extends to northern, western and southwestern France as far as the Pyrenees. The Central Plateau (with the highest point at 6,188 feet) forms about one-sixth of the area of the country. Between the Central Plateau and the Alps and the Jura on the east there is the Saône-Rhône valley.
CHIEF PRODUCTS: Wheat, potatoes, oats, barley, sugar beet, fruit, vegetables, wine, butter, cheese; coal, iron ore, potash salt, rock salts, bauxite, sulphur.
LEADING INDUSTRIES: Iron and steel, motor vehicles, shipbuilding, aircraft, electrical machinery, cement, textiles, perfumes and cosmetics.
IMPORTANT TOWNS Regional capitals: Paris, Marseilles (Marseille), Lyons (Lyon), Toulouse, Bordeaux, Nantes, Strasbourg, Lille, Rennes, Dijon, Clermont-Ferrand, Rouen, Montpellier, Limoges, Amiens, Metz, Besançon, Caen, Orléans, Poitiers and Chalons-sur-Marne. Other important towns are Nice, Saint-Etienne, Le Havre, Toulon, Grenoble, Le Mans and Nancy.
EDUCATION: Children must attend school between the ages of 6 and 14.

---

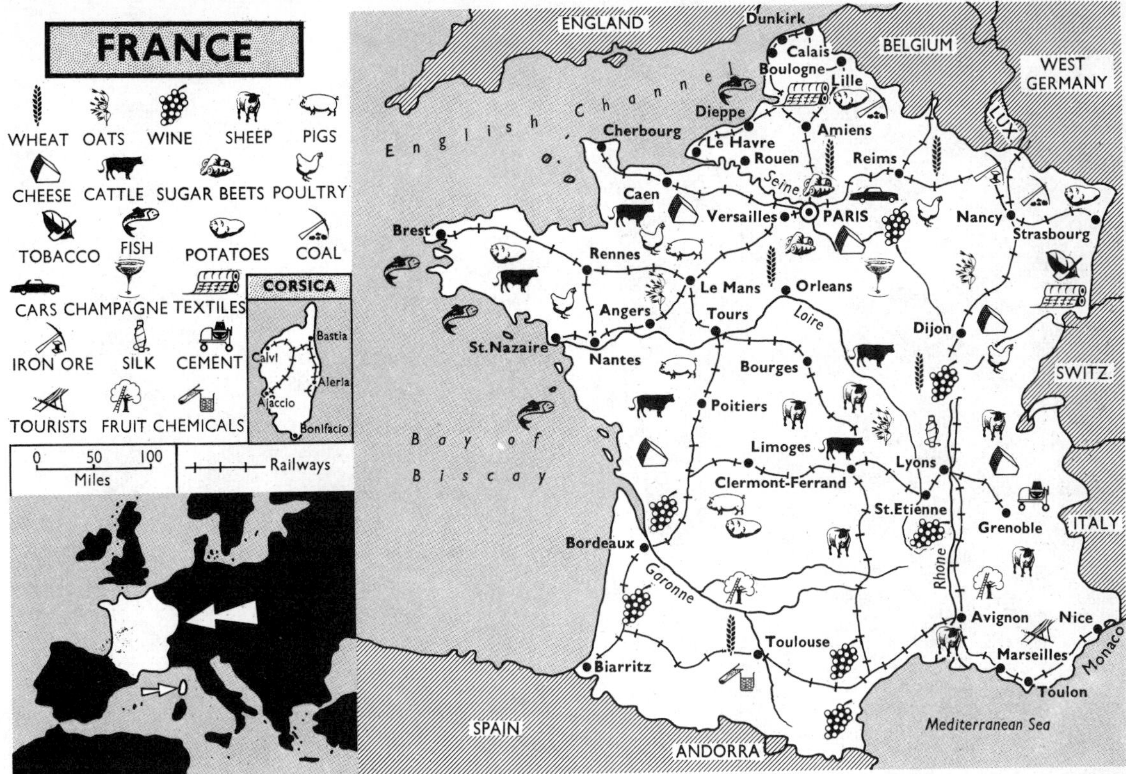


In some parts of the country, especially in Dordogne in the southwest, a kind of fungus called a "truffle", which is considered delicious to eat, grows under the ground, usually among the roots of oak trees. Truffles are eagerly sought but are hard to find, so people train dogs and pigs to sniff them out.

The chief fishing ports are those along the north and west coasts, those on the Mediterranean being less important. Herring, mackerel, tunny and sardines are caught off the coasts and in the Bay of Biscay, and French trawlers join those of other countries in catching cod in the waters around Iceland and Newfoundland.

## Mines, Factories and Transport

French farms and fisheries produce most of the food the people need and give work to many of them. This is one reason why factories are less important in France than in most other western European countries. Another reason is that not only is France short of coal to provide power to drive machines, but also that the coalfields and ironfields in the east have sometimes been damaged in wars. Although there are a number of large factories, French industrial plants are generally smaller than those in Britain.

Three-quarters of the coal comes from pits near the Belgian frontier in the northeast and in Lorraine. The coal shortage is to some extent made up by supplies of electricity obtained from water power from the rivers, particularly in the Alps and Pyrenees and on the central plateau. The River Rhône is also an important source of water power. France has nuclear energy centres at Pierrelatte and Marcoule in the Rhône valley and produces atomic weapons. There are several nuclear power stations. Natural gas obtained near the Pyrenees is piped to several large cities, and impurities extracted from the gas yield quantities of valuable sulphur.

France has abundant supplies of iron ore in Lorraine. Some of this is made into iron and steel in Lorraine itself and some sent to works in the northeast coalfield for that purpose, and a good deal of it is sent abroad. Bauxite, the ore from which aluminium is obtained, is mined in the southeast and turned into the metal in

*Courtesy, Direction Générale du Tourisme*

The Eiffel Tower, 1,001 feet high, is the most famous landmark of Paris. It was built in 1899.

works near the Alps and Pyrenees. Most of the heavy engineering factories making products such as locomotives and railway carriages and wagons are in the northeastern towns, but by far the biggest district for factories is Paris and its suburbs, where the large population means that there is plenty of labour. Paris is placed like the hub of a wheel with the roads and railways radiating from it; its factories make motor cars, aircraft, electrical machinery and other goods.

Textiles are an important French industry. Lille and other towns in the northeast make cotton, linen and woollen goods, and these are also made in Alsace and Lorraine. Lille gives its name to *lisle* thread used for hosiery and gloves, and the town of Cambrai not far from it to the fine white linen called *cambric*. The silk industry was brought into the valley of the lower Rhône by settlers from Italy in the 15th century, and is now centred in Lyons, where artificial silk is also produced.

Some towns in big agricultural districts have their own special trades. Limoges makes porcelain and boots, Grasse perfumes and Grenoble gloves and cement. Sugar is refined and chemicals are produced in Toulouse. Shipbuilding is not of great importance, but there are shipyards at St. Nazaire and Nantes on the Loire estuary and at Le Havre and Harfleur on the Seine.

There are small-scale industries throughout the country. In the mountainous districts of the Jura and the Vosges, people make wood carvings, furniture, toys and watches, and in the cattle-breeding districts skins and hides are prepared for making into leather goods in the towns near by.

The French merchant fleet is not big enough to carry more than half the country's seaborne trade, for which the chief ports are Marseilles, Le Havre, Rouen, Dunkirk and Bordeaux. Most of the French airlines are run by the state and their overseas services start from Paris. The railway system also belongs to the state and was carefully planned to radiate from Paris as a centre. The lines around Paris and those running to the Spanish frontier and Lyons are electrified. There are many good main roads in France and there is a big network of canals (in places joining up with the rivers) used chiefly for carrying coal and petroleum. It is possible to travel in a boat over these waterways from the English Channel to the Mediterranean.

## Language, Education and Sport

The French language, which from 1066 to the end of the 14th century was much used in England, is pleasant to listen to and has a large vocabulary. In the 18th century it was spoken by educated persons all over Europe, and because of its clearness it has often been used for important messages between governments to ensure that the meaning cannot be muddled. There are some dialects, or local languages, such as Corsican, Breton and Alsatian, but they are gradually disappearing. (See DIALECT.)

Most of the schools in France are controlled by the state and are free. Depending on the result of an examination taken when they are 11, children may go on to a secondary college for seven years, and if they succeed in further examinations can go on to one of the national universities. School is taken very seriously in France and less importance is attached to games than in schools in Great Britain.

Sport in France is increasing, particularly

*Courtesy, French Government Tourist Office*

A beach in the South of France.

among the town dwellers, tennis being the favourite game. Association and Rugby football are both popular, as also are horse racing, climbing and skiing, and shooting and fishing, but the great popular spectacle is the bicycle race round France called the "Tour de France".

## History

France has a long and full history. The Romans conquered the country (which they called Gaul) by about 50 B.C. and their language and customs were adopted by the different tribes, who became Christians in the 2nd and 3rd centuries. As the Roman power grew weaker the barbarian tribes beyond the Rhine became bolder, and during the 5th century they poured into Gaul. The strongest of these tribes were the Franks, who gave France its present name, and their king Clovis, by becoming a Christian, obtained the support of the church and the Gauls and so won the whole country.

In the 8th century the great King Charlemagne (on whom there is a separate article) pushed the boundaries of France well into what are now Germany and Italy. In 800 he was crowned Emperor of the West, thus becoming the first ruler of what came to be called the Holy Roman Empire. (See HOLY ROMAN EMPIRE.) Charlemagne gave his people law and order and encouraged trade, but after his death the Empire was split into three. During the 9th century the Vikings, or Norsemen, invaded France and settled in the north, and the French king allowed them to call themselves Dukes of Normandy. These dukes soon became more powerful than the king himself. In 1066 Duke William invaded England and made himself king of England, soon after there began the long struggle between the crowns of France and England which lasted almost to the end of the middle ages, in the 15th century.

First one side gained the advantage and then the other. In the 12th century the English captured nearly two-thirds of France, only to be driven out again, and in the Hundred Years' War (1338–1453) the English started well but by 1380 held only Calais and some other towns on the French coast. After the victory of Agincourt in 1415 (see AGINCOURT, BATTLE OF) the English under Henry V regained most of northern and eastern France, but when he died the French were led to victory by Joan of Arc, the heroic and saintly Maid of Orléans. (See HUNDRED YEARS' WAR; JOAN OF ARC.) The end of the war saw France victorious, for the English had been driven out from everywhere except Calais. Nevertheless, the country was exhausted by war, famine and plague and made wretchedly poor by heavy taxes.

By the end of the 15th century France recovered under stronger kings, and with the revival of learning that spread from Italy (see RENAISSANCE) art, architecture and literature flourished. However, during the 16th century religious and feudal quarrels led to bitter civil war (see REFORMATION). Order and peace were brought back for a time under Henry IV, but remained very uneasy even under the strong government of the great cardinals Richelieu and Mazarin. It was only under the greatest of the French kings, Louis XIV, who reigned from 1643 to 1715, that the nation found relief from the quarrels of feudal lords and from provincial uprisings (see FEUDALISM). Louis XIV raised his kingdom to a position of power and influence in Europe, though he led it into so many costly wars that he left it much poorer than he found it.

It was under the cardinals and Louis XIV that the attitude of France to other countries took the shape that lasted until recent times. France wished to have the Rhine as her eastern frontier, and thought it dangerous that the Low Countries should be held by a strong country. She wished to keep Germany divided into many small states, and to have enough power at sea and overseas to keep her colonies and trade safe from Britain. Most of the wars in which France took part were fought for one of these reasons.

During the 18th century French influence everywhere in Europe was very great. The ruling classes of most other countries in Europe knew French and read French writers, but France's condition became steadily worse, and the crushing burden of taxes and a very wasteful government caused discontent. Her thrifty, hard-working peasants and her intelligent middle-class people had no way of controlling their extravagant government. France had no parliament such as the English, and the states-general (or assembly representing the three "estates" of nobles, clergy and people) did not even meet between 1614 and 1789. When at last the king allowed the states-general to meet and realized how many reforms the people were demanding he gave way, and a republic was formed in 1792 with the motto "Liberty and Equality". (See French Revolution.) From then until 1815, except for short intervals of peace, France was at war, and its armies under the command of the Corsican general Napoleon Bonaparte were almost everywhere victorious, though the British command of the seas kept the French from spreading beyond Europe. The French invasion of Russia in 1812 was disastrous and Napoleon, who made himself Emperor in 1804, was driven from the throne in 1814. He escaped from exile in the island of Elba, off the west coast of Italy, for 100 days but was finally defeated by the British and Prussians at the Battle of Waterloo in 1815. (See Napoleon I; Napoleonic Wars; Waterloo, Battle of.)

The Revolution and the rule of Napoleon that followed it made a new France out of the wreckage of the old. The whole system of government and tax-collecting, of justice and administration, was remodelled. The peasants owned much more of the land, and were freed from the old burdens. Middle-class people took a bigger share in government. The people could never forget the experiences of the Revolution or the glories and conquests of Napoleon.

After the Battle of Waterloo the other European countries agreed that France should again be ruled by kings. The new kings, the nobles and the church tried to get back some of the power they had lost, but there were revolutions in 1830 and 1848 ending in a Second Republic under a nephew of the great Napoleon. This nephew made himself Emperor and in 1870 he plunged into war with Prussia, the strongest of the German states. France was quickly defeated and had to give up Alsace and Lorraine, at the same time becoming a republic again.

After that France enjoyed more than 40 years of peace and became prosperous, gaining new colonies in North Africa, West Africa and Indo-china, and making much scientific progress through the discoveries of such great scientists as Louis Pasteur and Pierre Curie. World War I (on which there is a separate article) broke out in 1914, and France, although helped by Belgium and Great Britain and later by the United States, found itself facing much stronger German armies than those of 1870. The Germans came near to taking Paris in the first two weeks of the war, after which there was a bitter struggle that lasted for four years and cost many French lives.

Although the Germans were defeated by the end of 1918 and had to give back Alsace and Lorraine, the peace left France once again exhausted and ruined. Huge tasks of reconstruction had to be tackled with too few men and not enough money, and the weakness of France in the 1930s gave the German dictator Adolf Hitler the opportunity to prepare for yet another war. Finally the German armies invaded Poland, which France and Great Britain were bound by treaty to help, and so World War II began in September 1939. In May 1940 the Germans attacked in the west and in six weeks drove the British from the continent and forced France to surrender. (See World War II.)

However, some Frenchmen who escaped to Great Britain and many of those in the French colonies were eager to continue the war, and they banded themselves together under the title of the Free French (later Fighting French), with General Charles de Gaulle as their leader. They formed new armies and helped the British and United States troops drive the Germans out of North Africa and France, and at the same time many patriotic men and women in France carried on a secret "resistance" warfare. (See Underground Resistance Movements.)

When the Germans were driven out of Paris in August 1944, General de Gaulle set up a temporary government and took charge of the country, though he resigned in January 1946.

Between the years 1944 and 1958 France had 25 different governments. There were a number of political parties and usually no one party was strong enough by itself to win more than half the seats in parliament. The Communists stirred up strikes among the workers, and there was discontent at home over high prices and heavy

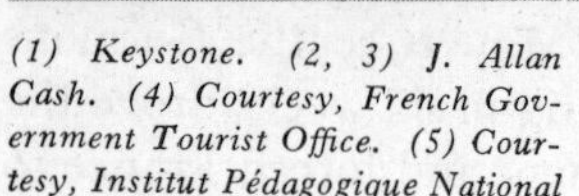

*(1) Keystone. (2, 3) J. Allan Cash. (4) Courtesy, French Government Tourist Office. (5) Courtesy, Institut Pédagogique National*

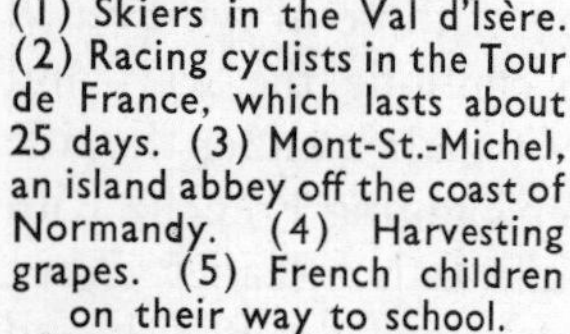

(1) Skiers in the Val d'Isère. (2) Racing cyclists in the Tour de France, which lasts about 25 days. (3) Mont-St.-Michel, an island abbey off the coast of Normandy. (4) Harvesting grapes. (5) French children on their way to school.

taxes. The people in some of the French overseas territories sought independence or were encouraged by the Communists to rebel. These troubles led to war in Indochina from 1946 to 1954 and in 1954 to a rising in Algeria which grew into a serious rebellion in 1958.

The disorders in Algeria caused not only a change of government in France but also a change in the French constitution. This came about when it was thought that the government might grant complete independence to Algeria, where there were many French settlers. In May 1958 French civilian and army leaders in Algeria called upon General de Gaulle to take charge of affairs. He became Prime Minister and asked the people to vote for a new constitution designed to give more power to the President. The people voted for the new constitution and after the elections De Gaulle became President of the Fifth French Republic in 1959.

De Gaulle did not set a high value on parliament, preferring to make decisions himself. After a bitter struggle in Algeria in which some French soldiers formed a secret army aimed at preventing any settlement there, De Gaulle granted independence to Algeria in 1962. He did not favour belonging to a western alliance led by the United States and in 1966 announced that France would leave the North Atlantic Treaty Organization (Nato). De Gaulle wished France to be the leading nation in Europe and he opposed Britain's efforts to join the European Economic Community (Common Market).

France and some of its former overseas possessions are linked in an organization called the French Community. (See French Community.)

## Literature and Art

The things of the mind are important to French people. Books, poetry, plays, films, paintings, sculpture and architecture—even dresses and hats, for Paris is the fashion centre of the world—all these things the French understand better than most, and their standards are very high. French actors and actresses are among the finest in the world, as can be seen by watching a French film.

The French interest in poetry probably started with the wandering minstrels and poets of the 11th and 12th centuries, who sang or recited verses about the gallant deeds of heroes and knights and their adventures in war and love. The early plays were usually about religious subjects—scenes from the Bible or the lives of the saints—and as time went on they became very long and complicated. One called the *Acts of the Apostles,* played at Bourges in 1536, had 500 performers and lasted 40 days.

In the 16th century French literature, like that of other countries, changed somewhat because of the rebirth of learning known as the Renaissance. The religious outlook of the middle ages later gave place to a spirit that rejoiced in the beauties of the world and had confidence in man's future. Something of this feeling had already appeared in the poems of François Villon, and it increased in the work of the group of poets called the Pléiade (after the group of seven stars) who also brought in new forms of verse and even new words from ancient Greek and Latin poetry. Pierre de Ronsard, the leader of this group, was however at his best in quite simple poems about love and nature. Another of the Pléiade translated the old Greek plays and wrote imitations of them, thus beginning a new kind of drama or stage play in France. Prose writing too was greatly improved, and in his rather rollicking stories François Rabelais combined this new love of life and learning with a certain amount of clowning. Another great prose writer was Michel de Montaigne, who invented the form called the essay—a short piece giving the author's thoughts and reflections on one subject.

In the 17th century appeared three great dramatists or writers of plays, Pierre Corneille, Jean Racine and Jean Baptiste Molière. Corneille is famous for his tragedies (plays with an unhappy ending), Racine took the subjects for his plays from legends or ancient history and Molière wrote the finest comedies—that is, plays which are not too serious and have a happy ending. Another writer who lived at the same time wrote pieces that many children know—the *Fables* of Jean de La Fontaine such as "The Raven and the Fox".

The wars and hardships of the 18th century made people think about the evils of the time and suggest remedies for them, and perhaps the greatest writer of this kind was Voltaire, who wrote attacks on the church and the government and pleaded for freedom of thought and reforms of all kinds. Other writers such as Charles Montesquieu criticized French life and customs by disguising the facts as fiction in novels. Serious authors of the time were Denis Diderot, who with others put together the first French encyclopaedia, and Jean-Jacques Rousseau. Rousseau taught that men should be free and equal in their rights and that most of the ills men suffered came from bad conditions and bad government. He made people think afresh about things that had been taken for granted before. His ideas had a great influence on the French Revolution. (See ROUSSEAU.)

In the 19th century French literature turned away from the rather stiff and starchy writing of the previous century, which had little use for sentiment—that is, it hardly ever dealt with people's private feelings. The new writers were not afraid to express their feelings and to set them down in rich and colourful language. Poets of this type were Alfred de Musset, Alfred de Vigny, Alphonse de Lamartine and Victor Hugo, although Hugo is better known for his wonderful novels such as *The Toilers of the Sea* and *The Hunchback of Notre Dame*. Another novelist whose books are not likely to be forgotten was Alexandre Dumas, who wrote *The Three Musketeers* and *The Count of Monte Cristo*. Honoré de Balzac, in a series of novels grouped under the title of *The Human Comedy,* left a detailed and not very pretty picture of all kinds of French people—nobles, middle-class and poor folk, soldiers, lawyers, priests and peasants. Later in the 19th century appeared a new kind of writing in which the authors took as their subject the stranger and less pleasant sides of human nature and described it in detail with the exactness of a photograph. The leader of these writers was Emile Zola and among them was Guy de Maupassant, famous for his short stories. Alphonse Daudet, on the other hand, wrote about cheerful things and created the great comic figure Tartarin of Tarascon—a sort of caricature of a Frenchman from the south. Jules Verne, who wrote *20,000 Leagues Under the Sea,* was the first writer of what is now known as science fiction.

The novel has been the most important branch of French literature during the 20th century. Pierre Loti, a sailor, wrote about foreign lands, and Anatole France told very good stories in very graceful French. Marcel Proust gave a detailed picture of the French noblemen, and later novelists such as Henri Barbusse and Georges Duhamel wrote of the horrors of trench warfare in World War I. André Gide was perhaps the most interesting and understanding critic of the modern world in his *Journals*; he also wrote several novels. Among modern writers should be mentioned the playwrights Jean Cocteau and Jean Anouilh and the novelists Jean-Paul Sartre, François Mauriac, Albert Camus, Georges Bernanos and Françoise Sagan.

French painting has also been extremely important. The early rulers of France encouraged it chiefly for decorating churches, but the later artists painted landscape pictures and portraits of people. Jean Fouquet was a wonderful painter of portraits and miniatures (tiny portraits) in the 15th century. In the 16th century pictures, landscape very often formed only a background to portraits of people, but it became important and popular with the pictures of Claude Lorraine. In his paintings the golden sunlight looks so real that one can almost feel its warmth. Antoine Watteau (1684–1721) peopled his landscapes with dancers and sweethearts, Joseph Vernet (1714–1789) painted pictures of nature in its wilder aspects and Eugène Delacroix (1793–1863) pictures of historical and religious scenes. Jean Millet (1814–1875) and Jean Courbet (1819–1877) painted the daily lives of peasants, and Jean Corot (1796–1875) the misty landscapes of dawn and dusk. Later in the 19th century appeared the Impressionist painters, who painted things as they appeared to them at the moment of painting and not as they actually knew them to be. Among them were Edouard Manet, Claude Monet, Paul Cézanne and Paul Gauguin, whose works are worth going a long way to see. France has not lacked fine musicians and composers, such as François Couperin, Hector Berlioz, Claude Debussy and Francis

Poulenc, but they have not as a rule been of the great importance of those of Germany. (See MUSIC; PAINTERS AND PAINTINGS.)

French architecture grew out of that left behind by the Romans and began in what is called the Romanesque style, with its rounded arches and lively sculpture. (See ARCHITECTURE.) The soaring Gothic style is seen at its best in the cathedrals of Paris, Amiens, Chartres and Reims. Carcassonne in the south is a wonderful example of a fortified city of the middle ages, and at Avignon, with its famous bridge, can be seen another walled town and the palace built by the Popes when they lived there. The castles along the River Loire are very fine, and nearly all of them are still lived in. Of much later date are the great palace of Versailles built for King Louis XIV and the Luxembourg Palace in Paris. Buildings of this style were greatly admired and copied in other countries.

(There are separate articles on most of the people mentioned in this article.)

**FRANCIS OF ASSISI, Saint** (?1181–1226). The boy who grew up to become the founder of the order of friars known as the Franciscans (see MONKS AND FRIARS), and who was made a saint (see SAINT) two years after his death was born in 1181 or 1182 at Assisi in the province of Umbria, Italy. His father, Pietro Bernardone, was a wealthy merchant who dealt in rich silks and velvets. Francis had as much money as he wanted and was a gay young man, the leader of the other young men in their pranks and revels. Until he was 20 he helped his father with the business. In 1202, during a dispute between Assisi and Perugia, a nearby town, he was taken prisoner while fighting for Assisi and spent the next year as a hostage.

After his return home Francis became seriously ill, and during his illness began to examine his life and decided that money and worldly pleasures meant nothing to him. He devoted himself to solitude, prayer and helping the poor, and before long went on a pilgrimage to Rome. Soon after his return to Assisi he passed a leper who was begging. Having always had a special horror of lepers he passed him by, but suddenly returned, gave the leper his money and kissed his hand. From that day onwards he gave special care to lepers and the sick. (See LEPROSY.)

Wishing to show his gratitude to God for calling him to such a life, Francis restored the half-ruined chapel of St. Damian, on the outskirts of Assisi, and later also restored the chapel of St. Mary of the Angels, generally called the Portiuncula. This chapel became the centre of the life of the Franciscan friars. Francis had a few followers who lived in poverty like himself and spent their time helping the sick and poor. In 1209, when there were 11 of them (12 including himself), they all went to Rome to ask the Pope for permission to start a brotherhood. The Pope gave permission and Francis was elected their superior, or head. Later on he started an order for those who wanted to follow his way of life but had to go on earning their living in the world.

Around the Portiuncula they built themselves huts of branches and twigs, and from there they wandered in pairs over the country round Assisi, preaching and helping people. They wore peasant clothes, worked in the fields for their daily bread and slept wherever they could. They aimed to live in exactly the way that Christ had lived, and made it a rule to have absolutely no possessions. More men joined them and new settlements were started. Francis himself went to teach Christianity in Spain and then in eastern Europe, Egypt and the Holy Land.

A highly born girl of Assisi, named Clare, was influenced by Francis' teaching and in 1212 was permitted to start an order for women on much the same lines as the Franciscan order for men, except that they did not go out preaching. The chapel of St. Damian was their headquarters and they were in close touch with the Franciscans at the Portiuncula. They became known as the "Poor Clares" and spread throughout Italy, France and Germany.

Francis had a great love for all God's creation and spoke to birds and flowers and even streams. It is said that once he was preaching to the people of Assisi and the swallows were twittering so loudly that people could not hear him.

"My sisters, the swallows, you have chattered enough," he said. "It is my turn to speak now. I pray you keep silence and listen to what I have to say to the people." Immediately the swallows were silent and every one of them sat still in its place during the sermon.

Two years before he died, Francis went up Mount Alverno in the Apennines and there saw a vision of an angel nailed to a cross. When the vision disappeared Francis felt sharp pains and found that his body had suddenly taken on the marks of a person who had been nailed to a cross. On October 3, 1226, he died, worn out by pain and almost blind. A church in Assisi dedicated to him contains beautiful frescoes, or wall paintings, by two Italian artists, Cimabue and Giotto, which tell the story of his life. It is a story that is repeated in some way every day, for the Franciscan friars and the Poor Clares carry on his work.

**FRANKLIN, Benjamin** (1706–1790). The people of the United States think of Benjamin Franklin as one of the greatest Americans. The youngest of 17 children, he was born in Boston (Massachusetts) of English parents, and spent only two years at school. Then, after two years learning his father's trade of soap and candle making, he became an apprentice in a printing shop belonging to an elder brother. He used to slip under his brother's door articles he had written in disguised handwriting. These his brother printed in his newspaper, but when he found who had written them there was a quarrel, and at the age of 17 Benjamin found another job in Philadelphia.

*National Portrait Gallery*

Benjamin Franklin.

He became such a good printer that the governor of the province offered to set him up on his own, and persuaded him to go to England to buy presses and type. The governor failed to keep his word and Franklin found himself stranded penniless in London, but he soon found work in a printing house and stayed in England nearly two years. Returning to Philadelphia, he continued printing and in 1729 he purchased a dull newspaper which had only a few readers. He soon turned it into a lively, amusing and popular one. After this he wrote and printed each year, beginning in 1732, an almanac which was full of wit and wisdom and made him a fortune. (See ALMANAC.) The almanac was famous for the sayings of "Poor Richard", some of which are still repeated today such as "Early to bed and early to rise makes a man healthy and wealthy and wise".

Franklin had many interests. He started a subscription library, a debating society, a fire service, a street-cleaning department and a college which later became the University of Pennsylvania. He also invented a heating stove which Americans found very useful during their cold winters. Yet he still found time to teach himself to read several foreign languages and to play a number of musical instruments. He was deeply interested in science and he proved by flying a kite in a thunderstorm that lightning is a discharge of electricity. Later he invented the lightning conductor.

In 1753 he became postmaster general of the British colonies in North America, and made the postal system both efficient and prosperous. In 1755 he took a leading part in defending the northwest frontier against the French and the Indians. In 1757 he was sent to England to try to settle the quarrel that had sprung up between the people of Pennsylvania and the Penn family who owned most of the land there. He succeeded in this, and returned to Philadelphia in 1762, but two years later he had to go once more to England to argue with the king's ministers about the taxes they wished the American colonists to pay. He saw that war could not be avoided (see AMERICAN WAR OF INDEPENDENCE) and sailed home to help the colonists in their struggle. In 1776, when the colonists decided to free themselves from British rule, he helped to draw up the Declaration of Independence and was one of those who signed it. (See DECLARATION OF INDEPENDENCE.) In the following year he went to ask the French to help with money and supplies, and succeeeded even in persuading France to become an ally of the colonists. When the war ended he helped to draw up the peace treaty, and finally in 1787 he was a member of the Constitutional Convention which met to work out the method of government that should be adopted by the United States.

**FRANKLIN, Sir John** (1786–1847). Few men have explored in so many parts of the world as John Franklin. He was born at Spilsby (Lincolnshire) and as a boy of 15 he sailed in 1801 with his cousin Matthew Flinders on his great Australian voyage. His first polar expedition was in 1818 when he was in command of one of two ships which sailed north beyond the islands of Spitsbergen. Between 1819 and 1821 he led a canoe party in Canada, starting at York on Hudson Bay, travelling to the Great Slave Lake, and from there to the Coppermine River and then down that river to the Arctic. He then explored—still by canoe—550 miles of the coast of northern Canada.

Three years later he led another expedition in Canada, following the Mackenzie River to the Great Bear Lake and then in only six days travelling the rest of the way to the sea. There he divided his party into two groups; one followed the coast eastwards, while Franklin himself led the other westwards to try to meet a sea expedition sent from the other direction through the Bering Sea. Between them, these two expeditions explored 1,200 miles of coast line for the first time. When he returned to England Franklin was made a knight.

From the age of 14 until his death, Franklin was first a midshipman and then an officer in the Royal Navy and he took part in the battles of Copenhagen and Trafalgar. From 1830 to the beginning of 1834 he commanded the frigate "Rainbow" in the Mediterranean, and from 1836 to 1844 he was Governor of Van Diemen's land (now Tasmania). On returning to England in 1844 he found that preparations were being made to try once more to find a passage from the Atlantic to the Pacific Oceans by sailing round the north of America. He asked the First Lord of the Admiralty if he might command this expedition and when his lordship pointed out that Franklin was 60 years of age, he protested "No, no, my lord; only 59". His wish was granted and in 1845 he set out with two ships, the "Erebus" and "Terror". Although this expedition was better equipped for the job than any before, it ended in disaster. Apart from the Eskimoes' stories, the only record of what happened was on a small sheet of paper found years afterwards. It seemed that the ships had been frozen in the ice in Victoria Strait from September 1846 until April 1848, Franklin dying halfway through this period. His crew then abandoned the ships and tried to reach Canada on foot, but all perished of hunger or disease.

Most people give Franklin the full credit for discovering the North-West Passage, for he came within a few miles of places reached by expeditions travelling from the other end.

**FRAUD.** A fraud is a dishonest trick by means of which one person does harm to or cheats another. It is treated as a crime. Fraud is practised in many forms, the commonest probably being that by which one person tells another a lie in order to get money from him.

One kind of fraud practised in England today is the mock auction. The men who cheat people in this way buy many imitation or useless goods, open a shop, announce that they are disposing of valuable goods and then hold a sale. Men who are working with them, or confederates, bid high prices for the goods, and so the public joins in, thinking that something valuable is being sold. When a high price has been reached, the confederates stop bidding, and so the public is left with something quite useless.

Sometimes people selling goods mix an article with a cheaper one and sell the two together for the price they would have got for the most valuable article. An example of this is the grocer who mixes sand with sugar. In the middle ages a form of fraud rather like this one was the weighing of goods by false weights.

No one who is travelling should ever play cards for money with strangers, for they may be card-sharpers. These people have packs of cards which are generally marked in some way, and during the game they take cards out of the pack and play various dishonest tricks to make sure that they always win. First they let their victims win a little money to give them confidence, but the card-sharpers end by winning all the money.

Racehorses are sometimes "doped" (given drugs) to make sure they win or lose a certain race. The criminals who do this hope to make money by betting on the result of the race. Greyhound racing has also produced a number of frauds. The dogs have been given drugs that either increase or lessen their speed, or they have been hampered by having chewing gum put between their toes.

Frauds have been committed throughout history, some with the intention of cheating someone of money and others as jokes. Many large business companies have been the victims of money frauds. A great company called the South Sea Company got into the hands of dishonest men who persuaded thousands of people to put their money in it. In 1720, however, the company was proved not to have the money it was supposed to have, and many people were ruined when the "South Sea Bubble" burst. (See South Sea Bubble.)

Some years ago there was a very remarkable fraud, or fake, as a fraud is also called. This which was evidently done as a joke, was called the "Piltdown man". A skull and jaw found at Piltdown in Sussex were thought to be the remains of a primitive man. In 1953, however, it was discovered that the jaw was that of an ape and the skull was not nearly as old as had been thought. Someone had collected the bones together, staining some of them to make them seem older, and had buried them at Piltdown.

Another kind of fraud is personation. This has been done many times in history when an important person, such as a prince or a duke, has disappeared. A man will come forward saying that he is that person in order to have his position and wealth. In the reign of Henry VII two young men said that they were important members of the House of York, which Henry had overthrown. The first of these, Lambert Simnel, personated the Earl of Warwick, the nephew of Richard III, and the second, Perkin Warbeck, said that he was the Duke of York, the youngest of the Princes in the Tower. Both these men were defeated by Henry when they led rebellions against him.

A very well known case of personation was the Tichborne case in the 19th century. Roger Tichborne, who was the heir to a baronetcy (in other words he was the son of a baronet and would succeed to the title when his father died), was shipwrecked on a voyage to Australia and apparently drowned. Some years later a butcher called Arthur Orton, who was living in Wagga Wagga in Australia, declared that he was Roger Tichborne and came to England, where he claimed Tichborne's title and property. This claim was brought before the courts, and during the trial Orton became known as the Tichborne Claimaint. He was extremely fat, whereas Tichborne had been thin, and his education was not as good as it should have been if he were really Tichborne. Although Tichborne's mother said that Orton was her son, he lost his case in 1872 and was later imprisoned for perjury (giving false evidence).

## Punishment of Fraud

After the Tichborne case, parliament passed an act which made personation punishable by imprisonment for life. Many other acts of parliament have been passed laying down penalties for almost every kind of fraud, and in most cases the punishment is severe.

In 1869 the Debtors Act was passed, providing that a person may be imprisoned for one year if he has "obtained credit under false pretences or by means of any other fraud". A person who eats a meal in a restaurant when he cannot pay for it, but lets it be supposed that he can, may be punished for fraud. The intent to defraud is criminal.

By the Gaming Act of 1845, cheating at cards or at any other kind of play may be punished by imprisonment for up to five years. By the Money Lenders Act of 1900, a money lender who persuades a person to borrow money by a false promise or dishonest hiding of fact (such as pretending that the loan costs the borrower less than it really does) can be punished by two years' imprisonment.

In 1916 a most important act, the Larceny Act, was passed. Under this, the offence of obtaining from any person by any false pretence any kind of valuable goods with the intention of cheating or deceiving him or her became punishable with imprisonment for up to five years. A person can only be found guilty if it is proved that he deliberately intended to cheat someone. If he acted for some quite innocent reason he cannot be convicted.

**FREDERICK II** (Frederick the Great, 1712–1786). At the time when Frederick the Great became King of Prussia the country that we now call Germany consisted of many different states, each with its own ruler. Prussia was one of the largest of these and Frederick made it one of the great states of Europe.

His mother was Sophia Dorothea, daughter of George I of England, and his father was Frederick William I of Prussia, who was very strict and tried to turn his son into a hardy soldier. Frederick liked more scholarly things and at the age of 18 tried to escape to the English court. He was caught, his father had him tried by a military court and he was imprisoned in the fortress of Cüstrin, where his father forced him to watch the execution of the man who had helped him to escape, Lieutenant Katte. He gave in to his father's will and was put to work in one of the Prussian government offices. In 1733 his father gave him a country estate and he lived there, studying history, philosophy and poetry. He liked the French language and French habits, and exchanged letters with some of the most famous French writers of his day.

In 1740, when Frederick came to the throne, he inherited from his father a prosperous, well-run state and a well-trained army. In the same year the Emperor Charles VI died. (He had ruled over Austria and several other lands. See Holy Roman Empire.) Frederick took this opportunity to claim the territory of Silesia from Charles's heiress, Maria Theresa. She refused to give it to him and Frederick invaded Silesia and defeated the Austrians. In 1742, by the Treaty of Breslau, Maria Theresa was forced to give Breslau, Silesia and Glatz to Prussia.

After this, Frederick worked hard to develop his country. He had the Oderbruch marshes drained and turned into farmland, he encouraged agriculture and industry and did much for primary education as well as for the study of science. He called himself "the first servant of the State" and made the Prussian government extremely efficient. He paid great attention to the army and kept all his fortresses ready for war at a moment's notice.

In 1756 he attacked Saxony, another German state, because he considered that Saxony was about to attack Prussia. (A treaty had just been made between Saxony, France, Austria, Russia and Sweden because those countries wished to prevent Prussia from growing more powerful.)

*Radio Times Hulton Picture Library*

Frederick was one of the last kings to ride into battle.

This began the Seven Years' War (1756–1763). Great Britain was an ally of Prussia but most of the British fighting was against the French in Canada, in India and at sea. Frederick suffered several defeats, but his armies won the battles of Prague, Rossbach, Leuthen, Zorndorf and Minden, and Prussia was able to keep all its territory at the end of the war.

Prussia was exhausted by the war, with great losses of men and damage to towns and farms. Frederick threw himself into repairing the damage. At this time he saw another chance of enlarging his country, and although he had recently been at war with the Russians now made a treaty with them, and in 1772 Russia and Prussia forced Poland to give them some of its territory. Frederick took from Poland a large area round the Gulf of Danzig—an act which the Poles have never forgiven.

Frederick died at the age of 74, leaving a nation that later united all the other states of Germany into one country under its leadership (see GERMANY).

**FREE CHURCHES** are those churches in Great Britain which, at various times since the Reformation (see REFORMATION), have broken away from the Church of England. Usually they broke away because they wanted to be free in one or more of three ways: free to decide what they should believe, free to organize their church life (especially the way in which people should worship God) and free to decide how their churches should be governed. For example, the Congregationalists broke away because they believe that the congregation of each local church should decide how its life and work are to be carried on, whereas in the Church of England it is a bishop who has the final authority over these matters. At one time the Free Churches were more often called Nonconformists, this name showing that they did not conform to (follow) the teaching and customs of the Church of England.

The most important Free Churches are the Baptists, Congregationalists, Presbyterians and Methodists. (There are separate articles about each of them.) There are several smaller ones, among them the Quakers (see QUAKERS). In Great Britain they work together through the Free Church Federal Council.

During the last 50 years the differences between the Church of England, on the one hand, and the Free Churches, on the other, have become very much smaller. Their ideas about what Christians should believe (the Creeds) and about the gospel they should preach (the Bible) are now much the same. They differ mostly over their ideas about how the church should be governed and, particularly, whether it is necessary to have bishops. Both types of church have learned much from the other and, over many matters, work together through the World Council of Churches (see WORLD COUNCIL OF CHURCHES).

**FREEMASONRY** is a word used to describe the beliefs, customs and organization of the Freemasons. The Freemasons are a society of men (no women are allowed to join) whose beliefs are given as "brotherly love, relief and truth", who have joined together to put their beliefs into practice. There are Freemasons in many countries of the world, and they are organized in local branches, known as "lodges", with a Grand Lodge at the head of the lodges in each country. Sometimes there may be a Grand Lodge for each part of a country; for example, there are Grand Lodges at the head of the Freemasons in England, Scotland, Ireland and in each state of the United States of America. Wherever they are, Freemasons undertake much charitable work for members and their families—in England they run boys' and girls' schools for the orphans of members, they maintain the Royal Masonic Hospital and have a home for aged members and their relatives. They also help many charities not connected with Freemasonry.

A mason is a man who works in stone, and Freemasonry grew from guilds formed by the masons who travelled the country in the middle ages, building cathedrals and castles. (See GUILD.) Unlike some other people at that time, such people were free men and were not bound to any master, hence the term free-masons. They were also unlike the town craftsmen, whose guilds had proper meeting places in the cities where they worked. The masons moved about and often worked in lonely places, so they started guilds near the building where they were working. In these circumstances they had to be very careful that no intruders or unskilled workmen should learn their trade secrets. This probably explains why modern Freemasons keep their ceremonies so secret.

About 1650 the masons' guilds were opened to people who were not masons, and they ceased to be specially connected with the trade of mason and began to take on work for the relief of the poor. An important date for Freemasons is 1717, for in that year the representatives of four lodges met in the Goose and Gridiron Tavern in the City of London and formed the first Grand Lodge of England, which developed into the governing body of Freemasonry in England, now called the United Grand Lodge.

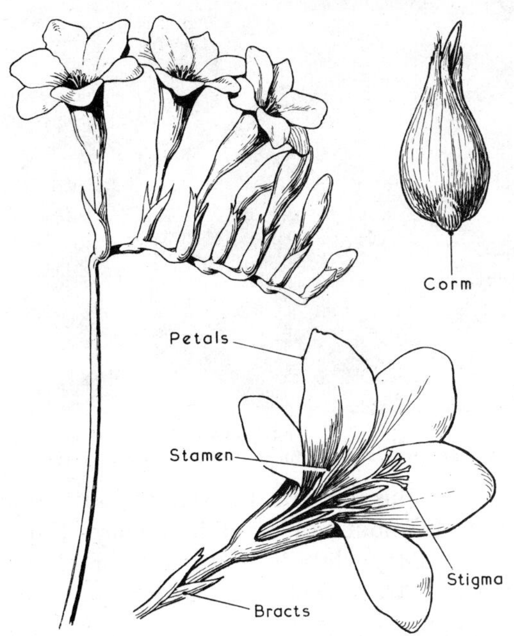


Freesia, with corm and drawing of a flower head.

**FREESIA.** One of the flowers most greatly prized for their scent is the freesia, which comes from the Cape of Good Hope in South Africa but is often grown in English greenhouses. The flower heads, which are funnel-shaped, opening into six petals, grow along one side of a slender bare stalk. The leaves are long and narrow and the plants are about 18 inches high.

There are at least three and possibly four different kinds of freesia and many varieties have been bred. Besides the original colours—white, cream and yellow—these are apricot, pink, red, mauve and blue. Freesias belong to Iridaceae, the iris family.

Freesias grow from corms, which are underground stems in which food for the plants is stored. However, they can be raised from seed sown in frames. As they grow the stems have to be supported.

**FREETOWN** is the capital of Sierra Leone, a former British colony which became independent in 1961. It is situated at the foot of a cluster of steep hills and looks out over one of the world's finest natural harbours. Both the hills and the harbour are unusual on the west coast of Africa, most of which is monotonously flat and beaten by surf. Damp heat and heavy rains make Freetown unpleasant at some times of the year, but it no longer has the reputation of being "the white man's grave", for malaria is not a common disease there now.

Many of the people of Freetown are descendants of freed African slaves. When an English court decided in the 18th century that slaves brought to England were free men from the moment they stepped on shore, many of those freed found themselves without any means of support. In 1787 some English people bought the land where Freetown stands so that the Africans could go back to their own country. Other early settlers were Negroes who had fought for the British during the American War of Independence, and also slaves who had been freed on the high seas by British naval patrols.

*Shell Photographic Unit*

In Freetown, the capital of Sierra Leone. It is strange to see road signs here just like the British ones.

Today the people of Freetown form a thriving community and the city's affairs are managed by a mayor and councillors, as in English cities. The population is about 100,000.

**FRÉMONT, John Charles** (1813–1890) is best known as an American explorer although he was later a politician, a general and a state governor. He was born in Savannah, Georgia.

Radio Times Hulton Picture Library

Frémont's party in rough country on the Oregon trail during the expedition of 1842.

In 1842, Frémont, then a young army officer, was chosen to lead an expedition to survey the Oregon trail which ran from Independence on the Missouri for about 2,000 miles to the Columbia River in Oregon. At that time Oregon was owned jointly by Great Britain and America, while Mexico claimed Texas and California. The Americans were keen to open up the West, but their knowledge of the country west of the Missouri came mainly from the confused accounts of trappers and explorers.

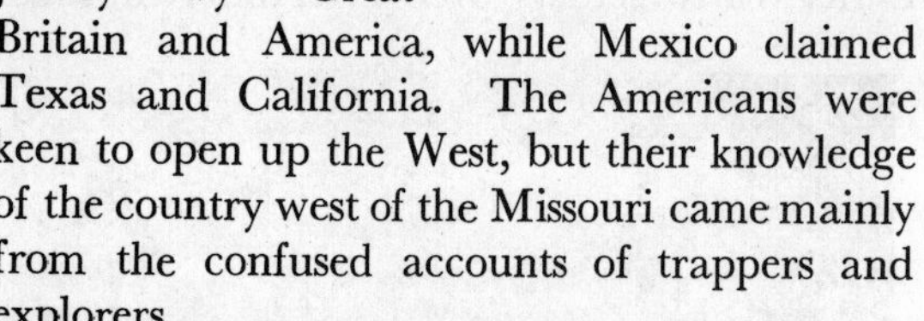

On his first expedition to the West Frémont and his party, with the famous trapper and hunter Kit Carson as guide, surveyed the Oregon trail as far as South Pass in Wyoming. The next year they penetrated to the mouth of the Columbia River and then daringly crossed the Sierra Nevada mountains in midwinter. They came home the following spring by way of Great Salt Lake. Frémont's reports of his two expeditions encouraged hundreds of settlers to set off on the Oregon trail. Although not the first to explore the trail, Frémont was the first to chart and describe it accurately and in detail. He gave practical advice about the sort of equipment needed and the dangers travellers might meet.

In 1845 Frémont helped the American settlers in California in their rebellion against Mexico, but he was accused of disobeying orders and sent back to Washington for trial. He was not punished, but angrily resigned from the army. He returned to California to hear that gold had been found on his estate and in a few years he became a millionaire. He was strongly against slavery and during the American Civil War was made a general in the Union Army. He was unsuccessful as a general and resigned to try to build a railway to the Pacific by a southern route. The finances of this undertaking were unsound and by 1870 Frémont had lost all his money. From 1878 to 1881, while he was governor of the territory of Arizona, he wrote an account of his explorations.

**FRENCH COMMUNITY.** The *Communauté Française*, or French Community, is a group of countries consisting of France and lands overseas that once belonged to France or are linked to it. It was founded in 1946 under the name of the French Union, which replaced the old French colonial empire. In 1958, when General Charles de Gaulle came to power in France, he decided that the links joining the union needed to be strengthened. A new constitution, or form of government, was prepared and the various countries (including France itself) were asked to vote whether or not they agreed to it. All of them agreed except French Guinea (Africa) which was therefore granted complete independence and changed its name to Guinea. (See GUINEA.)

The remaining overseas countries became members of the French Community. They were given the choice of becoming *départements* or of becoming territories or republics. France itself is divided into *départements*, which are roughly the same as British counties. In 1960 most of the African states in the Community became independent, and a law was passed in the French parliament allowing independent states to be members of the Community.

The French Community corresponds roughly to the Commonwealth of Nations. The overseas members of the Community are linked to France in several ways. Many of their peoples are French-speaking and they benefit from agreements on trade and on military help if attacked by other countries. They also receive help from French experts in improving their agriculture and setting up industries, and most of them use money based on the French franc.

In the 1960s several of the African republics which had formerly been members left the Community, including Algeria, Dahomey, Ivory Coast, Mali, Mauritania, Niger and Upper Volta. Although some of these countries continued to have special trading relations with France, the Community's importance grew less.

The table sets out the overseas countries of the French Community, arranged under continents or regions, Oceania being the central part of the Pacific Ocean. There are separate articles on many of these countries. (The New Hebrides Condominium, ruled jointly by Great Britain and France, is not part of the Community.)

| *Country* | *Capital* | *Class* |
|---|---|---|
| **Africa** | | |
| Central African Republic | Bangui | Republic |
| Chad | Fort Lamy | Republic |
| Comoro Archipelago | Moroni | Territory |
| Congo | Brazzaville | Republic |
| French Territory of Afars and Issas | Jibuti | Territory |
| Gabon | Libreville | Republic |
| Malagasy Republic (Madagascar) | Tananarive | Republic |
| Réunion | Saint-Denis | *Département* |
| Senegal | Dakar | Republic |
| Southern and Antarctic Lands | Paris | Territory |
| **America** | | |
| French Guiana | Cayenne | *Département* |
| Guadeloupe | Basse-Terre | *Département* |
| Martinique | Fort-de-France | *Département* |
| Saint-Pierre and Miquelon | Saint-Pierre | Territory |
| **Oceania** | | |
| French Polynesia | Papeete | Territory |
| New Caledonia and Dependencies | Nouméa | Territory |
| Wallis and Futuna Islands | Mata Utu | Territory |

**FRENCH CRICKET** is a game played by two or more players. The batsman is his own wicket. He stands in the middle of the ground surrounded by the rest of the players in a wide circle. They throw the cricket or tennis ball at him, aiming at his legs. He must not move from his spot and when he hits the ball he scores runs

by circling the bat round his waist—one run for every circle—before the ball is thrown in again.

He is out if he moves his feet, or if the ball strikes him anywhere below the knees, or is caught without the ball bouncing by one of the fieldsmen. The player who puts him out takes over the bat. The ball is bowled at the batsman by any of the players from the point where it comes to rest. This may be quite close to the batsman if he succeeded only in blocking the previous ball, but the batsman may appeal against "pegging in"; that is, throwing the ball at him too hard.

**FRENCH REVOLUTION.** One of the greatest uprisings of the people of a country against the whole of the old order and form of government was that which began in France in

1789, and which is known as the French Revolution. England had had a revolution and other great political changes in the previous century and, after the troubles were over, had become a fairly orderly country. The relations between the English sovereign and parliament had been settled for the time being and the sovereign often had to fit in with the wishes of parliament.

In France there was no proper parliament. The States-General, something like the English parliament but much less powerful, had not met for 175 years and during all this time the kings had ruled the country through men who were responsible only to them. They did not know what their people were thinking. The government was not efficient because it was impossible to rule such a big country without keeping in closer touch with what people wanted, and in any case the king was becoming very short of money. The peasants and small farmers were wretchedly poor because they had to pay heavy taxes to their feudal lords (see FEUDALISM), and the workers in the towns were nearly as badly off. Although people like merchants and lawyers were capable and well informed they could take no part in the making of laws. The French clergy had many special rights, but many of the parish priests sympathized with the people against the king and the nobles. The nobles paid hardly any taxes and often did no work, living off their lands and off pensions or offices bestowed by the king. By 1789 many people in France were living in miserable conditions and were ready to revolt.

In that year the King, Louis XVI, decided to call a meeting of the States-General and to ask its advice. For the purpose of sending representatives to the States-General the people of France were divided into three groups, called estates: the nobles, or first estate, the clergy, or second estate, and the rest of the people, or third estate. This last group consisted of very different kinds of people, including merchants and professional men such as lawyers, as well as tradesmen, farmers, and labourers. As the States-General had last met in 1614 nobody knew what would happen when it met on May 5, 1789.

The King promised to make some changes if the States-General helped him to raise the money he needed so badly. The representatives of the third estate demanded that France should have a constitution; that is, a set of rules by which it would be governed and which even the King would have to obey. To begin with, the first two estates were against this demand but gradually some of the nobles and many of the clergy supported it. Then Louis dissolved the States-General, declaring that its meetings were finished. However, the representatives of the third estate swore not to separate until they had given France a constitution, and took the title National Assembly.

On June 23 the Comte (Count) de Mirabeau defied the King's order to close the Assembly, saying to the messenger, "Go tell your master that we are here by the will of the people and nothing but bayonets shall drive us out". Disorder broke out in Paris. On July 14 the mob stormed the Bastille, a famous prison, and freed the prisoners (see BASTILLE). Throughout France the people rose against their masters. The National Assembly announced its ideas—liberty and equality—in a document called the Declaration of the Rights of Man. The church and the nobles had their property taken away from them and lost their special rights. In October a mob of people from Paris marched to Versailles, the King's palace just outside the city, and Louis XVI, his Queen, Marie Antoinette, and their son were taken back to Paris.

On June 20, 1791, before France could calm down after these changes, the King and his family tried to escape from the country. They were caught at Varennes, in eastern France, and had to return. This proof that they were not loyal to the new France changed everything, for it made the people of Paris begin to think it was not necessary to have a king. The next year war broke out with Austria and Prussia, who were planning to invade France in order to support the King. Five hundred members of the National Guard (a kind of army of civilians) from Marseilles and other parts of France came marching into Paris to celebrate the fall of the Bastille in 1789. They were singing their new war song, the "Marseillaise", and the people of Paris once more got out of control. The mob broke into the Tuileries, the palace in Paris where the King was

*Mansell Collection*

Girondists on their way to the guillotine, after the Convention had been overthrown by the people of Paris.

living, and forced him to wear the famous red cap worn by people who supported the Revolution.

The royal family took refuge with the Assembly but it was too late, for its members dethroned the King and imprisoned him and the royal family. The Assembly gave a vote to every adult male citizen and ordered that a general election should be held. General La Fayette, who was in charge of the army, tried to march on Paris to rescue the King but he acted half-heartedly and fled.

On September 20, 1792, the French army defeated the Austrians (and some French who were fighting with them because they were against the Revolution) at the Battle of Valmy, in north-eastern France. In November it defeated them again and at the same time conquered Belgium, which was put under French rule. These victories encouraged the supporters of the Revolution and filled them with excitement.

Also on September 20, 1792, the new assembly, now called the Convention, met for the first time after the general election, and the period known as the Reign of Terror began. Louis XVI and his Queen were sent to the guillotine (see GUILLOTINE), and the men who had started as lovers of freedom turned into tyrants who ruled as they wished. They had hundreds of people guillotined and ruled by threatening death to all who did not agree with them. Wanting to make France bigger and more glorious, they invaded the Netherlands and soon were also at war with Britain and Spain.

In May 1793 the Convention was overthrown by the people of Paris. Its milder members (known as the Girondists), who did not agree with violent methods of government, were imprisoned and later executed. Thus its more violent members (called Jacobins or Montagnards) now controlled France. They formed a small group, called the Committee of Public Safety, to govern the country. Its chief members were Georges Jacques Danton, Jean Paul Marat and Maximilien Robespierre.

The next two months were months of great activity. The Committee of Public Safety was determined to throw the foreign armies out of France and worked furiously raising armies and supplying ammunition. It inspired the people to fight, in spite of their lack of food (by this time supplies were running out). People were guillotined in great numbers and were often condemned to death in groups, without trial. Robespierre got the upper hand and had Danton guillotined. Then people became tired of all the bloodshed and ended it by sending Robespierre himself to his death in the same way. The more moderate, wealthier people set up a new assembly, and five of its members were entrusted with the government of the country. They were known as the Directory.

This government, however, was corrupt and not very efficient and people did not like it. In 1799 a young army officer called Napoleon Bonaparte took advantage of its weakness to seize power himself and to become the master of France. The system of government was changed—the new government consisted of three members, called "Consuls", and Napoleon was First Consul and the real ruler of the country. Shortly after this he became the only Consul and then, in 1804, the Emperor of France. (See NAPOLEON I.)

The Revolution thus came to an end but the ideas that had inspired it—the idea that everybody should be free and that all men should be treated equally—lived on, and from France they spread to many other countries.

**FRESCO.** When you look at reproductions of some of the famous paintings in the world, many of those by Michelangelo for example, it is difficult to remember that they are wall-paintings and that for many centuries in Europe most large pictures were painted directly on to walls. The most common method of wall-painting is

The preparations for a fresco: the uneven surface of the wall (A) is first covered by a coarse coating (B) of rubble and bitumen; this is then covered by a smoother layer of plaster and fine pebbles (C); a thin coat of fine plaster and marble dust is applied and polished to a smooth hard surface (D); on this the wet working surface (E) is floated, with a small trowel, a little each day.

known as fresco, an Italian word meaning "fresh". This method, which was developed chiefly in Italy during the Renaissance, consists of applying the pigment (colour) mixed only with water (or water and lime) on to a surface of wet lime plaster. The lime in the plaster mixes with the pigment and as the plaster dries binds the paint permanently to the surface. The fresco lasts almost as long as the wall on which it is painted; in fact in Italy there are fine examples more than 500 years old.

The chief difficulty in fresco painting is that the paint can be put on the wall only while the plaster is wet. As wall-paintings are usually large this means that the artist can paint only a limited area before the plaster hardens. He therefore applies just so much plaster as he can paint over in a day. No corrections are possible once the paint is put on and since the colours in fresco become much lighter as they dry great skill is required to match one day's work with the next. To overcome these difficulties the Italian artists carefully planned their compositions before starting the fresco. They made a full-sized working drawing (see CARTOON) and transferred its main outlines on to the plaster. This made it easier to paint quickly while the plaster was wet.

In fresco the tones are light (the colours can be neither very bright nor very dark) and it is difficult to obtain deep effects of shadow. This simplified and graceful style of painting, however, was especially suited for covering the large wall spaces in the churches and palaces of the Renaissance. Among other great artists besides Michelangelo, who used the method, were Giotto, Raphael and Piero della Francesca. In modern times probably the best known fresco painter is the Mexican, Diego Rivera.

**FREUD, Sigmund** (1856–1939). Freud (pronounced "froyd") was the founder of the modern science of psychoanalysis, which means the analysis or examination of the mind (see PSYCHOLOGY). Few men have done more to reveal the innermost workings of the human mind than this great Austrian doctor. He was born of Jewish parents in Freiberg, Moravia, in what is now Czechoslovakia. When he was four his parents moved to Vienna, where he lived most of his life. An early interest in scientific research led him to study medicine and eventually to become a specialist in nervous diseases.

In those days very little could be done to cure nervous illness beyond giving the patient drugs. Freud discovered that a cure was possible if the patient could be made to talk about his past. At first this was done by hypnosis (see HYPNOTISM); later he found that with sympathy and understanding the patient could talk quite freely and reveal memories hidden in that part of the mind which Freud called the "unconscious". Such memories, often of some unhappy experience in childhood, had been suppressed (hidden) because they were linked with unhappy feelings. By bringing the hidden past out into the open Freud found he could help people to recognize the possible cause of their troubles. One way of doing this was to ask them to tell him their dreams, for he believed that dreams can reveal a person's hidden memories and desires.

Freud met much opposition and it took many years for his ideas to become widely known and accepted. Two of his important followers, C. G. Jung and A. Adler, disagreed with his methods and founded systems of their own.

In 1938 the Nazis seized Austria and Freud, being a Jew, was in danger. He took refuge in England and died in London the next year.

**FRICTION.** When a heavy wooden box is pushed along the floor, resistance is set up between the box and the floor. This resistance is called friction. Friction comes from a Latin word meaning "rub" and it always occurs when two articles are moved so as to rub or chafe against one another. In engines and most machinery friction is harmful and wasteful and everything possible is done to reduce it by lubrication, or oiling. However, friction can be useful. Without it people could not walk, as is shown by the difficulty of walking on ice—when the friction is small. Without friction nails and screws would not hold and the brakes and clutch of a motor car would not work.

In sliding the box along the floor, more force is needed to start it than to keep it moving. The heavier the box, the greater is the force needed to move it. If it has a smooth base and the floor

It takes many men to drag a stone on a rough surface.

Fewer are needed to pull the same stone on rollers.

Four men can pull it in a cart over a rough surface.

Two can pull it on a smooth path if the axle is greased.

With the best equipment one man can move the same load.

is smooth there is less friction than if either or both were rough. It makes no difference to the force needed to move the box whether it stands on its base or its side or its end. The main rules are therefore: (1) starting friction is greater than running friction; (2) friction and the force needed to overcome it depend only on the weight squeezing the articles together and the kind of surfaces they have.

It is easier to move the box along the floor by turning it end over end, and easier still to move it if it is put on rollers or wheels. Rolling depends on friction, otherwise the wheels would spin without gripping. The ancient Egyptians used wooden rollers to move the huge stone blocks for the pyramids. When wheels are used they turn on an axle and the friction is reduced either by oil or (as in a bicycle) by ball bearings.

Whenever friction has to be overcome work is needed. For example, when riding a bicycle in the ordinary way little effort is needed because the friction is very small, but if the brakes are put on the friction is increased, the brakes and the wheel become very hot and pedalling becomes really hard work. This work is wasted as heat, and in a motor car about a fifth of the power of the engine is wasted just in overcoming the friction of the moving parts. Besides causing waste, friction can do damage. If the bearings of a machine go short of oil they can become so hot that the metal of them melts and they jam; this is called *seizure*. Oil and grease reduce the friction and the metal of which the parts are made is also important in doing this. Some metals such as brass are more slippery than others, and generally speaking two parts made of the same kind of metal should not be allowed to rub together.

When a boat moves through water or an aeroplane through the air there is a resistance to be overcome caused by *viscosity*, which is like friction although more complicated. It is easier to waggle a spoon about in water than in treacle and easier still in air, for treacle has the greatest viscosity of the three. When water flows down a river it tends to cling to the banks and therefore the water nearest the middle of the river flows faster. Air too offers a resistance akin to friction if an article is moved through it, and in high speed aircraft great care is taken to make the outer skin as smooth as possible.

## FRIESE-GREENE, William (1855–1921).

Friese-Greene was a British photographer who tried to find a way of photographing moving objects and afterwards showing the photographs on a screen so that they seemed to move. He thus helped towards the invention of the cinema.

Friese-Greene was born in Bristol and went to school there as plain William Green. Later he joined his wife's name to his own and added an "e", and so became William Friese-Greene. As a young man he met the famous William Henry Fox Talbot, who had discovered a method of taking still photographs on paper. Friese-Greene became a photographer, opening a studio in Bristol but also travelling a good deal. He worked with John Arthur Roebuck Rudge, a Bath photographer, who was trying to produce moving pictures by taking photographs on glass plates fixed to a revolving disc. Later Friese-Greene came to London, living at 39 King's Road, Chelsea. He had a workshop at 20 Brooke Street, Holborn, and also a shop, first at 69 Bond Street and later in Piccadilly.

In 1889 Friese-Greene worked with an engineer named Mortimer Evans to make a camera to take rapid photographs of animals and insects. This camera probably took three or four pictures a second. Friese-Greene then tried to show his pictures on a screen rapidly one after the other so that they seemed to move. This experiment could not have been very successful, as photographs must be taken at the rate of at least 16 every second (a modern film has 24 pictures a second) and shown at the same speed to get a smooth result. One of the difficulties is to find a material on which to take the photographs; it must be light and strong enough to be moved through the camera at high speed.

Friese-Greene realized that celluloid film was the best material and now began to work with another engineer named Frederick Henry Varley, who had invented a camera in 1890 which could use celluloid film. In 1893 Friese-Greene produced a camera which was a close copy of Varley's, but again the camera worked too slowly, taking only about four or five pictures a second, and the result when the film was shown on the screen must have been very jerky. Nevertheless, this was a step in the right direction.

In later years Friese-Greene lost most of his money and moved to Brighton, where he opened a small shop. In 1921 he was taken suddenly ill and died during a meeting at the Connaught Rooms, Holborn, in London. He was buried in Highgate cemetery and his tombstone has written on it, "William Friese-Greene, Inventor of Kinematography". This word comes from the two Greek words *kinematos*, which means "of movement", and *graphe*, meaning "picture". Usually it is spelt "cinematography", and from it comes the word "cinema".

Friese-Greene was only one of the many inventors who helped to make moving pictures possible, but he had a lively mind and besides his experiments already described he tried out many other ideas. He tried to make stereoscopic (3D) films as early as 1893 and later experimented with colour films. He was also interested in "talking pictures" and in 1889 he wrote to Thomas Alva Edison, inventor of the phonograph, suggesting that the Friese-Greene camera and the Edison phonograph might be put together to make a sound film machine.

*Radio Times Hulton Picture Library*

William Friese-Greene with one of the cameras he invented.

**FRIGATE.** At different dates the name frigate has stood for different kinds of ship. The Mediterranean frigate of the 16th century was a sort of galley, or low narrow ship either with oars or sails, used more for carrying dispatches (important papers and messages) than fighting. The Spaniards gave the name to the fast sailing vessels bringing treasure from America, and ships like these were later used by the privateers, or semi-pirates, of Dunkirk, which then belonged to Spain. They were fairly small ships, as were the first frigates built in England soon after 1640 to fight them. The new fashion, however, soon spread to larger vessels, so that by 1655 a big three-decker was called a frigate while men-of-war of the older type were "ships". Then the word "frigate" was dropped.

The word came into use again soon after 1750

Frigates through the ages.

as the name for another new type of ship, the so-called "true frigate" of Nelson's day. This was really a two-decked ship but had no guns on the lower deck (though this was still called the gun deck). It had some 30 guns or more on the upper deck, quarterdeck and forecastle and was the next class below the ship-of-the-line or battleship.

Such frigates lasted until the end of sailing men-of-war, having by then become large enough to carry up to 60 guns. Wooden steam frigates were similar and the first iron-built armoured ship, the "Warrior" of 1861, was still called a frigate, though it was obviously meant to do the work of a battleship. After that the name lasted a little longer for what would now be called a cruiser. Then it disappeared altogether until World War II, when it was used again for a vessel something like a small destroyer, used mainly for protecting convoys of merchant ships against submarines.

**FRIGATE BIRD.** The large sea birds known as frigate birds have very long wings and spend most of their lives in the air, cruising over the tropical seas. Their tails are forked and they have very short legs and long slim bills with a hook at the end. There are five kinds of frigate birds. Most of the males have glossy black plumage, while the females have white under parts. All young frigate birds can be distinguished by their white heads. There is a patch of bare skin under the beak and the males can blow this up into a bright red bag to attract the females during the breeding season.

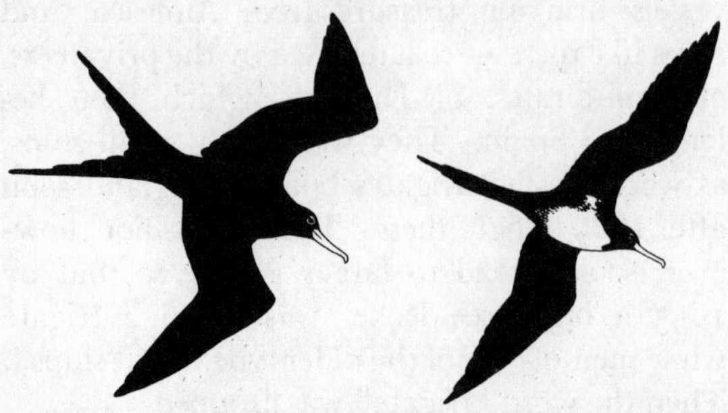
The slender frigate bird never alights on the sea.

These birds were given the name of frigate bird or "man-o'-war hawk" because they generally pursue other birds to make them drop the fish they are carrying and then catch it themselves in mid-air. They can also pick up food from the surface of the sea while still in flight, and indeed they never land on the water at all. At night they collect together and roost in trees near the coast.

Frigate birds breed on islands such as Christmas Island in the Indian Ocean, Ascension in the Atlantic and the Galapagos in the Pacific. They make their large nests of twigs in trees, bushes or on the rocks, and lay only one white egg. When the youngster is hatched it is naked; later it becomes covered with white down.

A young female of the magnificent frigate bird was found in the Island of Tiree in the Scottish Hebrides on July 10, 1953. This is the only British record of a frigate bird.

**FROBISHER, Sir Martin** (?1535–1594). One of the first people to try to reach India and China and the other countries of the East by sailing round the north of the American continent was Martin Frobisher. Earlier, this great Yorkshire seaman had taken part in the attacks being made on the ships of Spain, but he had long been interested in the possibility of reaching the East by sailing west, and in 1576 he left London on a voyage of discovery with two tiny vessels. One soon returned but Frobisher went on in the other to Greenland and Baffin Land, to the north of Canada. When he entered the long narrow bay now called Frobisher Bay, he thought he had found the channel he was looking for, but he was wrong. He returned, bringing back with him a piece of rock which was thought to contain gold. His next two expeditions did little but bring back cargoes of this rock, which turned out to be useless.

In 1585 Frobisher sailed to the West Indies with Sir Francis Drake and three years later in the "Triumph" he helped to defeat the Spanish Armada, being knighted for his services. It was from a wound received while attacking a Spanish fort in 1594 that he died at Plymouth.

**FROG AND TOAD.** The group of cold-blooded animals which can live both on land and in the water are known as amphibians, and the most familiar ones in Great Britain are the frog and the toad. They are found in most parts of the world, and in the tropics it is often difficult to tell them apart. In the case of those found in Britain, however, it is quite easy. Frogs are smooth and shiny and they have long hind legs with which they are able to make long hops. Toads have dry, rough skins with growths like warts on them and they can only make small hops because of their short legs. Also nearly all frogs have teeth, while toads have none.

Most frogs and toads feed on small creatures such as insects and worms. They have broad mouths with tongues fastened at the front of their mouths so that the tip points back towards the throat when the mouth is closed. When an insect comes near, the tongue is flicked out at great speed, the end, which is sticky, hits the insect and the tongue is brought back into the mouth with the insect attached. The frog's eyes, which are large and bulging, press inwards into the mouth cavity when the animal swallows. When eating a worm the frog uses its front legs to centre the creature in its mouth and thus make it easier to swallow.

Frogs and toads have lungs but they do not breathe in the same way as mammals. Air is sucked into the mouth through the two nostrils by lowering the throat. The nostrils are then closed and, by lifting the throat, the air is pushed into the lungs. This process can be seen by watching a frog's throat, which pumps up and down all the time.

Like other amphibians, frogs and toads do not drink water with their mouths, but swim in ponds or rivers or sit in the rain so as to absorb water through their skins. It is dangerous for a frog to stay away from water for a long time, for its skin may dry up and it will die.

Frogs and toads defend themselves against larger animals by means of poison glands. If they are roughly handled they will give out a poisonous stuff which varies in strength according to the species the animal belongs to. The common British toad gives out such unpleasant stuff that a dog that picks one up in its mouth will never touch another. The poison given out by some highly coloured South American tree frogs is used by the natives of that region to tip the points of their arrows.

In northern countries frogs and toads hibernate, or sleep during the winter. When the weather grows cold frogs bury themselves in the leaves and mud at the bottom of a pond, or, like toads, find a hole in a bank or under a log where they remain until the weather becomes warmer. During this time they need little oxygen and their blood almost stops circulating.

The eggs of frogs and toads are known as spawn. Each egg is surrounded by a transparent, jelly-like substance which is so slippery that if a duck, for example, tries to get hold of it and eat it the spawn slips back into the water. The jelly also helps to let the sun's warmth through to the egg inside. Frog spawn is laid in large masses which float on the surface of rivers, lakes and ponds. Toad spawn is fastened together in the form of long strands or ribbons which are wound among water plants.

Frogs and toads pass through three stages of development, which can be very clearly seen—egg, tadpole and adult frog or toad. The tadpoles grow from the round black dot that can be seen inside each blob of jelly, and while they are developing they feed on yolks also contained

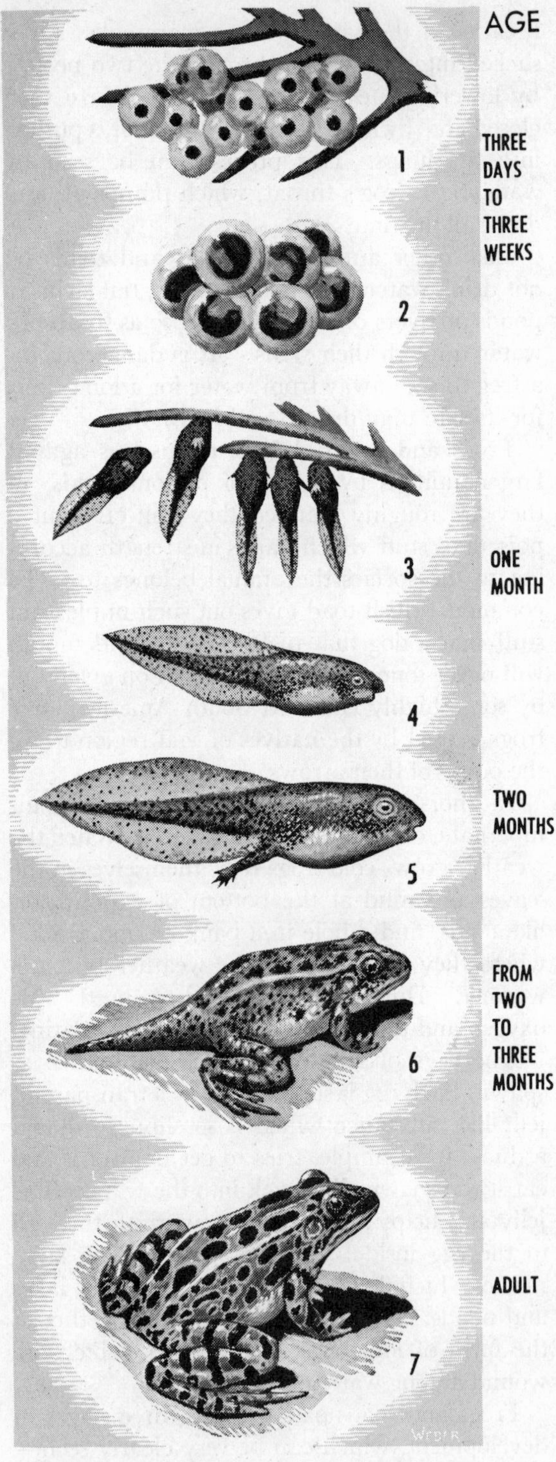


Here are some of the stages in the development of a frog. (1 and 2) The eggs are surrounded by a jelly-like substance. (3, 4, 5) In about a month they become tadpoles. (6) Gradually they develop legs and lose their tails. (7) The fully developed frog will reach its full size in three or four years.

inside the jelly. Tadpoles have a head and body all in one and breathe through gills. At first they have no legs and swim by means of a long tail. Gradually, however, legs begin to sprout and the tail shrinks and is absorbed while they also lose their gills and develop lungs, until they have become tiny frogs or toads.

It is quite easy to watch all this taking place by keeping some spawn in a bowl or tank at home and watching the tadpoles as they emerge from their eggs, lose their tails and grow legs. Frogs take from three to four years to reach their full size and often live as long as 40 years. During the breeding season they make a good deal of noise and can be heard croaking all night.

Although the frogs and toads in Britain lay their eggs and leave them to look after themselves, some kinds in other countries take great care of them. The male of the European midwife toad winds the string of eggs round his back legs and carries them until they are ready to hatch, when he takes them to the water.

In the tropics live amphibians known as tree frogs, which have pads on their fingers and toes which help them to climb trees. Some tree frogs lay their eggs in a frothy nest in a bush overhanging water, and when the tadpoles hatch they drop into the water from this nest.

The Surinam toad in South America hatches out her eggs in holes in her back. The holes are covered by skin and filled with a liquid in which the young remain while they are passing through the tadpole stage.

A relation of the English common frog is the edible frog, which is also found in England, and in France the legs of this frog are eaten as food. In America one of the several kinds of frogs known as bullfrogs is also eaten, and is even bred on special frog farms.

**FROGMAN.** An ordinary diver has to rely on air pumped from the surface through a long pipe, but the frogman carries his own breathing apparatus with him. On his body he carries a cylinder, from which a short tube takes oxygen to his face mask. This has a "window" through which the frogman can see, and he can control the flow of oxygen by means of a tap. He is dressed in a rubber suit with a close-fitting

*Courtesy, U.S. Navy*

"Sealab II" was a 45-day experiment to test man's ability to live and work for long periods under the sea. Here frogmen adjust the bundle of pipes that connected their underwater chamber with the surface.

rubber headpiece, and on his feet he wears long flippers. These look like a frog's feet and help to explain the frogman's name.

This kind of oxygen apparatus was used during World War II because no bubbles escaped from it, as they do in the most modern equipment designed for use in peacetime. The reason for this was that if bubbles were seen rising to the surface in an enemy harbour they would have aroused suspicion. When breathing oxygen, the frogman cannot go into very deep water, but his great advantage is that he can move upwards or downwards as he likes, whereas the ordinary diver must walk on the bottom of the sea in heavy boots, stirring up the mud so much that he may not be able to see. Frogmen are particularly useful for taking underwater photographs of things like fish and fishing nets, and for such jobs as inspecting the underwater part of the piles which support bridges.

Naval frogmen carry out a variety of tasks. Here the ship's diver receives his orders on board a destroyer.

During World War II the Germans had put great obstacles in the shallow water on the coast of Normandy, France, and arranged for mines to go off at a touch. However, in 1944, British frogmen cleared a wide space by first making the mines harmless and then blowing up the obstacles. This allowed landing craft to approach close to the beach for the Allied invasion of Normandy. (See also DIVERS AND DIVING EQUIPMENT.)

**FROISSART, Jean** (1338–1410?) The *Chronicle* in which the French writer Jean Froissart gave an account of his own times, of war and chivalry, of knights and ladies, is one of the most famous histories ever written. One story in it tells how, when Edward III of England was besieging the town of Calais, he agreed to spare it if six of the burghers, or leading citizens, would surrender themselves to him with rope round their necks. Six burghers came forth, but they were saved from death when King Edward's wife Philippa pleaded for them.

Froissart, like almost all writers in those times, had been ordained as a priest, though he liked the life of courts with its pageantry and banquets. He was born near Valenciennes, a rich city of France, its streets filled with men at arms and bright with their banners. Outside, along the river banks, were the knightly castles. Froissart began by writing verses to a lady, but he longed to see the world. He came first to England with an introduction to Queen Philippa, and it was she who suggested and paid for his journey to Scotland in 1365.

Most of the information for the *Chronicle* was gathered by word of mouth. In his own way, Froissart was extremely careful. If he wished to describe a particular battle and he knew knights from Brittany had taken part in it, he would travel to Brittany to interview them. In this way he travelled over a great part of France, Spain and Italy, always asking questions. A passage in the *Chronicle* describes a ride Froissart had in southern France with a knight called Espaing de Lyon. Every turn in the road showed a new castle and the knight knew the history of each. "*Sainte Marie!*" cried Froissart, "How pleasant are your tales and how much they profit me! . . . They shall all be set down in memory and remembrance in the history which I am writing."

**FROST.** When the earth's surface cools below freezing point (32 degrees Fahrenheit) on a clear cold night, a beautiful white coating of frost forms on trees and grass and windows. Frost is less likely on a cloudy night because the clouds act as a blanket and keep the earth warmer. When there is no wind the air remains longer against the cooling land, helping frost to form.

The white frost called "hoar frost" is caused by the tiny droplets of moisture in the air turning into ice crystals when they touch the trees and grass and window panes. The fern-like patterns are caused partly by the way the little ice crystals are made up (see SNOW) and partly by slight air currents and dust particles. A black frost, when few white crystals are to be seen, is caused by the freezing of a big mass of air at all levels instead of just a layer near the ground.

The likelihood of frost depends greatly on the exact situation of a place. Although the air generally gets colder as one goes higher, making frost more likely on really high ground, it is also true that cold air is heavier than warm and tends to flow downhill into valleys and hollows. Farmers and fruit growers with crops or orchards in such places often have to take special measures to protect against frost damage by using oil burners that give heat without smoke or by lighting smoky fires (called "smudge" fires) which act like clouds in keeping the air near the ground warm.

**FROSTBITE** is brought about by extreme cold, usually below freezing-point, together with wetness, tiredness and poor food and too tight gloves or boots. The skin, usually of the face, the fingers or the toes, feels pleasantly numb and looks waxy-white. Painful swelling follows, and in bad cases the skin goes a purplish-black. During the stoppage of the circulation of the blood, a finger or toe may be lost.

A frostbitten hand is treated very gently and warmed by someone else's hand or by a warm glove. A sling is then put on, or a stretcher used to carry anyone with frostbitten toes.

**FRUIT.** The fruit of a plant is its ovary, which contains the seeds, and it takes many different forms. Marrows, peas and beans, which we call vegetables, are known to the botanist as fruits; so are acorns, burrs, poppy-heads and even dandelion "clocks". All are fruits because they each contain seeds which are there for producing new plants.

The ovary develops after the flower has been pollinated (the way in which this is done is described in the article FLOWER). After pollination the ovary of the flower becomes the fruit, while the ovules inside the fruit develop into ripe seeds. Sometimes the sepals and the bracts, which are special kinds of leaves outside the flower petals, remain after the petals of the flower have fallen and may enclose the fruits, as in acorns and beech nuts.

Some fruits are actually made up of several smaller ones, each containing seeds. An example of this is the columbine. In other cases these fruits join together to form a single ovary which becomes one fruit, like the tomato, wallflower and horse-chestnut. The number of seeds in a fruit may vary from one to many thousands. Some of the fruits which contain only one seed—such as the acorn—are often mistaken for the true seed, which is inside the ovary wall.

One of the most important jobs a fruit has to do is to scatter the seeds it contains, for if they fell on the ground directly beneath the parent plant the young plants would crowd the parent plant and each other as they grew. The seeds of most fruits are therefore carried away from the parent plant, sometimes only a few yards, sometimes quite a distance, and the shape, structure and colour of the fruit all help to bring this about.

Some fruits actually fly away from their plants by means of "wings" or "parachutes" which are attached to the seeds. Winged seeds include those of the elm and the sycamore, which have papery parts attached to them that cause them to whirl along on the wind. Lighter seeds, such as the dandelion, have a crown of

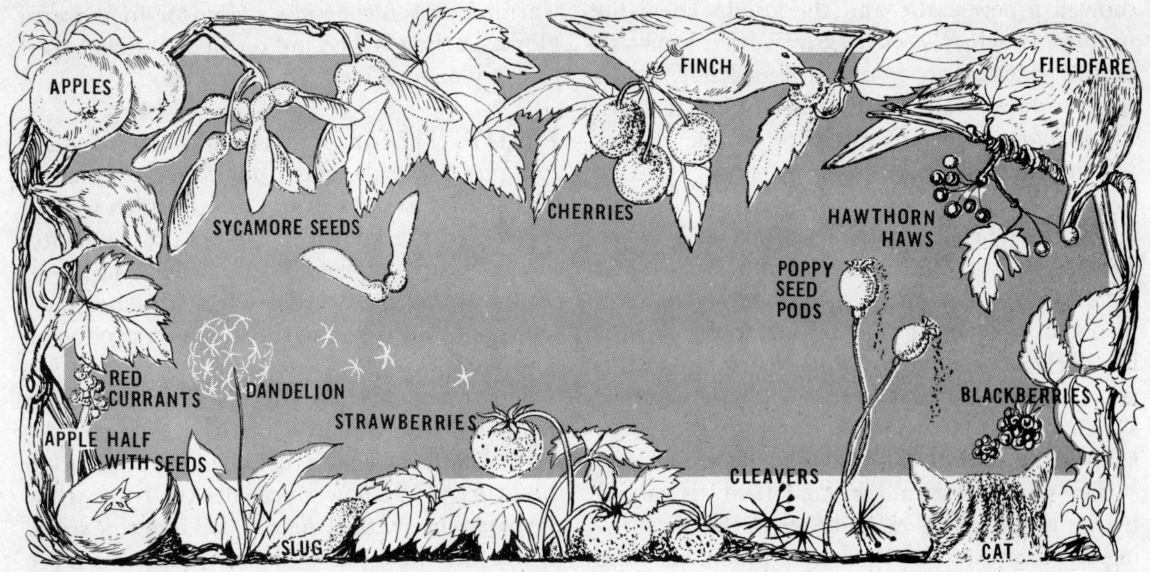


The seeds in fruit must be scattered so that new plants can grow. The wind carries away the sycamore seeds on their papery "wings" and the dandelion seeds under their filmy "parachutes". It also makes the dry poppy heads sway and shake their seeds out. The hooked burrs of the cleavers will cling to the fur of the cat as it brushes past them, and may be carried for miles. Other fruits are eaten by birds that will scatter the seeds in their droppings.

silky hairs like a parachute which can float on the faintest breeze, and the fruit of the wild clematis or traveller's joy has a feathery part attached to each seed to help it to fly.

Other fruits have dry walls and contain many seeds. The walls of the fruit may open up by splitting, like those of bluebells and violets, so that the seeds are shaken out as the plants sway in the wind. Or else the seeds escape through holes in the fruit walls, like the poppy fruit, which looks very like a pepperpot.

The pods of some plants of the pea family, such as broom and gorse, split open so suddenly that the seeds are shot out. On a warm afternoon this may be heard, like the cracking of tiny rifle shots, in the heathy country where these bushes grow.

Then there is the large class of fruits which are carried away from their parent plants by animals or birds. The fruits of cleavers and dog's mercury are covered with hooks which cling to the animals that brush against them so that the animals carry away the burrs, as these hooked fruits are called. People, too, may find burrs caught on their clothes when they have been out in the woods.

In the autumn, squirrels prepare stores of food to eat during the winter, and they collect together numbers of acorns, hazel nuts and sweet chestnuts and bury them in the woods. Some of these are eaten, but many are left in the ground and grow.

Birds are attracted by certain fruits with bright colours or pleasant smells, among them being the cherry, blackberry, rose hip and rowan (mountain ash) berry. They swallow these fruits and, after digesting the soft outer part, pass the seeds out of their bodies, by which time the bird may be several miles away from the parent tree.

## Kinds of Fruit

Many ripe ovaries that we call fruits in everyday speech are more correctly known as drupes, or stone-fruits. They have a fleshy outer covering and a hard inner layer, forming what is called the stone, which contains the seed. The plum, greengage, cherry and peach are all drupes, so are the walnut and almond, although their outer walls are not eatable and split open to release the stone, or nut. The coconut is also a drupe and has a thick outer layer of fibres outside the fruit wall. This layer soaks up water so that the seed inside can grow. Blackberries

*Courtesy, Agent-General for Tasmania*

FRUIT GROWING. Heavily laden apple trees at Lilydale in Tasmania, where fruit growing is a major industry.

FUNGI. Some of the many different kinds of fungus found in Great Britain. (1) blusher; (2) field mushroom; (3) fairy ring toadstool; (4) oyster mushroom; (5) shaggy ink cap; (6) wood blewits; (7) chanterelle; (8) fly agaric; (9) death cap; (10) sickener; (11) leaden entoloma; (12) common puff-ball; (13) common morel; (14) devil's boletus; (15) scaly polyporus; (16) spindle-shaped clavaria; (17) orange peel fungus.

and raspberries are collections of tiny drupes or drupels, forming a compound fruit made up of several parts developed from a single flower.

A berry, on the other hand, can be described as a fruit with seeds enclosed in pulp. The ovary wall becomes fleshy and the seeds are often embedded in pulp or pith. This is the case with black and red currants, tomatoes, pomegranates and cucumbers, in all of which there is soft and juicy pulp inside the outer wall of the fruit. The orange is a berry and so, strangely enough, is the banana. It can be seen, therefore, that the usual idea of a berry as a small, round fruit is quite a wrong one.

What are known to botanists as false fruits are those that are not developed from the ovary. The strawberry is a good example, as it is formed from a swollen, juicy stem, or receptacle, on the surface of which are the true fruits, which are generally known as the pips. The rose hip is a fleshy, hollow receptacle with the small fruits on the inner surface. In apples and pears, which are known as pomes, the ovary walls are leathery and form the core, while the outer part, which we eat, is a swollen receptacle. The haws, or fruit of the hawthorn, are also false fruits, with woody ovary walls forming stones.

Normally the ovary is able to develop into the fruit only after fertilization (the union of the cell in the pollen with the cell in the ovule), but in some cases pollination without fertilization may take place, and the result is a fruit with unripe seeds or no seeds at all. Some grapefruit and grapes are among these—grapes with no seeds are generally made into seedless raisins. The cucumber, if allowed to grow naturally, would produce seeds with such tough skins that the centre of the fruit could not be eaten. The stamens and ovaries of the cucumber are produced by separate flowers on the same plant, and if the flowers with the stamens are picked off before the pollen is shed, the ovaries will develop into the seedless fruits normally sold.

Fertilization releases what is known as a hormone, and it is by the hormone that the fruit is able to develop. Hormones or hormone substances are sprayed on to the flowers of certain plants, such as tomatoes, by gardeners and fruit growers, so as to make them produce good fruits.

**FRUIT GROWING.** What is more attractive than the bright pyramids of apples, oranges and pears arranged on the fruit counters and market stalls? And then there are peaches, plums, bananas, melons, grapefruit, pineapples and cherries in season. Some of this fruit may have been grown in nearby orchards, but a lot of it has come from other countries.

Great Britain is not a big fruit-growing country, but the climate in the south of England suits many *kinds* of fruit. Thanks to this variety, half the fresh fruit people want can be grown at home. The most important English fruit is apples, followed by plums, cherries and pears.

The fruit that cannot be grown in England comes from all over the world, chiefly from countries with a hot climate. Citrus fruits (oranges, lemons, tangerines and grapefruit) come from Israel, South Africa, Brazil, Spain and the United States, and fruits such as apples, pears, peaches and plums from Italy, Argentina, Australia, New Zealand and South Africa. Bananas come from the West Indies and pineapples from South Africa.

Many thousands of people both at home and abroad make their living by fruit growing. It is not an easy life because fruit trees have to be carefully looked after if they are to bear fruit regularly during their life of 40 years or so. Besides this, fruit trees do not "earn" any money for some years. Unlike the farmer who grows wheat and who can sow, harvest and sell his grain in a few months, the fruitgrower has to wait for years before the fruit from any particular tree makes a profit; that is, for instance, before an apple tree produces enough apples to earn more money when they are sold than it has cost to buy the tree, plant it, prune it and keep it healthy. It is five to seven years before there is a profit from apple, pear, plum, orange and grapefruit trees, and at least 12 years before there is one from cherry trees. Ever since the trees were planted, however, the fruitgrower has had to spend money on them.

For these reasons fruitgrowers take great care about where they plant their orchards. In Great Britain and the cooler countries one of the greatest dangers to their crops comes from late spring frosts, for if the trees are in bloom when the

*Above, Left: Courtesy, "The Grower". Right, Below: Radio Times Hulton Picture Library.*

**Above: A Kentish cherry orchard in blossom. Right: Picking fruit. Below: A machine for spraying chemicals to kill insects and fungi. Left: Pruning apple trees in Essex.**

frost occurs the flowers are destroyed and no fruit can form. Orchards are therefore planted in the places most likely to escape spring frost, such as on the top of undulating, or rolling, ground, and on the slopes of small hills, for the cold air is heavy and falls down to lower areas. The trees must also have as much sunlight as possible as this gives colour to the fruit and thus helps it to sell well, for people do not buy pale fruit. It is better to have too little rain rather than too much, because the trees can always be watered artificially. Too much rain when the blossom is out washes the pollen away, which means that new fruit cannot develop. Heavy rain is also a great nuisance when the fruit is being picked.

The fruitgrower must take care to plant his trees in a place where there is enough soil for the roots to grow properly. At least two feet of soil is necessary, and more still is needed if there is a bed of unbroken rock beneath the soil, without holes and cracks for the roots to enter. The soil must be fairly sandy, or light, as heavy soil holds too much water and rots the tree roots.

Even after the fruitgrower has planted his trees in the correct place he still has to protect them from fungus disease (see FUNGI) and insect pests. The fungi can spread very quickly and the insects appear throughout the spring and summer. These things sometimes attack the fruit, making holes in it or discolouring it and making it difficult to sell; sometimes they attack the tree itself, eating its leaves and sap and thus making it less able to produce a good crop of fruit.

The best way of killing fungi and insect pests is to spray them with chemicals. This is the most important summer work in an orchard, for up to eight sprayings may be necessary between March and July. Very often the chemicals are mixed so that both fungi and insects can be killed at the same time. The chemicals are sprayed on to the trees from a machine that has a tank to contain the liquid and a powerful fan to spread it. The machine is driven up and down the rows of trees and a blast of air from the fan blows very fine droplets of the chemicals on to the trees and wets them thoroughly.

As well as protecting his trees in this way, a fruitgrower also has to feed them by adding certain substances to the soil in which they are growing. Fruit trees need large amounts of nitrogen, phosphorus and potassium (see FERTILIZER), but if they are given too much of these foods—or too little of certain others—they will not grow properly and will not produce as much fruit as they should. Therefore it is not always easy to know exactly which fertilizers ought to be used. If the soil is kept bare, animal manure has to be added every few years, but if grass is grown under the trees this is not necessary. If the grass were left to grow long it would rob the trees of food and water in the soil, so it has to be kept short by frequent mowing. The cut grass is left to decay and helps to build up a healthy soil.

Even when he has fed his trees properly the fruitgrower's work is not finished, for he has to prune them by cutting off certain twigs or branches or parts of them. (See PRUNING.) Pruning is necessary because it makes the trees grow each year, and it is only growing trees that produce large crops of fruit. Pruning is very skilled work and is carried out in the winter while the trees are dormant, or resting. Young trees (up to five years old) are pruned for a different reason—to make them grow into the proper shape. A properly shaped tree is one that has four to six main branches growing out from the trunk. If the middle of the tree is full of branches, light and the chemicals used against pests will not reach the leaves there and the fruit in that part of the tree will be of low quality.

One thing more is necessary for a good crop of fruit, and that is proper pollination. (Pollination is explained in the article FLOWER.) The flowers of the citrus trees are self-pollinated. The ovules of each flower of an orange tree, for example, can develop into an orange after pollen from the same flower has fallen on them. In these cases, therefore, the flowers are easily pollinated. The flowers of many apples and pears, however, are best pollinated by the pollen of other types of apples and pears. Thus, in England, the fruitgrower often grows Worcester Pearmain apple trees in order to have his Cox's Orange Pippins pollinated. The pollen is carried by the wind, by small insects or by bees.

When the fruitgrower has seen to all these things he can hope for a good crop of fruit.

**FRY, Elizabeth** (1780–1845). Elizabeth Fry did much work for prisoners at a time when they were hardly treated as human beings at all.

Her maiden name was Gurney and she belonged to a Quaker family. (See QUAKERS.)

*Mansell Collection*

Elizabeth Fry reading to the prisoners in Newgate.

When she was only 15 she first showed interest in prison work in her home town of Norwich. As a girl she was fond of dancing and other amusements, but she gave them up after hearing a sermon by an American Quaker called William Savery. When she was 20 she married Joseph Fry, a London merchant, and had a family of 11 children.

In 1813 she was told by friends that women in Newgate prison in London were herded together, criminals being put with girls who had not been proved guilty of crimes, and that they were all living under terrible conditions. She therefore went to Newgate to see if she could make things better.

Elizabeth found that all the stories were true. The prison was overcrowded and dirty and the women so disorderly and violent that even the prison governor was afraid to go among them. Many of them had their children with them, and these children were allowed to mix with the worst criminals.

Elizabeth Fry first gave the poorer women clothes and then set up a school for the children. A committee of Quakers visited the women and read to them. Elizabeth also found useful things for the women to do. She had an extraordinary influence over the prisoners, who crowded round and obeyed her almost as soon as she first appeared. An American visitor reported: "The wretched outcasts have been tamed and subdued by the Christian eloquence of Mrs. Fry."

She worked to improve conditions in other prisons, and helped homeless people and beggars. She also visited prisons in Europe and was welcomed by the kings of Holland, Denmark and Prussia.

**FUCHSIA.** The word fuchsia (pronounced *fewsha*) is easier to spell if one remembers Dr. Leonhard Fuchs, the 16th-century German botanist after whom this graceful shrub was named. The fuchsia most often seen in Great Britain has flowers drooping from long stalks, each one consisting of four red sepals surrounding a funnel of purple petals, out of which hang the style and the stamens. The fruit is a berry with many seeds. Other kinds of fuchsia vary in colour, some having red petals, and there are white fuchsias and fuchsias that give a dye. The shape, too, is not exactly the same in all kinds. In some species the petals are like little scales, and others have no petals at all.

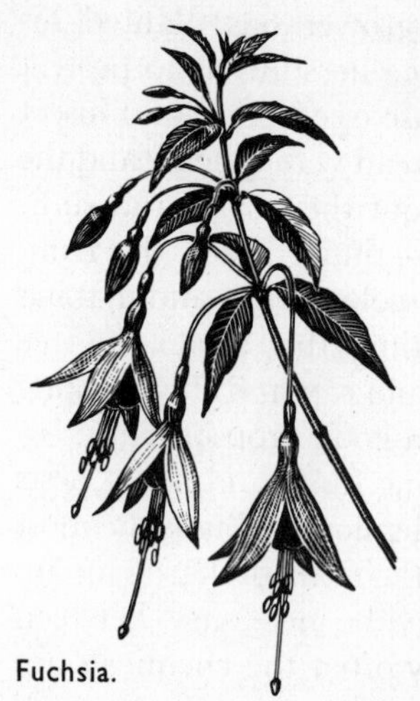
Fuchsia.

The fuchsia originally came from South America and New Zealand, but it is related to the English clarkia, godetia and evening primrose. Some fuchsias are rockery plants, while others cannot live out of doors. In Devon and Cornwall and the Isle of Wight, where the climate is mild, fuchsias are grown as hedges, which are scarlet when the flowers are out. The buds of the fuchsia pop when they are pinched.

**FUEL.** Substances that give heat when burnt are called fuels, and the process of burning is sometimes called *combustion*, on which there is a separate article. A fuel may be a solid, a liquid or a gas, and the heat from it may be used either directly, as in warming a house, or indirectly under a boiler to make steam for driving an engine. Sometimes the fuel is burnt in the engine (see INTERNAL COMBUSTION ENGINE).

About half the fuel used in the world is coal, on which there is a separate article. Coal can be used in lumps or ground to powder and taken through pipes to the furnace as is sometimes done in factory and power-station boilers. Wood supplies about one-twelfth of the world's fuel and is important in countries without coal. *Charcoal* is wood that has been charred by heating in an oven without air and is sometimes used for cooking because it is smokeless. Peat is partly formed coal dug out of bogs and marshes (see PEAT); it burns rather like wood but gives more heat.

The most important liquid fuels come from petroleum, which is natural oil found underground (see PETROLEUM). It is not much used in its natural state but made into fuels such as petrol, paraffin (kerosene), vaporizing oil and diesel oil. (See DISTILLATION.) The world's supply of petroleum may not last for many years longer and oil shale—a clay-like rock which gives off oil when heated—may become important as a fuel, since there is a great deal of it in many countries, including Scotland. *Benzole* is a liquid fuel like petrol obtained when coal is made into gas.

The fuel called natural gas, often found where there is petroleum, is a combination of hydrogen and carbon known as methane. It was discovered beneath the North Sea in 1965, and by 1975 is expected to provide about one-seventh of all Britain's energy requirements. (See NATURAL GAS.)

**FUJIYAMA,** or Mount Fuji, is a volcanic mountain on the south coast of Honshu in Japan and the highest in the country (12,388 feet). It last erupted in 1707 but steam still comes from the crater at the top and there are many hot springs near its foot.

It has long been looked on as a sacred mountain by the Japanese, who hope to climb it in a pilgrimage at least once in their lives. Part of the climb can be done on horseback but even so it takes ten hours. The most popular way is to spend the night in one of the rest houses near the top and then go to the summit in time to watch the sun rise.

*Camera Press*

There is always snow on the top of Fujiyama.

Seen from a distance it is a mountain of great beauty, having a very even, conical shape. Its lower slopes are thickly wooded and the upper ones covered with snow, which never wholly melts even in the hottest summer. The lovely summit cone sometimes seems to be floating in mid air when seen from the streets of Tokyo 60 miles away. The Japanese think of Fujiyama as an opened fan held down from heaven, and their artists never tire of painting pictures of it.

**FUNERAL RITES.** All the peoples of the world have special customs, or rites, which must be carried out very carefully at funerals. Many of the customs of other people may seem very strange to us, but it is easier to understand them if we remember why the customs have grown up at all. Almost every people believes that when a person dies he does not stop living altogether. His body stops living, so it must be buried or burnt or got rid of somehow, but another part of him, more important than his body, goes on into some other kingdom or kind of life. We call this part of him the soul. All the complicated customs of funerals have grown up because of the idea that the dead person still has a living soul or spirit.

Many of these customs come from two very important beliefs. One is that when the spirit goes into its new life it needs the same sort of things as people need in this life, such as food and drink. When people believe this they carry out special actions out of kindness to the spirit, so that it shall be comfortable in its new life. However, the second important belief is quite different—this is that the dead person's spirit will try to come back and do harm of some kind to the people who are still living. People who believe this will do everything they possibly can to keep the spirit away.

Among the most famous tombs are the pyramids of ancient Egypt. (See PYRAMID.) They were the tombs of the Egyptian pharaohs, or kings, and each pharaoh had his pyramid built while he was still alive. Beside each pyramid was a temple, and sometimes a waterway for the dead Pharaoh to be brought along it in a sacred boat. Later on, the Egyptians gave up building pyramids and instead made tombs in the rocks of deep valleys. The funeral ceremonies probably took place in the temples, and then the bodies were buried in secret. This was to prevent anyone stealing the precious objects that were put into the tombs or harming the body itself—for the Egyptians believed that if the dead body were destroyed the spirit would not be able to go on living in the other world.

In Britain nowadays people are usually buried in graves in cemeteries, but other peoples have had different customs. For instance, the Chinese people have always felt a great respect for the family, and until recently, whenever possible they buried their dead in ground which belonged to the family. When this was impossible, some earth from their land was taken to the place where the body was to be buried, even if this was in a foreign country. All this care was taken because the Chinese believed that the family land belonged to the spirits of the dead as well as to the people now living. Nowadays, however, these traditional burial ceremonies are no longer held in China.

Some peoples do not bury their dead at all. Many people in Great Britain and in other countries cremate (burn) the bodies, and when this is done the ashes may be put into a special jar to be kept, or else scattered. Some tribes put the dead bodies up in trees, the Parsees of India put them in sacred buildings called the Towers of Silence, where vultures come and eat the flesh, and some peoples place the bodies in boats which are sent out to sea.

In ancient times a man's tools or a woman's saucepans would often be put in the grave. Children were buried with their toys and kings with their treasures. Kings were supposed to need looking after in the next world, so in some countries their servants and wives were killed and buried with them. In many countries, however, the idea later grew up that models are just as good as the real thing. In China money made of silver paper, paper models of people, houses, horses and carriages, were carried in the funeral procession; then they were burnt, so that they might go to the spirit world with the dead person. In India the custom of killing a man's wife to go with him into the other world was kept up until only a century ago. The dead man's body was burned on a wood pile, and his wife had to throw herself into the flames as well. The practice was called *suttee*.

People try in many ways to prevent the spirits of the dead from coming back after the funeral to haunt or harm the living. The funeral may take place in the dark so that the spirit finds it hard to catch the living. In some countries the body is not taken out through the door of the house, but a special hole is made in the wall; often this hole is quickly shut up again to stop the spirit getting back in. The body is in many places carried out feet first, so that the spirit cannot see the way.

In Sweden people used to scatter seeds outside their house, believing that the spirit would stop to count them, and so not try to get into the house. In other places the dead were often buried on the other side of some water, for spirits were supposed not to be able to come back across water.

Nevertheless, most funeral rites are carried out to show respect and love for the dead person and his family's sorrow at losing him.

**FUNGI.** The great fungus family consists of oddly shaped plants that contain no chlorophyll and so are not green, as other plants are, and depend on living or dead substances to supply them with food to enable them to grow. Everywhere in the world where life is possible fungi are found growing on living or dead animals or plants in the air, the soil and the water, but many of them are so small that they are invisible. Other kinds of fungi, besides the mushrooms eaten for breakfast and the toadstools in the woods, are found on rotten fruit, decaying wood, mouldy leather, paper and fabrics and diseased crops. At the same time, however, life would hardly be possible for man without fungi, for they are largely responsible for the decay of dead plants and animals which enriches the soil. (See the articles MUSHROOM and TOADSTOOL.)

The fungi are very simply formed. They are made up not of stems, leaves and roots but of fine branching threads called hyphae, which are delicate, thin-walled structures containing the living substance protoplasm. Protoplasm is made up, among other elements, of oxygen, hydrogen, carbon and nitrogen. The hyphae grow rapidly in wood, jam, soil or whatever the fungus is feeding on. Sometimes, as in the tree-destroying honey fungus, quite thick, stringy branches can be seen growing under the bark of the tree.

Like ferns, fungi reproduce themselves by spores, not seeds. Each spore is a very tiny cell which has a protective coat and contains protoplasm. They are so light that they can be carried by the slightest breeze to every part of the earth's surface, and they are even found in the air over the North Pole. Spores are able to remain alive for some time but only when they alight on damp substances are they able to develop and put out branched hyphae.

Mushrooms and toadstools are the spore-producing parts of some of the larger fungi. They only grow at certain times of the year when conditions are just right, which is why they are found in the damp woods and fields of autumn. If a toadstool is placed on a piece of paper and covered over with a jar to prevent air currents from blowing the spores away, after an hour or more a dusting of spores will be found on the paper in the exact arrangement of the gills of the toadstool. (Gills are the thin plates or ribs on the underside of the toadstool.) A ripe mushroom can produce 40,000,000 spores an hour, while the giant puffball, which is the size of a football, is said to produce 7,000,000,000,000 spores. It is not surprising that fungus spores are always present in the air, and when a piece of germ-free soil is exposed to the air for a few minutes a growth of fungus appears on it.

As fungi possess no chlorophyll and so cannot build up their own food by a process known as photosynthesis (see PLANT), they live on what is called organic food, which means food that has already been made by a living plant or animal. They give out chemical substances called enzymes which help to change the food into liquid. The liquids are then absorbed into the fungus and broken down to supply energy for growth, in the same way that coal or wood is burned to release energy in the form of heat. Fungi which live on *dead* organic substances, such as the remains of plants or animals, are called *saprophytes*, and among them are the mushroom, pin-mould and many mildews. Fungi which live on *living* plants or animals are called *parasites* (see PARASITE). Plant parasites include rusts, which do a great deal of damage to crops.

A few parasitic fungi attack people and cause disease. In Great Britain the two most common are athlete's foot and ringworm, about each of which there is a separate article. There is also thrush, which causes white patches to appear on the lips or inside the mouth. More serious fungus diseases are found in the tropics.

Fungi do great damage to crops, and it is thought that £500,000,000 is lost each year from attacks of downy mildew on the grape vine alone. Then there is the dreaded potato blight, which in 1846 and 1847 brought about a potato famine in Ireland and caused many thousands of Irish people to die of starvation. In a rainy summer the spores from infected potatoes in the west of Ireland could be carried on the south-west wind during May and reach the potato-growing district of eastern England in July.

The fungus that causes the disease known as rust of wheat spends part of its life growing on the wheat and the other part growing on the barberry plant. The barberry is a thorny shrub with yellow flowers and, later, blue-black berries. It grows in hedges and woods which may be quite near a wheat field. The disease has been much reduced in England by clearing away the barberry plants. Other common fungus diseases are the green moulds on fruits, the grey moulds on vegetables, black rot of fruit and dry rot.

There are two main ways of preventing the spread of fungus diseases. One is to spray special solutions or dust powders over plants so that a thin poisonous film prevents the spores of the fungus from developing. The other method is to breed strains of crop plants which do not get fungus diseases.

The study of fungi is called mycology, and today there are mycologists at all large universities and agricultural research stations. The fungi are grown on transparent jelly in glass dishes and their growth, life-history and decaying effects are studied. This "controlled growth" is called a culture, and it was from a culture of *Penicillium,* the very common green fungus that grows on fruit and jam, that the existence of what is now known as the drug penicillin was discovered. (This is explained in the articles FLEMING, SIR ALEXANDER, and PENICILLIN.)

Penicillin is a recent discovery, but for many thousand years people have used fungi to make cheese and alcoholic drinks. The Old Testament mentions leavened bread, which is bread that has risen and become light by the production of carbon dioxide gas from yeast, which is a type of fungus, in the dough. Other yeasts produce enzymes, which break down sugar into alcohol in beer and wine making and so bring about what is called fermentation (see YEAST). The green mould *Penicillium* is used to ripen some cheeses.

No doubt, however, the most important activity of fungi is that of feeding on organic material and causing decay. The dead leaves of plants, for example, are slowly decayed by fungi and bacteria, first into a brown humus, or leaf-mould, then into smaller particles and finally into the simple mineral parts of the soil such as potash, phosphate and nitrate. These minerals are then taken up by new plants, which in their turn die and decay and provide more minerals for food. At the same time the carbon in the dead plants is released into the air and used by living plants in photosynthesis to build up more material. Man uses fungi to decompose, or break down, leaf-mould and other substances when he builds a compost heap.

**FUNNY BONE** is the name generally given to the lump at the very tip of the elbow. Although it is called the olecranon by doctors, it has got the name of funny bone because a light bang on it gives a "funny" feeling. The bone is just below the skin, and next to it there is an important nerve which is often touched when the funny bone is hit and causes a curious tingle to run right down to the little finger.

The funny bone is the end of the ulna, which is one of the bones of the forearm, on the same side as the little finger.

**FURIES, THE.** In their legends the Romans gave the name *Furiae*, the Furies, to the avenging spirits which the Greeks called Erinyes. With serpents wreathing round their heads instead of hair, carrying whips and burning torches, the three Furies were said to pursue and punish evil doers, especially anyone who had murdered a member of his family.

**FURNACE.** A furnace is a kind of oven giving a very great heat. It is used chiefly either for *smelting*—that is, getting metals out of the ores (earth and rock) containing them, or for melting metals so that they can be cast (see FOUNDING). The heat depends on the fuel used and the rate of burning it, and as all burning needs oxygen the heat is increased by blowing more air (which contains oxygen) through the furnace. This can be done by having a tall chimney up which hot gases from the fire rise, sucking in more air behind them. Often, however, a furnace has *forced draught* made by a blower or powerful fans which push air into it.

A blast furnace for smelting iron is a giant hollow tower about 100 feet high. It is *charged* (loaded) from the top with iron ore, coke and limestone, and when it has been lit hot air is led into the lower part and blown up through it. The iron melts out of the ore and trickles down to the bottom and the earthy part of the ore melts to become what is known as slag. The limestone makes the slag more fluid and also draws impurities out of the iron. The slag floats on top of the molten iron so that each can be run off separately through holes in the wall. Such a furnace may work for five years, fresh charges being continually put in.

Most steel is made in *open hearth* furnaces from pig iron (cast iron lumps) obtained from a blast furnace. A huge shallow tank surrounded by a roof and walls of fire-resisting brick is charged with 100 tons or more of iron, and hot gas and hot air are blown in through holes above the tank, where they burn as a raging fire. When the iron is melted, iron oxide is added to it. This combines with the carbon in the iron to make the gas carbon monoxide, which burns off leaving steel.

Furnaces for melting metals are often heated

electrically, by passing electricity either through elements called "resistors" rather like the bars of an electric fire and surrounding the metal, or through the metal itself. In overcoming the resistance the electric current produces enough heat to melt the metal (see ELECTRICITY).

**FURNITURE.** Human beings have made and used furniture ever since they have lived in settled homes instead of wandering about from place to place. All furniture is either for human beings to rest on or for them to put things into or on to, but there are great differences in the furniture of different times and countries. In ancient times much splendid furniture was made, but nearly all of it has perished and now it is only from drawings, paintings or carvings that we know anything about the elaborate wooden furniture used by the ancient Egyptians or the fine metal, stone and marble pieces of the Romans.

Every country has its own style of furniture. Lands as far apart as Great Britain and China make furniture that looks very different, and even near neighbours like France and Italy have designs and fashions in furniture that are specially their own. In various periods one country has taken the lead in furniture designing over others. For instance, in the 18th century France led the rest of Europe in the design of graceful but ornamental and luxurious furniture, and pieces made then, in the reigns of Louis XV and Louis XVI, are very valuable.

The story of furniture in England really begins about the end of the 15th century. English furniture has nearly always been made of wood, and because it is not a very long-lasting material (as stone is, for instance) most of the examples of earlier furniture have perished. Another reason why we see hardly any furniture made before the 15th century is that during the middle ages, which were times of much danger and trouble, people did not feel inclined to make their homes more comfortable when there was every chance that they might be burned or plundered by an attacking army.

In early days the man who tackled almost every job in woodwork was the carpenter. He was accustomed to large joinery work such as house-building and so the furniture he made was rough and ready. At the end of the 17th century, nearer to our own times, it became the custom for certain woodworkers to specialize in making furniture only, and these cabinet-makers, as they were called, began new ways of working and showed great skill in the making of elegant furniture. Later still, about the middle of the 18th century, came the time when individual designers of furniture led the way.

Yet it is important to remember that styles

changed much more slowly in earlier times than they do now. Because roads were bad and transport was difficult, country districts were very often cut off from the outside world and a man might pass his whole life without travelling more than a mile or two from his home. So furniture made in the country by a local craftsman was often a great deal behind the style of the towns; sometimes it was made in an old style, sometimes in a new style but in an old-fashioned wood.

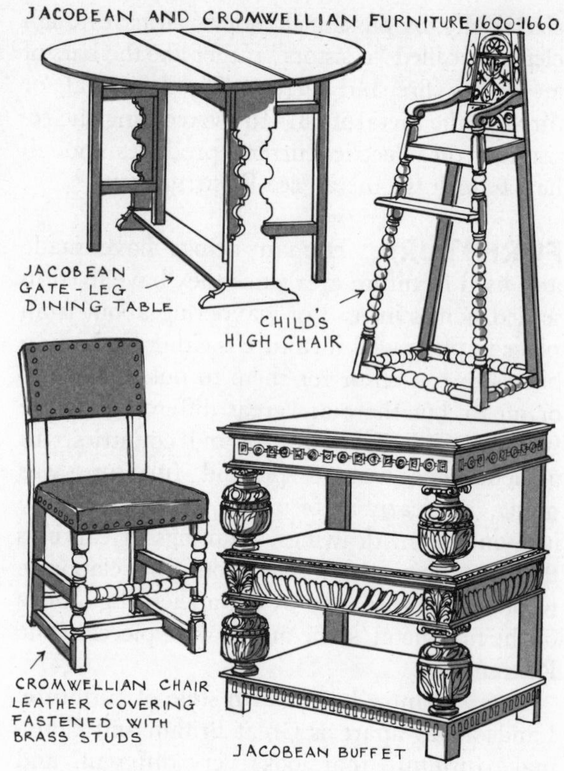


## The Age of the Carpenter

In the 15th and 16th centuries furniture was rare and even a wealthy home contained very little. For hundreds of years the chest was the most generally useful and the most common article. It was usually made of oak, a very strong and sturdy wood, and it served many purposes. It was used as a seat, as a table or shelf, as a treasure store or wardrobe and often as a bed as well. At first chests were merely hollowed-out tree trunks, later they were made of planks roughly fixed together, but in the 16th and 17th centuries they were often richly carved and were a prized possession in the household.

A chest did not make a very comfortable seat and at some time towards the end of the middle ages a clever craftsman thought of fitting one with a back and with pieces at the sides as arm-rests. This became the first kind of chair. Later still, the chest part underneath was no longer wanted, but for a long time carpenters still made a framework as an underneath part of their chairs, for this kept them steady and firm. At first chairs were only for the head of the household and other people sat on stools or benches. Another piece of furniture that developed from the chest was the settle, which provided seats for two or three people. It stood against the wall or by the fireplace.

Up to the 16th century tables in England were merely boards set up on trestles so that they could be taken down when not in use. In fact the early name for a table was a "board" and a sideboard was just another table at the side of the room, to put extra things on. Later, as life in the home became more settled, houses were built with separate rooms for different purposes, instead of everyone living and sleeping in the large hall. Fixed tables were made and others with pieces called leaves that could be drawn out, or with what are called "gate-legs" (legs that support flaps of the table but are not fixed to them and can swing inwards to let the flaps be folded down). Thus where space was limited the table could be made smaller when it was not being used.

Another kind of board was a "cup board". A cup board was an open structure of shelves or "boards" like bookshelves, used to hold drinking cups and other small things. Later it had doors fitted and fixed legs and top, and became the kind of cupboard we know today.

Bedsteads of wood were made in the early 16th century. Before that time people slept either on a chest or on a mattress on the floor, or even on just a pile of rushes. There were two kinds of bedstead, that with a panelled head and foot and the four-poster. By the time of Queen Elizabeth I four-poster beds were often huge structures, elaborately carved and surrounded with heavy embroidered curtains, so the sleeper was really lying in a room inside the bedroom.

It was close and unhealthy but houses were very draughty and it must have been very difficult to keep warm. These bedsteads were very expensive and we can tell that they were highly valued from the fact that people often mentioned them specially in their wills.

All this oak furniture was strong and long-lasting and a good deal of it has survived until now. It was often richly carved, at first with rather stiff patterns copied from church ornaments and later with less regular ones copied from nature. It is difficult for us, when we look at a piece of old oak furniture, to remember that oak in its natural state is a light-coloured wood and that therefore all the early furniture was light yellowish-brown in colour, sometimes with the carving painted in brighter colours. The dark brown colour which we now think of in connection with old oak furniture is simply the result of hundreds of years of use in people's homes and constant polishing.

In the early 17th century, which is called the Jacobean period because James I was the king and Jacobus is Latin for James, people wanted to make their furniture more comfortable. Chairs began to be upholstered (padded and covered) and chairs were made without arms as well as those with arms. Furniture was now much more plentiful and chairs were often made in sets of six, eight or a dozen of a kind, perhaps two or four of which would be with arms and the rest without. Beech was much used at this time for furniture and, as it is not such a solid, heavy wood as oak, it was carved more easily. Many chairs and settles were made with the carving of the back in a kind of openwork pattern. At this time, too, cane-work began to be used for the seats of chairs and often for a strip down the middle of the back.

The time of Oliver Cromwell, in the middle of the 17th century, was a dull period in furniture, when luxury was discouraged and plain, simple oak furniture was the fashion. Chairs were often covered with thick leather nailed on to the wooden frame with big brass-headed nails. Many country craftsmen, however, were not affected by the new fashion and continued to make oak furniture very like the kind which had been made for many generations before.

## The Age of the Cabinet-Maker

The period beginning with the return of Charles II to the throne of England was a remarkable one as far as furniture was concerned. It was the period when some craftsmen called cabinet-makers began to specialize in making furniture much more skilfully and finely than the carpenters had been able to do. They used a new wood, walnut, which has a far finer grain, or texture, than oak, is more easily worked and

is altogether a lighter, gayer kind of wood. They introduced a new process into furniture-making called veneering. Veneering consists of sticking a thin sheet of wood, usually very beautifully marked, on to a strong but less interesting wood. This process was something entirely new and enabled many patterns and decorations to be made which had not been possible when only solid wood was used. Many of the new ideas for furniture-making came from Europe, where Charles II had lived during his exile (see Charles II), and many French and Dutch craftsmen returned to England with him to make beautiful-looking furniture.

Many new types of furniture began to be required, for the design of grand houses developed considerably and there were now dining-rooms, libraries and salons (drawing-rooms where guests were entertained) for which furniture was needed. Cabinets, bookcases, bureaux (writing desks with drawers), chests of drawers, clocks and other pieces were in great demand for middle-class households as well as for those of the wealthy. Lacquered furniture (lacquer is a type of coloured varnish which was used mostly in China, Japan and other Eastern countries) became very popular, although it was never as well done in Europe as in the East. Furniture was also painted and it became extremely fashionable to decorate furniture by inlaying, or embedding, coloured woods in the surface. This is known as marquetry. Instead of wooden bedsteads, carved or panelled, there were now bedsteads with very high bedposts covered in fabric hangings, often with an ornamental top decorated in gilt.

The furniture made during the later 17th century and the first half of the 18th century was light and elegant to look at, very different from the solid and heavy pieces made in the 16th and early 17th centuries. Legs and columns of furniture were often "twist turned" like curly sticks of barley sugar and there were all sorts of other elegant details which showed how greatly the skill of the cabinet makers had surpassed that of the earlier carpenters. Among the new details were cane seats and backs, cabriole (curved) legs and "ball-and-claw" feet shaped like an animal's claw grasping a ball.

Walnut is a wood with a beautiful grain, so it was left plain to show its own pattern and carving was no longer used. Chairs could now be made without rails joining the legs underneath, and the backs were usually shaped to make them more comfortable to lean against.

From about 1720 yet another wood was used for furniture-making—mahogany. This was imported from the West Indies, though it was called Spanish mahogany, and it is a hard, heavy, very reliable wood. It was not used as a veneer as walnut had been, for the pattern of the grain is not particularly interesting. The cabinet-makers did not just make the same shapes in the new wood, but made new shapes suited to the plain, less decorative material. Doors were shaped in panels once more instead of being decorated with bands of veneers of different kinds of wood, carving was used again and most of the furniture was very solid-looking. Yet although it was solid it had curves; it had nothing like the square shapes of the oak period, but was also very different in form from the tall and graceful shapes of the walnut period.

## The Age of the Designer

The 18th century was a prosperous time during which some very fine furniture was produced by very famous makers and designers of furniture, especially Chippendale, Adam, Hepplewhite and Sheraton.

It is important to remember that although these great men were working out styles in their own individual way, they were not the only people using such styles and not every piece of furniture in those styles was made by the famous designers. The name "Chippendale", for example, has come to be used for a style of furniture of the type that was made so particularly well in the workshops of Thomas Chippendale, but not all pieces of furniture now called Chippendale were actually made or designed by Chippendale himself or even by his assistants.

There are many types of Chippendale furniture, some influenced by French ideas, others in Chinese style and some with square shapes. Chippendale himself was a practical cabinet-maker who published drawings of his designs, many of which are very fine. One new feature in chairs introduced during the Chippendale period was the square leg, either left completely plain or shaped in grooves. The splats (the middle pieces) of the backs of chairs were often carved in very elaborate, curly patterns. Bureaux, bookcases, settees, grandfather clock cases and tables are among other typical examples of the Chippendale style. All were made in mahogany. (See CHIPPENDALE, THOMAS.)

George Hepplewhite worked during the second half of the 18th century, which is often called the golden age of cabinet-making. His style was simple, with only a few touches of decoration. He used inlay, painting and gilding as well as carving. Famous types of chair made by Hepplewhite were the shield-back and the hoop-back. The front legs of his chairs were always tapered, which gave an impression of lightness, though these chairs were extremely strong as well.

Robert Adam was an architect and not a practical cabinet-maker. However, when he designed a house he also designed furniture to go with it and he required every detail, even the ornament of a sideboard, to fit in with the whole design. For decoration he used light carving, marquetry and inlay in delicate woods such as satinwood, rosewood and harewood. Sometimes he would decorate pieces with small painted or china plaques. He liked to copy the shapes used in Greek and Roman architecture in his designs for furniture. (See ADAM, ROBERT.)

Thomas Sheraton was the last of the great 18th-century furniture designers. His work is in

many ways similar to that of Hepplewhite, though his chairs were usually lighter, with low backs and arms which came from the back in a continuous sweep instead of being separate pieces. He used inlay and painted panels as decoration. Towards the end of his life Sheraton produced many not very good designs, overladen with unnecessary ornament. The finest period of English furniture was ended.

## The 19th and 20th Centuries

At the beginning of the 19th century, when the Prince Regent, later to be King George IV, was ruling, some charming furniture was made, in what was called the Regency style. It was light and elegant and one of its typical features was its striped upholstery.

Gradually, however, as machines were invented that could cut and fix together pieces of wood much quicker than was possible by hand, there were many changes in furniture-making. A great deal of furniture was mass-produced by machines in factories instead of being made by individual craftsmen, and although some of it was solid and well made a great deal was not well designed and was spoilt by having far too much decoration and ornament. The furniture manufacturers copied all sort of styles of decoration from the past and used them on pieces of furniture that were not suited to them.

The rooms of Victorian times were often overcrowded with this dark, heavy, ornate furniture—chairs and tables with heavy legs, sofas with curved arms and a great deal of upholstery, frequently in dark-coloured plush or velvet and fringed with bobbles. Upholstered furniture was now much more comfortable owing to the invention of coiled metal springs.

There were some designers who were not content, however, and towards the end of the century William Morris, who hated the shoddy factory-made goods, tried to encourage craftsmanship and good designing once again. Before very many years had passed, in the 1930s, a new kind of furniture was beginning to appear—inexpensive furniture in simple shapes, decorated only with the natural colour of the wood and the pattern of the grain.

Twentieth-century furniture is very varied because of the use of many kinds of new materials—beautiful woods from all over the world, and also plywood, laminated board (thin layers of wood stuck together), metal, plastic and glass. New processes, such as steaming, pressing or moulding wood, have made new shapes in furniture possible. Because many people today live in flats and small houses where there is not a great deal of space, built-in and "unit" furniture (in which various items, such as bookcases, desk and cupboards, are made in the same kind of pattern and can be bought separately) has become very popular.

As well as the new designs, copies, or reproductions as they are called, of older "period" styles are also produced. Some of these are well made, but many are badly designed with decoration stuck on to imitate hand-carving. Good modern furniture, however, is not necessarily

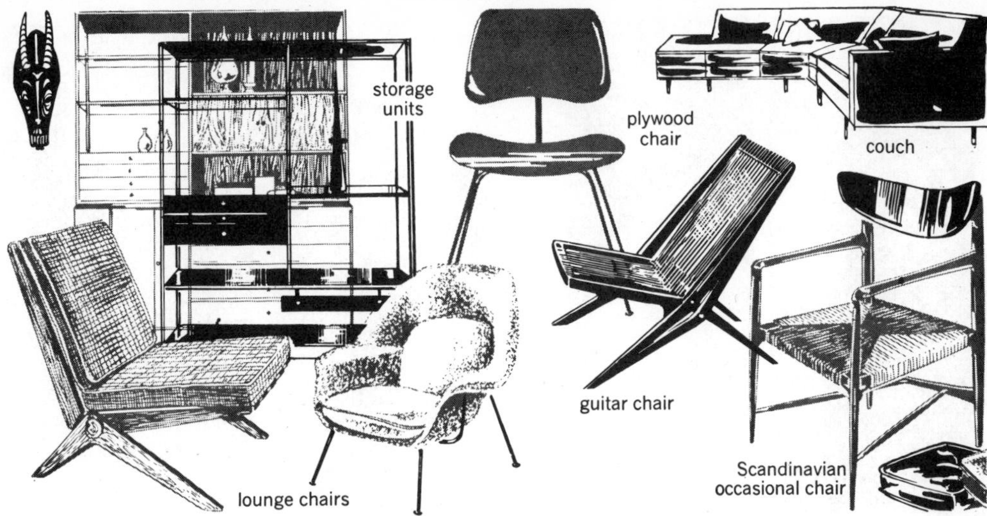


expensive, whereas the beautiful hand-made pieces of the past were all made for the few wealthy people who could afford them. Today for the first time, because of modern mass production methods, people can furnish their homes with furniture that is reasonably cheap, looks pleasant and is hard wearing.

**FURS.** Animal skins with the hair still on them were the earliest form of clothing and are known as furs. They are both warm and beautiful, and the finest have been used on the robes of kings and nobles since the 8th century.

The skins of tame animals, such as sheep and lambs, kids and the domestic rabbit, have been used for furs for a long time. Some other animals are kept on farms for their skins, among them being silver foxes and minks.

Wild animals are killed for their fur, and the leading fur trading company in the world is the Hudson's Bay Company, which has been sending traders into Canada to seek furs since the 17th century. Canada has many fur-bearing animals, but some valuable ones also come from the United States, South America, Africa, Australia and Siberia.

Seals are usually killed by being clubbed when they are on land, and land animals are trapped. They are generally caught at midwinter in cold countries, as their fur is then thickest and best. The furs are sent to the main fur trade cities—London, New York, Montreal, Leningrad—where buyers come from all over the world. The prices depend upon the kind of fur, its quality and colour, and upon the season's fashion, as furs are now mostly made into women's coats.

## Dressing and Dyeing

Furs have to be dressed, or prepared, before they can be made into coats. First they are soaked in water and any flesh left on the inside of the fur is cut away with a sharp knife. The furs are then put into vats of chemicals which make them soft and easily stretched. After drying, the furs are cleaned with sawdust in large revolving drums. Some furs, like beaver, mink and silver fox, are used in their natural colours, but many cheaper ones like rabbit, squirrel and marmot are dyed.

Dressed and dyed furs are bought by the furrier or coat manufacturer. He selects the number required for a coat, matches them carefully for quality and colour, cuts them to a pattern and then sews them together with special machines. The coat is then damped with water and stretched and shaped on a large wooden board by driving in small nails all along the edge. After it is dry, the coat is removed from the board, softened in a revolving drum with sawdust and then finished.

The number of skins in a coat depends on the size of the fur. A coat of sealskin needs only 5 or 6 skins, a mink coat about 60, Persian lamb about 25 and ermine about 300.

The value of the fur varies according to its

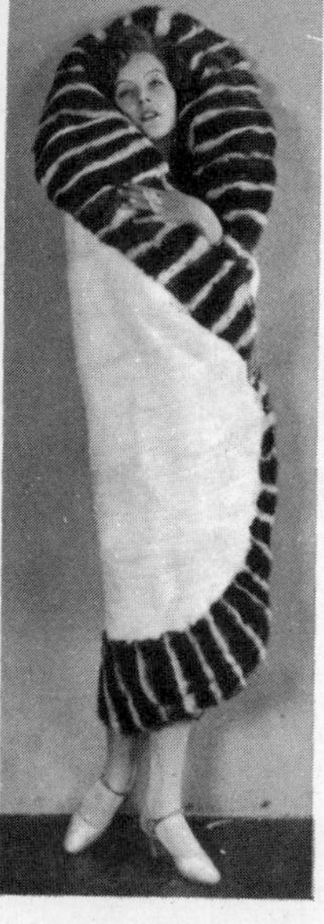

Fashion in furs: Russian sable (about 1905); ermine with black and white trimming (about 1925); wild mink (the 1930s); modern Italian lamb.

*Left: Courtesy, Mander and Mitchenson. Other photos: Radio Times Hulton Picture Library.*

quality, its colour and the needs of fashion. The most valuable furs are the Russian sable and the chinchilla (once very rare but now being farmed in several countries). The cheapest furs are rabbit and mole. A silky fur is worth more than a coarse one, and a thick, dense fur more than one with comparatively few hairs. In the list below are given the more important furs and the countries from which they come. There are separate articles on most of the animals whose fur is described.

*Beaver* was the first fur sold by the Hudson's Bay Company in 1671 and it is still supplied by Canada.

*Chinchilla* are found wild in the Andes Mountains of South America. Many are reared on farms.

*Ermine.* The small, white, silky ermine is used on royal robes. It comes from Canada and Siberia. (Ermine is the name given to the stoat and other members of the weasel family when they are in their white winter coats.)

*Leopard* comes from Africa.

*Marmot* fur is usually dyed and comes from Russia and China.

*Marten* is another Canadian fur. It is coarser than the more valuable Russian sable.

*Mink.* There are now more mink reared on farms than are caught in the wild state. There are many farms in the United States, Canada and Great Britain, and the total number of mink produced each year is about 7,000,000.

*Mole* is the only fur which comes from the British Isles. Millions are caught every year.

*Musquash.* Another name for the musquash is muskrat, and it is a rat-like animal living in water. The United States supplies up to 10,000,000 musquash furs every year.

*Nutria* comes from the South American animal called the coypu.

*Ocelot.* The beautifully marked ocelot is also a South American fur.

*Opossum.* The United States and Australia supply opossum furs.

*Otter.* Some of the best fur comes from the Canadian otter. The sea otter, which comes from the Bering Sea, is very rare and valuable.

*Persian Lamb.* Persian lambs do not come from Persia. The best are farmed in Turkestan and Afghanistan and several millions are bred in South-West Africa.

*Rabbit.* Large numbers of tame rabbits are provided for fur by France and Belgium.

*Red Fox* fur comes either from Alaska or Siberia.

*Russian Sable.* The most prized of all fur is the Russian sable, which comes from Siberia.

*Skunk* fur comes from the United States and is black with a broad white stripe.

*Seal.* Like the sea otter, the fur seal comes from the Bering Sea, off the Alaska coast. It is always dyed either black or brown.

*Silver Fox.* Nearly all silver fox fur comes from farms in Canada.

*Squirrel.* The red Canadian squirrel is used in large numbers and is always dyed. The best come from Alberta. The Siberian squirrel is large and grey and is of fine quality.

*White Fox.* Sometimes called the Arctic fox, this fur comes from northern Canada and Greenland.

# FUN WITH PHYSICS

*by Alison Crawshaw*

*Don't think that physics is only for people who smash atoms or fly to the Moon—remember that even they had to make a start once. All the experiments described can easily be done in your own home. Most of them cost nothing to prepare and none costs more than a shilling or two. For convenience, there are six sections in this article:* GENERAL PHYSICS; HEAT; SOUND; LIGHT; MAGNETISM; and ELECTRICITY.

# GENERAL PHYSICS

You may be surprised to learn that the PRESSURE OF THE AIR all round you is nearly 15 pounds on every square inch. You might suppose that this would be enough to shatter windows and knock people over. So it is if it is one-sided, but fortunately it usually is not. For example, an empty tin can is supporting this pressure all over its surface, both outside and inside. The pressures therefore balance and cancel each other out. But if the air inside is removed or partly removed with a pump, the outside pressure becomes so much greater than the inside pressure that the can collapses. It is crushed by the air pressure outside it. The pressure of the air is known as the *atmospheric pressure*.

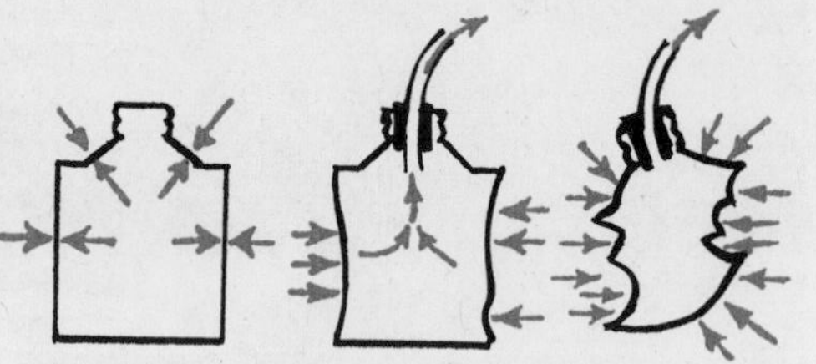

## 1. To show that air exerts an upward pressure

The atmospheric pressure anywhere is the same in all directions – downwards, upwards and sideways. Our first experiment shows that this pressure – and therefore the *upward* pressure – will support the weight of a full glass of water.

Fill a drinking glass with water, and place a piece of card or stiff paper over the top when the glass is absolutely full (this is important). With your hand over the paper, carefully turn the glass upside down. You will find that you can take your hand away without the paper falling off. Now put the glass and paper on a smooth-topped table. You will be able to slide the glass off the paper.

To empty the glass without spilling the water, hold a bowl at the edge of the table. Slide the upturned glass until it is just over the edge of the table and catch the water.

You can also do this experiment with a handkerchief instead of paper.

## 2. Peeling a piece of banana by air pressure

Chop a piece an inch long out of the middle of a banana, leaving the peel on. You also need a cake candle, a few inches of fuse wire, and an empty quart bottle whose mouth is narrower than the banana. (A wine bottle will do.)

Hang the cake candle on the fuse wire, light it, and lower it half way to the bottom of the bottle. Then immediately hold the piece of banana over the mouth of the bottle. The banana will glide out of its skin into the bottle with a sucking noise.

Why? The burning candle uses up some of the air in the bottle and so lowers the pressure inside. The greater atmospheric pressure outside is enough to push the banana out of its skin and into the bottle.

## 3. To make a siphon

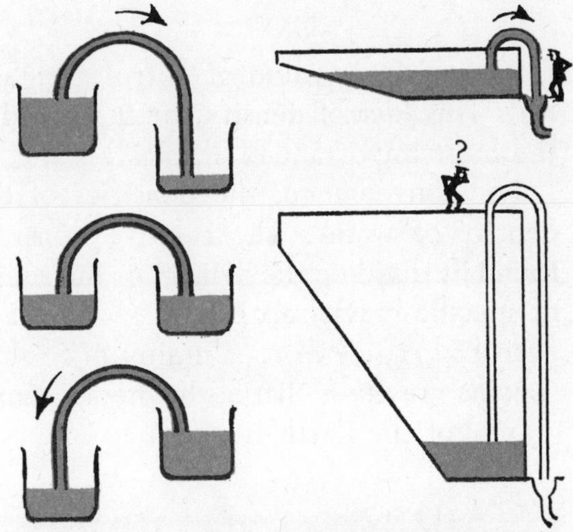


For this experiment you need a rubber tube and two glasses. Fill the tube with water either by laying it in a bowl of water or by sucking through one end. Pinch one end of the filled tube and place the open end in the higher glass A (see diagram) and the pinched end in the lower glass B. When you let go of the pinched end, water will flow from A to B as long as the level of the outlet in glass B is lower than the level of the water in glass A. To stop the flow, keep both ends under water and raise B until the levels of water are equal, as in the diagram. To reverse the flow, raise B until its water level is higher than that in A.

You can make this experiment more interesting by colouring the water with red or blue ink, or by starting off with one glass half full of water tinted blue and the other glass half full of water tinted pink.

By using a hose pipe as a siphon a swimming pool can be emptied, as long as the outlet is lower than the deepest part of the pool.

When using a siphon it is not possible to raise water to a height greater than about 34 feet above the level in the vessel that is being emptied. The downward pressure of a 34-foot column of water is greater than the atmospheric pressure, which would then not be enough to push the column "round the bend". So if the swimming pool were deeper than 34 feet (fortunately they never are) a siphon would not empty it completely.

OSMOSIS. Our next experiment shows another kind of pressure. When two liquids are separated by a porous membrane (that is, a skin through which liquid can seep), some of the weaker liquid will pass through the membrane into the stronger liquid. This movement is called osmosis, and the pressure exerted by the weaker liquid is osmotic pressure. In our experiment the weaker liquid is water.

## 4. To show osmosis with an egg

Remove a little shell from the sharp end of a raw egg, punch a hole with a skewer and push a straw about one inch into the egg. Then drop melted candlewax round the join so that it forms a seal. Next, carefully remove a small piece of shell (about the size of your little finger nail) from the blunt end, leaving the inner membrane undamaged. Place the egg in a glass of fresh water and leave it. After an hour or two you will see egg oozing out of the top of the straw. This is because the water has pushed through the membrane of the egg.

The roots of plants draw water from the soil by osmosis.

DENSITY. A gallon of petrol weighs less than a gallon of water: its density is less. This idea of density, or the weight of a unit volume of a substance, is one of the most important in physics.

For convenience, the densities of different substances are compared with the density of water. The relative density, or specific gravity, of any substance is found by dividing the density of the substance by that of pure water. Some examples of specific gravity are: cork 0·25 (that is, cork is one quarter as heavy as water,) petrol 0·75, ice 0·92, aluminium 2·70, lead 11·34, gold 19·3. The highest known specific gravity is that of the metals osmium and iridium, 22·6 The average specific gravity of the Earth is 5·52.

## 5. Salt water and fresh water have different densities

Place an egg in a glass and add tap water. The egg should remain at the bottom. (If it floats, it is *bad*. Try another!) Remove the egg, add salt to the water, and stir until you have a strong salt solution. You will find that the egg floats. Objects float when they are less dense (that is, have a lower specific gravity) than the liquid in which they are placed. A strong salt solution therefore has a greater density than an egg, and an egg has a greater density than tap water.

If you are very careful, you can adjust the strength of the solution until it has exactly the same density as the egg. The egg can then be placed anywhere beneath the surface, neither floating nor sinking.

## 6. A puzzle with moth-balls

This experiment, like the last one, depends on using something whose density is very close to that of water.

Pour a bottle of soda-water into a tumbler or a glass jug and add some moth-balls. They will sink to the bottom, only to rise again very shortly. After floating for some time at the top, they will once again sink. This will continue for several hours.

The explanation is that the soda-water gives out bubbles of carbon dioxide gas which tend to settle on the surface of the moth-balls. When enough bubbles have settled, the average density of the balls and bubbles together becomes less than that of the soda-water, so the balls rise. At the surface they lose their bubbles and sink again. In the end, the balls will stay on the bottom because there is no longer enough carbon dioxide to bring them up.

## 7. To weigh an apple without scales

For this experiment you need a measuring jug marked in fluid ounces and another larger jug. Fill the large jug to the brim with water, and place the smaller jug underneath the spout of the larger one so that it will catch overflowing water. Now float the apple in the large jug and catch the overflow. The weight of water caught is equal to the weight of the apple.

This result depends on the famous Principle of Archimedes, which states that when an object is weighed in a fluid, the apparent loss of weight is equal to the weight of the displaced fluid. If the object floats, *all* its weight is apparently lost. So the weight of the displaced fluid must equal the weight of the object.

Since a fluid ounce is the volume occupied by one ounce of water, a measuring jug measures not only volume but also weight of water, and in this case gives the weight of the apple.

Archimedes was a Greek mathematician who lived in the 3rd century B.C. It is said that he thought of his Principle when he stepped into a full bath, and that without bothering to put on his clothes he rushed into the street shouting *Eureka*! ("I have found it!")

CENTRE OF GRAVITY. Although the pictures showing the next three experiments are difficult to believe, the strange-looking balancing systems they show are quite easy to make. Each depends for its balance on the unusually low position of its centre of gravity.

The centre of gravity of an object is the point at which one may imagine the whole of the weight of the object to be concentrated. An object will balance when a vertical line through its centre of gravity passes through the point of support.

## 8. The balancing penny

Arrange a penny and two forks on the edge of a tumbler as in the diagram. One would expect the whole system to fall outside the tumbler. The reason why it does not is that the handles of the forks, being backswept, bring the centre of gravity of the whole system directly beneath the rim of the tumbler.

## 9. The hesitating diver

Push one end of a pencil through a potato and then stick a fork into the potato as shown in the diagram. Now adjust the pencil and fork so that the point of the pencil balances on the edge of a table. Cut out or draw a little paper figure of a high-diver and gum the foot of it to the pencil. The diver will bob up and down on his pencil diving-board if you rock it slightly.

## 10. The swaying fisherman

Make the fisherman by using a large and a small cork for his body and head and four pins for his legs and arms. The two corks should be gummed together. Draw a face on the small cork. Now push one end of a piece of stiff wire into the fisherman's chest and the other end into a fairly large potato. (A coat hanger made from untwisted wire will do for the wire.) Place the fisherman on the table or mantelpiece so that the potato hangs below his feet. He will rock backwards and forwards for a long time when given a little push. With care, you can even make him balance on one leg.

# HEAT

To understand what is meant when we talk about heat it is necessary to know a little about the structure of matter.

WHAT IS MATTER? The matter which forms all substances – whether solid, liquid or gas – is made up of atoms. There are more than 100 different kinds of atom and each different kind is called an element. Examples of elements are: hydrogen, oxygen, nitrogen, sodium, calcium, chlorine, carbon, iron, lead, tin, mercury, copper, silver, gold, radium and uranium.

Now when atoms of different kinds are bound together, they form what is called a compound. Some familiar compounds are: water, which is composed of hydrogen and oxygen; common salt, composed of sodium and chlorine; chalk, composed of calcium, carbon and oxygen; and sugar, composed of carbon, hydrogen and oxygen.

The smallest possible unit of a compound is called a molecule. A molecule must contain at least two atoms. Both atoms and molecules are so tiny that they cannot be seen with a microscope. A cubic inch of water contains many millions of molecules.

HOT AND COLD. Although it may seem surprising when we consider the solid nature of the objects round us, all molecules and atoms are in a state of continual movement. For example, the average speed of molecules in the air at ordinary temperatures is as much as 1,000 miles an hour.

When we boil a kettle we give the molecules of water more speed; and as this speed increases so does the temperature of the water. At a certain point, some of the molecules move so fast that they escape from the water and leave the others behind. The water is then boiling; that is, changing from a liquid to a gas or vapour.

On the other hand, if we cool water until the speed of its molecules has fallen sufficiently, it freezes; that is, the molecules no longer move fast enough to keep the water liquid.

All the elements can exist in the three states of solid, liquid and gas. Like water, many compounds can also exist in these three states, though some are decomposed (broken up) by heating, either into simpler compounds or into their elements.

You may wonder what happens to substances as they are cooled to lower and lower temperatures. Does there ever come a point when the molecules are so cold that they are completely still? The answer is that this point, which is called the absolute zero of temperature, has never been reached, although scientists have come extremely close to it – close enough for nitrogen and oxygen, the chief gases making up ordinary air, to become solid!

EXPANSION. The application of heat to nearly all substances – whether solid, liquid or gas – causes expansion; that is, the substance swells. This has many important consequences in everyday life. For example, railway lines must be laid with gaps between the ends of the rails to allow for expansion, as they would otherwise buckle and twist in hot weather. Because of expansion, the lines from London to Edinburgh are sometimes 330 yards longer in summer than in winter. (Of course, they cover the same distance, but in hot weather the gaps are reduced.)

When a substance is cooled it contracts, or shrinks. Use of this is often made in engineering. For example, the steel bands forming the tyres of railway carriage wheels are made slightly smaller than the wheel. The tyre is then heated and expands enough to allow it to be fitted over the wheel. When it cools it grips the wheel tightly.

The forces set up by expansion may be enormous. For this reason, one must never heat a sealed vessel (whether empty or not). A stoppered bottle will explode if heated over a gas-ring because of the expansion of the air inside, and the flying glass may injure someone seriously. Water as it freezes to become ice increases in volume by about one-tenth, which is why water pipes sometimes burst in very cold weather.

## 11. The expansion of air

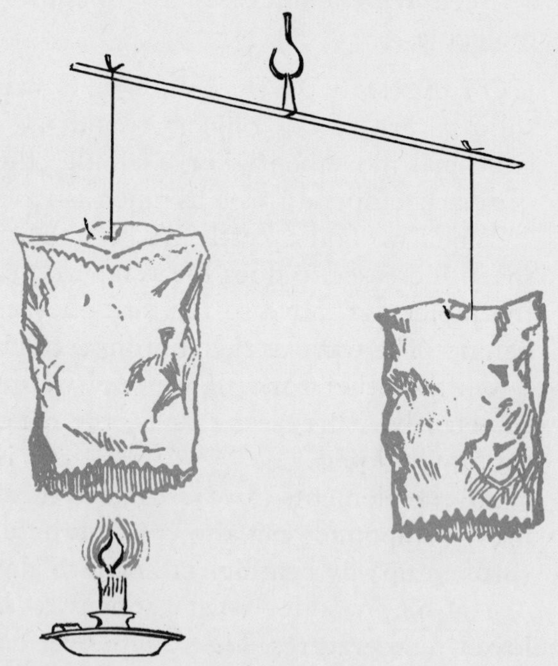

Using thread, hang two paper bags of the same size and weight mouth downwards on the simple balance shown in the diagram. Adjust the balance so that it is level, then hold a lighted candle under one of the bags. (If you find the bags won't balance exactly, hold the candle under the lower one.)

You will see the bag above the candle rise – mainly because of the upward flow of hot air. But the interesting thing is that the bag stays up for a while after the candle is removed. This is because the air in the bag above the candle expands and some air is pushed out of its mouth. There is then less air – and less weight – in that bag than before, so the balance is upset. Balance is restored when the air in the bag cools and contracts (shrinks) and more air is drawn in from outside.

**WARNING. Fire can be dangerous. Ask a grown-up to help you to set up this experiment safely.**

## 12. Ice and water – the great exception

Fill a four-ounce flat-sided bottle absolutely full of water, and tie the cork in firmly. (The bottle must be flat-sided. A medicine bottle will do.) Put the bottle inside a plastic bag and leave it overnight in the freezing compartment of the refrigerator. Next morning you will find that the bottle has broken, showing that the volume occupied by the ice is greater than the volume of the same weight of water.

This is very strange behaviour. We know that objects usually expand when they get *hotter*. Water obeys this rule in general, but close to its freezing point it actually expands on cooling. It is at its greatest density, or its heaviest, at a temperature of 4 degrees Centigrade, and a given weight of water then occupies its least volume.

The world would be a very different place if ice were heavier than water. Thick ice layers would form at the bottom of lakes, rivers and seas, with disastrous consequences for the fish and plant life. Icebergs would no longer float, and huge mountains of ice would form on the ocean bed.

HOW HEAT TRAVELS. There are three ways in which heat travels from one object to another: conduction, convection and radiation.

*Conduction* is the spreading of heat by simple contact. It takes place in solids, liquids and gases. Some substances, however, conduct heat much better than others. Thus metals are good conductors of heat; water, paper and fabrics are poor conductors of heat.

*Convection* is the movement of heat in liquids and gases caused by the currents set up by the upward movement of molecules from a hotter and less dense region to a cooler and denser region. This can be best understood by imagining a column of air heated at the bottom. As the air is heated it expands, and because of this expansion the air near the flame becomes lighter. This light air tends to rise and float on the heavier air that was above it. As this upward motion of molecules takes place, so the colder and heavier air above moves downwards to replace the heated and lighter air.

Because of convection currents, the air in a hot oven is hotter at the top than at the bottom, even though the bottom is nearer to the source of heat. If you don't believe this, make two pies or puddings of the same kind and cook them at the same time, one on the top shelf and the other on the bottom shelf. The one on the top shelf will be burnt by the time the one below is cooked.

*Radiation* is the method by which heat travels through empty space. Heat reaching an object by this method (such as that which reaches us from the Sun) is called *radiant heat*. Radiant heat travels in rays which are straight lines. It travels at the same speed as light, which is 186,000 miles a second.

## 13. The conducting penny

You have probably noticed that metal is a much better conductor of heat than wood. This is why one stirs with a wood spoon instead of a metal one, when cooking in a saucepan.

You can easily show the high conductivity of metal with a handkerchief and a penny. Wrap the handkerchief around the penny, stretching the fabric tightly. Get someone to press the hot end of a lighted cigarette against the wrapped coin. The heat is conducted to the coin and the handkerchief does not burn.

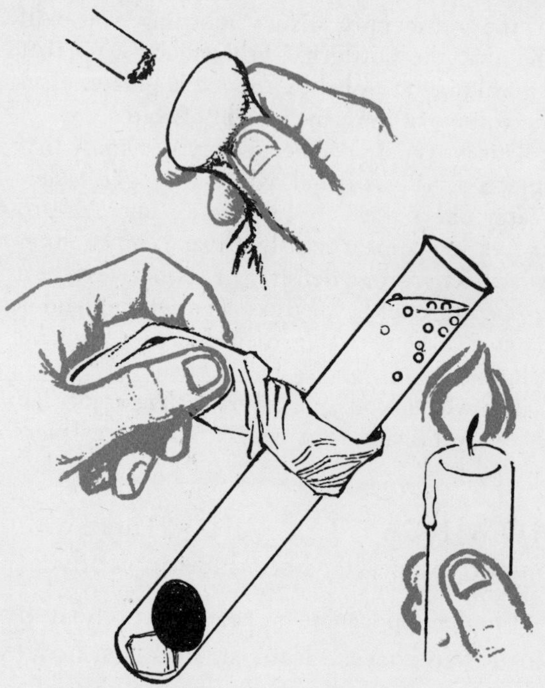

## 14. A poor conductor

Place a lump of ice in a test-tube full of water and add a pebble to keep the ice at the bottom of the tube. Make a holder for the test-tube from a strip of paper.

Hold the test-tube over a flame as in the diagram. You will find that you can actually boil the water at the top of the test-tube without melting the ice at the bottom. This shows how poorly water conducts heat.

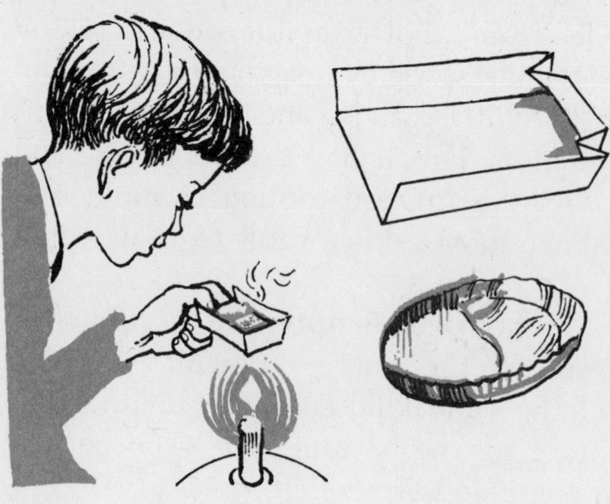

## 15. A paper saucepan

Although water is a poor conductor of heat, paper is an even worse one, as the following experiment very clearly shows.

Take a piece of paper and fold it and fold it as shown, so that it will hold a little water when tilted. Holding the paper "saucepan" in your hand, heat the water over a candle flame. You will find that you can boil the water at one end while the other remains cool enough for you to hold.

If you try the same thing using the metal top of a jar or a milk-bottle top as the "saucepan", you will soon learn the difference between a good and a bad conductor of heat. You will probably scorch your fingers long before the water boils!

# 16. An ink volcano

You can show the existence of convection currents in a liquid very easily with the help of some ink, two milk bottles and a small card.

Put four tablespoons of ink (or a little cochineal) into one of the empty milk bottles and fill to the top with hot water. Now fill the other bottle with cold or iced water. Make a small hole about a quarter of an inch across in the piece of card and place this over the milk bottle containing the cold liquid so that the hole is *not* over the water. Turn the bottle and card upside down, and place them over the other bottle so that their mouths are opposite. Now carefully pull the card so that the hole lies between the two bottles. You will immediately see a fine "volcano" as the hot coloured liquid rises through the hole by convection into the heavier, colder clear water. The ink will continue to mix until there are equal amounts in each bottle.

If you feel that this is exactly what would happen in any case, whatever the temperature of the water in the two bottles, you can easily do what scientists call a *control* experiment, to convince yourself that convection currents really do exist. To do this, simply repeat the experiment, using tap water in both bottles and tinting the water in one bottle with ink. This time, the movement of the coloured liquid into the upper bottle (though certainly still present) will be very much slower. However, after a time the ink will spread equally through both bottles.

This kind of mixing which is not caused by convection currents is called *diffusion*. It also takes place in gases.

# 17. The spinning snake

Hold a thimble firmly on a piece of writing paper and draw a circle by running a pencil round the base of the thimble. Then draw a slightly smaller circle inside this one. Cut out the inner circle. Draw the snake, with his eyes, tongue and mottled skin. Cut out the snake, whose length should be about one foot. Fit the thimble into the hole in the centre of the snake. Make a support by placing a long pencil (point upwards) into a cotton reel, and place the thimble on the point of the pencil.

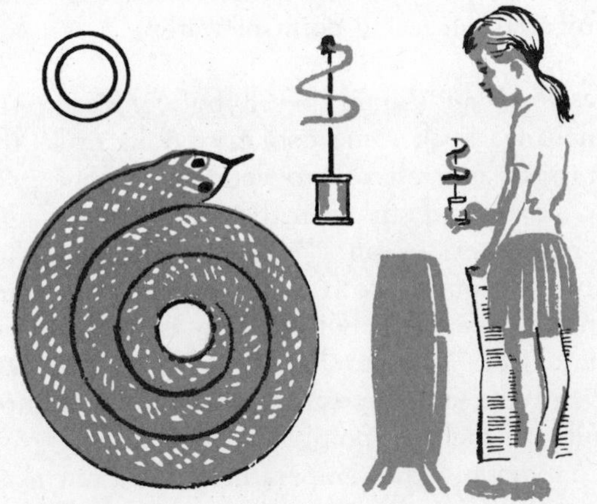

Now hold the reel above a radiator or oil heater. The rising hot air will make the snake spin round briskly. You can also make him spin with the heat from a lighted candle or match. Do not try holding him over an open fire or you may burn yourself as well as setting the snake alight.

## 18. Making a fire with a magnifying glass

As you may know, it is easy to use a magnifying glass to focus the sun's rays on paper or match-heads and set them on fire. This principle of focusing the radiant heat rays from the sun may be also used to cut a piece of string inside a corked bottle.

Attach a small piece of thin string to a cork with a drawing-pin and tie a weight (such as a small key) to the other end. Push the cork *lightly* into the bottle and focus the sun's rays on to the string with a magnifying glass. The string will catch fire and break within a few minutes.

For safety, the cork must not be pushed tightly into the bottle. Expansion of the air could blow out a loosely fitting cork, but if tightly corked the bottle might burst.

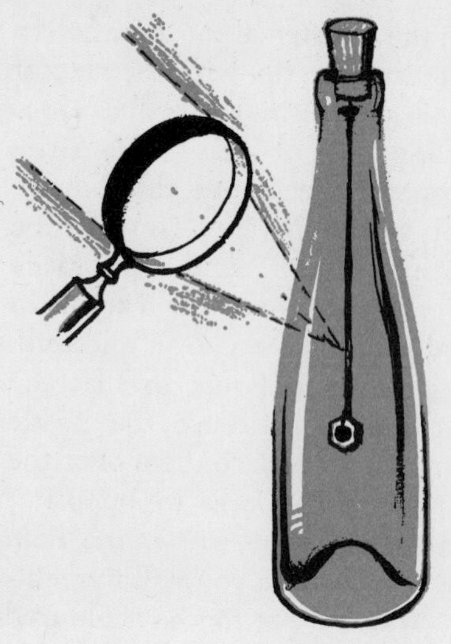

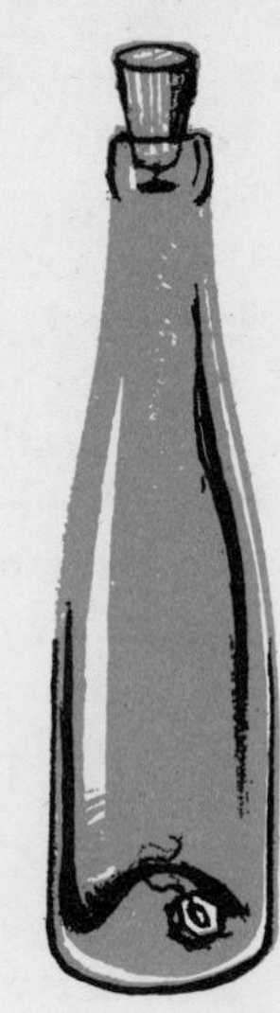

## 19. A trick with a lump of ice

You can play this trick on a friend. All you need is an ice cube, a cup of water, some table salt and a piece of string.

Produce the cup of water with the ice cube floating in it. Ask your friend if he can get the ice out of the cup by using the string. He must not touch the ice cube with his fingers or use any cutlery. When he has given up, wet the string, lay the end of it on the ice and sprinkle salt along each side of the string. In a few seconds you will be able to lift the ice with the string.

The explanation is that salt lowers the freezing point of water and so causes the ice to melt round the string, drawing heat from the nearby ice and the wet string. The string sinks in this layer of water, and when the water re-freezes the string is embedded firmly enough to support the weight of the cube.

Not only salt, but all dissolved substances lower the freezing point of water.

*Dissolving* should never be confused with melting. Even some cookery books make this mistake and tell you to "add the orange juice to sugar, and stir until the sugar has melted", when they mean "dissolved". Dissolving always requires both a solvent and something to be dissolved; but melting is a change of state from solid to liquid. Salt, for instance, dissolves readily in water at room temperature, but its melting point is about 800 degrees Centigrade – the temperature of red-hot iron.

# SOUND

Sound is produced by vibrations, or rapid to-and-fro movements, which are loud enough to be heard. Sound travels through gases, liquids and solids.

Sound will not travel through a vacuum. This can be shown in a laboratory by shaking a bell in a jar from which the air is gradually removed by a pump. As air is pumped out the sound becomes fainter and fainter, and if all the air is removed the bell cannot be heard at all.

The speed of sound in air is about 1,125 feet a second or 770 miles an hour. Sound travels more than four times as fast in water, and in steel its speed is fifteen times as great as in air. Light, on the other hand, travels at the amazing speed of 186,000 miles a second. This is why thunder is heard after a flash of lightning, although they take place at the same instant.

A pure musical note consists of vibrations of a single frequency or rapidity. The greater the frequency of vibration, the higher is the note. Thus middle C has a frequency of 264 vibrations a second; its octave, the C above middle C, has a frequency of 528 vibrations a second, or twice that of the lower note.

## 20. Spoon and fork music

Take a piece of string or (better) thin wire three or four feet long, and tie a spoon or fork to the middle. If you use string, make loops at each end for your fingers as shown in the diagram. Now put the ends of the string or wire to your ears and let the spoon or fork swing so that it strikes the edge of the table. You will hear chiming sounds. In particular, a spoon gives a bell-like note, rich in octaves.

The sound made by the vibrating spoon or fork is carried directly to your ears by the string or wire. These vibrations are stronger than those in the air and so a louder sound is heard. (You can easily check this by *not* putting the string to your ears.) You will find that larger spoons give lower notes; that is, their vibrations are of a lower frequency. You can also try this experiment with *pairs* of spoons and forks.

Nearly all metals, if free to vibrate, will produce notes rich in octaves when struck. Lead, however is an exception to this rule.

## 21. To make a string telephone

To make a string telephone you need two empty tins or (better) two paper cartons of the kind in which cream or yoghurt are sold. (Use a larger carton in preference to a smaller one.)

Make a hole in the centre of the base of each container and pass the ends of several yards of string through these holes. Fasten the string with a match inside each container. Now stretch the string quite tight and have a conversation with a friend at the other end of the "telephone". You will be surprised how well you can hear and be heard.

## 22. A trick with sound

Tell your friends that you are able to carry sound between your finger and thumb. Now hold a metal fork in the middle with the first finger and thumb of your left hand, and pluck the outer prongs with the first finger and thumb of your right hand. Pretend to carry the sound and to drop it into a glass. As you "drop it", touch the butt end of the fork on the table, so that the sound is amplified (magnified).

The table top acts as a *sounding-board*; that is, it is set in vibration by the fork. As the table top has a much larger area than the fork it sets a great deal more air in vibration.

## 23. Home-made orchestra

This experiment is fun if you make several "instruments" of different pitch and organize your friends to play a simple tune with them.

Flatten a drinking straw at one end for about half an inch and cut off two slanting corners as shown in the diagram. Put about $1\frac{1}{2}$ inches of this end into your mouth and blow hard. You will produce a musical note rather like that of a saxophone. (The flattened end of the straw, however, must not be completely flat; there must be room for the vibrating air to be set in motion.) If you make the straw shorter the note becomes higher, as the vibrating column of air becomes shorter. Find a tune with not too many different notes (such as "Good King Wenceslas") and make a straw for each note. Give one straw to each friend and conduct the orchestra.

# LIGHT

Light travels at the enormous speed of 186,000 miles a second. This speed is so great that it is impossible for us to imagine it, but we may think instead of the time taken by light to travel from one place in the heavens to another.

Light from the Moon, which is about 240,000 miles away, takes nearly $1\frac{1}{2}$ seconds to reach the Earth. Light from the Sun, which is about 93 million miles away, takes more than eight minutes to reach the Earth. Light from the nearest star, Alpha Centauri, takes more than $4\frac{1}{4}$ years to reach the Earth, or (as scientists say) Alpha Centauri is 4·3 light-years away. A light-year is a distance of nearly 6 million million miles.

## 24. The refraction of light

You may have noticed that water appears shallower than it really is. This is because the light rays are *refracted*, or bent, at the surface.

Look down into a glass full of water and put your finger on the outside where the bottom appears to be. (It helps to put a coin inside.) Now measure what this apparent depth is and compare it with the real depth.

You may make these measurements with various different vessels, such as milk bottles of different sizes, but you will always find that the real depth is about $1\frac{1}{3}$ times the apparent depth.

This ratio (that is, the number obtained from dividing the real depth by the apparent depth) is called the refractive index of the substance. For water it is about 1·33. For air it is of course 1·0. Other examples are: plate glass 1·52; turpentine 1·47; diamond 2·42. The greater refractive index of a substance, the slower does light travel in that substance and the more are light rays refracted on entering it.

Thus the speed of light travelling through a diamond is slowed down to a mere 77,000 miles a second. The diamond's refractive index is one of the highest known, and accounts for the brilliance of well-cut stones.

## 25. Rising penny and rising fish

## 27. Your master eye

You may not know it, but just as we are all either right-handed or left-handed, so are we all either right-eyed or left-eyed. It is easy to find out which you are. Look at a small distant object, such as the catch on a sash window, and try to cover this object with a finger held at arm's length. You will find that you cannot do this while you have both eyes open. Now shut your left eye. If your finger stays in the same place you are right-eyed. If your finger jumps to the left, you are left-eyed.

Your master eye is the one that leads your vision; the other eye follows. When you are doing something with only one eye, you will find it easier to use your master eye.

Place a penny at the far side of the bottom of a saucepan and fill up with water. Now step back, keeping your eye on the penny, and notice how it appears to rise. The water looks less and less deep as you step back. This effect is very striking if the saucepan is about six inches across and your eyes are about two feet higher than the saucepan.

If we now imagine that the penny is a fish, we can understand how refraction helps a fish to see fishermen. Without water, the fish in the drawing could not see the angler nor could the angler see the fish, but with the help of the refraction of water, both see each other. Like the penny, a fish appears to an angler to rise as the angler walks away.

## 26. Another rising penny

Place the penny in an empty cup and walk away until the penny is just out of sight. Now ask a friend to add water to the cup. The penny will come into view again. Stop your friend from adding water and step back until the penny has disappeared from sight again. Adding more water will then bring the penny back into view.

## 28. The Cheshire Cat

If you have read *Alice's Adventures in Wonderland* you will remember the grinning Cheshire Cat who kept appearing and vanishing suddenly.

Below is a Cheshire Cat who will appear and vanish as you please. Close your right eye and look steadily at the spot on the right. Bring the book slowly towards you from about a foot away and you will find that at a certain point the Cheshire Cat simply disappears. On bringing the book still closer, he will appear again.

The reason for this mysterious behaviour is the existence of the *blind spot*, a tiny area of eye where the optic nerve enters the retina. (The retina is the "camera film" of the eye, which records the pictures.)

# MAGNETISM

The ancient Greeks knew that the mineral lodestone, which is a kind of rock containing iron with magnetic properties, would attract and support small pieces of iron. The Greeks, who were not great scientists, even had stories of "magnetic mountains" whose attraction was so powerful that it would pull the nails out of passing ships. The use of a magnetic compass to indicate direction appears to have been understood by the Chinese in the 11th century A.D. and by Europeans in the 13th century.

MAGNETS, if they are hung up so that they are free to point in any direction, tend to turn so that they point north and south. This direction is called the magnetic meridian. We say that the end of a magnet that seeks the north is the north pole of the magnet; the other end is the south pole.

Now the magnetic meridian is not quite the same as the true geographic north-south line. The Earth behaves as if it contained a huge magnet inside it and the interesting thing about this "Earth magnet" is that its poles are not the same as the geographic north and south poles round which the Earth spins. For many purposes, however, this difference is not enough to be important.

## 29. To find the north pole of a bar magnet and a horseshoe magnet

If you are wearing a watch it is a good idea to remove it before experimenting with magnets, otherwise it may be magnetized and damaged. Hang both magnets as shown in the diagram, using thread about a yard long. It is best to hang them in separate rooms (or one at a time), otherwise one will attract the other. Wait until the magnets have come to rest completely (overnight if necessary). They will lie along the magnetic meridian, and the end pointing northwards is the north pole of the magnet in each case.

For this experiment it is necessary to know the difference between north and south. You will be able to tell this by remembering that the Sun is in the south around mid-day.

If your magnets are not marked already, make a scratch or an ink blob to show which is the north pole.

## 30. A floating compass

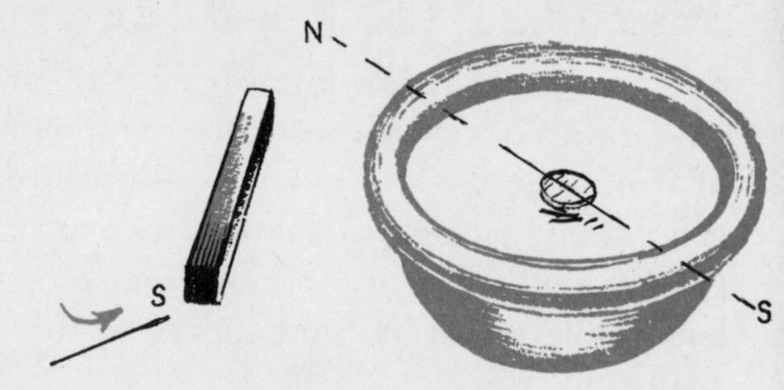


For this you need a darning needle, a cork, a bowl of water and a bar magnet.

Using the same end of your magnet, stroke the needle in the same direction repeatedly, lifting the magnet high in the air after each stroke. If you wish the eye end of the needle to become the north pole, stroke as shown in the diagram, so that the south pole of your bar magnet touches the eye end of the needle last.

Now balance the needle on a slice cut from the cork, in water. The cork will turn so that the needle lies along the magnetic meridian. No matter how you turn the bowl, the needle will continue to point in this direction.

## 31. To make a magnet by using a horseshoe magnet

Lay a needle across the horsehoe magnet as shown in the left-hand diagram. Then tap the needle about 50 times. Shift the needle to the position shown in the right-hand diagram and repeat the tapping. Float your new magnet as in Experiment 30. Its north pole will be at the eye end.

## 32. Like and unlike poles

Bring the north pole of a bar magnet close to the north pole of a floating or hanging magnet or to the needle of a pocket compass, and observe what happens. The poles *repel*, or push one another apart. Try all four possibilities: north to north; south to south; north to south; and south to north. You will find that *like poles repel each other; unlike poles attract each other.*

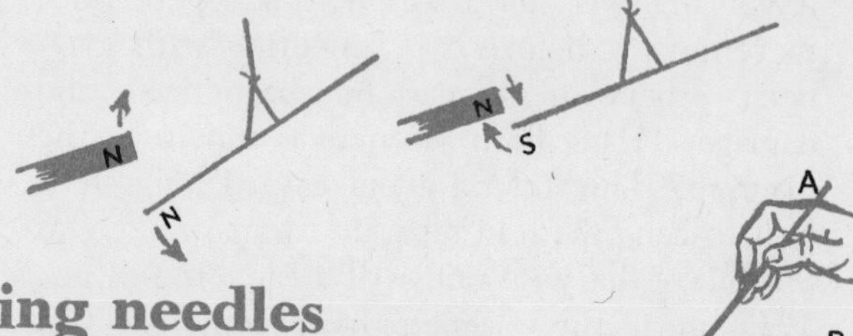


## 33. A trick with two knitting needles

Take two steel knitting needles of the same size and magnetize one of them. Then ask someone if he can tell you which one is magnetized. He is not allowed to hang up the needles on threads, float them on corks, or touch other metal objects with them.

This trick has been known to puzzle people who thought they knew quite a lot about magnetism. Touching the tip of one needle with the tip of the other does not give the answer because the attractor and and attracted have an equal pull on each other!

The secret is to touch the *centre* of one needle with the tip of the other. If the tip of needle A attracts the centre of needle B, then A is the magnetized needle. This is because there is little or no magnetism at the centre of a magnet; so if the tip of the unmagnetized needle touches the centre of the other there is no attraction.

## 34. A magnetic squadron

Take four darning needles of the same size and magnetize them so that all the eyes are north poles. Stick each needle vertically through a slice cut from a cork. (Use the smallest piece of cork that will support the needle.) Now float all the magnets, eye upwards, in a basin. You will find that they all go to the edge because they are all repelling one another.

Now bring the south pole of a bar magnet to the centre of the bowl. The magnets will become "excited" because they are pulled towards the bar magnet but still repelled by each other. When they settle down at last, you will find they form a square.

If you are patient and make a lot of magnets you will find that there is a pattern for every number – sometimes more than one pattern. Five magnetic corks, for example, will usually form a ring but may form a square with one at the centre.

## 35. Which are the magnetic materials?

Bring a magnet close to various metal objects and observe which of these are attracted. Try for example pins, tacks, paper clips, drawing pins, a tin lid, a milk-bottle top, a gold ring, a silver spoon, an aluminium saucepan, a penny. You will find that anything which is drawn to the pole of your magnet contains iron or steel. (There are other magnetic metals, such as nickel and cobalt, but they are not often found in the home.)

Tins are attracted to a magnet because the "tin" is really sheet steel with a thin coat of tin.

## 36. What will mask a magnet?

Cover one end of a bar magnet with a piece of paper and test whether the magnet will still attract tacks or pins. Now test the attractive power through other materials such as glass, a penny, a ruler, a slice of cork, cardboard, a silver spoon, a stainless steel spoon, an aluminium saucepan and an enamel saucepan.

You will find that the magnetic forces pass through all these things, except the stainless steel spoon and the enamel saucepan, which are made of iron or steel. The forces do not pass through iron or steel, but are turned aside so that they travel inside these materials. Depending on the strength of your magnet and the thickness of the spoon or saucepan, you may find that the attraction does not quite disappear.

## 37. A magnetic theatre

In a magnetic theatre the actors are cut-out figures stuck into slices cut from corks, in the base of which there is a steel drawing-pin. As a stage use a cardboard box such as a shoe box, and move your actors by using a strong magnet under the stage.

# ELECTRICITY

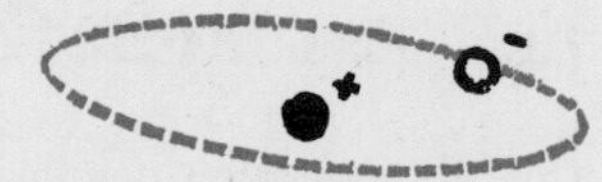

The experiments in this section are divided into two groups: static electricity and current electricity. Both kinds of electricity are caused by the movement of electrons, which are the tiny negatively charged particles which surround atoms. As was explained in the section HEAT, all matter is composed of the atoms of more than 100 different kinds of elements. Each atom consists of a nucleus – a central core carrying a positive charge of electricity—and a number of electrons. Each element has a different number of electrons. Electrons are even smaller than atoms, and each element (that is, each different kind of atom) has a different number of electrons which are all spinning rapidly round the nucleus. Electrons each carry a negative charge of electricity, and ordinarily their total charge is equal and opposite to the positive charge on the nucleus, so that the whole atom is electrically neutral, or balanced. Let us see what happens when the charge is unbalanced.

STATIC ELECTRICITY. Some pairs of materials become electrically charged very readily; that is, on rubbing, electrons are transferred from one material to the other. For example, when sealing wax is rubbed with wool, electrons are knocked off the wool and picked up by the wax. The wax then becomes negatively charged because it now has too many electrons; the wool becomes positively charged because it now has too few.

As in magnetism, there is a simple law of static electricity: like charges repel each other, unlike charges attract each other. This law is shown by the next five experiments.

## 38. The jumping snow-flakes

Rub a piece of sealing wax with a dry woollen garment to make it negatively charged. Bring it close to some small scraps of dry newspaper.

The scraps of paper will be attracted to the sealing wax.

Although the paper starts off by being electrically neutral, it is attracted to the negatively charged wax because the wax repels some negative electricity from the paper, leaving the paper positively charged.

## 39. The dancing balls

Cut two pieces of metal foil about the size of half-crowns and roll them into balls. Thread and knot some *silk* thread about 16 inches long and push the needle through both balls.

Remove the needle, knot the free end of the thread, and draw the balls along it so that one ball is at each end. Now comb your hair and bring the comb close to the balls. The balls are first attracted to the comb, and then repelled from it and from each other. Watch carefully for the attraction of the balls to the comb, as it lasts only a very short time.

As with the sealing wax and paper scraps, the negatively charged comb first attracts the balls because it has repelled the electrons from them, leaving them positively charged. The balls then pick up the charge from the comb and become negatively charged themselves.

A silk thread is necessary because silk is a poor conductor of electricity. If the thread were a good conductor, the charge on the balls would immediately escape to the Earth through your fingers and body. Materials such as silk which do not conduct electricity well are

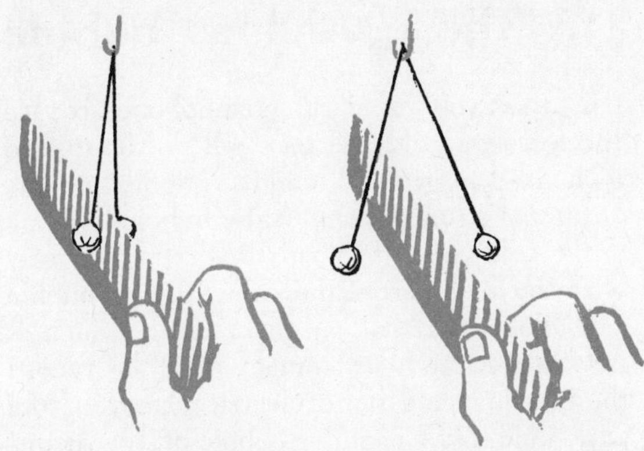

called *insulators*. Broadly speaking, poor conductors of electricity are also poor conductors of heat, and the other way round.

Examples of good insulators are air, oil, glass, rubber and plastics. However, no insulators are quite perfect, and because of this an electric charge cannot be stored for very long, as in time it will always leak away to the Earth.

## 40. The rotating ruler

Balance a ruler on an egg in an egg-cup and bring your charged comb close to it. The comb will attract the ruler, which can be made to spin round quite fast by circling with the comb. Balance a teaspoon on a needle stuck into a cork and repeat the experiment.

The following list will help you to try some of the many substances with which experiments can be made to work: photographic film; polished glass; wool; nylon; cotton; silk; sealing wax; polystyrene; and hard rubber.

Any two of these materials will produce static electricity when rubbed together. The material earlier in the list will become positively charged and the other negatively charged. The farther apart the two materials are in the list, the easier the charge will be created. For example, polished glass gives better results when rubbed with silk than when rubbed with wool. The materials must be as dry as possible, because if they are damp the charge leaks away as soon as it is created.

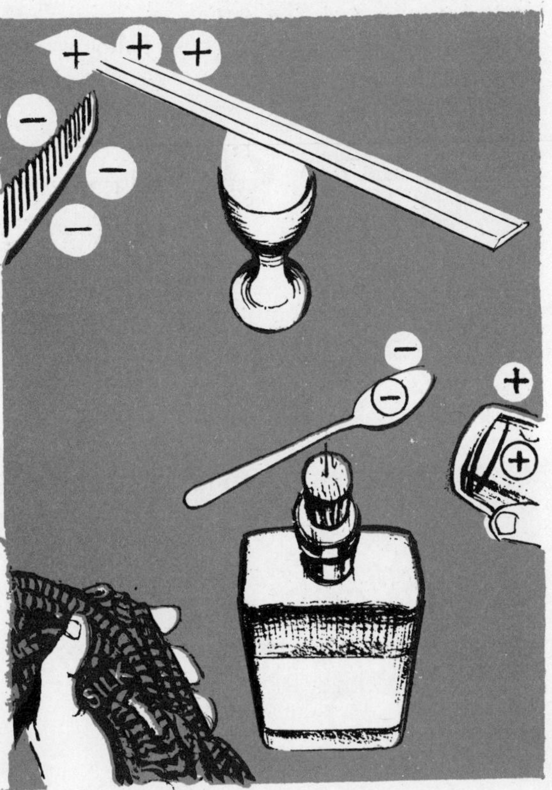

## 41. The suspicious bubble

For this you need a gramophone record (preferably an old one that will not be missed if it is damaged), a child's bubble-blowing outfit and a fur glove. Get the bubble-blowing outfit ready and then rub the record briskly with the furry part of the glove. Blow a bubble and allow it to fall on the record, which is held in one hand. By contact with the record the bubble gets a static electric charge of the same kind. Now flick the bubble off the record into the air. As it floats down, try to catch it on the record again. You will not be able to, because the record will repel the bubble.

## 42. The unfriendly balloon

Blow up two large balloons, and rub them one after the other against your jersey or pullover. Lay one balloon on the carpet and then try to touch it with the other. As both balloons now carry a negative charge of static electricity, they repel each other. The one on the carpet will roll away as soon as the other balloon is brought near it.

It is sometimes possible to produce sparks by the following method. Stick the melted end of a piece of sealing wax to the centre of a cake-tin lid to form an insulated handle. Stroke a rubber hot-water bottle briskly about 60 times with a woollen garment and press the lid on to the bottle. Then lift the lid by its handle and bring one finger close to it. You should be able to hear and feel the snap of a spark as it jumps from the lid to your finger. To make this work, however, all the articles used must first be thoroughly dried, and the attempt should be made on a dry day. (A cold dry day in winter is often best.)

CURRENT ELECTRICITY is the kind that flows continuously. There are two sorts: direct current (D.C.), and alternating current (A.C.). A direct current is one whose direction of flow is constant; an alternating current is one in which the direction of the current is continually being reversed. In most places the current from the mains is alternating. We shall be concerned only with direct current for our experiments.

You will find it easier to understand this section if you have done the experiments in the magnetism section.

## 43. How to detect a direct current

For this you need one cell of a torch battery, some copper wire (either bare, or insulated with the ends stripped) and a pocket compass.

Touch one end of the wire to the cap at the top end of the cell and the other end to the zinc base. Hold the wire over the compass so that the wire points roughly north and south (that is, parallel to the compass needle) and watch the needle. It will deflect, or shift its direction slightly. Now turn the battery and wire through 180 degrees and again observe the needle – it will deflect the other way.

The compass has detected the flow of an electric current, and this principle is sometimes used in the instrument called the *galvanometer*. The current creates a *magnetic field*, which is a region of magnetic forces in its neighbourhood. The direction of this field, which is shown in the diagram, is the direction in which the field deflects the north pole of a compass needle. The needle when left to itself settles north-south because of the Earth's magnetic field. In this experiment, however, the current in the wire sets up another field at right angles to the Earth's field, so the needle takes up a position between the two.

This relation between magnetism and electricity was discovered by the Danish scientist Hans Christian Oersted (1777–1851) in 1820, when he was showing some electrical experiments to his pupils. It was a discovery of enormous importance, because it led not only to the construction of *electro-magnets* but also to the development of the dynamo for producing electricity and of the electric motor.

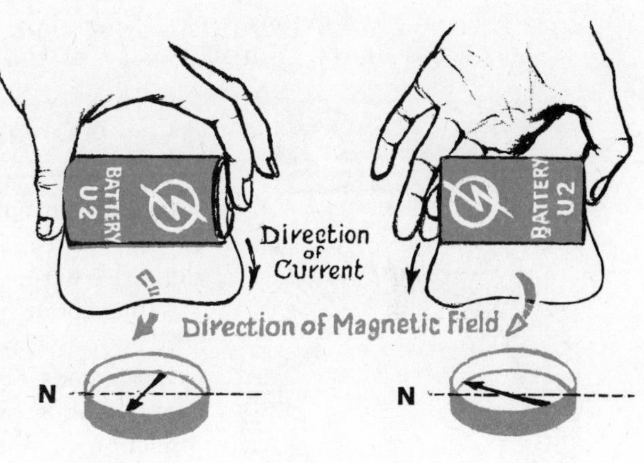


**WARNING. On no account try to use the mains electricity as a source of current for experiments. That would be very dangerous.**

## 44. To make a permanent magnet

Permanent magnets of steel and temporary magnets of soft iron can be made by placing an unmagnetized piece of steel or soft iron in the magnetic field of an electric current. (A permanent magnet keeps its magnetism when the magnetic field is removed, but a soft iron magnet loses most of its magnetism.)

Take a strip of card or stiff paper about two inches wide and wrap it round a long pencil. Now wind 160 or more turns of insulated wire (ten yards is not too much) round the card and remove the pencil. Put a steel knitting needle (or a steel skewer) in the place of the pencil and connect the stripped ends of the wire to a $4\frac{1}{2}$-volt bell battery for a few seconds – not longer, or the battery will soon be exhausted.

Remove the needle and test for magnetism by bringing it close to pins, tacks, paper clips, washers and so forth. You will find that the needle has become a magnet, and by using a compass or a permanent bar magnet whose poles are known, you will be able to discover which are the north and south poles.

By placing the needle in the coil the other way round, or by exchanging the connections so as to reverse the direction of the current, you will be able to reverse the poles of the needle.

A coil of insulated wire *without* a steel or iron core is called a *solenoid*.

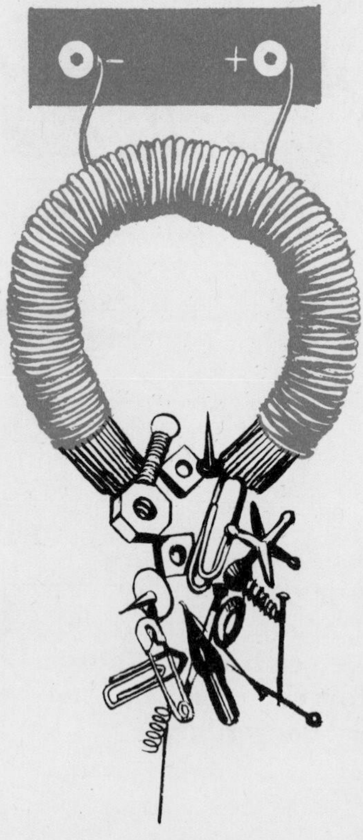


## 45. To make an electro-magnet

An electro-magnet consists of a piece of soft iron wound with insulated wire. It becomes a magnet only when a current flows along the wire.

Wind about 100 turns of insulated wire on a long soft iron bolt or rod, leaving about one inch bare at each end. Touch the stripped ends of the wire to the terminals of a bell battery for a few seconds, while bringing one end of the bolt close to your collection of small iron and steel objects. You will see that the bolt becomes a strong magnet. When you disconnect the wire, the bolt immediately loses all or most of its magnetism. By connecting up in the opposite direction you reverse the position of the poles.

A horseshoe electro-magnet is made in exactly the same way as the straight electro-magnet, but this time the core is 10 to 15 ten-inch lengths of soft iron wire (galvanized iron will do). The gap between the two ends of the horseshoe should be small. A curved electro-magnet is stronger than a straight one of the same length, but both of them are considerably stronger than a permanent magnet made with the same battery and the same winding.

# EXPLORING A VILLAGE

*by Colin Davies*

**PARISH CHURCH.** Very few old village churches now look exactly as they did when they were built. Over the centuries there may have been fires, collapsing roofs, enlargements and restorations. For this reason, you can usually find traces of several of the styles of building described in the *Children's Britannica* articles ARCHITECTURE and CHURCH. Some small villages built very large churches in the middle ages because there was good local stone and rich sheep farmers or wool merchants to provide the money. Tall imposing towers are to be seen in Yorkshire and Lincolnshire, graceful spires in Northamptonshire, round towers in Norfolk and Suffolk and the Perpendicular (late Gothic) towers, with much decoration in the top storeys, in Somerset and Cornwall. In Wales and the northwest, churches are normally smaller and plainer because the soil was poorer and the people therefore less wealthy.

Most churches have a tower or spire at the west end, like Boston Stump or Heckington, which are both in Lincolnshire. Occasionally the plan of the church is cruciform (cross-shaped), with a tower or spire at the crossing. A very fine example of this is Patrington in Yorkshire. At Wymondham the church, once an abbey, has a west tower and another farther east. Some churches have separate bell towers (St. Clement's Church at Terrington in Norfolk), or two west towers as at Melbourne in Derbyshire. Most churches have a west door which is rarely used because of draughts, so that there is usually a door or porch on the south side, sometimes with a room called a parvise over the porch. Many Gothic churches have visible traces of Saxon or Norman work. At Repton in Derbyshire there is a Saxon crypt, while at Barfreston in Kent there is a Norman doorway with rich carvings of animals and figures.

Inside any church there is always a great deal to see, from the style of building to small decorations such as faces carved on pillars or doorways. Fonts are often old and some 15th-century font covers are great wooden spires, elaborately carved. The bench ends and pews are sometimes the original mediaeval ones, as at Ufford in Suffolk and Bishop's Lydeard in Somerset. Family pews or box pews (pews with a door and high wooden sides), pulpits and carved screens (either to a side chapel or separating the nave from the choir) are other interesting furnishings. Some mediaeval churches have intricately carved wooden roofs, as at March in Cambridgeshire, with its flurry of angels' wings. Unspoilt mediaeval stained glass is rare, but at Fairford in Gloucestershire the church has some superb glass, especially in the great west window. Such windows often tell a

biblical story, or the lives of the saints, like the paintings with which many of the walls were once covered and of which a few remain. Other things to look for are the shapes of the tracery in the windows (the patterns made by the stone divisions) and the decoration on the pillars in the nave. In the chancel there is probably a bishop's throne and perhaps some early choir stalls with carved tip-up seats called misericords. Tombs vary from the brasses of the middle ages (usually a "portrait" in brass set in the stone floor), to the heavy alabaster tombs of Elizabethan and Jacobean times and the elegant monuments of the 18th century.

The tombs in the churchyard may also be interesting. At Wisbech in Cambridgeshire there are some fine 17th- and 18th-century tombstones and most churchyards have some lavish and heavy Victorian examples. On leaving the churchyard you may go out by a—

**LYCH-GATE.** The word lych comes from a Saxon word meaning "corpse" and a lych-gate is where the parish priest used to receive the coffins and read part of the burial service. Usually lych-gates are of wood, with benches at the side and with a tiled roof over the gateway, forming the main entrance to the churchyard.

**CHAPELS** belonging to one or other of the Free Churches can be seen in many villages. The religious groups that built them broke away from the Church of England at different times and were described as Nonconformist. They generally called their places of worship chapels, though the word church is also used. The earliest of these Nonconformist chapels were built in the 17th century and are very like the private houses of the time, though perhaps with larger windows. Later, as the Nonconformist churches grew, their chapels became larger. In the later 18th and early 19th centuries chapels were usually built in the classical style, whereas the parish churches were often Gothic buildings. A common design was a central doorway with a large round-topped window over it and two similar windows on each side. In Wales the name of the chapel was often carved or painted on the outside. Later the Gothic style was also used in Nonconformist chapels.

The inside of all chapels is plain, with simple oak or pine chairs or benches and without any decoration on the white walls. The building is dominated by the organ and the pulpit. This is because hymns and sermons play a larger part in Nonconformist services than they do in those of the Church of England. A few chapels have enough ground around them for a graveyard, but many are hemmed in on both sides by other buildings. Chapels are more numerous and prominent in the north and west of Britain than elsewhere. Chapels are quite noticeably plain, because Nonconformists disapproved of decoration and had less money than the Church of England to spend.

**TITHE BARNS,** another type of building connected with the parish church or a monastery, can still be seen in some parts of the country. They were built to store the tithe or tenth part of the year's produce which farmers had to give to the church as a tax in the middle ages. The monasteries have long disappeared but many of the barns are still used. Larger than ordinary barns, they were also more sturdily built than most houses in the middle ages. Many are long stone buildings, as at Bradford-on-Avon in Wiltshire, Glastonbury in Somerset and Great Coxwell in Berkshire. The inside is often like a roughly built church with massive wooden pillars dividing the barn into a "nave" and two "side aisles". The roof itself is made up of lots of rough-hewn timbers, supporting tiles, slates or thatch. The timber work becomes even more intricate if there are gables over the entrance at the side, or wings set at right-angles to the main line of the roof. These great barns are still used for storing hay or root crops, though nowadays they often house tractors and other farm machinery.

**BRIDGES** in country areas are often surprisingly old. The earliest type was just a plank or fallen tree trunk across a narrow stream. Then rocks, rolled into the stream, were joined by flat stones laid on top of them. This was called a clapper bridge and there is one at Tarr Steps in Devon which may have been made in the Bronze Age. All over Britain there are narrow, rough bridges over shallow rocky streams. They are known as packhorse bridges because they were built in the middle ages for horses carrying loads. At Croyland in Lincolnshire there is a steep three-way stone bridge, where three roads meet at the crest of the bridge. This is most unusual as a design, but many places have ordinary stone bridges of the 15th or 16th centuries. They are usually recognizable by their massive shape. The roadway is narrow and flanked by thick stone walls, and the arches are low and often pointed in the Gothic style. Between these, V-shaped projections called cutwaters were built to protect the bridge from rushing flood-waters. At the road level these cutwaters formed alcoves where pedestrians could stand when heavy traffic passed. The River Medway in Kent has bridges like this at Teston and East Farleigh, and at Swarkeston in Derbyshire there is a long bridge of this type, which also acts as a causeway over low and often flooded land. Barnstaple in Devon has a famous mediaeval bridge with arches of different shapes and sizes.

Later, arches became larger and more elegant and the stonework more finely finished, sometimes with balustrades (ornamental railings) at the top. A fine example of this is Greta Bridge in Yorkshire. In the late 18th century Thomas Telford built some splendid iron bridges in the West Country and during the following century road and railway bridges were often built in stone, brick, iron or steel, or in a mixture of several of these materials. (See the article BRIDGES in *Children's Britannica.*)

**TOLL HOUSES.** In the 18th century roads were looked after by the local parish councils and, as a result, most roads were in a shocking state. Bumpy and muddy, they sometimes had ruts deep enough for highwaymen to hide in. Road traffic was increasing, so groups of men all over the country set up committees called turnpike trusts. These trusts kept the roads in some state of repair, and charged travellers for the pleasure of a slightly less uncomfortable ride. Cottages, called toll houses, were built at each end of the turnpike, or where other roads joined it, and there was usually a bar or gate across the road, at which traffic had to stop and pay the toll. Toll gates have almost completely disappeared but many toll houses still exist. They are usually small circular or six-sided buildings looking rather like dolls' houses, and were built beside the road, with large windows so that the keeper could see oncoming traffic. They are often found by the older main roads or on others which were once important but have now become minor roads.

**HALF-TIMBERED HOUSES** were most common in areas which lacked brickworks or good local stone. Some of these houses survive from the 15th century and many from the 16th century. The style went out of fashion during the 17th century and was re-introduced by Victorian architects because it looked picturesque. The buildings have a wooden framework of upright, horizontal and diagonal beams and the gaps are filled in with plaster or brick. There are some very fine half-timbered houses at Lavenham in Suffolk, Chiddingstone in Kent and Tewkesbury in Gloucestershire. Among the largest and most elaborate buildings of this type are those in Cheshire, such as Moreton Old Hall, and many of the buildings in Shrewsbury. Sometimes the beams have been left in their natural colour but often, in Warwickshire, Shropshire and Cheshire, they have been stained black to contrast more strongly with the whitewashed plaster. Many villages in England have examples of this type of building, although the wooden framework is sometimes hidden underneath plaster or even tiles.

**LOCK-UPS AND POUNDS.** Lock-ups, which can still be seen in some villages, were local prisons where anyone who committed a "breach of the peace" could be kept while awaiting trial. They belong to the days before modern police forces were organized and as the alternative names, "roundhouses" and "blind houses" suggest, they were round and had no windows. They were small buildings, often with a domed roof, and stood on the village green or on spare ground. Pounds were enclosures with high walls, usually near water, where animals were "impounded". That is, they were put in the pound, a sort of prison for animals, until they were claimed by their owners, who were then fined for allowing their animals to cause trouble.

**GREENS AND COMMONS** date from the days when everyone grazed his animals on common land and the surrounding fields were cultivated in strips. (This is explained in the article AGRICULTURE, HISTORY OF in *Children's Britannica.*) As more land became enclosed with hedges or fences, commons were used less, but some survived as areas of poorer land not worth enclosing, or because the poorer villages had managed to hold on to their right to graze animals on the common. The green is usually in the centre of the village, with the main roads leading to it and the chief buildings grouped round it. Nowadays it is just an attractive open space which may be used by visiting fairs or circuses. The common is often rough land studded with heather, gorse, brambles and trees. In the west and north, commons may be areas of hilly moorland above the village, while in the sandy and gravelly parts of Surrey, Dorset and Hampshire they are open areas often with a few houses scattered round the edge. Good examples of greens are at Finchingfield in Essex and Milburn in Westmorland. Commons cover about 1,500,000 acres in England and Wales, and there are still some in the London area, for example at Clapham, Wimbledon and Ealing.

**SHOP FRONTS.** In general, the more modern a shop is, the simpler its front and the larger its windows—though some village shops are just the front room of a cottage. Until the end of the 18th century, many shops had bow windows with small panes of glass in a wooden framework. In the 19th century large sheets of plate glass were used, because glass of this sort had become easier and cheaper to make. From a stone or wooden base, a rectangular window rose to a board running right across the shop front on which was painted the name of the owner or the type of shop. Often narrow side windows were added, set at an angle and flanking the doorway to lead the customer's eye—and the customer—into the shop. This is still the commonest type of shop front. Only since about 1950 has it become fashionable to have doors all of glass and windows down to the level of the floor.

There are many other things which you can look for in a village. The names of some streets may seem strange, until you know the village's history. Wells, pumps and fountains may be seen. Farther afield you might come across windmills, watermills, quarries, weirs or an old Roman road.

# OPTICAL ILLUSIONS

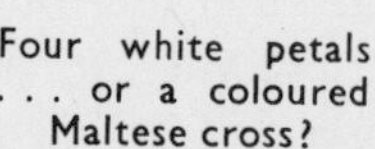

Four white petals . . . or a coloured Maltese cross?

In the diagram below, the length of A looks shorter than B, but actually they are equal. This is an optical illusion. The science of light and its behaviour is called optics, and an illusion is a deception or false belief. So an optical illusion happens when the eye deceives the mind and makes a person believe something that is false.

In the illusion below, the two long lines in each diagram are parallel. They do not look it, because of the effect of the short slanting lines that meet them.

The eye is not a perfect instrument. The German scientist Hermann Helmholtz (1821–1894) once said that if his instrument-maker were to send him an instrument as badly designed as the human eye, he would send it back and refuse to pay the carriage. The eye actually sees everything upside down—it is the brain that turns the image (picture) right way up. Also the eye has a "blind spot". This can be proved by drawing on a piece of paper a bold **X** and, about two inches to the right of it, a spot or blob. Shut the left eye and, with the paper held about one foot away, gaze firmly at the **X** with the right eye. Then slowly move the paper towards you. For a little while your eye, although looking at the **X**, will see the spot too. Then suddenly the spot will disappear but, as you continue to move the paper closer, the spot will re-appear.

In the days when stage performances of "magic shows" were common, the optical illusion known as "Pepper's Ghost" was a popular trick. The audience saw the shadowy figure of what was clearly a real person moving and dancing about on the stage. Yet this figure was transparent and the brighter parts of the background could be seen through it.

In its simplest form this "Pepper's Ghost" illusion was really very simple indeed. The stage was prepared by standing a large sheet of plate glass on it. The sheet was vertical and at an angle of 45 degrees with the line joining the stage and the audience. Thus anyone in the audience could see the background (which was rather dimly lit) through the glass.

The actor playing the part of the ghost stood in the wings—that is, at one side of the stage out of sight of the audience. Then a spotlight was shone on him and he could be seen in the glass. This was because the surface of the glass acted as a mirror, and the rays of light from the actor reflected at 90 degrees passed straight towards the audience. In fact, what the audience saw was a "virtual image" which seemed to be at the back of the stage. It was arranged that this virtual image should appear just in front of the background, which the audience could see through the glass.

One of the commonest optical illusions is seen at the cinema. The images of people, cars and aircraft that seem to move smoothly on the screen are created by showing "still" photographs rapidly one after the other, usually at the rate of 24 "frames" (pictures) a second. The succession of jerks is not noticeable.

The part of the brain that controls the messages sent by the eyes is called the *perceptual mechanism*. In ordinary conditions this mechanism works well; thus if you hold your hands before you, one twice as far away as the other, they appear almost the same size. Yet the actual image of the nearer hand on the eye's retina (which corresponds to the cinema screen) is twice the size of that of the farther hand. In this case, the perceptual mechanism has made allowance for the different distances; but it does not always do so. The harvest moon, which is the full moon that occurs nearest the autumn equinox, is

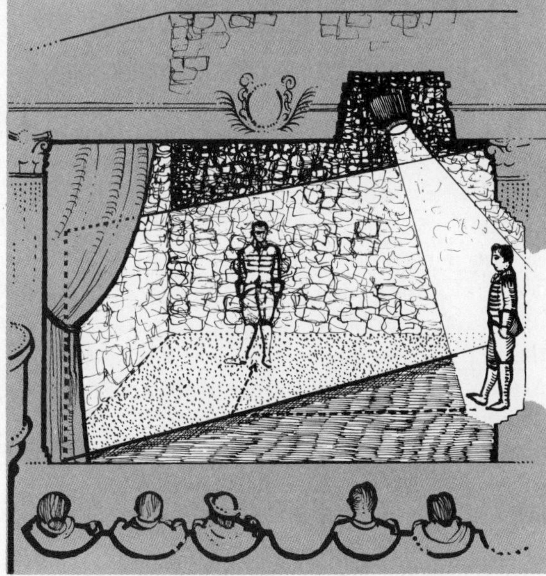

In the "Pepper's Ghost" illusion, the audience could not see the actor (shown on the right under the spotlight) who played the part of the ghost.

always low down in the sky. It looks much bigger than a full moon high in the sky because it is seen above a background of treetops and roofs. Here the perceptual mechanism cannot entirely disentangle the harvest moon from the treetops, and the brain is to some extent deceived into believing that the moon has a connection with the treetops and therefore that it is quite near. It has misjudged the perspective. (Perspective is explained in EYESIGHT in *Children's Britannica*.)

Sometimes the perceptual mechanism misjudges badly. The story is told of a man sitting in his room at twilight, who saw what he thought was a huge and horrible beast outside the win-

dow and nearly died of fright. It was really a moth crawling across the window pane. It is fairly certain that primitive peoples and savages see feathers on the wings of aeroplanes, because they think the aeroplane is a bird and therefore expect to see feathers. It has been said that the sightings of the Loch Ness monster and of the somewhat similar Canadian monsters in Lakes Okanagan and Manitoba can be explained by perceptual misjudgements of seals or otters.

Make a drawing of a lattice-work cube (that is, a cube with its 12 edges made of wire). Stare at it for some time. You will find that it appears to topple over; at one moment you are looking up at the cube and at the next you are looking down on it. The sudden change from one way of looking to the other is called *perceptual reversal*. The same kind of change can be seen in the illustration of the cellar steps. At one moment the observer seems to be looking down on them; then suddenly he finds himself in the cellar looking at the steps from below.

Optical illusions of this sort might create difficulties and even dangers for astronauts. The Moon, for example, has practically no atmosphere and therefore no particles of moisture such as form a haze and give an effect of distance

---

In the lettered examples on the next page, the circle in (A) appears flattened and the square frame in (B) looks crooked. In both cases the slanting lines trick the eye, as they also do with the upright parallel lines in (D). Perceptual reversal can be seen in (C). The height of the top hat in (E) is not in fact greater than the width of its brim, though it seems to be. The four horizontal lines in (F) are actually parallel.

Which of the inner squares looks the larger?

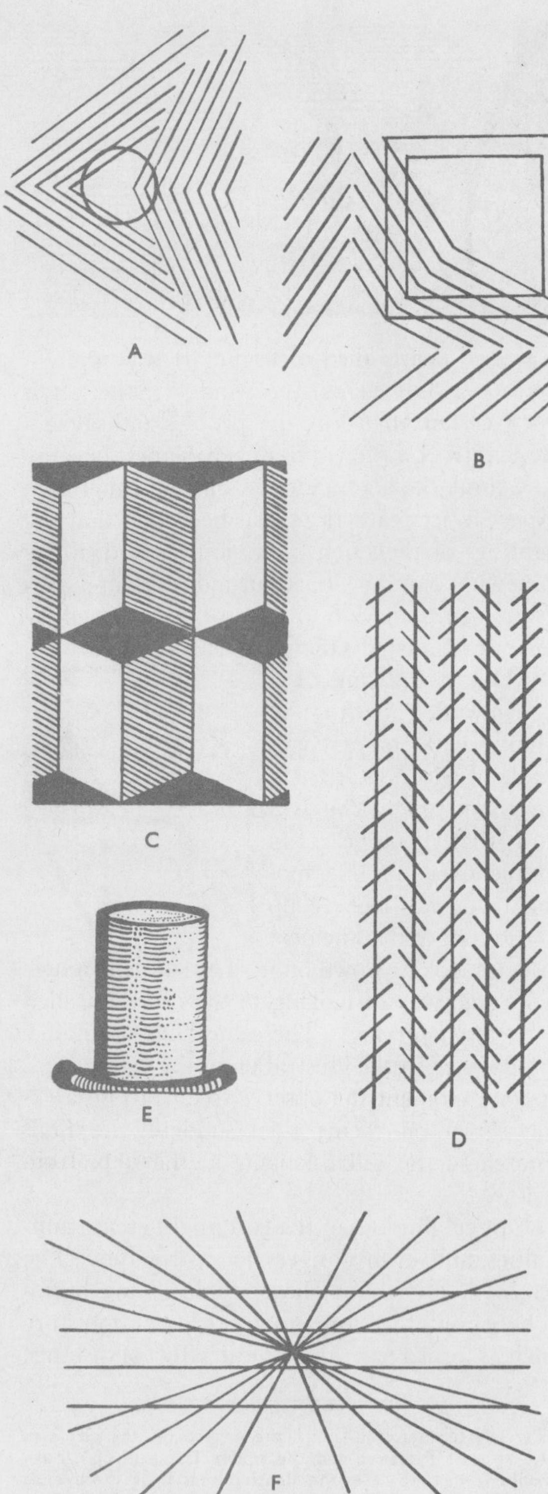


Here are six optical illusions. Can you say what appears to be odd in each of the illustrations? The answers are on the previous page.

on Earth. Everything on the Moon's surface is in glaring light or deepest shadow. The absence of haze will cause objects to appear too small and farther off than they are, and the absence of the soft shadows to which the astronauts' eyes are accustomed may lead to misjudgements. The harsh black shadows may easily be mistaken for solid features. Even while the astronauts are looking for a landing place as they approach the Moon in their spacecraft, perceptual reversal may cause them to mistake a mountain for a crater.

The perceptual mechanism when faced with a row of faint points tends to join them together into a line. Probably the best example of this is the report of *canali* (channels) on the planet Mars, made in 1877 by the Italian astronomer Giovanni Schiaparelli (1835–1910). These channels were seen by other astronomers observing through telescopes, but they have never been distinguishable on any photograph of Mars.

## After-images

Shut your eyes for half a minute, then gaze for half a minute at a bright electric light bulb. Now shift your gaze to a dull background, and you will see a bright image known as an after-image. The closer the background is, the smaller the after-image appears. Try this by shifting your gaze to a distant wall and to the night sky, and you will notice the effect of the perceptual mechanism.

Optical illusions occur with colours as well as with shapes and sizes. If you stare at a small coloured object for half a minute and then shift your gaze to a dull background, you will see what is called a negative after-image. If the object was green the after-image is pink; if the object was red the after-image is blue-green; if the object was dark the after-image is pale.